D1259550

THE PAPERS OF
Andrew Johnson

Sponsored by

The University of Tennessee

The National Historical Publications and Records Commission

The National Endowment for the Humanities

The Tennessee Historical Commission

Frontispiece: Andrew Johnson
Carte de visite based upon photograph
by C. C. Giers of Nashville, April 1869
Courtesy National Park Service,
Andrew Johnson National Historic Site,
Greeneville, Tennessee

THE PAPERS OF
Andrew Johnson

Volume 15, September 1868–April 1869

PAUL H. BERGERON
EDITOR

PATRICIA J. CABLE   GLENNA R. SCHROEDER-LEIN

MARION O. SMITH   LISA L. WILLIAMS

RICHARD M. ZUCZEK

THE EDITING STAFF

1999

THE UNIVERSITY OF TENNESSEE PRESS

KNOXVILLE

Library of Congress Cataloging in Publication Data
(Revised for volume 15)

Johnson, Andrew, 1808–1875.
    The papers of Andrew Johnson.
    Vols. 8—edited by Paul H. Bergeron.
    Includes bibliographical references and indexes.
    Contents: v.1. 1822–1851.—v.2. 1852–1857—[etc.]—
       v.15. September 1868–April 1869
    1. United States—Politics and government—1849–
1877—Sources. 2. Johnson, Andrew, Pres. U.S., 1808–
1875. 3. Presidents—United States—Correspondence.
I. Graf, LeRoy P., ed.   II. Haskins, Ralph W., ed.
III. Bergeron, Paul H., 1938–   . IV. Title.
E415.6.J65   1967   973.8'1'0924 B 67-25733
ISBN 1-57233-028-7 (v. 15)

TO

The Families of the Johnson Project Staff

Contents

Illustrations

Introduction

Andrew Johnson moved from being "president in limbo" (Hans Trefousse's label) to ex-president to campaigner during the eight months covered by this volume.[1] Rejected by the Democratic nominating convention in July in favor of Horatio Seymour, Johnson had little to do in the fall months and had scarcely any involvement in the national election. Despite the alleged comment by Horace Greeley that "the President will do something to make us all d——d mad before November," Johnson seemed fairly innocuous in this period.[2] Not until December did he "do something" to agitate the political and financial establishment.

Correspondents informed the President about their concerns over the possible replacement of the vice-presidential nominee, Francis P. Blair, Jr.[3] They also worried about election results in various states that showed Republican strength. Late in the campaign, Johnson publicly urged Seymour to become more actively involved in the canvass, so that "the mass of the people should be aroused and warned against the encroachments of despotic power. . . ." Some friends even begged the President himself to hit the campaign trail, but he would not.[4] Election day brought the expected news: by carrying twenty-two of the thirty states which participated, Grant easily swept the electoral vote.

When Congress returned to Washington in December, Johnson sought their attention—first with his Fourth Annual Message. In

---

1. The introductory essay is based upon documents published in this volume and also upon three monographs: Hans L. Trefousse, *Andrew Johnson: A Biography* (New York, 1989); Albert Castel, *The Presidency of Andrew Johnson* (Lawrence, Kans., 1979); and James E. Sefton, *Andrew Johnson and the Uses of Constitutional Power* (Boston, 1980). Trefousse's Chapter 18 is entitled, "President in Limbo."

2. Lewis E. Parsons to Johnson, Sept. 2, 1868.

3. In mid-October the *New York World* suggested that Blair should be replaced on the Democratic ticket, on the grounds that he had alienated moderates in the party with his earlier letter endorsing the use of force to restore white rule in the South. The *National Intelligencer* joined the plea for Blair's removal. Andrew J. Wilcox to Johnson, Sept. 18, 1868; Alexander Delmar to Johnson, Oct. 18, 1868; Edward G.W. Butler to Johnson, Oct. 28, 1868; Castel, *Presidency of Johnson*, 201.

4. Johnson to Seymour, Oct. 22, 1868; John Haviland to Johnson, Oct. 24, 1868; Edward G.W. Butler to Johnson, Oct. 28, 1868. Examples of letters seeking Johnson's active involvement include: George W. Parks to Johnson, Oct. 12, 1868; Horace H. Day and William H. Sylvis to Johnson, Oct. 27, 1868; and Nathaniel P. Sawyer to Johnson, Oct. 30, 1868.

it he again railed against the Reconstruction acts but moved beyond that to attack the fiscal policies of Congress and the Treasury Department. In good Jacksonian style, he lamented the national debt, charging that it imposed a new form of slavery upon the people. He recommended a scheme whereby the bondholders would be paid off in less than seventeen years, a proposal interpreted by outraged Congressional Republicans as a repudiation of the debt.[5]

Although his Fourth Amnesty Proclamation, issued on Christmas Day, was not overly controversial, the Senate demanded an explanation. About three weeks later, Johnson sent a defense of it to that chamber and the matter blew over.[6]

It was predictable that Johnson would not end his presidency without issuing more veto messages. Even though neither of the two pieces of legislation involved was of great moment, the President seemingly had to flex his executive muscle in the waning days of his administration. The first bill provided that the governing of the District of Columbia's black schools should be transferred from a board appointed by the Secretary of the Interior to the board that governed all other public schools in the District. Johnson rejected this proposal out of hand, alleging unfairness to the black citizens of the District.[7] The second measure concerned a tariff on imported copper; it stirred controversy and attention in business and financial circles. Johnson objected to it largely on economic grounds, believing it would eventually have a negative impact upon federal revenues and that it constituted special legislation for the benefit of the mining industry of the Lake Superior region.[8]

Oddly enough, on a matter of great importance the letters and documents sent to and from the President make no mention of the Fifteenth Amendment. This measure passed both houses of Congress in late February, yet Johnson refrained from any public message or state-

5. See Fourth Annual Message, Dec. 9, 1868; also Castel, *Presidency of Johnson*, 209–10; Trefousse, *Johnson*, 345–46. One of the favorable responses to Johnson's message claimed that as a result of it, "the name of Andrew Johnson will equal if it does not excel that of Andrew Jackson." See William H. Wesson to Johnson, Dec. 10, 1868.

6. Fourth Amnesty Proclamation, Dec. 25, 1868; To the Senate, Jan. 18, 1869. This final pardon document encompassed those remaining ex-Rebels who had not been included in the previous three proclamations.

7. Veto of Washington and Georgetown Schools Act, Feb. 13, 1869.

8. Veto of Copper Bill, Feb. 22, 1869. Charles J.W. Gwinn was the most persistent correspondent who advocated the rejection of the copper bill. See Gwinn to Johnson, Dec. 19, 1868, Jan. 11, 19, Feb. 8, 1869. Two who asked Johnson to approve the bill were Henry R. Linderman to Johnson, Feb. 13, 1869; and Nathaniel P. Sawyer to Johnson, Feb. 13, 1869.

ment (unlike his reaction to the Fourteenth Amendment). In fact, he made only a fleeting reference to the Fifteenth Amendment in a rambling interview conducted a few days after its passage by a reporter from the *New York World*.[9]

Another vexing problem that further demonstrated Johnson's ineffectiveness, if not weakness, was the whiskey frauds investigation in New York, an examination that had commenced in the summer. Beginning with a September 2 document and continuing through December, there are approximately thirty documents in this volume concerning this matter. The investigation was complex by any reckoning, but made more so by the unreliability and even criminal actions of some of the investigators. Thus the Johnson administration found itself in the predicament of defending its investigators. The original intent had been to uncover damaging evidence about Internal Revenue Commissioner Edward Rollins, in order to justify his removal; but Rollins remained in office.[10]

Meanwhile the President received numerous reports from the South. If these documents from public officials and private citizens are creditable, violence marked the latter months of 1868. In early September, for example, a special legislative committee from Tennessee arrived at the White House to report on Ku Klux Klan activities and general violence and to seek federal troops.[11] Concurrently, there were reports from North Carolina concerning various outrages in that state. Information about violence in Alabama, however, was disputed by different citizens.[12] Much attention focused upon Louisiana and especially New Orleans. General Lovell Rousseau repeatedly sent messages to Johnson regarding the situation there, but his death in January ended that source of information.[13] Late in 1868 and at the beginning of the new year, wide-

9. Interview with *New York World* Correspondent, Feb. 28, 1869.

10. Two of the most avid correspondents, as well as participants, in the frauds investigation were John M. Binckley and Samuel G. Courtney. Many of the complications of this matter may be followed by tracking their letters to Johnson.

11. Edmund Cooper to Johnson, Sept. 1, 1868; Mary M. Ferguson to Johnson, Sept. 4, 1868; Michael Burns to Johnson, Sept. 9, 1868; Jacob J. Noah to Johnson, Sept. 10, 1868; William H. Wisener, Sr. et al. to Johnson, Sept. 11, 1868; George P. Cabler to Johnson, Sept. 20, 1868.

12. Concerning North Carolina, see John W. Sharp to Johnson, Sept. 7, 1868; Dixon Ingram to Johnson, Sept. 13, 1868. With regard to Alabama, see Thomas G. Jones and Henry T. Walker to Johnson, Sept. 22, 1868; Montgomery, Alabama Citizens, Sept. 24, 1868; Peyton T. Groves et al. to Johnson, Sept. 26, 1868.

13. Walter M. Smallwood to Johnson, Sept. 6, 1868; Edward G.W. Butler to Johnson, Sept. 20, 1868; Lovell H. Rousseau to Johnson, Sept. 26, Oct. 4, Nov. 10, 20, 1868; Johnson to Rousseau, Oct. 31, 1868; John M. Schofield to Johnson, Oct. 30, 1868.

spread atrocities apparently erupted in Arkansas.[14] But there, as elsewhere, the President took no direct action.

On the patronage front, however, Johnson did take action, prompted by an unrelenting stream of entreaties for federal appointments. Remarkably for a "president in limbo," there was little diminution of requests; in fact, there are nearly 140 letters published in this volume that deal with patronage—a number comparable with other periods in his presidency. From September 1 through February 27 (five days before the end of the administration) written pleas for jobs arrived at the White House; likewise many visitors came to plead their cases in person. Johnson made some recess appointments but mainly he forwarded scores of nominations to the Senate. Congress, of course, was not in a friendly mood about confirming his recommendations. There was truth in Thomas Ewing, Jr.'s observation, when he recommended General Granger for an appointment: "He would probably be rejected—so will anybody who even professes to be your friend & has not carried water on both shoulders."[15]

But the prospect of possible rejection did not inhibit scores of office-seekers. Not surprisingly, numerous prominent individuals, such as William Evarts, Edmund Ross, William Groesbeck, Horatio Seymour, and William T. Sherman, interceded in behalf of their friends.[16] Of the thirty-five different women who corresponded with Johnson during the September–April period, approximately one-third of them sought federal jobs for family members or friends. One of the most poignant was Maria Rousseau, who, a few days after her husband's death, sent two letters to the President in behalf of military appointments for her sons.[17] Meanwhile Ann S. Stephens and Anne M. Deen persisted in their pleas in behalf of family as well as friends.[18] Two of the last three letters requesting patronage (on February 27) were from women: Margaret Spencer resigned as postmaster and recommended someone else; and Lily

14. Augustus H. Garland to Johnson, Dec. 7, 1868; Benjamin C. Brown et al. to Johnson, Jan. 1, 1869; Arkansas Citizens, Jan. 2, 1869; Thomas Black to Johnson, Jan. 14, 1869.

15. Ewing to Johnson, Jan. 17, 1869.

16. See, for example, William M. Evarts to Johnson, Sept. 3, 1868; Edmund G. Ross to Johnson, Jan. 20, 1869; William S. Groesbeck to Johnson, Sept. 3, Dec. 29, 31, 1868; Horatio Seymour to Johnson, Sept. 24, 1868; William T. Sherman to Johnson, Nov. 28, 1868.

17. Maria Rousseau to Johnson, Jan. 12, 14, 1869.

18. Ann S. Stephens to Johnson, Oct. 16, Dec. 11, 26, 1868, Jan. 22, 1869; Anne M. Deen to Johnson, Dec. 18, 1868, Feb. 1, 17, 1869.

G. Yeaton asked for an appointment for her brother.[19] In an unusual twist in the patronage story, the President, unsolicited, offered an appointment as deputy collector in a North Carolina district to Millington P. Lytle, the son of a man who years earlier had befriended Johnson.[20] Contrary to what one might have expected, the quest for public office simply did not abate during the closing months of his presidency. And evidently Johnson did not recognize or acknowledge his own impotence in patronage matters.

Be that as it may, the calendar moved relentlessly on toward early March, when Johnson would end his embattled administration. Feeling compelled to defend his presidency one more time, he issued a "Farewell Address" on the day when, as he described it, "the robe of office . . . falls from my shoulders. . . ." At the conclusion of this document Johnson expressed his devout conviction that "I have nothing to regret"—a view not shared by very many political leaders and observers.[21] Refusing to go to the Capitol to sign documents, he remained at the White House, where he attended to the final items of business. That accomplished, he unceremoniously vacated the premises, determined not to attend Grant's inauguration.

Johnson took up temporary residence at the home of John F. Coyle and did not actually leave Washington until March 18. His trip home to Tennessee was something of a triumphal progression, with stops along the way (Charlottesville and Lynchburg, for example) to be cheered by throngs of citizens and to deliver speeches. An exhausted but immensely satisfied Johnson arrived at his hometown of Greeneville on March 20, his first visit since the secession crisis had forced him to leave in 1861.[22] But once the shouting died down, Johnson quickly came to the realization that Greeneville held few charms for him. He simply could not quietly retire there to live out his days.

Instead, he was seized by the desire to rehabilitate or revitalize his political fortunes. After all, for months numerous correspondents had

19. Margaret Spencer to Johnson, Feb. 27, 1869; Lily G. Yeaton to Johnson, Feb. 27, 1869.

20. Johnson to Millington P. Lytle, Oct. 25, 1868.

21. Farewell Address, Mar. 4, 1869.

22. While still in Washington, Johnson made a trip to Baltimore, where he attended a dinner given in his honor and offered brief remarks. See Response in Baltimore, Mar. 11, 1869; Speech at Charlottesville, Mar. 18, 1869; Speech in Lynchburg, Va., Mar. 18, 1869; Speech at Greeneville, Mar. 20, 1869.

been urging Johnson to run for governor of Tennessee in 1869 or else for a seat in the U.S. Senate.[23] He could not turn a deaf ear to those beguiling entreaties. Only a serious attack of kidney stones (some sources even reported that he had died) postponed his new agenda. Once he recuperated, however, he ventured forth on the campaign trail, in an attempt to reestablish his viability as a statewide political figure.[24]

A speech at Knoxville on April 3, followed four days later by one in Nashville, launched Johnson's new search for vindication. Afterwards he visited Memphis, where he gave a major speech on April 15; from there he moved into northern Alabama for speaking engagements at Huntsville and elsewhere.[25] The warmth and enthusiasm of the crowds confirmed Johnson's strategy to position himself for election to some office in the near future.

But suddenly the dark cloud of family tragedy hovered over his plans for a new political career. As Johnson was departing from Alabama, he received the shocking news that his much-troubled thirty-five year old son, Robert, had committed suicide. The former president immediately took the train back to Greeneville.[26] Since there are no extant documents that reveal his reactions to this sad turn of events, the extent of his grief can only be imagined. Yet one should be reminded that Johnson's family, with the exception of his two daughters and their children, had seldom been a source of happiness or pride for him.

23. Examples of such letters include: Edward I. Golladay to Johnson, Nov. 10, 1868; P. Donan to Johnson, Jan. 8, 1869; Absalom A. Kyle to Johnson, Jan. 16, 1869; Francis H. Gordon to Johnson, Feb. 4, 1869; Natus J. Haynes & Sons to Johnson, Feb. 8, 1869; Joseph H. Thompson to Johnson, Feb. 9, 10, 1869; Johnson to Natus J. Haynes & Sons, Feb. 15, 1869; Interview with *New York World* Correspondent, Feb. 28, 1869. There were at least two letters that encouraged Johnson to seek the presidency in 1872: Nathaniel P. Sawyer to Johnson, Sept. 1, 1868; William Davidson to Johnson, Nov. 16, 1868. In March and April 1869, Johnson received letters that continued to press him to seek either the governor's office or a seat in the Senate. See, for example, Albert A. Fagala to Johnson, Mar. 4, 1869; Louis B. Weymouth to Johnson, Mar. 14, 1869; Augustus H. Garland to Johnson, Mar. 19, 1869; George H. Locey to Johnson, Mar. 27, 1869; John Black to Johnson, Apr. 12, 1869; John Campbell to Johnson, Apr. 15, 1869.

24. Alexander Delmar to Johnson, Mar. 26, 1869; Annie Coyle to Johnson, Mar. 27, 1869; Ellison E. Duncan to Johnson, Mar. 27, 1869; George H. Locey to Johnson, Mar. 27, 1869; Sarah Magruder to Johnson, Mar. 29, 1869; James F. Irvin to Johnson, Mar. 30, 1869; John F. Coyle to Johnson, Mar. 31, 1869.

25. Speech at Knoxville, Apr. 3, 1869; Speech in Nashville, Apr. 7, 1869; Speech in Memphis, Apr. 15, 1869; Trefousse, *Johnson*, 355–56.

26. Robert A. Bennett to Johnson, Apr. 24, 1869; Sam Milligan to Johnson, Apr. 25, 1869; Robert Avery to Johnson, Apr. 26, 1869.

Reverses never deterred Johnson for long, however; and he would bounce back from this family crisis, much as he had rebounded from troubles during his administration. Before long he resumed his campaign to restore his political fortunes in Tennessee, as he set his sights on a return to Washington, either as a representative or as a senator. For Johnson the future lay ahead. As he had declared, he had no regrets about his presidency and now he wished to press forward. Vindication might be gained in a renewed political career.

ACKNOWLEDGMENTS

Once again it is a privilege to recognize those persons and institutions that have been and continue to be vital to our editing enterprise. We are indebted for financial and other support to the National Historical Publications and Records Commission, to the National Endowment for the Humanities, and also to the Tennessee Historical Commission. All three of these agencies have offered support beyond monetary grants. Persons affiliated with said entities who have lent special assistance include Timothy D.W. Connelly and Michael T. Meier of the NHPRC, Daniel P. Jones of the NEH, and Herbert L. Harper of the THC. Needless to say, the University of Tennessee has played an indispensable role in providing financial assistance to our project.

As always we continue to be dependent upon the resources and research support offered by various libraries, archives, and historical societies. These institutions are indicated in our various footnote citations. We are most indebted to the Library of Congress, the National Archives, the Lawson McGhee Library (Knox County Public Library), and the University of Tennessee Library (particularly the Special Collections and the Interlibrary Services departments).

In the College of Arts and Sciences we continue to be supported in a variety of ways by Dean Lorayne W. Lester, for which we are grateful. In the History Department there has been a change of leadership, but not a diminution of interest and encouragement. Professor Russell D. Buhite left the headship of the department in the summer of 1997 to move to an administrative post at another university. His successor is Professor John R. Finger, who serves this academic year as acting head. We are also indebted to our fellow laborers in the editing vineyards, namely, the editors and staffs of the Andrew Jackson Papers and the Correspondence of James K. Polk. The University of Tennessee Press continues to be an invaluable partner with us.

Our connection with Andrew Johnson's hometown of Greeneville remains vital and significant. During the time that we have worked on this volume we have had a close and mutually beneficial relationship with the staff of the Andrew Johnson National Historic Site, particularly with Mark Corey and Jim Small. We cannot comment about Greeneville without acknowledging our appreciation for the longtime financial and moral support provided to us by Ralph M. Phinney.

No expression of gratitude would be complete without directing attention to the editing staff of the Johnson Papers. The names of these five persons are provided on the title page of this volume, a necessary but inadequate recognition of their talents and labors. These same staff members have worked together on Volumes 12 through 15, a remarkable record by anyone's reckoning. Unfortunately, one of the five, Lisa L. Williams, left our staff in the summer of 1997. This is the eighth volume completed under my direction as Editor; I readily concede that I could not have accomplished this without the highly competent and devoted work of this staff.

I close with a personal word of thanks to my family for their continuing encouragement, in a variety of ways, and steadfast affection. To my wife, Mary Lee, and to our sons and daughter-in-law—Pierre and Jennifer, Andre, and Louis—I am forever grateful.

Paul H. Bergeron

Knoxville, Tennessee
February 1998

Editorial Method

Our editorial procedures have been spelled out in previous volumes; see particularly Volume 11 for an updated summary. At this late date in our project we know of no compelling reason to deviate from our established practices. As with all the volumes that deal with the presidential years, we have far more documents than we could possibly include in Volume 15. Compelled therefore to be selective, we have attempted to include documents that represent the various kinds and types of letters, telegrams, etc., that were received at or sent from the White House. We continue to believe that the main focus of Johnson and his presidency was politics, broadly construed. In any event, hundreds of documents have been published in this volume and still hundreds of others have been referred to in the footnotes.

This volume, like many of our previous ones, reflects the limited number of documents *from* Johnson. To deal with that situation we have searched for and included newspaper interviews, speeches, proclamations, and official messages. Through these kinds of materials we offer a more complete record of Johnson and his presidency.

As before, we again have engaged in tremendous amounts of research in order to identify and/or explain references to persons, places, and developments mentioned or referred to in the multitude of documents published in this volume. We have been successful most of the time, but there are scattered examples where we have not been able to identify the subject in question. In such instances we have raised the white flag. Persons identified in previous volumes are *not* identified again in this volume. Instead, the reader should consult the Index to Volume 15 to ascertain whether a person has been earlier identified and the exact location of that identification. Occasionally we have found it necessary to provide updated or corrected information for certain previously identified subjects.

We have endeavored to offer an accurate and faithful rendering of the text of all the documents included in this volume. But we should remind the reader that the overwhelming majority of these documents are nineteenth-century *handwritten* letters or telegrams that we have transformed into twentieth-century *printed* ones.

SYMBOLS AND ABBREVIATIONS

REPOSITORY SYMBOLS

DLC   Library of Congress, Washington, D.C.
DNA   National Archives, Washington, D.C.
       RECORD GROUPS USED*
       RG48 Records of the Office of the Secretary of the
             Interior
       RG56 General Records of the Department of the
             Treasury
       RG59 General Records of the Department of State
       RG60 General Records of the Department of
             Justice
       RG75 Records of the Bureau of Indian Affairs
       RG94 Records of the Adjutant General's Office,
             1780s–1917
       RG99 Records of the Office of the Paymaster
             General
       RG107 Records of the Office of the Secretary of
             War
       RG153 Records of the Office of the Judge Advo-
             cate General (Army)
       RG204 Records of the Office of the Pardon Attorney

*We have also used a number of microfilm collections from the Na-
tional Archives, all of which are parts of the various Record Groups
listed here.

CLU-S/C   University of California, Los Angeles,
             Department of Special Collections, Los
             Angeles, Calif.
CSmH   Henry E. Huntington Library, San
             Marino, Calif.
InFwL   Lincoln National Life Foundation, Ft.
             Wayne, Ind.
NHi   New York Historical Society, New York, N.Y.
NjMoHP   Morristown National Historical Park,
             Morristown, N.J.
NRU   University of Rochester Library, Rochester,
             N.Y.
NWM   U.S. Military Academy Library, West
             Point, N.Y.

PHi   Historical Society of Pennsylvania, Phila-
                  delphia, Pa.
PPRF   Rosenbach Museum and Library, Philadelphia,
                  Pa.
TU   University of Tennessee Library, Knoxville

MANUSCRIPTS

AD   Autograph Document
ALI   Autograph Letter Initialed
ALS   Autograph Letter Signed
ALS draft   Autograph Letter Signed, draft
Copy   Copy, not by writer
Draft   Draft
L   Letter
LBcopy   Letter Book copy
L draft   Letter, draft
LS   Letter Signed
PD   Printed Document
Pet   Petition
Tel   Telegram

ABBREVIATIONS

ACP   Appointment, Commission, and Personal Branch
Adj.   Adjutant
Appl(s).   Application(s)
Appt(s).   Appointment(s)
Arty.   Artillery
Asst.   Assistant
Atty. Gen.   Attorney General
Bk(s).   Book(s)
Brig.   Brigadier
Btn.   Battalion
Bty.   Battery
Bvt.   Brevet
c/ca.   circa
Capt.   Captain
Cav.   Cavalry
Cld.   Colored
Co.   Company
Col.   Collection/Colonel

Commr.	Commissioner
Comp(s).	Compiler(s)
Cong.	Congress
Corres.	Correspondence
CSA	Confederate States of America
CSR	Compiled Service Records
Dept.	Department
Diss.	Dissertation
Dist(s).	District(s)
Div.	Division
Ed(s).	Editor(s)
Enum.	Enumeration
Ex.	Executive
fl	flourishing
Gen.	General
Gov.	Governor
Inf.	Infantry
JP	Johnson Papers
Let(s).	Letter(s)
Lgt.	Light
Lt.	Lieutenant
Maj.	Major
Mil.	Military
Misc.	Miscellaneous
No(s).	Number(s)
n.d.	no date
n.p.	no page; no place
p./pp.	page/pages
Pet(s).	Petition(s)
Prec.	Precinct
Pt.	Part
Recd.	Received
Recomm.	Recommendation(s)
Regs.	Regulars
Res.	Reserve
Rev.	Revised/Reverend
Rgt.	Regiment
Sec.	Secretary
Ser.	Series; Serial
Sess.	Session
Subdist.	Subdistrict

Subdiv.	Subdivision
Tel(s).	Telegrams(s)
Tr(s).	Transcriber(s)
Trans.	Translator/Translation
Twp.	Township
USCT	United States Colored Troops
Vet.	Veteran
Vol(s).	Volume(s); Volunteer(s)

SHORT TITLES

BOOKS

American Annual Cyclopaedia	*American Annual Cyclopaedia and Register of Important Events* (42 vols. in 3 series, New York, 1862–1903).
Appleton's Cyclopaedia	James G. Wilson and John Fiske, eds., *Appleton's Cyclopaedia of American Biography* (6 vols., New York, 1887–89).
Alexander, *Reconstruction*	Thomas B. Alexander, *Political Reconstruction in Tennessee* (Nashville, 1950).
Alexander, *T.A.R. Nelson*	Thomas B. Alexander, *Thomas A.R. Nelson of East Tennessee* (Nashville, 1956).
Altshuler, *Cavalry Yellow & Infantry Blue*	Constance W. Altshuler, *Cavalry Yellow & Infantry Blue: Army Officers in Arizona between 1851 and 1886* (Tucson, 1991).
Ames, *Pioneering the Union*	Charles Edgar Ames, *Pioneering the Union Pacific: A Reappraisal of the Builders of the Railroad* (New York, 1969).
BDTA	Robert M. McBride et al., comps., *Biographical Directory of the Tennessee General Assembly* (6 vols. to date, Nashville, 1975–91).
BDUSC	*Biographical Directory of the*

United States Congress, 1774–1989, Bicentennial Edition (Washington, D.C., 1989).

Beale, *Welles Diary* Howard K. Beale, ed., *Diary of Gideon Welles* (3 vols., New York, 1960).

Bennett and Rae, *Washington County Tombstone Inscriptions* Charles M. Bennett and Loraine Bennett Rae, comps., *Washington County, Tennessee, Tombstone Inscriptions* (3 vols., Nashville, 1977–79).

DAB Allen Johnson and Dumas Malone, eds., *Dictionary of American Biography* (20 vols., supps., and index, New York, 1928–74).

Dawson, *Army Generals and Reconstruction* Joseph G. Dawson, III, *Army Generals and Reconstruction: Louisiana, 1862–1877* (Baton Rouge, 1982).

DNB Leslie Stephen and Sidney Lee, eds., *The Dictionary of National Biography* (22 vols. and supps., London, 1938– [1885–1901]).

Doughty, *Greeneville* Richard H. Doughty, *Greeneville: One Hundred Year Portrait (1775–1875)* (Greeneville, 1975).

House Journal . . . 1868–69 *House Journal of the Adjourned Session of the Thirty-Fifth General Assembly of the State of Tennessee, for the Years 1868–69* (Nashville, 1868).

Hunt and Brown, *Brigadier Generals* Roger D. Hunt and Jack R. Brown, *Brevet Brigadier Generals in Blue* (Gaithersburg, Md., 1990).

Johnson Papers LeRoy P. Graf, Ralph W. Haskins, and Paul H. Bergeron, eds., *The Papers of Andrew Johnson* (14 vols. to date, Knoxville, 1967–).

NCAB	*National Cyclopaedia of American Biography* ... (63 vols. and index, New York, 1893–1984 [1–18, Ann Arbor, 1967]).
NUC	Library of Congress, *The National Union Catalog: Pre-1956 Imprints* (754 vols., London, 1968–).
OR	*War of the Rebellion: A Compilation of the Official Records of the Union and Confederate Armies* (70 vols. in 128, Washington, D.C., 1880–1901).
Powell, *Army List*	William H. Powell, *List of Officers of the Army of the United States from 1779 to 1900* (Detroit, 1967 [1900]).
Randall, *Browning Diary*	James G. Randall, ed., *The Diary of Orville Hickman Browning* (2 vols., Springfield, 1925–33).
Richardson, *Messages*	James D. Richardson, comp., *A Compilation of the Messages and Papers of the Presidents, 1789–1897* (10 vols., Washington, D.C., 1896–99).
Simon, *Grant Papers*	John Y. Simon, ed., *The Papers of Ulysses S. Grant* (20 vols. to date, Carbondale, 1967–).
Sobel and Raimo, *Governors*	Robert Sobel and John Raimo, eds., *Biographical Directory of the Governors of the United States, 1789–1978* (4 vols., Westport, Conn., 1978).
Tyler et al., *New Handbook of Texas*	Ron Tyler et al., eds., *The New Handbook of Texas* (6 vols., Austin, 1996).
U.S. Off. Reg.	*Register of the Officers and Agents, Civil, Military and Naval in the Service of the United States* ... (Washington, D.C., 1851–).

Van Deusen, *Seward*	Glyndon G. Van Deusen, *William Henry Seward* (New York, 1967).
Warner, *Blue*	Ezra J. Warner, *Generals in Blue* (Baton Rouge, 1964).
Warner, *Gray*	Ezra J. Warner, *Generals in Gray* (Baton Rouge, 1959).
Who Was Who in America	*Who Was Who in America* (11 vols. to date, Chicago, 1943–).
Wiese, *The Woodville Republican*	O'Levia N.W. Wiese, comp., *The Woodville Republican: Mississippi's Oldest Existing Newspaper* (5 vols., Bowie, Md., 1990–96).
Williams, *Great and Shining Road*	John H. Williams, *A Great and Shining Road* (New York, 1988).

JOURNALS

AHQ	*Arkansas Historical Quarterly*
Con Vet	*Confederate Veteran*
KSHS Colls.	*Collections of the Kansas State Historical Society*
LH	*Louisiana History*
MHSP	*Massachusetts Historical Society Proceedings*
PSQ	*Political Science Quarterly*
SHSP	*Southern Historical Society Papers*
THQ	*Tennessee Historical Quarterly*

Chronology

1808, December 29	Born at Raleigh, North Carolina
1826, September	Arrives in Greeneville, Tennessee
1827, May 17	Marries Eliza McCardle
1829–35	Alderman, then mayor
1835–37, 1839–41	State representative
1841–43	State senator
1843–53	U.S. Representative, First District
1853–57	Governor
1857, October 8	Elected to U.S. Senate
1862, March 3	Appointed military governor of Tennessee
1864, November 8	Elected Vice President
1865, March 4	Inaugurated as Vice President
1865, April 15	Sworn in as President
1865, May 29	Amnesty Proclamation
1866, February 19	Vetoes the Freedmen's Bureau Bill
1866, March 27	Vetoes the Civil Rights Bill
1866, July 16	Vetoes the Freedmen's Bureau Bill
1866, August 28– September 15	Trip to the Northeast and Midwest
1867, March 2	Vetoes the First Military Reconstruction Act and the Tenure of Office Act
1867, March 23	Vetoes the Second Military Reconstruction Act
1867, July 29	Vetoes the Third Military Reconstruction Act
1867, September 7	Second Amnesty Proclamation
1867, December 7	House defeats impeachment resolution
1867, December 12	Message to Senate *re* suspension of Stanton
1868, February 21	Removes Stanton; replaces with Lorenzo Thomas as *ad interim*
1868, February 24	House votes to impeach Johnson

THE PAPERS OF
Andrew Johnson

September 1868

From John P. Dodd [1]

[September 1868][2]

Concrete   De Witt County   Western Texas

Dear Sir

We are an old neighbor & county man of yours. Our Father[3] was a blacksmith by trade in Old Green Co Tennessee & used to support you in your early political career. And we take the liberty to ask a favor of a poor mans friend. We engaged in the mercantile business here two years ago or nearly three—with an aristocratic old Planter who is a haughty old Virginian[4] & who would like to make his carriage driver whip evry man of my de'cent & degree. The business has been gone through with & settled up & now with his aristocratic friends around him he has sued us & wants to rob us outright & we fear with his great influence in this county on account of family connections &c he may crush us & ruin our little business—on account of some informalities in the business which was brot about by his despotic & overbearing conduct. He has made a move to ruin us. And we would appeal to you for justice as It cant be had among such aristocrats. The final settlement of our business which was made in Feby last he wants to do away—& probably will solely by his influence here. He hates men of Plebian stock & is *connected* with many of the most aristocratic families in the South—& some men who occupy high positions on the bench. We know little of law but know what justice is. And if this Aristocratic Friend should influence the court to our ruin—we would appeal to you for yr decission in the matter.[5]

J. P. Dodd

ALS, DLC-JP.

1. Dodd (*c*1833–*fl*1880) was a dry goods merchant by 1880. 1870 Census, Tex., DeWitt, 2nd Prec., Clinton, 26; (1880), Williamson, 157th Enum. Dist., 2.

2. The Library of Congress, for reasons not obvious, has assigned a September 1868 date to the letter. We are not able either to dispute or confirm that date.

3. In the 1850 census, Thomas Dodd (*c*1799–*fl*1850) was listed as a farmer. 1850 Census, Tenn., Greene, 9th Div. E. Dist., 532.

4. Perhaps Madison G. Jacobs (*c*1813–*fl*1880), a farmer from Virginia. His partnership with Dodd has not been confirmed, however. 1860 Census, Tex., DeWitt, 10; (1870), 2nd Prec., Clinton, 10; (1880), 2nd Prec., 47th Enum. Dist., 6.

5. Nothing further is known about this case.

From Rock Island Employees Committee[1]

[Rock Island, Ill. ca. September 1868][2]

We the under signed committee of the employes at the U.S. Arsenal on Rock Island would respectfuly represent that Congress having enacted a law aproved June 25 1868[3]—constituting Eight hours a Legal days work for all Laborors workmen or Mecanics employed by or on behalf of the Government of the United States the benefit of whitch we have not received except in the shortened time of labor while our wages was reduced one fifth so that many of the workmen here were forced to work ten hours to suport their families so receiving no benifit from this reformatory law.[4] We feel this to be injustice as it is contrary to our understanding of the law and Atourney General Evarts explanation of the same[5] and more especialy so as near as we can ascertain eighteen out of twenty one Government posts receive the same remuneration for a days work under the Eight as under the ten hour systim. Therefore your petitioners would most respectfully yet earnestly pray that sutch order or orders may be ishued as will secure to the day workmen employed in the U.S. arsenal on Rock Island a full days wages for a full days work dateing from June 25th 1868 to beter enable them to suport their families and free themselves from the debts whitch many of them have been forced to contract on account of their diminished wages. And whereas the President in his inaugural adress states that the laws are to govern all alike therefore we would also pray that such order or orders may be issued as will place all civilian laborers workmen and mecanics employed by or on behalf of the government subject to the same regulations regarding compensation of wages to the end that harmony peace and good will may exist between the diferant departments of the government and its employes and thus your petitioner will ever pray.[6]

Pet, DNA-RG60, Office of Atty. Gen., Lets. Recd., President.

1. A seven-man committee signed this petition.

2. This date has been chosen because it is after Attorney General Evarts expressed his preliminary opinion on the eight-hour day (August 23) and because the issue was still of concern in early September. *Washington Evening Star*, Aug. 24, 1868. See also Albert M. Winn to Johnson, Sept. 4, 1868.

3. The bill (H. R. No. 365), which passed Congress on June 25, was signed by Johnson on July 3. *Congressional Globe*, 40 Cong., 2 Sess., pp. 3466, 3731.

4. When, on August 4, Gen. Thomas J. Rodman, commanding the Rock Island arsenal, announced the policy that the workers could choose whether to work ten hours for ten hours' pay or eight hours for eight hours' pay, only 100 men agreed to work ten hours. The other 400 walked out. *National Intelligencer*, Aug. 8, 1868.

5. Evarts's opinion was that the intention of the law was to decrease the number of hours worked without decreasing the workers' pay. *Washington Evening Star*, Aug. 24, 1868.

6. The situation was apparently not resolved under Johnson, but Ulysses S. Grant issued a proclamation on May 19, 1869, directing that no wages should be decreased. Simon, *Grant Papers*, 19: 189.

From Mattie Anderson[1]

Corner North Capitol & "I" Streets

Washington, D.C.   Thursday, Septr. 1. 68.

Sir;

I have the honor very respectfully to apply for a situation as Clerk in the United States Treasury. My father Mr Anderson[2] (of Louisiville Ky. where you have doubtless heard of in connexion with the Campbellite Sect, and his new version of the Testament) suffered much from his devotion to the cause of the Union; and finally found it necessary to leave at great pecuniary sacrafice. I am the eldest of a large family and I have thus far failed in my efforts to obtain a situation where I might give tuition in music, singing, &c. and as a last alternative make this application to you. There is no need to enter again into particulars which I explained during the interview which you kindly granted me.

Hoping that your kind offices in my behalf may prove successful.

Mattie Anderson

ALS, DNA-RG56, Appls., Positions in Washington, D.C., Treasury Offices, Mattie Anderson.

1. Anderson (b. c1845), a native of Kentucky, was the third child of Henry T. and Henriette Anderson. An older sister and brother must have died by 1868, thereby leaving Mattie as the eldest of the remaining five girls and two boys. There is no evidence that she received a treasury appointment, despite Johnson's hearty endorsement of her request. 1860 Census, Ky., Mercer, Harrodsburg, 68.

2. Henry T. Anderson (1812–1872) was a Disciples of Christ clergyman, scholar, and New Testament translator. *DAB*.

From Edmund Cooper

At Home. [Shelbyville]   September 1st 1868

My Dear Mr President.

The enclosed letter from S. R. Cockrill of Nashville, Tennessee, explains itself.[1]

If you can consistantly grant to him the special pardon asked for—

"with restoration of all rights of property or proceeds of property, not paid into the Treasury of the United States," I would esteem it as a great favor to me personally.[2]

Mr Cockrill was a school mate of my father's.[3] When in affluent circumstances he bestowed on me many favors, whilst I was a college student at Nashville—and I would be delighted now to be able to repay some of them.

I can see no reason why the pardon should not be granted as asked for—when by so doing something can be saved and no wrong done to the Government.

If you think favorably of the application—please have it made out, and forwarded first to S. R. Cockrill Nashville, Tennessee, under your own frank so as to shew, that the act comes from your own great clemency.

Of course, I make no charge against Mr Cockrill for asking you to grant his request.

Edmd Cooper

P.S. I have been overwhelmed with my legal business, since my return home—having been in the court House during the entire month of August. The court is yet in session.

On Saturday last, I spoke to a large concourse of people at Richmond in this county.[4] It was a Berbacue.

You may rest assured that your administration was warmly defended; and the Brownlow dynasty opened up to merited scorn and detestation.

The Tennessee legislature are going to send a committee to you.[5] The instruction to General Buchanan and others, with Atty General Evarts[6] letter, will afford them much useful political wisdom?

However, the Radicals in this state are wiked—illustrating the old saying "that those whom the Gods wish to destroy, they first make mad."

Edmd Cooper

ALS, DLC-JP.

1. Cockrill to Cooper, Aug. 23, 1868, Johnson Papers, LC. Cockrill indicates in the letter that he seeks Cooper's assistance with a special pardon from the President for the release of a special fund of money. The fund derived from a marshal's sale of some of Cockrill's real and personal property during the war. Cockrill seeks resolution of the question whether the fund belongs to him or to the U.S. government.

2. Johnson's response or action has not been determined.

3. Matthew D. Cooper (1792–1878) was a longtime Maury County merchant. Fred Lee Hawkins, Jr., comp., *Maury County, Tennessee Cemeteries* (2 vols., Columbia, Tenn., 1989), 2: 637; 1870 Census, Tenn., Maury, 9th Civ. Dist., Columbia, 86.

4. On August 29 the Democrats of Bedford County staged a barbecue at Richmond. An advance announcement indicated that Edmund Cooper and George W. Jones would be among the speakers on that occasion. *Shelbyville American Union*, Aug. 28, 1868.

5. The special legislative three-man committee—William H. Wisener, Thomas A. Hamilton, and James H. Agee—left Nashville on September 1 for Washington. Hamilton (1823–1905) served only one term in the legislature and was a cotton factor and commission merchant in Memphis. Agee (1827–1899) represented Campbell County for several terms in both the lower house and senate. A physician, he moved to Indiana during the war and served in an Indiana infantry unit. The committee met with Johnson on September 11 and 12 and presented a petition calling for federal troops to help suppress violence. *BDTA*, 2: 5, 375; James W. Patton, *Unionism and Reconstruction in Tennessee, 1860–1869* (Chapel Hill, 1934), 198; *Washington Evening Star*, Sept. 12, 14, 1868. See William H. Wisener, Sr., et al. to Johnson, Sept. 11, 1868.

6. Bvt. Maj. Gen. Robert C. Buchanan had received instructions in August after inquiring about the use of the army to quell disturbances in his Department of Louisiana. Similarly, William M. Evarts had written in August to a Florida marshal, explaining how civil officials might call upon the military to help execute the laws. E. D. Townsend to R. C. Buchanan, Aug. 10, 1868, *House Ex. Docs.*, 40 Cong., 3 Sess., No. 1, pt. 1, "Annual Report of the Secretary of War," pp. xx–xxi (Ser. 1367); J. C. Kelton to Buchanan, Aug. 25, 1868, ibid., pp. xxv–xxvi; William M. Evarts to Alexander Magruder, Aug. 20, 1868, ibid., pp. xxiii–xxiv.

From Nathaniel P. Sawyer

Republic Office

Pittsburgh   Sept 1st 1868

My Dear Mr President

I understand R. H. Kerr of this County leaves here to day for Washington.[1] He is no friend of yours in any way shape or form. I trust you will treat him accordingly. You are still a young man. If we cannot elect you President in 68 we may be able to do it in 72. Therefore so far as it is practicable I don't want you to put any but Johnson men on gaurd.

N P Sawyer

ALS, DLC-JP.

1. In a September 5 letter to Johnson, Kerr makes no mention of a visit and no evidence of his appearance in Washington has been found. See Robert H. Kerr to Johnson, Sept. 5, 1868.

From John M. Binckley

New York, 2 September 1868[1]

Mr. President,

I hasten to inform your Excellency that I have good reason to apprehend that the cause of criminal justice might be impeded in the

Brooklyn District should it be deemed expedient at this time to suspend Mr. Welwood,[2] Assessor, assuming, as I do, that nothing has been established against that gentleman incompatible with the performance of public duty. I therefore respectfully recommend that no further action be taken at present in his case. I beg also to express the opinion that no selection should be made for supervisor of the Southern District of New York,[3] until further progress be made in certain important criminal proceedings.[4]

John M Binckley   Solicitor of Internal Revenue

ALS, DLC-JP.

1. A second page bore the note, "This letter was sent under cover to Col. Moore, who being absent, my communication has not reached him, but has been returned to me." This message, initialed by Binckley, was dated September 11, 1868.

2. Thomas Welwood, assessor of New York's Third District. In August, President Johnson sent Binckley to examine evidence that Welwood claimed to possess with reference to revenue frauds. Binckley's suggestion notwithstanding, Johnson suspended Welwood around October 14, 1868. Johnson to Binckley, Aug. 25, 1868, *Johnson Papers*, 14: 540; *New York Herald*, Oct. 15, 1868. See also Asahel N. Cole to Johnson, Oct. 10, 1868, and George G. Reynolds to Johnson, Oct. 22, 1868.

3. Secretary of the Treasury Hugh McCulloch selected S. B. Dutcher as supervisor on November 19, 1868. It is not known if Binckley had any role in the selection or its timing. *Washington Evening Star*, Nov. 19, 1868.

4. Probably a reference to the "whiskey fraud" investigations being conducted by Binckley. For more on these cases, see Edmund Laubie to Johnson, Aug. 26, 1868; Asahel N. Cole to Johnson, Aug. 27, *Johnson Papers*, 14: 543–45, 549–52; and the many documents contained in this volume.

From Asahel N. Cole

Brooklyn, September 2d 1868

My Dear Sir:

I confess to have been hasty in my judgment, and to having accordingly done injustice to Solicitor Binckley, in my communication of last week.[1]

Mr. Binckley *may* fail in making a case against Thomas Harland and others,[2] but I think not. *Should* he fail, it will be no fault of his. He is evidently in earnest, and doing all in his power to expose fraud, and break up the whiskey ring.[3]

A. N. Cole

LS, DLC-JP.

1. Cole met with John M. Binckley when the latter arrived in New York to begin his rev-

enue investigations. Their initial meetings were less than cordial. See Cole to Johnson, Aug. 27, 1868, *Johnson Papers*, 14: 549–52.

2. In early September Binckley charged Daniel Murray, collector Thomas E. Smith, deputy revenue commissioner Thomas Harland, and commissioner Edward A. Rollins with conspiracy to defraud the government. *National Intelligencer*, Sept. 3, 1868; *New York Herald*, Sept. 4, 1868.

3. Binckley did in fact fail. By late September he had been removed as prosecutor, and in mid-October the case was dismissed. Ironically, many of Binckley's sources and witnesses were thereafter charged with perjury, and at least two were convicted. See Binckley to Johnson, Sept. 25, Oct. 7, 1868, Jan. 8, 1869; George W. Greene to Johnson, Nov. 26, 1868.

From John McClelland

Nashville   Sept 2 /68

Dear sir & friend

I have just learned that a fellow by the name of T. O. Crawford,[1] has been appointed detective for this district. Crawford was an Inspector in the 4th district. He was found guilty before the U.S. Court, Judge Trigg[2] presiding, of swindling the Gov't. on several counts, one was of selling his brand.[3] He is an arrant scoundrel. He was a Rebel soldier, and yet took the usual oath of office. After great trouble he has succeeded in getting a New Trial. He has just returned from Washington, and must have had some good voucher there.[4]

It is hard that men of his character, as well as "Bummers" from all parts of the North, can get situations, when well known honest men who are well known as such, can get nothing.

Jno McClelland

ALS, DLC-JP.

1. Thomas O. Crawford (*c*1845–*fl*1870) was still identified in 1870 as a revenue collector in Coffee County. 1870 Census, Tenn., Coffee, 13th Dist., Tullahoma, 11.

2. Connally F. Trigg.

3. According to the newspapers, Crawford was convicted in mid-July of conspiring to defraud the U.S. government of the revenue from the sale of distilled spirits. But a day or two later Crawford was granted a new trial in federal court. The case was continued to the next term. *Nashville Republican Banner*, July 16, 18, 1868.

4. President Johnson endorsed McClelland's letter thus: "The writer of this letter is well known to me and would make no statement but what is correct." Obviously, Johnson forwarded the letter to the Treasury Department, for Secretary McCulloch added an endorsement on it to report that the Revenue Bureau suspended Crawford on May 23 and therefore he no longer had a connection with the government.

From Isaac Newton, Jr.
Personal

Washington   Sep" 2d 1868

Sir

I have no doubt that the report of Gen Cox[1] in the Heustis matter will reach you to day:[2] and I regret to say that I believe it will be weak and unsatisfactory: Not mr President because there is any lack of testamony to convict Heustis of immorality, dishonesty and incompetency, but because that testimony has not been brought out. Before this examination took place, so eager were a number of these Guards to disclose his conduct, believing that he would have to go out, and that they would be protected, they were constantly coming to me and repeating what they would sware to if protected: and I can only give you an idea of the character of their statements, by recalling to your mind the disclosures made to you by Mr Noyes.[3] Others spoke to me just as freely, and with quite as much force as did Mr Noyes,—But the informal manner in which they were calld. before Gen Cox, or some other influence, evidently frightened them and put them on their guard and they concluded to testify to nothing not elicited by a question. This has been told me by the witnesses themselves, since they were before Gen. Cox. Therefore I feel confident in saying *that the truth of the matter* has *not been reached at all.* I am inclined to the opinion that such answers as they gave were not reduced to writing in their own words. These men would also have been willing to have written out their statements and sworn to them if they had been assured of protection.

I will not say why this matter has been conducted in this slipshod way, but so far I regard the investigation as a farce. Should Mr Heustis be *suspended at once* there would come forth—testimony so ample and overwhelming that no man or body of men would even think of sustaining him thereafter.[4]

I deem it my duty to state this much to you, that you may be advised of the manner that this examination has been conducted.

Isaac Newton

ALS, DLC-JP.

1. John C. Cox (1817–1872), a commissary of subsistence during the war, had been brevetted brigadier general in 1863. A lawyer, farmer, and railroad executive, he served as chief clerk of the interior from 1866 to 1869. No report by him has been found. Hunt and Brown, *Brigadier Generals.*

2. Although Cox's report has not been found, Newton had submitted seven, supposedly

substantiated, charges against William H. Huestis. See Newton to Johnson, Aug. 10, 1868, Appts. Div., Misc. Lets. Recd., RG48, NA.

3. Joshua Noyes was a guard at the jail but is not further identified.

4. Huestis served through the remainder of Johnson's presidency. However, Newton was nominated to replace Huestis as warden on December 18, 1868. No decision was made by the Senate for, despite a favorable report from the committee, his nomination was recommitted on January 7, 1869. *Senate Ex. Proceedings*, Vol. 16: 408, 426. See also William H.C. Duhamel to Johnson, Dec. 27, 1867; John H. Campbel to Johnson, Jan. 10, 1868; John Lang to Johnson, June 15, 1868; Newton to Johnson, June 22, 1868, *Johnson Papers*, 13: 372, 460–61; 14: 225–26, 248–49; Newton to Johnson, Sept. 22, 1868; Josephine S. Griffing to Johnson and Thomas T. Johnson to Johnson, Oct. 10, 1868; William Kennedy to Johnson, Feb. 18, 1869.

From Lewis E. Parsons

Washn.   Sepr. 2 /68

Dear Mr President

Permit me to say that I have certain information that Senator Morgan[1] is opposed to the reassembling of Congress on the 21st inst.—so also is Mr Greely,[2] but the latter gentleman is certain "the President will do something to make us all d——d mad before November." He also thinks it is best to keep talking about it—i.e., the reassembling of Congress but it will not do to have another session.[3] The members cannot brave their respective Districts. I hope to be able to give you the views of Genl. S.[4] in a short time, & perhaps others.

Lewis E. Parsons

ALS, DLC-JP.

1. Edwin D. Morgan.

2. Horace Greeley.

3. When Congress adjourned at the end of July, its members arranged to convene on September 21, October 16, and November 10, should they feel the need of an extra session in response to any actions by the President. As matters turned out, a quorum was present on each day and voted to adjourn until the following preset date. On November 10 the quorum voted to adjourn until the regular session beginning the first Monday in December. *Congressional Globe*, 40 Cong., 2 Sess., pp. 4518–23.

4. Not identified.

From William S. Rosecrans

New York   Sept. 2. 1868

I earnestly appeal to your excellency for an exercise of Executive clemency in behalf Brt. Maj. John F Skelton 1s Lt 45th U.S. Infantry who has been dismissed the service for violation of the act of

Congress which forbids officers from depositing their private with
the public funds in their hands.[1]

The grounds of my request are that the evidence in the case it stated
shows no improper use of public funds nor any thing prejudical to his
character as an officer and gentleman, that he was a very brave and gallant officer and lost his right eye and received several wounds while
fighting for his country under my command in the army of the
Cumberland.

He has a wife and child[2] dependent upon him for support, and as
his offense is not criminal but technical it seems very hard that an
innocent family should be disgraced instead of wearing honors justly
earned by its head in the service of our Country.[3]

W. S. Rosecrans

Brt. Majr. Gnl. USA & Mex Minister

ALS, DNA-RG94, Lets. Recd. (Main Ser.), File P-595-1868 (M619, Roll 651).

1. In June 1868 a court martial found Skelton guilty of violating "An Act to Regulate and
Secure the Safe-keeping of Public Money Intrusted to Disbursing Officers of the United States,"
approved June 14, 1866. The court claimed he had used government funds to pay private debts.
Report of Joseph Holt, July 27, 1868, Lets. Recd. (Main Ser.), File P-595-1868 (M619, Roll
651), RG94, NA; *Congressional Globe*, 39 Cong., 1 Sess., Appendix, p. 328.

2. At least two individuals, in affidavits of July 1868, claimed that Skelton had told them
that he was not married to his "wife," that their daughter was illegitimate, and that his "wife"
had a husband living elsewhere. In an 1898 pension claim Skelton reported, in fact, that he had
only been married once, in 1875, and he had no children. The dependents Rosecrans referred
to have not been identified. ACP Branch, File C-1120-CB-1868, Peter J.A. Cleary, RG94,
NA; Pension File, John F. Skelton, RG15, NA. See also Joseph Holt to Johnson, July 25, 1868,
Johnson Papers, 14: 424–25. Skelton's flourishing date given at that document is not accurate;
his pension file reveals he died on January 4, 1899.

3. In early October Johnson ordered the removal of the disabilities resulting from Skelton's
dishonorable discharge. He was not reappointed to the service. Endorsement, Report of Joseph
Holt, July 27, 1868, Lets. Recd. (Main Ser.), File P-595-1868 (M619, Roll 651), RG94, NA.

From William M. Evarts
Private

Windsor Vt.   Sept. 3. 1868

My dear Sir,

I have felt quite as desirous as you could be that there should be a
new Commissioner of Internal Revenue, and yet, wholly indisposed
to submit to the unseemliness of Mr. Rollins being suffered, under
the pressure of the public interests, to impose upon the Executive a
nomination of his own. I have therefore taken some interest in try-

ing to fix upon a suitable man for the office, that should not be open to any just objection from Mr. Rollins, within the rule that he has seen fit to adopt for his own conduct, and yet should not be, in the least, a candidate of his selection or of the suggestion of any of his advisers.

I believe Genl. Hillhouse,[1] late Comptroller of the State of New York, to occupy this position, while his character, ability and excellent public reputation would make his appointment most useful to the public service, and most creditable to the Administration.

Mr. Hillhouse is a Republican but unobjectionable, wholly, to the sound and sensible men of that party, and, for that reason, was left off the State ticket of the party last year. His great reputation for probity and capacity, it is true, compelled the party to correct this mistake of the Convention and place him on the ticket, in the hope of helping its success.

I cannot suggest a better solution of the embarrassment in which the public service is placed, than this & I have ventured to commend it to your attention.

I hope you will not allow yourself to be defrauded of some little recreation this season and I apprehend no disturbance in public affairs that should interfere with such a purpose.

Wm. M. Evarts

ALS, DLC-JP.

1. Thomas Hillhouse (1816–1897) of New York was a skilled agriculturist before entering politics. In 1859 he was elected to the state senate. Two years later Gov. E. D. Morgan appointed him adjutant general and then President Lincoln named Hillhouse assistant adjutant general of volunteers on the staff of Maj. Gen. E. D. Morgan, commanding the Department of New York. From 1865 to 1867 Hillhouse was state comptroller before serving as U.S. assistant treasurer in New York (1870–82). He was never nominated for commissioner. *NCAB*, 8: 247.

From William S. Groesbeck

Cincinnati   Sept. 3. 1868.

President Johnson:

Allow me to make another recommendation. The friends of Hon: O. F. Moore of Portsmouth, Ohio,[1] are presenting him for appointment as Commissioner of Internal Revenue, and I have been asked to join them in the movement.[2]

I do so most willingly, believing that Mr. Moore would make an

excellent officer and that his appointment would reflect credit upon
your administration.[3]

W. S. Groesbeck

ALS, RG56, Appls., Heads of Treasury Offices, Oscar F. Moore.

1. Oscar F. Moore (1817–1885), a Portsmouth lawyer, served in the Ohio legislature in the
early 1850s and thereafter in the U.S. House for one term. During the Civil War he was
lieutenant colonel and then colonel of the Thirty-third Rgt., Ohio Vol. Inf. *BDUSC*.

2. In his application file, there are letters recommending Moore from a number of important Ohio leaders.

3. Johnson did not appoint Moore to the post of Commissioner.

From Henry A. Smythe

Private

New York, 3 Septr. 1868

My dear Sir.

The Secy of the Treasury has given me an unusual amount of work
this week—in the way of *removals*[1]—at the same time I am subject to
the *usual* anoyances that I am in the habit of experiencing from that
man Guthrie[2]—(with regard to the matter of Carting[3]—& in fact
whenever he can in any way anoy, & embaress me in my office—) so
that I propose to defer my visit to you for a few days—unless you are
about to leave Washn.—or *prefer* to see me *now*—and in that case
will you please advise me? Not hearing, I will delay my visit for a
week or ten days.[4]

H. A. Smythe

ALS, DLC-JP.

1. The *New York Herald* reported that as a cost-saving maneuver over one hundred employees of the customhouse had been removed. *New York Herald*, Sept. 1, 3, 1868.

2. Probably John B. Guthrie, special agent of the treasury.

3. Smythe may have meant Samuel J. Carter, who was seeking a position in the customhouse. See Laura C. Holloway to Johnson, Sept. 7, 1868.

4. Smythe arrived in Washington on September 13 and met with Johnson the same day.
New York Herald, Sept. 14, 1868.

From Mary M. Ferguson[1]

Mount Hope [Tenn.], Sept. 4, /'68

Mr. President:—

I concluded to send you this token of my remembrance that it may assure you, that your many little acts of kindness and courtesy to me while in Washington[2] are not entirely forgotten.

You have no doubt many correspondents trespassing on your time, and interfering into your important duties, the knowledge of which has caused me to forego taxing you further even though the desire to write you a friendly greeting, has prompted me to effort sooner than the present moment.

Since my arrival home my health has not been good—mentally, however I have often called up the reminiscences of my trip, and as my thoughts wander from one little incident to another connected with it; I can imagine at times that I can see your good face reflected in them, and wonder whether or not the future will ever reward you for the burdens you bear in the present.

Whether our country is again to be preserved from the many perils environing it, and in such preservation, of her people will ever be made to appreciate the causes of such redemption, or the trusty agent who bequeathed it.

You can not imagine what a change for the worse has taken place in *our* native State, public affairs are indeed fast becoming more alarming every day. Were you placed in our midst, unknown, and unobserved, as some more obscure individual, Your noble good heart would become alarmed for the safety of your kind, and your indomitable *will* would instantly seek for the most speedy solution to avert its impending calamities.

I do not doubt but that numerous memorials are forwarded you, and that the plainest facts are brought to your knowledge—yet notwithstanding all this you must fail to see the immediate threatened dangers of our situation as a people.

The Southern people after their great sufferings in the past desire peace above every other consideration, and their hope is directed toward maintaining it by their trust in the final triumph, of the Democratic party. Had we wisely tempered conservative *military commander* over the different departments—, *relief would* be immediate and order preserved. Partizans such as Genl. George H Thomas who commands the United States forces in this department are not calculated to aid in restoration or to sustain authority.

We need the stamp of a Hancock, or Rosecrans[3] to command the extreme elements in this State, to prevent mischief, and assuage troubles. You will no doubt say after reading this that women have grown to be politicians, but I shall even be content with this rebuke, if you do not charge me with giving impertinent advice. I have written you all my doubts, and fears, and have given you all the facts as they come to a woman's perception. It is my first effort at approaching the chief Magistrate of a nation in such a disguise, and yet I feel that you will appreciate me by saying Mary has written to her friend, to acquaint him with troubles he already knew,—to suggest changes that perhaps he has weighed seriously!

The oldest of Poets has said: "a well advised messenger brings most honor to every deed."[4] Such a General we need from you!

Dear Mr. President,—

> I do feel, Thou art the Leech, the times require.
> And Paean speed thy skill profound;
> Now with stern hand, our country's Sire!
> Soften and heal our People's wound.
> The worst, the weakest from the base.
> A State, with ease may skake; but to replace,
> The falling pile is power indeed.
> Unless some guardian Spirit in his love,
> Seize the loose helm, the leaders lead,
> For thee that grace the favoring fates have wove.
> Oh! dare for thy Country's weal
> Strain all thy strength, use all thy Zeal.

May you be long spared to our people and may they again call you to be their chief, which I devoutly believe they will.

Permit me to subscribe myself with highest respect.

Mary M. Ferguson.

ALS, DLC-JP.

1. Daughter of Jesse B. Ferguson, Mary M. (c1844–ff1870) lived with her parents and siblings in 1860 and 1870. 1860 Census, Tenn., Davidson, Nashville, 4th Ward, 146; (1870), 21st Dist., 17.

2. Information about Ferguson's Washington visit has not been uncovered.

3. Winfield S. Hancock and William S. Rosecrans.

4. The poet has not been identified.

From Charles T. Sherman

Cleveland, Sept 4. 1868.

Sir

From the Organization of the Union Pacific Rail Road Co[1] to the month of October last Mr Ashmun of Mass.—Mr Williams[2] of Ind. Mr Carter of Ill. Mr Springer Harbaugh[3] of Penn. and myself were the Government Directors of the Company. In that month I retired & declined a reappointment. Mr Harbaugh & Mr Carter were replaced by others[4]—leaving of the old Board, only two Mr Ashmun & Mr Williams.

The Constitution of the Board of Directors is a peculiar one. The Majority of the Directors are members of a great Contracting Company who are constructing the Road at large & excessive profits. The Government Directors can & have proven obstacles to their plans & have directly & indirectly been of great service to that important national work.

The old Government Directors were familiar with all the details & history of the Company & were largely instrumental in forwarding the rapid construction of the Road, and preventing improper & undue demands upon the Treasury.

Mr Harbaugh was one of the most active & intilligent of the Directors. He gave more time & attention to the details, and oftimes visited the work on the Plains, than either of us. We always considered & treated him as more reliable & better acquainted with the work & management than either of the others.

I have therefore considered that his failure to be reappointed, last October, to have been unfortunate, and that the interest of the Government was prejudiced by the appointment of another, who otherwise worthy enough, but was ignorant of the work and of the men who were managing it.

As the Road will probably be completed, during the next year, and at that time the interest of the Government should be pecutiarly watched, and guarded, I cannot too highly recommend and urge upon you, the appointment of Mr Harbaugh as one of the Government Directors for the ensuing year.[5]

By associating him with Mr Ashmun & Mr Williams, I feel assured that the interests of the Government, and of that great National work will be properly protected.

Mr Harbaugh is a gentleman of high standing in the business, social & Rail Road world, but I base my recommendation in addition to thiss upon his peculiar fitness for the position founded upon his familiar knowledge of the history & details of the work and of the men who control the construction and management of the Road.

Charles T. Sherman

ALS, DNA-RG48, Appts. Div., Misc. Lets. Recd.

1. Although both houses of Congress passed a bill chartering a prospective Union Pacific Railroad in June 1862, the company was not actually organized until October 1863. Ames, *Pioneering the Union Pacific*, 11.

2. George Ashmun and Jesse L. Williams. Williams (1807–1886), an Indiana civil engineer, held surveying, locating, and supervisory positions with a number of canal and railroad companies. He was appointed government director of the Union Pacific in July 1864 and resigned in October 1869. *NUC*; *Valley of the Upper Maumee River* (2 vols., Madison, 1889), 2: 61–62; *A Biographical History of Eminent and Self-made Men of the State of Indiana* (2 vols., Cincinnati, 1880), 2: 12th dist., 75–77.

3. Timothy J. Carter (c1813–fl1869), a civil engineer, was apparently associated with an Illinois railroad and lived in New York City during the late 1860s. Harbaugh (c1816–fl1880), of Pittsburgh, was a dealer in wool and hides and a member of Pittsburgh's Board of Viewers for street improvements (1877–80). Appointed in October 1863, Carter and Harbaugh were the first government railroad directors. Roy P. Basler, ed., *The Collected Works of Abraham Lincoln* (8 vols., New Brunswick, 1953), 6: 497, 504–5, 545; Ames, *Pioneering the Union Pacific*, 19; New York City directories (1865–69); Pittsburgh directories (1861–81); 1860 Census, Ill., Sangamon, Springfield, 148; (1870), Penn., Allegheny, Pittsburgh, 22nd Ward, 222.

4. The three new members of the board were James Brooks, Samuel McKee, and James S. Rollins. Ames, *Pioneering the Union Pacific*, 178.

5. Harbaugh was not reappointed. Ibid., 240.

From Samuel J. Tilden
(Confidential)

Utica [N.Y.]   Sept. 4th 1868

My Dear Sir

Coming here to stay over night, after our state convention;[1] I have the pleasure of meeting Genl. McQuade, Gen McMahan and Col O'Beirne.[2] They wish me to ask of you to signify the appropriate leave of absence to enable Genls. Hancock & Grainger to visit Maine[3] in connection with some Ex officers[4] who prepere to do so; and also to intimate to them such encouragement as you may deem proper. We feel the more emboldened to make this request inasmuch as the issues on which the democracy and their conservative allies are making the contest are those which will make you illustrious in history. I may add that Gov. Seymour has been consulted and appreciates the value of the suggestion, and recognizes as we all do the devoted patriotism with which you are dealing with the present situation of our country.[5]

S. J. Tilden

ALS, DLC-JP.

1. The New York state Democratic Convention was held at Albany on September 2 and 3. Delegates chose John T. Hoffman, mayor of New York City, as their gubernatorial nominee, and he was elected in early November. *American Annual Cyclopaedia* (1868), 549–50; *New York Herald*, Sept. 3, 4, 1868.

2. James McQuade, Martin T. McMahon, and James R. O'Beirne. A Utica native, McQuade (1829–1885), a banker and merchant, ended the war as a brevet major general of volunteers. He was probably the McQuade chosen at the convention as presidential elector for the 21st district of New York. Hunt and Brown, *Brigadier Generals*; *New York Herald*, Sept. 4, 1868.

3. Winfield S. Hancock and Gordon Granger. On September 10 Hancock was at a Democratic gathering in Missouri, while Granger appeared with Horatio Seymour in Saratoga. There is no indication either officer received a leave of absence or campaigned for the Democrats in Maine. *National Intelligencer*, Sept. 14, 1868.

4. Sources only mention one prominent military officer speaking on the Democrats' behalf, Gen. Thomas Ewing. *New York Herald*, Sept. 7, 8, 1868.

5. The Maine election, held on September 14, resulted in a sweeping victory for the Republicans and their gubernatorial incumbent, Gen. Joshua L. Chamberlain. *Boston Advertiser*, Sept. 15, 1868; *American Annual Cyclopaedia* (1868), 449–50.

From Albert M. Winn [1]

San Francisco, Sept 4th 1868

Dear Sir,

I am directed to send you a copy of my communication and the resolutions passed by the council last Wednesday night.

Copy

Office of Mechanics State Council

San Francisco   Sept 2d /68

Gentlemen

I have the pleasure of informing you that since our last meeting the news from Washington is encourageing. We requested the President of the United States to consider and change the order of General Schofield as to his construction of the eight hour law.[2] The Telegraph tells us that he laid the subject before the atorney general who renders a decission adverse to the opinons of the Secretary of war, and in accordance with our opinion expressed a few weeks ago.[3]

Mr. Evarts Atorney General is one of the ablest Lawyers in the United States and his decission will secure us the full effect of the eight hour law, leaving the price to be regulated according to the demand and supply for labor at the different localities of public works. I congratulate you upon the result.

Your obt Svt.

A M Winn Pres. M.S.C.

Whereas the following resolutions were unanimously adopted.

Resolved That we return our thanks to the President of the United States, for his prompt action in refering the eight hour Law to the Atorney General.

Resolved That we return our thanks to Mr Evarts Atorney General of the U S for his promt and just decission in favor of the toiling thousands that are engaged on our public works.

Resolved That copies of these resolutions, and the Presidents communication, be sent to the President of the U S, and the Atorney General, and that they be published for the information of the Leagues.

A M Winn Pres. M.S.C.

Wm. D. Delany Secy.[4]

Permit us the pleasure of assureing you, that we admire and approve your independence of character, as shown in the many attempts you have made to save the Constitution and the Country.

California will cast her vote for the Democratic Party. Our only hope is that Seymore may be elected President of the U.S. and that public opinion may come back to its original purity.

A M Winn Pres. M S.C.

ALS, DLC-JP.

1. Winn (1810–1883), a general in the California militia during the 1850s, was a real estate dealer and president of the House Carpenters' Protective Union. San Francisco directories (1851–53, 1867–72); *NUC*.

2. H.R. No. 365. See Rock Island Employees Committee to Johnson, ca. Sept. 1868. Secretary of War John M. Schofield interpreted the law to mean that the workers would be paid proportionally, only receiving pay for eight hours' work and thus taking a pay cut. *Washington Evening Star*, Aug. 8, 1868; *National Intelligencer*, Aug. 8, 1868.

3. The President had referred the question to Attorney General William M. Evarts before August 22. *Washington Evening Star*, Aug. 22, 24, 1868. See Rock Island Employee Committee to Johnson, ca. Sept. 1868.

4. Delany (c1835–f1881) was a ship carpenter. San Francisco directories (1867–81); 1870 Census, Calif., San Francisco, San Francisco, 9th Ward, 42.

From John D. Freeman

Jackson [Miss.]   Sept. 5 1868

The undersigned has the honor to enclose herewith a correspondence between the Commanding General of the 4th Military District and the writer,[1] in reference to the Presidential Election in this state, the result of which is that the General refuses to cause or permit said Election to be held.

The people of Mississippi, therefore, have no remedy for this great wrong to them and to their co states but by an appeal to the General of the Army and to the President. This appeal has been demanded as the President will see by the papers enclosed.[2]

Having stated our reasons for the refusal of the order of the Commanding General in the printed Enclosure, we have but to ask the attention of the President to this appeal, and if the same is not promptly allowed and the decision of the local Commander rebuked by Genl Grant, to ask of the President the exercising his Supreme Constitutional Prerogative on all matters pertaining to the Existence of the Executive Department of the federal government.

The federal Constitution has designedly placed the election of President and Vice President beyond the power of Congress to prevent the same.

If therefore Congress has passed any act or joint resolution designed to have this effect & which might be regarded by the General of the Army as binding on him, the President, as his superior officer, is supposed to have the power to supervise the action of the General in this particular and to cause the Constitutional requirements for the Election of Electors of President and Vice President to be faithfully executed by the local Commanders in the several states affected by such enactments.

Remarking that the people of Mississippi feel a deep solicitude for the speedy solution of this question . . .[3]

John D Freeman
Chm. Dem. Ex Com Missi.

ALS, DLC-JP.

1. Not found enclosed. Freeman's August 15, 1868, letter to Gen. Alvan C. Gillem and Gillem's reply of a week later via a staff officer, were published in newspapers. *Nashville Press and Times*, Sept. 10, 1868.

2. The reply to General Gillem's letter of August 22, 1868, was not found enclosed. Freeman to Gillem, Sept. 4, 1868, Johnson Papers, LC.

3. Johnson saw the papers on October 3, 1868, and seven days later General Orders No. 82 was issued by his direction. This order forbade military commanders to interfere in the presidential election. On October 19 Freeman again urged Gillem to allow the election, but Gillem replied that the order "positively prohibited" him to interfere "in any manner with the election." Ibid.; *Washington Evening Star*, Oct. 13, 1868; *American Annual Cyclopaedia* (1868), 516; *House Ex. Docs.*, 40 Cong., 3 Sess., No. 1, p. 526 (Ser. 1367).

From Robert H. Kerr

Pittsburgh   Sept 5th 1868

Respected Sir.

I have the honor to send you copy of my remarks at the Democratic meeting.[1] Where ever your name is mentioned it is hailed with shouts of applause by the People. I trust we will be successful in redeeming the Country from the grasp of fanatics who hold power to the wrong of the masses.[2]

R H Kerr

ALS, DLC-JP.

1. Copy not found enclosed. Probably Kerr is referring to his speech given at the Democratic Cass Club meeting held at McClure Township. There he issued a strong plea in behalf of support for the national ticket of Seymour and Blair. Kerr also praised Johnson and his administration. *Pittsburgh Post*, Sept. 5, 1868.

2. For a very different view of Kerr's allegiance to Johnson and the party, see Nathaniel P. Sawyer to Johnson, Sept. 1, 1868.

From Robert W. Latham

New York, Sept 5, 1868

My Dear Sir

I have not troubled you since the New York Convention, because I did not see how I could serve you, and because I have had very little heart to engage in political matters sine my disappointment on that occasion.

I saw how easy it would have been to nominate you, if you have been surrounded by your friends in Washington. In all my life I have never felt such an interest in the success of any administration as I have felt in yours. This feeling took possession of me the moment you became President, and from that time I never laboured for one man as I have done for you.

It was as plain to me more than 12 mo. ago as it is now, that the enemies around you in your administration would defeat, if they did not destroy you. I therefore wrote, and got others to write, saw you twice in person, and appealed to you in the strongest terms that I could command, *to put your friends on gaurd.*

I continued this up to the N. York Convention when your friends on the out side, were completely routed by your enemies on the in side. Few or none of your friends had position or power, while your enemies weilded the whole influence of the Govenment against you.

It can be truly said, that no man ever lived who sustained himself as you have done, under the circumstances by which you have been surrounded.

It is perfectly plain what would have been the result, if you had been otherwise situated; sustained and aided by men whose sentiments were in accord with the wise, constitutional and national views promulgated by yourself. Had you been thus sustained and thus supported, your success, and tryumph would have been inevitable; and this day you would stand before the world, as the Greatest, and wisest statesman, the truest and boldest patriot, and the most fearless defender, and champion of constitutional Liberty that has ever lived in any age.

I shall continue to do all I can for you, as long as you remain in office, and when you retire, will let no oppertunity pass to advance your interest. I hope you will get rid of Rollins and all your enemies before your good name is injured by them.

R W Latham

ALS, DLC-JP.

From Walter C. Maloney, Jr.[1]

Key West Florida
September 5th 1868,

The undersigned most respectfully submits to the consideration of the President, the papers herewith enclosed.[2]

Believing that it was the gracious and patriotic purpose of the President to include within the benefits of his proclamation of 4th July last, the individuals within named,[3] and who as will appear by charge 1 exhibited against them (a copy of which is hereto annexed) come within the language of that proclamation as persons "who directly or indirectly participated in the late insurrection or rebellion" and as such are entitled to the benefits of the pardon therein proclaimed, but who as will appear by the opinion of the Judge of the District Court of the United States for the Southern District of Florida[4] are not in the opinion of the said Judge therein embraced and there being no prospect of a session of a Circuit Court in said District for any reasonable length of time to which an appeal might be taken. The undersigned presents to the President the case of these unfortunate men with the hope that if he correctly understands the intention which actuated the President in setting forth his last aforesaid proclamation, that special pardon might be granted in the premises.[5]

The undersigned subscribes himself with true and loyal affection to the government of the United States.

W. C. Maloney Jr
Atty at Law

ALS, DNA-RG204, Pardon Case File B-596, Samuel A. Mudd.

1. Maloney (1839–1894) was a longtime Key West lawyer. He saw duty in the Confederate army (7th Fla. Inf.) during the war. Subsequently, he published a Key West newspaper (1867–72). In the 1880s Maloney was involved with establishment of a trolley system for Key West. David W. Hartman and David Coles, comps., *Biographical Rosters of Florida's Confederate and Union Soldiers, 1861–1865* (6 vols., Wilmington, N.C., 1995), 2: 769; Walter C. Maloney, *A Sketch of the History of Key West, Florida* (Gainesville, 1968 [1876]), xvii, 46.

2. Not found enclosed.

3. According to the file cover sheet, Maloney had written in behalf of Samuel A. Mudd, Samuel Arnold, and Edward Spangler.

4. Thomas J. Boynton (*fl*1870) had served as U.S. district attorney (1861–63) and then as U.S. district judge for the Southern District of Florida (1863–70). Mudd, Arnold, and Spangler had applied to Boynton for a writ of *habeas corpus* and the judge had apparently just issued his opinion in early September. He declared a difference between Mudd's case and *ex parte Milligan* and stated that the three prisoners were not included in Johnson's latest amnesty proclamation. Harold W. Chase et al., comps., *Biographical Dictionary of the Federal Judiciary* (Detroit, 1976), 28; Frederick B. Wiener, "His Name Was Mudd," in John Paul Jones, ed., *Dr. Mudd and the Lincoln Assassination: The Case Reopened* (Conshohocken, Pa., 1995), 149–51.

5. Johnson did pardon Mudd, Arnold, and Spangler just before he left office. See, for example, Pardon of Samuel A. Mudd, February 8, 1869.

From Algernon Sidney Robertson[1]

New Orleans   September 5, 1868

Sir

The difficulty of such of our citizens, who command the respect and confidence of our people in taking the oath of office prescribed by Congress, precludes nearly all of our best men from accepting positions under the Government.

On the 20th July last, Congress having passed an act relieving me, with several others, of my "Political disabilities"[2] I respectfully solicit at your hands an appointment in Louisiana[3] or elsewhere promising that my best energies shall be used in faithfully discharging any duties which may be confided to me.

I was for several years U. S. Marshal of La. under the administration of President Tyler,[4] & refer to the settlement of all my accounts in 1845, on file in the Treasury Department as evidence of the satisfactory manner in which my duties were discharged.

The Petition & accompanying papers sent to Mr. Trumbull,[5] chairman of the Senate Committee, asking Congress to remove my "Political disabilities," will show that in the fall of 1860, altho I was confined to a sick bed & unable to walk, I was carried on a bed Eleven miles to our place of voting in order that I might record my vote *against* secession, so important did I consider *one vote in such an issue.*

But at the same time I must say, that I have never had any sympathy with the Radical majority who have placed us in the Southern States, under such humiliating oppression.

I consider their defeat in Nov. most essential for the restoration of the Union & the equality of the States.

Like every true man in the south, I shall always cherish towards you the most grateful recollections for the bold & patriotic course you have pursued in defence of the Constitution, and hope you may survive long enough to see it appreciated by the whole country. Bad as is our condition, but for your interposition it would have been far worse.

In addition to the endorsement of every Judge of the late Supreme Court of this State which was forwarded to Senator Trumbull, in June last, I respectfully refer you to the Hnbl. Wm. L. Sharkey of Mississippi & Col. James G. Berrett of Washington City, both of whom have known me for twenty five years.

With my ardent wishes that you may triumph over your and the countrys enemies.

A. Sidney Robertson

I should have stated that I held no office under the Confederate Govmt. & took no part whatever in the war.

ALS, DLC-JP.

1. Robertson (*c*1809–*fl*1870) was a steamboat owner, captain, and, later, a planter. John Rowan to William Henry Harrison, Mar. 6, 1841, Lets. of Appl. and Recomm., 1845–53 (M873, Roll 74), RG59, NA; 1860 Census, La., West Baton Rouge, Hermitage, 638; (1870), Assumption, Napoleonville, 4th Ward, 198.

2. Perhaps H.R. Bill No. 1353 relieving various unnamed persons of their political disabilities, which was introduced on July 3, 1868, and signed by the President on July 20. *Congressional Globe*, 40 Cong., 2 Sess., 3724, 4255.

3. Robertson was nominated for the collectorship of internal revenue of the second district of Louisiana on January 12, 1869, but the Senate apparently took no action on the nomination. Ser. 6B, Vol. 4: 204, Johnson Papers, LC.

4. Robertson was marshal just over three years and was removed by President Polk because he was a Whig. Robertson to John M. Clayton, May 23, 1849, and Robertson to Millard Fillmore, Oct. 9, 1851, Lets. of Appl. and Recomm., 1845–53 (M873, Roll 74), RG59, NA.

5. Lyman Trumbull. The papers have not been found.

Notes on the Purchase of Alaska

[ca. September 6, 1868][1]

On the 6th Sept Sundy 1868 Mr Seward and myself rode out some seven or eight miles on the Road leading to Malsboro Md. Near place called old fields, we drove out into a shady grove of oak trees. While there taking some refreshment, in the current of conversation on various subjects, the Secretary asked the question if it had ever occurred to me how few members there were in congress whose actions were entirely above and beyond pecuniary influence. I replied that I had never attempted to reduce it to an accurate calculation, but regretted to confess that there was a much smaller number exempt than at one period of life I had supposed them to be. He then stated you remember that the appropriation of the seven $ million for the payment of Alaska to the Russia Govnt was hung up or brought to a dead lock in the H of Reps. While the appropriation was thus delayed the Russian minister[2] stated to me that John W. Forney stated to him that he needed $30,000 that he had lost $40,000, by a faithless frind and that he wanted the $30,000 in gold. That there was no chance of the appropriation passing the House of Reps without certain influence was brought to bear in its favor. The 30,000 was paid hence the advocacy of the appropriation in the Chronicle. He also stated that $20,000 was paid to R. J. Walker and F. P. Stanton for their services—N P Banks chairman of the committee on foreign relations $8000, and that the incoruptable Thaddeous Stevens received as his "*sop*" the moderate sum of $10,000. All these sums were paid by the Russian minister directly and indirectly to the respective parties to secure appropriation of money the Govmt had stiputed to pay the Russian Govmt in solemn treaty which had been ratified by both Govmts.

Banks and Stevens was understood to be the counsel for a claim against the Russian Govmt for Arms which had been furnished by some of our citizens—known as the Perkins Claim[3]—Hence a fee for their influence in favor of the appropriation &c. Banks was chairman of the Committee on foreign retions.[4]

AN, DLC-JP.

1. This date has been assigned to the document because it appears that Johnson wrote his memorandum soon after the conversation.

2. Baron Edward de Stoeckl.

3. During the Crimean War Benjamin W. Perkins (*c*1824–*c*1863), an American sea captain from Worcester, Massachusetts, provided arms to the Russians for which he claimed he was not paid. He and, eventually, his widow, Anna B. Perkins, attempted for years to get the U.S. government involved in the claims. Congress finally decided negatively in 1886. William A. Dunning, "Paying for Alaska: Some Unfamiliar Incidents in the Process," *PSQ*, 27 (1912): 390–91; 1850 Census, Mass., Worcester, Princeton, 799; Worcester directories (1853–67); *NUC*; *Senate Reports*, 49 Cong., 1 Sess., No. 1304, p. 1 (Ser. 2361).

4. Dunning's article discusses this Johnson document and the circumstances surrounding it in great detail. At least one Stevens biographer maintains that there is no evidence for something so clearly out of character for Stevens. Dunning, "Paying for Alaska," 385–98; Hans L. Trefousse, *Thaddeus Stevens: Nineteenth-Century Egalitarian* (Chapel Hill, 1997), 214, 280.

From Walter M. Smallwood

New Orleans, La.   Sept. 6— 1868

Sir:

A careful inquiry has convinced me that there is imminent danger of a riot in this city at almost any moment. All intelligent citizens agree with me in this opinion. The Radical party seem determined to carry out their whole programme at every hazzard, even to legislating our people out of all such avocations as auctioneers, forbidding all persons except such as may be named by the Governor from following that and kindred callings. Mixed schools, enforced by fines against such as refuse to send their children to such schools, and other legislation equally obnoxious, leaves but little for the white people here to contend for except their honor as men. The colored people have been thoroughly educated up to the fearful issue of an "irrespressable conflict" of races. On all occasions both white and black Radicals openly proclaim black supremacy and their determination to maintain and perpetuate that supremacy by legislation and if necessary by an open and exterminating war against the white people. Mr. President, this state of case does not admit of any argument respecting results. It is here only what it would be at the North under similar circumstances—the whites will not be put down without a struggle. Even before our late election I entertained the opinion that the adoption of the Black & Tan Constitution would seal the fate of the colored man. In the interest of the general peace and of the colored man, I urged that class to cast their lot with the whites, vote the constitution down, and having done that they would then have a well grounded claim upon the white people for such legislation as would promote the interest of the colored race, and I firmly believe the claim would have been honored to the extent of all that true wisdom and statesmanship would dictate.

On next Saturday night, by common consent, will come a crisis in our affairs here. Scarcely a demonstration has been made by the Radical negroes, which has not been followed by outrages instigated by the irresponsible white men that lead them, from pillaging stores to murder. On the day referred to it is proposed to fill the city with a large importation of negroes from the country, for whom no provision can or will be made for food or shelter. I am told that Gov. Warmouth has said there will be not less than 10,000 such brought here. No sufficient provision can be made to keep so large an assemblage of ignorant and excited men quiet, especially when acting un-

der the promptings of hunger and poverty. With respect to that meeting the most intense anxiety is felt, for we all know that the entire
city is but a magazine which the lighting of a match may inflame.[1]
Under these circumstances I think Gen Rousseau ought to be here.
His simple presence in the city will do more to preserve order than
any other one thing within the compass of your authority.

W. M. Smallwood

ALS, DLC-JP.
    1. The Radicals had scheduled a torchlight parade for Saturday night September 12. At the
request of Col. Edward Hatch, superintendent of the Louisiana Freedmen's Bureau, Secretary
of War John M. Schofield ordered Gen. Robert C. Buchanan, commanding in New Orleans,
to provide troops to protect the marchers. Buchanan used seven companies of troops along the
parade route to guard property from the marchers. The more than 6,500 blacks and whites
who participated were not involved in any violence or damaging of property. Dawson, *Army
Generals and Reconstruction*, 83.

From Horace H. Day[1]

New York   Sept. 7 1868.
    I have just finished reading for the third time your financial views
published today in our Truly democratic paper of this city.[2] I note in
it some entirely new suggestions—strong arguments—points—which
have not been before presented for public consideration. I have been
writing publishing and talking on this financial subject a long time
aided by the wise ones with whom I hold council.
    Over Six months ago I pressed repeatedly upon your frinds Philo
Duffy, Richard S Spofford Mr Wells of Detroit[3] & Two of the Editors of the National Inteligencer[4] to get Andrew Johnson to come
out in favor of the people on this financial question well-knowing
that It would become the controlling issue. I failed to effect what I
so much desired yet kept working—and when the critical moment
arrived—(The Republican party having adopted a bond holders platform)—and the Democratic Nat Convention was coming off I gathered through the machinry of the Labor Union a great power into
our hands and hurled it against the Convention to such extent as to
compel the adoption of the financal platform it has—and altho not a
well arranged one it is in the direction of the Truly Wise and philosophical position of the Labor Union Platform or Theory.[5]
    If the intentions wishes, and efforts of the Belmonts[6] of Wall St,
had then and there prevailed the great present strength of the Demo-

cratic party to which you have added so much by your published views today would have given no hope for the South—for the National Union—or for the continu of a Democratic Republican Govemnt in North America—for we should have had a repetition of the Bond holders platform such as Chicago put forth with a necessary consequence Anarchy & National Ruin.

The act of President Johnson in arresting at the last hour of the Session that monstrous attempt at Wholesale Robery, in the funding Bill[7] and his present noble stand on this question as today published will become historical events of larger significance in the future.

The financal plank in the present Democratic platform was made under the pressure brough by Pendleton[8] which would have been swept aside but for a greater pressure brought in at the right moment by us who held the ballance and evidence the work of unskilled hands and as it stands is weak. Fair men of all parties are afraid—while it suits only those who would repudiate.

Had the resolution as drawn by S. F. Cary & myself[9] and passed in the Labor Union Council have been adopted—Greely[10] & Co would have been disarmed of argument. I am at work to remedy this and have assurance it will be done in the right quarters. *If it is not the great party of the people will* NOT *win the Election.*

A low rate of Interest—cheap money—low rate for the use of money—to be established by law of Congress to apply only upon its own obligation—will do more to restore & save the nation than all other Legislation—3 pct. without Taxation would restore old rates for the use of money, less the fair amount it should bear of Taxation equal about 4 1/2 pr cent. This would bring back old prices and it matters not whether governmt stamps paper or coin, it is the goveremt Stamp which makes it money.

This would do more to restore to the South its just relation than has all the attempts heretofore made. The present financial System is a greater curse—a greater load on the back of the South than would be a standing army of 200,000 men to be supported by the South itself.

The South can never recover its power—its propper relation to the Govermnt—till we get the rate of Interest fixed at 4 1/2 pct with Taxation equal to other property or 3 pct Interest without taxation. This would be the greatest boon to give the south. It would do more to break the back bone of the infamous party of Congress than any one thing.

The payment of the 5.20 in greenbacks then fund them as proposed by Hon S. F. Cary's bill[11]—is the true way: to bring this about.

England from 1823 to 1861 increased her wealth at the avrage rate of only 2 pct per annum. For 80 years past the U.S. has increased hers at the average rate of 3 1/3 pct. England paying only 2 pct can never pay the principal of her Debt—has not—and cannot reduce it. With us now the RATE OF INTEREST is every thing—of importance.

Horace H. Day

ALS, DLC-JP.

1. An inventor, manufacturer, and pioneer in the processing of rubber, Day (1813–1878) spent years defending his patents against alleged infringements by Charles Goodyear. After the courts backed Goodyear's claim to the vulcanization process in the mid-1850s, Day spent the next two decades constructing a "power canal" at Niagara Falls and experimenting with compressed air power generators. *DAB*.

2. Not found.

3. Philo Durfee and William P. Wells.

4. Probably John F. Coyle and Chauncey H. Snow.

5. Enclosed was an extract from the National Labor Union Platform of Principles, which claimed that the government's fiscal policies were oppressing the working classes. Among the goals expressed were the taxation of government bonds and the exclusive use of legal tender notes as national currency. The National Democratic Platform also called for "one currency," for the repayment of the national debt with the "lawful money of the United States," and "equal taxation" of all property, including bonds. See also the *National Intelligencer*, Aug. 29, 1868.

6. August Belmont, the national chairman of the Democratic Party and a hard money proponent, opposed the so-called Ohio (or Pendleton) Plan, which among other things called for repayment of the debt in greenbacks. Jerome Mushkat, *The Reconstruction of the New York Democracy, 1861–1874* (Rutherford, N.J., 1981), 121, 136; Charles H. Coleman, *The Election of 1868: The Democratic Effort to Regain Control* (New York, 1933), 39–40, 204.

7. The Funding Bill provided for the sale of bonds and the reappropriation of import duties to repay the national debt. Congress passed the bill on July 27, 1868, the last day of the session, but Johnson pocket-vetoed it. *Congressional Globe*, 40 Cong., 2 Sess., p. 4517, Appendix, pp. 483–84. See also Alexander Campbell to Johnson, July 20, 1868, *Johnson Papers*, 14: 385–86.

8. George H. Pendleton of Ohio.

9. Samuel F. Cary spoke at the National Labor Union meeting held in New York on July 3, 1868. Resolutions included payment for the debt by legal-tender notes, equal taxation of property, a termination of corporate land grants, and support for an eight hour day. *New York Times*, July 4, 1868.

10. Horace Greeley.

11. Cary proposed two bills related to repayment of the national debt, one on January 27, and one on May 25, 1868. Apparently neither made any headway. *Congressional Globe*, 40 Cong., 2 Sess., pp. 779, 2571, 3885.

From Edward H. East

Nashville   Sept 7th 1868

Dear Sir

I have the honor to introduce to you the bearer of this Mr E. Levy[1] of this city. I wish particularly to recomend him for the appointment of collector for the Territory of Alaska.[2] He is a Russian by birth and understands the language, and besides a gentleman of high standing, and accomplishments, strict honesty and integrity. I am satisfied will make the gov't an efficient and worthy officer and will discharge faithfully any trust which may be committed to him.

I will consider it as a personele favor if you will give Mr Levy the nomination and if one has already been made for that position give him some other appointment corresponding his ability and standing.

Edward H. East

ALS, DNA-RG59, Lets. of Appl. and Recomm., 1861–69 (M650, Roll 29), E. Levy.

1. Levy was a Nashville merchant who became president of a Jewish anti-Grant club in that city during the summer of 1868. Fedora S. Frank, *Beginnings on Market Street* (Nashville, 1976), 67–68; John C. Burch to Johnson, Sept. 7, 1868, Lets. of Appl. and Recomm., 1861–69 (M650, Roll 29), E. Levy, RG59, NA. For Jewish opposition to Grant see Moritz Niedner to Johnson, June 12, 1868, *Johnson Papers*, 14: 205–6.

2. There is no evidence that Johnson nominated Levy for any post in late 1868 or early 1869.

From Laura C. Holloway

34 East 19th St.
New York   Sept 7th 1868

My Friend,

Your kindness to me heretofore is my excuse for taking the liberty of writing to you now.

On my return home I immediately presented your letter to Mr Smythe[1] and a few days since he gave my Father a position as Store Keeper with a salary of $1400. The duties of the office requiring the closest attention from *Sunrise* till after dark. The position was declined on account of the small pay and labor. My motive in writing is not to complain of Mr Smythe but to assure you that we all feel deeply grateful to you for your exertions in our behalf. Pa is growing old and there are but few positions he could hold, but there are several offices in the Custom House such as Inspector Weigher &c that are more *exalted*, less laborious and better pay that Pa could hold with credit to himself and justice to the government. I renew my request for any positions you may deem proper to bestow. He is out of buisness, and it is my plain duty to do my best to aid him.

It is right that I should thank you, and it makes me happy to tell you how grateful I am for every kind word and thought you have ever given me. There is ever with me an abiding sense of your friendly feelings and it encourages me to tell you my troubles and ask you to assist me.

Should you honor me with a reply your thoughtfulness will be appreciated. I write without the knowledge or consent of any one and if there is any impropriety I am alone responsible.

But knowing you entertain for me most friendly feelings . . .[2]

Laura C. Holloway.

ALS, DLC-JP.

1. New York customs collector Henry A. Smythe had already informed Johnson that he had received the President's recommendation for Holloway's father, Samuel J. Carter. See Henry A. Smythe to Johnson, Aug. 22, 1868, *Johnson Papers*, 14: 536.

2. As late as the end of January 1869 Johnson was still interceding on Carter's behalf. There is no evidence Carter received another position. William G. Moore to Carter, Jan. 29, 1869; Moore to Smythe, Jan. 29, 1869, Johnson Papers, LC.

From John W. Sharp[1]

Selma   Johnston Co [N.C.]   Septr 7— 1868.

Dear Sir,

W W. Holden appointed Colonels all over this State a few days ago consisting of men wholy irresponsible and to day I learn that they received their *Commissions*.[2] He evidently intends to organise a police force or Malitia throughout the state under his own Control and for the purpose of intimidating and keeping away from the Polls the respectable and peacible white men throughout the State whom he well knows are opposed to his Career. Therefore in Veiw of your Construction of the laws under the *Constitution*, which is evidently correct, and the duty the Goverment owes to a peacible law abiding people, we do most earnestly request and respectfully ask that prompt and Efficient Measures be at once taken to surpress and put down such unwarrantable and unlawful acts—and that the good people of N C now in peace be permitted to remain so. Hoping that something for our relief may be done in the premises . . .

J W. Sharp

ALS, DLC-JP.

1. Sharp (*c*1823–*fl*1870) was a farmer, merchant, and lawyer. During the 1868 presidential campaign, Sharp served as head of Selma's Seymour and Blair Club. 1870 Census, N.C., Johnston, Selma Twp., 16; *Raleigh Sentinel*, Sept. 9, 1868.

2. In mid-August 1868, at Holden's request, the North Carolina legislature passed a law, whereby all male citizens between twenty-one and forty were liable for service in the militia, unless they were exempted by a physician or paid an annual payment of two dollars. By early September the governor had appointed an adjutant general, major generals of the eastern, middle, and western divisions, and colonels for each of the eighty-nine counties. However, units were actually activated in only two counties, Halifax and Robeson. By mid-October Holden suspended his militia order. Horace W. Raper, *William W. Holden: North Carolina's Political Enigma* (Chapel Hill, 1985), 106–7; William C. Harris, *William Woods Holden: Firebrand of North Carolina Politics* (Baton Rouge, 1987), 249–51; *Raleigh Sentinel*, Aug. 29, Sept. 4, 1868; *Washington Evening Star*, Oct. 19, 1868.

From James B. Bingham

Memphis, Tenn., Sept. 8. 1866[1868][1]

My Dear Sir—

Having understood that under a late Treaty between the United States and Mexico,[2] commissioners would be appointed to settle claims between the two Governments, the friends of *Col. Robertson Topp* have urged him to apply for the appointment of Commissioner on the part of the United States.[3]

Col. Topp is not a mere office seeker. He has resided here thirty seven years. He has been urged, again and again, by his numerous friends, to run for office, which he could at any time have obtained; but, for twenty-five years, he has persistently refused. He only consents now because his large fortune has passed out of his hands, in consequence of the late revolution, which at all times he steadily opposed. His opposition to Secession brought upon him heavy losses. By Beauregard's order,[4] for debt due him, he with others was forced to take large sums of Confederate Money, which, as he had no confidence in it, he invested in Cotton. Some twenty-five hundred bales, worth half a million of dollars, was destroyed by the rebels with peculiar pleasure, because he had opposed Secession. With the war, his large planting interest, worth $400,000, was likewise destroyed. He is now reduced to poverty. He is qualified, by high talents, to fill any office whatever. I write to urge his appointment. I was sorry when I learned that you had promised the Mexican Mission to another,[5] before he became a candidate, and therefore could not appoint him. I hope it will be in your power to give him this office, and that you will do so. He has firmly, steadily and persistently sustained you in your noble struggle to uphold the Constitution and the liberties of the people, and that too when many pretended friends had deserted you. At the late Convention in New

York, although not a delegate, he exerted his influence to secure your nomination, and he will sustain you to the end, whether you appoint him or not. On all questions he makes up his mind, and rarely changes, come what will, whether popular or unpopular.

Late unwise statements of Gen. Forrest to the correspondent of the Cincinnati *Commercial*[6] have caused much apprehension here, lest their influence in the Northern States may injuriously affect our friends. Articles have appeared in both the *Avalanche* and *Bulletin* advocating the annexation of Mexico and the Central American States.[7] The proposition meets with universal approbation in this section. There may be difficulties in the way which we do not understand, but, if agreeable, your friends here would be pleased to see you take hold of this great measure and push it through, and thereby close your illustrious administration with the greatest measure of the age. The Mexican nation cannot subsist of themselves. They have not the requisite virtue and intelligence to govern themselves. By annexing Mexico to the United States we should benefit its people, as well as ourselves, to an incalculable degree, and not ourselves alone, but all the commercial nations of the world besides.

I have some hope yet that as Patterson has been *rejected* as one of the Supervisors,[8] and as I had the endorsement of Hon. D. A. Nunn, for the position, that the appointment which I solicited may yet be conferred upon me.[9] If however, that is not possible, perhaps *you* may have need of a good man in some other capacity.

Wishing you the greatest success, with all my heart . . .

J. B. Bingham

ALS, DLC-JP.

1. Although Bingham clearly wrote 1866 as the date, internal evidence confirms that the correct date is actually 1868.

2. On July 4, 1868, Mexico and the United States signed an agreement to establish a claims commission that would adjust the claims of citizens from either country for the period since 1848. Frederick S. Dunn, *The Diplomatic Protection of Americans in Mexico* (New York, 1971 [1933]), 92–93.

3. For letters in support of Topp for appointment as commissioner see Lets. of Appl. and Recomm., 1861–69 (M650, Roll 49), Robertson Topp, RG59, NA. According to one source, Topp's application as commissioner was referred to the secretary of state on September 23. There is no evidence, however, that Topp received the nomination. Ser. 6A, Vol. E: 262, Johnson Papers, LC.

4. Perhaps Bingham refers here to P.G.T. Beauregard's order in May 1862 to force all persons to accept Confederate money in all business transactions or else risk arrest. Likewise all banks were compelled to accept Confederate money. *Memphis Appeal*, May 11, 1862.

5. William S. Rosecrans. See *Senate Ex. Proceedings*, 16: 363–64, 385. See William S. Hillyer

to Johnson, June 23, 1868, and Rosecrans to Johnson, Aug. 5, 1868, *Johnson Papers*, 14: 253–54, 481–82.

6. Nathan Bedford Forrest's statements to the *Cincinnati Commercial* were reprinted in the *Nashville Press and Times*, Sept. 3, 1868. In his somewhat rambling remarks Forrest talked about the Klan, even giving estimates of the numbers of followers, about black suffrage which he opposed, and about General Grant. Although Forrest opposed Grant's election, he believed that Grant would make an effective president.

7. We have been unable to examine extant issues of either the *Memphis Avalanche* or the *Memphis Bulletin* that might have had articles about the Mexican and Central American annexation.

8. Robert F. Patterson. See Tomeny to Johnson, Aug. 8, 1868, *Johnson Papers*, 14: 490–91.

9. See Bingham to Johnson, Mar. 7, 1868, ibid., 13: 615; Bingham to Johnson, May 23, 1868, ibid, 14: 107.

From John Heart
(Private)

Columbia [S.C.], September 8, 1868.

Dear Sir:

In transmitting to you the accompanying paper[1] I avail myself of the opportunity to respectfully call your attention to the anomalous and somewhat embarrassing position of the Governor.[2] Denounced by the extremists of one party as a "copperhead," and by those of the other as a "carpetbagger," he has pursued a wise and liberal policy in his administration of affairs, looking only to the establishment and enforcement of the laws, the protection of the life, liberty and property of every citizen, and the development of the material resources of the State. That his efforts have not been altogether unsuccessful or unappreciated may be learned from the fact that he has not only the confidence of the moderate men of his own party, but nearly if not all the Democratic members of the Legislature. These gentlemen are with but one exception (Horry county) from the upper districts of the State, between which and the Democracy of the lower portion of the State, as you are aware, there has always been more or less of antagonism. They are conservative in their views, and their moderation is exemplified in the fact that most of them are largely indebted to colored voters for their election. The entire press of the State takes its cue from the newspapers at Charleston, led by the *Mercury*, which, true to its rule or ruin antecedents, advocates and urges the most extreme and violent policy. But this while responded to, and sometimes acted on, by the thoughtless and designing, is disapproved and discountenanced by a large portion of the moderate men of the party, and it is by the aid of these that the restoration and renovation of the State is to be accomplished. Much of the prevailing excitement is attributable to the old party leaders—the Bourbons of the State, who learn nothing and forget nothing—whose struggles are as much for personal position as on party account. But even if their party should be successful, there is much doubt whether they will be permitted to retain a position in which they have shown themselves signally incompetent, and in which their policy and counsels were so disastrous to the State and the Union.

I have presumed upon our long acquaintaince and friendship to intrude thus much upon your time and attention to place you in possession of the policy of Gov. Scott and the obstacles by which he is surrounded. My position with him enables me to speak authoritatively on the subject, and you may be assured I would not retain it a moment had I not full faith in his sincerity and patriotism.

Jno. Heart

ALS, DLC-JP.
   1. Not found.
   2. Robert K. Scott.

From John S. Ward[1]
(Private)

Nashville, Tenn., Sept 8 1868.

My Dear Sir

As the interests of minors are involved in the case to which I wish to call your attention, I will refresh your memory in regard to it by referring to a conversation you once had with Hon Ed East about it.

The late Judge John S Brien sued me as the administrator of Ben. C Robertson decd for a $10,000 fee, for his services in procuring Mr Robertson's release from Prison and the remittal of the fine imposed by the Court Martial.[2] The papers were sent to Washington by Judge B. and Mr East says that at one time when you were on the eve of leaving for Washington he (Mr East) requested you to see Mr Lincoln and use your influence with him in having Mr Robertson released. This request was complied with by you and Mr East says that it was through your representation of the case that Mr R. was released, which fact he learned from a conversation with you on your return. Judge B. did his duty in the premises and has been paid $1000, which we think is enough. Interrogations will be forwarded to you to day touching this matter. I hope you will answer them immediately as the case will come up for trial in two weeks. I regret to trouble you with such matters, but duty requires that I should use diligence to prevent a monstrous fraud.

Hoping to hear from you soon ...

John S Ward

ALS, DLC-JP.

1. Ward (c1835–fl1892) became editor of the *Ladies Pearl* in the spring of 1868, a post he held for several years. Before the war he had been associated with the *Banner of Peace*, a magazine owned and edited by the Rev. William E. Ward. 1870 Census, Tenn., Davidson, Nashville, 10th Ward, 79; Nashville directories (1859–77); *Nashville Union and Dispatch*, Apr. 19, 1868; John Shirley Ward, "Did the Federals Fight Against Superior Numbers?" *SHSP*, 20 (1892): 238.

2. See Petition of F. M. Carter, July 16, 1863, *Johnson Papers*, 6: 293.

From Michael Burns

Nashville   Sept 9" 1868

Sir

A Radical delegation left here for Washington[1] in order to confer with you in reference to Stationing United State troops in Tennessee. These men I believe without Exception are bitter opponents of yours and if they can they will misrepresent you.

No troops are wanted in the state but If troops are to be Sent on us for Mercy Sake Send united states troops. I fear the result of the Militia being called out. The State is not able to pay them and our Security will go down; the peace of the state is above money. If troops are to be Sent U S. will preserve the peace best.[2]

M. Burns

ALS, DLC-JP.

1. The legislative delegation included William H. Wisener, Thomas A. Hamilton, and James H. Agee. See Edmund Cooper to Johnson, Sept. 1, 1868.

2. See William H. Wisener, Sr., et al. to Johnson, Sept. 11, 1868.

From John W. Leftwich

Memphis, Tenn., Sept 9th 1868

Sir

I have just returned from a visit through the counties of this district and take the liberty of saying I have never seen more reliable evidences of not only a desire for peace but I may say a determination on the part of the people to have it at any cost.

There may be here and there—not one in a hundred—individuals who having all to gain & *nothing* to lose by a revolution would like to see it inaugurated but the masses of the people are just the reverse. After a year of unprecedented privation and hardship they have been blessed with abundant crops the prices for which promises to be satisfactory and remunerative and their hearts are now set on a peaceable enjoyment of the fruits of their labor. The negroes are not less happy and hopeful than the whites and if appearances are not unusually deceptive they are properly estimating radical influence and are determined to be influenced by them no longer. Barbecues which are participated in by both whites and blacks are very prevalent and the utmost good feeling prevails between the races.

Mr Nunn[1] the Radical Candidate for Congress has just said to a reliable gentleman hitherto and stil recognised as a radical that he will certainly have the militia here before the election and that without them in such counties as Madison where there are many negroes and no white Radicals to control them he would be left almost without a vote. There is a company of regular Troops at Somerville and though they have been there many months the commanding officer[2] says no necessity has ever existed for their presence and that they are well received and politely treated by the entire community.

Such would be the case with Federal Troops throughout this end of the state but a militia sent upon the evident purpose of creating disturbance would in my opinion accomplish their end.

Jno W Leftwich

ALS, DLC-JP.
  1. David A. Nunn.
  2. Not identified.

From John M. Binckley

Washington   Sep. 10th 1868

Mr. President.

I hasten to submit the following report:

The subjoined order[1] of your Excellency reached me on the day of its date.

Executive Mansion
Washington, Aug. 25th 1868

Sir,

You will at once proceed to the City of Brooklyn, New York, and examine certain evidence said to be in possession of Assessor Wellwood,[2] and report whether, in your opinion, the same substantially implicates, in violations of law, any officer of the internal revenue service.

Respectfully yours,
Andrew Johnson.

John M. Binckley Esq.
Solicitor Internal Revenue Bureau
Washington, D.C.

Accordingly, I proceeded at once to New York, and appointed an interview with Assessor Wellwood to whom I showed this order. I was strongly impressed with that gentleman's love of justice, but as it became manifest that he was extremely apprehensive of falling into some position of indelicacy, I thought it reasonable to afford him opportunity and time, to form for himself such an opinion of my object as would relieve him from what I afterwards learned to regard as an excusable hesitation. I disclaimed any motive but a strictly official one, and cordially adopted his own expression under that head. Yet I was much surprised to discern, in the conversations I had with several persons, including Mr Wellwood, that it was not considered credible that any attempt would be made in good faith to enforce the penal sanctions of the revenue laws in New York irrespectively of persons or parties. Mr. Wellwood pointed out a man formerly a revenue inspector named McHenry[3] as likely to be conversant with the documents and facts which had engaged our conference. Treating this suggestion as a substantial compliance with my demand upon Mr. Wellwood in person, I sent for McHenry. His personal knowledge included several important facts implicating Revenue officials of the highest grade, but not indicating that general prevalence of corruption of which I shall speak hereafter. Meantime, my presence in the city became known, and was popularly, but as you know, erroneously taken to be for the purpose of general investigation with the sole object of collecting plausible data upon which to predicate a suspension of Mr. Commissioner Rollins.

Under this mistaken hypothesis, I was called upon by large numbers of persons, some accredited, some total strangers, but mostly of a mercenary and unprincipled class, who were desirous of employment in the work of detecting crime. I need not say that the very different character of my mission left me at liberty wholly to discountenance all such persons; and I deemed it admissible to refuse to hear revelations they would propose to make as an earnest of the value of their services. What amount of point-blank evidence may possibly have been thus rejected, I have, of course, no means of reckoning.

But another class of persons approached me with a different object. They were deeply impressed with a wide-spread and apparently irremediable demoralization in the revenue service, and had come to ascertain what prospect existed of a reform. Without exception, they were discouraged upon ascertaining by my frank declarations that there was nothing extraordinary in my powers, and that I held myself exonerated, on this occasion, from noticing any criminal transactions beyond such as were, at least, in some degree, cognate to the matters supposed to be in Mr. Wellwood's reach. From every direction came the substance of this strong expression: "Let it once appear by demonstration that the government will really make a bold and honest attack on the whiskey ring, and every safe in the city will furnish documentary evidence."

According to the best sagacity I could command, these expressions came from persons having access to, or control of proof. Frequently papers were described, and facts stated, reserving indicative particulars. In some instances, the coincidence of numerous statements enabled me to determine the actual existence, and the custody of the paper, and on a pledge of honor to return it on the spot, to have it exhibited for my inspection. In a word, through those sources of knowledge on human affairs which transcend all mere legal verification, I came to share to some extent, the melancholy but universal opinion of all classes in New York who are acquainted with internal revenue business, that it has been for years substantially a business of malversation among the higher grades of officials.

This astonishing conclusion is undoubtedly the actual belief of all whose opportunities have enabled them to form a correct opinion. It is needless to remark that with my very recent introduction to Revenue business, those who were better informed by experience were not more incredulous of a real purpose of public duty, than I was of their narratives of crime. I exhorted them to make their communications to the proper officers, and insist upon public justice. They replied with instances of private ruin arising from similar attempts.

I reproached their timidity, and they ridiculed my simplicity. Every where the same sentiment was uppermost—"I cannot risk it—if the government were able to protect me, I would speak out. A thousand investigations of revenue fraud have been made, but always for the purpose, or at least with the effect, of better concealing and promoting bribery and corruption—this will end the same way." &c &c. Such a sentiment seems to be unaccountable upon any hypothesis but the sad one that the combinations of politicians, officials, tradesmen, and speculators, that go under the name of the "whiskey ring" actually exert the power to disable the zeal of the local prosecuting officers and other agents of criminal justice.

Upon the whole, I realized that in pursuing a very restricted inquiry, I had fallen upon startling discoveries that I did not know what to do with. To submit them to the President for disposition and action according to the usual course of business, would be simply putting them back where I found them. On the other Hand, it was manifest to my best judgment that the general desire of honest citizens for an earnest of real work would be easily kindled into active support, and that as soon as a real effort should be publicly recognized, evidence without end would come forward; the Press would unanimously sustain a reform, partisanship would no longer be imputed, and the dignity and power of the law would revive.

This was abundantly confirmed by the visible commotion among the suspected classes, in consequence of the report that an official was engaged in investigating frauds. But who was to take the first step? No officer of the government could have been called upon to take that great responsibility who might not have pertinently asked me "Why do you not do it yourself? You are a revenue official, and the only one who, by designation, is a law officer: if you shrink from attacking the 'whiskey ring' under circumstances which implicate the heads of your office, and which show the futility of relying upon the District Attorney,[4] what other official is obliged to do it?" I considered this matter anxiously, and finding no worthier motive for resigning my office than a fear of consequences of right action in it, I resolved to do what I could to break the spell of domination which has kept the truth out of court for years in New York.

My plan was simple—to collect evidence enough to justify the prospect of commitment under ordinary circumstances, trusting that as it actually entered the record and the public prints, the corrupt and desperate resorts of the so-called ring to suppress and discredit it would be frustrated by a great quantity of point blank evidence to be encouraged, by the resolute good faith of the proceeding, to come forward in the hands of honorable and notable witnesses. A combination of just men for their own vindication against this abominable organization of crime would destroy its fearful power in a week. I then took the step, by instituting proceedings before a United States Commissioner[5] arresting two of the accused,[6] and entering upon their examination. I had engaged, to come in at a suitable moment, the assistance of an untarnished practical lawyer,[7] whose unavoidable failure considerably disconcerted me. As I had not, at that time, reasonable grounds, for publicly accusing the District Attorney, I invited him to impart the authority of his office to the prosecution. To avoid the indecency of a more direct understanding we acted in a tacit relation of mere formal participation in the case on his part, of actual control on mine. Subsequently, evidence which I could not affect to ignore, rendered it extremely irksome to proceed together. Circumstances affecting the conduct of the case *out* of court, were rendering it a pertinent question for me which side of the issue he was prosecuting *in* court. The purity of the proceeding required an immediate end to his connexion with the matter. The hour was coming for a full development of the magnitude of the case, and the number of defendants, to include the District Attorney himself.[8] There was urgent use for able and numerous Counsel, and the public were about to be astonished by a proof that the government had made a real and resolute attack upon the defiant and powerful enginery of corruption and intimidation, notwithstanding the most unprincipled and shameless practises had been employed with the countenance of the District Attorney against the effort, through mercenary and degraded men appearing as counsel. It was at this stage that I called upon the Honorable Secretary of the Treasury[9] for the necessary authority to enter systematically upon the work. I had been assured that he had publicly and strongly discountenanced my proceedings[10] but with proper respect for that gentleman, as he could have no other opinion of them than what could arise in total ignorance of my grounds of action, which were known to no one but myself, I could not suppose he would run the risk of allying the Government with the so-called "whiskey ring." Nevertheless, with whatever regret he may now realize it, that is the practical effect of his action in the premises, and it is my duty to express that opinion.

Finally, in court yesterday morning I was surprised by a dispatch which on some representations not made known at the time, the District Attorney had procured from Mr. Assistant Attorney General Ashton,[11] which was promptly, and not erroneously, recognized as an authoritative repudiation of the prosecution by the United States; except as far as Mr. Courtney might be pleased, to continue it against his own particeps criminis.[12] The court, however, at my instance, adjourned the proceeding till this day week, when it will be in order for further hearing. My object in asking this postponemnt, (granted against the wishes of counsel on both sides, as formally opposed) was less for the purpose of reappearing myself, than because it was my duty to do what I could to contravene a sham prosecution in the name of the United States by motion in court.

The govenmnt having suppressed the proceedings instituted by me as a citizen and law officer, it would be incumbent upon me, if I could, to stand corrected before my superiors and my country. This I cannot do because I believe I was right and consequently, nothing remains for me but to retire from the govenmnt in favor of some person in better harmony with the preferred methods of such business as this. The Honorable Secretary has received my resignation.[13]

John M. Binckley
Solicitor of Internal Revenue

ALS, DNA-RG60, Office of Atty. Gen., Lets. Recd., President.

1. See also Johnson to Binckley, Aug. 25, 1868, *Johnson Papers*, 14: 540.

2. Thomas Welwood. See also Binckley to Johnson, Sept. 2, 1868.

3. John D. McHenry (*c*1842–*fl*1872) was currently in the fancy goods business, and later worked as a carpenter. On August 29 McHenry swore in an affidavit that Daniel Murray, a New York distiller, claimed to have bribed revenue collector Thomas E. Smith and revenue commissioner Edward A. Rollins. After the dismissal of that case in October, McHenry was indicted on perjury charges, convicted, and sentenced to five years' imprisonment. It does not appear he served his sentence. New York City directories (1867–72); *New York Herald*, Sept. 8, 1868; *New York Tribune*, Sept. 3, 1869; *New York Times*, July 1, 2, 1869. See also Binckley to Johnson, Oct. 7, 1868.

4. Samuel G. Courtney, the district attorney for the southern district of New York.

5. Joseph Gutman, Jr. (*c*1835–1889), who had been appointed commissioner by Abraham Lincoln, later gained reknown as a patent lawyer. *New York Tribune*, Oct. 16, 1889.

6. Thomas E. Smith and Daniel Murray. Murray (*fl*1869), a marble dealer, was also part owner of a New York City distillery. *National Intelligencer*, Sept. 9, 1868; New York City directories (1867–69).

7. Not identified.

8. For Courtney's rebuttal, as well as a scathing critique of Binckley's investigation, see Courtney to Johnson, Oct. 1, 1868.

9. Hugh McCulloch.

10. On September 2 the *Washington Evening Star* reported that McCulloch was upset over rumors that an arrest warrant had been issued for Edward Rollins. However, no public statements directly concerning Binckley's investigation have been found.

11. J. Hubley Ashton (*c*1836–1907), assistant attorney general since July 1868, resigned in 1869. A one-time professor of law at Georgetown University, Ashton was also a founding

member of the American Bar Association. *Senate Ex. Proceedings*, Vol. 16: 345, 369; Vol. 17: 286, 352; *New York Times*, Mar. 16, 1907.

12. Courtney had asked to be relieved, claiming he could not cooperate with Binckley. Ashton refused Courtney's request, assured him that he was chief prosecutor, and that Binckley had no authority, but was there only at Courtney's "sufferance." Binckley withdrew temporarily, but returned to New York in a supervisory capacity following another order by Johnson. *New York Tribune*, Sept. 10, 1868; *Washington Evening Star*, Sept. 10, 1868; Beale, *Welles Diary*, 3: 435. See Johnson to Binckley, Sept. 19, 1868.

13. In a September 8 letter Binckley demanded that McCulloch either support his efforts with political and financial backing or accept his resignation. Following the appointment of a special counsel and further prompting by Johnson, Binckley withdrew his resignation and returned to the investigation. Binckley to McCulloch, Sept. 8, 23, 1868, Johnson Papers, LC. See also McCulloch to Johnson, Sept. 16, 1868, and Johnson to Binckley, Sept. 19, 1868.

From Jacob J. Noah[1]
Private

Washington D.C.   Sept 10" 1868

Have conversed with the delegation ('desultory') but sufficient to ascertain that the programme is to make *you responsible for the calling out of the militia, and the passage of the bill through the Senate*. They have prepared an address of about eight pages, setting out the grievances of the Unionists and outrages of the KuKlux.

Wisener is conservative and evidently non-commital—Agee fair, but Hamilton *violent*.[2] I am of opinion that they fancy you *are opposed* to Gen. Thomas—checkmate this by expressing confidence in Thomas. I think this will be a *Staggerer*. They will be up to see you tonight, if you will see them.[3] I have no doubt you will be able to "weather the capes," and I have expressed to them my opinion that you will be able to satisfy all reasonable and just demands.

J.J.N.

ALI, DLC-JP.

1. The handwriting of this letter matches that of other Noah documents.

2. William H. Wisener, James H. Agee, and Thomas A. Hamilton.

3. Attached was a note from the Tennessee delegation to Johnson, dated September 10, in which the men indicated their desire to meet with the President that night or the next day.

From William S. Rosecrans
Personal

New York   Sept 11, 1868

Without entering into details I wish to tell you that the great head centre of the Whiskey Ring in New York—S. N. Pike[1] and friends feebly [pretend?] that Col. Thom R. Dudley[2] was an applicant for the Supervisorship of Internal and out of 129 applicants the appointment seemed to lay between him an Jas Worthington,[3] first through an agent then to scare him off the track then to bribe him by an offer of $10000 to give way to Worthington—then if he would [?] to go to Men who had the proper power and influence to ensure success—viz *Pike* [Dr?] *Long*[4] Etc. When these felt of him they flew into a violent fit of war for him and prefered—(they said to all others[)]. Meanwhile they have secretly dispatched their principal agent[5] some where to work against his appointment. They fear him and will move all that millions at stake will inspire them to do to prevent his appointment.

I write all this because if you have him appointed you will do a very great good to the public.[6]

W. S. Rosecrans

ALS, DLC-JP.

1. Samuel N. Pike had been accused of bribing government officials to avoid whiskey taxes. Additional suspicions concerning Pike's involvement in the whiskey business can be found in Joseph R. Flanigen to Johnson, July 20, 1868, *Johnson Papers*, 14: 387.

2. During the war, Thomas R. Dudley (b. *c*1838) had risen from lieutenant in the 2nd Ind. Cav. to assistant quartermaster of volunteers. After the war he was associated with a Cincinnati tobacco firm. CSR, Thomas R. Dudley, RG94, NA; Cincinnati directories (1867).

3. Although the nature of his current occupation is unclear, James T. Worthington (*fl*1869) had earlier been revenue agent at Cincinnati, a position he held again in 1869. Both Worthington and Dudley were seeking the position as supervisor of the southern district of Ohio. Two weeks after Rosecrans's letter, John M. Binckley, who was investigating revenue frauds in New York City, wrote to Johnson with a warning that Worthington was "utterly unfit" for the position. *House Ex. Docs.*, 40 Cong., 2 Sess., No. 144, p. 7 (Ser. 1337); Cincinnati directories (1868–69); Binckley to Johnson, Sept. 26, 1868, Johnson Papers, LC.

4. Possibly Lawson A. Long (*fl*1869), a New York City physician. New York City directories (1867–69).

5. Not identified.

6. Neither Dudley nor Worthington received the position; in early December treasury secretary Hugh McCulloch appointed Gen. Thomas L. Young supervisor. *Washington Evening Star*, Dec. 12, 1868.

From William H. Wisener, Sr., et al.

[September 11, 1868][1]

We have been appointed a Committee by the Legislature of Tennessee to wait upon you and "place fully before you the present condition of affairs in that State and urge upon you to take steps to give protection to the law abiding citizens of the State under the provision of the Constitution of the United States." We now address you in discharge of the duty imposed on us by the action of the Legislature of that State.

The first thing required to be done by us is to place before you fully the present condition of affairs in Tennessee. To do this, Mr. President, would take more time and space than is consistent with a written Communication prepared as this necessarily has been. We can only touch upon the more prominent "affairs" of our State.

First, Mr. President, you are aware that the Legislature of Tennessee has been called together in Extra session and has not yet adjourned. The main object in calling them together by the Governor, as indicated in his message,[2] was that it might pass laws for calling out troops for the protection of the people against a secret organization known as the "Ku Klux Klan," which were deemed necessary by His Excellency to suppress such illegal association. In the necessity for military protection in some portions of that State the Legislature and Committee fully concur. That there is such an organization as the "Klu Klux Klan" is now beyond question or peradventure. By a recent publication made by authority, or with the assent of a distinguished general officer* of the so called "Confederate States," it is stated there are forty thousand members of this association in Tennessee.

As to the objects and purposes of the organization they can only be known by their acts and sayings, whilst in their "masks and ghostly uniforms." Whilst thus engaged they take out citizens and kill them, some by hanging, some by shooting, and some by the slower and more certain plan of whipping. Whilst some are whipped not until death, but severely and disgracefully. In some parts of the State they are travelling at night as often as twice a week, and visiting the houses of union men and Federal soldiers, some of whom they kill, others they whip and order from the Country on pain of being Killed if they do not leave, whilst others are ordered under promise of violence if they remain after their being warned to depart. This is carried on by greater or less numbers, according as the objects to be effected on the particular night are of greater or less magnitude. They rarely appear in their masks and uniforms in daylight. It is in the night when they mostly travel and perpetrate their acts of violence and bloodshed. The most peaceable, orderly, quiet and, we may say, the most exemplary members of the Church are not exempt from their midnight visits, and are the objects of their personal violence.

Instances are known where the most orderly and pious men of a neighborhood have been waked from their slumbers and beaten by them for no other reason than their political sentiments. Murders are common, particularly among the colored people against whom the "Klan" seems to have a peculiar and mortal hatred. Many colored people have been whipped—some of them badly and some until they have died from its effects, and many of them have been murdered for no other reason or offence than their political opinions and sentiments.

Many people who had hired for the year or engaged to work for a portion of the crop, have been compelled to leave their homes for their personal safety, and flee for their lives, leaving their employers or their crops. And unless something be done for their relief they cannot go home and will, of course, loose their earnings; with starvation in the gloomy future for themselves and families.

In the class of cases above there is no excuse or palliation for the wrongs perpetrated on the citizen. But there is another class of cases where the "Klan" take the law into their own hands, where although there is no justification, there are circumstances of alleged palliation. These are where a murder has been committed under circumstances of aggravation, as in the case of young Bicknell,[3] in the County of Maury. He was foully murdered and the guilty agent[4] was arrested by the civil authorities, lodged in jail and afterwards by the "Klan" taken out and hung. There seems to have been no doubt as to his guilt, but that was no justification to those who hung him without trial. There are some other cases where they have hung men for an alleged crime. These cases we mention for the reason that we are sent here to place before your Excellency "the present condition of affairs" in our State. These parties should be tried and punished according to law. It is true in some of these cases it is said, and the fact may be, that the guilt of the party is beyond question or doubt. Assume this to be so, as we concede it to be in some of the cases where they have hung the offender, it is the more certain that they will be convicted and punished.

These cases of punishment for crime are referred to by the friends of the order to justify its existence when they are assailed in the newspapers or otherwise.

We will further add that most, if not all persons engaged in these violations of law, and who belong to the "Klan," so far as known, were enemies of the government of the United States during the late civil war. But we are able to state, and do so with pleasure, that many

of the "Confederate soldiers and officers," who fought gallantly during the war, disapprove of and condemn the "Klan" and its acts of
unprovoked violence.

We have thus far spoken of the acts of this organization. Their
object, they say, is to overturn the State Government of Tennessee,
and many of them declare that they are now as willing to fight the
Government of the United States as they were at the Commencement of the Rebellion. The more discreet ones of them however, do
not say "Government" in this connexion, but say the "Yankees."

Many of them declare the State Government of Tennessee is illegal, and they have legally a right to resist and even to overturn it.
This is not confined to the masses, but finds advocates in distinguished men, high in the estimation of those forming the late so
called Confederate States.

Resistence to the Government of Tennessee and the laws passed
by her Legislature since the war is, in the opinion of the Committee,
as criminal as to attempt to overthrow or resist the Government and
laws of the State of New York or any other state in the Union.

But it may be said the Courts can punish these offenders and therefore no military force is necessary. To this we reply that as a fact no
one in any of the Counties in Tennessee, as far as we have been able
to ascertain, has ever been tried or punished for any of the offences
or class of offences mentioned above. And so long as public opinion
remains as it is, none will be, especially in those counties where the
order is numerous. No person dare prosecute, for if he should, his
life would be endangered thereby. People are apprehensive that should
they prosecute, that they would be murdered by the "Klan." Indeed
they tell persons upon whom they inflict violence, that if they should
know any of them and disclose it, they will be killed. With this state
of alarm and apprehension no one will prosecute. Hence the civil
authorities are powerless.

Again should any one have the courage and firmness to appear
before the grand juries, there is no assurance that an indictment would
be found. Few grand juries, it is apprehended, have none of the "Klan"
on them, enough at least is generally there to defeat an indictment.
As they go in masks and disguises it is not known who is or is not, in
the order, and hence they get on juries and defeat the laws, if per
chance any of them should be known and prosecuted.

The Committee will in this Connexion state, as a fact, that when
the present Legislature met in regular session in October last, they

were disposed to be liberal, and in a spirit of liberality, substantially repealed the military law[5] passed by their immediate predecessors, in the hope and expectation that the promises made by those who were opposed to them politically, that soldiers were unnecessary. In this they regret to say, they were disappointed, for no sooner was the law repealed and soldiers discharged, than this "Ku Klux Klan" sprang up in Tennessee, and commenced their midnight travels and depredations. The "present condition of affairs" as given above, is sustained by the sworn testimony taken before the Committee of military affairs of the Legislature of Tennessee, of witnesses from various Counties in that State, and is corroborated by the personal observation of the Committee and confirmed by the history of Tennessee troubles.

We regret, Mr. President, not being able to furnish you with a printed copy of that report and the testimony on which it is based. When we left Nashville they were in the hands of the printer and we were unable to procure one.

We come now to the other part of our instructions which is, "to urge upon you to take steps to give protection to the law abiding citizens of the State (of Tennessee) under the provisions of the Constitution of the United States." This we now respectfully do. Not because we believe, as the Legislature and Governor believe, that that State is unable to overcome by military force the opposition to the State Government there and the "Ku Klux Klan," and punish the offenders, but because they (the Legislature) and we deem it better to have Federal troops there to aid in the enforcement of the laws and suppress any riots or insurrections that might be attempted or occur. Federal troops are preferred on another ground. They have no local personal likes or dislikes to influence them to commit wrongs on the peaceable citizens. Nor be subject themselves, after discharge from the service, to wrongs and outrages for having been in the state military service.

Further, this "Klan" threaten that no more elections shall be held in Tennessee, in counties where they have the power to prevent it. If this should be the principle upon which they act in the absence of a proper force, then probably no election could be held in Tennessee, for the Republicans in the counties where they have the numerical strength might drive the Conservatives from the Polls. What we desire is a sufficient force to aid the civil authorities in holding elections, so that every man who is entitled to exercise the Elective Franchise may exercise it, no difference for whom or for what party he may choose to vote.

That this is the determination of the "Klan," is evidenced by their continued night travels, and their saying to the Union men, as well white as colored, that they shall not vote unless they exercise the privilege in a particular way. They are disarming the white and colored men wherever they can.

The Legislature hoped that the numbers of the "Klan" would decrease and that their outrages would diminish. But in this they were mistaken. It has delayed action, having a well founded hope and expectation that the efforts of certain prominent and distinguished representative men, who pledged their honest endeavors to effect as far as possible such a desirable result. Their efforts thus far have, although well intended, been crowned with no beneficial results. On the contrary their numbers and violence in many localities are on the increase. Nothing is therefore left but to resort to the military, and the Legislature prefer for the reasons above stated, that Federal, instead of State troops, be used.

We therefore on behalf of the Legislature of Tennessee, respectfully urge that you send, as early as practicable,—the sooner the better—a sufficient Federal force to that State to aid the civil authorities, to act with them, in suppressing these wrongs, and bringing to trial the guilty parties, giving assurance to all that the laws will be enforced, crime punished, and protection extended to such officers and citizens as may attempt to execute the laws or prosecute for their violation.[6]

The Legislature of Tennessee in sending us to make the request we have, did so upon the ground that she is part of the great American Union, contributing to the support of the common Government, enjoying its benefits and blessings, and that they were asking of the Government of the United States that which they believed they had a right under the Constitution, to expect.

We respectfully request as early an answer from your Excellency as it is convenient for you to give it, for the reason that the Legislature has adopted a resolution fixing Monday next as the day of adjournment, and it is important for them to know the result of our application before that time.

Hoping a favorable result to our application we subscribe ourselves, . . .

Wm. H Wisener Sr.
On the part of the Senate

Thos. A. Hamilton   J. H. Agee
On the part of the House.

*Genl. N. B. Forest.

LS, DNA-RG107, Lets. Recd., Executive (M494, Roll 104).

1. Although no date was affixed to this document, other supporting documents indicate that September 11 is the correct date. See John M. Schofield to Wisener et al., Sept. 11, 1868, in *Report of the Legislative Committee... in Regard to the Troubles in Tennessee* (Knoxville, 1868), 7–8. See also Edmund Cooper to Johnson, Sept. 1, 1868.

2. See Brownlow's Legislative Message, July 28, 1868, in Robert H. White et al., *Messages of the Governors of Tennessee* (10 vols. to date, Nashville, 1952–), 5: 609–10.

3. John Bicknell (*c*1846–1868), son of Samuel T. Bicknell of Columbia, traveled about the Maury and Lawrence county area to sell subscriptions to various publications which he represented as an agent. He was murdered on Friday, February 28. *Nashville Press and Times*, Mar. 1, 2, 1868; *Nashville Republican Banner*, Mar. 1, 1868; 1860 Census, Tenn., Blount, 9th Dist., Maryville, 46.

4. The alleged murderer was a man named Walker, alias Powell (*c*1843–1868). He himself was murdered, as indicated in the delegation's letter, by a group of angry men. Walker, alias Powell, was apparently a native of South Carolina and had served in the Confederate army at the battle of Gettysburg. *Nashville Republican Banner*, Mar. 2, 4, 1868; *Nashville Press and Times*, Mar. 2, 4, 5, 1868.

5. See Brownlow's July 28, 1868, message.

6. Johnson, through Secretary Schofield, made federal troops under General Thomas's command available for special duty in Tennessee. On September 17 General Thomas contacted Governor Brownlow, asking where troops were most needed. He then requested an additional regiment from the War Department, and arranged these and other soldiers according to Brownlow's recommendations. See Schofield to Wisener et al., Sept. 11, 1868, and Schofield to Thomas, Sept. 11, 1868, in *Report in Regard to Troubles*, 7–8; Thomas to Brownlow, Sept. 17, 1868, and Thomas to Schofield, Sept. 23, 1868, *House Ex. Docs.*, 40 Cong., 3 Sess., No. 1, pt. 1, "Annual Report of the Secretary of War," pp. xxx–xxxi (Ser. 1367).

From George A. Fitch

Washington   Sept 12th 1868.

Sir:

I charge Samuel G. Courtney, United States District Attorney for the Southern District of New York with having conspired with the Attornies[1] for the defense, in the case now pending in said District before U.S. Commissioner, Joseph Gutman, against E. A. Rollins, Thos. Harland, Thos. E. Smith, *et al*, and with sundry and diverse other persons in the city of New York, for the purpose of acquitting said offenders, and to prevent their conviction and punishment, in violation of his oath of office, and in gross disregard of his official duties as said United States Attorney.

I charge the said Samuel G. Courtney with felony, in this, that he, the said Courtney while acting as a Member of the Metropolitan Internal Revenue Board, of the city of New York, accepted a bribe of ten thousand dollars from the Kentucky Bourbon Company or from some person acting for said Company as a full or partial consideration for the release of the property and effects of said Company then under seizure for a violation of the Internal Revenue Laws of the United States, and for a discontinuance of the suits for the sequestration of the goods, chattels and effects of the said Kentucky Bourbon Company, then pending in the United States Dist. Court for the said Southern District of New York.[2]

I charge the said Samuel G. Courtney with attempting to shape the testimony of witnesses for the Government in the case against E. A. Rollins, *et al*, now pending in said United States District Court in New York, so as to destroy its legal effect and usefulness and bearing—with having obstructed the course and efficiency of the prosecution—for the purpose of overthrowing said prosecution and compelling its discontinuance, and with other acts of personal and official turpitude which are unbecoming the high and dignified office he holds—destructive of the enforcement of the laws of the United States in that Judicial District—are disgraceful in a law officer of the Government—and fatal to his character as a citizen.

I charge the said Samuel G. Courtney with having, on the 8th of Sept. inst., at his office and room at the Astor House, New York, commited a violent personal assault upon J. M. Binckley,[3] Solicitor of Internal Revenue, an officer engaged in prosecuting high crimes and misdemeanors against the Government—whose official position and character he was, at all times and under all circumstances, bound to respect and defend as the chief law officer of a coordinate branch of the Government—and with having at sundry times and on various occasions done such acts, and used such violent, disgraceful and unwarranted language as was well calculated to bring the said Binckley into ridicule and contempt before the public, and I firmly believe for the sole purpose of impairing said Binckley's usefulness and efficiency in carrying on the prosecution for the Government in which he was then engaged.

I therefore pray your Excellency to suspend the official functions of the said Samuel G. Courtney until these charges may be made the subject of legal inquiry and investigation, to the end that the enforcement of the laws of the United States in the Judicial District aforesaid may no longer be impeded or obstructed by him—that important suits brought by the Government may no longer be imperilled, and that, if the allegations herein contained are found true, he, the said Samuel G. Courtney, may be brought to punishment.[4]

Geo. A Fitch

ALS, DNA-RG60, Office Of Atty. Gen., Lets. Recd., President.

1. John H. White was counsel for Thomas E. Smith, and John Sedgwick for Thomas Harland. White (d. c1878) apparently continued to practice law until his death. Sedgwick (d. c1898) later became a superior court judge, a position he held until at least 1897. New York City directories (1867–99). See also John M. Binckley to Johnson, Sept. 10, 1868.

2. For similar charges, see Binckley to Johnson, Sept. 25, 1868.

3. Allegedly Binckley, dissatisfied with Courtney's handling of the case, reproved the district attorney on the evening of September 8. An altercation ensued, but questions about the instigator and victor remained in dispute. *Washington Evening Star*, Sept. 10, 1868. For Courtney's version of the fight, see Courtney to Johnson, Oct. 1, 1868.

4. Courtney remained in office until the Grant administration and, in fact, took over the whiskey case from Binckley in late September. After the case was dismissed in mid-October, Fitch was arrested for perjury and later testified before a congressional committee that his charges against Courtney were unfounded. Fitch claimed Binckley had misled him into falsely accusing Courtney. *New York Times*, Dec. 22, 1868; *House Reports*, 40 Cong., 3 Sess., No. 3, p. 4 (Ser. 1388). See also John M. Binckley to Johnson, Oct. 7, 1868.

From Dixon Ingram[1]

New Forestville [N.C.]   Sept 13 1868

Dear Sir

I hope you will pardon me for the liberty I have taken in writing to you.

Nothing but an earnest desire, for peace could induce me to do so and I am encouraged from the fact that I have been assured by Honr. O. H. Dockery of N C and William B. Ingram[2] of Fall Branch Ten. who is by the by my oldest son that you are a *gentleman* in the fulles acceptation of that term and that you are allways ready to assist those who call upon you in a proper maner for redress.

I am a member of the legislature from Anson County N.C. and I can assure you that the union men in my part of the Country are in great danger. Outrages of the worst kind are common and on last Saturday at a public meeting where both parties had a fair hearing I was most grossly insuled an a pistol drawn and my life threatend and had I not submited to the insult there is no telling how many lives would have been lost.

On yesterday as I was returning from the baptist Church of which I have been a member about 36 years I was met in the publick road by 4 young men in an open carriage and in a most profain and abusive manner ordered to stop and one of them said that he had a good mind to blow seven balls through my body and all this because I was and am yet a friend to the government of which you are the executive.

Pardon me for saying that in 1860 and during the war I and you ocupied the verry same ground and permit me to call your attention to some litle things.

In 1860 you went to Fall Branch and stoped with Dr. Catrel[3] and while making your speach a Beuket was thrown you by a lady,[4] this was daughter of your old friend J. H. Crouch[5] and the wife of my son with whom you got better acquainted at Knoxville.

I do most earnestly implore you to use your influance in behalf of peace. I can *assure* you that the republicans are not the aggressors and one word from you would do more good than any force that we could bring to bear.

Must we allways submit to such things and at last perhaps be murdered in cold blood and have an afflicted wife and five helpless daughters without thier legal protector.

One at least of my neighbors has been murdered in his own home in presence of his wife and helpless children, and as far as I know not one effort has been made to bring the murderer to justice—and my life and others are constantly threatened and no one would be suprised at any time to hear that I was shot.

I would address you as the confiding Indian does "Father of your Country" if I could only believe that it would in any way contribute to the *peace* of *our* distracted country.

I can say in all *good* concience that I would not hurt one of Gods creation but again I *implore* your good offices in behalf of our common country.

For the truth of what I say I would most respectfully refer you to Hon. A. Dockery Rockingham N.C. Gov. Holden Honr. J. C. Abot Wilmington N C J H Crouch Fall Branch Ten. Honr. David Heaton New Bern N.C.[6]

D. Ingram

ALS, DLC-JP.

1. Ingram (*c*1807–*fl*1870) was an Anson County railroad contractor and farmer. 1860 Census, N.C., Anson, Lilesville Dist., 141; (1870), Lilesville Twp., 379.

2. Ingram (*c*1837–*fl*1870) was a carpenter with a wife and four children. 1870 Census, Tenn., Washington, 13th Dist., Fall Branch, 11.

3. John B. Cottrell (1806–1874), a native North Carolinian, was a physician. Fall Branch was the site of a mass meeting on October 31, 1860. 1860 Census, Tenn., Sullivan, 15th Civil

Dist., Fall Branch, 3; Bennett and Rae, *Washington County Tombstone Inscriptions*, 3: 5; Johnson to Robert Johnson, Oct. 4, 1860, *Johnson Papers*, 3: 667–68.

4. Martha Crouch (*c*1842–*fl*1870) married William B. Ingram sometime prior to 1862. 1850 Census, Tenn., Washington, 4th Subdiv., E. Dist., 483; (1870), 13th Dist., Fall Branch, 11.

5. Jesse H. Crouch (1808–1878) was a well-to-do minister, merchant, and farmer. *History of Washington County, Tennessee, 1988* (Salem, W. Va., 1988), 303; 1850 Census, Tenn., Washington, 4th Subdiv., E. Dist., 483; (1870), 13th Dist., Fall Branch, 11.

6. Alfred Dockery, William W. Holden, Joseph C. Abbott, Jesse H. Crouch, and David Heaton. Dockery (1797–1875), a planter, served in the North Carolina state senate (1836–44) and U.S. House (1845–47, 1851–53). Abbott (1825–1881), a lawyer and Civil War brevet brigadier general, edited several newspapers and served as New Hampshire's adjutant general (1855–61), U.S. Senator from North Carolina (1868–71), and in a variety of treasury posts. *BDUSC.*

From Ellen Keizer[1]

Phila.   Sept. 13th /868

Hon Sir

Please pardon the liberty I have taken in addressing you thus, but having over heard a conversation between two men, some few weeks ago, concerning Yourselfe and the Honorable Horatio Seymour of New York which has been praying upon my minde ever since, I would have told, You immediately, only I was fearfull You might think it was a scheme or plan of some kinde to make you notice the letter I wrote about one year ago[2] to your Honored selfe. Having those *fears*, I came to the conclusion I would never mention it but it is troubling me so much, and I feel that it is my duty to tell *You*, And humbly beg *You* to think kindely of it, as it is *Your*, wellfare I have at heart. *Only* this prompts me to do this.

Having been an invalid for five months, I became quite low spirited, and when I recovered sufficiently to get out, I went to the park, hunted out a quiet lonely spot as I could bear no excitement or noise, thinking as I sat alone that I woud not be disturbed by any one, but presently I heard footsteps coming behinde me and looking around I saw to men approaching. They came very near me but could not see me for the bushes then sat down on the otherside. I would have left immediately only I was afraid of attracting thier attention as I was alone and a distance from the main walks and therefore remained perfectly quiet and heard every word they was saying. I should not [?] have feared them from thier looks as they were very genteel looking men. At first thier conversaton was very trifling. At last one said to the other looking all around, Well now Bill we will resume our conversation, as we are alone and I want You to tell me if You think that is the best thing for our Countrys good.

His answer was I do and the Boys are just right. That attracted my attention, and I payed particular attention to what they was saying and the other again asked, do you realy intend to stick to that promise and keep that Oath.

His reply was I do and by all that is holy and sacred I honestly swear that Andy Johnston days are numbered and are few and by God by this he must die at the same calling you a dreadfull name. I did not see what he had I was to much frightned to look. The other said O hush not so loud. You are right, and I to have solomnly sworn if Seymour is elected he shall never take his seat at Washington. In fact the Boys have all sworn that to and so help me God I'll keep my word any how then they may have me as quick as possible. They still talked on but I was to much frightened to listen any longer. I did not know what such wicked wretches might do to me if they saw me for they would know I had heard all they had said, and it was such a releif when they got up and walked away. I would know those men if I ever was to meet them again. Had I been able at the time I would have gone to Washington and not have taken this plan to inform You and was also fearfull I could not get to see you. Honored Sir You may think this trifling but I don't; and I couldn't rest untill I told You, and sincerely hope you will pardon the liberty I take in writing . . .

                                                        Ellen Keizer

No 1818 Bellevue st Phila.

ALS, DLC-JP.

   1. Keizer (c1835–fl1886) was the wife of John L. Keizer, a Philadelphia machinist. 1870 Census, Pa., Philadelphia, Philadelphia, 45th Dist., 15th Ward, 617; Philadelphia directories (1868–87).

   2. No other letter from Keizer has been found.

From J. Warren Bell

                                      Austin Texas   Sept 14, 1868.
My dear Sir

You requested me when in Washington, to give you information from time to time of the state of things in this country, so far as I could ascertain. Since that time I have travelled over much of the interior of the state, and have endeavored to learn truthfully the actual condition of the public mind and the causes of the present condition of the things. I shall not weary you with a long letter. I will say in all candour that certainly there is much lawlessness and disregard of what is right, based perhaps upon the hope, that something will come to pass, to relieve the pressure felt in consequence of the attempt of Congress to put the ballot into the hands of the Negro.

I am forced to the beleif that were it not for the military authority exerted a *very bad* state of things would exist. In fact there is no denying that murders are committed, and that all sorts of outrages have existed, and still are resorted to by the reckless; and the citizens are not anxious to have the guilty arrested and punished, but rather to a great extent encourage such violence. I have got along quietly but I am cautious & watchful. I cannot do otherwise than commend the course of Genl Reynolds[1] now in command of this district. I met him last year while at Brownsville, and I have been watchful of his course. I am disposed to think him an upright justice loving man, and firm to do what he believes to be right, and I also think he has a clear & comprehensive view of the actual condition of things and of the responsible duties devolving upon him. He is not more radical than seems to be demanded by the condition of things here. While on this point I will call your attention to the enclosed "order" and "extract" from his requisition for a military commission for the trial of offenders.[2] I am no advocate for military commissions, where it is possible for trials to be had by civil authority. But I hesitate not a moment in saying to you the President of the U.S. that I am satisfied from what I have learned in this state, that were there no military authority here there would be few arrests and trials of offenders in capital offenses. You may set it down as certain that the knowlege existing that offenders will be tried by military law, induces the courts of the state to take cognizance of the hundreds of cases which would pass unnoticed were there no military authority to demand trial. Withdraw the military from this state and there would be but little done by the civil courts towards punishing the guilty. I was in Waco a few days since and court in session a verdict was rendered against a criminal for murder, and it seemed to me every person was astonished, that a man could be in Texas sentenced to be hung. An appeal was taken and I presume he will yet come clean. Such is the state of Society here.

Genl Reynolds is not in favor of negro suffrage negro equality, nor of negroes holding office. Neither will he permit them as "*Registrars.*" I want you to think occasionally of the condition of things away down here and remember that not all men are equal to the requirements of the unsettled condition of affairs in Texas. When men tell you that the country here is perfectly quiet, and that life is safe, just you remember *such is not the case*. Gov Hamilton is very bitter against you. Gov Pease[3] is not quite so much so. Genl. Reynolds is far otherwise than hostile towards your views and I am of opinion he is doing as much to save the country as any commanding officer you have. Remember what I have said in this, and see if I am right in my views. I have written thus plainly concerning matters here, and Genl Reynolds in order that you may know of the men commanding and holding high authority, that those who are striving to do right, may be sustained, and not wrongly judged of for want of reliable information in the premises.

While these things are as herein stated, I am not prepared to state, nor do I desire to argue the causes, which have produced them. It is enough that they exist. Nor am I without hope for the future. I believe confidently that the course being pursued by Genl. Reynolds, if sustained, will work out salvation yet. He strives to quell both extremes.

J Warren Bell

LS, DLC-JP.

1. Joseph J. Reynolds.

2. Not found enclosed. Reynolds believed that, due to unstable legal conditions in Texas, military commissions were the only way to provide a fair trial. Reynolds supervised the commissions carefully. William L. Richter, *The Army in Texas During Reconstruction, 1865–1870* (College Station, Tex., 1987), 149.

3. Andrew J. Hamilton and Elisha Pease.

From Edmund Cooper

Shelbyville Ten.   Septr. 14 1868

My Dear Mr. President.

Honl. Robertson Topp, of Memphis, desires the appointment, as one of the commissioners, on the part of the Government of the United States under the Mexican Treaty—to adjudicate outstanding claims between the citizens of the Republics.

If there is such a commission, and the commissioners have not been selected, I would most earnestly recommend for the appointment my friend.[1]

Honl. Robertson Topp of Memphis—is one in every respect fully qualified for the performance of the duties.

A man of energy and integrity, he will reflect credit upon the administration.

May I hope that you will take his name into consideration?

Edmund Cooper

ALS, DNA-RG59, Lets. of Appl. and Recomm., 1861–69 (M650, Roll 49), Robertson Topp.

1. See also John M. Lea to Johnson, Sept. 10, 1868, and James B. Lamb to Johnson, Sept. 18, 1868, Lets. of Appl. and Recomm., 1861–69 (M650, Roll 49), Robertson Topp, RG59, NA; James B. Bingham to Johnson, Sept. 8, 1868.

From F. S. Richards et al.[1]

Nashville Tenn   Sept 14 1868

Sir:

The undersigned citizens of Nashville respectfully represent that they believe the interests of the Federal service in Tennessee would be greatly promoted by the retention of Bvt Brig Gen Duncan in this Dept and at this point,[2] he having been recently ordered to report to Omaha.[3] He has proved himself a wise firm and discreat officer and has earned thereby the confidence of the entire community—peace and order being the great desideratum. We believe that no one could exert a better influence for that result than Gen Duncan and we earnestly solicit if compatible with the general interests of the service that he be continued in command at this point.

Tel, DLC-JP.

1. At this time Richards was serving as speaker of the lower house of the legislature. Eighteen other names were affixed to the telegram.

2. For an earlier document about Thomas Duncan, see John C. Gaut to Johnson, July 22, 1868, *Johnson Papers*, 14: 403–4.

3. Duncan left Nashville in late October to take his assignment to the Department of the Platte (which included Nebraska). His first post of duty was Fort McPherson in Nebraska. *Appleton's Cyclopaedia*; *Nashville Union and American*, Oct. 25, 1868.

From Hugh McCulloch

Treasury Department. Sept. 16, 1868.

Dear Sir:

I requested Mr. Evarts[1] by letter on Monday to employ additional counsel according to the arrangement which was made in your presence. After Cabinet meeting yesterday, I wrote him again suggesting the name of Judge Fullerton.[2] Before the letter was mailed I received a telegram from Mr. Evarts advising me that he had received my letter, and would give the subject immediate attention. As I desired that he should have the name of Judge Fullerton before him before selecting the assistant counsel, I telegraphed him at once to make no selection until he received my letter of yesterday.

I take it for granted that everything is going off according to the programme, and that the prosecution will be conducted thoroughly and vigorously.

H McCulloch

P.S. Since writing the above the following telegram has been received from Mr. Evarts:—

"Your Second letter recd. I shall be in Washington on or before Friday morning. Wm. M. Evarts"

LS, DLC-JP.
    1. William M. Evarts.
    2. At a September 14 meeting, President Johnson, Treasury Secretary McCulloch, and District Attorney Samuel G. Courtney decided to add another counsel to help investigate the whiskey revenue frauds. After consulting Evarts, they selected William Fullerton (1818–1900), a former justice of the New York state supreme court who was currently partner in a New York City law firm. *New York Tribune*, Sept. 15, 1868; *New York Times*, Sept. 21, 1868; *New York Herald*, Sept. 22, 1868; *Senate Ex. Docs.*, 40 Cong., 3 Sess., No. 51, pp. 1–2 (Ser. 1360); *NUC*.

From James H. Hoblitzell

Baltimore   Sept. 17 /68

Dear Sir,

Schenck & Morgan calling Congress togather!![1] Have we no President? No people have ever been more insulted & yet I am afraid we will have to endure another four years Radical rule. The thought almost maddens me.

McColloh has the power to save us—and if he is honestly opposed to the Radicals he will do so. He must have long seen how futile is his efforts to keep gold down. All efforts in this way must only be temporary. Sending our Bonds abroad only increases the gold debt against us. I repeat Mr. McColloh has it in his power to destroy this Radical Party in thirty days. Will he do it?

J H Hoblitzell

ALS, DLC-JP.

1. Sen. Edwin D. Morgan and Rep. Robert C. Schenck, chairmen of two radical congressional committees, were acting in accordance with concurrent resolutions calling for Congress to meet and adjourn on various dates should no business require a special session. However, only the President was supposed to have the power to call for a special session. See Lewis E. Parsons to Johnson, Sept. 2, 1868; Beale, *Welles Diary*, 3: 437.

From Morris S. Miller

Sept. 17, 1868, Washington, D.C.; ALS, Morris S. Miller Papers, Spec. Coll. Div., NWM.

Miller responds to an August 18, 1868, letter from Quartermaster General Montgomery C. Meigs to Secretary of War John M. Schofield which Johnson had shown to Miller. In his letter Meigs objected to Johnson's revoking an order sending Miller to a post in Texas.

Miller deals with Meigs's points in order. The officer sent to Texas is to be responsible for only a part of the duties previously performed there by Miller's junior in rank, Brevet Brigadier General Charles H. Tompkins, who will retain the more important district headquartered in New Orleans. While Meigs believes that "all the Colonels of the Department have by their onerous duties in the War earned the right to remain undisturbed" in their present positions, Miller believes that not all are "properly engaged."

Miller, as the senior-ranking lieutenant colonel, feels that Meigs has singled him out "as the only one of that grade who has not had heavy duties to perform and who is not now employed on duty important and for which he is capacitated." Meigs's account of Miller's assignments is inaccurate as he did not work in the quartermaster general's office until after the war. Miller wants to remain at his current duties of examining and correcting quartermaster accounts, tasks more important and relevant than the assignment in Texas.

Even a reduced clerical staff requires supervision. Miller challenges General Thomas's statement that Miller did not need an assistant. He discusses Thomas's experience and skill as an organizer.

Miller disputes the quartermaster general's version of how long Miller had been working in Washington. Meigs failed to take into account the six weeks when Miller was a prisoner of war or the seven months when he suffered a "political punishment." Miller does not think his time in Washington should be counted against him, given that he had applied to become a Brigadier General of Volunteers but was not appointed. Neither should Miller be sent elsewhere just because he has been in Washington for quite a while.

Miller protests that it is not his "turn" for frontier service "until my juniors have had theirs." Even more galling, the young officer assigned to relieve him in Washington had never had frontier duty, whereas Miller had served in Texas after the Mexican War. If, because of his "rank and experience," he deserves "an important and useful station," he should be allowed to remain in Washington, which is a more important post than Texas.

Meigs claimed that he knew no officer besides Miller "who is competent and can well be spared from his present duties" to go to Texas, but Miller recommends the younger officer who was supposed to replace him. This officer Stanton advanced from captain directly to lieutenant colonel ahead of thirty-two others who ranked him. "He should surely not be overlooked when an occasion, such as this, offers for him to prove himself worthy of the extraordinary promotion conferred on him." If General Joseph A. Potter is relieved from his post in Texas, it should be by someone younger than Miller.

Miller suggests that the real reason for the change of assignment is that Meigs is a Republican, as is the younger officer scheduled to replace Miller, while Miller is a Democrat. The younger officer's partisan activities have included staying with Stanton while the latter refused to vacate the War Department, participating in the funeral of Thaddeus Stevens, and keeping Republican campaign literature in his office to distribute.

Miller stresses his own firm support of Johnson, especially during the impeachment crisis, relating such symbolic actions as putting Johnson's picture in a prominent place in both his office and his living room. Perhaps "for these and other, similar, high crimes and misdemeanors, I may have been impeached and banished." If Johnson does not oppose Meigs's order sending him to Texas, however, Miller will obey it with his customary "alacrity."

From James M. Spellissy
Personal

Philadelphia   Sept. 17 —68

This brief but full editorial from the Universe of the 13th. inst. is respectfully sent.[1] It is a sample of the way in which the Universe is out in evry issue for the President.

The Editor hopes his application for the Supervisorship of East. Pa. is still the best.[2]

Jas. Spellissy Ed.

ALS, DLC-JP.

1. The enclosed newspaper article lauded Johnson for his vetoes as president and minimized the discussions about Johnson and his connection with John Binckley of whiskey frauds notoriety.

2. A longtime applicant for federal appointments, Spellissey did not receive the requested post of supervisor of internal revenue for eastern Pennsylvania.

From Andrew J. Wilcox

Baltimore   Sept 18th 1868

Mr President.

I to-day mailed to your address several copies of the Sun newspaper published here containing articles published by me which you will find marked.[1] Under the 3rd Section of the 2nd Article of the Constitution, the President of the United States is required "from time to time to give to the Congress *information* of the State of the Union & recommend to their consideration such measures "as he shall judge necessary and expedient." The letters that I have published have I suppose & will hereafter, I judge be regarded as the inside working of a crazed brain yet I do not feel so and the conclusions I arrive at seem to me so manifestly just and certain that I do not see how any sane man could doubt them. May I therefore have the privilege of asking that you make them (excluding personal matters) a part of your message to Congress when it meets on Monday next if you deem it necessary to send in a message to Congress on that day & that you recommend to Congress the adoption of the policy indicated in those letters so far as it is now applicable to Congress under the section of the Constitution above referred to and that you institute such a line of policy in regard to the other matters referred to in those letters as shall seem to you best to accomplish the ends desired. Blackstone[2] and he is supported by all the authorities and the best lawyers & statesmen lays down this rule that in order to make equitable & just laws it is necessary first to understand the law as it is, Secondly to ascertain wherein consists the defects of the law & thirdly to ascertain and apply the correct remedy. This although not the exact words is at least the substance of the rule. I think I have very clearly shown what is the law & wherein consists its defects, will any one doubt the efficaciousness of the remedy.

Members of Congress certainly of their own knowledge have correct information of the dangerous condition of the country & could not therefore regard the recommendation by you of the adoption of this policy as of being of any personal interest to either you, or myself, I am no candidate or applicant for office. The end of your tenure of office is certain which you cannot prolong except by revolutionary measures which I am sure are altogether foreign to your patriotism & nature. Congress can only hasten the end by the same means which I do not believe it has the least inclination of resorting to, but may it not be that unless this policy be adopted the next Congress in the event of the election of Gen Grant (who is regarded as being committed to a certain policy) & the Republican majority in the next Congress be as great as in the present, that it will be controlled by the extreme men of the party and an extreme policy, the outline of which has been frequently indicated, be adopted & carried out, which will inevitably result in war. Then take the other horn of the dilemma suppose the democratic ticket is successful, although it be true that at least one branch of the legislative department be of the opposition as Gov Seymour has shown may not the extreme men of that party require that the policy indicated in Gen Blairs letter (prior to his nomination to Colonel Brodhead)[3] & which it is believed secured him the nomination will be made the policy of that administration which also must inevitably result in war, both of these views of the case are certainly possible & I think more than probable.

Gen Grant has said "let us have peace," the party organs respond "We will have peace and you, the opposition, must submit to our terms of peace even if we be compelled to have a peace at the point of the bayonet.["] Gov Seymour has said I believe "we will not have war" (both very similar to Napoleon when he means war all the time yet I do not put this interpretation upon the personal meaning of either of these gentlemen). The party organs respond "we will not have war because *if necessary* we will use the army & navy to oust the governments now in existence in the Southern States, which we believe are clearly unconstitutional & void. Are not these queer ideas of peace to you Mr President and is not the thing so palpably false on its face that the most casual observer could not fail to see it. Now under my line of policy which certainly has the merit of being very simple & practical would it not be physically impossible to have anything else but peace accompanied by very great prosperity in & by which we would be able "to repair the waste places" both of the goverment & country? Does not prudence & wisdom to say nothing of the exegincy of the times therefore *demand* that we shall have peace even if it be only acquired under terms dictated by an humble individual?

Andrew J. Wilcox

(*Confidential*) Would be much pleased to have an answer to the above letter to publish so as to throw the onus upon Congress of accepting it or not.[4]

Andrew J. Wilcox

ALS, DLC-JP.

1. See the *Baltimore Sun*, Sept. 2–5, 12, 15, 1868, for Wilcox's views on a variety of topics involving the federal government.

2. William Blackstone (1723–1780), British jurist, taught at Oxford, served in Parliament, was solicitor general to the queen, and was a judge of the Court of Common Pleas. *New Columbia Encyclopedia* (1975).

3. In a June 30 letter to James O. Broadhead, Francis P. Blair, Jr., argued that congressional reconstruction was unconstitutional and the next executive must use the army to "disperse" the southern governments and allow whites to create new ones. *New York Herald*, July 3, 1868. See also E.G.W. Butler to Johnson, Oct. 28, 1868.

4. No evidence of an answer from Johnson has been found. On September 21 and 25 Wilcox sent a revised copy of this letter and asked what he might be authorized to say at its publication. On January 2, 1869, Wilcox again wrote concerning the contents of this letter and requesting information. See Wilcox to Johnson, Sept. 21, 25, 1868, Johnson Papers, LC; and Wilcox to Johnson, Jan. 2, 1869.

To John M. Binckley

Washington, D.C.   Sept. 19th 1868

Sir:

You will proceed to New York for the purpose of investigating alleged frauds on the internal revenue laws, and obtaining such information as it may be believed will result in exposing and suppressing them. You will supervise, within the sphere of your office, any prosecutions which may arise from your investigations, first, however, reporting the facts, for instructions, to the property authority.[1]

Andrew Johnson

LS, DNA-RG56, Misc. Records Recd. from Treasury Officers.

1. Newspaper accounts to the contrary, this order authorized Binckley to "supervise" in only the most general way. The investigating and prosecuting of the whiskey fraud cases had actually been turned over to district attorney Samuel G. Courtney and special counsel William Fullerton. *Washington Evening Star*, Sept. 22, 1868; *New York Herald*, Sept. 22, 1868.

From Hugh McCulloch

Treasury Department. Sept. 19, 1868.

Dear Sir:—

I enclose Mr. Seymour's letter.[1] I intended to hand it to you at the Cabinet meeting yesterday; but forgot to do so.

It will afford me pleasure to appoint Mr. Lewis[2] Supervisor of the Virginias (as he is Strongly recommended by the Conservative men of those States) if I can get his name before me.

H. McCulloch

LS, DLC-JP.

1. Horatio Seymour wrote a letter recommending W. M. Lewis. Seymour to Johnson, Sept. 3, 1868, Johnson Papers, LC.

2. Possibly Wellington M. Lewis (c1841–1874), former lieutenant colonel of the 89th N.Y. Inf., who lived in Petersburg, Virginia, after the war. Lewis was not nominated for the position. Pension Records, Annie [Nannie B.] Lewis, RG15, NA.

From Nicholas E. Paine[1]

Confidential

Rochester N.Y.   Sept 19 /68

My Dear Sir,

Mr Lewis Selye[2]—member of Congress from this District—intends making a *very especial* effort for the removal of Saml P. Allen Esq. collector of Revenues at this place. I need not inform you that Mr. Selye is an *inveterate Radical* and our most *active & persistent adversary*, while Mr Allen is not only eminently conservative but has faithfully & ably sustained all the measures of your administration and is now doing so. Mr. Seward will understand this and will fully confirm my statement. Mr. Selye would rejoice to effect Mr Allen's removal and have in his place some pliant party whom he can control. May I ask your Excellency to watch this case & guard the rights and interests of your friends here. I have no motive but to prevent Mr Selye in his object. I have ben and am your firm friend—and have done all in my power to promote your able & patriotic administration. I trust you may remember me but if not, our mutual friend—Capt. Maguire[3]—in whose care I send this that he may deliver it *personally*—will inform you who I am & that you can *rely* upon me.[4]

N. E. Paine   Late mayor of Rochester

ALS, DLC-JP.

1. Paine (c1810–fl1886), a lawyer, had been district attorney (1846), mayor (1851), and postmaster (1858–60) of Rochester. Sometime in late 1868 or early 1869 he moved to New York City, where he continued to practice law. William F. Peck et al., *Landmarks of Monroe County, New York* (Boston, 1895), 109, 126, 217; New York City directories (1868–86); Rochester directories (1861–68); 1860 Census, N.Y., Monroe, Rochester, 4th Ward, 331.

2. Selye (1803–1883), elected to his only term in Congress in 1867, had previously been Rochester alderman and county treasurer. In 1868 he established the *Rochester Chronicle. BDUSC.*

3. Not identified.

4. Paine's letter was evidently enclosed in a letter from James Maguire to Johnson. Maguire vouched for Paine's character and also asked that Allen be retained. By September 1869 Allen was no longer serving as collector, but it is unknown if his removal was a result of Selye's intervention or merely the new presidential administration. Maguire to Johnson, Sept. 23, 1868, Johnson Papers, LC; *U.S. Off. Reg.* (1867–69).

From John R. Pitkin

Sept 19. 1868.

My Dear Sir.

I address you as one of the People of this great Country: To Express my gratitude for your firm Support of the CONSTITUTION, of our Fathers.

Will you Join the People in their choice of Candidates for the coming Elections in Nov 1868, as expressed in my Printed Circular No 1. Enclosed: dated Sept 3d 1868.[1] The only or princple objection is the want of time: To Elect Mr Chase & General Sherman as President & Vice President (U S.)

But the Little Monitor Surprised the *Country*, and the *world*!! And the *People* of the *US*; May do the *same*, by taking matters into their own hands as a corrective eliment in a Rule of Government now so much required to Restore the Union to its original purity.

Please Say; or convey, my hope to Mr Chase & General Sherman— That they will allow us to make an effort to Elect them, to the offices named in said Circular.

John R Pitkin of Woodhaven L I.   N Y

ALS, DLC-JP.
1. The circular, entitled "Political and Business Convention," called for the establishment of a third party which would have Salmon P. Chase and William T. Sherman as candidates. Ser. 20, pt. 1, Johnson Papers, LC.

From Edward G. W. Butler

Dunboyne, La., Sept. 20, 1868.

My dear Sir:

I take the liberty to send you the N. Orleans *Crescent* of the 11th & *Picayune* of the 18th Instant;[1] & from the statements of the Sheriff of the Parish of Franklin,[2] contained in the former, you will perceive how false are the statements of Govr. Warmouth, in his letter to you;[3] which the telegrams of Genl. Buchanan to the Adj. General,[4] of 12th & 14th Instant, will prove to you how false and mischievous is the report of Gen. Hatch to the Secretary of War,[5] that there was "danger of an assault upon a torchlight procession," which took place on the night of the 12th;[6] when, as you will perceive from the Crescent's advice to "keep quiet," the only danger apprehended was that the negro procession would, as usual, prove riotous, and carry out the threat of the negro Senator, Pinchback—to "lay waste the city."[7]

Gen. Buchanan's testimony before a General Court Martial, would convict the miserable tool of Genl. Howard[8] & his negro Bureau of "Conduct unbecoming an officer and a Gentleman," under the 83rd article of war, and end the service of one of the many poor creatures who now disgrace it.

Not content with his infamous letter to you, Gov. Warmouth recently handed to Gen. Lee[9] (Banks' Red Hair Cavalry Commander, & now Editor of the New Orleans *Republican*,) an anonymous letter, over the signature of "Iberville,"[10] for the correctness of whose statements he vouched, charging the Democratic Club of Plaquemine with making negroes drunk, and causing them to commit outrages upon "loyal men"; and, when called upon by a committee from the club, he denied all knowledge of the letter, & Genl. Lee refused to give up its author; who is said to be the Bureau Agent at Plaquemine.[11]

Pardon me, my dear sir, for thus obtruding upon your valuable time; especially at the moment when you are about to have the Rump-Congress again inflicted upon you; but, you are the only friend we have to look to in this hour of our great trial and vexation.

Congratulating you upon the glorious prospects of the Democracy, and wishing you a happy termination to your administration . . .

E.G.W. Butler

P.S. The negroes are tired of the Carpet Baggers & *Free* negroes, and I think the Democracy will carry this State.

ALS, DLC-JP.

1. Not found enclosed.

2. A. W. Moore.

3. Henry C. Warmoth to Johnson, Aug. 1, 1868, *Johnson Papers*, 14: 471–74.

4. Lorenzo Thomas. See Robert C. Buchanan to J. C. Kelton (assistant adjutant general), Sept. 12, 1868, and Buchanan to adjutant general, Sept. 14, 1868, *New Orleans Picayune*, Sept. 18, 1868, morning. The telegram of the twelfth, responding to one from Kelton of the same date, gave Buchanan's opinion that there would be no trouble at the torchlight procession and the message of the fourteenth assured the authorities that there had been no trouble.

5. Gen. Edward Hatch's report to Secretary of War John M. Schofield has not been found, but Kelton's telegram to Buchanan of September 12 indicates that Hatch, as quoted by Butler, had warned of the danger of an assault on the procession. Ibid.

6. On the day preceding the Republican parade, New Orleans mayor John R. Conway issued a proclamation asking liquor dealers to close their premises from Saturday evening (September 12) through the morning of September 13. According to newspaper reports, the parade lasted about an hour and allegedly had few spectators, besides black women. Ibid., Sept. 12, 13, 1868, morning.

7. Pinckney B.S. Pinchback (1837–1921), the free-born son of a white planter and his former slave, raised a company of black volunteers during the Civil War, and was elected to the state senate in 1868. In the meeting of the legislature on September 3, Pinchback protested against certain newspaper articles critical of him and of attacks against blacks. The next white outrage, warned Pinchback, "will be the signal for the dawn of retribution . . . that will cause ten thousand torches to be applied . . . and this city will be reduced to ashes." *DAB; New York Times*, Sept. 6, 1868; *New Orleans Picayune*, Sept. 4, 1868, morning.

8. Oliver O. Howard and presumably General Hatch, who was the assistant commissioner of the Freedmen's Bureau.

9. Albert L. Lee.

10. Not found.

11. Perhaps agent and subassistant commissioner of the Freedmen's Bureau in Louisiana, E. Charles Merrill, who served from January through December 1868. He has not been otherwise identified. Elaine Everly and Willna Pacheli, comps., *Preliminary Inventory of the Records of the Field Offices of the Bureau of Refugees, Freedmen, and Abandoned Lands* (3 pts., Washington, D.C., 1973–74), pt. 1: 229.

From George P. Cabler[1]

Rome Tenn   Sept 20th 1868

Dear Sir,

I take the liberty of writeing to you, asking your advice and opinion in regard to the expected troubles of our now agitated State. From a recent Proclimation issued by the Govener of our State,[2] we see that he intends to call out the melishia entirely from East Tenn, and from a report of a commity from the legislator we see that they have a vebal promise from you to assist and if nescesary to furnish aditional troops from the regular Armey, to act in conjunction with the Goveners troops. We the People of Smith County are entirely ignorent for what pourpose this array of armed men are for. Peace and Quietude have reigned heare suppreme since the ending of the rebelion. The good Citizens of this county who have ever been and who now are your staunch friends, would be greatly releaved to heare some thing direct from you in reguard to this question. Hopeing that you will answer, with some good advice . . .

Geo P. Cabler

ALS, DLC-JP.

1. Cabler (*c*1846–*fl*1870) was the son of a Nashville saddler (William D. Cabler), who moved to Rome, Tennessee, shortly before the outbreak of the war. In the immediate aftermath of the war, the younger Cabler moved back to Nashville and lived with relatives. In 1870 he was listed as a druggist there. 1860 Census, Tenn., Smith, 12th Dist., Rome, 123; (1870), Davidson, Nashville, 6th Ward, 44; Nashville directories (1855–70).

2. On September 16 Governor Brownlow issued a proclamation in which he explained that the violence prevalent in so many areas of the state had prompted him to call the legislature

into special session. He then outlined the provisions of the law enacted by that body to provide for raising and enlisting of the "Tennessee State Guards." Brownlow called upon loyal citizens, black and white, of every county in the state to raise companies, although he expressed a preference for troops from East Tennessee. *Nashville Press and Times*, Sept. 17, 1868; E. Merton Coulter, *William G. Brownlow: Fighting Parson of the Southern Highlands* (Chapel Hill, 1937), 362–63.

To John Quincy Adams
Private

Washington, D.C.   Septr 21st 1868.

Dear Sir:

I have just read in this morning's Intelligencer, your letter of the 14th instant, accepting the nomination of Governor of Mass.[1] Without commenting upon the various propositions which it states with such remarkable force and clearness, and in such exact accordance with the first principles of the Govm't, I desire to thank you for a paper of so much ability, issued at a time so opportune. It cannot fail to exert a powerful and salutary influence upon the mind of every sound thinker who has at heart the welfare of the Nation, and entitles you to the gratitude and respect of every sincere patriot. You have, in a few words, correctly stated the question—that the battle is between the Constitution and Congress, and thank God! you have taken your stand for the Constitution. If, in this bitter struggle, that sacred instrument can be preserved, all will yet be well.

(Sgd.) Andrew Johnson

Copy, DLC-JP.

1. Adams's lengthy letter to Henry W. Paine, president of the Massachusetts Democratic state convention, dated September 14, was printed in full in the *National Intelligencer*, Sept. 21, 1868.

From Ephraim R. Eckley et al.[1]

Washington D.C.   September 21 1868

Sir

In view of the vast rapidity with which the Territory of Wyoming is filling up and becoming populated and the large amount of property including several hundred miles of Rail Road[2] and the thousands upon thousands of passengers and the millions of dollars worth of freight passing over this great national thoroughfare monthly and in view of the fact that robberies and murders are of daily and nightly occurrence and that they have petition since the adjournment of Congress for protection and that the wildest anarchy prevails there and they have no protection except that afforded by the vigilence Committee[3] we would respectfully ask that the organization of the Territory be completed by the appointment of the usual Territorial officers that the tide of lawlessness and crime may be stayed and that there may be some security to life & property in that distant Territory.[4]

LS, DNA-RG59, Territorial Papers, Wyoming (M85, Roll 1).

1. Ephraim R. Eckley (1811–1908), a lawyer and a member of the U.S. House of Representatives from Ohio, along with ten other senators, representatives, and territorial delegates to Congress, signed this letter. Eckley had previously served in the Ohio state senate and house and as a colonel with Ohio troops during the Civil War. *BDUSC*.

2. On September 21, 1868, the Union Pacific Railroad tracks reached Point of Rocks, Wyoming, not far from the western edge of the territory. Ames, *Pioneering the Union Pacific*, front end papers, 287.

3. Much of the violence centered around the railroad construction towns, populated by saloon keepers, gamblers, prostitutes, and other crooks who preyed on the construction workers. Several towns defended themselves with vigilantes before the arrival of more standard forms of justice. Hubert H. Bancroft, *History of Nevada, Colorado, and Wyoming* (San Francisco, 1890), 738–39.

4. For the result of this and other pleas for the organization of the Wyoming Territory, see Wyoming Citizens to Johnson, Aug. 25, 1868, *Johnson Papers*, 14: 543.

From Stephen J. Field

San Francisco   Sept. 21 1868

Col Hently[1] is absent but I am authorized by him to say that he withdraws his opposition to the commissioning of Coey.[2] This will aid us.

Stephen J. Field

Tel, DLC-JP.

1. Thomas J. Henley.

2. James Coey had been nominated, confirmed, and commissioned for the collectorship of internal revenue at San Francisco. See Samuel B. Axtell to Johnson, Aug. 15, 1868, *Johnson Papers*, 14: 509.

From Thomas G. Jones and Henry T. Walker[1]

Montgomery, Ala., Sept 22nd 1868

Sir.

Deeply interested in the peace & prosperity of Alabama—we have taken the liberty of enclosing an article in our today's issue bearing upon the mission of those who leave here from this Legislature to ask for troops.[2] It gives some insight in to the character of one of the leading members of the deputation. Hoping you will excuse the liberty taken . . .

Jones & Walker   "Eds Picayune"

LS, DLC-JP.

1. Jones (1844–1914), a Confederate staff officer who after the war became a lawyer and had a long public career, serving as Montgomery alderman, legislator, governor, and U.S. district judge. Walker (1844–*fl*1902), originally from Columbia, Tennessee, was a Confederate captain. After the war he moved permanently to Montgomery, where he became Jones's law partner. Sobel and Raimo, *Governors*, 1: 24; Emma S. White *Genealogy of the Descendants of John Walker of Wigton, Scotland* . . . (Kansas City, 1902), 522, 536; 1870 Census, Ala., Montgomery, Montgomery, 3rd Ward, 2.

2. The article was not found enclosed, but on September 23, 1868, Governor William H. Smith and a legislative committee left Montgomery for Washington. On the 28th they met with the President and the next day they met with him in the presence of Secretary Schofield. Johnson reportedly promised to assist them and to have General Meade instructed to that effect. Officially, Johnson referred the legislature's resolutions to Schofield, who in turn sent them to Meade. The latter was to be guided by the August 25 War Department instructions concerning military aid to marshals or sheriffs. *New York Herald*, Sept. 29, Oct. 1, 1868; *Washington Evening Star*, Sept. 28, 29, 1868. See also Peyton T. Groves et al. to Johnson, Sept. 26, 1868.

From Isaac Newton, Jr.
Personal

Washington   Sepr 22d 1868

Sir

The investigation in the case of Mr Heustis[1] Warden of the jail has closed I think as far as the action of Genl. Cox[2] is concerned. I am unable to say with what result, but I fear that the truth has not been elicited only in part—and I must say that I am confident that the greater part of the truth is still behind. I do not know what Gen. Cox proposes to do with the case; if his report is made out and I think it is, I desire very much that it should be PLACED in YOUR *hands at once*. For, Mr Heustis attempted on Sunday last, to persuade or force his Guards to sign a paper exonerating him from all CHARGES of whatever character that had been made against him. His Guards, or a majority of them refused to sign any such paper, and *did not sign it*; and they are anxious that *you* should give them a hearing, their names are Mr Noyes, I. Ross, Rust, & Bell.[3] I am sure Mr President that if you could get at half of the truth in this matter you would not allow him to retain his place for a single day.[4]

Isaac Newton

ALS, DLC-JP.

1. See Isaac Newton, Jr. to Johnson, Sept. 2, 1868.

2. John C. Cox, chief clerk of the Interior Department.

3. Joshua Noyes; Isaac W. Ross (*c*1802–*fl*1881), a New Jersey native; Benton Russ (*c*1833–*fl*1901) of Maine who became deputy warden in 1872; and John Bell. All but Noyes remained employed at the jail. Washington, D.C., directories (1868–1901); 1870 Census, D.C., Washington, 3rd Ward, 613; 4th Ward, 659; 5th Ward, 32.

4. Despite Newton himself being nominated in December, Huestis retained the post.

From Joseph Powell

Washington D C.   Sept 22d 1868

Dear Sir:

I learn that R. R. Butler is working very hard to try and defeat any payment the House may make, in my contest with him for a seat in Congress.[1] I have already expended too much money to give up this claim, and therefore must wait here until Congress meets in December. As I am necessarily hard pressed, I beg of you the favor of some small clerkship in the Departments somewhere, that will enable me to meet personal expenses until I can either sink or swim in my matters. I am frank with you and earnestly hope you will extend to me your kind consideration.

Joseph Powell

ALS, DLC-JP.

1. For an earlier discussion of the dispute between Roderick R. Butler and Powell over a Tennessee congressional seat, see Powell to Johnson, June 25, 1868, *Johnson Papers*, 14: 268. There is no evidence that Congress considered any resolution concerning payment for Powell during the third session of the 40th Congress.

From Rae Burr Batten

Philada   Sept 23d 1868.

Dear President

I hope you will excuse me for troubling You. The office of Measurers to which brother J. Earl Burr was appointed through Your kind request has been abolished. Brother had an interview with Collector Cake[1] and he assured him that it would afford him pleasure to comply with any request Your Excellency might make.

I sincerely hope that you will do brother the especial favor to write a line or indorse the application. I have taken the liberty to write to Col Cake in his behalf.[2]

Brother has always faithfully and honestly discharged his duties with satisfaction to the Goverment & Merchant—as You will see by the enclosed. I do assure you Dear President Your kindness would be highly appreciated by brother as well myself. Trusting to Your generosity to favour this request and that you may be enjoying Your usual good health . . .

Mrs Rae Batten

811 Race St

ALS, DNA-RG56, Appts., Customs Service, Subofficer, Philadelphia, J. Earl Burr.

1. Joseph W. Cake remained as collector of customs until March 1869. Johnson had nominated Cake's replacement in December 1868. An earlier reference to Cake's tenure as collector erroneously stated that he left that post in March 1868. See Wilson C. Swann and William H. Holloway to Johnson, Feb. 13, 1868, *Johnson Papers*, 13: 559.

2. Evidently Johnson did in fact write to Cake. See Rae Burr Batten to Johnson, Oct. 21, 1868.

From William W. Duffield

Belmont [Mich.]   Sept 23, 1868

My Dear Sir

I promised never to solicit any office of profit or trust and I still retain the pledge thus given But I find many whom I instructed in the school of the soldier, now ranking me by brevet. If you can without inconvenience, brevet me Major General it will incur no expense to the Government and as it carries neither command nor pay it is not an office either of profit or trust.[1]

I served eighteen months upon colonels pay, doing a general officers duty and subject to the expenses of that rank, as commander of forces at Murfreesboro Tennessee and subsequently in command of the state of Kentucky prior to being relieved by Genl Boyle.[2]

If you wish to state any particular occasion for the brevet, you can assign the pursuit, attack and destruction of John Morgans forces at Lebanon Tennessee in the spring of 1862. You are probably familiar with this attack being then military Governor of Tennessee. Genl

Dumont[3] claims the credit of this movement, but the forces engaged during the five days pursuit were those of my command, and I was not under Dumonts orders and he only accompanied me with but one member of his staff Capt Braydon.[4] His report however gives me full credit, and Genl Michler[5] who is now in Washington can give you all particulars of my service during the rebellion.

If you can do this without inconvenience or subjecting you to any annoyance please do so, but if not then I do not care enough for it to subject you to trouble on my account.

William W. Duffield

P.S. I was at the time of Lebanon [?] colonel of 9" Michigan Infantry in command of 23d Brigade, and the post at Murfreesboro Tennessee.

ALS, DNA, RG94, ACP Branch, File D-194-CB-1868, William W. Duffield.

   1. Duffield was never brevetted.

   2. Jeremiah T. Boyle.

   3. Ebenezer Dumont. See Dumont to Oliver D. Greene, May 5, 1862, *OR*, Ser. 1, Pt. 1, p. 884.

   4. T.P.M. Brayton served as assistant adjutant general. See Duffield to Brayton, May 6, 1862, ibid., pp. 885–86.

   5. Nathaniel Michler.

From Jared B. Waterbury[1]

Brooklyn L.I.   Sept. 23d /68

Dear Sir,

Two years ago, on application through Mayor Hoffman endorsed by Genl. Dix,[2] you gave my son, Wm. M Waterbury,[3] the appointment of 1st. Lieut. in the army. He had served through the late war, and was honorably mustered out; having a high record for military skill and fidelity from the Generals, under whom he served.

So soon as he was passed by the Examining Board, he proceeded to Arkansas, where he has been doing duty in all the responsible positions to which he has been assigned. He has served on Court martials—has acted for a time as post-adjutant; and for several weeks had the entire command of a company of rough recruits alone in Fayetteville Arkansas. In all these positions, he has shown himself the energetic and faithful officer.

Something like a year ago he asked me to request Senator Morgan to present his name to the then Secy. of War—Mr. Stanton[4]—for the hon: title of Brevt: Major, as several of his fellow officers had been thus honored. The Senator did so at once; and that was the last we have heard of it. Probably the late Secy. was so much engrossed in more weighty affairs, that no notice was taken of it.

But you are well aware Mr. President that what wd. seem of little importence to such a man as the late Secy. would be considered a valuable honor to one in the circumstances of my son. He is a very modest young man; but a purer—more upright and faithful officer, there is not I venture to say, in the army.

If then, dear Sir, you will give him this honor,[5] you will encourage modest merit, and oblige yours truly.

J. B Waterbury.

His address is Lieut. William M. Waterbury 19th Infantry. Fort Smith, Arkansas. And mine is Rev J B Waterbury D.D. Brooklyn, N.Y.

ALS, DNA-RG94, ACP Branch, File 4903-ACP-1873, W. M. Waterbury.

1. Waterbury (1799–1876) pastored various Presbyterian and Congregational churches in Massachusetts, New Hampshire, and New York, finally serving as city missionary in Brooklyn (1860–76). He was the author of eight books. *Appleton's Cyclopaedia.*

2. John Hoffman to Johnson, endorsed by John A. Dix, Aug. 28, 1866, ACP Branch, File 4903-ACP-1873, W. M. Waterbury, RG94, NA.

3. Waterbury (1841–1914) had been second and first lieutenant with the 4th N.Y. Arty. and was mustered out of service on January 3, 1865. He was appointed first lieutenant in the 19th U.S. Inf., effective July 1866, and was retired from the service for disability, with the rank of major in July 1895. Powell, *Army List*, 657; Pension File, Elizabeth S. Waterbury, RG15, NA.

4. Edwin D. Morgan and Edwin M. Stanton.

5. Jared B. Waterbury had already written to Johnson on February 18, 1868, about a brevet for his son. The letter was referred to General Grant who, on April 1, disapproved the application. ACP Branch, File 4903-ACP-1873, W. M. Waterbury, RG94, NA.

From Thomas W. Egan

Washington, D.C.   September 24, 1868.

My dear Mr. President

Since my interview with you this morning, I have seen General Sturgis,[1] and he is anxious to have you grant him the favor of an interview, together with myself, to-morrow.

Any hour convenient for you would suit us. If agreeable to you, I would suggest either 2 or 7 P.M. I am anxious to leave town to-morrow evening if possible.

I would remind you that Gen. Sturgis' regiment is now in Texas, which seems to render his assignment to duty according to his brevet rank consistent with propriety and usage.

Gen. S. is an old officer, and has a splendid record. He is and has been an ardent Democrat and a firm supporter of your Administration.

His would seem to be a creditable appointment in every way.

T. W. Egan.

ALS, DLC-JP.
　1. Samuel D. Sturgis (1822–1889) was a West Point graduate and a career army officer. During the Civil War he moved rapidly in rank to that of brigadier general of volunteers in 1861. In 1865 he was brevetted brigadier and major general but, once mustered out in August 1865, his regular army rank was lieutenant colonel of the 6th Cav. In May 1869 he became colonel of the 7th Cav. Thereafter he was stationed at various western forts. Warner, *Blue.*

From George W. Long[1]

Washington D.C.　September 24th 1868

Sir,

I called yesterday to thank you for the appointment you had directed the Secretary of the Navy to give me. I enclose a copy of his letter of the 27th ult,[2] granting me permission to report to Commodore J. B Marchand,[3] at Philadelphia Penna, for examination as to my qualifications for the position; in compliance with the same I reported, and passed a satisfactory examination. I desired to know what was next to be done in the matter, and called on the Hon Secretary to ascertain, but could not get to see him. Mr Edgar Welles, however, thought the appointment could not be made until the next meeting of Congress, his answers were indefinite, and left me in doubt as to whether the appointment would be made at all if left to the Navy Department. I intended returning to Saint Louis last evening, letting the matter rest for the present, but Col Morrow[4] advised me to see or communicate with you before leaving; he thought the appointment could be made at once, and that if I did not attend to it now, might never get it.[5]

Geo. W. Long

ALS, DLC-JP.
　1. In 1869 Long was in St. Louis, where he served as U.S. Navy paymaster. St. Louis directories (1869).

2. Not found enclosed.

3. John B. Marchand (1808–1875) was a career naval officer, first entering service in 1828. During the Civil War he held a variety of posts, including service with Farragut in the Gulf of Mexico. In 1866 he was promoted to commodore; he retired from the Navy four years later. *DAB.*

4. Robert Morrow.

5. On September 25, Long learned from Morrow that Secretary Welles had decided that no appointments could be made during the recess of Congress. Long's name would be forwarded to the Senate at the next session, however. Indeed, that was the case, for on December 7, Johnson presented Long's name to the Senate for appointment as assistant paymaster, from October 22. The Senate agreed to the nomination on December 18. Long to Johnson, Sept. 25, 1868, Johnson Papers, LC; *Senate Ex. Proceedings*, Vol. 16: 404, 412–13.

From Montgomery, Alabama, Citizens
September 24, 1868, Montgomery, Ala.; Pet, DLC-JP.

A meeting of the citizens of Montgomery, Alabama, held on Wednesday, September 23, 1868, chaired by Dr. Alfred A. Wilson with Micah Taul as secretary, unanimously adopted a preamble and resolutions and ordered a copy sent to Johnson. The "Radical party of the So-called legislature of Alabama" prepared a memorial stating that in Alabama there was "such domestic violence as prevents the due execution of the law, and such as creates apprehension of bloodshed at the approaching election in November." Gov. William H. Smith approved the memorial and agreed to be one of the party taking the document to President Johnson, despite the fact that the governor had never stated that there was any such violence, nor called out the militia to combat it, and had actually said that predictions of violence tended to make the Republicans look ridiculous. In fact, "the condition of Alabama was never more peaceful than at the present moment," and the Democrats had resolved "to obey the laws of the *de facto* State Government." Therefore, the meeting resolved: 1) that the memorial was false "in every particular"; 2) that the entire state was "peaceably disposed"; 3) that the partisan spirit demonstrated in the memorial would "plunge" the state into civil war; 4) that the stationing of U.S. Army troops in Alabama would be a constitutional violation and "an unjust imputation upon . . . character & conduct" of the citizens; 5) that the letter of Robert E. Lee and others to William S. Rosecrans be endorsed; 6) that the members of the legislature are mostly "strangers in the State," elected when two-thirds of the adult males, due to misinformation, did not vote, and that these legislators are robbing the state treasury, trying to deprive the people of the ballot, and slandering the state; 7) that the members of the legislature are corrupt and "capable of perpetrating even greater outrages."

From Jacob J. Noah

No. 139 F bet. 20th & 21st Sts.
Washington D.C.   Sept. 24 1868

Dear Sir

This will introduce my brother, Mr. R. P. Noah,[1] for whom you so kindly interested yourself with Secretary Welles. He will make some explanations touching the Rio Janiero Storekeepers' matters. Your consideration in his behalf will be gratifying to . . .

J. J. Noah

ALS, DLC-JP.

1. Robert P. Noah (*fl*1900) was a correspondent in Washington and subsequently a lawyer in New York City. Washington, D.C., directories (1869–70); New York City directories (1871–1900).

From Horatio Seymour

Utica   September 24 1868

My dear Sir

I am advised that no General officer is at this time credited to the State of New York. I am ignorant of the rules which govern military promotions and of the claims of individuals but I deem it proper to say that Bvt. Brigadier General Stoneman[1] has many warm friends in this State who will be gratified with his promotion to the vacancy made by the retirement of Genl Hooker.[2] It will give me great pleasure to learn that he is commissioned to a position he has earned by gallantry in war. I take the liberty of adding my name to the list of those who desire the advancement of General Stoneman.[3]

Horatio Seymour

ALS, DLC-JP.

1. George Stoneman, a New York native, held the regular army rank of colonel and commanded the 1st Mil. Dist. from the fall of 1866 until his regiment moved west in 1869. Altshuler, *Cavalry Yellow & Infantry Blue*, 320–21.

2. Joseph Hooker retired on October 15 because of disability. Several persons other than Stoneman were recommended to fill the vacancy. But in anticipation of congressional action to reduce the army, Johnson delayed a nomination. On January 20, 1869, Johnson finally forwarded nominations for the two existing brigadier general vacancies occasioned by Hooker's

retirement and Lovell Rousseau's death. They were Robert C. Buchanan and Alvan C. Gillem. But the Senate tabled the nominations. Daniel Butterfield, *Major-General Joseph Hooker* (New York, 1896), 29; Simon, *Grant Papers*, 19: 297; *DAB*; *Washington Evening Star*, Nov. 13, 1868, Jan. 20, 1869; *New York Tribune*, Jan. 11, 1869.

3. Among those recommending Stoneman were Perez Dickinson and John Williams of Knoxville, and John Gittings of Baltimore. Dickinson and Williams to Johnson, Sept. 25, 1868; Gittings to Johnson, Sept. 26, 1868, Johnson Papers, LC. There are a number of other documents in Volume 15 concerning the replacement of Hooker.

From John M. Binckley

New York, 25 September 1868

Mr. President:

In your Excellency's order whereby I am here, I am directed to "supervise, within the sphere of your <my> office, any prosecutions which may arise from your <my> investigations; first, however, refuting the facts for instructions, by the proper authority."[1]

The following state of facts has arisen: the Attorney of the United States for the Southern District of New York[2] has been informed officially by the then Acting Attny General of the United States,[3] in effect, that he could not accede to his request to be relieved from appearing in the case of the United States v. Rollins and others, and that the Attny General[4] had not the power to grant such a request; and moreover, that not having any information on the subject of my being authorized to represent the United States in said action, he felt competent to advise the court, on behalf of the government, that I was an intruder. The court therefore recognizing the right of the Executive, through the Attny General, to define the status of counsel for the government, promptly, though respectfully, decided that I must desist from participating in the conduct of the prosecution.[5] Subsequently, able special counsel[6] was employed to "assist" the District Attny in said prosecution, which is now in progress under such supervision on my part as my orders authorize. Meantime, evidence is in my reach directly showing that the District Attorney aforesaid has violated the statute against bribery.[7] It is not an unnatural presumption under those circumstances, that such an office should not be trusted with the control of any criminal litigation of the government. On the other hand, as I understand the decision of the court in the pending case, given exclusively in deference to the position assumed by the government, through the then Acting Attorney General, no counsel, official or special, can be qualified to institute and conduct a complaint against the District Atty without his own co-operation and control. Your Excellency has no doubt of my personal views on this point of law, nor of what I should promptly do, were I not exonerated from moral and legal responsibility in the premises by the concluding clause of my orders. That the United States cannot appear in their own courts to vindicate their own sovereignty against crime without the authority of the malefactor himself, appears to me to be the mortifying but logical result of the strange position that the consent of the District Attny is necessary to the standing of a prosecutor for the government.

I respectfully submit the case of the District Attny in this city for practical determination; my opinion just expressed being, of course, subject to the better judgment of my superior law officers.[8]

John M Binckley
Solicitor of Internal Rev

ALS, DLC-JP.

1. See Johnson to Binckley, Sept. 19, 1868.

2. Samuel G. Courtney.

3. J. Hubley Ashton.

4. William M. Evarts.

5 See Binckley to Johnson, Sept. 10, 1868, and Samuel G. Courtney to Johnson, Oct. 1, 1868.

6. William Fullerton.

7. George A. Fitch, who was involved in initiating the whiskey fraud investigations, also accused Samuel G. Courtney of receiving bribes. Fitch later recanted, but was arrested for perjury nonetheless. See Fitch to Johnson, Sept. 12, 1868, and Binckley to Johnson, Oct. 7, 1868.

8. Courtney continued as prosecutor and district attorney. For his rebuttal, see Courtney to Johnson, Oct. 1, 1868.

From Samuel G. Courtney

New York, Sept. 25, 1868

Sir:

I received a copy of the report of the Solicitor of Internal Revenue,[1] (heretofore filed in the Executive Department) through the office of the Attorney General.

I have the honor to inform you that shortly, and just as soon as my pressing official duties will allow, I will submit to you an answer to the statement of Mr. Binckley,[2] as far as said report refers to me; and, in the mean time, to say to you, that all the statements, inuendoes, insinuations or imputations in said report contained, derogatory to, or in any manner reflecting upon, me, personally or officially, are utterly false.

> Samuel G Courtney,
> U.S. Atty.

LS, DLC-JP.
   1. On September 15 Courtney wrote to Johnson, requesting a copy of Binckley's report on the whiskey fraud investigation. Courtney to Johnson, Sept. 15, 1868, Johnson Papers, LC. For Binckley's report, see Binckley to Johnson, Sept. 10, 1868.
   2. See Courtney to Johnson, Oct. 1, 1868.

From Samuel N. Goodale[1]

Washington D.C.   Sept 25", 1868.

Sir:

I am desirous to introduce among the Indians of the Frontier— Hand Looms, to be made attractive by colored yarns & rolls for which they have a natural fondness, & with a view of teaching them to fabricate their own blankets, and lead them to habits of industry.

Wishing to secure Letters of Authority from the Executive, (The Commissioner[2] being absent, from whom I have received preliminary directions), herewith find a copy of the commissioner's first instructions,[3] since which I have transmitted many reports, corroborated by Indian Superintendents and agents, who urge the importance of its adoption.[4] Also, find Senator Ross' letter of recommendation,[5] he alludes to my being the inventor of the Loom. In justice to others, I must disclaim that, or any pecuniary interest in it. I am instigated by a desire to promote industry among an unfortunate class of the Govts. wards, hoping thereby to improve their condition.

This may be surely though gradually achieved, by furnishing me with authority to visit such tribes as are submissive to our Govt. and leaving with them one hand-loom, after teaching them its use,— with such material as is necessary to accomplish the object, with authority to take a receipt for the cost of such machine, & materials with the agreement that the amount may be deducted from annuities now or which may hereafter be due them. Such Letter of Authority will enable to enter at once, upon the duties contemplated.

Allow me to add that Senators Henderson & Doolittle and others of the committee[6] with whom I have talked, express themselves warmly in favor of the plan, & trust the same will meet with Executive incouragement.[7]

S N Goodale

LS, DNA–RG75, Gen. Records, Lets. Recd. (M234, Roll 461).

1. Goodale (c1818–f1870), a native of Massachusetts, was a Lawrence, Kansas, wool merchant. 1870 Census, Kans., Douglas, Lawrence, 4th Ward, 365.

2. Commissioner of Indian Affairs Nathaniel G. Taylor.

3. Not found.

4. Not found.

5. Edmund G. Ross to Johnson, Sept. 5, 1868, Gen. Records, Lets. Recd. (M234, Roll 461), RG75, NA.

6. John B. Henderson, James R. Doolittle, and other members of the Senate's Committee on Indian Affairs.

7. There is no known response to this request.

From William J. Barker[1]

Black Hawk Colorado   Sept 26th 1868

Dr Sir

We have been having some unpleasant feelings with the Poor Indians for the past few months and the result has been about one hundred and fifty whites have been killed or carried away Captives and I am pained to Say some twenty five Braves have been Slain by the white settlers.[2] I learn that the Indian Commissioners are on their way to treat with the Indians also provided with presents for them. I have also learned that Some few Indians are not provided with long range breach loading rifles. I would suggest that the Commissioners be provided with say fifty of the best rifles to be given to those who are not well armed. I think that number will supply all not already provided for by the Commissioners in their visits. Perhaps it would be well to send a few of Colts Revolvers. Do not fail to have a generous supply of Blankets & provisions as winter is Comming on. Also an extra amount of Amunition as most of the western settlers are so cruel as to refuse to sell the Indians any Since their unpleasant troubles.

Wm. J. Barker

ALS, DLC-JP.

1. Barker (c1832–1900), a Republican, was a feed dealer in Central City, Colorado, and then in Denver. He was mayor of the latter in 1874–76. Denver Republican, Mar. 28, 1900.

2. From August through October there were a substantial number of raids, mostly by Cheyenne and Arapaho Indians, in Kansas as well as Colorado. They ran off much stock and killed seventy-nine settlers. *American Annual Cyclopaedia* (1868), 381–82; Robert M. Utley, *Frontier Regulars: The United States Army and the Indian, 1866–1891* (New York, 1973), 143–44.

From Charles A. Eldridge

Washington   Sept. 26, 1868

Mr. President.

I called this evening with Mr. C. H. Snow[1] to see you. I feel that the Intelligencer has done much to defend & protect us. I dined this afternoon with Mr. Snow. I learn that he has put in to that concern all that he has, all that his wife[2] has & all that his Father[3] has. It seems as though they ought to be protected if they can be. Waht I wanted to talk with you about was, if there was any way to aid them & make them whole. It will be a calamity to the country & the cause of constitutional republican government for the Intelligencer to go down. It has been our most reliable & earnest defender. Is there not some way that it can be helped & sustained?[4]

I write this after learning that it is not probable that you will be able to see me this evening. I leave on tomorrow evening for the Campaign in Pennsylvania.

C A Eldridge

ALS, DLC-JP.

1. Chauncey H. Snow.

2. Not identified.

3. William R. Snow (*fl*1869), a former steamboat agent who operated a coal company with his son in 1866–67. Washington, D. C., directories (1863–69).

4. The *Intelligencer* received no further patronage. See John F. Coyle to Johnson, July 25, 1868.

From Peyton T. Groves et al.[1]

Hayneville, Ala.   Sept. 26. 1868

Honored Sir:

At a meeting of the citizens of this County on this day—composed of over three thousand citizens of all political parties and of both races, white and black, the following resolutions were unanimously adopted and a copy ordered to be forwarded to your Excellency, duly certified, to wit:

"Whereas the body styling itself the General Assembly of Alabama, on the 21st instant did adopt, by a partisan vote, a preamble and resolutions, memorializing the President of the United States to detail troops for the preservation of law and order within the State[2]—and

Whereas the peaceable deportment of our people under the repeated injuries and humiliations to which they have been subjected prove them to be law abiding and forbearing beyond precedent therefore be it

Resolved, that we, a portion of the people of Alabama, in mass meeting assembled irrespective of party ties and predilections hereby declare that said memorial is false in fact, and is a reflection and libel upon all the people of the State.

Resolved further, that it can only be regarded as a measure to create political capital for the Radical party at the North, and that it was palpably and deliberately designed for that purpose.

Resolved further; that while our people do not object to the mere presence of federal troops in their midst, they utterly deny the necessity; for they are deeply impressed with the importance of peace and repose for their oppressed section.

Resolved that the Executive Committee of Lowndes County be instructed to forward a copy of these resolutions to the President of the United States, the Governor of this State, and that all the newspapers of the State be requested to give them circulation."[3]

(Signed) Peyton T. Groves

Copy, DNA-RG107, Lets. Recd., Executive (M494, Roll 104).

1. In addition to Groves, three secretaries, John Enochs, Cecil D. Whitman, and Robert M. Michael, signed the document. Groves (c1823–ff1880), a Confederate legislator in 1863, was a farmer. Enochs (c1841–ff1880) was a lawyer. Whitman (c1842–ff1870) owned a livery stable. Michael (c1848–ff1870) was a "publisher." 1870 Census, Ala., Lowndes, 1st Beat, 9; 2nd Beat, 4, 33; (1880), 108th Enum. Dist., 39; 110th Enum. Dist., 31; Willis Brewer, *Alabama: Her History, Resources, War Record, and Public Men* (Tuscaloosa, 1964 [1872]), 336.

2. The Alabama legislature's resolution indicated that in portions of the state, civil authorities had not yet begun their duties, and consequently, in many counties laws were "neither respected nor obeyed, and violence has been committed." Therefore, "the cause of peace, law and order" required "an armed force to be detailed by the President." *Washington Evening Star*, Sept. 28, 1868; *New York Herald*, Sept. 29, 1868. See also Thomas G. Jones and Henry T. Walker to Johnson, Sept. 22, 1868, and Montgomery, Alabama, Citizens to Johnson, Sept. 24, 1868.

3. An endorsement indicates that on October 5 Johnson referred the Hayneville resolutions to Secretary Schofield "for immediate reference to *Maj. Gen'l. Meade* . . . for his information."

From Lovell H. Rousseau

New Orleans, La., Sept 26th 1868.

Sir.

I cannot give you in a letter a very accurate account of the condition of affairs here. I wish I could. But, I can only say that it could not be much worse, and yet, I do not despair of keeping the peace. The public mind is in a continual state of excitement, looking constantly for a riot. The wildest reports on that subject are received, and credited, causing the assembly of crowds of people and keeping up the most intense excitement. Nothing could more fully show the state of the public mind here than the credence given to these reports, as it evinces the fact that the people expect a Mob and that the expectation is based on a full knowledge of the same condition of affairs.

I can compare the population here to nothing so apt as a volcano, ready for an explosion at any moment. There is no confidence among the people in the Civil Authorities and these Authorities have very little in themselves, antagonistic as they are to nearly all the white population of the city and state. Both people and authorities persist in looking to the Military to keep the peace, and this in spite of their constant tendency to break it. The Chief of Police[1] and two thirds of his force are partisan Radicals, the balance are partisan Democrats and I have no doubt that both Radicals and Democrats would take sides according to political bias in any riot that occurs. All the respectable whites and people of property are entirely forbearing and submissive desirous of and hoping for peace on almost any terms. Seven tenths of the Niggers are of the same mind. In fact there would be very little trouble with the Niggers, if left to themselves, though some of the Leaders and Strykers of that race in this city and state are of the worst possible character, and many of the Radical leaders from abroad soarjouning and filling responsible positions do all they can to influence the minds of the Niggers in order to keep them completely Radical.

But there is so much to excite and irritate occurring every day and hour that none but the most hopeful would expect to pass through the next forty days without the most terriffic Mob and riot that ever occurred on this continent.

I have busied myself assiduously in keeping the peace and to that end have become acquainted and conferred with the "Govenor" the "Mayor"[2] and "Chief" of Police together with the leading men of both parties. The Radicals have not been much inclined to the afiliation except the "Govenor" "Genrl. Lee" "Senator Ray"[3] and a few others. I have endeavored to deserve and obtain the confidence of all parties and think I have succeeded pretty well, though each party has hertofore demanded that the Military commander here should be wholly with one side or the other.

I have told plainly all parties that the Civil Authorities must keep the peace, That the Military could not be called out until after an honest effort to do so had failed, That the Army was not here as a Police, but if called upon by the Authorities or the necessity of the occasion it would discharge its duty to put down the aggressors no matter who they might be.

There is little or no division among the white residents of the City or State in politics. They are all Democrats. They have constant processions in the city often half a dozen a night. They uniformly carry United States Flags and are uniformly without exception as far as I have heard peaceful, decorous, and well behaved and this notwistanding the irritation caused by offensive Laws, enacted by for the most part strangers of extreme political views antagonistic to them, and ignorant Negroes and enforced in the most offensive manner. These people are greatly impoverished and yet their state taxes in addition to the National are *Enormous* levied by a Legislature the leading Men of whom they say have no interest in common with them, and the balance have neither interest or capacity.

The Legislature as at present constituted is but a shamefull and disgraceful burlesque upon Republican institutions. No Man can fully appreciate this assertion without an actual view of that body.

In the belief that they have an overwhelming majority of Conservatives in the City and State, They have little hope that the vote will be either taken or counted if taken. Baker[4] an unnaturalized Englishman is chairman of the Board of Registrars. All concede him to be an unmitigated scoundrel and the rules of registering he had adopted would exclude his opponents almost in a body. As one of these rules in substance regects all who did not vote the Republican ticket.[5] In this view they can see no end to their dilemma as they wake up every morning and find a new trick adopted by those in power to deprive them of their share in self Goverment—another Nail rivetted in their shackels.

You can immagine the state of mind of a people thus situated Goaded hourly by such anoyances and means of irritation as a Political party in power composed as before stated would offer.

I can give no assurance of the future except that I shall endeavor to do my duty as an Officer of the Army. Col. McKibben[6] can tell what else you would know of affairs here. If the vote was fairly taken in the State it will go Democratic by twenty to thirty thousand.

Lovell H Rousseau

LS, DLC-JP.

1. John J. Williamson (c1840–fl1892), a 1st lieutenant and captain in the 128th N.Y. Inf. and chief ordnance officer for Gen. Gordon Granger at the end of the Civil War, apparently served briefly as New Orleans chief of police in 1868. In the early 1870s he may have been a railroad agent. He lived in Boston later. *New Orleans Picayune*, Sept. 18, 1868; New Orleans directories (1868–71); *OR*, Ser. 1, Vol. 49, pt. 2: 25, 133; 1870 Census, La., Orleans, New Orleans, 2nd Ward, 165; Pension File, John J. Williamson, RG15, NA.

2. Henry C. Warmoth and John R. Conway.

3. Albert L. Lee and John Ray.

4. William Baker (fl1873) had been registrar of voters under Sheridan and then served as street commissioner, in which post he had been charged with misconduct in office. He was appointed registrar by Warmoth in early September 1868. Later he may have been deputy customs collector and commissioner of the Metropolitan Police Board. *New Orleans Picayune*, Sept. 9, 25, 26, 1868, morning; New Orleans directories (1868–73).

5. See "Baker's Instructions to Supervisors of Registration," *New Orleans Picayune*, Sept. 26, 1868, morning.

6. Probably Joseph C. McKibbin (1824–1896), a Pennsylvanian who moved to California in 1849, where he practiced law, served in the state senate, and was elected to a single term in Congress (1857–59). At the outbreak of the Civil War he was one of the first cavalry officers appointed by Lincoln and he served as a colonel and additional aide-de-camp on the staff of Gen. George H. Thomas and several other generals. After the war he settled in Washington, D.C. *BDUSC*.

To Henry A. Smythe

Executive Mansion, September 26, 1868.

Dear Sir

I hope that you will be able to make provision for General Egan.[1] It is not necessary that I should refer to his services during the war, or to his capabilities; for you are yourself familiar with both. He deserves the appointment which he seeks, and I sincerely hope will receive it.

Andrew Johnson

ES, InFwL.

1. There is no evidence that Thomas W. Egan received a position at Smythe's hands. He did receive a customhouse appointment under Ulysses S. Grant, and worked as either weigher or deputy collector for several years. *New York Times*, Feb. 25, 1887; Egan to Grant, May 1870, Simon, *Grant Papers*, 20: 431.

General Lovell H. Rousseau. By Mathew B. Brady.
Courtesy National Archives

General Joseph Hooker. By Mathew B. Brady.
Courtesy National Archives.

From Bernard A. Maguire[1]

Geo. Town College, D.C.   Sep. 27th 1868

Dear Sir

In a conversation with Your Excellency a few days ago you desired me to state in writing a request which I then made. Two of our Fathers Revd. Joseph O'Callaghan & Revd. Joseph Keller[2] are about to visit Rome on matters concerning the Church. They desire, if consistent with usage or in your power, to receive a letter from the State Department which might save them from annoyances in the various Custom houses in France and Italy.

If Your Excellency can do any thing in the case you will add another to many past favors and greatly oblige . . .[3]

B. A. Maguire   S.J.

ALS, NRU.

1. Maguire (*fl*1877), a Jesuit priest, served two different terms as president of Georgetown (1852–58, 1866–70). *NUC*; Joseph T. Durkin, *Georgetown University: First in the Nation's Capital* (Garden City, 1964), 36–40, 42–43, 140.

2. Keller (1827–1886) became a Jesuit priest in 1844 and taught in a variety of Jesuit colleges. In 1868 he represented his order at a convention in Rome. He was provincial of the Maryland province (1869–77) and afterward president of St. Louis University and then Woodstock Seminary in Maryland. O'Callaghan is not identified. *Appleton's Cyclopaedia.*

3. On October 2 Johnson endorsed this letter to Seward hoping "he may not find it inconsistent with the public interests to grant the request of the Reverend Dr. Maguire."

From Philip B. Fouke

New Orleans   Sept 28th 1868

My Dear Sir

Your uniform kindness to me assures me in the privilege of writing. You have very many very warm friends here. In the Canvass be assured Sir that your name is never forgotten. The mere mention of it draws forth warm and hearty applause from every conservitive heart. We have a very stormey & exciteing town—but I assure you that there is not the least danger of an outbreak if the negroes behave themselves. The Conservitives are *determined* to have peace & quiet if posible. They will submit to insult—*anything* but blows. Our excellent friend Major Perry Fuller has arrived and taken charge of his office.[1] He has gone to work in good earnest. The change is already manifest. He will become one of most popular as well as eficient offercers that has been here for many years—but even *that* will not protect him from the shafts of malice and vindictiveness. He is firm just and obliging. The business community here hail his advent with more than pleasure.

P B Fouke

ALS, DLC-JP.
1. Perry Fuller had assumed the post of collector of customs at New Orleans on September 21, 1868. *New Orleans Picayune*, Sept. 22, 1868, morning. See Fuller to Johnson, Aug. 21, 1868, *Johnson Papers*, 14: 530; Fuller to Johnson, Sept. 30, 1868.

From Charles C. Yeaton

PRIVATE

[New York]   8. P.M., Sept. 28th, 1868.

Mr. President:—

Since my arrival here this morning I have been very busily occupied.[1] I have not only conversed with the leading and honest citizens of this great metropolis, with a view to learn their sentiments regarding this investigation, but have ventured into the very midst of the so-called "Whiskey Ring." I have seen Messrs. Binckley and Fullerton, several Editors-in-chief of the daily journals and last— and by no means least—the senior Editor and proprietor of this paper,[2] with whom I had an hour's interview. I found him disengaged, in a remarkably happy frame of mind and delighted to see me.

Before proceeding further I would say that although Mr. Bennett is past seventy six (76) years of age, he is in the full vigor of health and evinces the deepest interest in every event of the day; and especially all such as pertains to the growth and welfare of our Country. It should be remembered that at this ripe age which Mr. Bennett has attained, and with those peculiar advantages which have been at his command—having been the leading journalist of this Country for many years—his knowledge and experience must necessarily be very great and extensive; and whenever he expresses his views, upon any subject, in all *candor* and *sincerity*, and from a *disinterested standpoint*, I have always listened to his teachings with profound reverence, and rarely ever found him mistaken'd in his predictions.

To day he talked much of you, your persecutions and of the manfulness with which you have borne them all through out your administration. I will not enter into details, for I am writing in much haste: This much I will say he is to be numbered among your admirers, and is undoubtedly your very warm and sincere friend.

In the matter of investigating the internal revenue frauds Mr. B.

says he will support you with all his strength; the people seem to have believed that all your characteristic traits of earnestness and bravery had been swallowed up in the impeachment trial, and that you had not sufficient ambition left to rise again to the fullness of your power. While this feeling was allowed to exist, but little enthusiasm on the part of the people or press could be expected, and comparatively no encouragement tendered you to go on in the great fight. Now since you have shown a persistent disposition to ventilate these frauds—in the matter of sending back Mr. Binckley to 'face the music'[3]—not only *his* paper but the whole press and honest people of the country will rally to your support. He furthermore said: "Give the President my compliments, and impress upon him the necessity of prompt, determined and powerful action. This is his opportunity—his last chance before retiring from office—let him embrace it! If he is successful in his efforts he will have achieved much to perpetuate his name; and it will be a great and crowning glory to all else he has accomplished to popularize his name in future ages."

I shall enclose for your perusal an editorial,[4] clipped from today's Herald, to which Mr. Bennett called my attention as a proof of his sincerity to support you in—what he calls—"the most gigantic and laudable undertaking known to the age."

I took Mr. Binckley to the Tribune Office this evening, where I introduced him to Horace Greeley, who also gave assurances of earnest support.

Mr. G. remarked that "while he did not believe Mr. Rollins was a dishonest man he regarded him as a very weak one, and hoped you would succeed in removing him from office, as he had already done all *he* could in order to accomplish that end."

I have stated to Messrs. Binckley and Fullerton what you said to me yesterday relative to protecting witnesses and the employment of detectives. That appears scarcely satisfactory; but what is more requisite now (I mean immediately) than anything else is a *proper* fund for them to draw from.[5] If this cannot be furnished the prosecution must fail, while the malefactors, stimulated by this assault, redouble their hold upon the means of escaping criminal justice. The question is very suggestive: shall the "Whiskey Ring" conquor the Government, or, shall the Government conquor the "Whiskey Ring"? This question I know can be solved by no one so promptly as by you.

The Secretary of the Treasury has allowed Mr. Binckley to draw but one thousand.[6] The Secretary must be aware of such an absurdity. It is virtually an impliment to impede the way of justice and appears to me as rediculous as the Massachusetts legislature when—after the declaration of independence—it appropriated twenty thousand pounds with which to support American independence against the power of the British Empire.

Messrs. Binckley and Fullerton want at least, to start with, a fund of twenty five (25) thousand dollars to draw against. This is a trifle compared with the amount at the command of the Whiskey Ring. This Ring is a powerful institution by itself and keeps a set of books upon which are shown the amount of its receipts, expenditures and to whom paid. Judge Fullerton is in possession of knowledge where these books can be found; and today employed detectives to bring them to him; but before they had actually proceeded ten squares they had been bought over by the "Whiskey Ring." This state of affairs is most deplorable and alarming.

This evening Mr. Odway,[7] Sargent at Arms, House of Representatives, served papers upon Messrs. Binckley and Fitch[8] to appear before the "Smelling" Committee,[9] on the first of October, to meet, I understand at the Astor House.

Chas. C. Yeaton

LS, DLC-JP.

    1. Yeaton was in New York City, serving in some semi-official capacity as an assistant in the whiskey fraud investigations. *New York Herald*, Nov. 3, 8, 1868; *New York Times*, Nov. 15, 1868. See also K. L. Hodges to Johnson, Nov. 23, 1867, *Johnson Papers*, 13: 254–55. For an unflattering opinion of Yeaton, see K. L. Hodges to Johnson, Nov. 6, 1868.

    2. James G. Bennett, Sr., of the *New York Herald*.

    3. See Johnson to John M. Binckley, Sept. 19, 1868.

    4. The clipping, not found enclosed, praised Johnson for his attempt to break up the "whiskey ring" which had been defrauding the government of revenue. A note on a September 22 letter from John M. Binckley to Johnson read: "Mr Bennet flatly promised to support me with the Herald," another indication of that paper's stance. *New York Herald*, Sept. 28, 1868; Binckley to Johnson, Sept. 22, 1868, Johnson Papers, LC.

    5. Other interested parties also stressed the need for increased financial support. For instance, see A. B. Ely to Johnson, Sept. 30, 1868; Henry S. Fitch to Johnson, Oct. 3, 1868; Binckley to Johnson, Oct. 9, 1868.

    6. Although McCulloch did extend to Binckley a credit line of $1,000, Binckley wrote to him on October 9 arguing that a substantial increase was necessary to continue the prosecution. John M. Binckley to Hugh McCulloch, Oct. 9, 1868, Johnson Papers, LC.

    7. Nehemiah G. Ordway (1828–1907) was sergeant-at-arms from 1863 until 1875, after which he returned to his native New Hampshire and served in the state legislature. For four years he was governor of the Dakota Territory (1880–84). Thomas A. McMullin and David Walker, *Biographical Directory of American Territorial Governors* (Westport, 1984), 87–89.

    8. George A. Fitch.

    9. A subcommittee of the House Committee on Retrenchment traveled to New York City to investigate, quite literally, the investigation. The December report, produced by the Republican-dominated subcommittee, criticized Binckley severely and concluded the investigation

was intended to implicate revenue commissioner Edward A. Rollins in revenue fraud, thus allowing Johnson to remove him from office. *House Reports*, 40 Cong., 3 Sess., No. 3, pp. 1–14 (Ser. 1388); *New York Times*, Dec. 22, 1868. For a rebuttal of the subcommittee's findings, see the letter by Binckley, published in the *New York Times*, Dec. 28, 1868. See also Binckley to Johnson, Oct. 9, 1868.

From Cynthia Elliott Morris[1]

Memphis   Sept 29th 1868

Dear Sir—

I have again presumed, to appeal to your kindness—for redress and remuneration—relative to my property used by the U S forces at "Ft. Pickering" Col McClary,[2]—appointed Commissioner at your request, awarding me—8000$ dollars—as damages on same. Congress, having made no appropriapriation, to meet this—I will await the issue of the future, trusting, that "Republics may not prove ungreatful" in all cases to the daughters of her gallant vetrans of "1812." I hold a receipt from Genl. Wm. T Sherman handed me by *his order*, when in command of the Post Head Qtr— Memphis for the Sum of 1,400$ dollars. The amt was so small that I have withheld it 'till now. May I ask a letter from you to Genl Wm. Sherman, coroperating this statement and ask throug you that the Govement allow this. As *taxes are now due*, to state of *Tennessee*, on the *same property* used by the *Fedral Govement*, and left in a *condition*, that *denies all income* from *rent*.

I trust it may yet be my happy privilidge to thank you in person when you return to a "Hermitage" of private life as a daughter of the late Col Geo Elliott[3]—for your kindness.

Mrs Cynthia Elliott Morris

Adress me care Messrs Mosby & Dorion[4] Memphis.

ALS, DLC-JP.

1. Morris (b. c1807) was married to Walter B. Morris, who died sometime during the 1850s. By 1860 she was living with her son, Calvin. 1850 Census, Tenn., Shelby, 14th Civil Dist., 178; (1860), Chickasaw City, Memphis, 98.

2. Not identified.

3. Elliott (1780–1861) was a long-time resident of Sumner County, where he was a successful farmer. He had distinguished himself in the War of 1812 in battles in Alabama and at New Orleans, where he was wounded. He was long active in Democratic party politics. *Gallatin Examiner*, Feb. 9, 1861; Walter T. Durham, *Old Sumner: A History of Sumner County, Tennessee from 1805 to 1861* (Nashville, 1972), 10, 78; 1860 Census, Tenn., Sumner, 11th Dist., 26.

4. Mosby and Dorion was a cotton factor firm in Memphis. Samuel Mosby (1809–1886) was a principal partner in this firm. Charles H. Dorion, Jr. (fl1871) was the other member of the firm's leadership. *Memphis Appeal*, Mar. 4, 1886; Memphis directories (1860–71).

To John M. Schofield

Washington, D.C. Sept. 29 1869

Will the Honorable the Secretary of War please furnish me, at his earliest convenience, with a copy of any charges preferred during the war against Colonel C.H.B Collis,[1] of Pennsylvania, and especially with a copy of those preferred against that officer by General Birney,[2] immediately after the battle of Chancellorsville?[3]

Andrew Johnson

LS, DNA-RG107, Lets. Recd., Executive (M494, Roll 104).

1. Charles H.T. Collis (1838–1902) served as colonel of the 114th Pa. Inf. He was brevetted brigadier general, October 1864, and major general, March 1865. Collis was a lawyer by profession. Hunt and Brown, *Brigadier Generals*.

2. David B. Birney (1825–1864) was in business and the practice of law in Philadelphia until the outbreak of the war. He quickly advanced in rank from lieutenant colonel to colonel to brigadier general. Promoted in May 1863 to major general, he saw action at Chancellorsville and Gettysburg. Warner, *Blue*.

3. According to a report written at the time by Birney, Collis and others left their command posts and withdrew to the rear. For this action Collis was arrested; he was subsequently tried on the charge of misbehavior before the enemy but was acquitted. See Reports No. 112 and 119 in *OR*, Ser. 1, Vol. 25, Pt. 1: 407–10, 422–25.

From Alfred B. Ely

Boston Mass   Sept 30. 1868.

Sir.

I have just returned from New York, where I have facilities for getting at the bottom of some things, and having taken some pains to ascertain regarding the movements of Mr Binkley, (whom you have sent there in relation to frauds upon the revenue,) I feel constrained to say to you that I am persuaded he is on the right track, and will prove it, if he is only cordially and properly sustained. It will rest with you to make his work a success or a failure. He will need large assistance in men and money, and he will need *prompt* and energetic action. His great obstacle is the government, that is, government officials. He will be thwarted in every way; but he has pluck and confidence and honesty, and he deserves success. He is working for the people, against the official thieves and politicians, and I trust you will give him every assistance he may require.[1]

A. B. Ely

ALS, DLC-JP.

   1. Ely was not alone in calling for financial assistance for the whiskey fraud investigations. See Charles C. Yeaton to Johnson, Sept. 28, 1868.

From Perry Fuller

New Orleans, La.   Sept 30th, 1868.

Dear Sir:

After one week of labor in my new position,[1] I take the liberty of making a statement of the condition of affairs, for your information. I found the office in a bad condition, having been made by my predecessor a political machine for his election,[2] and all the most important positions under his control used for political purposes only. I think Sec'y McCulloch is deceived in Capt. Stockdale[3] who was first deputy, for although a good business man as far as the duties of the office are concerned, I found he had combinations and arrangements for his own benefit, in connection with other officers, that were disgraceful, and he is now doing all in his power to aid men who were removed by me at once upon my arrival.

The removals and appointments I have made,[4] after consulting your friends here, and your true friends in this city are very many. Your unceasing defence of the rights of the people have endeared all men to you in the South whose friendship is worth having, and they look to you alone to carry them through the trials & tribulations they so patiently endure.

The Democrats are making a very vigorous canvass, and the political excitement is intense. The young men are full of fire and enthusiasm and nearly all organized into different clubs,[5] and it is with difficulty that the older citizens can keep them within bounds. After long untiring urging by influential conservative citizens, the Governor[6] has vetoed the Social Equality Bill,[7] which gives great satisfaction.

I called on him yesterday in reference to the miserable registry regulations now being enforced by Baker,[8] who is particularly obnoxious to the citizens, and the Gov. promised me to have a bill passed at once correcting the regulations. If it is not done and Baker and the Gov. do not act fairly in the matter, I would not as a Life Insurance agent take any risks on either of their lives at a small premium. Of one thing I am quite convinced, and that is that the Democracy of the country will have to consent to negro suffrage before they can control their votes. They realize that the Radicals are only their friends to secure their votes, and would act with the Democrats if accorded half the same privileges.

Gen'l. Steedman is working very earnestly making telling speeches all about the City. Gen'l. Rousseau is gladly received and much liked. Col Foulke[9] is doing all he can—in fact all are exerting themselves but the Assessor of Int. Rev.[10]

Perry Fuller

LS, DLC-JP.

1. Fuller assumed his duties as collector of customs at New Orleans on September 21, 1868. *New Orleans Picayune*, Sept. 22, 1868, morning.

2. William P. Kellogg had recently been elected to the U.S. Senate.

3. Sidney A. Stockdale.

4. As of September 22 Fuller had appointed W. C. Grey as deputy collector and Fred A. deWolfe as second deputy. A newspaper report on September 30 projected extensive changes to take place at the customhouse that day. Sixty-five "Union men" were summarily discharged and allegedly replaced by 150 Democrats and former rebels. *New Orleans Picayune*, Sept. 22, 30, 1868, morning; New Orleans directories (1869); Petition of C. B. Young et al., Oct. 2, 1868, Johnson Papers, LC.

5. Among these clubs were the Chanticleers, Seymour Cadets, Seymour Southrons, and Minute Men of '68. One newspaper editorial commented that 15,000 Democratic club members would turn out for major events. *New Orleans Picayune*, Sept. 28, Oct. 1, 1868, evening.

6. Henry C. Warmoth.

7. The bill provided punishment for the owner of any public place, such as a hotel or steamboat, which did not provide equal accommodations for whites and blacks. Warmoth vetoed the bill on September 25, and, for so doing, lost a good deal of his black support. Richard N. Current, *Those Terrible Carpetbaggers* (New York, 1988), 128; Joe Gray Taylor, *Louisiana Reconstructed, 1863–1877* (Baton Rouge, 1974), 209; *New Orleans Picayune*, Sept. 27, 1868, morning.

8. William Baker, head of the board of registration, was trying to enforce more stringent regulations than the law required, which would prevent many white Conservatives from being able to vote. Ibid., Sept. 24, 26, 1868, morning.

9. James B. Steedman, Lovell H. Rousseau, and P. B. Foulke.

10. Probably Lewis Wolfley. Ser. 6B, Vol. 4: 203, Johnson Papers, LC.

From Alvan C. Gillem

Vicksburg, Miss., Sept 30 1868.

Dear Sir:

I learn that Brigadier General Joseph Hooker is to be retired from active service. Should such be the case, I respectfully request to be promoted to fill the vacancy created by his retirement.

I have endeavored to secure no recommendations—in the conviction that no person is better acquainted with my character, capacity & services, than your Excellency.

Should I be promoted, I shall endeavor by an honest and faithful discharge of the duties devolving upon me, to justify your confidence. I am aware that there will be great competition for the position I seek, and do not desire it, if confering it on me would in any manner embarass you.[1]

Alvan C. Gillem

ALS, DLC-JP.

1. Gillem was not promoted. On January 22, 1869, Johnson asked Secretary of War Schofield to assign to duty both Robert C. Buchanan and Gillem, "according to their brevet rank of Major General." But this was not done. Congress reorganized the army, and early in the Grant administration, on March 15, 1869, Gillem, was ordered to Texas as colonel of the new 11th (consolidated 24th and 29th) U.S. Infantry regiment. Johnson to Schofield, Jan. 22, 1869, Lets. Recd. (Main Ser.), File W-49-1869 (M619, Roll 761), RG94, NA; *Washington Evening Star*, Mar. 17, 1869. See also Horatio Seymour to Johnson, Sept. 24, 1868; Robert A. Hill to Johnson, Nov. 6, 1868; W. L. Sharkey to Johnson, Nov. 7, 1868; and Joseph S. Fowler to Johnson, Nov. 13, 1868.

October 1868

From Mary Dean[1]

270 P. Street between 14' & 15 Street
Washington City   [Oct. 1868][2]

If the President of the United States retains any pleasant memories of his residence in *Laurensville* So. Car. some Forty years ago, he may perhaps recall the names of Lawyer Patillow Farrow,[3] and his student nephew, afterwards co-partner, H. J. Dean;[4] both of whom knew, and esteemed, Mr. Andrew Johnson, when his own Life, and Character, consetuted his sole claim to respect.

In this case, now that the developement of that life, and character, hase elevated their possessor to the very first place on earth, it is not impossible he may find pleasure in rendering a service to the widow, and family, of one who recognized *nature's* nobeleman, years before office, and honors, had affixed the stamp of public appreciation upon him.

The widow of H. J. Dean most respectfully asks (if she can furnish satisfactory testimonials of character, and competency,) that President Johnson will endorse her application for a position as writer, in the "Dead Letter Dept." of the General Post Office, to furnish her means of support in this city, where important interests of her self, and children, require her presence for some time.

It may *prejudice*, or recommend, the applicant to the President, as his *real* feelings on this subject may be—to know that tho' occupying for many years a *first* place, in the best society of the upper part of the state of S. C—it has been held not by virtue of the golden calf— "family," which has heretofore been the idol of that state's worship, but by an humble measure of the same qualities which have—in spite of aristocratic (?) opposition, elevated President Johnson, immeasurally above those who affect to look down upon him.

Tho' the birth place of her husband, and children, is the dearest spot on Earth to her, the writer is a native of the city of London, born in almost precisely the same circumstances as any children the President may have had in So Car.

The first time she ever heard the name of "Andrew Johnson" was hearing her husband Maj Dean reprove his eldest son a lad of 12 for inattention to his studies, arising from being told that "having three rich, and childless uncles, whose wealth he would inherit there was no need of his studying"—Maj Dean said

"My son! *money*, will never make you respected—but virtue and intelligence, will. The man who is to day Governor of Tennessee, has made himself what he is—without fortune or family."

"Who is it Sir"? I asked—"*Andrew Johnson*["] he replied, and then related to me his acquaintance with, and employment of you—while he was studying and practicing Law in Laurens. A removal to a better world, spared him the horrors of the past seven years, but his family inheriting from him respect for the man, have been warm supporters of the administrative policy of the President, and earnestly *pray* that if not now, yet *in the end*, his principles may be triumphant, and *History* do justice to him who would fain have been the Savior of his Country.

The writer, is the bearer of this, but unwilling to trespass upon the time of the President will be grateful if a line of reply, if addressed (to day if possible) to her—(as below)—Mrs. Dean can furnish testimonials from Gov Orr, Chancellor Dunken[5] & any number of men in the first position in S C. but fears any thing from that latitude would be prejudiceal, and names Dr. Allen President of Girard College Phila.[6] Genl. Duff Green—and Mr. Geo Reggs Banker of this city.[7]

Trusting for forgiveness for the liberty to the dictates of a heart which has itself suffered—the petitioner submits her case without attempt of enlist his sympathy for personal suffering from injustice.

Mrs. H. J. Dean

ALS, DLC-JP.

1. Dean (c1825–fl1874) served for a number of years in the 1860s and 1870s in the Internal Revenue office of the Treasury Department in Washington as copyist and "lady clerk." Previously, she had married Hosea J. Dean in 1840 and afterwards lived in South Carolina for a number of years. Some sources indicate that she was born in New York and was appointed to her Treasury Department job from Ohio. But the census report of 1870 notes that she was born in Ohio. Of course her letter claims that she was born in London. She did not secure an appointment in the Post Office Department. J.B.O. Landrum, *History of Spartanburg County* (Spartanburg, 1960 [1900]), 257–60; Washington, D.C., directories (1870–74); *U.S. Off. Reg.* (1865–71); 1870 Census, D.C., Washington, 2nd Ward, 186.

2. The Library of Congress has assigned this date to the document.

3. Patillo Farrow (1797–1849), a lawyer in Laurensville until his death, had been associated with Hosea J. Dean for a short time. Brent Holcomb, comp., *Marriage and Death Notices from Upper South Carolina Newspapers, 1843–1865* (Easley, S.C., 1977), 54.

4. Hosea J. Dean (1806–1855), a lawyer in Laurensville and Spartanburg, served in the South Carolina legislature in the early 1850s. Landrum, *Spartanburg County*, 254–57.

5. James L. Orr and Benjamin F. Dunkin.

6. William Henry Allen (1808–1882) became president of Girard College in 1850, after a number of years at Dickinson College. He left Girard's presidency in 1862 but returned to that institution in 1867, where he remained until his death. *DAB.*

7. George W. Riggs (1813–1881) became a partner in the banking firm of Corcoran & Riggs in Washington in 1840. Fourteen years later he bought out Corcoran's interest and renamed the institution Riggs & Company. He also built and owned the Riggs House, a famous Washington hotel. *DAB.*

From Charles A. Yancey[1]

Washington D.C.   Oct 1868

Mr President

I have the honor to inform you that I came to *Washington* desiring to obtain an inteview with your Excellency; for the purpose of *soliciting your favorable* Consideration and *endorsment* of a *National Educational Enterprise* inaugerated and *exclusively managed* by the *leading responsible Colored* men of the Countery for the *Education* and *Elevation* of our *race; free* from *bias* on account of *Sect* or *party* adhering *only* to the general principles of *Christian Morality*, and the cultivation of *Self-reliance*: and known as the *National Reform Educational Association.*

The enclosed documents[2] will inform you of its Success, and who its active membrs are. With the *hope*, that you may *regard* the *enterpise worthy* of your *aid, influence*, and *endorsement*.

C. A. Yancey

Business Manager   N.R.E. Association

P.O. Box 44 New Albany Indiana

ALS, DLC-JP.

1. Possibly the Yancey (d. 1870) who lived in Ohio and Canada prior to the Civil War. He attended black conventions in Ohio in the 1850s and in 1865. A Republican congressional committee employed Yancey in 1867 as a speaker in the South. Three years later he represented Panola County in the state legislature of Mississippi. Eric Foner, *Freedom's Lawmakers: A Directory of Black Officeholders during Reconstruction* (New York, 1993).

2. No related documents nor any further information about the association have been found.

From Samuel G. Courtney

New York, October 1, 1868.

Sir.

I have been furnished with a copy of a report addressed to yourself by John M. Binckley,[1] Solicitor of Internal Revenue, purporting to give a history of what was done by him in pursuance of an order issued by yourself on the 25th August, 1868, directing him to "proceed to the City of Brooklyn, (Eastern Judicial District,) New York, and examine certain evidence said to be in possession of, Assessor Wellwood,[2] and report whether in your (his) opinion, the same substantially implicated, in violations of law, any officer of the internal revenue service."

Any general criticism, as to the manner in which the special service designated in this order has been performed, it is not in my province to offer, but I must be permitted to notice this extraordinary document so far as relates to the utterly unfounded accusations and insinuations against myself, contained therein.

This gentleman came to this city, and commenced a series of investigations, certainly not contemplated by the terms of the order under which he professed to act, and undoubtedly without precedent in the manner in which they were conducted.

Without any communication with me, whom official courtesy and decency should certainly have impelled him to, at least, advise of his proceedings, he caused a prosecution to be instituted against the two chief officers of his own bureau,[3] an ex-collector,[4] and one Daniel Murray, charging them with a conspiracy to defraud the United States. This charge was based upon the testimony of one man alone,[5] of whose character Mr. Binckley seems to have had no knowledge, and to have taken no steps to acquire any.

It was not till these charges had been made, and some of the defendants already arrested, that I was notified that any such action was contemplated. I then found that a man, without the slightest authority so to do, of his own motion, had sneaked surreptitiously into my district, and attempted, in total ignorance both of law and fact, to usurp functions, which your Excellency and the Senate of the United States had seen fit to devolve upon me.

I might surely have been pardoned if, smarting under this wholly gratuitous and unprovoked insult, I had peremptorily refused to have any connection whatever with a prosecution, which, it now seems, was instituted, as a mere fishing enquiry, which might induce "Evidence to come forward in the hands of honorable and notable witnesses."[6] This admission in Mr. Binckley's report confirms the opinion which my intercourse with him, while it lasted, produced, viz: that he was wholly without legal testimony by which to support or establish the charges which he had made.

I know, however, the sensitiveness of the public mind in regard to frauds in the Internal revenue service. I was determined that I would not allow any possible opportunity to bring to light corruption in any quarter, to be defeated, through the ignorance or discourtesy of the man who affected to know something of importance. I therefore waived all sense of the gross insult I had received, and, upon seeing in the papers that his conduct was repudiated by yourself and the Secretary of the Treasury, I applied to the latter by telegraph to know whether I was expected to take charge of the prosecution.[7] On being informed that I was, I immediately cooperated with Mr. Binckley as cordially as his offensive and arrogant manner would permit, determined that if there was any truth at the bottom of his vague and misty accusations, no personal feeling of mine should stand in the way of its development. I found it, however, impossible to learn any thing from him, which was of value as legal proof in establishing the charges he had made; but the prosecution of which, my official position, and the special instructions of the Secretary devolved upon me. He seemed to have no idea of the relevancy or competency of evidence, no conception of the legal scope of such an investigation as he had begun. He seemed to think that such a proceeding might legally be used as a drag net, with which to rake up any insinuations that scandal or malice might give birth to, in regard to any transactions in the internal revenue service, or any officers connected therewith, whether mentioned in the warrant or affidavits in this case or not. He seemed to have not the smallest notion of any legal rules, which would confine the investigation to the particular charge, or particular defendants specified in the warrant. I could not discover that he had any knowledge whatever of even the simplest principles of criminal law, and I labored in vain to impart any to him. His report displays this utter ignorance of law in a very striking manner, when he says, "The hour was coming for a full development of the magnitude of the case, and the number of defendants, to include the District Attorney himself." A child's knowledge, had he possessed it, would have taught him that the rules of evidence must necessarily confine the testimony to be introduced within the limits marked out in the warrant, and that the number of the defendants could not be increased in the way he proposed.

Here then, our difference of opinion began, and if this man had, even in his own mind, any ground whatever for charging me with lack of co-operation with him, it arose wholly from my entertaining some regard for the long-established rules of evidence and principles of law, and my unwillingness to peril all my reputation as a lawyer, by following the wholly unwarrantable and absurd mode of proceeding which he desired, and which, without producing any beneficial result, would have exposed the prosecution and all concerned in it, to the just scorn and ridicule of the profession and the public. He could follow that course if he chose, I could not.

These and none other are the circumstances which "rendered it a pertinent question which side of the issue he (I) was—prosecuting in Court."[8]

The impudence of this question, put to me in the most offensive manner by this man, at the very time when I had been patiently enduring his ignorance and arrogance, in order that a full investigation might be made, was more than I could bear, and I expressed to him, in the plainest terms my opinion of his intellect and attainments, and rose to leave his room, that I might be no longer subjected to his insults. He attempted to compel me to remain, by closing the door upon me, and his violence obliged me in self-defense, to resort to force.[9] I immediately telegraphed to the Attorney General,[10] that I would no longer be associated with Mr. Binckley, and desired that somebody else might be designated to conduct this prosecution. The Attorney General declined to relieve me from the duty, and advised me that Mr. Binckley had no right or power in the premises, that he had been authorized by nobody to do what he had done, and that he, and not I, was the one to retire from the case.

This is my connection with this case and with Mr. Binckley, through the time embraced in his report. I submit to your Excellency, whether my course has been that of a man who dreaded examination into his own conduct, or sought to stifle inquiry into that of others. In view of my official career and record, and what I am confident would be the testimony of every officer of the Government with whom I have ever been brought in contact, I feel that it can hardly be necessary to add to this statement, that every insinuation and charge contained in this extraordinary report, in any way assailing my official or personal conduct or integrity, is wholly, maliciously, and basely false, without shadow of foundation, and originating only in the slanderous imagination of its author.

The history of the case since, abundantly vindicates me. The counsel[11] designated for the purpose by the Attorney General, and myself have exhausted all Mr. Binckley's resources of testimony, and sought earnestly to effect the most thorough search into all the matters as to which he has affected to have proof. I desired some one to be associated with myself, not because I felt that the case needed it, but in order that the public and yourself might be abundantly satisfied of the utter falsity of Mr. Binckley's charge that I was disposed to stifle investigation.

I am happy to find in Mr. Binckley's report and the order of your Excellency under which he professed to act, that his action was wholly unauthorized, and that upon him, and him alone, rests the responsibility of having initiated a proceeding, which in its utter failure and absurdity thus far (the case is not closed) can only tend to weaken the confidence of the public in the utility of any criminal proceedings against Government officials for frauds upon the revenue, and to impair the administration of public justice by bringing its proceedings into contempt.

I enclose herewith copy of the affidavits on which the warrant was granted, and copy warrant.[12]

Samuel G Courtney
U.S. Atty.

LS, DLC-JP.

1. Binckley to Johnson, Sept. 10, 1868. Consult that document for details about the whiskey cases and the individuals involved.

2. Thomas Welwood.

3. Commissioner of Internal Revenue Edward A. Rollins and deputy commissioner Thomas Harland.

4. Thomas E. Smith.

5. John D. McHenry.

6. This quotation is taken from Binckley to Johnson, Sept. 10, 1868.

7. In early September the attorney general's office ruled that Binckley had no legal authority to prosecute the whiskey cases, and that the investigation had to be turned over to district attorney Courtney. Although Johnson continued to use Binckley in a supervisory capacity, newspapers reported that both the President and Secretary of the Treasury McCulloch had largely abandoned Binckley. See Johnson to Binckley, Sept. 19, 1868; *New York Times*, Sept. 15, 1868; *New York Tribune*, Sept. 15, 16, 1868; *Washington Evening Star*, Sept. 24, 1868.

8. Binckley, unhappy with Courtney's lack of cooperation, made this comment to Courtney at a meeting on September 8. Ibid., Sept. 10, 1868.

9. The much publicized scuffle, which exacerbated tensions between the investigators and further hurt Binckley's image, probably contributed to his removal from direct involvement in the case. Ibid.; George A. Fitch to Johnson, Sept. 12, 1868.

10. Actually, on September 8, Courtney had telegraphed the acting attorney general, J. Hubley Ashton, who replied that same night that Binckley had no jurisdiction and Courtney had to prosecute the whiskey cases. See the telegrams published in the *New York Tribune*, Sept. 10, 1868.

11. William Fullerton. See Hugh McCulloch to Johnson, Sept. 16, 1868.

12. Not found enclosed. A published version of the affidavit of John D. McHenry, who claimed knowledge that would implicate Thomas E. Smith and Commissioner Edward A. Rollins in revenue frauds, appeared in the *New York Tribune*, Sept. 3, 1868.

From William S. Groesbeck

Cincinnati   Oct. 1, 1868.
President Johnson:

You may remember that I spoke to you, when I was in Washington, in behalf of Mr. Preston[1] of Kentucky, asking that he might be pardoned.

In July last, you issued a general pardon,[2] but it did not cover the case of Preston, because he was under indictment. He has been indicted I am told, and I am further told and believe that there is no disposition or intention to try his case. Can he not be pardoned, Mr. President? It seems to me very improbable that he will ever be tried, and that he is entitled to the same favor and kindness, that have been shown to those with whom he was associated.

You did wisely, in my opinion, in granting a general pardon in July last, and I shall take it as a personal favor, if you can extend the same treatment to Mr. Preston. His papers on file in the office of the Attorney General show the signature of Mr. Speed[3] of Kentucky, formerly one of your Cabinet.

Hoping you can grant this pardon[4] and with the best wishes for yourself and, your administration . . .

W. S. Groesbeck

ALS, DNA-RG94, Amnesty Papers (M1003, Roll 26), Ky., Wm. Preston.

1. William Preston (1816–1887), a lawyer by training, entered politics and served in the Kentucky legislature (1850–55) and as U.S. minister to Spain (1858–61). During the Civil War he served in the Confederacy both in the army, attaining the rank of major general, and in the diplomatic service, being named in 1864 minister to Maximilian's government in Mexico. Forced temporarily to reside abroad following the war, he returned to Kentucky in 1866 and to the state legislature in 1868–69. *DAB*.

2. Third Amnesty Proclamation, July 4, 1868, *Johnson Papers*, 14: 317–18.

3. In addition to James Speed's written support was that of Montgomery Blair. Amnesty Papers (M1003, Roll 26), Ky., Wm. Preston, RG94, NA.

4. Preston himself had written the President on February 7, 1868, requesting pardon. Johnson pardoned him October 19, 1868. Ibid.

From Carlos Butterfield

October 2, 1868, New York, N.Y.; LS, DLC-JP.

Professing an earlier acquaintance with Andrew Johnson, Butterfield writes about his concern over the loss of Latin American trade to Europe. The

United States has ignored this lucrative market, claims Butterfield, while exploring Asian trade interests. He notes that the United States gets only $114 million out of the total of $503 million in trade from the Latin American countries; the remainder goes to Europe. The completion of the Union Pacific Railroad and the development of new steamship lines from the west coast should greatly enhance the position of the United States in relation to Latin American trade opportunities. Moreover, "the cost to our Government . . . would be trifling compared with the sums expended in other directions for similar objects." Butterfield alludes to the fact that Great Britain has special commissioners in virtually every part of the globe who investigate trade possibilities; he urges that the United States do much the same. He then offers himself as an extremely well qualified person to fill such a proposed post. Indeed, he is eager to come to Washington for a personal interview with Johnson on the matter.

From George H. Staring[1]

Alexandria [La.], October 2d 1868.

Sir,

The undersigned begs leave to say that being an assistant assessor now, he was appointed to the office in 1866 by the Friendly Influence of the Honorable, The Treasurer of the United States,[2] removed by representations of Knaves both Federal & Confederate or Rebel because he would not consent to steal with them from the United States Treasury Department; that during the late terrible war he saved about $2000, which was all lost in consequence of the above mentioned removal from office; that though he has done his duty well & faithfully as assistant assessor he is to day *poorer* by $2000, than he was the day he entered the Revenue Service; with all decent economy; that he is a Democrat, or has been; that he will always be a Democrat, if, by that term or word is meant that *It Is An Imperative Duty*, under ALMIGHTY GOD, that Every Man Have An Independent Opinion *on the subject of* Politics; & that *no man* has a right either under the Laws of *God* or Man to question him on the subject of his Opinion *so formed*. Thus, I am a Democrat. What the Honorable The Treasurer Of The United States may think of me politically, I know not. But I think this, that he is a Gentleman of more knowledge than to beleive that Politics have much if anything to do with FITNESS for office or a position as Servant Of The People.

If Your Excellency Will Permit me, I would say, that my position as assistant assessor is now become almost intolerable. I am about 50 years of age, have a wife & four fine little ones[3] looking up to me; I wish, if Your Excellency Please, to be appointed to some other position, as Assessor or in any other capacity in this State or in any other state. The tax being removed from Cotton & Sugar, the difference to your humble servant is about $500, per annum. Living where I do, Rent & Necessary Domestic or House-hold Expenses require so much that at even $6 50/100 per day, the Hollidays always excluded whether you work or not, I find it a close affair to make "Two Ends Meet" at the end of the year. I beg leave to impress upon the Mind of His Excellency, The President Of The United States, that an Assistant Assessor in this Portion of the United States has, if *He Does His Duty*, A MOST UNGRATEFUL TASK TO PERFORM. Compared with the service he is obliged under his OATH to perform his Pay is *indifferent* & he is hated by those amongst whom he is compelled to perform his duty. I do therefore respectfully solicit your Excellency to place me in a better Position, officially; or, if you please effect an improvement of my pay through the Honorable Secretary of the Treasury. If my application to His Excellency, the President seem something short of propriety, I beg leave to state that though the remaining portion of Your Presidency may be short you may greatly subserve the Interests Of The United States, or The People Thereof, by *securing as far as your Excellency* may have opportunity to do so the services of *every honest man now in the Treasury Department*. Whether I am or am not *An Honest Man I will not take upon myself to say*. But this much *Your Excellency* I will take upon myself to say, that, if it be not too much trouble for those whose duty it may be to make the required investigation to compare my Work as Assistant Assessor with any Predecessor of mine I will venture to say that I am Honest & Worthy so far as they are concerned. I hope Your Excellency Will Give Me An Answer.[4]

Geo H. Staring   Ass't Asser.

ALS, DNA-RG56, Appts., Internal Revenue Service, Assessor, La., 2nd Dist., George H. Starling[*sic*].

1. Staring (*c*1819–*fl*1870) was a native of New York. 1870 Census, La., Rapides, Alexandria, 10.

2. Francis E. Spinner, who was also from New York.

3. Elizabeth Staring (*c*1832–*fl*1870) was a native of England. She and her husband had three sons and a daughter who, in 1870, ranged in age from two to nine years. Ibid.

4. There is no known answer from Johnson and Staring was not nominated to any other post in Louisiana. By 1870 he was a teacher in Alexandria. Ibid.

From Henry S. Fitch

New York Oct 3rd 1868

Sir:

Circumstances have called my attentive observation to the progress of the Internal Revenue infestigation instituted in this City. I am satisfied that no candid man familiar with the manner in which the examination has thus far been conducted can arrive at any other conclusion than that stupendeous frauds have been committed and that measures commensurate with the magnitude of the officers have been adopted to conceal the criminals. It is due to the dignity of the Government—it is due to you as custodian of the Constitution—it is due to every honest citizen of the Republic that this matter be probed perseveringly to its foundation. You will, I am sure excuse me for suggesting that in my opinion Mr Binckley is the *only* man here really in earnest in this matter and that to him and to him *alone* should the service money be transmitted. The Secretary[1] has as yet placed at his disposal only the trivial sum of 1000$ scarcely enough to pay his hotel bill much less the expenses of necessary witnesses and detectives. It is said however that other counsel[2] for the Govt have had large sums at their disposal—if so Mr. B. has never been informed of the fact, nor has he ever been consulted as to its disposition—a fact in my humble judgement of considerable significance.

Henry S. Fitch

ALS, DLC-JP.
  1. Treasury Secretary Hugh McCulloch.
  2. The "other counsel" were district attorney Samuel G. Courtney and William Fullerton. Nothing is known about their financial arrangements.

From John McGinnis, Jr.

New York, Octo. 3d 1868

My dear Sir:

I hand you some slips cut from our leading Journals[1]—and will remark that with one single exception—every daily in N.Y. has come out in the same tone and spirit. I commend this matter to your *careful consideration*. If you *desire* my opinion thereon, I will be pleased to give it.

Jno: McGinnis Jr.

ALS, DLC-JP.

1. Two articles from the *New York Herald* of October 3 were enclosed. One complained of Treasury Secretary Hugh McCulloch's ill-timed sale of gold, while the other called for his suspension for official misconduct.

From Lewis E. Parsons

Washn   Oct 3/68.

Mr President

If Secretary McCulloch will reject Mr. Saffold[1] who has been recommended by the Court for Supervisor of Internal Revenue for the district of Ala, Ga. & Fla. I beg to *assure* you that Col. W. D. Mann will be recommended to day.

The Secy. said some days since he would confirm him if his name was sent in.

While I have nothing to urge against Mr Saffold as a man I have, & I think all your friends in Alabama have, serious objections to his appointment to that office.

1. His education & habits as a student of *books* rather than men do not fit him to deal with the shrewd men of the world with whom he will come in contact & conflict in the discharge of its duties.

2d. His political position & influence are now & have been adverse to your policy. This I know to be so. It has occasioned much hostility to him personally & he is to day one of the least influential men in Alabama.

On the other hand Col. Mann is in all respects not only well qualified for the office (& for the evidence to support this I appeal to the Internal Rev. office itself), but he is also one of the most energetic friends & supporters of the policy of your administration. He came to the state at the close of the war (in which he was a Federal Col.) & settled among us, bringing with him the means to purchase & carry on the best paper in Alabama[2] & as good as any in the South West.

He is a *Union man*. He & his paper will stand by you with your friends in the present & future. In helping him to this office Mr. President you are ading the cause for which you have struggled so long & with such unparalelled devotion.[3] In giving it to the other the Secy. will strengthen one who has never ceased to oppose yourself, your policy & your friends.

A word or line from you to the Secy. *to day* will secure your friend & the supporter of your principles.

Lewis E. Parsons

ALS, DLC-JP.

    1. Milton J. Saffold. There is no evidence that Johnson actually nominated him for the supervisor position, although a newspaper account indicated that McCulloch had approved Saffold's appointment. See *Washington Evening Star*, Nov. 11, 1868.

    2. William D. Mann was proprietor of the *Mobile Register*.

    3. There is no evidence that Mann was nominated for this post.

From Joseph H. Thompson

Shelbyville, Tennessee   Oct. 3, 1868

Dear Mr. President

The enclosed note from our mutual friend E. H. East explains itself.[1] Aware that I was an applicant to be made one of the *supervisers* under the new law he was good enough to tender me a note to you. I now inclose it.

In the discharge of my duties as a "special agent" and in obedience to instructions from Mr McCulloch I was in Memphis this week and am glad to tell you that unless Brownlow *wipes* out the registration our friend Jno W Leftwich will be elected to Congress.[2] Indeed I should not be at all surprised to see the state carried by Seymour.[3] Cooper speaks in Knoxville on to day and will on Monday speak at Greenville—your old home.[4]

We understand here that Gordon Granger will be in command of the troops sent here.[5] This is to *your friends*, in this state very gratifying. We believe that he will act justly—protecting the people from *rebelism* on the one hand and *red* republicanism on the other and thus ensuring peace.

In obedience to instructions from Mr McCulloch I start today for Savannah Georgia.

Joseph H. Thompson

ALS, DLC-JP.

    1. In his October 2 note to Johnson, East "with full assurance and complete endorsement" recommended Thompson for whatever federal position he might seek. In mid-December 1867,

Johnson had nominated Thompson to serve as U.S. consul at St. Thomas. The Senate finally rejected that nomination in mid-June 1868. *Senate Ex. Proceedings*, Vol. 16: 106, 266.

2. Actually, in November Leftwich received a plurality of the votes (40.6 percent) in a three-man race; the Republicans succeeded in recounting enough ballots to give the election to Republican challenger William J. Smith, who had initially secured only 34 percent of the total vote. *Guide to U.S. Elections*, 621; Alexander, *Reconstruction*, 210–12.

3. Thompson's prediction about the presidential election in Tennessee was hopelessly inaccurate. Seymour captured only 31.6 percent of the statewide vote; in other words, Grant won a landslide victory in Tennessee. *Guide to U.S. Elections*, 273.

4. See Edmund Cooper to Johnson, Oct. 5, 1868.

5. Perhaps Thompson is referring to the fact that General Granger had just been ordered to the command of the Department of the Cumberland with the intention of making his headquarters at Memphis. The word "here" in Thompson's letter probably refers to Tennessee, rather than Shelbyville or Bedford County. See *Memphis Appeal*, Oct. 3, 6, 7, 1868.

From Lovell H. Rousseau

New Orleans, La., Oct 4th 1868.

Mr President

All is quiet here now and likely to be. The veto of the negro equality bill & the abrogation of the rules adopted by the registration board[1] have had a good effect & quieted the public mind.

I exerted myself to attain these two objects. The ascendancy of the *negro* in this state is approaching its end—the white Republicans are heartily sick & tired of it & have resolved against it. A *division* & *disentions* naturally follow.

Genl Smith[2] of Ark. has leave of absense for 20 days with permission to renew & apply for extension. Three days ago two *carpet bag* Senators[3] telegraphed to know if he was *releived*, which shows how they watch.

I did not go to Ark. Genl Ayres,[4] Assistant Inspector Genl came soon after my arrival with a full & favorable report of affairs there and I thought it best to remain here & watch. For if I had left and a riot had occurred it would have been said I ran away from it & left to avoid it—tho I had hoped to get away from the city during the hot & sickly days of Sept & Oct.

The riot here some ten days ago[5] amounted to very little tho very threatening. I think we are pretty safe now.

A fair vote will give the state to the democrats[6] & I now believe a fair vote may be had. And that is the opinion of some of the leading democrats. The people here are quietly registering white & black.

Lovell H Rousseau

ALS, DLC-JP.

1. For information on the Negro equality bill and Warmoth's veto of it, and for the registration rules, see Perry Fuller to Johnson, Sept. 30, 1868. See also the *New Orleans Picayune*, Sept. 26, 1868, morning.

2. Charles H. Smith.

3. Not identified.

4. Romeyn B. Ayres (1825–1888) was a career army officer who served in the Army of the Potomac throughout the Civil War, achieving the brevet of major general. At the time of this letter he was lieutenant colonel of the 28th Infantry and inspector general of the Department of Louisiana. *DAB*; Warner, *Blue*; *New York Herald*, Feb. 8, 1869.

5. On September 22 a political procession of mostly black members of Republican clubs was harassed by some whites. In the resulting altercation several blacks were killed and a number of persons on both sides were injured before troops and city police restored order. Melinda Meek Hennessey, "Race and Violence in Reconstruction New Orleans: The 1868 Riot," *LH*, 20 (1979): 78–79; Joseph G. Dawson, III, "General Lovell H. Rousseau and Louisiana Reconstruction," ibid., 380.

6. As a result of Democratic intimidation, Seymour did win Louisiana with 80,225 votes to Grant's 33,225. Taylor, *La. Reconstructed*, 172.

From Edmund Cooper

Knoxville, Ten.   Octr. 5 1868.

My Dear Mr. President.

I am in the performance of my duties as Elector for the state at large—and have reached this place, in the list of my appointments.

I find the public mind perfectly quiet, without the slightest excitement in this end of the state.

In the middle and western part of the state, the public mind is aroused, and we hope to be able to accomplish something—but I can hope for nothing so long as the purpose of the state Government continues in this end of the state so powerful and omnipotent.

I go from here to Morristown; thence to Greenville; and thence to Jonesboro.

I hope that I may be able to do some good—but I cannot tell until the canvass is over and the result is announced.

The reception that I have met with has been continuing although not enthusiastic.

Hoping that good may come to the state—I will persevere to the end—and then go home to the quiet of professional life.

Every day proves to the satisfaction of the true friends of constitutional liberty, the folly of the Democratic Convention, in failing to nominate you as their candidate.

If such had been its action, the mountains would have been on fire—and the country in a blaze.

Now I presume we will see what comes of it?

Edmd Cooper

ALS, DLC-JP.

From Edmund Cooper

Knoxville Ten.   October 5th 1868.

My Dear Mr. President.

At the request of Mr P. Dickinson[1] whose guest I am, and of Col John Williams, I write you this note in behalf of Col George Stoneman, who is an applicant as they inform me, for the Brigadier Generals place in the regular army made vacant by the retirement of Genl Jo Hooker.[2]

They speak in such high terms of him, whilst in command at this place; of his kindness to the citizens, of his urbanity as a commander and of his skill and courage as a soldier that I cheerfully join with them in an earnest request if not in conflict with your own views, to confer the honor upon Col Stoneman.

They say that he is your friend—and that he has always been true to you, and your administration. If such are the facts and I have no reason to doubt them, I can the more cordialy endorse his application.

Edmd. Cooper

ALS, DLC-JP.
    1. Perez Dickinson.
    2. For an earlier recommendation of Stoneman as a replacement for Hooker, see Horatio Seymour to Johnson, Sept. 24, 1868.

From Henry E. Knox[1]

New York, Oct 5th 1868.

Respected Sir:

After leaving you last Friday[2] I saw and had an interview with the Secretary of the Treasury on the subject spoken of to you.

The Secretary expressed himself unable to make any advances without the opinion of the Attorney General as to whether any of the present appropriations are properly applicable to the purposes referred to and which if any were so applicable.

We trust that this matter will be adjusted immediately on the return of the Attorney General. Every moment is of importance and nothing satisfactory can be accomplished until funds are provided. As I stated to you at Washington neither Judge Fullerton nor Mr Binckley have any doubt of entire success in fully disclosing the Govts frauds on the revenue in this city if means are promptly supplied. Every hours delay is used to advantage by the enemy.

Henry E. Knox

ALS, DLC-JP.

1. A law partner with William Fullerton and college friend of James A. Garfield, Knox (*fl*1902) was still practicing law in New York as late as 1902. He seems to have served briefly as U.S. marshal in the early 1880s. New York City directories (1868–1902); Theodore Clarke Smith, *The Life and Letters of James Abram Garfield* (2 vols., New Haven, 1925), 1: 84; 2: 844, 1081.

2. In a letter to "Madame," written earlier on the 5th, Knox made reference to his visit to Washington, apparently to discuss the financial needs of the whiskey fraud investigation. Knox to "Madame," Oct. 5, 1868, Johnson Papers, LC.

From David Looney

New York   October 5th 1868

Mr. President

I recieved the Enclosed a few days since.[1] *I made no such application* about the time referred to. I wrote you asking you to appoint me collector of the Port of New Orleans or Marshall of Kentucky. Subsequently I asked you to use *your influence* with Secretary McCulloch to appointment me Superviser for the district of Kentucky.[2] I learn from the newspapers Col D. S. Goodloe has recived the appointment.[3] I have good reason for saying he has been among the most active of your *Enamies* in that State.[4]

David Looney
No 219 East 17 Street. N.Y.

ALS, DLC-JP.

1. No enclosure has been found with Looney's letter. It could be, however, that he refers here to the September 23 letter which he received from the Treasury Department. That letter informed Looney that his September 19 letter seeking an appointment in the customhouse in

New Orleans had been referred to the collector of customs there. See William H. West to Looney, Sept. 23, 1868, Johnson Papers, LC.

2. See Looney to H. M. Watterson, Aug. 31, 1868, Johnson Papers, LC. In this letter Looney asked Watterson to talk with Johnson about seeking the Kentucky supervisor appointment from McCulloch.

3. Newspapers of early October carried the news of Goodloe's appointment. See, for example, the *New York Tribune*, Oct. 2, 1868; *Washington Evening Star*, Oct. 2, 1868.

4. In late December Looney's son, Robert, wrote to Johnson in behalf of his father's quest for a federal appointment. Robert Looney to Johnson, Dec. 20, 1868, Johnson Papers, LC.

From John McGinnis, Jr.

New York, Octo. 5th 1868

My dear Mr. President:

Mr. Rollins has sent in to Secty McCulloch, the name of Genl. West,[1] for Supervisor of the New Orleans District. West is the tool of Kellogg[2] and for some dirty work done for him, Kellogg promised positively that West should have that position. There are two reasons why West should not be appointed. First he would use his office, *vigorously* & without scruple—in the interest of the Radical party in Lousiana & other states of his District—and 2d he is Kellogg's candidate—and Kellogg has sworn to defeat Perry Fuller's confirmation—and has promised to make Genl. Herron[3] the Collr of Port of N.O. If Mr. McCulloch will promptly reject Mr. West— Rollins will nominate John B. Andeson[4]—who is a *true* and *devoted* friend of yours & a good Democrat.

Jno: McGinnis Jr.

ALS, DLC-JP.

1. Joseph R. West (1822–1898) lived in New Orleans several times before the Civil War, served in the Mexican War, and edited a newspaper in San Francisco during the Gold Rush. A member of the 1st Calif. Inf., he attained the rank of brigadier general and the brevet of major general. After the war he held various offices in New Orleans, including deputy U.S. marshal, auditor for customs, and U.S. Senator from Louisiana (1871–77). Glenn R. Conrad, ed., *A Dictionary of Louisiana Biography* (2 vols., New Orleans, 1988); *BDUSC*.

2. William P. Kellogg.

3. Francis J. Herron.

4. Anderson has not been identified. No apparent attempt was made to nominate West, Herron, or Anderson. On November 24 McCulloch appointed C. E. Creecy to the post. *Washington Evening Star*, Nov. 24, 1868.

From Sam Milligan

Greeneville Tenn   Oct. 5 1868

Dear Sir:

You well remember when I was at Washington[1] I requested you, at Dr Jas F Broyles'[2] instance, to unite in a recommendation with me of his son in law, Mr A. F. Naff,[3] and you declared to do so, but said for me to draw up a recommendation, and you would indorse me.

I have since seen Dr Broyles, and he has urged me to forward the recommendation, which I herewith send.

If you will oblige me so much as to make the indorsment spoken of, I shall feel under renewed obligations.

The letter to Naff is properly addressed, and you will after the endorsment, seal the envellope & let it go to the mail.[4]

All well.

Sam Milligan

ALS, DLC-JP.

1. We have not been able to confirm the dates of Milligan's visit to Washington.

2. Broyles (1801–1884) was a Greene County physician, trustee of Tusculum College and Greeneville Female Academy. In 1870 he was president of the Farmers and Mechanics Association of Greene County. Broyles was the Johnson family's physician. *Historic Greene County, Tennessee and Its People, 1783–1992* (Waynesville, N.C., 1992), 43; Doughty, *Greeneville*, 173, 251, 256.

3. Adam Ferdinand Naff (1837–*fl*1905) married Broyles's daughter in 1865. He served in the Civil War as a private with the I Co., 60th Tenn. Mounted Inf. (CSA). In 1870 Naff was a newspaper editor and also corresponding secretary of the Farmers and Mechanics Association of Greene County. *Historic Greene County*, 43; Doughty, *Greeneville*, 251; *Tennesseans in the Civil War: A Military History of Confederate and Union Units with Available Rosters of Personnel* (2 vols., Nashville, 1964–65), 2: 300; 1870 Census, Tenn., Greene, 13th Civil Dist., Greeneville, 7; CSR, A. F. Naff, RG109, NA; Tennessee Confederate Pension Applications, No. 7639, Adam F. Naff, TSLA.

4. There is no evidence that Johnson actually nominated Naff for any federal position.

From Edward A. Pollard

personal

New York City. 58 Liberty Street

October 5. 1868.

Sir,

Collector Smythe has yet done nothing for me. I think he certainly will or should do something, if you were to do me the very great kindness of writing a line, recalling the matter to him.[1]

I take the liberty of enclosing an article from my pen.[2] It contains nothing more and nothing less, than my sincere opinions, and what I think will be the plain and obvious verdict of History.

Be assured, Sir, of my respectful admiration and gratitude. In any event, I shall not cease to be grateful for your kind expressions and encouragements to me in a recent interview[3] and to be proud of your good opinion.

With respect the most profound and unaffected . . .

Edwd. A. Pollard

ALS, DLC-JP.

1. In mid-September Johnson wrote a letter of introduction to Smythe in behalf of Pollard. The President entreated Smythe to give Pollard "some aid in an enterprise which I think is well calculated to accomplish some public good." On October 3, Pollard complained to Johnson that Smythe "has done nothing." Johnson to Smythe, Sept. 19, 1868; Pollard to Johnson, Oct. 3, 1868, Johnson Papers, LC.

2. No article has been found enclosed with this letter.

3. According to at least one newspaper, Pollard was in Washington in mid-October, but a report of an earlier interview with Johnson has not been located. There was a controversy in early 1869 in the New York customhouse about Pollard's assignment there; in fact, according to one report Pollard was slated for removal from the staff. *New York World*, Oct. 11, 1868; *Louisville Courier-Journal*, Feb. 4, 1869.

From William B. Reed

Chestnut Hill near Philadelphia   Oct. 5, 1868

Dear Sir,

I beg leave to call your attention to the following statement of facts.

On the 9th of September last the Hon: W. D. Kelley in the course of a political speech which has since been reported[1] asserted in the most positive manner that the surrender of the United States troops in Texas by General Twiggs in 1861, was made with the assent of President Buchanan, and that this could be proved by a Mr. Shippen[2] of this city whom Judge Kelley described as Twiggs' Executor and the custodian of his papers.

The trust which the late President confided to me[3] authorised me at once to ask for the proof of this sharp assertion which I know to be groundless.

I addressed a note to Mr. Shippen who at once assured me that he was not Genl. Twiggs Executor and had not and never had his papers.[4] There was however an impression on his mind that he had seen copies of a correspondence between Twiggs and the Executive which to some extent justified Mr. Kelley.

I at once addressed an inquiry to the Adjutant General and to Judge Holt—Mr. Buchanan's Secretary at War. Both informed me no such correspondence existed or ever had taken place.[5] None such exists among the Ex-President papers.

Desiring for the sake of the truth of history to have the proof of all the facts connected with the Twiggs surrender, I addressed a letter to the Adjutant General requesting him if consistent with the public interests to furnish me with copies of all the correspondence of the War Department and General Twiggs anterior to the surrender and after Mr Lincolns election.[6]

This morning the Adjutant General informs me that the Secretary of War[7] does not deem it expedient to furnish the copies.

Deeply solicitous as I am to ascertain the whole truth and in doing so to vindicate the memory of the dead I have no alternative but to appeal to you.

The Secretary at War may be under the impression that I contemplate some publication on this subject during the exciting canvass now in progress, while Mr. Kelley is a candidate. I beg to assure you that I do not; having given my personal assurance to one of the friends of Mr. Kelley that I would publish nothing till the election shall be decided.[8]

I hope it will be consistent with your sense of duty to direct these copies to be furnished me.[9]

William B. Reed.

ALS, Buchanan Papers, PHi.

1. Kelley's speech at a Republican mass meeting on September 8, was printed in the *Philadelphia Press*, Sept. 9, 1868.

2. David E. Twiggs, James Buchanan, and Edward Shippen. The Philadelphia city directory shows two Edward Shippens. The lawyer (1821–*fl*1888) was very involved with the board of education of Philadelphia, and the Sanitary Commission during the Civil War. He also served as consul at Philadelphia for Argentina and several other Latin American republics. The other Edward Shippen (*fl*1878) was a physician. Philadelphia directories (1868–79); *Appleton's Cyclopaedia*.

3. Buchanan had hired Reed to write his biography but Reed never finished it. Philip S. Klein, *President James Buchanan: A Biography* (University Park, Pa., 1962), 419.

4. The administrator of Twiggs's estate was his son-in-law Abraham C. Myers. Henry Stanbery to Johnson, Jan. 5, 1867, *Johnson Papers*, 11: 590–91.

5. Lorenzo Thomas and Joseph Holt. This correspondence with Reed has not been found.

6. Reed to Adjutant General, Sept. 19, 1868, Lets. Recd. (Main Ser.), File R-396-1868 (M619, Roll 655), RG94, NA. Reed quotes a letter from Twiggs claiming that he requested instructions five times but received none. Reed wants copies of those five letters. The endorse-

ment on Reed's letter dates the letters as December 27, 1860, January 2, 7, 18, and 23, 1861. The request was forwarded to the Secretary of War on September 24, 1869. The five letters are in Lets. Recd. (Main Ser.), File T-5-1861 (M619, Roll 62), RG94, NA. The *Official Records* also contains a number of letters from Twiggs requesting instructions. *OR*, Ser. 1, Vol. 1, pp. 579-82, 585.

7. John M. Schofield. See E. D. Townsend to Reed, Sept. 30, 1868, Lets. Sent (Main Ser.), Vol. 48 (M565, Roll 35), RG94, NA.

8. In 1868 Kelley was reelected to Congress for the fifth of his, ultimately, fifteen terms. *BDUSC*.

9. On October 7 Johnson referred Reed's letter to the Secretary of War requesting him to give Reed the desired papers. May 1993 Sale Catalog, Gary Hendershott, Little Rock, Ark.

From Alexander D. Febuary[1]

Tailor Shop, Jonesboro, Tenn.

October 6th, 1868.

Dear Sir:

I have been on the eve of writing to you many a time, then I thought that you was pestered and annoyed so by so many people, asking you to help them in one way or another, that I thought I would not trouble you. But my circumstances have at last forced me to ask you *if you remember your old friend A. D. Febuary*, who came across the Mountains with you in 1826 with a wagon, with your Step-father and Mother as a Journeyman tailor. Do you remember the Panther that came and knocked the skillet off the fire where we camped one night? And do you remember on the top of the Blue Ridge when you snapped your Shot-gun so often at a *bear*?

I remember all these incidences, and the hard time we had on our journey. I remember what long hard days of travel we had through the Mountains. Since that time you have been fortunate in your pursuits in life—some how, I have been rather unfortunate, but have always worked hard and provided for my family. I have ever been your friend—and whilst others have been against you in politics I have Stood square up for you, and am yet your undying friend. My Son[2] was a Lieutenant in the Union Army for over three years, and was with you when you made speeches to the East Tennessee boys, and encouraged by your words of cheer to Stand up for the Union Cause. I now take a leaf out of my old account book to write to you and ask you—if it be possible to aid me by giving a position of *Some Kind* that will help me, as Masons say, "the better to provide for my family."[3] Is there not some humble place where you can place me as an old confidential friend, where I can make something for my family. My eyes have greatly failed me, & I am getting too far advanced in age to make anything at my trade. I think there is something due me in France, of my father's estate, & I may be able some day to repay you for your kindness. For God's sake, and the sake of our former friendship, please help me. I can bring the best citizens of this country to prove that I have ever been your warm friend and political adherent.

If you cannot help me, I have a son named Joseph A. Febuary 23 years of age in this place, who was a Lt in the U S. Army—a good soldier. Can you not help him—so he can care for me in my old days? I lost *two* sons in the U.S. Army besides. One was killed at Chicamauga and the other died at Knoxville from disease contracted on Campaign at Perryville Kentucky.[4]

Do not let me be a trouble to you. I would not cause you the least trouble, for I know you are annoyed enough. But if in your kind heart, you can help an old man or his son, who has been your live-long friend, I shall ever feel grateful to you for your Kindness, and return my heart-felt thanks for so doing.

Will you be so kind as to let me hear from you? Please write to me at this place.

A. D. Febuary—
Tailor

ALS, DLC-JP.

1. Febuary (1801–1873), a native of France, moved to the United States at a young age. Shortly after arriving in East Tennessee he married Sarah Williams. Sometime in the 1840s Febuary married his second wife, Ann Maria Snayd. *History of Washington County*, 49, 142; *Carter County, Tennessee and Its People, 1796–1993* (Waynesville, N.C., 1993), 311–12; 1870 Census, Tenn., Washington, 15th Dist., Jonesboro, 36.

2. Evidently Febuary refers here to Joseph A. Febuary (1845–1915), who served with Co. G of the 4th Tenn. Inf., USA. In 1870 he was listed as a deputy U.S. marshal; in fact, he assisted with taking the census of that year. In the 1880s he served as postmaster of Jonesboro. Ibid.; Bennett and Rae, *Washington County Tombstone Inscriptions*, 3: 138; *History of Washington County*, 105; James P. Brownlow, *Report of the Adjutant General of the State of Tennessee of the Military Forces of the State, from 1861 to 1866* (Nashville, 1866), 92.

3. There is no evidence that Johnson offered Febuary any sort of federal appointment.

4. Possibly Febuary is referring here to two sons from his first marriage: George B. (b. 1831) and Mordecai W. (b. 1835). *Carter County, Tennessee*, 312.

From Ann S. Stephens

National [Hotel]   Oct 6 1868

My Dear Sir,

I am informed by a telegram, sent at the request of Mr. Binkly, that he is very busy preparing a Synopsis of the evidence he has secured against Rollins and will probably forward his report tomorrow.[1]

I enclose a Letter[2] to myself enclosing one which, I think, the writer desired that I should bring to you, as he has reason to distrust both mails and Telegraphs, but I am reluctant to claim any portion of your time unnecessarily. The possibility that this information may not have been already recieved by you and that it may be of some importance will I hope be my excuse for obtruding it upon you.

A S Stephens

ALS, DLC-JP.

1. Although John M. Binckley did eventually accuse Edward A. Rollins of impeding his investigation, other developments forced a delay in delivering his full report, including the dismissal of his case, the arrest of his witnesses, and the demands of the congressional subcommittee on retrenchment. For Binckley's charges against Rollins, see Binckley to Johnson, Nov. 5, 1868.

2. No letter was found enclosed.

From John M. Binckley
Confidential

New York   7' October 1868

Mr. President,

I hasten to report confidentially that I expect to have in a condition to lay before your Excellency very strong evidence against sundry officials, including Mr Rollins, within five days hence. The evidence itself would be more acceptable than a promise of it, but I thus anticipate because the unavoidable though universal misapprehension respecting the actual condition of the business in my charge is about to operate for the apparent benefit of the guilty with fresh energy.[1] The proceeding in court, for which I was expressly deprived of all responsibility by Mr. Attorney General Evarts in his letter to Mr. Fullerton,[2] has been conducted simply as a sham, subservient to the wicked purpose of making a ground for false prosecutions. They have already arrested McHenry,[3] on whose affidavit the warrants were originally issued, on the charge of perjury. The object is, by convicting him of perjury to institute against me a prosecution for subornation of perjury. His protection is, therefore, my protection, and I have resolved to stand by him to the last extremity. They have also arrested Mr. George A. Fitch,[4] and he is now in jail. He is not charged with any offence, nor has even a suit been brought against him. But being a non resident of New York, a statute of this state makes it practicable to require a heavy bail bond to remain within the jurisdiction where a suit is contemplated. The threatened suit is for libel, in submitting to your Excellency the sworn charges against Mr. Courtney of which they have in some manner got possession. The suit is only a pretense. But it affords the newspapers a theme. The discharge of all these prisoners[5] today by Commissioner Gutman is, of course, regarded by the public as a proof that I have failed. It is an error, not only because I was wholly excluded from the matter which was committed to the defendants themselves, in effect, but because in spite of great discouragements and obstacles I have made good progress. This the public will learn in the most satisfactory manner at no distant day.

But the object most likely to be realized by these alarmed and desperate malefactors is the intimidation of witnesses by the remorseless and cruel assault on McHenry for daring in New York to speak the truth about a revenue fraud implicating the wealthy and powerful. So common is this resort here that McHenry from the first had lively apprehensions.

His sincerity is believed in by every candid man who has spoken on the subject. But I think if I can demonstrate the strength of McHenry's support, the intimidation will not be great enough to defeat my arrangments for the strong evidence referred to, after which, the doors will open wide.

My own arrest on I know not what false charges, may occur at any moment. It will be but a sensation, and I beg to add, Mr. President, I am conscious of the fortitude to withstand any thing they contemplate against me with ease, except only unadvised interference from Washington. Trust me.[6]

John M. Binckley.

ALS, DLC-JP.

1. On October 7, 1868, U.S. Commissioner Joseph Gutman, Jr., dismissed the whiskey fraud case against Rollins, Thomas Harland, and Thomas E. Smith. *New York Tribune*, Oct. 8, 1868.

2. William Fullerton was serving as special counsel, assisting district attorney Samuel G. Courtney following Binckley's removal from direct involvement in the case. The letter has not been found, but for information on the composition of the prosecution, see Hugh McCulloch to Johnson, Sept. 16, 1868; Binckley to Johnson, Sept. 25, 1868; Courtney to Johnson, Oct. 1, 1868.

3. Immediately after dismissal of the government's case, several defense witnesses swore out affidavits against the chief government witness, John D. McHenry. McHenry was arrested,

and in June 1869 was convicted of perjury. *New York Tribune*, Oct. 8, 1868; *New York Times*, Oct. 8, 1868, July 1, 2, 1869.

4. Following the dismissal, district attorney Courtney filed libel charges against Fitch. Fitch, unable to produce bail, was ordered jailed. Still in jail in late October, Fitch claimed his earlier charges were mistaken, and alleged he had been duped by Binckley and Ann S. Stephens, who believed the removal of Courtney would facilitate the removal of Rollins. Fitch made the same allegations before a congressional subcommittee investigating the whiskey cases. *New York Times*, Oct. 23, 1868; *House Reports*, 40 Cong., 3 Sess., No. 3, p. 4 (Ser. 1388); Fitch's charges against Courtney are in Fitch to Johnson, Sept. 12, 1868. See also Ann S. Stephens to Johnson, Aug. 7, 1868, and Asahel N. Cole to Johnson, Aug. 27, 1868, *Johnson Papers*, 14: 489–90, 549–52.

5. Perhaps Binckley meant defendants, being Rollins, deputy commissioner Thomas Harland, and Thomas E. Smith.

6. Binckley's investigations met with no success, due to, according to Binckley, a lack of funds, the interference of the congressional subcommittee, and deliberate obstructions by Rollins and McCulloch. Binckley to McCulloch, Oct. 9, 1868, Johnson Papers, LC; Binckley to Johnson, Oct. 9, Nov. 5, 1868.

From Hugh McCulloch

[Washington, D.C.]   Oct 7th 68

The President has doubtless noticed this article[1] in the Intelligencer of this morning. I will advise him, some day, who inspired it.

The President must yield to the Secretary the palm of being the "best abused man in the Country."

H. McCulloch

ALS, DLC-JP.

1. The enclosed article from the *National Intelligencer*, Oct. 7, 1868, concerned the nation's indebtedness and expressed disapproval of those in the government who wished to deny the payment of claims of private individuals against the federal government.

From Thomas H. Reeves

Tennessee   Oct 7th 1868.

Your petitioner would respectfully represent that by direction of your Excellency he was retired from service (Copy of the order herewith) on the Fifth day of June 1868 for the reasons stated in said order[1]—That said incapacity is the result of disease contracted in the line of duty, and in consequence of which he has to rely wholy upon his salary, the pay proper alone of Captain for the support of himself and family, which when unassigned to duty is inadequate for that purpose.

He would therefore humbly request, if the circumstances of the case, his services and conduct as an Officer warrant such a proceeding, that the order retiring him from service be so amended, as to retire him with the full rank of Lieutenant Colonel, now held by him by Brevet;[2] which will give him the pay proper of that rank, when unassigned to duty, and increase his pay nearly one third; for which he will ever humbly pray.[3]

T. H. Reeves
Bvt Lieut Col U.S.A.   Captain (Retired)

ALS, DNA-RG94, ACP Branch, File 1260-ACP-1873, Thomas H. Reeves.

1. The attached statement, signed by Edward D. Townsend, indicated that the President had directed that Reeves be retired because of sickness not related to military service. His condition had been determined by a board of examination. Special Orders No. 133, June 5, 1868.

2. Another attached document, signed by five prominent East Tennessee citizens (including Roderick R. Butler and Thomas A.R. Nelson), asked that Reeves be brevetted colonel for his "gallant and meritorious service with his Regt in repulsing the Rebels at Greenville Tennessee February 22d 1865." This document, dated June 28, 1867, bears a Jonesboro, Tennessee, provenance.

3. There is no indication that the President took any action on the Reeves case. Reeves continued to reside in Washington County, where he subsequently enjoyed a prominent career in public service, elected and appointed. See *Johnson Papers*, 6: 117.

From David D. Belden[1]

Black Hawk Colorado Ter.
October 8th, 1868

I take great pleasure in recommending to you, Hon. Saml. E. Brown,[2] of this Territory, as a suitable person, for the Office of Supt. of the U.S. Mint, at Denver Colorado, and earnestly do I hope that he will receive the appointment.

Mr. Brown is a gentleman in whose integrity and ability the people of Colorado have the highest confidence, and I believe his appointment would give the fullest degree of satisfaction to all classes of our people.

In politics Mr. Brown was formerly a Republican, and was a staunch supporter of the late war for the Union, but since the war closed there have been no stronger supporters of your administration. As a public advocate of Democratic policy, he did noble service in the political campaign just closed in this Territory.[3]

D. D. Belden

ALS, DNA-RG56, Appls., Asst. Treasurers and Mint Officers, Denver, S. E. Browne.

1. Belden (1832–1888), a lawyer, was living in Denver in the 1870s and was associated with spiritualism. Denver directories (1876–79); *NUC.*

2. Browne (1822–*fl*1881), a former Ohio legislator, was U.S. attorney for Colorado (1862–65) and then continued to practice law in Denver. Denver directories (1876–81); *History of the City of Denver, Arapahoe County, and Colorado* (Chicago, 1880), 341–42.

3. Browne was not appointed superintendent. The chairman of Colorado's Democratic Central Committee recommended Browne. See George W. Purkins to Johnson, Oct. 18, 1868, Appls., Asst. Treasurers and Mint Officers, Denver, S. E. Browne, RG56, NA.

From Orville H. Browning

Washington, D.C.   Oct 8th 1868.

Sir.

I acknowledge receipt by reference from you, of sundry papers[1] relating to a marble statue of Washington now in the Patent Office, and its return to the State of Louisiana, to which it belongs.[2]

I instituted an enquiry with the view of ascertaining when and by what authority the statue was deposited in the Patent Office, but could obtain no satisfactory information upon the subject. A former Commissioner of Patents[3] reports, orally, that it was found on the Georgetown wharf by a Mr. Lyon,[4] and, the fact reported to President Lincoln, who ordered it to placed where it now is. The files of the Department contain no information whatever upon the subject.

That the statue belongs to the State of Louisiana, and that it was brought away from there during the war of the rebellion,[5] are facts about which there is no doubt or dispute; and that it is the duty of the government to restore it to the state does not admit of question or debate.

I respectfully ask for authority to cause it to be delivered upon the official order of the Governor of Louisiana.[6]

The papers are herewith returned.

O H Browning   Secretary

ALS, DNA-RG48, Patents and Misc. Div., Lets. Recd.

1. Several documents, dating from 1866–68, are found in the files that accompany Browning's letter.

2. The statue, which had been displayed at the old state capitol building in Baton Rouge, was sculpted by Hiram Powers in 1852. *Louisiana: A Guide to the State* (St. Clair Shores, Mich., 1976 [1940]), 256.

3. David P. Holloway, commissioner of patents (1861–65). See J. M. Clarke to John C. Cox, Oct. 7, 1868, Patents and Misc. Div., Lets. Recd., RG48, NA.

4. Not identified.

5. Gen. Benjamin F. Butler had ordered the statue removed from Baton Rouge. *Louisiana:*

A Guide, 256; *National Intelligencer*, Oct. 13, 1868.

6. On October 9 Johnson endorsed Browning's letter, authorizing return of the statue to Louisiana.

To George H. Nixon[1]

Washington D. C   October 8 1868

Dear Sir:

I am in receipt of your letter of the 1st instant,[2] and regret that there is no vacancy at the Military Academy to which your son[3] can be appointed. The ten appointments at large within the gift of the President are now made one year in advance of the time of their admission and under this law the selections for 1869 were all made in the month of June last.

Andrew Johnson

LBcopy, DLC-JP.

1. Nixon (1822–1887) served in both the lower and upper houses of the Tennessee General Assembly in the 1850s. He practiced law in Lawrenceburg for a number of years and was elected judge of chancery court, serving from 1870 to 1886. Nixon recruited and commanded several different Confederate regiments. *BDTA*, 1: 555.

2. An October 1 letter from Nixon to Johnson has not been located.

3. Nixon had more than one son, but in all likelihood the person in question here was Henry (*c*1851–*fl*1870), who was approximately seventeen years old in 1868. 1870 Census, Tenn., Lawrence, 9th Civil Dist., Lawrenceburg, 12.

From John M. Binckley

New York, Oct 9th 1868

Mr President,

I have the honor to forward herewith a copy of my hurried report of this date, to the Hon Secretary of the Treasury,[1] & a copy of a communication of this date, also addressed to my counsel the Hon David Dudley Field of this city.[2]

From the former your Excellency will learn the present condition of my business here, as far as it is practicable to expedient to describe it in a letter, at this hour of multiplied engrossments. I trust my action may be approved, or that if any of it may appear obscure the nature of my duties will suggest probable explanations.

From the communication to Mr Field you will perceive the delicate & responsible position in which I was placed by the action of a member of a congressional committee,[3] clothed with the authority of the whole, & will concede, I trust, that without exercising a scarcely warranted assurance, I ought not to have deemed my solitary judgment adequate to the occasion, distracting & pressing as were the circumstances & duties of it. The committee expect me to morrow & upon their demand, I shall act in conformity to the advice of my counsel; and continue so to act until I shall receive your instructions in the premises.[4]

Notwithstanding discouragements both of kind & degree beyond all example of which I have ever heard, against a solitary individual, I have but a single apprehension of failure—and that is a strangely mistaken & inopportune economy of funds. I declare seriously that I believe the expenditure forthwith of a few thousands of dollars under my direction, with a corps of counsel, clerks & detectives properly organized, & all of my personal selection, would work an increase of many millions of revenue within a few months.

John M Binckley
Solicitor of Internal Revenue

LS, DLC-JP.

1. In the letter, which was not found enclosed, Binckley informed Hugh McCulloch of the arrest of John D. McHenry. Binckley also stressed the need for additional funds, in order that he could continue his investigation of the New York City revenue frauds. Binckley to McCulloch, Oct. 9, 1868, Johnson Papers, LC. See also Binckley to Johnson, Oct. 7, 1868.

2. Not found enclosed. There is a letter in the Johnson Papers, however, from Binckley to an unknown recipient, dated October 8. This may be the communication in question, since it discusses Binckley's predicament over providing information to the congressional subcommittee investigating the whiskey case. Binckley, who claimed to have sensitive material implicating high-level officials, wanted to know if the subcommittee could compel him to divulge such information. Binckley to Unknown, Oct. 8, 1868, Johnson Papers, LC.

3. Charles H. Van Wyck, chairman of the congressional subcommittee on retrenchment. See also Charles C. Yeaton to Johnson, Sept. 28, 1868.

4. Two days after the subcommittee subpoenaed Binckley, he wrote to Johnson asking if he should comply. Johnson replied on October 1, stating that the attorney general could offer better advice. According to Binckley's above-mentioned letter of October 8, Attorney General Evarts refused to give Binckley a clear answer. It is not known if Field responded to Binckley's request, and there is no evidence Johnson offered any assistance. Johnson to Binckley, Oct. 1, 1868; Binckley to McCulloch, Oct. 9, 1868; Binckley to Unknown, Oct. 8, 1868, Johnson Papers, LC; *House Reports*, 40 Cong., 3 Sess., No. 3, pp. 1–14 (Ser. 1388).

From William M. Evarts

Washington, October 9, 1868.

Sir,

I have the honor to enclose a copy of a letter received by me some weeks ago from the Hon. Richard H. Dana, Jr.,[1] of Mass., associate counsel for the United States in the prosecution against Jefferson Davis now pending in the District of Virginia, giving his (Mr. Dana's) views, in a careful and deliberate form, as to the propriety of the Government's remitting further prosecution of the pending indictment against Mr. Davis.[2]

Mr. Dana was associated with me as counsel for the Government in this prosecution, about a year ago, and we acted together in making the preparations for the trial of Mr. Davis, which we both expected would take place last spring. The opinions which Mr. Dana expresses were a subject of conference between him and myself while we occupied this common relation of counsel for the Government, and, had I remained in a private professional relation to the case and to the Government, his communication probably would have borne my signature also. The circumstance of my having been placed in an official relation to the case and to the Government, has occasioned the present form of Mr. Dana's communication, and I respectfully submit the same to your attention.[3]

Wm. M. Evarts
Attorney General.

LS, DLC-JP.

1. See Dana to Evarts, Aug. 24, 1868, Johnson Papers, LC. Dana (1815–1882), a prominent lawyer and author, taught at Harvard (1839–40, 1866–68), was one of the founders of the Free Soil party, and served as U.S. district attorney for Massachusetts (1861–66)). *DAB*.

2. Dana's letter expressed the belief that because the trial would be conducted in the unrestored state of Virginia, it would be very easy for Davis to emerge the winner and the U.S. government to be humiliated. Even if the U.S. won the case, Dana believed that the people would not support a death sentence for treason and that to impose a minor punishment would be beneath the government's dignity. Dana also believed that there was no longer any great interest on the public's part in pursuing the trial.

3. In February 1869, the U.S. Supreme Court, at the request of Evarts, dismissed the case against Jefferson Davis. *Washington Evening Star*, Feb. 20, 1869.

From Fred Tate

Huntsville Ala   Oct 9th 1868.

My Dear Sir

I beg to state to you that Lt. A J. Kelley[1] has been forced to resign his position in the army on account of his political sentiments.[2]

He is a firm and steadfast advocate of your policy & has been and is now being persecuted on account of his adherence to the great principles of Constitutional liberty. I beg that if you can aid him in any way that you will do so.[3]

Fred Tate

ALS, DLC-JP.

1. Andrew J. Kelley (c1843–ff1911), who resided with his family in Greeneville, Tennessee, in 1860, enlisted as a private in the 1st Tenn. Cav., USA, in August 1862, but spent most of the war either as a prisoner of war or in a hospital. He was appointed a 2nd lieut. in the 33rd U.S. Inf. in June 1867. CSR, Andrew J. Kelley, RG94, NA; 1860 Census, Tenn., Greene, 9th Dist., Greeneville, 9; Powell, *Army List*, 407; *U.S. Off. Reg.* (1911).

2. Kelley resigned on October 2, 1868, but no further explanation has been found. Powell, *Army List*, 407.

3. There is no known response from Johnson. By at least the late 1870s, Kelley resided in Chattanooga, where he worked for years with the railway mail service between Chattanooga and Meridian, Mississippi. Chattanooga directories (1880–1906); *U.S. Off. Reg.* (1887–1911).

From Nathaniel G. Taylor

Chicago, Illinois, October 9th 1868.

At a meeting of the Indian Peace Commission held this day, the following resolutions, embodying the views of the Commission were adopted;[1] to wit,

Resolved, That this Commission recommend to the President of the United States and Congress, that full provisions be at once made to feed, clothe and protect all Indians of the Crow, Blackfeet, Piegan, Gros Ventres, Sioux, Ponca Cheyenne, Arapahoe, Apache, Kiowa and Comanche Nations of Indians who now have located or may hereafter locate permanently on their respective agricultural reservations.

Resolved, That the treaties of said tribes with the United States, whether ratified or not, should be considered to be and remain in full force as to all Indians of such tribes as now have or may hereafter have their homes upon the agricultural reservations described in their respective treaties, and others.

Resolved, That in the opinion of this Commission, the time has come when the Government should cease to recognize the Indian tribes as "domestic dependent nations," except so far as it may be required to recognize them as such, by existing treaties and by treaties made but not yet ratified; that hereafter all Indians should be considered and held to be individually subject to the laws of the United States, except where and while it is otherwise provided in said treaties, and that they should be entitled to the same protection from said laws as other persons, owing allegiance to the Government enjoy.

Resolved, That the recent outrages and depredations committed by the Indians of the plains,[2] justify the government in abrogating those clauses of the treaties made in October 1867, at Medicine Lodge Creek, which secure to them the right to roam and hunt outside their reservations; that all said Indians should be required to remove at once to said reservations and remain within them, except, that after peace shall have been restored, hunting parties may be permitted to cross their boundaries with written authority from their agent or Superintendent. And Resolved, further that military force should be used to compel the removal into said reservations of all such Indians as may refuse to go, after due notice has been given to them that provision has been made to feed and protect them within the same.

Resolved, That, in the opinion of this Commission, the Bureau of Indian Affairs should be transferred from the Department of the Interior to the Department of War.

N. G. Taylor
President of the Indian Peace Commission

Copy, DNA-RG48, Indian Div., Special Files *re* Negotiations with Indians, Land Matters, Investigations, and Other Matters.

1. Seven of the eight commission members attended the October 7–8 meeting in Chicago which was the commission's last. These resolutions became their final report. See the proceedings of the meeting, Oct. 8, 1868, and Taylor to Johnson, Dec. 11, 1868, Indian Div., Special Files *re* Negotiations with Indians, Land Matters, Investigations, and Other Matters, RG48, NA; Utley, *Frontier Regulars*, 138–39. For more about the work of the peace commission, see Taylor to Johnson, Nov. 12, 1867, *Johnson Papers*, 13: 231–33.

2. For more about these Indian depredations, see Samuel J. Crawford to Johnson, Aug. 22, 1868, and Orville H. Browning to Johnson, Aug. 24, 1868, ibid., 14: 531, 539.

From Charles W. Woolley

Cinti.   Oct 9th '68

My information from Gen'l Butler's district makes me Confident of his defeat, if the democrats there will keep faith with me and make no nomination against Dana.[1]

The medicine administered to Bingham—Schenck—Ashley and Eggleston[2]—has so weakened them that the "distance flag"—will probably be flouted in their faces. Our enjoyment may be a short one—but we are happy now. If we succeed here, I shall emigrate to Massachusetts—and give a little Con amore work there. It will probably not distress you or myself very much if the people should repudiate at the hustings your persecutors and my Slanderers.

C. W. Woolley

ALS, DLC-JP.
1. Richard H. Dana, Jr., vied unsuccessfully with Benjamin F. Butler in 1868 for a seat in Congress from Massachusetts. Dana had been nominated on October 5 by the anti-Butler Republicans. *DAB*; *Washington Evening Star*, Oct. 5, 1868.
2. John A. Bingham, Robert C. Schenck, James M. Ashley, and Benjamin Eggleston. This is probably a reference to their involvement in the failed impeachment ordeal.

From Asahel N. Cole

Brooklyn, Oct. 10th 1868.

My Dear Sir:

I take the liberty of again writing to you a personal letter, and, I am confident that, under the circumstances, you will pardon me for so doing.

You know fully the circumstances under which an investigation into internal revenue affairs has been brought about. I say an *investigation*, and yet, no investigation has yet been had, and, I fear, never will be.

Suffice it to say that the proceedings had before the Commissioner in New York have been mortifyingly farcical.[1] I can but say that my worst fears have been realized, and I am again led to the conclusion that all attempts to break in on the Whiskey Ring will only result in ruin to those who attack it. I know but one way to reach the operations of this Ring, which is, by a Congressional Investigating Committee, and, even this is a source of doubtful success.

But, to the occasion of this letter. I am associated in this office, intimately associated as Chief Clerk, with Mr. Thomas Welwood, Assessor of this District. I know Mr. Welwood, and I know him too, intimately and well, and I give it as my opinion that Mr. Welwood is one, of a very few *honest*, I will say, *strictly honest* revenue officers in this Metropolitan District.

Mr. Welwood's unswerving fidelity, and his determination to see the revenues in his own immediate district fully and honestly assessed and collected, together with the fact, now well known, that, in common with thousands of other good citizens, he is desirous of seeing fraud exposed, and the parties brought to justice if possible who are engaged in defrauding the Government of its revenues, has brought upon Mr. Welwood's head the direct vengeance of the parties *hit*, together with their friends, irrespective of party.[2]

Though Mr. Welwood is a Republican, he is just as ready to aid in exposing a Radical, as a Democratic plunderer. There is a fraternity of this gentry here, and this gentry are by no means all of one political faith.

Now, Mr. President, you and I do not agree in politics, and, as I on an occasion long ago wrote, which you *may*, and again, *may not* have forgotten, I think, and have always thought your reconstruction policy a mistaken one.[3] I believe nevertheless, that you are honest in your political opinions, and in your official action.

Believing this, permit me to also hope, that no amount of pressure can be brought to bear to induce you to punish Mr. Welwood for simply doing what he feels to be his duty. Of course, the Internal Revenue Department will do its utmost to bring about Mr. Welwood's discomfiture. In this, they will be aided by certain men of both parties. Holding, as you do, the ultimate power, I am sure you will see justice done, though the Heaven's fall.[4]

A. N. Cole

LS, DLC-JP.

1. U.S. Commissioner Joseph Gutman, Jr., dismissed the government's case in the whiskey fraud investigations on October 7, 1868. See John M. Binckley to Johnson, Oct. 7, 1868.

2. Welwood was purported to have information implicating high-ranking officials in revenue fraud. Welwood was also charged with misconduct in office, which Cole evidently believed was retribution for the assessor's stand against the "whiskey ring." See Cole to Johnson, Aug. 27, 1868, *Johnson Papers*, 14: 549–51; Binckley to Johnson, Sept. 2, 1868.

3. An endorsement by Secretary McCulloch describes Cole as "an extreme Republican" but also calls him a "truthful man." Besides an 1866 letter wherein Cole admitted Johnson's policies "more frequently elicit my approval than disapproval," no references to Johnson's program have been found. Cole to Johnson, June 14, 1866, *Johnson Papers*, 10: 585–86.

4. Despite McCulloch's endorsement and Cole's protestations, Johnson suspended Welwood around October 14, 1868. See Binckley to Johnson, Sept. 2, 1868, and George G. Reynolds to Johnson, Oct. 22, 1868.

From Josephine S. Griffing[1]

Wash.   Oct. 10" 1868.

Sir

From a common sympathy with the unfortunate, and a desire to ameliorate the condition of Prisoners in the public jails and penitentiaries throughout the country I desire to express my earnest conviction that the present Warden of the Jail of this Dist. Mr Heustess,[2] because of his own dissolute habits, is unfitted to exert a moral influence over the Prisoners entrusted to his care, and from well authenticated statements of his business transactions since he has fitted his place in the jail it is evident that he neither regards his oath of office nor the public trust—and therefore, ought to be removed.

I hope your Excellency will take steps to secure a favorable change, in behalf of the prisoners, and the public welfare, in which event I would respectfully name Mr Noyes[3] now on duty as Guard in the said jail, as a man most eminently qualified by a life of purity, temperance, & uprightness, to act in the capacity of Warden of the prison.

Josephine S. Griffing

ALS, DNA-RG48, Appts. Div., Misc. Lets. Recd.

1. Griffing (1814–1872) was a prominent social reformer involved throughout her career with the causes of antislavery, freedmen's relief, and women's suffrage. In March 1869 she was an applicant for postmaster of Washington. *DAB*; *Washington Evening Star*, Mar. 11, 1869.

2. William H. Huestis.

3. Joshua Noyes.

From Simeon M. Johnson

Washington   Oct 10 1868

Sir—

If you should determine to make any change in the Govt. agency of the Pacific R Road, or have occasion to supply any vacancy therein, I am convinced B H Cheever Esq, will be found to be the very best man for employment. He is, perhaps, the best posted citizen in the country on the subject, perfectly honest universally respected and peculiarly fitted for a govt office having the affairs of the Road to supervise.[1] I am convinced the public interests as I suggested to you the other day, might be promoted by some change.

S M Johnson

ALS, DLC-JP.

1. No appointment of Cheever was made by Johnson. For another letter in support of Cheever's railroad appointment, see Henry A. Smythe to Johnson, Oct. 12, 1868, Caleb Cushing Papers, LC.

From Thomas T. Johnson[1]

Washington City, DC   Oct 10th 1868

Sir

The affidavit sworn to by me charging Mr Heustis[2] with boasting of his intimacy with Nicholson's wife[3] &c also that the Guards at the jail would swear for him that white was black &c has already received your notice. I wish here to state that while the case of Heustis was before Genl Cox[4] for investigation I offered to bring witnesses to prove every Statement made in my affidavit also to bring the man who hauled two loads of Potatoes from the Jail to a Store on Capitol Hill but Genl Cox thought it was, not necessary, and also the case of Bundy[5] a Prisoner at the Jail who was allowed to go out and in at will and while out stole a horse from Dr. Howard,[6] also the man Jackson[7] another Prisoner who Mr Heustis had out on his farm and allowed to run away and who Mr Heustis says is Dead, can be proved to be still liveing. In regard to the charges made by Mr Newton[8] I can assure you thay are all true and most of the witnesses can readily be found to prove them beyond a doubt.

Messrs Noyes, Russ, Corey, and Bell,[9] Guards at the jail are anxious to state some facts to you since Mr Heustis has tried so hard to make them perjure themselves by signing a paper exonerating him from all the charges.[10]

Mr President I have nothing to expect Personally in makeing this Statement and ask only to aid in removing a dishonest and disreputable Goverment Officer as in my opinion no man so abusive and foulmouthed and criminally guilty as Mr Heustis ought to rest outside of the walls of the Penitentiary.

Hoping this will received your immediate attention . . .

Thos. T. Johnson

ALS, DNA-RG48, Appts. Div., Misc. Lets. Recd.

1. Johnson (c1822–fl1894) of Virginia, served as a guard at the district jail from late March 1869 until 1894. During the war he served under General L. C. Baker. 1870 Census, D.C., Washington, 4th Ward, 670; Washington, D.C., directories (1870–94); *Washington Evening Star*, Mar. 22, 1869.

2. William H. Huestis, warden.

3. Not identified.

4. John C. Cox.

5. Anthony Bundy was in jail for assault and battery. On February 17, 1869, Huestis was indicted for misconduct in office for allowing Bundy and his fellow prisoner Samuel Jackson to escape during June and July 1868. *Washington Evening Star*, Feb. 18, 1869.

6. Not identified.

7. Samuel Jackson was in jail for larceny. *Washington Evening Star*, Sept. 2, 22, 1868.

8. See Isaac Newton, Jr. to Johnson, Sept. 2, 22, 1868.

9. Joshua W. Noyes, Benton Russ, George H. Corey, and John Bell. Corey (*c*1838–*fl*1871) remained a jail guard until 1870. The following year he was a census clerk. 1870 Census, D.C., Washington, 5th Ward,, 33; Washington, D.C., directories (1869–71).

10. At the end of October, in addition to facing seven charges placed by Newton, Huestis had to face charges of raping a female inmate. In turn he instituted charges of libel against eleven persons. On November 12 the rape case was dismissed and on November 18 the libel case was also dismissed. Later in April 1869 Thomas Johnson was found guilty of assaulting Huestis but was fined only court costs because of Huestis's provocation in the situation. *National Intelligencer*, Oct. 28, 1868; *Washington Evening Star*, Oct. 29, Nov. 1–18, 1868, April 16, 1869.

From John W. Leftwich

Memphis, Tenn.   Oct 10th 1868

Sir

A paragraph in one of the morning Papers[1] informs us that an opertunity presents itself for you to reward with promotion some one of the Army officers and I beg to join in the request that Genl. Gordon Granger receive the same.[2] I know your proverbial unwillingness to bestow such favors on personal friends but this is such an opertunity to reward a most efficient officer and at the same time a personal friend that I hope you will not allow it to pass unimproved.

Jno W Leftwich

ALS, DLC-JP.

1. We have not been successful in identifying which of the three daily Memphis papers Leftwich is referring to.

2. Leftwich is probably referring to the pending retirement of General Hooker and the possibility of promoting Granger to that rank and position. Johnson did not nominate Granger. See Horatio Seymour to Johnson, Sept. 24, 1868; Connally F. Trigg and Davidson M. Leatherman to Johnson, Jan. 7, 1869.

From Thomas C. Durant

Salt Lake City   Oct. 11th 1868.

The Union Pacific Rail Road company has been informed of the appointment of a special commission to re-examine their road.[1] If the Commission included all the roads receiving similar Government subsidies and bonds, this company will regard the appointment with satisfaction, but if no other road than this is included, it becomes evident that the government has listened to representations unfavorable to the character of our work and which justice requires that I should contradict.[2] I think it my duty therefore to assure your excellency that the Union Pacific Rail Road is at least equal to any of these other lines in construction, appointments and permanent improvements, and that you can easily ascertain the thoroughness and efficiency of our work by reference to Generals Grant, Sherman and Sheridan who have lately been over the line. I can also furnish you the names of many of the most eminent practical Railroad men in the country also will corraborate these statements from personal knowledge. I respectfully request therefore that the Commissioners be instructed to include all these roads in their estimation and to report in detail the comparative qualities of each to any test of this sort. We shall respectfully submit only asking to be protected from unnecessary delays which are as hostile to the interests of the Country and the safety of the settlements along our route as they would be unjustly expensive to ourselves.[3]

Thos C. Durant   Vice President

Tel, DLC-JP.

1. On October 7, 1868, Secretary Browning appointed members of such a commission: Gen. James Barnes, Gen. Gouverneur K. Warren, and Jacob Blickensderfer, Jr. Barnes (1801–1869) was a civil engineer for various railroads (1836–61). Colonel of the 18th Mass., he was appointed a brigadier general in November 1862, serving in the Army of the Potomac. Warren (1830–1882) served in the topographical engineers both before and after the Civil War. A brigadier and major general during the war, his most important service was at the battle of Gettysburg. Blickensderfer (1816–1899), of Ohio, was a civil engineer who had located parts of the line for the Union Pacific. Evidently, in the 1870s he operated out of St. Louis for the Atlantic and Pacific Railroad. Williams, *Great and Shining Road*, 221; Warner, *Blue*; *DAB*; Ames, *Pioneering the Union Pacific*, 251–52, 266, 300; *NUC*; St. Louis directories (1872–74).

2. During the summer of 1868 government railroad director Jesse L. Williams had examined the Union Pacific line and estimated that it would cost at least three million dollars to correct the deficiencies in the railroad's construction. Williams, *Great and Shining Road*, 221.

3. Johnson referred Durant's letter to Browning, who replied that the letter did not need an answer. "Its suggestions have been anticipated, and the Commissioners have been instructed to examine and report upon all the roads which receive aid from the government." Durant would be so informed when the commissioners arrived. Browning to Johnson, Oct. 12, 1868, Johnson Papers, LC.

From John M. Ragan[1]

Benton Illinois   October 11th 1868.

Sir

I write you requesting information concerning Guerrillas. I desire to know if they were all pardoned under Proclamation made by you and if not I desire to know if there is a reward for the notorious Capt Moore who burned Lawrence Kansas[2] and was engaged in many other outrages and how much that reward is. Also I desire to know if there has been a murder or robery committed or engaged in by one Samuel J Starmer.[3] He is six ft one inch high, light hair dark eys and dark skin very heavy buit man. These men are here under fictitious names and I have good authority that one of them is Capt Moore The other Starmer. Please give the desired information.[4]

John M Ragan

ALS, DLC-JP.

1. Ragan (*c*1846–*fl*1870), a Tennessean who joined the 2nd Mounted Infantry, USA, in 1864 when he was eighteen and served for the rest of the war, was teaching school by 1870. CSR, John M. Ragan, RG94, NA; 1870 Census, Ill., Franklin, Benton Twp., Benton, 29.

2. William C. Quantrill's guerillas attacked and burned Lawrence on August 21, 1863. No information about a Captain Moore, among Quantrill's raiders or otherwise active in Kansas, has been discovered.

3. Not identified.

4. No response from Johnson has been found.

From Garrett Davis

Paris Ky   October 12th 1868

Mr. President,

I write you this note in all the frankness of the highest regard and truest friendship, and at the same time in the deepest Domestic affliction.

My late wife[1] had but one daughter, my step-daughter,[2] who is married to a Lieut Badger,[3] of whom I speaked in a note accompanying this one.[4] She was with her husband on the frontier, and a few days since, was summoned home to see her mother die of an incurable disease, who to day was summoned away by her Maker and left us overwhelmed with grief. A few hours after this sad affliction, Mrs. Badger received a despatch from her husband, which has induced me to address an application to you in his behalf.

For the meritorious husband of the only daughter of my late wife, one of the truest & noblest of her sex, who made your acquaintance at my house, who read & comprehended, I believe, beyond all other women, your veto messages, and who was one of the most appreciative and steadfast supporters of your policy, I bespeak your favor for her son-in-law, who is not less your friend & admirer.[5]

Garrett Davis

ALS, DLC-JP.
    1. Eliza J. Davis (*c*1805–1868), a native of Kentucky, married Garrett Davis in 1846; it was the second marriage for both. 1850 Census, Ky., Bourbon, 289; (1860), Eastern Div., 81; *DAB*.
    2. Mary A. Elliott Badger (b. *c*1842) was the daughter of Eliza and her first husband Thomas Elliott, a Paris, Kentucky, lawyer. 1850 Census, Ky., Bourbon, 289; *DAB*.
    3. Nicholas D. Badger (*c*1837–1882), a native of New York, was a career army officer who served from April 1861 until his retirement in 1878. He died in Jackson, Michigan. *Jackson Citizen*, July 19, 1882; Powell, *Army List*, 172.
    4. On the same day, October 12, Davis wrote another letter to Johnson asking that Badger be detailed to replace a recently deceased officer in the Department of the Missouri. Davis to Johnson, Oct. 12, 1868, Lets. Recd. (Main Ser.), File 313-D-1868 (M619, Roll 661), RG94, NA.
    5. While Johnson endorsed Davis's request on October 15, the position had already been assigned by Gen. Phillip Sheridan to another lieutenant. Ibid.

From Joseph Holt

October 12, 1868, Washington, D.C.; LS, DNA-RG94, ACP Branch, File M-29-CB-1869, T. D. Murrin.

Holt submits the petition of Thomas D. Murrin, late 2nd lieutenant, 30th U.S. Infantry, for reinstatement. He had been court-martialed and dismissed from the service for irregularities of his accounts associated with selling subsistence stores to post trader T. D. Woolley (at Fort D. A. Russell, Dakota Territory). But Murrin insists that "he has been guilty not of fraud but of technical irregularities merely; and that the Government has lost nothing." Holt reports that Murrin submitted a recommendation signed by six officers who had served on his court-martial, asking "that his sentence be mitigated," as well as several other letters of recommendation.

Holt claims that the so-called "technical irregularities" consisted of falsified accounts, which "were prepared for the single purpose of covering up deficiencies, and correcting errors in the returns of previous months." The evidence and also Murrin's admission of what he had done support this view, according to Holt.

Murrin apparently did not realize that reinstatement can only occur through Senate confirmation and his petition must therefore be seen as a request for nomination to the Senate. Holt, however, believes that Murrin's "irregularities," were "written falsehoods . . . committed with an intent to deceive the authority which had placed him in a place of trust." Consequently, Murrin deserves "the penalty affixed by law to such acts of misconduct"—dismissal from the service.

[Murrin explained to Johnson that the accounting irregularities arose because Woolley could not pay his bill promptly, thus requiring an adjustment of the figures. Murrin also protested, as did his principal supporter Gen. T. W. Egan, that the court-martial itself was irregular and biased. At the end of January, Johnson revoked the court-martial verdict and ordered, subsequently, that Murrin should be reappointed; but President Grant canceled this order in early March.]

From Max Herris Langenschwartz

New York   October 12th 1868.

Honorable Sir,

I am preparing to go to Europe where I have to superintend the publication of some new historical works (in which of course the life and endeavors of Andrew Johnson will not be omitted).

At the same time I intend to exercise all my influence to foster, direct, and protect respectable Immigration from abroad into our Southern States,—a work the importance of which needs no comment.

I refer Your Excellency especially to honorable Salmon P. Chase for nearer information about my person. I also refer to Governor Fenton, George B. McClellan, Gerrit Smith and to the kind, friendly memory of hon. William H. Seward etc. etc.

In fact I was invited by some of Your "*Truest friends*" to go forthwith to Washington in person, and, considering the influence of my pen in Europe, to begin and realise the intended good work without losing one moment. But my position would not allow to incur just now the perhaps great extra expenses of a *prolonged* sojourn without having received before some reliable assurances of higher assistance and support.

Of course, all personal sacrifices I am *able* to offer and to bear, I will joyfully submit to; my time and my life are at all hours ready for my adoptive country the "Manifest Destiny" of which is so intimately in rapport with the future welfare, march and liberty of the "old" World.

I shall lay before Your Excellency letters from Governor Fenton,— as also from South Carolina, Florida, Arkansas, Nebraska etc.

The People of all classes in Europe know me, and even Governments abroad will not hesitate to heed my directions in regard to the object, and to seriously consider my opinion or advices if my fundamental condition of mutual honesty, fairness and absolute uprightness receives authoritative support and guarantees.

I would therefore be happy to know Your Excellencies kind views, and to be encouraged by the possibility of governmental assistance and Consent.

Dr. Max Herris Langenschwartz
Chairm. U.S. Peoples League

ALS, DNA-RG59, Lets. of Appl. and Recomm., 1861–69 (M650, Roll 28), M. H. Langenschwartz.

From George W. Parks[1]

Chicago   Oct. 12th 1868

Distinguished Sir

The seeming indiference of the N.Y. Convention to your undoubted claims upon the democracy for the nomination for the Presidency for the next term, I hope, will not make you indifferent in your efforts to secure the election of H. Seyour; as that result will undoubtedly secure your future success as our standard bearer.

You are not forgotten by the people and If God is with us in this campaign it will yet appear that your able administration is appreciated by the People.

Give us success in this election and the mutterings of the people which is heard upon all sides advocating your right to the nomination will burst out in thunder tones and insure your triumphant march again to the White House.

It is the earnest wish of my heart that justice shall be done you in the future, for the stupendious efforts made by you in your fight for the Constitution and the law.

May God give us victory and the people place again upon your brow the wreath of honor that has been so gallantly won by you in your past administration.

It may be presumptious in a stranger to present these views, but our President is not a stranger to those who love the constitution of Washington, and every emotion of my being struggles for the consumation of the hopes herein expressed.

Not until Andrew Johnson by the sufferages of the american people is again elected as Chief Executive, can I consider the constitution, law, and equity triumphant.

George W. Parks

ALS, DLC-JP.

1. Parks (*fl*1873) was a Chicago lawyer. Chicago directories (1868–73).

Proclamation re *Thanksgiving*

[October 12, 1868]

A PROCLAMATION

In the year which is now drawing to its end the art, the skill, and the labor of the people of the United States have been employed with greater diligence and vigor and on broader fields than ever before, and the fruits of the earth have been gathered into the granary and the storehouse in marvelous abundance. Our highways have been lengthened, and new and prolific regions have been occupied. We are permitted to hope that long-protracted political and sectional dissensions are at no distant day to give place to returning harmony and fraternal affection throughout the Republic. Many foreign states have entered into liberal agreements with us, while nations which are far off and which heretofore have been unsocial and exclusive have become our friends.

The annual period of rest, which we have reached in health and tranquillity, and which is crowned with so many blessings, is by universal consent a convenient and suitable one for cultivating personal piety and practicing public devotion.

I therefore recommend that Thursday, the 26th day of November next, be set apart and observed by all the people of the United States as a day for public praise, thanksgiving, and prayer to the Almighty Creator and Divine Ruler of the Universe, by whose ever-watchful, merciful, and gracious providence alone states and nations, no less than families and individual men, do live and move and have their being.

In witness whereof I have hereunto set my hand and caused the seal of the United States to be affixed.

Done at the city of Washington, this 12th day of October, A.D. 1868, and of the Independence of the United States the ninety-third.

ANDREW JOHNSON.

Richardson, *Messages*, 6: 660–61.

From *Thomas Ewing, Jr.*

Oct 13. [1868]

Please read enclosed.[1] Mr. Camden is an Candidate for Govr.

Troops are wanted by Govr. Boreman for, I think, a bad purpose. I will call to see you about this tonight.[2]

Thomas Ewing Jr.

ANS, DLC-JP.
    1. Two telegrams from Johnson N. Camden to Ewing, both dated October 13, were enclosed. Camden warned that Gov. Arthur I. Boreman was in Washington to seek federal troops for West Virginia and urged Ewing to block or prevent this request. Camden to Ewing, Oct. 13, 1868, Johnson Papers, LC.
    2. See also Camden to Johnson, Oct. 14, 1868.

From Hiram Ketchum, Sr.

New York   Oct 13, 1868

My dear Sir

I take the liberty of sending you two communications expressive of my views on a preliminary question entering in the present Canvass, which appeared in the N.Y. Express.[1] How far these views or, more properly, this view may coincide with your own I can only conjecture.

I suppose your duties, as you draw near the close of your term, are light in comparison with those which have hitherto pressed upon you. I look for an able resume of the policy and acts of your administration, in your next message to Congress; that policy and those acts cannot fail in my judgment to hand your name with approbation and honor to posterity.

Hiram Ketchum

ALS, DLC-JP.
    1. Not found.

From James W. Nesmith

Salem Oregon   October 13th 1868

Dear Sir,

It is expected here that Genl Hooker is ordered before the retiring board. In the event that he is retired[1] there will be a vacancy in the Rank of Brig Genl. and it is important that a proper selection should be made. During my service of Six years on the Military Committee in the Senate[2] I had opportunities to judge of the character and worth of our military men, and I desire to say to you that I know of no officer in our Army more worthy of promotion than Genl George Crook. His present rank is Brevet Maj Genl. while his lineal rank is that of Lieut Col.

Crook is a young man, modest of deportment, conservative in politics, and a *real soldier* who knows the *rights of the citizen*. He is likely to outlive all of your Radical Generals, and if promoted *now* may at some time command the Army. He is one of the few men that I would trust to fight for me and at the same time would not hesitate to trust with my rights as a citizen.

His eminent ability in bringing our Indian troubles to a close has endered him to the people of this Coast.[3] I have not the space in a letter to discuss his merits, and can only say give him the first promotion within your power.[4]

J. W. Nesmith

ALS, DLC-JP.

1. Joseph Hooker retired on October 15, 1868. *DAB.*

2. Nesmith was U.S. Senator from Oregon from 1861 to 1867. *BDUSC.*

3. Crook was involved in various western Indian campaigns from the 1850s to the 1880s but apparently won his reputation during a campaign in Idaho in 1868. Altshuler, *Cavalry Yellow & Infantry Blue*, 87.

4. Crook was not promoted to brigadier general until October 1873. Ibid. For the outcome of the attempt to replace Hooker, see Horatio Seymour to Johnson, Sept. 24, 1868.

From James W. Nesmith

Rickwall, Polk Co   Oregon   Oct 13th 1868

Dear Sir,

Some time since I telegraphed you in relation to Col Eddy,[1] who is the Chief Quartermaster of this District. At that time he had been superseded, by the Efforts of a clique of corrupt radical politicians in this state, who desired the appointment of one of their pliant tools for the two fold purpose of swindling the govmnt, and geting controll of the politics of the State.

The patronage of the Quartermaster department here is great, and is a powerful political engine when prostituted to that purpose.

Our friends here want it kept out of Radical hands, and to simply remain neutral. Col Eddy who has been reinstated[2] is an old officer, and an honest man, and we all hope that you will either allow him to remain, or have some honest competent man who is not a politician sent in his place.

J W Nesmith

ALS, DLC-JP.

1. Nesmith's telegram concerning Asher R. Eddy has not been found.

2. The issue of Eddy's removal or retention was discussed in Johnson to Grant, May 29, 1868, and Grant to Johnson, June 1, 1868, *Johnson Papers*, 14: 134–35, 147–48. See also Grant to Christopher C. Augur, Sept. 29, 1868, Simon, *Grant Papers*, 19: 49.

From Margaret Pennybacker[1]

Mount Jackson [Va.]   Oct 13th 1868

Dear Sir

Allow me to introduce myself to you as Miss Pennybacker who called on you in company with Mr. Bowyer.[2] I hope you will excuse me for the liberty I take in addressing you, but I believe you to be the only person that can recover the money for me, and I feel embolden to ask from your kind reception of me, & the many blessings you have been instrumental in conferring upon the South. I am the youngest daughter of Judge Joel Pennybacker[3] who held office for a number of years in Washington and during that time had his life insured. He died here in April 1861 and could not meet the payment which was due in Feb. as the Federal Army was in Winchester, and there was no communication between here and Washington, by the non payment of which we forfeit it all. Mr. Wm. Kilgore[4] No. 517. 7th St. Washington has the papers and if desired will wait upon you with them. My object in writing is to know if it cannot be gotten legally, if you would favor the payment of all or a portion, if the company could be induced to present it to my single sister[5] and myself. There are seven heirs. My parents[6] designed willing she and myself the property, but unfortunately died without wills, and the estate consisting of slaves, leaves us entirely without means. I made application for a situation in one of the Departments at Washington, also as governess, but failed in both. I have the energy and ambition of my Uncle I S Pennybacker[7] but unfortunately nature has clothed me in the form of a diminutive female, and I feel perfectly powerless. I will be under great obligations if you would aid in getting the money, and if my presence would be of any advantage will gladly go to Washington.

I hope you will excuse me for asking the favor of you, but ignorance of what is due a Prest. and the desire to have some means are
my apologies. Would be pleased to hear from you on the subject.[8]

Margaret Pennybacker

Mount Jackson   Shenandoah County   Va

ALS, DLC-JP.

    1. Pennybacker (*c*1836–1919). 1860 Census, Va., Shenandoah, Mount Jackson, 89; Duane
L. Borden, comp., *Tombstone Inscriptions: Shenandoah County, Virginia* (8 vols., Ozark, Mo.,
1981–88), 8: 174.

    2. Possibly John C. Bowyer (*c*1804–*fl*1876), a lawyer, who later served as a government and
internal revenue agent. 1870 Census, D.C., Washington, 1st Ward, 45; Washington, D.C.,
directories (1871–76).

    3. Joel Pennybacker (1793–1861) served in the Virginia senate (1830–35), as president of
Valley Turnpike Company, and as marshal of the District of Columbia. Borden, *Shenandoah
County Tombstone Inscriptions*, 6: 276; John W. Wayland, *A History of Shenandoah County, Virginia* (Strasburg, Va., 1927), 263, 553, 628; B. L. Boyan to James K. Polk, Nov. 10, 1847, Lets.
of Appl. and Recomm., 1845–53 (M873, Roll 67), RG59, NA.

    4. Kilgour (*c*1834–*fl*1878) was an attorney who sometimes resided in Alexandria, Virginia.
1870 Census, Va., Alexandria, Alexandria, 1st Ward, 4; Washington, D.C. directories (1868–
78).

    5. Rebecca J. Pennybacker (1834–1881). Borden, *Shenandoah County Tombstone Inscriptions*,
6: 277; 1860 Census, Va., Shenandoah, Mount Jackson, 89.

    6. Joel Pennybacker married Margaret Stribling (*c*1800–1861) in 1823. Borden, *Shenandoah
County Tombstone Inscriptions*, 6:276; Wayland, *Shenandoah County*, 553; 1860 Census, Va.,
Shenandoah, Mount Jackson, 89.

    7. Isaac S. Pennybacker (1805–1847), an attorney, served as a U.S. Representative (1837–
39) and Senator (1845–47) from Virginia and as U.S. district court judge for the western
district of Virginia (1839–45). *BDUSC*.

    8. No response from Johnson has been found.

From David Tufts[1]

Pittsburg Pa   Oct 13th 1868

Dear Sir

My vote was rejected this day in this City on the grounds that I
could not produce a special pardon from you. Before the war I lived
in the State of Arkansas, served in the confederate army, was a non
Commissioned Officer,[2] was paroled by maj Gen E R S Canby U.S.A.
Since the war have lived two years in this City. When I offered my
vote I produced my tax receipts and cited your amnesty proclimation
of July 4th 1868. If it be in accordance with your will I would respectfully ask a pardon granting the right of suffrage.[3]

David Tufts

ALS, DNA-RG94, Amnesty Papers (M1003, Roll 14), Ark., David Tufts.

1. Tufts (also Tufft or Tuff) (*c*1844–*fl*1890), a clerk, was a wholesale liquor dealer in 1880. Pittsburgh directories (1867–90); 1880 Census, Penn., Allegheny, Pittsburgh, 16th Ward, 2nd Prec., 214B.

2. Tufts was a native of Pennsylvania and Pittsburgh resident who had moved to Arkansas in the early 1860s and served as quartermaster sergeant with Captain Thrall's company of the Arkansas Light Artillery. 1860 Census, Pa., Allegheny, Pittsburgh, 5th Ward, 59; CSR, David F. Tuffts [*sic*], RG94, NA.

3. There is no indication that Tufts received a special pardon, nor is there any obvious reason why he needed one.

From Johnson N. Camden

Parkersburg W Va   October 14 1868

I have fully canvassed this State and feel authorized to vindicate the people of all parties against any charge of lawless intentions or violence at the approaching election. No troops are needed to preserve order here and it would be detrimental to the character and good name of our state to have them sent.[1]

J. N. Camden
Democratic Candidate for governor

Tel, DLC-JP.

1. See also Thomas Ewing, Jr. to Johnson, Oct. 13, 1868.

From Robert W. Johnson

personal

Washington   Oct 14th, 1868

Mr President.

I can not resist the inclination to send you the enclosed or following extract of a letter of Oct 3/68 from a citizen of Memphis of very high characters and of sound practical sense.

"Gordon Granger arrived from Washington. I am glad he is here, for only his troops can prevent a damned row. There are 5,000 stand of arms here, on St Boat, and on there way here, to arm Negroes in Arkansas, sent it is supposed by the Loyal Leagues of the north.[1] If these arms are put in the Negroe's hands, you can guess what a state of things will exist there. In New Orleans a row is imminent. It seems that we stand on a thin crust under which is an abyss of fire ready to explode and shatters every thing to peices. Such is about to be the culmination of Radical *policy*."

How dark is the prospect that hangs over and envelopes the land in these last days of your government, when *all* the power and *all* the will, even if exercised in desperation, would be none too great to save us.

R. W. Johnson

ALS, DLC-JP.
1. The Memphis newspapers were full of reports about a shipment of arms arriving there by steamboat. It was alleged that at least some of the shipment was intended for use in Arkansas. There seems to have been some difficulty about securing a boat to take arms on from Memphis to Arkansas; subsequently, however, one was secured. *Memphis Appeal*, Oct. 4–9, 14–17, 1868.

From C. H. Bostwick[1]

New York.   Oct 15th 1868

Mr. President Sir

You will please excuse me but nesesity compels me to appeal to your Presidency. I have been in the Servis from the year /61 to the close of the ware, was Scout & under Major J. R. O.Berne & was one of the officers under Majr O.Berne. During the Booth affare was at the Kirkwood House with Major O.Berne & took a very active part in the capture of Booth & his confedrates.[2] I have papers to show conserning my Good Servises During the ware & in the Booth matter in particular. I have just returned from Texas. I was Custom House inspector but have been unable to return. I would like so to doo a gain but there has been so many changes that I cannot procure an appointment without a Letter to the collector at Brownsville Texas.[3] All the officers have had positions for there Servises renderd but I never have asked for any thing yett. I have a Family & I would like a position if it is no more than $2, Per Day. Mr. President I should not of trobled you but thy will promis & that is all. Now Mr. President please doo something for me. I can show you papers that will justify my appointment let it bee ever so humble. I am capable of filling any thing in my line. Mr President thre lines from You will give my Family & my self a living.[4]

C. H. Bostwick
406 Broon St.   N Y

ALS, DNA-RG56, Appts., Customs Service, Subofficer, New York, C. H. Bostwick.

1. Not identified.

2. While Maj. James R. O'Beirne and his troops pursued John Wilkes Booth, they remained in Maryland following leads and were not part of the group which finally tracked down the culprit. William Hanchett, *The Lincoln Murder Conspiracies* (Urbana, Ill., 1983), 167–68, 176–77.

3. Robert A. Crawford.

4. There is no known response from Johnson. Bostwick apparently did go back to Texas, where he served as a detective in the town of Jefferson in early 1869. He got into considerable trouble for allegedly ordering a squad of soldiers to shoot an escaping man, Capt. William Perry, who died as a result of the gunfire. *Louisville Courier Journal*, Feb. 12, 1869.

From Austin S. Cushman[1]

New Bedford, Mass.   October 15th 1868

Upon the breaking out of the late rebellion I left a good practice as a lawyer and as a Lieut in Co. E 3rd Mass. Infy Vols took the field with nothing but my uniform, so suddenly did I respond to the call for troops. On the assembling of the Regiment I was appointed Adjutant. When we advanced into Hampton I was the first to make a landing and posted the pickets. After a service of three months I was discharged & mustered out with the Regt.

In August 1862 when Pope[2] had been driven back upon Washington I felt it to be incumbent upon every patriot to rush to arms, and accordingly I raised a company under very adverse circumstances and was on the 19th September following commissioned as Captain Co. D, 47th Mass. Infy. Vols. I was subsequently promised the Lt. Colonelcy of the Regiment, but to secure the colonelcy for one who had been most active in its formation[3] I waived my claims and was Commissioned as Major on the 8th day of November following. The Regiment was ordered to New Orleans, and in a short time after arrival there I was detached as an aid on Maj Genl. Bank's[4] staff and ordered for duty on the Sequestration Commission of which Genl. Beckwith[5] was President. The greater part of the duties of that commission devolved upon me and though my position afforded me excellent opportunities for emolument yet I gave my entire attention to the duties of the office and left it poorer than when I entered it. That it was successfully conducted I have had the satisfaction of learning from Genl. Banks and Genl. Beckwith.

Since my discharge in September (1st) 1863 I have neither sought nor been offerred promotion, but now I desire it, for the reason that certain Republicans in my vicinity are unscrupulously and violently opposing me on account of my efforts to secure official employment for some of my shattered comrades during the present administration, and whatever I can do to increase my influence among the soldiers I intend to do, and to use that influence for the success of their cause and their interest.

I was formerly a private secretary of President Fillmore during the last year of his administration,[6] and could refer to him for my social standing and ability were it necessary so to do. I have also been the presiding officer of an association of soldiers and sailors in this state for more than a year[7] and my efforts politically to secure employment for the deserving and competent has made me many enemies in my own party.

I desire, if compatible with the proper discharge of your duty, to obtain the Brevet of a Brigadier General.[8]

A. S. Cushman

ALS, DNA-RG94, ACP Branch, File C-405-CB-1868, Austin S. Cushman.

1. Cushman (1827–1907), a Massachusetts lawyer, moved to New York in 1879. *Who Was Who in America*, 1: 288.

2. Probably John Pope's defeat at Second Manassas or Bull Run, August 29–30, 1862.

3. Lucius B. Marsh (1818–1901), colonel of the 47th Mass. Inf., was a Boston importer of woollens. Boston directories (1861–81); *NUC*; *OR*, Ser. 1, Vol. 26, Pt. 1: 531.

4. Nathaniel P. Banks.

5. Edward G. Beckwith (1818–1881) was the Chief Commissary of Subsistence for several Union armies during the Civil War and received the brevet of brigadier general for his services. He remained in the regular army, retiring in 1879 due to ill health, having attained the rank of major. Hunt and Brown, *Brigadier Generals*; Boatner, *Civil War Dictionary*.

6. Cushman served during 1852. *Who Was Who in America*, 1: 288.

7. Probably the Grand Army of the Republic in which Cushman was a prominent figure. Ibid.

8. Cushman did not receive a brevet.

To George W. Childs

Washington, D.C.   Octr. 16th 1868

My dear Sir

I thank you for your kind letter of the 15th instant.[1] Fully reciprocating its friendly expressions, I assure you nothing would afford me greater pleasure than to be able, upon your return from Europe, to accept the invitation which you so kindly extend to me, to visit you in Philadelphia.

With my best wishes for a pleasant voyage and a safe return . . .

Andrew Johnson

LS, NjMoHP-L. W. Smith Coll.

1. In his letter of the 15th, Childs informed the President that he expected to sail for Europe in a few days and invited Johnson to stay with him at his home in Philadelphia once he returned from Europe. Childs also complimented the President. Childs to Johnson, Oct. 15, 1868, Johnson Papers, LC.

From John W. Fairfax

New Orleans, Oct. 16th, 1868.

Your Excellency:

I have delayed a solemn and painful duty because the loss of so true and warm a friend could be recurred to only with anguish. I was charged by the late W.H.C. King,[1] than whom you possessed no more ardent admirer or sincere well-wisher, to convey to you his grateful appreciation of your kindness in crowning with success his efforts to have Col. Lewis Wolfley made Assessor in this District.[2] Upon the accomplishment of this purpose, having once engaged therein, he had set his heart. It was regarded by many as a test of your esteem for him—he felt that failure would condemn him as without place in your good will—and even upon what subsequently proved his deathbed, the knowledge of victory was a consolation and a pleasure. So the last moment of life your dear friend blessed you as the country's bravest and best defender.

It may not be inappropriate in this connection to say that Col. Wolfley is proving, as an officer, all that his friends claimed for him or could wish. With an eye single to his duties and the welfare of the Government, he disowns partizanship in selecting subordinates, makes business efficiency and a good name the qualifications for appointment, and is doing much to redeem the character of the Internal Revenue Service, in this city, from the obloquy which past mal-administration engendered. I feel strongly assured, Mr. President, that Col. Wolfley will never give you the slightest cause to regret the confidence you reposed in him.

J. W. Fairfax.

ALS, DLC-JP.

1. William H.C. King had died of cancer at his residence at Pass Christian, Mississippi, on August 27, 1868, at age 43. *New Orleans Picayune*, Aug. 28, 1868, evening.

2. Wolfley was confirmed for the second time on July 27, 1868, but his commission was delayed until sometime after August 13. King's last telegram to Johnson, dated July 29, 1868, was a recommendation of Wolfley. King to Johnson, July 29, 1868, Johnson Papers, LC. See James E. McBeth to Johnson, Aug. 13, 1868, *Johnson Papers*, 14: 506–7.

From Ann S. Stephens

National Hotel   Oct 16 1868

My Dear Sir

I cannot force myself to press my own affairs upon you, when I am granted the honor of an interview and so must write what I always shrink from saying. It is not that I doubt your goodness, but I cannot help a painful reluctance to ask favors, which are only to benefit me or mine. It is now five months since I first made a promise to obtain some appointment under the government for my son.[1] I persuaded him to leave Wall St, where he had been in business five years, because I did not wish him to spend his life in a situation so precarious and full of temptation. During the winter he had lost a great deal of money there and I persuaded him to settle up everything and come away. He did this, honorably paying all obligations, leaving himself nothing but his own energies to depend on.

It was then I asked your kindness for my boy—a kindness it is my own fault that you have not already extended. But all the time I have been hoping that some change in the Departments would leave a Supervisors position open to him, and save me from pressing my wishes more directly upon you. This may happen yet and probably will; but I am told that Rollins has just nominated a Mr Tracy[2]—formerly, and perhaps now, District Attorney of Brooklyn—as Supervisor of New York, and that the Secretary is disposed to confirm him—though Mr Fullerton[3] informed him that Tracy's name had been connected with the whiskey frauds. If this man is confirmed, of course there will no hope for my son in that direction. The enclosed letter from my son,[4] who has waited all summer for me to do something for him, will tell you how necessary it is that I should redeem my promise.

There is, I am told—the appointment of Commissioner of Mexican Claims at your disposal.[5] Could you give that to him? Or would you kindly hold it in reserve if no appointment is open to him elsewhere within a few days? I am afraid to wait longer, without some certainty. The result would be very humiliating to me and injureous to my son if I did. But I am very reluctant to urge anything selfish upon you. The Mr Gregory he speaks of is his wife's grandfather—the Hon. Dudley L. Gregory[6] whom you will possibly remember as a member of Congress from New Jersey, a republican now. My son is in every way capable of performing the duties of commissioner. He has studied the Spanish Language and I judge myself that you will be satisfied with him and the testimonials he can produce when you require them. Indeed there is very few positions which the young man has not the ability to fill. I have for some time, been very anxious about him, but would not annoy you.[7] Now I cannot help it. Still I only force myself into willingness by remembering that it is not altogether The President that I am writing to but a kind friend, who will to the end of life find me his friend.

Ann Stephens

ALS, DLC-JP.

1. Edward "Ned" Stephens. Johnson had once nominated Stephens as consul to Manchester, England, but the Senate did not act on the nomination. Ser. 6B, Vol. 2: 317, Johnson Papers, LC.

2. Though nominated by Edward A. Rollins, Benjamin F. Tracy did not receive the appointment. The two supervisor positions for New York were filled by John B. Smyth and Silas B. Dutcher. Tracy remained district attorney for the eastern district of New York until at least September 30, 1871. *U.S. Off. Reg.* (1869–71); *New York Times*, Oct. 22, 24, 1868.

3. William Fullerton was serving as special counsel in the government's investigations into the New York whiskey frauds. Although Tracy appeared at times as a witness during the trials, he was never accused of any wrongdoing. *New York Tribune*, Oct. 7, 1868. For Fullerton's role, see Hugh McCulloch to Johnson, Sept. 16, 1868, and George W. Greene to Johnson, Nov. 26, 1868.

4. Edward Stephens to Ann Stephens, Oct. 12, 1868, was enclosed.

5. No one was nominated for the position during the remainder of Johnson's term. The commissionership was eventually filled by William Henry Wadsworth of Kentucky. *U.S. Off. Reg.* (1869).

6. Gregory (1800–1874), a banker, was three times mayor of Jersey City, a director of sixteen different railroads, and a U.S. representative for New Jersey (1847–49). *BDUSC.*

7. Ann Stephens persisted in her quest for an appointment for her son. See Stephens to Johnson, Dec. 26, 1868.

From Charles C. Yeaton

PRIVATE

New York, Oct. 16th, 1868.

Mr. President:—

I observe by the newspapers that Rollins has nominated as Supervisor for the Southern District of New York, District Attorney Tracy of Brooklyn. He is a radical republican, and was formerly a leading member of the (corrupt) Metropolitan Board. He would neither be acceptable to your friends or command confidence with first class merchants of this city.

Chas. C. Yeaton

ALS, DLC-JP.

From John M. Schofield

Washington City, Oct. 17. 1868

Mr. President

In reply to your note of this morning,[1] I have the honor to inform you that no application has been made to this Department by the Governor of North Carolina for additional forces to be sent into that state.[2]

J M Schofield   Secty of War

ALS, DLC-JP.

1. An October 17 communication between Johnson and Schofield has not been found.

2. William W. Holden. For earlier comments about the governor and his appointment of state militia officers, as well as reports of various outrages in North Carolina, see John W. Sharp to Johnson, Sept. 7, 1868, and Dixon Ingram to Johnson, Sept. 13, 1868.

From William P. Wells

Detroit, 17 Oct. 1868

To the President:

I beg to say a word in behalf of the application of Bvt. Maj. Gen. John C. Robinson for the appointment of Brigadier General in place of Gen. Hooker, retired. Gen. Robinson's services and sacrifices in the war are well known to you. His life has been spent in diligent devotion to his profession, and in the war, his courage and talents were conspicuous.

I know that in political matters Gen. Robinson has held, and now holds, views in entire opposition to the reckless course of the Radicals. If any word of mine can commend his application to Executive favor, I earnestly urge it. And I know that your friends in Michigan greatly desire his appointment.[1]

William P. Wells.

ALS, DLC-JP.

1. Robinson was not nominated. For the outcome of the attempt to replace Joseph Hooker, see Horatio Seymour to Johnson, Sept. 24, 1868.

From Alexander Delmar[1]
Personal

New York   Oct 18 1868

My dear Sir:

I left Wash. on Friday night to ascertain the condition of affairs here *definitely*. I learn that the article in the World of Thursday[2] was unauthorized by and unknown to the Executive Committee; that the suggestion it contained will not be entertained for an instant; that the World and the Wash. Intelligencer and their designs *all and Every*, are rejected and repudiated by the party managers; and that the latter are now out of the city with the object of inducing Gov. S.[3] to come to N.Y. and straighten the party line by a great meeting and a campaign Speech.[4]

I had no opinion to express on any of these matters; and merely give you the facts, supposing they may interest you to know.

Alex Delmar

ALS, DLC-JP.

1. Delmar (1836–1926) established a reputation as a mining engineer, economist, and historian. He served as director of the Bureau of Statistics (1866–69). *DAB*.

2. Following Democratic defeats in several October state elections, the *New York World* of October 15 subtly suggested replacing vice presidential nominee Frank Blair, Jr., arguing that his controversial letter to James O. Broadhead had alienated many moderates. The *National Intelligencer* reprinted this and several subsequent *World* editorials, and openly supported the suggestion. *New York World*, Oct. 15, 19, 20; *National Intelligencer*, Oct. 16, 17, 19, 20; Homer A. Stebbins, *A Political History of the State of New York, 1865–1869* (New York, 1913), 380–81. See also Andrew J. Wilcox to Johnson, Sept. 18, 1868, and Edward G.W. Butler to Johnson, Oct. 28, 1868.

3. Horatio Seymour.

4. Although Seymour did not travel to New York City, he did begin actively campaigning across the North in an effort to rejuvenate the Democratic campaign. See Johnson to Seymour, Oct. 22, 1868.

From Oden Bowie[1]

Fair View   Collington P.O.
Pr. Georges County Maryland
Oct 19. 1868:

My Dear Sir:

General Hooker having been placed on the retired list I beg to ask the appointment of Col. Robt. C. Bucchanan, now on duty at New

Orleans, to the vacant Brigadiership. Col Bucchanan is a native of this State[2] and belongs to one of our oldest and most influential families. He is a high toned, honorable, intelligent gentleman, and a gallant and accomplished soldier, as I *know* from having served under him during the Mexican War,[3] where he commanded the Regiment from this State and the District of Columbia after the death of Col Watson,[4] killed at Monterey.

I have a very extensive acquaintance among the officers of the Army, and I know no one more deserving and more competent than Col. Bucchanan.

Knowing the pressing demands upon your time at present I forbear to urge Col B's claims in person, but I *do hope* Mr President, that you will authorize me to write to Col. B. of his success.[5]

Oden Bowie: Gov elect of Maryland.

ALS, DLC-JP.

1. Bowie (1826–1894), a railroad president, served in the Maryland house of delegates and state senate and was also governor (1869–72). Sobel and Raimo, *Governors*, 2: 670.

2. Buchanan was born in Baltimore. Warner, *Blue*.

3. Bowie served initially as a private but was promoted to lieutenant for gallantry in action. Sobel and Raimo, *Governors*, 2: 670.

4. William H. Watson (*c*1808/1809–1846), a lawyer who had served three terms in the state legislature and been speaker of the house, was killed at the Battle of Monterrey on September 21, 1846. George C. Furber, *The Twelve Months Volunteer; or, Journal of a Private, in the Tennessee Regiment of Cavalry, in the Campaign in Mexico, 1846–7* (Cincinnati, 1848), 119; *National Intelligencer*, Oct. 13, 1846.

5. See Bowie's further plea in behalf of the appointment of Buchanan, Bowie to Johnson, Dec. 15, 1868, Johnson Papers, LC. Johnson did eventually nominate Buchanan.

From Orville H. Browning

Washington, D.C.   Oct 19th 1868

Sir.

I have the honor to acknowledge receipt of the letter of Hon J. W. Grimes[1] in relation to the issue of Bonds to the Union Pacific Rail Road Company by reference from you of this date.

Permit me to say in regard to the subject of the letter of Mr. Grimes, that the course recommended by him has already been anticipated by the action of the President and Secretary of the Interior this morning.[2]

The letter being marked "Personal" is herewith respectfully returned.

O H Browning

LS, DLC-JP.

1. Grimes to William M. Evarts, Oct. 13, 1868, Johnson Papers, LC.

2. Grimes did not think that the bonds could legally be withheld from the Union Pacific Railroad once the commissioners had approved a stretch of rail as required by law. While Browning's diary indicates no contact with Johnson on October 19, on the following day at the cabinet meeting, Browning advised that 800 miles of the Union Pacific be accepted and the commissioners sent to examine twenty more miles. Ibid.; Randall, *Browning Diary*, 2: 221–22.

From Massachusetts

Boston   Octo. 19, 1868.

Pray do what you possibly can to defeat General B. F. Butler in his attempt to elect himself to Congress in District No. 5. in Massachusetts—thus Secure the *good faith* & maintain the deserved high credit of the Government of the United States. The Services of your friends Henry A. Smythe Collector of the Port of *New York* & the Honorable Mr. Evarts your Attorney General are with me.

Mr. McCullochs interest in the Same direction would be most desirable.

The Candidate whom I have been instrumental in putting in opposition to General Butler is the Honble Richard H. Dana Jr. he being a householder at Manchester in that District.

The Democratic Candidate in that District Otis P. Lord[1] is a most respectable man & *I believe* would be influenced for the right viz— by opposing repudiation & favoring the election of R. H. Dana the republican Candidate provided he could not be elected *himself.* If he could be induced to make effort against Genl. Butler by taking from him all Democratic Votes then Mr. Dana has only General Butler to oppose him for Republican votes.

In this way Butlers defeat is possible.

Please advise with Mr. Evarts to use all possible justifiable means to oppose General Butler who I think an enemy to the best interests of his Country & Society.[2]

Massachusetts

L, DLC-JP.

1. A longtime attorney in Salem, Lord (1812–1884) had served in the state legislature prior to the Civil War and became associate justice of the state superior court in 1859. He held that post until 1875 when he became an associate justice of the state supreme court. D. Hamilton Hurd, *History of Essex County, Massachusetts* (2 vols., Philadelphia, 1888), 1: xliv.

2. Butler won the election. See Charles W. Woolley to Johnson, Oct. 9, 1868.

From William B. Dayton[1]

Austin   Octo 20th 1868

Sir

I am glad to see your order in relation to Gen. Reynolds order,[2] excluding the State of Texas from the Presidential Campaign. Our State has as good record as that from which "Gen" Reynolds hails from, or any of his party. You are a Democrat, and working honorably for the interest of the Country at large. Let your order be carried into execution by all means. Not only in regard to this state but Virginia and Mississippi, should have the same privaleges that the other States have, which compose our "free Country."

William B. Dayton.

ALS, DLC-JP.
   1. Not identified.
   2. In late September the state Democratic executive committee called on citizens to vote for electors for the upcoming presidential election, despite the fact that Texas had not yet been readmitted. In response, Gen. Joseph J. Reynolds, commander of the Fifth Military District, forbade the holding of an election or "any proceedings, or acts for such purpose." President Johnson responded with General Orders No. 82 of October 10, which cited various laws prohibiting the Army from interfering in elections. But these measures only applied to states within the Union. Eventually, the Democratic leadership in Texas cancelled its election plans. Soon afterward, Johnson replaced Reynolds with Edward R.S. Canby. *American Annual Cyclopaedia* (1868), 731; Charles W. Ramsdell, *Reconstruction in Texas* (New York, 1910), 237–38; Richardson, *Messages*, 6: 668–71; Richter, *Army in Texas*, 154–55.

From Samuel Lowery[1]

"Tenn Manl Labor University"
Near Murfreesboro Tenn   Oct 20th 1868

Most Respected Sir

I had the honor to receive from you a Subscription to the Tenn Man'l Labor University while in Washington D.C. several months since. We are now building & preparing our school premises—for increased usefulness,[2]—and would be greatly benefitted & encouraged to receive your Subscription $150.00—if you will please be so kind as to remit per mail.[3] Its receipt will be duly acknowledged privately & publicly &c.

Samuel Lowery
Asst Financial Agt

ALS, DLC-JP.

1. Lowery (1832–*fl*1887), a native of Nashville, was born of a slave father and a free black mother. He studied at Franklin College before the war and afterwards became a lawyer in Nashville. In 1875 Lowery moved to Huntsville, Alabama, where he opened a school while continuing his legal practice. He was the first black lawyer admitted to practice before the Tennessee supreme court; in 1880 he was admitted to practice before the U.S. Supreme Court. *Leslie's Illustrated Newspaper*, Mar. 13, 1880; *Nashville American*, Dec. 28, 1887.

2. In March 1869, Peter Lowery, president of the board of trustees of the Manual Labor School, revealed the expenditures to date for purchase of land, livestock, and equipment. His report indicated that some $20,000 was needed for the erection of suitable buildings and the purchase of more livestock and farm implements. Lowery also noted that sixty-six students were currently enrolled at the school. *Nashville Union and American*, Mar. 6, 1869.

3. The President immediately acknowledged Lowery's October 20 letter and request; he forwarded a gift of $50. Subsequently, in February, he sent another donation of $50. Apparently at some other date Johnson donated another $50 to match the total of $150. In his April 1869 Knoxville speech, Johnson referred to his $150 gift to Lowery's school. Robert Morrow to Lowery, Oct. 28, 1868, Feb. 2, 1869, Johnson Papers, LC. See Speech at Knoxville, Apr. 3, 1869.

From Hugh McCulloch

[Washington, D.C.]   Oct 20th 68

I fear that Fullers action is too sweeping for the good of the Service or the credit of the appointing power. The indiscriminate proscription of Union Soldiers is a blunder politically. The indications also are that the expenses of the Custom House will be considerably increased by Mr Fuller while those of all other Custom Houses are being reduced.[1]

McC

ANI, DLC-JP.

1. On September 30, 1868, a week after Perry Fuller assumed the post of collector of customs in New Orleans, he discharged sixty-five "Union men," replacing them with 150 alleged Democrats and former Rebels. C. B. Young et al. to Johnson, Oct. 2, 1868, Johnson Papers, LC.

From Anna Maria Watts

(*private.*)

Vienna [Austria]   Oct. 20th 1868.

My dear Mr. President,

Having arrived here from Paris, where I had remained a few weeks later than my Husband,[1] to replenish my wardrobe in that city of taste and extravagance, I found a letter from the Secretary of State to

my husband, asking him, at your kind suggestion, to name a successor for the Secretary of Legation here.

This additional proof of your friendship and consideration touched
me deeply and impels me to acknowledge through this imperfect
medium our sincere thanks.

In reply to Mr. Seward's letter my husband named my eldest son,[2]
and his appointment would be most agreeable to us, as well as to
himself.

My dear President, you *know* that I possess a heart capable of ap-
preciating, and holding in grateful remembrance for the rest of my
life all these acts of kindness,—and may I ask, has the poor friend
for whom I interceded when last in Washington, and for whom you
promised *your* all-sufficient aid, been made happy also? I allude to a
friends son Dr. Wm. L. Wheeler[3] of the *Navy*. I feel deeply interested in this case on account of his *parents*. They are nearly heartbro-
ken at his present position, and his Mother has fallen into a state of
melancholy bordering on insanity. Now, my dear Mr. President as
your whole administration has been signally marked for *leniency* and
mercy, (And for which the Nation will forever bless you) let this act
of *justice* to this gentleman be numbered among the rest. He only
asks for a re-examination and re-instatement into the *regular Navy*. I
have applied to Secretary Wells before, but he gave as a reason for
refusing that he had *passed* the *age* for re-examination. This may be,
but this rule has been waived before in other cases, and *I* PLEAD with
you to have it set aside in his case. You need *only* give the *order* and it
will be accomplished, and *I* will esteem it a *personal favor* and Kindness which I shall never forget, and I *know* that you will have the
undying gratitude of himself, his parents and a number of others. If
you knew the circumstances under which he failed in his examination I know you would say with me that it would only be an act of
justice to this gentleman, and to *you* will I look, and hope for this
result.

Now let me remind you of *another* promise you made me, when
last I had the pleasure of seeing you, which was, that you were to
make *me* a visit at *Vienna* next spring, after the arduous labors of
your administration are over. You will require recreation and rest—
you will find it here, and *warm friends* to welcome You. Believe me,
my dear President and friend ever sincerely yours.

Anna W.

ALS, DLC-JP.

1. Henry M. Watts.

2. Henry S. Watts (*c*1843/46–*fl*1870) was commissioned legation secretary on October 8, 1868, but served for less than a year. 1860 Census, Pa., Philadelphia, Philadelphia, 8th Ward, 435; (1870), Lancaster, Marietta, 407; *Register of the Department of State* (Washington, D.C., 1872), 75; William F. Johnston to Johnson, May 20, 1867, *Johnson Papers*, 12: 286.

3. Wheeler (b. 1834) had entered the navy in 1861 as an assistant surgeon and resigned in May 1864. In July 1864 he was once again in the navy as an acting assistant surgeon and was honorably discharged on November 15, 1868. Edward W. Callahan, ed., *List of Officers of the Navy of the United States and of the Marine Corps from 1775 to 1900* (New York, 1969 [1901]), 581; Personnel Records, Lets. from Volunteer Officers, 1861–71, RG45, NA.

From Rae Burr Batten

Philada.   Oct 21st 1868

Dear President

I have purposely delayed acknowledging the receipt of the letter you so kindly favoured us with in behalf of brother to Collector Cake, for which please accept many thanks.[1]

The department to which brother J. Earl Burr was assigned was abolished. The Surveyor finding it impossible to relinquish this the Measurer's department, wrote to Secretary McColloch asking him to rescind so much of the Order as would retain brother. Mr. Burr being reliable and Honest was selected from the four former Measurers on account of his worth. As brother is a Democrat and a true President Johnson man Collector Cake refuses to send his name to be confirmed altho' he professed so much interest in brother. The idea is this. Mr. Cake would be willing if he could couple some radical friend of his—with Mr Burr as Measurer.

Mr. Harbeson Surveyor thinks brother sufficient, and he has ordered him to duty. He has been doing the required duties since Mr. McColloch complied with Mr. Harbeson the Surveyor request.

Collector Cake informed brother he need not expect any pay—untill he was Confirmed altho' he is performing daily duties. The supposition is Collector Cake has never Sent J. Earl Burr's Name to Secretary McColloch for Confirmation as Measurer—altho' he pretends to brother he has—done so—he cannot think of replacing a democrat and leaveing out his three radical republican friends.

How can we learn whether Col. Cake has Sent J. Earl. Burr's name to be Confirmed?

Pardon me for troubling You. My prayers are that you may be blessed with a *long* and *happy life.*

Mrs Rae Batten

ALS, DLC-JP.
   1. A letter from the President to Cake has not been located. For an earlier discussion of Mrs. Batten's brother vis-à-vis the job in Philadelphia, see Rae Burr Batten to Johnson, Sept. 23, 1868.

From John S Gallaher
(Confidential)

Washington, October 21, 1868.

Dear Sir:

I live on Virginia Avenue, in the 7th Ward, where the negroes largely outnumber the whites, and where they are drilling every night. Two nights in the week, Tuesday and Friday, they are out with the drum. They "made night hideous," until after 12 o'clock last night, with drum and banners, yelling and shouting, greatly distressing the sick.

It means mischief evidently on the night of Grant's return, or on election night, if victorious. Negro women disclose occasionally the purpose of the hordes who now infest the City. One of them lately stated to my wife that the families and houses of the "soul drivers" were not safe, and one was named as "spotted."

The question is often naturally asked, "Why this drilling and parade of negroes?["] Is this the "Peace" promised us?

I understood the people of the First Ward (represented in the Councils by a negro alderman and a negro councilman) are annoyed as we are.

Pardon me for annoying you, but I feel sure, unless timely precautions are taken, there will be both *murder* and *arson* on the night of the Radical demonstration already advertised.

The negroes can be drilling for no other purpose.

John S Gallaher,

Q. M. Gen's Office

P.S. I understand some outrages were committed last night by the negroes.[1]

ALS, DLC-JP.
   1. There had been a fight between a police officer and a group of black Republicans who were parading along Pennsylvania Avenue. For an account of that event, see the *Washington Evening Star*, Oct. 21, 1868.

From Sam Milligan

Greeneville Tenn   Oct 22d 1868

Dear Sir:

At the repeated solicitations of our friend William S McGaughey[1] of this County—(Greene)—and who is a good man, I am induced to write you this note. Mr McGaughey's son David[2] is now in the Custom House at New York, on a night service and his father and himself desire it changed to a service in day time.[3] Mr McGaughey thinks if you would suggest the change Mr Smythe, the Collector, would readily do it. I told him you would not desire to interfere, I supposed, in such matters, but he urged me to write.

I am with great respect your friend.

Sam Milligan

ALS, DNA-RG56, Appts., Customs Service, Subofficer, New York, David McGaughey.

1. McGaughey (1821–1889) represented Greene County in the state legislature (1869–75, 1879–81) and was speaker of the House (1873–75). He was a planter. *BDTA*, 2: 575.

2. David R. McGaughey (b. *c*1845) was the second son of William S. and his first wife, Nancy. Ibid.; 1860 Census, Tenn., Greene, 13th Dist., Greeneville, 56.

3. There seems to be some confusion about which one of William S. McGaughey's sons was actually at New York. Although Milligan refers here to David, an earlier letter indicates that Thomas A. had gone to New York to take a job there. See John McGaughey to Johnson, Sept. 23, 1867, *Johnson Papers*, 13: 95.

From George G. Reynolds[1]

Brooklyn   October 22d 1868

Sir

Thomas Welwood assesser of the 3d District Brooklyn N.Y. having been suspended from his office by the President desires to be furnished with a copy of the charges on which such suspension is based.

Will the President be so good as to direct the same to be sent to Mr. Welwood, or to the undersigned as his counsel.[2]

Geo. G. Reynolds

ALS, DNA-RG56, Appts., Internal Revenue Service, Assessor, N.Y., 3rd Dist., Thomas Welwood.

1. A member of the Brooklyn bar since 1844, Reynolds (1821–1913) served as judge on the city court from 1872 until 1887. *New York Times*, Jan. 24, 1913.

2. The communication was forwarded to the Secretary of the Treasury, and was answered on November 5. Beyond that simple fact, nothing is known about its disposition. Ser. 4A, Vol. 5: 711, Johnson Papers, LC.

To Horatio Seymour

WASHINGTON D.C., October 22, 1868.

Hon. Horatio Seymour:

I see it announced in the papers of this morning that you will enter the Presidential canvass in person.[1] I trust this may be so, as the present position of public affairs justifies and demands it. It is hoped and believed by your friends that all the enemies of constitutional government, whether secret or avowed, will not be spared, and that their arbitrary and unjust usurpations, together with their wasteful, profligate, and corrupt uses of the people's treasure, will be signally exposed and rebuked. The mass of the people should be aroused and warned against the encroachments of despotic power now ready to enter the very gates of the citadel of liberty. I trust you may speak with an inspired tongue, and that your voice may penetrate every just and patriotic heart throughout the land. Let the living principles of a violated Constitution be proclaimed and restored, that peace, prosperity and fraternal feeling may return to a divided and oppressed nation.

ANDREW JOHNSON.

New York Times, Oct. 24, 1868.

1. The *National Intelligencer* of October 21 and the *New York Herald* of October 22 reported that Seymour had decided to embark on the campaign trail. This may have been a response to criticism from the *New York World,* which had suggested a change in candidates following a controversial letter of Seymour's running mate, Francis P. Blair, Jr. See Andrew J. Wilcox to Johnson, Sept. 18, 1868, and Edward G.W. Butler to Johnson, Oct. 28, 1868.

To Robert A. Crawford

Washington, D.C., Oct. 23d 1868

Dear Sir:

Mr. Stuart Nelson,[1] son of Hon Thos. A. R. Nelson, of Knoxville, desires some suitable position under you, and I write to express the hope that you will do all you can for him. I would be gratified to learn of his appointment and trust that you will give his case your special consideration.

Andrew Johnson

Cartes de visite for the 1868 presidential campaign. From Arthur Schlesinger, Jr., Fred L. Israel, and David J. Frent, eds., *Running for President: The Candidates and Their Images* (2 vols., New York, 1994), 1:296

Courtesy of the David J. and Janice L. Frent Political Americana Collection

Copy, DLC-JP.

1. Nelson (1843–*fl*1880) had served as a sergeant in Co. A, 60th Tenn. Mounted Inf., CSA, during the Civil War and spent some time as a prisoner of war. There is no indication that Nelson received an appointment with Crawford, who was collector of customs for the Brazos district in Texas. By 1880 he was teaching school. Alexander, *T.A.R. Nelson*, 18; *Tennesseans in the Civil War*, 1: 300; 2: 302; 1880 Census, Tex., Cass, 7th Prec., 16th Enum. Dist., 226; CSR, Stuart Nelson, RG109, NA. See also Hugh McCulloch to Johnson, July 24, 1868, *Johnson Papers*, 14: 418.

From S. Snyder Leidy

Philadelphia   Octr. 23, 1868.

My Dear Sir.—

Honestly, I confess to unkind treatment by parties who could long since have secured me through you or the Secretary of the Treasury some appointment. I am quite poor. I have been made so by a system of persecution and proscription levelled at me, because of my determined advocacy of your first Veto and your course of action as President ever since. From no interested motive did I support and defend, but wholly from a settled conviction in my mind that you were the friend of human liberty, the defender of the Constitution and Supporter of law. I am proud of my action. I am at this moment, as in the past, your warm friend and advocate, and nothing can absolve from my mind the distinguished ability you brought to bear upon all questions touching the rights of the people under the Constitution, and your resistance to unholy and wicked legislation.

I have many appeals by letter for some position. I am in no sense an obscure individual here. I am well known to all of our Congressmen and to every politician and others who visit Washington from this City.

I do pray, Mr. President that I may be remembered. I am capable of filling any position: And there is no man in our District here, more deserving of the appointment of "*Superviser*" under the new Internal Revenue Law than I am.

I would take any position here, or I would go South or even out of the Country if the President would do me the honor to appoint me.

I do trust the President will remember me.[1] *I am sadly in need of some appointment.* God bless the President.

S. Snyder Leidy
October 23, 1868.

ALS, DLC-JP.

1. On September 29 Johnson had written to Philadelphia collector of customs Joseph W. Cake requesting the post of "Superintendent of Petroleum Exports, or some other position suitable to him" for Leidy. Apparently nothing came of the request, however. Johnson to Cake, Sept. 29, 1868, Johnson Papers, LC.

From Moses Bates

Plymouth, Mass., Oct 24 1868

Dear Sir

Thankless as the task may be I enclose a report of the proceedings of the Radical convention[1] which nominated Mr Buffinton[2] for Congress, merely to show you the true character of Davis[3] whom we attempted to have removed, but who through Hanscom[4] substantiated his claim to be a friend of your administration. I need not say to you sir that the charge of ever having been *trusted* by an "Apostate President," further than to sacrifice a large sum to sustain an administration paper is groundless.

Moses Bates
Editor of the *Old Colony Sentinel*

ALS, DLC-JP.

1. No enclosed report was found. Probably Bates was referring to the meeting of the First Congressional District held in mid-October. For an account of that convention, see the *Boston Advertiser*, Oct. 14, 1868.

2. James Buffington (1817–1875) had earlier served four terms in the U.S. House (1855–63). He was internal revenue collector for his Massachusetts district from 1867 to 1869. Not only was Buffington nominated to run for Congress, but he was elected. In fact, he served as U.S. Representative from 1869 to 1875. *BDUSC*.

3. Charles G. Davis, internal revenue assessor of the First District.

4. Probably Simon P. Hanscom.

From John F. Coyle

Washington   Oct. 24 1868

My dear Mr. President

Enclosed please find letter recommending General Butterfield[1] for the vacancy occasioned by the retiring of Genl. Hooker. My letter from Mr Schell[2] desires me to urge the appointment, but as I do not feel that YOU *owe* these Gentlemen anything, I simply perform an act of courtesey in complying with their request. I will see you during the evening. Have remained away because I did not wish to have you charged with directing our course. It is so DEFINED NOW however, that I will call and I hope have your approval.

John F. Coyle

ALS, DLC-JP.
   1. Daniel Butterfield. No letter was found enclosed.
   2. Probably either Richard or Augustus Schell. Richard (1810–1879) was a New York City businessman, state senator (1857), and U.S. representative (1874–75). Augustus (1812–1884), younger brother of Richard, was a prominent New York lawyer and businessman. He served as collector of the port of New York (1857–61). He played a critical role in Democratic party politics in New York City, particularly after the reorganization of Tammany Hall. *BDUSC; DAB.*

From Hugh Douglas

Nashville Tenn   Octo 24th 1868

Dear Sir

As you know I have ever been your personal friend and Supporter in your political asperations, and have always rejoiced at your Successes; that no one of your many friends would have rejoiced more Cordially and Sincerely at your entire Success in your present position, that I have never asked an office or any favor for myself at your hands, I hope you will not now think that I am drawing too heavily on your bounty or liberality, in requesting you to Send me a complete set of the Congressional Globe and appendix with your proper Sign manual.

A mutual friend of ours, now present, who has been one of your most Consistent and uniform personal and political friends and Supporters, who had done all in his power to advance your interest & insure your Success, from the time you and he entered political life, thinks you should Comply with this request.

Please make my Kind regards to the ladies of the White House.

Hugh Douglas

ALS, DLC-JP.

To Thomas Ewing, Jr.

EXECUTIVE MANSION
WASHINGTON, D. C., Oct. 24, 1868

DEAR SIR:

In a recent conversation upon the subject of the finances, you expressed a desire to be furnished with some of the leading facts then mentioned touching the national expenditures and the public debt. I now comply with your request, regretting, however, that other and more pressing matters have prevented me from more clearly illustrating the absolute necessity for immediate reform in the financial operations of the Government. In 1776 our national independence was proclaimed, and after an exhaustive bloody struggle of seven years, was, in 1783, acknowledged by the parent Government. In 1787 the Federal Constitution was framed, and in 1789 the Government went into operation under its provisions, burdened with a debt of $75,000,000, created during the war of the Revolution. Immediately upon the organization of Congress, measures were devised for the payment of the national obligations, and the restoration of the public credit, and when, in 1812, war was declared against Great Britain, the debt had already been reduced to $45,000,000. It was then largely increased by the three years' struggle that ensued between the two nations, until in 1818 it had reached the sum of $127,000,000. Peace again established, provision was made for the earliest practicable liquidation of this indebtedness, in order that it might not become a permanent incumbrance upon the people. Under wise and economical legislation the entire amount was paid in a period of twenty years, and the extinguishment of the national debt filled the land with rejoicing, and was one of the great events of President JACKSON'S administration. Even after its payment a large fund remained in the Treasury, which for safe keeping was deposited with the several States on condition that it should be returned when required by the public wants. In 1849, the year after the termination of an expensive war with Mexico, we found ourselves involved in a debt of $64,000,000 and this was the amount owed by the Government in 1860, just prior to the outbreak of the rebellion. In the Spring of 1861 the war of the rebellion commenced. Each year of its continuance made an enormous addition to the debt, so that when in the Spring of 1865 the nation successfully emerged from the dreadful conflict, the obligations of the Government had reached the vast sum of $2,600,000,000. They had not yet, however, attained their highest point; for when the army any navy had been paid, the volunteer forces disbanded and the navy largely reduced, it was found in February, 1866, that our indebtedness exceeded $2,800,000,000. Having thus referred to the indebtedness of the Government at various periods of its existence, it may be well to call attention to a brief statement of facts connected with its expenditures. From the 4th day of March, 1789, to the 30th of June, 1861, the entire public expenditures were $1,700,000,000, although covering a period of seventy-two years. This amount seems small when compared with the expenses of the Government during the recent war of four years' duration, for from the 1st of July, 1861, to the 30th of June, 1865, they reached the enormous aggregate of $3,300,000,000.

An investigation into the disbursements since the 1st of July, 1865, further shows that by adding to the expenditures of the last three years, the estimate cost of administering the Government for the year ending the 30th of June, 1869, we obtain the sum of $1,600,000,000 as the amount required for the four years immediately following the cessation of hostilities, or nearly as much as was expended during the seventy-two years that preceded the war. It will be seen that from 1791 to 1861 our public debt was at no time more than $127,000,000, while subsequently four years of civil war expanded it to $2,800,000,000. It will also be perceived that while prior to 1861 the largest annual disbursement was not quite $74,000,000 for the year 1858, the expenditure during the last three years of peace have successively been $520,000,000, $346,000,000, and $393,000,000; $372,000,000 being the amount which it is estimated will be necessary for the year ending the 30th of June next. In making this comparison we should remember that during the long interval between 1787 and 1861 the Government was frequently required to make expenditures of an extraordinary character. Large sums were paid to Indians as annuities and for the purchase of their land, and expensive wars were waged against powerful tribes. Louisiana was acquired from France at a cost of $15,000,000. Florida, in consideration of $5,000,000, was ceded to us by Spain. California became part of our possessions on payment to Mexico of $15,000,000, while for $10,000,000 our Government secured from Texas the territory of New-Mexico. During these periods of our history we were also engaged in wars with Great Britain and Mexico—the first waged against one of the most powerful nations of the world; the other made additionally expensive by the prosecution of military operations in the enemy's territory.

The startling facts thus concisely stated suggested an inquiry as to the cause of this increase in the expenditures and indebtedness of the country. During the civil war the maintenance of the Federal Government was the one great purpose that animated our people, and that economy which should always characterize our financial operations were overlooked in the great effort of the nation to preserve its existence. Many abuses, which had their origin in the war, continued to exist long after it had been brought to a triumphant conclusion, and the people, having become accustomed to a lavish expenditure of the public money for an object so dear to them as the preservation of the integrity of their free institutions, have patiently tolerated taxation of the most oppressive character. Large sums of money continued to be extorted from them and squandered in useless and extravagant appropriations. Enormous expenditures are demanded for purposes, the accomplishment of which require a large standing army, the perversion of the Constitution and the subjugation of the States to negro domination. With a military establishment costing in time of peace not less than $100,000,000 annually, and a debt, the interest upon which draws from the Treasury each year nearly $150,000,000, making a total of $250,000,000 for these two items of expenditure alone. Retrenchment has become an absolute necessity or bankruptcy must soon overtake us, and involve the country in its paralyzing and disastrous results. If, however, a wise economy be adopted the taxes may soon be materially reduced, not merely for the benefit of a few, but in the interest of all. A revenue would yet remain sufficient for the administration of the Government, as well as for such a reduction of the public debt as would in a few years relieve the people from millions of interest now annually drawn from their resources. The idea that the debt is to become permanent should be at all times discountenanced as involving taxation too heavy to be borne, and payment of an amount in interest every sixteen years equal to the original sum. The gradual liquidation of the public debt would by degrees release the large capital invested in the securities of the Government, which, seeking remuneration in other sources of income, would add to the wealth of the nation upon which it is now so great a drain. This immense debt, if permitted to become permanent and increasing, must eventually be gathered into the hands of the few, and enable them to exert a dangerous and controlling power in the affairs of the Government. The debtors would become the servants of the lenders; the creditors the masters of the people. It is our boast that we have given freedom to three millions of slaves; it will then be our shame that by their own toleration of usurpation and profligacy forty millions of people have enslaved themselves, and exchanged slaveholders for new taskmasters in the shape of boldholders and tax-gatherers. Hence the vital issue—Whether Congress and its arbitrary assumptions of authority shall supersede the supreme law of the land; whether in time of peace the country shall be controlled by a multitude of tax-collectors and a standing army—the one almost as numerous as the other, and making the debt a permanent burden upon the productive industry of the people, or whether the Constitution, with each and all of its guarantees, shall be sacredly preserved; whether now, as in 1789 and 1816, provision shall be made for the payment of our obligations at as early a period as practicable, that the fruits of their labor may be enjoyed by our citizens rather than used to build up and sustain a moneyed monopoly at home and abroad. The contest is not merely who shall occupy the principal offices in the people's gift, but whether the high behests of the Federal Constitution shall be observed and maintained in order that our liberties may be preserved; the union of the States restored; that our Federal system may be unimpaired, fraternal feeling reestablished; that our national strength may be renewed. The expenditure diminished, that taxation may be lightened and the public debt once more extinguished, that it may not injuriously affect the life and energy, the prosperity and morals of the nation. Believing that for the redress of the great wrongs and that correction of these many abuses under which the country is now laboring, we must look to the American people, and that in them is our hope . . .

ANDREW JOHNSON.

New York Times, Oct. 26, 1868.

From John Haviland [1]

Custom House, Philada. Pa.
Oct 24, 1868.

Honored & Respected Sir.

Your Despatch of the 22nd inst. to the Hon. Horatio Seymore,[2] is universally spoken of among the masses of the people.

And I sincerely & firmly believe, it will do more towards the elec-

tion of Seymore & Blair, than all that has been said or written during the Canvas.

John Haviland—
Labourer at the C.H.

ALS, DLC-JP.
1. Haviland (c1811–ff1874), a Pennsylvania native, was usually listed as a clerk, although in
1867 he was a "marker" at the Philadelphia customhouse. *U.S. Off. Reg.* (1867); Philadelphia
directories (1861–74); 1870 Census, Pa., Philadelphia, Philadelphia, 20th Dist., 7th Ward,
550.
2. See Johnson to Seymour, Oct. 24, 1868.

To Millington P. Lytle[1]

Washington City D C   Oct 25 1868

Dear Sir

You no doubt my Dear Sir will excuse the liberty I have taken in
writing to you in this friendly off hand manner. When I explain the
cause I know it will be sufficient excuse.

In a recent conversation with ex gov Vance of your State, I made
enquiry after the health of your honorable father,[2] and he Stated to
me, that the old gentleman was entirely blind, and you your self was
lame and unable to pursue the ordinary labor of plantation life and I
was reminded of a debt of gratitude I owed you father and I know of
no way to cancel it but by Doing Some favor to his Son. When I was
a young man, penniless and friendless, making my way from North
Carolina to Tennessee I was kindly and hospitably entertained by
your Father and in the morning he gave me twenty five cents, which
made a lasting impression on me, and calling it to mind at this late
Day I declare to you Sir, it was more than any man ever done for me
in the State, and should not go unrewarded. I am told by ex gov
Vance that a vacancy at this time exists in the Revenue office at
Morganton, Burke County and I have the pleasure of offering you
the office of Deputy Collector of that District[3] and further Suggest
that you report at once to J. W. McAlrath at Morganton,[4] who is
entrusted by me with the arrangement.[5] I have written to him on the
Subject. The office will be worth about three thousand Dollars per
year. There is no reasonable doubt of Grants election and I would
advise you to Say as little as possible on the Subject of politics as
possible, and by the 4th day of March, next (at which time Grant

will be inaugurated[)] you can become So pleased with the new president that you will be able, to retain the office During Grants term, and be the means of Doing yourself and friends much good.

I have an opportunity of Sending this letter by Judge Nelson of Tenn[6] and directed him to drop it in the nearest post office to you, which gov Vance informs me is Swanonoa.

You will please remember me kindly to your venerable Father, and if you should visit Washington, I shall esteem it a personal favor to have you call on me at the Presidents Mansion.

A Johnson   Prest. U.S

Copy, DLC-JP.

1. Lytle (c1832–f1870) was a farmer and laborer in Buncombe County. He served in the Civil War with the 49th Regiment of North Carolina troops. 1860 Census, N.C., Buncombe, Swannanoa, 20; (1870), Swannanoa Twp. No. 8, 26; Louis H. Manarin et al., comps., *North Carolina Troops, 1861–1865: A Roster* (13 vols. to date, Raleigh, 1966–), 12: 35.

2. Millington Lytle (c1790–f1870) was a Buncombe County farmer. 1860 Census, N.C., Buncombe, Swannanoa, 20; (1870), Swannanoa Twp. No. 8, 26.

3. Evidence about Lytle's appointment has not been located. Given the 1870 Census report on Lytle, it is quite likely he did not receive such an appointment.

4. John W. McElrath (1819–1875) was a popular Monganton merchant. Edward W. Phifer, Jr., *Burke: The History of a North Carolina County, 1777–1920* (Morganton, 1982), 258.

5. See C. G. Bechtler to Johnson, Nov. 14, 1868.

6. Probably Thomas A.R. Nelson.

From Thomas W. Walker[1]

Groton Conn   Oct 25th 1868

Sir

Firmly believing that you would gladly do any thing in your power for the good of our common country and the preservation of our Constitutional liberties—And further believing that nothing short of Divine interposition can save our liberties in this crisis I would respectfully suggest to your Excellency the propriety of issuing a proclamation calling upon "all Christians throughout the Union to offer up public prayer in their respective places of worship on Sunday the 1st day of November 1868 for the guidance of Almighty God in the elections of Tuesday, Nov 3rd to the end that those men may be elected whose elevation to office will secure the greatest good to our Country."

The almighty has assured us that wherever "two or three" shall agree together as touching anything they shall ask, it shall be granted them. Then surely there are enough righteous in the land to secure, by a united effort, such interposition of Providence as to secure so great a blessing.

If I have presumed too much upon myself, in making this suggestion, which seems to me to be called for by the exigency of the occasion I would most respectfully beg your pardon for so doing.

T W Walker
Capt & Bvt Maj U. S. Army

ALS, DLC-JP.

1. Walker (1833–1890) was a professional soldier who saw active duty in various battles of the Civil War. Walker retired in September 1863 because of illness. He subsequently served as president of Norwich University in Vermont. Altshuler, *Cavalry Yellow & Infantry Blue*, 349.

From Thomas E.H. Cottman

Washington   Oct. 26th 1868

Mr. President

Since I had the pleasure of seeing you this morning, I have met many friends in this place. The general topic has been the mixed Commission with England.[1] Now you know I am in the habit of expressing any opinion I may entertain & I take the liberty of expressing to you mine in relation to this Commission should such be decided upon. There will be eight American to be appointed & I would suggest & recommend, without the knowledge of what may be his views on the subject, the United States Marshal under Mr. Lincoln Mr. Ward H Lamon for one of them. He has been a friend & unflinching supporter of yours—is a man of considerable ability, bred to the profession of Law, but has unfortunately made an association in business detrimental to his pecuniary interests. His connection with Judge Black[2] is visited upon him to such an extent as to interfere very materially with his successfully prosecuting Claims befor the different Departments. He has sacrificed his interests to his convictions of right. Being a Republican he might have expected favors from that party, but his course has unfortunately left him in a similar position to the one I occupy; outside of any organization & consequently without political friends. Allow me to submit: That you can in this matter favor an indubitable friend, who in my judgment is too proud to solicit the favor for himself. My opportunities of knowing his *real* sentiments, have been unmistakeable & I unhesitatingly say he has been your *friend* & think that few men of his age have warmer or more personal friends than he has. I learn that he is now doing but little in his profession & on the authority of Judge Davis of the U.S. Supreme Court his adaptation to the position of which I speak is equal to that of any man in the country. The strong personal friendship of the Judge for Mr. Lamon will command from him to you the strongest recommendation that he can pen. From what appears in the papers every one takes it for granted that *the* Commission has been decided upon & as a friend of yours, a friend of Mr. Seward, & a friend of your predecessor I earnestly hope he may recieve favorable consideration at your hands.

Thos. Cottman

ALS, DLC-JP.

1. Probably a reference to the 1868 negotiations conducted by Reverdy Johnson and British leaders for a resolution of several pending matters between the U.S. and Great Britain. The most important was the question of settling claims, including the *Alabama* claims. Seward revised the agreement and returned it to London, where it was signed in January 1869 by representatives of both governments. Each was to appoint commissioners to meet in Washington to hammer out final agreements on financial claims. President Johnson submitted the treaty to the Senate in mid-January; but certain Senate leaders blocked the treaty until an April vote which overwhelmingly opposed ratification of the treaty. Van Deusen, *Seward*, 508–9; Albert Castel, *The Presidency of Andrew Johnson* (Lawrence, Kans., 1979), 211.

2. Jeremiah S. Black.

From Daniel S. Curtiss[1]

Washington, Oct 26, '68

Respected Sir:

Without wishing to be obtrusive, upon your deeply engrossed attention, as an humble private citizen, I trust to be Excused for taking the liberty of Expressing my deep gratitude & high admiration, for the soundness and patriotism of your very clear & comprehensive Letter, of the 24th inst. to Gen. Ewing—which, in my opinion, presents the best showing of our National Debt, & obligations of Congress in regard to it, yet given to us; and if Every voter, in our Country, could see & read it, before the November elections, I have no doubt, they would give an overwhelming majority against the present usurping party, called the Republicans. I enlisted and fought cheerfully, being several times wounded, in the recent war,[2] for the purpose of maintaining the Union in its perfect harmony, & preserving the Constitution in its complete integrity. I supported Lincoln &

Johnson in 1864—and am *now*, unwilling to see the Radical party ruin the Country in its Constitutional barriers & bankrupt it in its finances.

Enclosed is an article—which I wrote for the leading paper of my State,[3] which I would be glad could you find time to do me the honor to read. With highest admiration for your Constitutional integrity & patriotic firmness & devotion . . .

D. S. Curtiss.

ALS, DLC-JP.

1. Curtiss (1814–1890), appointed from Wisconsin, was a clerk in the internal revenue office in Washington for a few years, at least until 1869. Sometime after that he landed a clerkship in the First Auditor's office in Washington, a position he held in the 1880s. *U.S. Off. Reg.* (1865–67, 1883–87); Washington, D.C., directories (1866–90); Pension File, Mary A. Curtiss, RG15, NA.

2. Curtiss, captain and major in the 1st D.C. Cavalry (1863–65), was wounded at Roanoke Bridge on June 29, 1864. Ibid.

3. No article was found enclosed. However, a Memphis newspaper took note of an essay written by Curtiss, a "Wisconsin man, a brave and patriotic soldier," who strongly criticized the Radical Republicans and announced he was leaving that party. See *Memphis Appeal*, Sept. 24, 1868.

From W.B.R.A. King[1]

St Louis Mo   Oct 26 /68

Dr Sir

On Reading your kind & hopfull Letter to the People[2] this morning it makes me think of your Goodness & Kindness to our falling Race.

I wish to ask you one favor it is a very Great favor not only to me—but to all & it is our Last hope—*that you will at this* Late *day—again—Declare* Amnasty to our Poor People & Give us—a Chance to Say who Shall (*be our Ruler and President*). We are cut off again Called Rebels Copper Heads & not all allowed to vote get our hard earnings taking from us (*Taxes*).

You will I trust forgive my Rashness in addressing you *thus* but it is on my mind & I can not get it out untill I have asked you.

O I hope if it Lays in your Power to Grant this to our People I hope & Pray you will.[3]

W.B.R.A. King

ALS, DLC-JP.

1. Not identified.

2. Johnson's letter to Thomas S. Ewing, Jr., of October 24, 1868, about finances was published in the *St. Louis Missouri Democrat* on October 26.

3. Johnson issued a fourth amnesty proclamation on December 25, 1868.

From Jonas R. McClintock

Pittsburgh   Octr. 26 1868

Dear Sir,

During the unusual excitement consequent to the threatening March of *Congressional radicalism*, I was unfortunate in departing from my Customary rule of avoiding any approach toward the infliction of personal wounds, especially to the prejudice, as in the case in point, of the closest personal relations.

The facts stated, and said to have called for your notice, had reference to the *Status* of Capn. Jno. E. Blaine, Mily. Store Keeper Q.M.Dt. have been charged as cause of refusal to assign Capn. Blaine to the Post at Pittsburgh. If so, I deeply regret my interference in putting on paper even to and old and valued Correspondent, the *import* of the incautious words of an impulsive *friend*, which I now believe would not have been spoken in his Cooler Moments.

I desire to make amends for my *Social offence*, and on the ground of my unfaltering admiration of your fearless opposition to "radical Assaults" on the Constitution, and in view of your triumph over unscrupulous enemies, I ask that you will enable *me* to *wipe out* even the *Shadow* of wrong.

Capt. B. is under orders for Fort Leavenworth, Whither he has gone leaving his family in Penna. for the present. No political or other reasons, Can now be urged to his transfer to the Post at Pittsburgh. I ask this as a *personal favor*. Indeed it would afford me great relief, if Your Excellency would instruct the proper Dept. to make the transfer, before his full installment in office in Kansas or Missouri.

I have written the foregoing without Consultation, & of my own volition, Confident that it will be in accord with the Wishes of the Honl. Edgr. Cowan[1] (& of Henry D. Foster[)],[2] & many Western friends.

Jonas R. McClintock

ALS, DLC-JP.

1. Several months earlier Cowan had successfully sought Blaine's appointment as military storekeeper at Pittsburgh. See Cowan to Johnson, May 28, 1868, *Johnson Papers*, 14: 126–27.

2. Foster (1808–1880) first served in the U.S. House in the 1840s and then in the Pennsylvania legislature in the 1850s. He was an unsuccessful candidate for governor in 1860. Foster later served again in the U.S. House (1871–73). *BDUSC.*

From Robert C. Trigg and John T. Harcourt[1]

Richmond Texas   Oct. 26 1868

The following order was received here by telegraph. "To Judge McFarland[2]—Richmond Texas—For reasons made known by the Governor[3] and Attorney General[4] You will continue until next term the *causes* involving the question of heirship to the estate of J. C. Clark[5] deceased. (signed) J. J. Reynolds Brevet Major General." We regard this order as a great military usurpation. It is addressed to a Judge of a civil court directing him how he shall decide—the question of continuance. Both parties are present and represented by counsel, case ready for trial. Shall the commander of the District control the Judiciary? We ask you to revoke the order. Answer.[6]

R. C. Trigg

Jno T. Harcourt

Plaintiffs Counsel

Tel, DLC-JP.

1. Trigg (*c*1828–1872), a graduate of the Virginia Military Institute and former colonel of the 54th Va. Rgt., was a Christiansburg, Virginia, lawyer, representing some of the Virginia plaintiffs in the Clark case. Harcourt (1825–*fl*1882), a Kentuckian who moved to Texas in 1850, practiced law in Columbus and Galveston and served in the state senate during the Civil War. *Con Vet*, 17 (1909): 65; *Richmond Dispatch*, Jan. 4, 1872; William S. Speer and John H. Brown, eds., *The Encyclopedia of the New West* (Marshall, Tex., 1881), 156–57; Galveston directories (1875–83).

2. Isaac B. McFarland (1818–1899), a Tennessean who moved to Texas in 1845, practiced law and served as a county judge, state legislator, and then as district judge (1865–75). *Biographical Encyclopedia of Texas* (New York, 1880), 183; Frank W. Johnson et al., *A History of Texas and Texans* (5 vols., Chicago, 1914), 4: 1758.

3. Elisha M. Pease.

4. Ezekiel B. Turner (1825–1888) moved to Texas in 1853 and practiced law in partnership with Andrew J. Hamilton. A Unionist, he fled Texas during the Civil War. After the war he held various posts such as U.S. district attorney, state attorney general (1867–70), and judge of both district and federal courts. Tyler et al., *New Handbook of Texas.*

5. John C. Clark (*c*1798–1862) went to Texas in 1822 and was one of Stephen F. Austin's "Old Three Hundred colonists." He owned substantial amounts of land and slaves, an estate worth nearly half a million dollars at his death. Assumed to have no heirs, Clark's estate was sold for nearly $478,000 in 1866 and the proceeds were taken by the state. Ultimately, however, there were four sets of claimants for the estate. The suit against the estate in the fall of 1868 particularly involved the claims of an alleged nephew of Clark's living in the New River

area of Virginia. Apparently Pease and Turner had asked Reynolds to delay the trial because the state was not ready to defend its case and it did not want to lose such a large amount of money to an heir. Lets. Recd. (Main Ser.), File P-627-1868 (M619, Roll 651), RG94, NA; Tyler et al., *New Handbook of Texas.*

6. Johnson referred the matter to Secretary of War Schofield, who referred it to General Reynolds for a report. Reynolds, protesting that he had "carefully abstained from interference in civil causes," indicated why he had agreed to the request of Turner and Pease for a delay of the trial. In fact, the contest for Clark's estate became even more complex when his three children by his slave Sobrina, with whom he had privately lived as husband and wife from at least 1837 until his death, sued for his estate under provisions of the 1869 Texas constitution legitimizing the children of persons who lived together as spouses until the death of one. The jury decided in favor of the children but the heirs were violently driven off their inheritance because of racial prejudice. Lets. Recd. (Main Ser.), File P-627-1868 (M619, Roll 651), RG94, NA; Tyler et al., *New Handbook of Texas*; E. M. Wheelock, *Reports of Cases Argued and Decided in the Supreme Court of the State of Texas . . . 1872*, vol. 37 (St. Louis, 1882), 686–709; Annie Lee Williams, *A History of Wharton County, 1846–1961* (Austin, 1964), 114–15.

From I. M. Blood[1]

Washington D.C.   Oct 27th 1868

Geo Savage Esq[2] & myself called upon you to ask a favor, viz That you would be kind enough to Surgest or intimate to his Hon Secretary McCulloch that by rejecting Chas. Hudson as Rev. Supervisor it would open the way for a friend of yours to be nominated. Mr Hudson has been recommended & his nomination urged by Charles Sumner & Ben Butler who are no friends of mine. I would respectfully refer to Col Moore & your messenger or Usher Mr[3]   in regard to the interest I took in your acquittal on the impeachment trial &et &et. Hoping you will be kind enough to favor me with your influence . . .[4]

I. M. Blood
at Bayley & Co   Cor 7th & F Sts

ALS, DLC-JP.

1. Blood (*fl*1870) apparently was employed at Bayley & Co. and was listed in the city directory as a patent agent. Washington, D.C., directories (1869–70).

2. Savage (*c*1804–*c*1879) was a hardware merchant in Washington. 1870 Census, D.C., Washington, 4th Ward, 300; Washington, D.C., directories (1869–81).

3. Blood left a blank space next to "Mr." We do not know to whom he is referring.

4. Blood's letter *suggests* a Massachusetts connection, but we are not certain of such. At any rate, there is an I. M. Blood in the Boston directories in the 1870s as an agent of a temperance association. See Boston directories (1871–76).

From Horace H. Day and William H. Sylvis[1]

Philadelphia, October 27th 1868

Dear Sir

Could you make it convenient to be in this city on Saturday night and address a Mass meeting of Workingmen? The meeting to be called by the National Labor Union. We are using all our energies to carry this state for Seymour, against the "Bondholders" and we know your assistance would be invaluable. Can you come? Answer by telegraph.[2]

H. H. Day
Wm. H. Sylvis,
Pres N. L. U.

Address 330 Harmony St

LS, DLC-JP.

1. Sylvis (1828–1869), a longtime labor leader and reformer, assembled a national convention of workingmen in February 1861 to oppose the war. After the war began, however, Sylvis helped recruit a company for the Union army. In 1868 he was elected president of the National Labor Union, representing some 600,000 workers. *DAB*.

2. No reply from Johnson has been found.

From Thomas S. Gathright[1]

Gholson, Miss., Oct. 27. A ∴ L ∴ 5868, A ∴ D ∴ 1868.

Dear Sir & Brother,

The Masons of this state, whose Grand Master I am, desire you to release J.H. McIlwaine and W. T. Hewitt[2] now undergoing the sentence of a Military Commission, cruel and outrageous. J. H. McIlwaine is a Master Mason and is suffering treatment too horrible for contemplation. Your brethern pray you for the release of these prisoners from the Penitentiary at Jackson, Miss.[3]

You have done many noble things—this request granted and you are forever enshrined in the hearts of your brethren of Mississippi.

Thos. S. Gathright.
Grand Master of Masons of Mississippi.

ALS, DLC-JP.

1. Gathright (*c*1829–1880) was a prominent Mississippi educator who operated a private school, the Summerville Institute, in Noxubee County. In the mid-1870s he served as the state

superintendent of education. 1870 Census, Miss., Noxubee, Twp. 13, 14; Wiese, *The Woodville Republican*, 4: 207; Richard A. McLemore, ed., *A History of Mississippi* (2 vols., Hattiesburg, 1973), 1: 624; 2: 414; *Jackson Clarion*, July 10, 1868.

  2. William T. Hewitt (*c*1845–1881), a private in the 10th Miss. Inf. during the war, became a lawyer in Natchez, where he died of consumption. McIlwain is not further identified. 1880 Census, Miss., Adams, Natchez, 1st Ward, 48th Enum. Dist., 11; CSR, William T. Hewitt, RG109, NA; Wiese, *The Woodville Republican*, 5: 37.

  3. Hewitt and McIlwain, convicted by a military commission of conspiracy to murder, were sentenced to a year of hard labor at the penitentiary. In November 1868, they were discharged by a federal judge on a writ of *habeas corpus*. *Memphis Appeal*, Nov. 12, 1868.

From Edward G. W. Butler

                                          Dunboyne, La.   Oct. 28, 1868

My Dear Sir:

Few things could afford me more pleasure than the perusal of your letter to Gov. Seymour;[1] for, tho' un influenced by the persistent efforts of the Radical press to place you in an antagonistic position toward the Democratic party & it's nominees for the Presidency & Vice-Presidency, my confidence was somewhat shaken by the editorial of the *National Intelligencer*, indorsing the treasonable course of the New York *World*,[2] recommending the withdrawal of the Democratic nominees; and, although you have not responded to my letters, heretofore addressed to you, I will not deny myself the gratification of thanking you for your letter of good advise & encouragement to Gov. Seymour at the moment when the clouds were looming upon the cause of Constitutional Government & Civil Liberty; when our columns faltered; and it became necessary for the Commander-in-Chief to lead them on to victory.

Tho the ways of the Almighty are inscrutable, I cannot believe that he will subject us to the inflictions, of another four years of Radical rule, of insult and injustice; and, pleasing myself with the hope & belief that the Democracy will triumph in the coming contest, and that you can have the satisfaction of retiring from your exalted position with the conviction that your brave and patriotic defense of the Constitution and of States' and individual Rights have not been in vain.

                                                          E.G.W. Butler

P. S. Pray have the kindness to present me kindly to our friend Genl. Lorenzo Thomas.

ALS, DLC-JP.

1. See Johnson to Seymour, Oct. 22, 1868.
2. The *National Intelligencer* and *New York World* had suggested changing the Democratic ticket. See Alexander Delmar to Johnson, Oct. 18, 1868.

From S. Snyder Leidy

Philada. Oct. 28. 1868.

My dear Sir

We have a great Country; as a patriot and Statesman, you know it. You have labored, heaven knows, as an honest, faithful, public Servant in your office, the highest, and noblest, and greatest in the gift of God's people on this earth, to protect support and defend it by and through the Constitution of the United States. The Constitution is truly the President's platform. He is given the veto power as a check upon any undue, or unholy, or wrongful legislation on the part of Congress. If he does not therefore thus use it; then it would be proper to abolish the Constitution and the office both, and thus save to the Country the payment of the Salary, pittance thought [*sic*] it is, it would fill some radicals pocket and compensate him for services.

My dear Sir, when I think of the honest and faithful course you have pursued since you were inaugurated into the office as the honored President of the United States, I appreciate it all. Your work was well commenced, well continued. The Constitution was protected with all the ability and power that it was possible for man to do. And although the majorities in both houses were against you, you maintained and preserved your integrity and manhood in a manner greatly to embarrass their action. To such an extent was this done, that you had the radical party demoralized and the result was, that in 1867 the democracy received the fruit of your Constitution Statesmanship over the radicals.[1] You opened the door of the White house and the Capitol that the Democracy might walk in and thus defeat these radical destroyers,—these consummate demoralizers of our great Country.

Here at the very door-way of success, the Democratic leaders of the party became greatly conceited, they felt that while they succeeded in 1867 by your maintaining and preserving the right for the people, that they could walk over the course in 1868 with Congressmen Legislative men President &c.—and in this conceited idea did they act at the New York Convention where the Cup was brimfull of Cream—where Success was certain: where the great door-way was open for them to enter—the Council of the leaders gained the ascendancy they got their foot, not upon the *native heath* prepared for them by you, but on the brim of the Cup of Cream—toppled it over, and lost—lost—yes lost greatly in October[2] and I fear, the rest in November.

S. Snyder Leidy

Please acknowledge this.

ALS, DLC-JP.

1. A reference to Democratic victories in state elections in the fall of 1867. See the many relevant documents in *Johnson Papers*, volume 13.

2. Earlier in the month, state elections in Pennsylvania, Ohio, Indiana, and Nebraska resulted in Republican victories. *New York Times*, Oct. 14, 1868.

From William H. Van Nortwick[1]

Personal and private.

Bordentown [N.J.], Octr. 28th 1868.

Mr. President:—

From 1861 until the past summer I have co-operated with the Republican party. From the commencement of 1863 until July 30th 1868, I was connected with the Internal revenue service, three years of the time being spent in the Office at Washington.

My personal knowledge of the management of that branch of the public service—the immense frauds committed and glossed over, or connived at, by prominent officials—the attempts to conceal the extent of the whisky frauds from the people by means of false official reports—the duplicity and dishonesty of the present Committee of Ways and means on the liquor question, coupled with personal wrongs received at the hands of said Committee, led me to take the stump against the Congressional Radicals during the present canvass.

I have briefly stated these facts preliminary to calling the attention of your Excellency to a matter that has recently come to my knowledge.

While speaking, during the present canvass, in the State of Pennsylvania, I learned that, after the passage of the late Internal revenue Act,[2] a certain dealer in the city of Philadelphia visited New York for the purpose of obtaining the advice of a house, with whom he was in the habit of dealing in relation to the liquor trade.

The New Yorkers advised him to invest all the means that he could possibly spare in whisky, giving as a reason that, they held seventy thousand (70,000) gallons which they had taken out of bond on account of certain members of Congress, and that after the Presidential election was over, it was the intention to restore the old tax of two ($2.00) dollars per gallon on whisky. That they had the personal assurances of members to that effect.

I also learned that, acting on the advice received, the Philada. party has made heavy investments in the direction indicated.

Should Your Excellency deem this matter of high handed and corrupt legislation worthy of Executive attention, it will give me pleasure to furnish the name of the Philada. dealer, and to give such further aid in the matter as may be deemed necessary to establish the facts.

Appended please find copy of a letter relating to myself.[3]

Wm. H. Van Nortwick.

ALS, DLC-JP.

1. Van Nortwick (c1823–fl1878), a clerk, had been editor of the *Bordentown Register* in the 1850s and served on the borough common council (1860–62). He worked for the internal revenue service at least 1863–65. 1870 Census, N.J., Burlington, Bordentown, 49; *NUC*; E. M. Woodward and John F. Hageman, *History of Burlington and Mercer Counties, New Jersey, with Biographical Sketches of Many of Their Pioneers and Prominent Men* (Philadelphia, 1883), 97, 491; *U.S. Off. Reg.* (1863–65).

2. See Joseph R. Flanigen to Johnson, July 20, 1868, *Johnson Papers*, 14: 386–88.

3. Attached was a copy of a letter from Revenue Commissioner Edward A. Rollins to Van Nortwick, dated September 7, 1868. Rollins commented on Van Nortwick's "retirement," caused by the new revenue law which abolished his position as inspector, and remarked on the "fidelity and efficiency" with which Van Nortwick discharged his duties.

From James Dixon

Hartford   Oct. 29, 1868

To the President,

I acknowledge with thanks, the receipt of your letter to Gen Thomas Ewing "upon the National Expenditures and the Public debt."[1] Like every thing from your pen it is production of great ability, and cannot fail to exert a wide & a beneficial influence. I also noticed with great pleasure your letter to Gov. Seymour,[2] approving of his appearance before the people to discuss the great questions of the day.

Every day's experience leads me to a more & more confident belief that we should have been more likely to succeed if you had been our Candidate for the Presidency.

But though the present day may seem dark & ominous, History will do you justice, and rank you with the great patriotic statesmen of the past.

James Dixon

ALS, DLC-JP.

1. See Johnson to Thomas Ewing, Jr., Oct. 24, 1868.

2. See Johnson to Horatio Seymour, Oct. 22, 1868.

From Thomas C. Durant

End Track U P RR   1868

Oct 29th

One of the Commissioners appointed to examine the Union Pacific Rail Road now completed and also to examine the location of the line thereof, has been here some time in the employ of this company as civil engineer and located that portion of the line above referred.[1]

I would therefore most respectfully suggest that the Commissioners be composed of disinterested persons believing their decision will be more satisfactory to the Government, the stock holders, and the public, and rival parties for unfriendly criticism.[2]

Thomas C. Durant

Vice Prest U P R R

Tel, DLC-JP.
   1. Jacob Blickensderfer, Jr.
   2. Blickensderfer remained on the commission.

From Henry R. Linderman

Phila.   Oct. 29. 1868.

Dear Sir,

Capt. Robert McKibbin,[1] has recently been tried by a court marshal for intoxication and sentenced to be dismissed from the army.[2] I do not know the details of the case but from my knowledge of the man I do not beleive that he is habitually addicted to the excessive use of strong drink. He served faithfully throughout the war and was twice brought home desperately wounded, & belongs to a family which sent six out of seven sons to the field. All of them served with distinction. The Father, Chambers McKibbin Esq, has very recently buried a beloved son[3] & is greatly depressed in spirits & if another blow is to come from the dismissal of Capt. McKibbin it will be more than he can bear. In view of these facts, & of the gallant services of the McKibbin family, I respectfully ask that all possible clemency consistent with duty may be exercised & that if possible the sentence be not approved & if it must be approved, deferred at least for the present.

The Father & Mother of this Young man are now over seventy Years old & bowed down with grief & I trust that the threatened disgrace of their son may be averted. With this hurried statement & appeal I leave the case to the good heart of the President.

H R Linderman

ALS, DLC-JP.

1. McKibbin (d. 1873) held a number of different ranks and appointments during the Civil War and was brevetted for service at Antietam and at Petersburg. By 1868 he was a captain, 4th U.S. Inf., and stationed in the Wyoming Territory. He eventually resigned from the military in 1870. Powell, *Army List*, 471; General Court-Martial Orders No. 77, Lets. Recd. (Main Ser.), File M-1527-1868 (M619, Roll 643), RG94, NA.

2. McKibbin's court-martial was held at Fort D. A. Russell, Wyoming Territory, in mid-October 1868. The charge of drunkenness was one of three charges brought against McKibbin; he was found guilty of that charge. The sentence meted out by the court was that McKibbin should be dismissed ("cashiered") from military service. But, according to the court-martial report from the adjutant general's office in Washington, the sentence was commuted to a mere reduction in rank for McKibbin. Ibid.

3. William C. McKibbin (*c*1822–1868), a dry-goods merchant who helped the family manage the Merchants' Hotel, succumbed to typhoid fever on October 3. *Philadelphia Press*, Oct. 5, 7, 1868; Philadelphia directories (1858–68); *History of Cincinnati and Hamilton County, Ohio* (Cincinnati, 1894), 753.

From Henry R. Linderman

Philadelphia   October 30th 1868.

Dear Sir.

I have received and read with much satisfaction a copy of your very interesting and instructive letter to General Ewing, upon the subject of "National Expenditures and Public Debt." The facts therein set forth are startling and should arouse the American People to a proper sense of the imminent danger of national insolvency with which we are unquestionably threatened. This timely ennunciation of facts and indication of inevitable results will I trust be productive of good. It is another evidence that You are generally in advance of the public men of the day in warning the people of impending danger, and indicating to them the path of safety.

The present financial system is vitally defective and must be speedily reformed or disaster will surely come. Of this I think there can be no reasonable doubt. The evils of an inflated and irredeemable currency must be apparent to every man of reasonable intelligence. By it the prices of nearly all the commodities of life,—especially those that are of an imperishable character—are kept at enormously high rates: and speculative combinations use the national Banks for purposes inimical to the interest of nineteen twentieths of the people.

A policy looking to the continuance of the present inflated and irredeemable currency, enormous public Debt, & heavy and unequal taxation, cannot but be regarded as ruinous to the material interests of the People, and you have done the Country a great service in calling their attention to the Subject.

H. R. Linderman

ALS, DLC-JP.

From Nathaniel P. Sawyer

Pittsburgh   Oct 30 1868.

Two speeches from you, one Saturday in Phila & one Monday in New York might elect Seymour & save the country. I beg you not to hesitate at this perilous moment of the Nations danger.

N. P. Sawyer
Personal

Tel, DLC-JP.

From John M. Schofield

Washington City, October 30, 1868

Mr President

Upon further consideration of Genl Rousseau's despatches of yesterday and to day, asking instructions relative to the New Orleans police,[1] and Gov. Warmouth's despatch of yesterday[2] (received today), upon the same subject, I would suggest that Genl Rousseau be directed to sustain the present police organization until the question of law involved is decided by the proper court, and then to sustain the decision of the court.

I enclose herewith the two despatches from Genl Rousseau, with my reply to the first, and that of Gov. Warmouth.[3]

J M Schofield   Secty of War

ALS, DLC-JP.
1. The New Orleans police situation had become very complex. The state legislature had recently established the Metropolitan Police, two-thirds of whom were black. Meanwhile, the mayor and city council of New Orleans established a rival force and Rousseau was concerned about the prospect of a clash between them. Rousseau had asked Schofield at what point he

should interfere. Dawson, *Army Generals and Reconstruction*, 88–90; Rousseau to Schofield, Oct. 29, 1868 (two telegrams), Oct. 30, 1868, *House Ex. Docs.*, 40 Cong., 3 Sess., No. 1, pp. 36–37 (Ser. 1367).

2. H. C. Warmoth to Schofield, Oct. 29, 1868, ibid., p. 37, requested that Rousseau be instructed to maintain order and keep the mayor's forces from taking control.

3. Schofield sent Rousseau two replies on October 29. The official reply asserted that "it is impossible to give instructions in detail from this distance in the short time allowed." Schofield claimed that Rousseau had "ample authority to do what is necessary to preserve the peace." In his unofficial reply of the same date Schofield said that Rousseau would have to judge which police force was the lawful one. His troops could "be a good temporary substitute for both the rival police forces." However, Rousseau did not use his troops as police substitutes. Schofield to Rousseau, Oct. 29, 1868 (two telegrams), ibid., p. 36; Dawson, *Army Generals and Reconstruction*, 90. See Johnson to Rousseau, Oct. 31, 1868.

To Henry H. Haight

Oct 31, 1868

Genl. Halleck[1] has been directed to take such action, in conformity with the Constitution & laws of the U.S., as may be necessary to aid the civil authorities of California in preserving the peace.[2]

Andrew Johnson.

Tel, DLC-JP.

1. Henry W. Halleck headed the Division of the Pacific with headquarters in San Francisco. Stephen E. Ambrose, *Halleck: Lincoln's Chief of Staff* (Baton Rouge, 1962), 204.

2. There had been several clashes, with resulting injuries, between Democratic and Republican campaign processions in San Francisco. These were probably the "sufficient reasons" which caused Gov. Haight to telegraph Johnson on October 31 requesting authority "to use United States troops to quell disturbance here if any occurs." On the same date Secretary of War Schofield telegraphed Halleck with presidential authorization "to take such action . . . as may be necessary to aid the civil authorities of California in preserving the peace." Haight to Johnson and Schofield to Halleck, Oct. 31, 1868, *House Ex. Docs.*, 40 Cong., 3 Sess., No. 1, p. 39 (Ser. 1367); *New York Times*, Oct. 30, 1868.

From John McDonald[1]

Hazlehurst Miss   Oct 31st 1868

Sir

I learned this day that W J Brittain[2] assessor of Internal Revenue for this 1st District of Mississippi has resigned and Mr T A Burdett[3] appointed by him to take charge of the office untill the said Burdett is commissioned or some other person. I made application by petition for the office when *A H Hall*[4] was relieved. Mr Brittain being in Nomination as it was believed it would not be confirmed by the Senate, my petition and recommendation was sent directed to you

about the first of February last. Recommended by Judge Wm. Yerger
Judge George T Swann Judge Hill U.S.D.C.[5] Thos. T. Swann auditor of public accounts and Capt *Estell* Treasurer of the State[6] &c
deeming those Gentlemen to be sufficient which I expect you received. If my petition was filed it will be seen that all these names are
on it. I could get all the prominant men of the District and the State
to certify to my capability integrity honesty sobriety and industry. I
am still an applicant for the *office*. I am 70 years of age injoying good
health but I was among the unfortunate who lost all by the war. Was
worth $40,000 nearly all slave property but now peniless have to
subsist by hard labor. I have five Grand *children orphans* without parents three daughters & two sons the oldest 12 years old parents all
died before the *war* except one he died in the army was forced by the
conscript Law &c to go. I have all these orphans to support the best
I can well to do before the war were wealthy but now peniless. I send
you this that you may put my name in nomination with the recommendation sent in Feby last. If the petition is lost I can get another if
necessary. Mr Burdett is a young man a good clerk and his wife[7] a
good music teacher a small family &c. I look on my situation to be
different to Mr Burdett. I am certain I can fill the office as well as
Mr Burdett having been assistant assr. for nearly 18 months and
from my experience as a book keeper. I merchandized before the war
and never employed no book keeper and my books will compare
with any in the Country. You will see from my application that I
filled several offices in the State for the last 38 years such as assessor
& collector of State Revenue *Sherriff; Deputy Marshall* and *Probate
Judge* &c. I was always a *Union Man* opposed to Seccession in days
gone by an old line Whig now a *Democrat* oposed to radicalism.

John McDonald

PS   If you send any communication to me please send it this place or
Beauregard Station N.O. & N. R R 10 miles before this station.

J McD

ALS, DNA-RG56, Appts., Internal Revenue Service, Assessor, Miss., 3rd Dist., John
McDonald.
    1. McDonald (*c*1800–*fl*1870), a former merchant, was later a farmer. 1860 Census, Miss.,
Copiah, 161; (1870), Copiah, Twp. 1 & 2, 133.
    2. During antebellum years William J. Britton (b. *c*1816) had been a planter. He had been
nominated in January 1868 to become assessor; the Senate confirmed the appointment the
following month. 1850 Census, Miss., Madison, 179; *Senate Ex. Proceedings*, Vol. 16: 127, 164.

3. Thomas A. Burditt (*c*1828–*fl*1870), a Massachusetts-born accountant, was nominated as assessor on December 18, 1868, for the permanent appointment. But the Senate Finance Committee reported adversely on the nomination on March 3, 1869, at the close of the Congressional session. Ibid., 415, 505; 1870 Census, Miss., Copiah, Hazlehurst, 6.

4. Alexander H. Hall (*c*1815–1895), physician and farmer, had been confirmed as assessor in May 1866. He was removed in late 1867 or early 1868 for "inefficiency and misconduct" in office and "habitual intemperance." 1860 Census, Miss., Covington, Williamsburg, 29; (1870), Hollidays Creek Beat, 22; Betty C. Wiltshire, comp., *Mississippi: Index of Wills, 1800–1900* (Bowie, Md., 1989), 82; *Senate Ex. Proceedings*, Vol. 16: 127; Ser. 6B, Vol. 4: 193, Johnson Papers, LC; McCulloch to Johnson, Jan. 6, 1868, Lets. Sent, Mail and Files Div. (L Ser.), Vol. 2, RG56, NA.

5. Swann (*c*1809–*fl*1870), a lawyer and former state auditor, was now a court clerk at Jackson. Robert A. Hill (1811–1900), a former resident of Tennessee, moved to Tishomingo County, Mississippi, during the 1850s. A lawyer, he served as United States judge of the first or northern district of the state for many years (1866–91). 1870 Census, Miss., Hinds, Jackson, 1; Robert Lowry and William H. McCardle, *A History of Mississippi* (Spartanburg, 1978 [1891]), 576; Wiese, *The Woodville Republican*, 4: 11; *DAB*.

6. Swann (1825–1870), a brother of George T. Swann, was a real estate agent. The state treasurer was John H. Echols (*c*1835–*fl*1881), listed in censuses as a planter and land agent. Mary C. Landin, *The Old Cemeteries of Hinds County, Mississippi* (Utica, Miss., 1988), 83; Wiese, *The Woodville Republican*, 4: 11; 5: 29; William C. Harris, *The Day of the Carpetbagger: Republican Reconstruction in Mississippi* (Baton Rouge, 1979), 36; 1860 Census, Miss., Hinds, Jackson, 29; (1870), 13, 41; (1880), North Ward, 1st Enum. Dist., 4.

7. Clara Burditt (*c*1829–*fl*1870), a Maine native, was the mother of at least three daughters and one son. 1870 Census, Miss., Copiah, Hazlehurst, 6.

To Lovell H. Rousseau

[Washington, D.C.]   Oct. 31, 1868

You are expected and authorized to take all legitimate steps necessary and proper to prevent breaches of the peace or hostile collisions between citizens.[1] Questions relating to the civil polity of the State must be left to the proper civil authorities for consideration and settlement. The object is to preserve peace and restore civil Govermnt to the people according to the principles laid down in the constitution.

You are referred to instructions hertofore given, which are deemed full and ample for all just and lawful purposes.[2]

[Andrew Johnson]

AL draft, PPRF.

1. For background on the New Orleans police conflict, to which this document refers, see John M. Schofield to Johnson, Oct. 30, 1868.

2. This telegram was in response to one of Rousseau's in which he asked: "Please inform me whether I must interfere in case there is no collision and no breach of the peace." He wanted to be sure to preserve the good relations existing between the military and the citizens. Rousseau to Schofield, Oct. 30, 1868, *House Ex. Docs.*, 40 Cong., 3 Sess., No. 1, p. 37 (Ser. 1367).

November 1868

From Allen M. Gangewer

Washington City D.C.   November 1868

Sir,

At the annual meeting of the Industrial Home School[1] it was found that the institution has not been able to pay its way during the past year, and that it is now about one thousand dollars in debt. Between sixty and seventy children are receiving the benefit of the school, and the Lady Managers do not feel at liberty to turn them out to the cold charities of an unsympathizing world, where, unless they are cared for, they will grow up as outcasts or something worse. Believing it to be far better to aid them to become useful and self-sustaining members of society, rather than criminals and pests, the managers appeal to you to aid them in the work of elevating these waifs of society. They ask a *thanksgiving contribution* to assist them in prosecuting their plans without embarrassment.

We are all Stewards of Heaven's bounty, and believing it to be true that "He that hath pity on the poor lendeth to the Lord, and that which he hath given will he pay him again["],[2] they confidently trust that this appeal will [?] from you a fitting response.[3]

A M Gangewer V Pres. & Acting Pres.

LS, DLC-JP.
1. A brief report of the October 31 meeting is found in the *Washington Evening Star*, Nov. 2, 1868.
2. A quotation from Prov. 19:17.
3. A response from the President has not been found.

From Albert W. Paine[1]

Washington D C   November 1868

I address you to solicit the appointment of Consul at Leeds, England.

The enclosed references,[2] to which I beg to invite your attention, furnish some information of my capabilities and fitness for the position. An earnest desire is added to this request with the highest respect of . . .[3]

Albert W. Paine

ALS, DNA-RG59, Lets. of Appl. and Recomm., 1861–69 (M650, Roll 37), Albert W. Paine.

1. Paine (1812–1907), a Bangor, Maine, lawyer, served as state banking and insurance commissioner (1868–73). In addition, he was president of the Maine Telegraph Company for twenty-five years. *Who Was Who in America*, 1: 929.

2. According to the file cover sheet, Paine had references from at least six different prominent persons, including Senators James R. Doolittle and Timothy O. Howe, and Alexander W. Randall.

3. Paine did not receive the appointment to Leeds. In December, still interested in the nomination, he submitted the required oath of allegiance to Secretary Seward. The next month, however, Paine wrote to withdraw his name from further consideration. Paine to Seward, Dec. 9, 1868, Jan. 6, 1869, Lets. of Appl. and Recomm., 1861–69 (M650, Roll 37), Albert W. Paine, RG59, NA.

From John Scott Payne[1]

Columbia Boone Co Mo.
Novembr 2nd 1868.

Mr President

I have the honor to request that an order may be issued from the War Department, revoking that by which my resignation as 1st Lieutenant 5th U S Cavalry, was accepted to take effect Septembr 12th 1868. The circumstances under which my resignation were of such a nature as to require some explanation in order that you may fully understand my course in taking that step. The Regiment of which I was an officer was under orders to proceed west without delay. I had just joined my company at Nashville Tennessee, having been detained in Washington during the month of August, pending my trial under charges preferred by Major Genl George H Thomas commanding Department of the Cumberland.[2] Previous to my arrest on said charges I had procured a leave of absence for three months to visit my mother[3] in the state of Missouri, who had been recently widowed by the death of my Father,[4] and placed in consequence in embarrassing circumstances.

At the time of my return to Nashville the necessity of visiting her, still existed, as the leave of absence before mentioned, had been revoked when I was placed in arrest; at the same time I had business of such a nature in Knoxville Tenn that it was absolutely necessary for me to be in that city for a short time. The alternative was then presented me, to telegraph asking a leave of absence or failing in that I was compelled to tender my resignation. Being so forced to act by circumstances, I was induced to so word the telegram to your Excellency, as to make the importance of the step I was taking apparent to yourself. I therefore tendered my resignation *conditionally*, and was surprised on the receipt of a telegram from the Adjutant General to see that those conditions were not complied with.[5]

From the decision of the Attorney General Mr Evarts, in the case of Mr E A Rollins Commissioner of Internal Revenue,[6] I am of the opinion that the acceptance of my resignation, *without a compliance* with its conditions, is null and void.

I therefore respectfully and earnestly ask, that your Excellency will give this matter your attention, and direct an order to be issued revoking that by which my resignation was accepted. I will here state that I have made application to the Secretary of War, to this effect.[7]

Hoping that this matter may meet your favorable consideration . . .[8]

J Scott Payne
Late 1st Lieut 5th U S Cav

ALS, DNA-RG94, ACP Branch, File P-156-CB-1868, G.[*sic*] S. Payne.

1. Payne (1844–1895) graduated from West Point in 1866, was appointed 2nd lieutenant in the 5th Cavalry, and was promoted to 1st lieutenant in 1867. Powell, *Army List*, 523; Nancy C. Baird and Carol Jordan, *Fauquier County, Virginia Tombstone Inscriptions: Volume 1* (Athens, Ga., 1994), 148.

2. Payne was court-martialed on rather petty charges stemming, he believed, from his support of Andrew Johnson while Payne was stationed in Knoxville, Tennessee. The court acquitted Payne but the verdict was returned on a technicality—Payne had pleaded guilty to some of the charges. The court then changed its verdict to attach no criminality to his actions. Court-Martial Records, File OO-3415, RG153, NA. For an anti-Payne account of his actions while in Knoxville, see the *Boston Advertiser*, Sept. 18, 1868.

3. Mary M. Hume Payne (*c*1825–*fl*1870) was the much younger second wife of Arthur M. Payne, whom she married in 1843. J. Scott Payne was her only child. By 1870 she was living with one of her step-daughters in Missouri. 1850 Census, Va., Fauquier, Ashby Dist., 238; (1860), Mo., Boone, Cedar Twp., 754; (1870), 5; John K. Gott, *Fauquier County, Virginia Marriage Bonds, 1759–1854 and Marriage Returns, 1785–1841* (Bowie, Md., 1989), 154.

4. Arthur M. Payne (*c*1805–1868), a fairly well-to-do Virginia farmer, had moved to Missouri by 1860. His 1829 first marriage to Mary C.M. Fitzhugh produced at least five children. Ibid.; 1850 Census, Va., Fauquier, Ashby Dist., 238; (1860), Mo., Boone, Cedar Twp., 754.

5. On September 11, Payne wrote a letter of resignation to take effect on December 1, 1868, if he could not be given the six-month leave of absence he needed to attend to business matters for his mother and himself. The next day J. C. Kelton of the adjutant general's office sent a telegram accepting Payne's resignation, effective that day, September 12. Payne to Johnson, Sept. 11, 1868, and other documents, ACP Branch, File P-156-CB-1868, J. Scott Payne, RG94, NA.

6. Rollins had resigned effective with the nomination and confirmation of his successor. When Johnson accepted the resignation immediately, Rollins objected and attorney general William Evarts ruled that the President could only accept the resignation with its conditions. Summary of Payne's case, ibid. See also Edward A. Rollins to Johnson, June 8, 1868, *Johnson Papers*, 14: 187.

7. No letter from Payne to the Secretary of War has been found.

8. Allegedly, Johnson brought the Payne case before the cabinet, which discussed it and

agreed with Payne's interpretation, although neither Secretary Browning nor Secretary Welles recorded such a discussion in his diary. On January 30, 1869, the War Department issued an order revoking the order of September 12, 1868, which had accepted Payne's resignation. Summary of Payne's case, ACP Branch, File P-156-CB-1868, J. Scott Payne, RG94, NA. For further developments, see William F. Switzler to Johnson, Feb. 20, 1869; J. Scott Payne to Johnson, Mar. 5, 1869; Mary M. Payne to Johnson, Apr. 26, 1869.

From James R. Doolittle
Confidential

Racine   Nov 3d 1868

Dear Sir

In the case of our Marshal[1] I gave a letter to Mr Lyon[2] to be forwarded in case it met the views of several other gentlemen. One of them has presented the name of another, and other persons advise to hold on for a while. They wish a little more time.

I do not wish to have premature action, and it is all well enough to let it rest a little while.[3]

J. R Doolittle

9 A M a beautiful day for election. God only knows the result. I fear all is lost.

ALS, DLC-JP.

1. The post was vacant due to the death of the previous occupant, Cassius Fairchild. Ser. 6B, Vol. 4: 337, 340, Johnson Papers, LC.

2. Probably Joseph M. Lyon (c1825–1868), a newspaperman who had been postmaster at Utica, New York (1859–61) before he moved to Wisconsin. At Milwaukee he and an associate bought a newspaper in 1862. *History of Milwaukee, Wisconsin* (Chicago, 1881), 629; *U.S. Off. Reg.* (1859–61); 1860 Census, N.Y., Oneida, Utica, 2nd Ward, 59.

3. For more on the search for a new U.S. marshal for Wisconsin, see Doolittle to Johnson, Nov. 19, 1868.

From Robert W. Latham

New York   Nov. 4 1868

My Dear Sir

The result of the Presidential Election, is a subject so painful, that I will not dwell upon it in this letter. Indeed but for the enclosed slip from the N. York Herald this morning,[1] I would not occupy a moment of your time.

In the last 18 months I have seen it often verified, that,

> "The wisdom of the poor man is dispised
> And his words are not regarded,"[2]

and I am unwilling to call up unpleasant reflections, by any reference to the past.

McCulloch has been the source of almost every trouble, and difficulty you have had since you became president. To convince you of this, I, in common with your other friends, have been unsuccessful. I shall however continue "to peg away" until the close of your administration.

If by any means you can, or rather if you will get rid of this man before you retire from office, it will remove a mountain of odium from your shoulders. It is painful to hear you charged with being a partner of his, in his Gold swindling, and stock jobbing opperations; and many assert that your keeping him in office, cannot be accounted for upon any other principle, but that of personal interest in his speculating transactions.

Rollins, as the tool of McCulloch, has done you incalculable injury, and if you could not remove him, you certainly could *suspend him*. As you cannot now be charged with favouring either political side, do for your own sake, and for the country's sake, make some changes, that will show the country, that the Executive Department still has, in your hands, a little life and vitality left.

I will again Suggest *Genl. Tho. Ewing* to take McCulloch's place.

R. W. Latham

ALS, DLC-JP.

1. The enclosed clipping concerned the latest rumors about the pending removal of McCulloch.

2. A variation of Ecclesiastes 9:16, "nevertheless the poor man's wisdom *is* despised, and his words are not heard."

From Edward A. Pollard

New York City. November 4. 1868.

Sir,

I have obtained a clerical situation in the Custom House here, although one of slenderest salary—only $1000 per annum. Yet, Sir, I thank you heartily for your consideration; you will always possess my gratitude, as you have already long since obtained my admiration. The situation will be an aid to me in the prosecution of some literary works, and in these I hope and aspire to interest you.

My most immediate literary work will be a Life of Jefferson Davis, appearing probably next January or February, of which the enclosed Announcement gives some account.[1] I beg to call your attention to it, Sir, because one of its most conspicuous chapters will be an account of your signal and dramatic defence of the Union against the array of Southern Secessionists. Whatever have since been the august fortunes of your life, permit me to say, Mr. President, that I think your stand on that occasion—in the debates preceding the war—the most marked and singular and sublime attitude in your history. I shall write this chapter with some ambition for dramatic effect, with a minute attention to details, and with an effort to develope the debates of the Senate in 1860–1 into a great historical picture.

It is, Mr. President, to further this effort—an effort at the truth and justice of history—that I venture to ask if you can furnish me with any personal recollections of this debate (the transcendent preface to the war, as I esteem it), or guide me to what you may consider the best references. I repeat that I am anxious to adorn and amplify it with as many details as possible. If I could obtain something more than your printed speeches and the common newspaper narrative, something of the secret history of the dramatic encounter of mind preluding the war, you may be sure, Sir, that I would use it with discretion, and in the interest of truth.[2]

Edwd. A. Pollard

ALS, DLC-JP.

1. The enclosed printed announcement indicated Pollard's intention to write and publish a Davis biography.

2. Johnson replied that the press of duties prevented him from providing the requested information to Pollard. The President suggested, however, a possible future interview with Pollard during which he could respond to direct questions about the secession debates. Johnson to Pollard, Nov. 5, 1868, Johnson Papers, LC.

From John Rosenberg[1]

La Grange, Texas   November 4th 1868

May it please Your Excellency,

To pardon an humble individual for troubling you at this time, but knowing, that you will not refuse a simple prayer I have made this request with full confidence in your justice.

About the beginning of last May being induced to send a petition to E. M. Stanton then forcibly holding the office of Secretary of War, to be appointed chaplain to one of the regiments then serving on the western frontier of this state. I am a licensed Lay-Reader and Missionary of the Protestant Episcopal Church of the U. States. The document was signed by Brevet Maj. Genl. Edward Hatch, Colonel of the 9th U.S. Cavalry, as also by Bvt. Brig. Genl. Mason[2] Maj 35th U.S. Infantry, inclosing a certified copy of my license, & original testimonials from other parties, since which time nothing has been heard from the War Department in relation to the matter.

Since writing my application, the chaplain of the regiment, the Revd. Mr. Jacobi[3] has resigned, and Genl. Hatch, as Colonel of the Regiment has expressed his wish that I might be appointed to the vacant chaplaincy. If I cannot obtain the appointment I am anxious to obtain my original documents; and although I have written for them, never received a reply.

May it, therefore, please your Excellency, if consistent with your duty, to grant my application or cause my papers to be returned, full well knowing, that should Genl. Grant unhappily succeed you, there would be no chance of receiving the appointment.[4] With every confidence in your justice & Kindness . . .

John Rosenberg

ALS, DNA-RG94, ACP Branch, File R-308-CB-1868, J. Rosenberg.
    1. Not further identified.
    2. John S. Mason (1824–1897) was an 1847 West Point graduate and career military man. He became major of the 17th Infantry in October 1864 and was transferred to the 35th Infantry in September 1866. Although he was brigadier general of volunteers during the war, his highest postwar regular army rank was colonel, achieved in 1883. Powell, *Army List*, 456; Warner, *Blue*.
    3. John C. Jacobi.
    4. Johnson did not appoint Rosenberg.

From W. Bakewell[1]

New York   5th Nov 1868.

Hond. & Respected Sir,

The great Conflict is ended and the result is only what we good democrats expected. It is useless to recapitulate here the reasons why we are unsuccessful, as you are just as well convinced as we are.

Now the reason why I take this liberty is that, first, I admire you *throughout all* your career and *Secondly*, I believe my suggestion would not only do *our* party an incalculable amount of good, but it would make *you* not only in the eyes of your supporters but also that of your enemies, one of the greatest patriots living. It would also take the wind out of, and entirely burst up the great beasts B. B. & Co.[2] My suggestion is and pardon me for it—That you vacate the Presidental Chair in favor of Grant say on New Years day alleging as a reason that *you have fulfilled* your mission—and that in order to heal the wounds of the Nation (as the villians have it) that you will transfer over the reigns of Government, to great *Pacifier* at once in order that *he* may loose no time in declaring *Peace*. By so doing the "Coup de Etat," would eclipse the great Nap IIIs of '48.

Always having been your firm Supporter & Friend.

W. Bakewell

ALS, DLC-JP.
  1. Perhaps William H. Bakewell (*fl*1874), a New York City sailmaker who resided in Brooklyn. Brooklyn directories (1868–74); New York City directories (1860–71).
  2. Benjamin F. Butler and Radical colleagues.

From John M. Binckley

Washington, 5" November, 1868.

Mr President,

It has become my duty to lay before the Executive information that the functions, duties and powers of my office have been, since the 21" ult—and still are, completely obstructed by the Commissioner of Internal Revenue with the consent of the Secretary of the Treasury.[1]

I herewith submit copies of the correspondence in which the case is developed.[2] My report to the Honorable Secretary, it will be observed, is dated twelve days ago. It may not have been received until the monday following, which is ten days since. I have received no letter in reply, and lest longer silence on my part be construed into acquiescence in the suspension of business with which I am expressly charged by law, I hereby signify my continued readiness to fulfil all my official duties.

John M Binckley
Solicitor of Internal Revenue

ALS, DLC-JP.

1. Edward A. Rollins and Hugh McCulloch, respectively.

2. Apparently the copies were attached originally, but have been rearranged in the Johnson Papers under Binckley's name. Binckley wrote to Rollins on October 21, claiming that a clerk had removed files from his office on Rollins's orders. Binckley wrote again on October 22 informing Rollins that the clerk continued to withhold the material. On October 24 Binckley explained the situation in writing to McCulloch, charging Rollins was interfering with the official duties of the solicitor. Binckley to Rollins, Oct. 21, 22, 1868, and Binckley to McCulloch, Oct. 24, 1868, Johnson Papers, LC. For other suspicions regarding Rollins's complicity in revenue fraud, see John H. Gilmer to Johnson, Nov. 11, 1868.

From John V.L. Pruyn

Albany, Nov 5th 1868

Dear Sir

I beg to introduce to your Excellency, the Revd. Thos W Haskins[1] of the Protestant Episcopal Church, for whom an appointment as Chaplain in the Army, will I learn be requested, from several quarters. Mr Haskins is one of the Clergymen who went out about two years ago with Bishop Tuttle[2] to Salt Lake City, where he has since that time resided. Their mission was the first among the Mormons, & has excited warm interest throughout the Country. An effort was made at that time in which I took part to procure a Chaplaincy for Mr Haskins, but there was no vacancy. I have known Mr H for many years and can say without hesitation that he will if appointed, be a faithful exemplary and zealous officer; doing good to all about him. Indeed he is just the person for such a post, and I hope you will at once give him the appointment asked for.[3]

John V.L. Pruyn

ALS, DNA-RG94, ACP Branch, File 2609-ACP-1872, Thomas W. Haskins.

1. In addition to his position as minister, Haskins (1840–1895) was also principal at St. Mark's School in Salt Lake City, and author of various religious tracts. Salt Lake City directories (1869); *NUC*; ACP Branch, File 2609-ACP-1872, Thomas W. Haskins, RG94, NA.

2. A native of New York state, Daniel S. Tuttle (1837–1923) had been serving as missionary bishop of Montana, Utah, and Idaho since 1867. In 1886 he became bishop of St. Louis, Missouri, and at his death was considered one of the city's most distinguished citizens. *DAB*.

3. Haskins received the appointment, effective November 16, 1868, and held it until his resignation in April 1872. Powell, *Army List*, 361.

From Thomas J. Rollins[1]

Marshall N.C.   Nov 5th 1868

Dear Sir

The election is over, and we had a quiet time in our county. The Republican majority is 70 votes. I am sorrow to say, that the so called Democratic party made an unfair display in their zeal to carry the election, and their conduct if persisted in will ruin the county and all fair minded men will leave this country. Every man who is opposed to the Government and its restroration to the Federal Union is with that party. The so called Democratic party of this county is mostly composed of rebel scouts, who are organized in bands trying to make the rebelion honorable and going at night destroying private property, by throwing down houses, and threatening lives, diging graves, and leaving [?] knives with letters of threats for Union Soldiers, and original Union men to leave, and wherever they have the power, they are organizing to cut all buisiness employment from those who will not join them in their destructive crusade. If this is not stoped, there will rise up bands of the same character on the other side and we will have bad times in this country. I write, this to you, because you acted so nolbly, when the enemies of this Government was trying to destroy it. I kept one of your speeches during the war, but had to keep it consealed. It was sought after, by some of these rufins, who are diging graves &c. They said then that your speeches ought to be destoyed and your tounge cut out &c. This is no exageration. I have not been interupted, nor have I any malice at any party. I am satisfied with the restroration of our government.

Now let us have law and order and make the law a terror to evel doers, and may the Lord bless you.

T. J. Rollins   Marshall Madison Co N.C

ALS, DLC-JP.
1. Rollins (c1817–f1870) was listed in 1860 as a preacher but in 1870 as a hotel keeper in Marshall. 1860 Census, N.C., Madison, 143; (1870), Twp. No. 1, Marshall, 36.

From W.E.P. Smith[1]

41 Wall St. New York   Nov 5 /68.

Sir,

Hon. Chauncey Shaffer[2] of this City has called upon me in reference to a cotton case involving upwards of a million dollars brought in the U.S. Court for this District.

Knowing all the facts and circumstances connected with said case, I am free to say that had the advice, counsel and suggestions of Mr Shaffer been carried out in said action, I feel confident that the Government would long since have realized said amount of money.

All the papers in said case were prepared in Mr Shaffers office and were the lamented Judge Betts[3] now living, he would bear testimony to the persistency and pertinacity with which Mr Shaffer urged the interests of the country in said case, and the laxness and negligence, (to designate it by no harsher term), of the U.S. District Atty[4] for this District which neutralized Mr Shaffers efforts.

W.E.P. Smith

ALS, DLC-JP.

1. Smith (*fl*1875) was a lawyer in New York City. New York City directories (1868–75).

2. Shaffer (*c*1818–*fl*1894) was a New York City attorney. Ibid. (1868–94); 1860 Census, N.Y., New York, New York, 17th Ward, 9th Dist., 84; Shaffer to Daniel Lamont, Sept. 17, 1888, Cleveland Papers, LC.

3. Samuel R. Betts (1786–1868) died just two days before Smith's letter. Many years earlier he had served one term in Congress. In 1826 he became a federal district judge, a position he held until 1867. *DAB*.

4. Samuel G. Courtney.

From Edgar Cowan

Greensburgh Penna   6 November 1868.

Dear Sir:

I take great pleasure in recommending J Harvey Jones[1] for the place of Government Director of the Pacific Rail Road Co. He has all that large experience in and about the management of Rail ways— and as the head of a principal manufactory of Hard ware in Pittsburgh can do to qualify any one for an intelligent performance of the duties of the above position. I can also say that his character for industry and integrity is without reproach, and that I sincerely desire his appointment.[2] The most prominent of your friends in Pittsburgh join me in this as you will see by the accompanying Letters.[3]

Edgar Cowan

ALS, DNA-RG48, Appts. Div., Misc. Lets. Recd.

1. Jones (*fl*1875), who also seems to have spelled his name Hervey, was involved in various

Pittsburgh hardware firms. Appointed a U.S. commissioner to the 1867 exposition in Paris, Jones resigned because of a family illness. Pittsburgh directories (1856–76); Pittsburgh Citizens to Johnson, Sept. 18, 1866, Lets. of Appl. and Recomm., 1861–69 (M650, Roll 25), J. Hervey Jones, RG59, NA; Jones to Johnson, Mar. 7, 1867, Appts., Lets. of Resignation and Declination, RG59, NA.

2. Jones was not appointed one of the government directors of the Union Pacific Railroad. Ames, *Pioneering the Union Pacific*, 240.

3. There were seven additional letters of recommendation from men and firms in Pittsburgh. Appts. Div., Misc. Lets. Recd., RG48, NA.

From Robert A. Hill

                                        Jackson Miss   Nov 6th 1868

Honorable Sir

Having for about two years been intimately associated with General A. C. Gillem now in command of this District, both socially and officially; indeed from our official relations few men have had a better opportunity to know his official course, in his different official positions, than myself. I take pleasure in testifying to his integrity and ability, as an Army Officer, and as the quasi civil Govenor, Legislator, and Judge of the State. His administration has been marked with soundness of judgement, integrity and firmness of purpose, doing as far as possible equal and impartial justice to all. Whilst a few extreme men of both parties have occasionally complained that he has not adopted their views, and subserved their purposes, his course stands approved by the sober minded and right thinking of all parties. I regard him in every way competent, and worthy for any position in the Army of the United States to which he may be appointed.[1]

                                        Robert A Hill
                                        U S Dist Judge for Mississippi

ALS, DLC-JP.

1. Gillem was being mentioned for the brigadier generalship vacated by Joseph Hooker in October. See Horatio Seymour to Johnson, Sept. 24, 1868, and Alvan C. Gillem to Johnson, Sept. 30, 1868.

From K. L. Hodges

                                        New York   Nov 6th /68

Dear Sir

I cut the enclosed from the N.Y. Herald of tuesday nov the 3rd.[1]

The man mentioned as having had an interview with you of five hours lenght—i.e Charles C. Yeaton, left N.Y. for Washington, if I rightly remember, sometime last spring or late in the winter. I knew him here, having boarded in the same house with himself & family for some months. He certainly is a very specious Gentleman. And has managed to decieve more astute persons than my self but I scarcely can believe that he has had the effrontery, considering the man he is—and how well he is known—to try to gain your confidence. If however there should be any truth in the enclosed paragraph, and he has made his way to your presence, Here in N.Y. where Mr Yeaton has spent his years, he is reckoned by those who know him well, one of the *Greatest* liars in the world, and one of the most unprincipled men, to be found.

At three places here, where I have known him to board—viz—Mr Carlocks, at "pleasant vally", Mrs Woods, 47 West 29th St. and Mrs Storms, 126 East 12th Street, He had his baggage detained for his bills. His goods and effects have been siezed, and sold by the Sheriff,[2] and his Wife's clothes were recently, and I think are still for sale at Madam Lavals on Broadway between 9th and 8th Sts. This last debt incured to a poor man whome he persuaded to trust him, Just before he left for Washington and who lent him $250. taking in pledge the dresses now for sale.

He has doubtless made some boast of his Connection with the "Alden Type Setting Machine."[3] Three months ago, I saw the decison in the public papers here that his whole Connection with that machine was a pretense and a fraud. Mr A. V. Stout[4] president of the Shoe & Leather Bank, Cor of Chambers St 7 Broad Way, was one of that Company, and I think is still. One of the parties I named above as having boarded Mr Yeaton—Mr Carlock—told me that Mr Stout was a friend of his—And he Stout hearing that Yeaton was going to his house to board, wrote to Caution him not to trust him, as he was a man of very bad character, and worthy of neither credence nor trust.

These are only portions of what Can be brought against Mr Yeaton here. Of Course he is vulnerable to attack and if he is one the parties engaged in discovering Rev frauds, he Can be soon assailed, and the whole thing brought into discredit, and redicule.

He went to Mr Courtneys Dist atty[5]—room at Washington, during that Gentlemans recent visit to that City—and told him—C— that I Said I knew of dishonest practices on the part of Mr Courtney & Mr Thurlow Weed, And that I could *make* either of them do anything I wished. Mr Courtney very kindly told me of it. Of course it was a falsehood. I neither know, or said I knew any thing of the kind. Mr Courtney has reckoned up Mr Yeaton, and they are ready here for anything, *he* is connected with.

I have been prevented from finishing this till now, Nov 8th. I enclose another paragraph Cut from to days "herald"[6] Also—one from yesterdays "Times"[7] which I think points to Mr Yeaton. Some months ago, I invited Mr Yeaton to leave my room here and not to again enter it—for what I deemed a good and Sufficient Cause—hence his hostility to myself.

It is not the knowledge of that hostility however that prompts me now to write as I am doing. For here, where Mr Yeaton is know, and his record can be found, hostility or kindness from him would be eaqually disregarded, but seeing paragraphs of the nature of the enclosed, And fearing that Contact with that person, may bring Good Men into rediculc, And that his participation in it, may bring scorn and defeat to a Just Cause, I write this in all Sincerity and good faith.

Proofs of much more than I write Can be found here against Mr Yeaton and those whose interest it is to do so Can eisily satisfy themselves.

Apolegizing for so great a trespas on your time, I beg you to believe I would not do so, but from the best motives.

K. L. Hodges

ALS, DLC-JP.

1. Not found enclosed, the article claimed that Charles C. Yeaton took part in a meeting with William Evarts, William Fullerton, and President Johnson. The topic probably concerned the New York whiskey frauds, as Yeaton was apparently assisting government lawyers in locating witnesses. *New York Herald*, Nov. 3, 1868; *New York Tribune*, Nov. 14, 1868; *New York Times*, Nov. 15, 1868.

2. James O'Brien (*c*1835–1907) had been elected sheriff in 1867. Earlier he had served in the state legislature. He was defeated in his bid for mayor of New York City. O'Brien became an arch foe of Boss Tweed and Tammany Hall. *New York Times*, Mar. 6, 1907.

3. A discussion of this, and a much more favorable view of Yeaton, can be found in K. L. Hodges to Johnson, Nov. 23, 1867, *Johnson Papers*, 13: 254–55.

4. At first a teacher and school administrator, Andrew V. Stout (1812–1883) eventually moved into the New York City business community with interests in banking, insurance, a gas-light company, and ferry operations. He was president of the Shoe & Leather Bank from 1855 until early 1883. *New York Times*, Sept. 6, 1883.

5. Samuel G. Courtney.

6. Although not found enclosed, the article mentioned that both Fullerton and Yeaton had visited Washington on November 7, and again met with Evarts and Johnson. The paper did not speculate as to the details of their meeting. *New York Herald*, Nov. 8, 1868.

7. The *Times* article, also not found enclosed, claimed that "persons" working under Fullerton were operating a blackmail scheme in New York, and other "principal operators" might have committed financial misconduct. It is not known to whom the article refers. *New York Times*, Nov. 7, 1868.

From William S. Rosecrans
personal

New York   Nov. 6. 1868

You seemed so much interested in the few remarks I made in your office about our Southwestern and Southern overland Rail road routes that I venture to inclose you two printed papers.[1] One, of a letter designed to impress on those who are promoting these lines the necessity of agreeing among themselves to select a line of policy in their application based on reason and justice and appealing by facts, figures and arguments properly displayed, to an elightened public opinion to sustain the government in giving the lines which deserve it subsidies instead of appealing to intrigue corruption to ensure sucess, where the public interests at stake would be amply sufficient.

The 2nd paper contains a few condensed reasons for the construction of our Southern overland South of the Gila.

If the policy of these papers or something substantially the same be adopted it would in 20 years transform the face of things south and lock the Pacific and Atlantic Coasts together, while it will draw all the trade of the table lands towards us and send our products to them beyond the reach of foreign rivalry.

This theme is fruitful of thought to the comprehensive mind of an american statesman who fathoms the full meaning of our motto of "*Many in one*" and sees that next to the preservation of the *unity* of the *nation* is that of the *autonomy of the* states. That as without the former we must have *anarchy* so without the latter we must have despotism. But with both liberty and law, self Government and indefinite expansion of political states with unity for "common defense" and "General welfare." You I think greatly appreciate these truths and look with hope and working power to the great destiny that awaits our system and people, and will duly consider the part that Rail Roads are to play in this future.

Heretofore settlement and civilizations have been based on the shores of navigable waters and diminished in grandeur and importance as they recede from these lines of transport and travel. In the future, Rail Roads will create more expeditious & effective lines of travel than even these lines formed by the hand of nature, and will civilize and harmonize peoples as remote from the great centres as was Abyssinia from the Capitals of the Grecian & Roman Empires.

Hence to the statesman they are more than matters of business convenience they are new powers of unity and civilization.

Begging pardon for the length of this letter . . .

W. S. Rosecrans

ALS, DLC-JP.
  1. Not found enclosed.

From Andrew J. Wilcox

Balto   Nov 6th 1868

Mr President

I infer from what I read in the newspapers that in the event of a change in the Presidential programme, that I am to be substituted for Gen Grant. This cannot be, for I am positively only *thirty-three* years and six months of age having been born on the 30th day of April A D 1835. And I am glad it is so for were I of the requisite age I would be compelled to preemptorily decline the position for the reason that I am sure that I am not sufficiently well qualified to fill the position with the dignity and credit that it should be filled. If I should be placed in the second position I can only say as I have heretofore said "that I would endeavor to conscientiously perform the duties of the position to the best of my ability and I hope to the credit of the nation but I would much rather prefer not to have any office at all.

If therefore there is to be any changes at all and there *certainly should be* I think Chief Justice Chase from his position experience and independence should be selected for the Presidency as he would have the support of all and be under obligations to none, neither being what strictly may be termed a Republican or a Democrat. If it was not for the fact that Gen Grant would be considered under obligations to the Republican party which would hold him to his promise not to have any policy of his own to contravene the policy of the party, at all events in the distribution of the offices under him, it would be well to let the election go as it has gone, but for the reasons just stated and for fear that we would get back again into the old ruts and the peace and prosperity that is now breaking over us be delayed and probably never realized and *for other grave reasons* I am of the opinion that the change should *positively* be made.

Andrew J. Wilcox

ALS, DLC-JP.

From Edwin F. Brown[1]

Vicksburg Miss   Nov 7th. 1868

Honored Sir—

In common with many other friends of Genl Alvan C. Gillem I desire to ask that you name him for the vacancy occasioned by the retiring of Genl Joseph Hooker. From an intimate, personal acquaintance of the facts it is not necessary to tell you that Genl Gillem proved himself a brave—patriotic & most exemplary soldier & an officer during the war of great service to the Government. On this point you will require no testimony as it is already a matter of History & a well established fact. In addition to his Military record—I desire to assure you that Genl Gillem, has shown superior tact & skill as a statesman while acting in the capacity of Commander of the "fourth Military District." As "Military Commander" he has established a high reputation for candor—truthfullness—efficiency—impartiality—and elevated statesmanship. In proof I desire to point you to the quiet condition of affairs in the state of Mississippi as compared with other reconstructed & unreconstructed States. I desire also to point you to the July Elections in this State—when political excitement was at *boiling heat*—& can assure you that our escape from riot & bloodshed is mainly attributable to the quiet—dignified & impartial manner of conducting the Election. It will be borne in mind that all the Orders for Registering & holding the Elections were issued by Genl Gillem—& although another held his position as Military Commander for a few days—yet his influence was alone the controlling & quieting influence during the Election.

In the exercise of his power—Genl Gillem has ever dealt manfully justly & impartially with all races, colors & conditions of men— doing his duty & his whole duty to all. Should your Excellency find it consistent to nominate him you will confer the honor upon a worthy & efficient officer and greatly gratify his numerous friends.

E. F. Brown

Late Col 28th Regt N.Y. V & Ex Mayor of Vicksburg

ALS, DLC-JP.

1. Brown (1823–1903) was a New York native who, after his Civil War duties, became governor of the National Home for Disabled Volunteer Soldiers at Dayton, Ohio. Following that he served as inspector general of all these homes (1880–1902). *New York Times*, Jan. 11, 1903; *New York Tribune*, Jan. 11, 1903.

From William L. Sharkey

Jackson Miss   Novr. 7th 1868

Mr President

It is understood that there is a vacant Brigadier Generalship in the United States Army, and it is hoped by the people of this State generally, that it may accord with your Excellency's views to appoint General Alvin C Gillem, now in Command at Vicksburg, to fill that vacancy. General Gillem has discharged the various and difficult duties which have devolved on him in his present position, with great satisfaction to the people of this State, and has shown himself to be not only a competent officer, but a high toned gentleman, and I sincerely hope he may be appointed to fill the vacancy.[1]

W. L. Sharkey

ALS, DLC-JP.

1. There was an obvious letter-writing campaign on behalf of Gillem, for there are several letters, all dated November 7 and all from Jackson, Mississippi. These individual letters, found in the Johnson Papers, LC, are from such prominent persons as William Yerger, Robert Leachman, E. G. Peyton, Thomas Shackelford, and E. Jefford.

From Allen G. Thurman

Columbus, Ohio, November 7. 1868.

Sir,

I am told that the retiring of Gen Hooker creates a vacancy in the office of Brigadier Genl. in the army, & that the friends of Brevet Maj. Gen. Crook,[1] now commanding the Department of the Columbia, have recommended, or will recommend his appointment to fill the vacancy. If this be so, I beg leave to join in the recommendation. You are aware what an admirable officer, Gen Crook proved himself to be in the war; and I am assured that his administration of the Department of the Columbia has been marked by great ability and given much satisfaction to the inhabitants. Gen Crook is a native of Ohio & has many friends in this state who would be highly gratified at his promotion. I beg leave to add that I am personally acquainted with him, and think him one of the best officers I know. I feel much interest in his welfare, and would be greatly pleased to see him promoted.

A. G. Thurman.

ALS, DLC-JP.
    1. George Crook.

From Edmund Laubie

Ludlow Street Jail, New York, Nov. 8 /68

Sir:—

In the matter of Revenue frauds I ask for the following a due consideration. I am detained here, by S. G. Courtney, U.S. Dist Atty, as a witness for the government. During the summer I wrote to Secretary McCulloch and yourself [1] concerning Revenue frauds in this city—since then I have come in possession of most astounding facts. I have at my disposal documentary evidence implicating leading Government officials in tobacco and whisky frauds in this City— Brooklyn—Philadelphia and Pittsburgh—evidence incontestible— and also nearly all the leading tobacco manufacturers in the cities above named. Testimony that cannot be got over or whitewashed. I would have communicated to you, sir—ere this, but seeing how Binckley was used and overslaughed here—and from what Fitch[2] told me while he was in this prison, I confess I was afraid. If it is your determination to *really* prosecute the men engaged in these frauds, irrespective of persons, I can produce the evidence (written) to develope a system of frauds on the part of government officers and others that will astonish you and the country. In November of last year I voluntarily gave information to the Hon. B. F. Tracy, U. S. Dist Atty. in Brooklyn who at once saw how valuable it was, and got me appointed in the Secret Service Division, and promised me immunity from the government for whatever I had done. I know that in my reports to the Treasury Dept.[3] I furnished much valuable information, and effectually broke up the bogus bonding in this city; saving to the government many millions, and *here I am in prison*, detained as a witness, in cases which never will be prosecuted, for not one of the parties implicated have yet been arrested, although I was put in here on Sept. 22d—and I know that at least some of the men are to be seen daily walking about the city. Mine, appears to be the fate of men who do give valuable information to the government. If the Revenue frauds are placed in the hands of Fullerton or some other honest lawyer, who will not be obstructed and frustrated in his action by the interference of government officials, I and my friend are the very men to aid him in bringing the guilty parties to condign punishment. If it is merely another Binckley fizzle—we are not wanted. If the government really wishes such testimony we cannot be got over—we can furnish it for New York and Brooklyn—Philadelphia and Pittsburgh. As a matter of course, we will not work for the government for nothing—we would expect to have positions given us with sufficient means to get along with, and when it was seen, how valuable and incontestible our evidence would prove to be we should certainly expect some recourse, and one thing we would look for, and that is that the government should protect us in good faith, and not leave us at the mercy of District Atty's, after we had been made use of. If you, sir, will send some one whom you trust these matters to, with full powers to act with us, I assure you, sir—that we can give him more information than he would scarcely credit.

In conclusion, sir I desire to say a word in my personal behalf. Mr. Tracy, of Brooklyn, promised me immunity for all my acts—and here I am. Mr. Tracy is the *only* truly honest man holding office under government, here. The whiskey and tobacco rings have never been able to buy him. I am 50 years old—am suffering grievously from consumption—heart disease—chronic diarrhaea and asthma—and have suffered from these for 8 years. I cannot eat the prison fare, and have no means to get in other food—and the consequence is I am dying for want of proper nourishment suitable for a man in my condition—can you not have something done to ameliorate my sufferings. However, I suppose, a certain person thinks it a good way to get rid of a troublesome witness. I am only kept here because of the letters that I wrote in confidence to the President and Secy. McCulloch having been shown to Mr Courtney. If Judge Fullerton is acting in concert with Mr. Courtney I want to have nothing to do with him, as it will only end in smoke. I write this in confidence, trusting in the honor of the President not to expose me to the enmity of him who has already put me in here.[4]

Edmund Laubie

ALS, DLC-JP.

1. No letter to McCulloch has been found. Laubie may have meant for his earlier letter to Johnson to include McCulloch as well. See Laubie to Johnson, Aug. 26, 1868, *Johnson Papers*, 14: 543–45.

2. George A. Fitch, who had been assisting in the whiskey fraud investigations. See Fitch to Johnson, Sept. 12, 1868, and John M. Binckley to Johnson, Oct. 7, 1868.

3. Not found.

4. Nothing further is known about Laubie's situation.

From Edward H. East

Nashville   November 9/68

Dear Sir:

I have been desirous of coming to Washington, for some time, but have found it impossible—to do so, owing more particularly to confusion of the Terms of our courts, and general bad health this summer.[1]

The Government of the United States holds the bond of the Nashville & Chattanooga Rail road Co. for about Fifteen hundred thousand dollars, held in the department of war. I am the Atty of that road, and know that the bond can never be paid. Between the debt due the state, and this debt, the road can never hope to see a solvent day. Is there any way to have this bond reduced, if so, who is empowered to act in the matter? Has the War Department, any power to make a reduction upon an equitable showing on the merits of the case? Is there any relief outside of Congress?[2]

I hear from Gillem[3] occasionally. I think he would like to have a Commission as Brigadier vice Hooker, retired. I would be very glad to see you, and hear your views of our future.

Edward H. East

ALS, DLC-JP.

1. See East to Johnson, Nov. 18, 1868.

2. See East to Johnson, Dec. 2, 1868, Johnson Papers, LC; Edmund W. Cole to Johnson, Dec. 19, 1868.

3. Alvan C. Gillem.

From Henry T. Helmbold [1]

N.Y.   Nov. 9th 1868

I presume ere this you have recd. letter from Mr Simeon Leland[2] Metropolitan Hotel also that of Father,[3] on the back of which I endeavoured to explain the whole matter. If I was undignified in my remarks please excuse For I was so much excited. I am still anxious to have the lad[4] released and I know he would not do a wrong if he was not half crazy to see his Mother.

My letter was written on back of Fathers and Mr Lelands contained that of Cousin now confined in Fort Macon North Carolina.

Pardon my presumption in addressing you.

H. T. Helmbold

P.S. Will you do me the kindness if you think him unworthy by returning his letter to Mr Simeon Leland Metropolitan Hotel N.Y. I am so anxious about the matter I must really try some other way if you are too much occupied.[5]

LS, DLC-JP.

1. Helmbold (c1832–fl1877) was a wealthy and prominent Philadelphia and New York druggist and patent medicine entrepreneur. He made a very generous donation to the Democratic presidential campaign in 1868 and later threw an elaborate post-election party at his drug and chemical warehouse in New York City. 1860 Census, Pa., Philadelphia, Philadelphia, 10th Ward, E. Dist., 243; Philadelphia directories (1868–74); New York City directories (1868–71); *Washington Evening Star*, Nov. 13, 1868; First Search-World Cat.

2. Leland (1812–1872) owned the Metropolitan Hotel and was a renowned hotel owner and keeper, as were his brothers. No letter from Leland has been located. *New York Times*, Aug. 6, 1872.

3. Not identified. No letter has been found.

4. Franklin Helmbold, a private in Company L, 5th U.S. Cav., since January 1867, was anything but a model soldier. He was tried by courts-martial no less than five times, and escaped from the guard house twice. His second escape resulted in the charge of desertion, and in April 1868 he was drummed out of service and sentenced to three years' hard labor. Headquarters 2nd Military Dist., Gen. Court-Martial Orders No. 60, Apr. 6, 1868, RG94, NA.

5. By Johnson's order, the remaining portion of Private Helmbold's sentence was remitted November 13, 1868, and he was actually released five days later. Headquarters of the Army, Special Orders No. 272, Nov. 13, 1868, RG94, NA; Returns of Military Posts, Fort Macon, N.C., Nov. 1868, RG94, NA.

From Phineas T. Scruggs[1]

Memphis   Nov 9th /68

Dr Sir

As I presume you have no knowledge of me a short apology is proper for troubling you with this letter. I have left with me by an estimable Lady friend who has been reduced to want by our late unfortunate war 36 pages of original manuscript of Genl Washington on ordinary size fool cap containing entries & directions for the government of his "River Union & Muddy Hole Farms." The manuscript is in good state of preservation but bears all the marks of age such as you would expect to see in paper of that age. It bears date 1800 Satisfactory proof can be given of its genuineness. I'm sure one inspection of the paper will convince any one of that fact. The Lady owner is actually in want of the ordinary means of living. Would the Gov take it for the Public Museum? If you can do any thing for her you would do her a great favor. For my self I refer you to Dr Leftwich Hon E Cooper Hon A O P Nicholson. In fact to any of our prominent men in the Middle or west end of the State. The document is in my possession & can be examined by any one whom you designate. Permit me to say in the close of this letter that although beaten in the late contest our people are still hopeful & trust that time & the good sense of the great Anglo American race will yet set things straight.

P T Scruggs

No 53 Union St   Memphis

ALS, DLC-JP.

1. Scruggs (c1806–1878) was a Methodist minister, lawyer, and judge during his career—in Mississippi and then in Memphis. J. M. Keating and O. F. Vedder, *History of the City of Memphis and Shelby County, Tennessee* (2 vols., Syracuse, 1888), 2: 70; J. M. Keating, *The Yellow Fever Epidemic of 1878 in Memphis, Tennessee* (Memphis, 1879), 233; 1870 Census, Tenn., Shelby, 16th Dist., 11.

From Mary P. Atkinson[1]

Brentwood [Tenn.]   Nov 10, [1868]

My Friend

I feel I can address you as such, for you were a kind friend to me during your stay in Nashville. I have been persuaded by some of my male Friends to drop you a few lines that it could do no harm if you could do me no good. I cant believe that the Government of these United States would be willing to take all I had and leave me distitute and make me no compensation. But few of my Friends know how very very poor I am. My first claim I swore to before Mr. Driver.[2] It was an expensive buisness to me and after all I was told he was not authorized by the Government and I could get nothing. The last battle at Nashville the Federals on their retreat from Franklin took all I had Corn Fodder Hay Hogs everything on the place excep my Pork Hogs and Hoods[3] Soldiers shot them in the [pen?] and I had no one to help me and there they stayed until I could hire a Negro man to take them off for the crows to live on. I have sworn to that

claim twice, costing me a Dollar every time and yet I can get nothing. Stokes's[4] cavalry the day of the Battle with Forest[5] took both my
Cows and the only Horse my Brother had. Colonel McCook[6] and
Captain Walker[7] took fifty Dollars worth of Hay at one time. General Mitchel[8] promised my Brother Allen A Hall that it should be
paid. General Miller[9] when in the chair told me both the officers
were at the St Cloud to go there and make them give me a receipt.
They would not see me but sent their Lieutenent and he had the gall
to say to me Madam a small Cavalry like that could not use that
quanty of Hay. I told him Sir you did not use it. What your Horses
did not eat you spread on the hill side to sleep on and the next morning you gave the Hay to a Nieghbour and he went with his wagon
and took it home, And when I sent to you for a recept you wrote one
and instead of giving it to the Negra man gave it to one of their own
men to take to the quarter Master. Now because I cant swear that all
they took from me was for the use of the army and not stolen by the
Soldiers I can get nothing. I can scarcely keep dry when it rains.
Sometimes in the night I am compelled to change my clothes and
not a dime to cover my House. Just one week before I was striped
the first time the carpenter had been here and taken the measure of
the house and I was to send the next week for what he needed, But
the army took every thing left nothing on the place except my family. Everything that I had to sell to enable me to cover my house was
taken, and now there are holes in the top of my house as big as my
head. I have just written to Mr. L. B. Fogg[10] to ask him and judge
Campbell[11] to apply to the Court in Kentucky to see if any of the
Childrens property could cover it as it belongs to them at my death.
I do not know what I shall do this winter. The dampness around me
must kill me. I am old and very infirm. Please forgive me for troubling you but you have often been remembered at the throne of Grace
by me. May God forever Bless you and yours.

Mary P. Atkinson

ALS, DNA-RG107, Lets. Recd., Executive (M494, Roll 104).

1. Atkinson (c1805–fl1870) was listed in Nashville in 1870 as presiding over a household
with three young children. 1870 Census, Tenn., 8th Dist., Nashville, 19.

2. William Driver.

3. John Bell Hood.

4. William B. Stokes.

5. Nathan Bedford Forrest.

6. Possibly Edward M. McCook.

7. Not identified.

8. John G. Mitchell (1838–1894), a native of Ohio who saw a variety of duty during the war, particularly with the 113th Ohio regiment. He went with General Thomas back to Tennessee and participated in the Battle of Nashville. He was appointed brigadier general of volunteers in 1865 but resigned shortly thereafter and went to Columbus to practice law. Warner, *Blue.*

9. John F. Miller.

10. Francis B. Fogg.

11. Probably David Campbell (1802–1889) who practiced law in both Williamson County and Nashville for a long period of time. He was in the state legislature for one term in the 1850s. Later Campbell served as a chancellor and as a special judge for several different courts. *BDTA,* 1: 115.

From Edward I. Golladay

Lebanon Tennessee   Nov. 10th 1868

President Andrew Johnson:

I do not know that you will remember my name or that these lines will reach and command your Eye, in the multiplicity of matters, which demand your time and attention. But I desire to send you greeting and my heart-felt thanks as an humble citizen of this great Republic, for the glorious and magnificent State papers you have from time to time given to the Country and for the lofty and patriotic efforts you have put forth in attempting a happy restoration of civil liberty, and the broken bonds of Union. Future ages will call you great and bless you for your labors. Radicalism had triumphed. A terrible mistake was made by the Democracy, in the ticket they put before the country. Andrew Johnson for Prest., W. S. Hancock for Vice Prest—the candidates of Freedom of the country, should have been placed before us. Before nominations were made anywhere, in an humble way, in a couple of public speeches in Wilson County such was my ticket. It found a deep lodgement in the hearts of this people. It was a *live* ticket. It should have carried in the New York convention. But other views prevailed. Perhaps Grant may not be as bad as Radical leaders would have him. We shall know by waiting.

But to, the point of this communication. In March next you resign a Chair which future time will say was never better filled—never occupied by a greater statesman or a finer or firmer patriot. Such I feel, will be the accepted verdict, of the coming time, and such my estimate of you. You will come back to your home in Tennessee, & dwell amid your own people. Now in the prime of life and in the full and vigorous possession of all your faculties your years forbid, that one so able, faithful and competent should be lost to the service of his country. "The sere & yellow leaf" have not come to you. Could

you not come home and be our Govenor in the coming canvas? And
on a platform of your own making too. I think all patriots in the
State would risk you, and your work, your intellect, your patriotism,
and your integrity. Redeem your own beloved state from the hateful
and abominable oligarchy which like mildew and rust is cankering
her soul. Lift up a downtrodden and oppressed people, set them once
more to bask in the sunlight of civil and religious freedom, & make
them again happy and content. And when you have redeemed the
State, ask and receive at her hands, a seat in the United States Senate, a field of dignity and usefulness scarcely inferior to your present
exalted station, where a vast nation may have the benefit, of your
mature and superior statesmanship and genuine patriotism. Would
not such a course be a fitting one to crown a life of public services?

Forgive this intrusive suggestion, & be assured it is made with the
best intention and out of the warmest admiration and respect for
you and by one entirely willing to commit his own and the destiny of
his country to your keeping.

I ask nothing for myself in this communication, & only desire the
good of all. Am content to pursue the duties and labors of my profession the law, & rest satisfied with its reward.

E. I. Golladay

ALS, DLC-JP.

From Columbus B. Guthrie and Henry G. Marquand [1]

Office Cairo & Fulton R.Rd. Co.
71 Broadway, New York   Nov. 10th, 1868

Sir:

Enclosed please find a map of the contemplated International Pacific Railroad and papers connected therewith.[2]

On behalf of the company I represent, I take the liberty of calling
your attention to this important work, that you may give it such
prominence in your forthcoming annual message to Congress as in
your judgement may be proper.[3]

You will perceive that this road has its initial point at Cairo, Illinois, with a northern Railroad connection extending in a direct line
to Indianapolis, the central radiating point for all the great eastern
& western roads. That south-wardly it passes through south-west-
ern Missouri, through the centre of Arkansas, and through the cen-

tre of the populous part of Texas to the Rio Grande. At the Rio
Grande, it is intended to connect with two Roads, one running to
the city of Mexico and the other to San Blas on the Pacific Coast. By
this road New York is brought one thousand miles nearer the Pacific
ocean than by the Union and Central Pacific Roads. Considering
this road as the great trunk line, the present existing Southern Roads
can make easy connection with it, first, at Little Rock by the Memphis & Little Rock Road, second, near Marshall, Texas, by the con-
tinuation of the Vicksburg & Shreveport road and third, by the
Berwick's Bay road from New Orleans. These would give to every
portion of the South an opportunity to participate in the direct trade
with Mexico and the Pacific coast.

Arkansas and Missouri have given the sanction of their legislation
to this subject and a bill looking to the same object has passed to a
third reading in the convention of Texas by a strong vote, and will no
doubt become law upon the reassembling of that body. The road
through Missouri and Arkansas has a land grant from Congress of
ten sections per mile and the bill in Texas contemplates a land grant
from that State, but in the present prostration of values in the Southern States, this aid is not sufficient to inspire capitalists with confidence necessary to secure the means for building this great international highway and a bill (senate No. 603) is pending in Congress[4]
to further aid the enterprise by granting to it a loan of the National
credit after the manner and upon the same security of that extended
to the Union and Central Pacific Roads. The amount of the grant
solicited, however is much less than that accorded to these corporations. We ask for only ten thousand Dollars a mile from Cairo to
Little Rock and sixteen thousand Dollars a mile from Little Rock to
the Rio Grande, the total loan not exceeding Fourteen millions of
Dollars.

The advantages of this route to the Pacific over all others, are obvious. It is 1000 miles shorter. It has no impediments to encounter
from frosts or snow, but is equally traversable at all seasons. It has no
difficult grades to over come, no mountains to tunnell and can thus
carry its passengers and freight with greater speed, greater safety,
less wear and tear and greater economy. Instead of crossing the continent upon a single parallell of latitude (counting the connecting
road between Indinapolis and Toledo) it forms a direct line from
Toledo to San Blas cutting, north and south, twenty parallells of
latitude, bringing the northern lakes in conjunction with the Pacific
tropics. It passes entirely through a country already settled and pro-

ductive, a country that is not spell bound by the chains of winter during six months of the year, but where nature labors with bounteous prodigality and the earth teems with her productions the whole twelve months through.

The effect of this road upon the Republic of Mexico will be equally beneficial. It will secure to the two governments the most intimate and friendly relations and will build up between the people of the two countries a large and remunerative trade. These will go far to strengthen the bonds of peace while they engender mutual national growth, while at any time, should war between the two nations unhappily arise, the value of the road for military purposes would be incalculable.[5]

C. B. Guthrie

in behalf of the Cairo & Fulton Rail Road

H G Marquand

V prest St Louis & Iron Mt. R R Co

ALS (Guthrie), DLC-JP.

1. Guthrie (fl1870), a New York agent and contractor, resided in New Jersey. Marquand (1819–1902) amassed considerable wealth through real estate and banking and became a noted philanthropist, especially supporting the Metropolitan Museum of Art in New York. New York City directories (1868–70); *DAB*.

2. No map was found enclosed, but the papers may have included a letter from Green Clay Smith to an unknown party discussing the railroad. Smith to Unknown, Nov. 6, 1868, Johnson Papers, LC.

3. Johnson did not mention any railroad companies besides the Union and Central Pacific lines in their role as constructors of the transcontinental railroad. Fourth Annual Message, Dec. 9, 1868.

4. Introduced in July 1868, Senate Bill No. 603 (to aid the construction of the International Pacific Railroad) was referred to the Committee on the Pacific Railroad but was not discussed again during the session. It was one of seventeen railroad bills and resolutions which that committee asked to be relieved from considering, since so little time remained before the expiration of the final session of the Fortieth Congress. A similar bill, HR No. 847, had been introduced in the House of Representatives in March 1868, and sent to the Committee on Roads and Canals. Brought up again in February 1869, the bill was ordered to be printed but no further action was taken during the session. *Congressional Globe*, 40 Cong., 2 Sess., pp. 1631, 3818; 3 Sess, pp. 798, 1363.

5. Gordon Granger endorsed the letter with the remark that he thought "it by far the best route yet named connecting the Atlantic & Pacific Oceans." For more on this proposed rail line, see W. G. Ford to Johnson, Nov. 25, 1868.

From Lovell H. Rousseau

New Orleans, La., Nov 10th 1868.

My Dear Sir

Genrl Tompkins[1] my Quarter Master will hand you this, and will tell you of matters here. I have been too busy to write you, at length but will do so in a few days.[2]

Affairs are entirely quiet here and likely to remain so, at least until the Legislature again assembles. Whether there will be an outbreak then or not remains to be seen. I shall not be surprised either way. Please dont forget "old Buck" and the Brigadiership.[3]

Lovell H Rousseau   U.S.A.

LS, DLC-JP.

1. Charles H. Tompkins (1830–1915) became a quartermaster with the rank of captain and brevets through brigadier general during the Civil War. A recipient of the Congressional Medal of Honor for actions at Fairfax Court House in 1861, he served on the military commission which tried the Lincoln assassination conspirators. He retired from the quartermaster department with the rank of colonel in 1894. Powell, *Army List*, 632–33; Hunt and Brown, *Brigadier Generals*.

2. See Rousseau to Johnson, Nov. 20, 1868.

3. Probably Robert C. Buchanan. Although briefly a brigadier general during the Civil War (his commission was not confirmed by the Senate) and the recipient of the brevets of brigadier and major general, Buchanan was a colonel. He was not promoted to any higher rank. Powell, *Army List*, 218.

From John H. Gilmer

Washington. Willards Hotel
November 11th 1868

Sir.

You will pardon the seeming liberty I take in addressing you this communication, covering a copy of the New York Herald, which contains a correspondence between the secretary of the Treasury, the Commissioner of Internal revenue, myself and others.[1]

The correspondence is on public matters, and discloses facts, circumstances and transactions which in them selves, contain subject-matter worthy of your official consideration and administrative action. It will speak for itself. It needs no embellishment or commentary. The subject of investigation—the results arrived at—the legal and administrative action which they invoke, have not only challenged your attention, but have awakened your official solicitude.

You stand sir, before the American people the pure exempler of honesty, fidelity, and purity of personal character. What in your person, you have so consistently illustrated, the American people expect, and have a right to claim—in your fearless, but firm—bold, but prudent administration of their affairs. You have their confidence: allow no paliative measures on your part, to throw a veil over your historic fame—as it is made up—and handed down to your successor, and posterity, by your official acts.

That purity of character and sense of representative ability which have always attended your public life, warrant me in thus addressing you. Where the executive is pure, his motive high and his aims patriotic, no private citizen, however humble, need fear wicked combinations and concurring action in officials, who seek to delude—oppress—and betray their trusts. As the Chief Magistrate of the American people—and as such—the living embodiment of the constitution—the laws—and the majesty of the people—I approach you—seeking that relief for the tax payer—which you, and you alone can give.

The reign of law is ever superior to the demands of mere party or temporary expediency. As the law is supreme in its power and severe in its majesty—so are the claims of the people superior, in their absolute dependence on its administrative functions. The spirit, life and power of the law, rest in the executive will—which is, under the constitution, authorised to enforce them. Without the will to punish and the power to execute—the franchises of the people derived from and abiding in the constitution—must ever be the mere play things of party, or the creatures of organised cupidity. In your hands sir, rests the power, as in your will repose the elements of those safe guards, enacted by the fathers of the republic. Shall they sleep while the spirit of liberty, cries aloud for their active operation?

The right to tax and the power to enforce the collection of the revenue, is the most delicate and responsible function of the administrative department of the federal government. Congress imposes the taxes. The treasury department is entrusted with their collection. If, in that department, any where, or in any way, or at any time, there is ascertained misfeasance, malfeasance, or neglect of duties imposed by law—there is but one remedy—and the constitution has wisely placed that remedy sir, in your hands.

Then sir, with a full appreciation of your powers, duties and functions, I, with becoming deference, submit the accompanying correspondence. Consider it I pray you. The incidents of the late civil war—are gradually passing away, to be harmoniously blended in a glorious unity of sympathy, interest and destiny—in all the coming future. The only dark and portentous cloud which overhangs the dawning brightness of a grand and successful nationality, is the impoverishment of the people by an insupportable weight of cumulative taxation. The department, bureau or functionary who seeks to burden the tax payer beyond the ascertained measure of the law, is an oppressor of the people—the enemy of the government,—and a culprit, in the eye of the law.

With these views I submit the accompanying correspondence to your enlightened judgement and wise discernment. If there are guilty or delinquent parties—the law is present, and speaks through you. Let not its potency be suppressed or its voice stifled. Let it not be said, that these facts are from "a private citizen." Let it not be urged that the voice of complaint comes from a state—once powerful but now prostrate. Let it not be argued that Virginia and Virginians have no right to be heard on such an issue. The law should be permanent, uniform and universal. The past, with its sad lessons is, it is to be hoped, about to be illumined—by a more perfect and harmonious unity—in the future—undisturbed by the passions and prejudices of our recent difficulties. Allow me to assure you sir, for myself, and state and people, that our first wish is that, the close of your administration may be as brilliant in the light of historic truth, as the advent, duration and close of the incoming administration, may be pure, high toned, conservative and constitutional: and that both—in view of the grand developements awaiting the immediate future, may so cooperate, as to reassure the American people and states—that constitutional republics are not failures—in the hands of a pure and honest administration.

John H Gilmer

ALS, DLC-JP.

1. Not found enclosed. The correspondence, which covers more than a page in the *Herald*, disclosed Gilmer's efforts to expose revenue fraud and seize distilleries in Richmond, Virginia. Gilmer, a lawyer assisting the Treasury Department, claimed that Edward A. Rollins, possibly with the consent of McCulloch, used revenue supervisors and detectives to obstruct his investigations. Binckley, to whom Gilmer wrote for advice, had made similar accusations about treasury officials. *New York Herald*, Nov. 11, 1868; John M. Binckley to Johnson, Nov. 5, 1868. For a defense of Gilmer and Binckley, see *New York Herald*, Nov. 10, 1868, while a scathing critique of Gilmer appears in the *New York Times*, Nov. 16, 1868.

From Robert W. Latham

Washington, Nov. 11. 1868

My Dear Sir

You have doubtless read the enclosed article from the Herald[1] which came in last night, but will you do *yourself* the justice to read it again, and *act upon it*.

I also refer you to the article in the Tribune of yesterday upon the same subject.[2]

It is with the deepest regret that I see your reputation injured, by a seeming toleration and endorsement of the villiany of those officials around you.

R. W. Latham

ALS, DLC-JP.

1. The enclosed editorial called on President Johnson to suspend any government official, including any cabinet officer, who might be interfering with the revenue fraud investigations. *New York Herald*, Nov. 11, 1868.

2. The *Tribune* piece praised Johnson for appointing William Fullerton as special counsel to investigate the whiskey revenue frauds in New York City. *New York Tribune*, Nov. 10, 1868.

To William H. Seward

Washington, D.C.   Novr. 11th 1868.

My dear Sir:

Mr. John Savage finds it necessary to visit Europe for the benefit of his health. Sincerely desirous of aiding him, I have requested him to see you, and explain his wishes, in the hope that you will not find compliance inconsistent with the public interests. Will you please do all you can to assist him, as I feel much interest in his welfare?[1]

Andrew Johnson

LS, NRU.

1. In early January 1869 Johnson nominated Savage for the post of U.S. consul at Leeds, but the Senate tabled the nomination. *DAB*.

From Leroy Chandler[1]

Cooper County Mo.   Nov 12 1868

Respected Sir

Some 2 or 3 years ago the subject of giving to the soldiers of the war of 1812 a pension was before Congress for 2 sessions & was favourably recd. & at last a bill was reported but being late in the session was sufferd to die from neglect. There are a few of us only left. Bending under the infirmities of age poverty & disease a pension would now be recd. as a charity & help to ease us down the steeps of time to our near but final resting place. Would it be impertinent to ask you as the head of the nation & one who seems disposed to right to all to bring the subject in some way before the councils of nation. A word or two from you would bring it to the attention of all more than any *mere* motion from an individual member & being no party measure might receive attention at an early day *now* that no impeachment election or probably any other all absorbing question is in discussion. Congress has acted with much liberality to the soldiers & widows of the war of the rebellion & we are its *only forgotten friends*. We cannot possibly want it long and few very few left to be the recippents of the bounty asked.

Leroy Chandler
for himself & 3 others

ALS, DNA-RG48, Patents and Misc. Div., Lets. Recd.
 1. Possibly the Leroy Chandler (b. *c*1800) who was a farmer in Cooper County. 1850 Census, Mo., Cooper, 23rd Dist., Being, 153.

From Robert Lowery[1]

Fort Wayne Ind.   Nov 12" 1868

Those applying thus far for vacancy in post office here are intense radicals and your bitter enemies. Hope no appointment will be made until your friends are heard from.

R. Lowery

Tel, DLC-JP.
 1. Lowery (1824–1904) was an Indiana lawyer who served as circuit court judge from 1864 to 1875. He was in the U.S. House of Representatives for two terms (1883–87). *BDUSC.*

From Hugh McCulloch
Private

Treasury Department. Nov 12 1868

My Dear Sir

I have been at a loss to account for the Savage attacks that have been recently made upon me by the Republican Press. The enclosed memorandum[1] sent me by one who knows, explains it. If any one of your Cabinet desires to retain his position under Gen Grant you need no assurance from me, that *I am not the man*. With your administration my connection with public life ceases. I send you the memorandum in order that you may understand that I am assaulted not because I ought to be, but because I am supposed (without any means for the suppostion) to be in somebodys way.

H McCulloch

ALS, DLC-JP.

1. The memorandum indicated that some Republican leaders feared that McCulloch might try to remain in the cabinet under the new administration and that therefore Seward, and possibly others, would also attempt to stay in the cabinet. Thus, in order to head this off, attacks were being launched upon McCulloch.

From James W. Taylor

St Paul, November 12. 1868.

I beg permission to resume the topics of a conversation which occurred about a year ago.

You are on record before the country in favor of the restoration of the Southern whites to their personal and political rights. It is not understood that you are hostile to the extension of the same rights to the Southern negroes; but to the manner and want of discrimination with which that great change has been effected.

As I regard the late election, it is an expression by the people that it would be neither right or expedient to deprive 500,000 colored men in the South of the ballot—that the extension of suffrage in the South must in some way be accepted as a *fait accomplished*. Granted that this extension was without constitutional authority, yet the practical question remains. How shall we make the most and the best of what is irrevocable.

Allow me to suggest that the Southern States and a large body of the people of the North would now concur in the following Amendment to the Constitution:

To add to the enumeration of the powers of Congress this clause: "To prescribe an uniform rule of suffrage."

By its adoption a constitutional warrant would be supplied to what has been done in the South, but Congress, in turn, *would be forced to extend the same rule of suffrage to the great central states of Pennsylvania, Ohio, Indiana, Illinois, Kentucky and Missouri.*

As an experienced politician you can see at a glance the advantages of such a position.

A year ago, I ventured to submit the enclosed paragraphs[1] with the hope that their substance would be incorporated in your Message of 1867. I hope you will pardon me if I now request that you will consider the propriety of such an expression after a years experience.

James W. Taylor.

ALS, DLC-JP.
1. Not found enclosed.

From Joseph S. Fowler

Vicksburgh Nov. 13" 1868.

Respected Sir,

The present vacancy in the office of Brigadier General will be filled by you. Without presuming to dictate to you or to influence that nomination I may suggest what no doubt has occurred to your mind befor this letter may reach you that the name of Alvan C. Gillem is entitled to the highest consideration.

I may also suggest the following reasons the force of which are well known to you.

His entire competency for the place has been demonstrated both in the office and in the field during the period of active hostilities.

He has since the close of the rebellion executed one of the most delicate and difficult civil trusts ever confided to any military man in this country. He has shown the highest capacity in that department for his responsible position. He has shown matured wisdom and a rare sense of justice patriotism and subordination to law and civil authority.

He has so governed his district as to compel the approbation of every fair minded man in either party.

After a careful examination of the state I am compelled to admit that it is in a better condition as respects peace good order and regard for law than any southern state. I am confident that this condition of things is due in a great degree to the foresight and prudence of Gen. Gillem.

You are well aware of his good morals his industry and devotion to his profession. I do also think that as he is the only Southern man that will be prominent and as the South has no representative man in high position that he is entitled for this reason to your consideration.

I hope that these suggestions may meet your approbation.

Jos. S. Fowler

ALS, DLC-JP.

From Christopher G. Bechtler[1]

Morganton North Carolina   Burke Co   No 14 1868

Dear Sir

Mr. M. P. Lytle of Buncomb Co arrivig here at this place In pursuance of orders receved from you, by letter[2] to report to J. W. McAlrath to obtain the office of the Deputy Collector of Revenue, conferred on him by your Excelency and to receve instructions from J. W. McAlrath which you said you had informed him as to the nesesary arrangements. Mr. Lytle did as you commanded him to do, and reported to J. W. McAlrath. But he refused to give him any informatn and further said that he had never receved any letter or anything concerig any arrangments from President Johnson. Therefore Mr. Lyttle did not obtain possesion of the office or necessry arragents and in excuse J. W. McAlrath told Mr Lyttle that the letter was not from you But that it was a Bogus letter written by some one in Buncomb County to tease him or in common phrase devil him And only made light of him with such conversation.

This is the reason why I addressed you on the Subject and I thought it prudent to enclose you a copy of the letter purportg to be from you which I belive is genuine. Therefore I hope you will be so kind as to give the Subject your kind attention as Mr. Lyttle is a lame man and his father is entirely Blind and has lost his former property by the late unfortunate war and is unable to do any ordinary Labor. He is verry thankful more than words can express for your kind and generous gratitude in bestowing the office on him which will give him a mens of Support for him and his aged Father. Mr. Lyttle firmly beleves the letter to be genuine as his Father recollects the circumstances of your staying at his house all night as stated in your letter, and he further asks if you will be so kind as to send him instructions how to obtain the office and if any other official papers are necesay to obtain it and how to proceed to obtain the office of Deputy Collector.

I will State that Mr. McAlrath may have his idea of obtaing the office himself I only conjecture so and that may be the cause why he denied recevng any instructions from you, or to obtain the same, and may say Mr Lyttle is incapable of filling the office. It appears so from his conduct to Mr Lyttle, though it is only conjecture.

I will say that Mr. Lyttle is a man fully capable. With a good Education and a good Scribe to transact the Busyness of the office, and a man of good sound sense and good morals character, he is fully capable of attending to it in the highest Degree. Mr. Lyttle came to this place almost a Stranger and unwell and therfore unable to write himself and therfore I offered him my Services gratutoly. I write for him and receve your Reply to him as he lives a great Distance from a post office, and therefore will more be convenient for me to send him your reply by hand.

In conclusion he presents his and his Fathers most kind regards to your Excellency & family.

You will be so kind as to give him an Early reply to this letter, and by his request address your letter to me, which, I will forward to him immedeatly on reception.

Hoping that you will pardon me for troubling you so much . . .

C. G. Bechtler, M.D.

Morganton, Burke Co. N.C.

signed M. P. Lytle

ALS, DLC-JP.

1. Bechtler (c1841–fl1870) was a native North Carolinian. 1870 Census, N.C., Burke, Morganton Twp., 14.

2. See Johnson to Millington P. Lytle, Oct. 25, 1868.

From Chauncey F. Black[1]

York Pa.   Nov 14, 1868

Mr President;

It is of great importance to Messrs Patterson and Murguiondo[2] that the records of the Executive Department should contain all the papers that were ever filed in relation to their claim, as American Citizens, to the possession of the Guano Island Alta Vela. As Mr Seward's pretended "report"[3] to you omitted several very valuable documents necessary to a proper understanding of the case, and as the Secretary took advantage of that omission to misrepresent and pervert the history and character of the claim to suit his own purposes, the claimants are led to believe that those papers have been *destroyed* by some one interested, directly or indirectly, in defrauding them. I hope you will pardon me if I address you again for the purpose of repairing that injury to the extent of replacing one paper whose absence has cost us something.

On p. 13, Ex. Doc. No 38, 40th Congress, 2d Session, the Secretary in the course of his "report" says:

DIPLOMATIC CLAIM INEXPEDIENT.

The political condition of the Republic of St Domingo has not essentially improved. It is still feeble, destitute of resources, and a theatre of military revolution. A special envoy is now here soliciting financial and moral assistance.

"The Secretary of State *adheres to the opinion that even if the justice of the claim of Patterson and Murguiondo were clearly and conclusively established,* YET *it would be inexpedient to urge it by Diplomatic representation under existing circumstances and at the present time.*

THE CLAIMANTS ACQUIESCE IN THIS DECISION

It has already appeared that Patterson & Murguiondo now *distinctly disclaim any expectation or desire* that the Executive of the United States shall apply to the Republic of St Domingo for *indemnity or any other form of redress sounding in damages in their behalf.*"

Farther on the Secretary emphasises this assumption with the phrase: "*There is no misunderstanding the claimants on this point.*"

It is at least certain, Mr President, that *he* did not misunderstand them "on this point," nor, perhaps, on any other. Instead his mind was so entirely unclouded by any misapprehension that when he came to this part of his "report" he took care, among the other documents he suppressed, to include that one which would have made this wretched pretense too obviously false for even *him* to employ.

I find among the copies of papers relating to this claim a "Draft of Letter to the Secretary of State" dated March 27, 1861. This was written and filed at the time of date. But "to make assurance doubly sure," I have also a copy of a letter of Judge Black's[4] of April 3, 1866, covering an additional copy of the letter of 1861. Please find both herewith.

They were addressed and delivered to the Secretary of State. They should be in his office now. I do not pretend to say why he excluded them from his "report," which contained the most trivial notes of Root, or Webster or Clark.[5] Other letters of claimant's counsel, equally plain and explicit, are not found there. Mr Pattersons report, made at the Secretary's own request, is not found there. General Cagneau's[6] first notice of the "outrage" to the Department is not found there— nor Mr De Roucerays[7] letter, nor a certain mysterious letter of Webster's. Whether they have been committed to the flames, or to the keeping of the "Alta Vela Guano Co," I do not know. It is possible they may be pigeon-holed in the custody of "Smith" in the "Bureau of Claims." At all events they were not thought worthy of a place beside the curious, and not very pertinent, literature which adorns the Secretary's report.

Chauncey. F. Black.

ALS, DLC-JP.

1. Black (1839–1904) served as lieutenant governor of Pennsylvania (1883–86) and was long active in Democratic party politics. For some time he was an editorial writer for the *New York Sun*. Black was the son of Jeremiah S. Black. *New York Tribune*, Dec. 3, 1904; *New York Times*, Dec. 3, 1904.

2. Abraham D. Patterson and Prudencio de Murguiondo.

3. See *Senate Ex. Docs.*, 40 Cong., 2 Sess., No. 38 (Ser. 1316). Seward forwarded his report to Johnson on February 12, 1868; the President in turn sent it on to the Senate on March 6, 1868.

4. Jeremiah S. Black.

5. Henry G. Root, Thomas A.R. Webster, and Lemuel B. Clark. For these documents, see *Senate Ex. Docs.*, 40 Cong., 2 Sess., No. 38, pp. 13–15, 57–58 (Ser. 1316).

6. William L. Cazneau (1807–1876) was very active in the early days of the Texas Republic, holding several different posts, including congress and the new legislature. He fought in the Mexican War and was subsequently involved in extensive land speculation. He served as special agent to the Dominican Republic in the 1850s. Tyler et al., *New Handbook of Texas*.

7. Charles DeRonceray, a native of Maryland, was appointed consul at San Juan by President Buchanan in the late 1850s after having earlier served as a clerk in the Treasury Department. *U.S. Off. Reg.* (1859); Washington, D.C., directories (1858).

From Thomas Ewing, Jr.

Washington, D.C.   Novr. 14 1868.

My dear Sir:

Hampton B. Denman, now Supt. of Indian Affairs for Nebraska, wants to be appointed Surveyor General of New Mexico in which office there is a vacancy. Mr. Browning favors his application, and I am quite sure he can be confirmed through the influence of his personal friends in the Senate. He is a staunch Democrat—& was on the stump for Seymour in Nebraska. He has lived in New Mexico, though more recently in Kansas and is very popular there—and I am sure you could hardly satisfy the people of the Territory better than by his appointment. He is too a practical Surveyor, a man of ability and high personal character, and a warm admirer & friend of yourself.

Denman and I have important interests in New Mexico, (unconnected with the office of Surveyor General however) and he seeks this appointment in part to look after those interests & with the intention of becoming a permanent resident of the Territory—expecting to hold the place under Grant because of its being out of the currents of National politics.

I therefore ask you to appoint him if you can, & shall regard his appointment as a special favor.[1] I am just back from Kansas, & am unexpectedly called to St Louis tomorrow—& therefore can not call to pay my respects & present the request in person.

Thomas Ewing Jr.

ALS, DLC-JP.

1. Johnson did in fact nominate Denman for the post of surveyor general of New Mexico. The nomination was referred to committee but no further action was taken before the adjournment of the 40th Congress. *Senate Ex. Proceedings*, Vol. 16: 418, 425.

From John Tyler, Jr.

Washington, Novr. 14th 1868.

Mr. President:

Permit me to invite your attention to a movement which I started some days ago, and which I regard as of essential importance to the future happiness of the people and the prosperity and welfare of the Country. At the same time suffer me to say, that it is in my power to show, that in July & August last, I saved the peace of the nation by preventing a collision with Great Britain, while contributing not a little to stay civil commotions at the South,[1] thus saving you from numberless additional troubles to those you have suffered with so much astonishing forbearance & fortitude. I pray you bear in mind also, that besides being covered by the terms of General Lees surrender and oath of allegiance that about that time I took in Petersburg, I have been *twice* pardoned & redeemed from all of the past by your Proclamations of Amnesty.

Under these circumstances may I not, with propriety, invoke your attention to the enclosed Legal answer to the Report made to you by Mr. Secretary Browning in the matter of the Claim of Col: William Selden, late Marshall of the District of Columbia, for keeping prisoners.[2] You will find the Report in the envelope with the Answer. This Legal reply to the learned Secretary will be found, upon examination, I am sure, exhaustive of the Case; and I am equally sure that it will convince your Excellency that not only Secretary Browning, but all of his Predecessors concerned, in the office of the Interior, including Mr. Jacob Thompson, who made the first erroneous & mischievous decision in the Case, while differing among themselves as to the Law governing the Case, in each & every instance entirely mistook the Law, placed the Government in a false position, and did injustice to the Claimant. Shall wrong continue to breed wrong is the question? The Petition in the Case filed in your private office some months since, submits the matter to Your Excellency *by way of appeal to the* CHIEF MAGISTRATE, and from the Answer to the Report of Mr. Browning now Submitted, it will be clearly seen that, *the final appellate Jurisdiction over the Case is not with the Secretary as alleged, and therefore, that it may be legitimately reopened by Your Excellency & referred back to the accounting officers of the Government for readjustment & settlement according to the actual Law & facts governing the Case.*

I am satisfied Mr. President, that you know me well enough to believe that, however impecunious I may be, and whatever my personal interest might be, I would not approach you in this business, nor make a demand against the Government, in any matter, unless I was fully persuaded that Right, Law & Equity, sustained me. And sincerely trusting that your Children & Grand-Children, as members of a Presidential Family, may never be reduced to that extremity of want visited upon me & mine, and that they may always meet, from the Executive of the Nation, with that generous & courteous regard always accorded by my Father, while occupying your Seat, to all who had been associated with that high office, whether political friends, or political Enemies, through a proper & becoming gratitude for Services rendered the Country, and through a true respect for the dignity of the position . . .

John Tyler, Jr.

ALS, DNA-RG48, Patents and Misc. Div., Lets. Recd.

1. It is unknown to what Tyler refers here.

2. Neither Browning's report nor Tyler's answer has been found. Selden, and later his heirs, sought reimbursement of expenses incurred by Selden during the war for use of his property and for accommodating prisoners (1858–61). Eventually the claims went before Congress but payment was delayed, despite committee recommendations and joint resolutions over the years that the claims be paid. A $5,000 payment for use of Selden's property was approved in 1870, whereas payment for his claims for care of prisoners was not approved until 1873. *House Reports*, 41 Cong., 2 Sess., No. 87 (Ser. 1438); *Senate Reports*, 42 Cong., 3 Sess., No. 418 (Ser. 1548); 46 Cong., 2 Sess., No. 511 (Ser. 1897); *Congressional Globe*, 41 Cong., 2 Sess., Appendix, p. 766; 42 Cong., 3 Sess., Appendix, p. 333; Records of Accounting Officers, Register of Misc. Claims, RG217, NA.

From Lewis Wolfley

New Orleans   Nov 14th 1868.

Honored Sir.

It is approaching three months since I entered upon the duties of my office.[1] The political Excitement and strife has given place to quiet and peace. Our Community are or have resumed their business occupations. During this time it has been impossible to make full and complete assessments, however I believe all Departments will give me credit for having done my duty.

Permit me to assure you Mr. President, that I have conscientiously kept my promise not to use my office politically nor have I forgotten your almost Fatherly advice. "Do not allow yourself to be carried away by party excitement; what you do, do upon principle, in after years, under any and all Circumstances you can look back upon the past with satisfaction and without regret. You go with my very best wishes."

I recall this now Sir, from the fact that lately Senator Kellogg has stated that he had received information of your dissatisfaction with me and a willingness and desire to change "even to a radical republican" provided he would Consent. There are but few circumstances under which I would place reliance in the Senators statements. Certainly not in this, for you were kind enough to say that I should have a hearing before any unfavorable action was taken against me. My actions are matters of facts and records, upon them I rely with implicit Confidence, that an investigation will but redouned to my Credit.

Lewis Wolfley

ALS, DLC-JP.
    1. Earlier in 1868 Wolfley had been nominated and confirmed for the position of assessor of Louisiana's First District. See William M. Daily to Johnson, Mar. 25, 1868, *Johnson Papers*, 13: 690–91.

From Nicholas E. Paine

New York   Nov 15 /68

My Dear Sir.

I have read, with much interest, the late attack upon Mr Courtney[1] and Several of his friends here and of the disposition you made of the case.[2]

My interest in the subject arises from the fact that I am not only well & favorably acquainted with him (Mr. Courtney) but have been a life-long friend of his father in law, the late Hon. D. S. Dickenson.

I know Mr. Courtney both socially and professionally and I assure your Excellency that up to this charge no man in the State has sustained a more elevated reputation and nothing short of the most positive proofs and from the highest source could induce me to distrust his integrity. In this case it is quite evident, Mr. Fullerton is moved by vindictive considerations and motives coupled with a purpose to *hedge off* his own iniquity. The sources from which he draws his proofs shows to what *extremities* he has resorted to make out his case *prima faciae*—and added to this fact, his own personal reputation, in this city, by no means improves his case. I am most happy to say to you that, as I am well informed, Mr Courtney will very shortly have it in his power fully to sustain each and every allegation he made before your Excellency upon the hearing, by proofs that are irrefutable. I am glad of this and believe your Excellcy will be also as it would be a source of the deepest regret to have a reputation as well earned, unfavorably affected.

Mr Courtney is and has been your friend and a warm and effective one too, throughout all the assaults upon you and he only asks, as I well know, & I only ask in his behalf what both he and I know that you will continue to sustain him until there be clear proof that he is answerable to censure.

I assure your Excellency that the whole community here sustain Mr Courtney and warmly affirm the disposition you made of the case.[3]

N. E. Paine

ALS, DLC-JP.

1. Samuel G. Courtney. As early as September William Fullerton, Courtney's partner in the whiskey fraud investigation, suspected Courtney of official misconduct. In early November, Fullerton requested Courtney's suspension, and Attorney General William M. Evarts ordered a halt to some of Courtney's cases, pending review of the charges. Evarts found no evidence of misconduct and authorized Courtney to proceed in late December. John M. Binckley to Johnson, Sept. 22, 1868, Johnson Papers, LC; *New York Times*, Nov. 13, 1868; *Senate Ex. Docs.*, 40 Cong., 3 Sess., No. 51, pp. 1–9 (Ser. 1360).

2. On November 13, after consultation with Attorney General Evarts, Johnson decided not to suspend Courtney. *New York Times*, Nov. 14, 16, 1868.

3. In what was becoming a typical pattern in the whiskey fraud investigations, William Fullerton, the government's special counsel, came under suspicion of misconduct at about this time. He was indicted on conspiracy charges on November 23, but the attorney general suspended his trial until March 1869. Courtney was never charged formally and remained in office until the Grant administration. *New York Herald*, Nov. 24, 1868; *New York Times*, Dec. 21, 1868; *New York Tribune*, Feb. 11, Mar. 12, 1869. See also George W. Greene to Johnson, Nov. 26, 1868.

From Moses Bates

Personal

Plymouth Mass.   Nov 16, 1868

Dear Sir

In view of the fact that during the *last* Winter and Spring, at your Suggestion, communicated by the Secretary of the Treasury, I devoted myself to procuring reliable information in regard to the condition and resources of the South, some of which I communicated from time to time for the information of the Administration,[1] I am extremely anxious, now that the democracy are defeated in the election,—as they need not have been—to visit a larger portion of the Southern States the coming Winter, partly with a view to compile information for publication in a *book form*,[2] and partly to institute a series of Land Offices, by which Northern capitalists will be induced to invest their money in the fertile lands of the South. All my own fortune has been lost in the Radical plan of re-construction, every thing having been invested upon plantations when the War closed, and though I devoted three months last year in the interest of the government,—at the request of the Secretary of the Treasury, I have never been able to recover even the money disbursed. Under all these circumstances I am induced to ask you to give me some duty to perform in the South, and the Comptroller of the Currency[3] will judge from the past year, how faithfully and how intelligently my *work* will be done.

Moses Bates
Editor Plymouth Mass *Sentinel*

ALS, DLC-JP.

1. See Bates to Johnson, Dec. 31, 1867, *Johnson Papers*, 13: 387–92.
2. No record of such a publication has been found.
3. Hiland R. Hulburd (*fl*1880) before the war was a clerk in the Ohio auditor's office. He served as deputy comptroller of the treasury (1865–67) before becoming comptroller of the currency. He left office in 1872, and later worked as a broker in New York City. Charles Lanman, *Biographical Annals of the Civil Government of the United States* (Detroit, 1976 [1876]), 217; *U.S. Off. Reg.* (1865–73); Columbus directories (1858–62); Hulburd to James A. Garfield, June 17, 1880, Garfield Papers, LC.

From Thomas M. Cook

No. 40. West Ninth Street,
New York, Nov. 16, 1868.

Mr. President:

Immediately after the evacuation of Richmond by the Rebel army, Mr. President Lincoln visited that city, and there held some conferences with southern men of prominence in regard to terms of peace. At one of these conferences held on board Admiral Porter's flagship[1] the late President handed to Judge Campbell a paper, unsigned and without address, remarking that it was an ultimatum for peace.[2] This paper was subsequently withdrawn from Judge Campbell's possession by military orders. You afterwards told me, in conversation upon the subject, that the original document was in your possession, or in the archives of the Executive Office. I have an abstract of it, made from a copy preserved by Judge Campbell; but I am very anxious to obtain a full and literal copy for use in some papers I am preparing on the closing events of Mr. Lincoln's official career. As these papers will, in fact, be a very strong defence of your administration, in bringing out the conservative purposes and intents of your predecessor, who had so remarkably strong a hold on the popular sympathies of the times, I feel confident that you will willingly aid me in securing the material I want. May I therefore ask you to cause a copy of this paper to be sent me if not inconsistent with the public welfare.

It will also occur to you, in this connection, that Mr. Lincoln, at the same time above referred to, in writing, authorized Gen. Weitzel, then in command at Richmond, to permit the assembling of "influential gentlemen"—meaning the Virginia Legislature—the call for which was issued but soon after revoked by orders from Washington.[3] If Mr. Lincoln's authorization to Gen. Weitzel is among the archives of the President's Office, as well as the letter of revocation, and any other matters bearing upon the subject, I would like them also. In case there is no valid objection to my having these papers (copies of them, I mean) and you consider that I am taxing your office too much in asking copies to be made for me, I will come and copy them myself, with your permission, or will pay for the extra labor of one of your clerks.[4]

With assurances of my highest regard and esteem . . .

T. M. Cook

ALS, DLC-JP.

1. David D. Porter. Lincoln was staying on board the *U.S.S. Malvern*, but the conferences were held on shore. E. B. Long, *The Civil War Day by Day: An Almanac, 1861–1865* (Garden City, N.Y., 1971), 666–67.

2. On April 4 and 5, 1865, President Lincoln presented John A. Campbell, assistant secretary of war for the Confederacy, with the same conditions he had done two months earlier at Hampton Roads, namely the restoration of national authority, the acceptance of Lincoln's decisions on slavery, and the disbanding of state forces hostile to the government. Lincoln added that any state meeting these terms would avoid future confiscation of property, other than slaves. Ibid.; Basler, *Works of Lincoln*, 8: 386–88.

3. Lincoln had authorized General Godfrey Weitzel to allow "the gentlemen who have acted as the Legislature of Virginia" to assemble if they decided to withdraw Virginia troops from the war. Lincoln rescinded his order after Campbell continued to push for an armistice and insist on the legitimacy of the Virginia legislature as a legal body. Ibid., 389, 406–7.

4. There is no evidence Johnson acted on this request.

From P. Curran[1]

Chicago   Nov 16th 1868

Sir—

About a month since I wrote to you[2] with regard to the presidential Candidacy. Matters did not turn out as favourably as we would have wished. It is not probable that I will be able to give a conscientious support to the incoming administration. I do not desire to give a factious one neither do I wish to give an indirect support to the extreme measures that may be adopted by the Radical party in allowing them to pass unnoticed. Under these circumstances I earnestly desire a government appointment, if possible in either Canada or Mexico. In that way I could leave the country without necessarily taking part in public affairs. It would moreover recompense for whatever damage I may have suffered during the late Campaign.

I do not have the names of any of my friends appended to this application, for the reason, that I am reluctant to let them know that I am at all an applicant for any office. However, if needed I can procure the most unexceptionable names in this city.

Leaving the matter to your consideration and action I have the honor to be . . .[3]

P. Curran

63 E. Polk st. Chicago Ills

ALS, DNA-RG59, Lets. of Appl. and Recomm., 1861–69 (M650, Roll 12), P. Curran.
1. Not identified.
2. Not found.
3. Curran was not nominated for any office.

From William Davidson

Oregon Herald Office

Portland   Nov. 16th 1868

Honored Friend

Having transmitted to your address, from time to time, various Editorial political articles published in our Daily and Weekly Herald, in vindication of your patriotic Constitutional National Administration of our General Government, as the honored President of our great Republic, permit me to express the hope that you will have approved of the course of our Paper in our faithful efforts in advocating all of your great measures for the promotion of the true interests of the whole people of our entire Country and allow me to assure you that the great mass of our citizens in this State, most cordially endorse and sustain your most noble conduct as our beloved President.

I have also forwarded to you several extracts from our Paper, upon the great importance of the election of our Candidate for the Presidency nominated by the National Convention at New York, and you may be assured that, while I most deeply regret the general result, it is a real satisfaction to be able to inform you that we have carried this State for the Hon. Horatio Seymour, as the enclosed article from our Paper will more fully explain to you.[1]

You are quite well aware of the fact, that the nomination of Mr. Francis P. Blair Jr. for the Vice Presidency was not satisfactory to the conservative men of our party, and it was the cause of great astonishment to most all of our democratic friends in this State that he should have received the nomination of the Convention, while Governor Seymour was a more prudent nomination for the Presidency.

Permit me to express the sincere hope that, four years hence, you will be our peoples Candidate for a re-election to the Presidency, and that you will be brought forward under circumstances which will secure complete success, as you have always been victorious before the mass of the people of our Country and as one of the indications of your great popularity with the people of this State, please find herewith enclosed an Editorial article from one of the Papers in the interior of our State, containing a reference to your telegraphic dispatch to me in June last,[2] alluding to the result of our State election at that time and I herewith enclose to you copies of communications addressed to me by your good friends Secretary Seward and Governor Seymour published in the News Papers of this State.

Having been engaged, during the past six years, in the News Paper business in this City and, although I have given constant attention to it, permit me to inform you that I have not been very fortunate in a pecuniary point of view, therefore, it is my intention to engage in other Business.

Referring you to my friends the Hon. J. S. Smith, our member elect to Congress from this State, and Senators Williams and Corbett,[3] now at the National Capital, will you do me the favor to appoint me to the position of Consul General, or a Consul at some one of the principal Commercial Cities in China, Japan, Central, or South America, or in England, in some port of Europe which favor will be fully appreciated.[4]

William Davidson

ALS, DNA-RG59, Lets. of Appl and Recomm., 1861–69 (M650, Roll 13), William Davidson.

1. None of the newspaper articles mentioned in the letter were found enclosed.

2. Johnson to Davidson, June 8, 1868, Johnson Papers, LC. See also Davidson to Johnson, June 15, 1868, *Johnson Papers*, 14: 222–23.

3. Joseph S. Smith, George H. Williams, and Henry W. Corbett.

4. There is no evidence of any attempt to nominate Davidson to a post.

From Hugh McCulloch

Personal

Treasury Department.   Nov. 16th 1868.

Dear Sir:—

Enclosed I hand you a copy of a letter just received from Gen. Jeffries.[1]

As the nomination of Fulton[2] seems to be approved by your friends in Baltimore, and as it is satisfactory to yourself, it will be confirmed.

I learn also that Judge Olney,[3] nominated for Supervisor of Illinois, was an *anti-impeacher*, and is a warm friend of Senator Trumbull[4] who had recommended his appointment. I shall, therefore, unless you see some objection to it, confirm his nomination.

H McCulloch

LS, DLC-JP.

1. His letter to McCulloch, enclosed to Johnson, indicated Noah L. Jeffries's withdrawal of objections to the appointment of Alexander Fulton. Jeffries to McCulloch, Nov. 15, 1868, Johnson Papers, LC.

2. Alexander Fulton (*fl*1899) was appointed supervisor of internal revenue for Delaware, Maryland, and the District of Columbia. He had served as one of the editors of the *Baltimore American*. Baltimore directories (1868–99); *Washington Evening Star*, Nov. 17, 18, 20, 1868.

3. John Olney (1822–*fl*1883) was an Illinois lawyer who actively served during the Civil War, rising to the rank of colonel before being honorably discharged in 1863. In 1867 he was elected judge of the circuit court in Illinois, a position he held until his resignation in 1869 to accept the appointment as supervisor of internal revenue. *The United States Biographical Dictionary and Portrait Gallery of Eminent and Self-Made Men. Illinois Volume* (Chicago, 1883), 759–60.

4. Senator Lyman Trumbull of Illinois.

From Bernard O'Kane

Boston   Nov. 16th 1868

Sir:

The following facts are addressed to your excellency, in order that they may be referred to the proper authority having charge of such cases, to be fully investigated. I held the office of Inspector of Internal Revenue, which was abolished by Act of Congress July 30th., whereupon I wrote to the Honorable Secretary of the Treasury, to give me a Warrant or Commission for protection as private detective, without pay, being satisfied that extensive frauds were being committed by dealers in spirits &c. The Hon. Secretary promptly authorized me to proceed on my own responsibility, which I did.

The first case brought before the U.S. Commissioner, Henry L. Hallet, Esq.,[1] was that of Michael G. Minon,[2] a man somewhat notorious for illegal connection with several illicit Stills, in and around this city, among which was one formerly reported by me to the Honorable Commissioner of Internal Revenue, in which I charged Collector McCartney[3] with complicity. The facts in this case proved the truth of my accusation. The case against Minon was that of non-erasure of inspection marks & repeated offers of bribery. When it came before the Commissioner, Mr. McCartney appeared in the capacity of private counsel for said Minon, & against the Government. The case was continued repeatedly, but it was evident that this was merely a mockery of justice, as McCartney's influence with the Commissioner was but too conspicuous. When the final hearing was to be had the third assistant U S. Attorney[4] who had the case in charge, left on business for New York. I appealed in vain to Mr. Hillard[5] & to his second assistant[6] to go into court to defend the Government. Mr. Hillard replied that the case would be postponed till his third asst., came home & guaranteed that the Government would be properly defended, but he failed to do so. The second assistant Mr. Hyde, said he had other more important cases to attend to. The evidence against Minon was direct, conclusive & irreputable, notwithstanding this the Commissioner Mr. Hallett in the absence of the Government Counsel, proceeded to deliver a most abusive tirade against me, eulogizing Mr. McCartney; & in violation of all law & all justice acquitted said Minon, merely because one of the counts in the indictment, was delayed, in his estimation, too long. My object in delaying the first charge, was to develop other more important charges. This reason was satisfactory to Mr. Dickinson, assistant attorney & also to Mr. Hallett when he issued the warrant. But ponder on the power which Collector McCartney exercised over this quasi judicial functionary. It is fearful to contemplate! I will venture no comment but submit these facts to your excellency's serious consideration, hoping you will not allow such matters to pass without proper investigation. Perhaps it will throw some light on this case, by relating some charges hitherto preferred against Collector McCartney to the Honorable Commissioner. In August 1866, eight or nine witnesses examined before a Commissioner of the Treasury charged McCartney with fraudulent practices by "black mailing" parties charged with non-stamping legal papers. The *modus operandi* was, McCartney employed collectors of bills to bring to him all such papers, whereupon instead of entering complaint, he referred the

parties to an accomplise named Dyer,[7] who advised them to settle
with the Collector. In this way large sums was collected. The question is, did he pay this money into the Treasury? These cases were
discovered by McCartney, refusing to pay commissions to "stool pi-
geons." What became of the report of the Treasury agent? McCartney
has a peculiar way of hushing up matters. Many other charges have
been preferred against this notorious character, which must be on
file in the Internal Revenue Department. One especially which occurred on the 10th. of June last, was that of extorting one thousand
dollars from S. C. Bocher & Co.,[8] of Boston for alleged selling of
rum below the tax. An U. S. Guager was employed to compromise in
this case. Did McCartney pay this money into the Treasury? Witnesses in this case can be brought up at any moment. I have preferred charges of corruption against him, all of which he has managed to cover up. The secret lies in this: that the power of compromise
gives such officials too much control of money which they can & do
use in bribing, I fear, too many persons in the employ of Government, who should spurn it.

Your Excellency will find it will redound to the honor of your career in office to have the cases above mentioned thoroughly investigated, that it may not be said hereafter you knowingly permitted
such unworthy persons to hold office during your administration.

Bernard O'Kane

late Revenue Inspector   Mass. 3d District

ALS, DNA-RG56, Appts., Internal Revenue Service, Collector, Mass., 3rd Dist., Wm. H.
McCartney.

1. Hallet (*fl*1881), a lawyer, had been U.S. commissioner since the mid-1850s. He held the
post until at least 1881. "The Trial of Anthony Burns, 1854," *MHSP*, 44 (1910–11): 332;
Boston directories (1865–81).

2. Minon (*fl*1881) was a Boston restauranteur and liquor merchant. Boston directories (1867–
81).

3. William H. McCartney. See O'Kane to Johnson, July 23, 1868, *Johnson Papers*, 14: 414–
16.

4. Marquis F. Dickinson, Jr. (1840–1915) was an assistant district attorney from 1868 until
1871. He then entered into private practice with another assistant district attorney, Henry D.
Hyde, and the former district attorney, George S. Hillard. Dickinson also held many local civic
posts, and continued to lecture and write on law. *NCAB*, 2: 507; *New York Times*, Sept. 19,
1915; Boston directories (1867–71).

5. A former state senator and city solicitor, George S. Hillard (1808–1879) served as district attorney from 1866 until 1870. Prior to the Civil War he edited several newspapers, and
cooperated with Charles Sumner in the publication of "The Jurist." *Appleton's Cyclopaedia*.

6. Henry D. Hyde (*fl*1896) had been an assistant district attorney since 1867. In 1871 he

entered into private practice, and was still working with Marquis F. Dickinson in 1881. First Search-World Cat.; Boston directories (1867–81).

7. Possibly Micah Dyer, Jr. (*c*1829–*fl*1881), who was admitted to the Massachusetts bar in the summer of 1868. Boston directories (1868, 1881); *Boston Advertiser*, June 10, 1868; 1850 Census, Mass., Suffolk, Boston, 3rd Ward, 317.

8. S. C. Bocher & Co. has not been identified.

From James E. English

New Haven, Nov 17— 1868.

Sir

I am induced by warm personal relations to write you in behalf of Henry Sherman, Esq.[1] soliciting for him the appointment of asst Secretary of the Treasury.

Mr. Sherman is well known in Conn. and has many personal and political friends here.

I beleive him to be a man of sound principles, honest and in accord with our friends.

Hopeing that your excellency will give his application thorough and if possible faverable consideration . . .[2]

J E. English

ALS, DNA-RG56, Appls., Heads of Treasury Offices, Henry Sherman.

1. Sherman (1808–1879), a lawyer by training, moved to Hartford from New York City in 1850. During 1861–68 he was employed in the Washington office of the Treasury Department. *Appleton's Cyclopaedia*.

2. Sherman was not nominated to any office. He remained in Washington practicing law. Washington directories (1870–74).

From Edward H. East

Nashville   Nov 18 /68

Dear Sir

Your Dispatch came to hand.[1] Your request for me to come to Washington and remain until spring was quite unexpected and but for our Supreme court that meets the 1st Monday in December, I would certainly comply. At all events I shall come, to Washington before spring[2]—and remain some time—as it is probably the last time, that I will ever be there, at least, with friends like yourself & others. I have several good cases in our Supreme court, and my circumstances demand that I should obtain the promised fees. I would much like to come to Washington, and would be very glad to see you, and have a conversation with you relative to our future—and the probabilaties of the country under the fixed change that the last election made. In Tennessee, we have no head, no organization, and no ambition, among that class of men, who are capable and worthy. I would be glad to hear from you.

Edward H. East

ALS, DLC-JP.
  1. No recent communication from Johnson to East has been located.
  2. Available evidence sheds no light on an actual visit by East to Washington.

From James R. Doolittle

Racine   Nov 19, 1868

Sir

Enclosed please find certain letters addressed to me in relation to the vacant Marshalship in our State.[1]

As there is no probability that the Senate would confirm Mr Lyon[2] it is probably best not to send in his name. Young Jackson[3] is well recommended, by the Judge[4] & many of the Bar.

He is a fine young man and our faithful friend. Mr Sholes[5] of Milwaukee is very earnest in his favor.

Others have recommended Mr Hooker[6] a man of fine standing of Milwaukee. While Genl. Bragg[7] who has done such efficient service, specially and urgently recommends Major Conklin,[8] who is a very worthy man.

The last three are Republicans but not of the savage kind.

Either of them would fill the office respectably.[9]

J R Doolittle

P. S. Mr Sholes letter perhaps had better not go on to the files as it is private.

ALS, DLC-JP.
  1. The only letter found is C. Latham Sholes to Doolittle, Nov. 11, 1868, Johnson Papers, LC. For an earlier discussion of the marshalship vacancy, see Doolittle to Johnson, Nov. 3, 1868.
  2. Probably Joseph M. Lyon whose nomination would have been useless in any case, since he died on November 25. *History of Milwaukee*, 629.
  3. Not identified, but perhaps related to former marshal Darius C. Jackson, who had been removed from office in 1866 after a brief tenure. Ser. 6B, Vol. 4: 337, Johnson Papers, LC.
  4. Probably U.S. district judge Andrew G. Miller (1801–1874) who, by virtue of his position, worked closely with the marshal. Miller was appointed an associate justice of the Wisconsin territorial supreme court in 1838 and served until statehood in 1848, when he became U.S. district judge, a post he held until his resignation in January 1874. *United States Biographi-*

cal *Dictionary and Portrait Gallery of Eminent and Self-Made Men: Wisconsin Volume* (Chicago, 1877), 12–13.

5. Christopher Latham Sholes.

6. Samuel T. Hooker (1816–*fl*1881) engaged in merchandising in New York and transportation on Lake Ontario before he moved to Milwaukee in 1855, where he established a grain business. Active in the city's Chamber of Commerce, he was also collector of customs (1869–71). *History of Milwaukee*, 1144–45.

7. Edward S. Bragg (1827–1912), a lawyer, moved to Fond du Lac, Wisconsin, in 1850. After commanding the "Iron Brigade" during the Civil War, he reentered politics and held a number of offices, including state senator (1868–69) and U.S. Representative (1877–83, 1885–87). Warner, *Blue*; *BDUSC*.

8. Probably James T. Conklin (b. *c*1829), undersheriff of Fond du Lac in 1860, who became 1st lieutenant, 14th Wis. Inf., and in August 1863 was promoted to captain, assistant quartermaster of volunteers. *Off. Army Reg.: Vols.*, 7: 184; *OR*, Ser. 1, Vol. 49, Pt. 2: 1097; *The History of Fond du Lac County, Wisconsin* (Chicago, 1880), 791, 998; 1860 Census, Wis., Fond du Lac, Fond du Lac, 3rd Ward, 67.

9. Johnson nominated Hooker for the post on December 16, 1868, but on the eve of adjournment the Senate placed his nomination on the table. Ser. 6B, Vol. 4: 340, Johnson Papers, LC; *Senate Ex. Proceedings*, Vol. 16: 407, 412, 505.

From Hugh McCulloch

Treasury Department. November 19th 1868

My Dear Sir

Comr. Rollins, sent me last evening, the name of S. B Dutcher[1] for Supervisor of the Southern District of New York in place of Spencer Kirby[2] rejected.

I cannot reject the nomination of Mr Dutcher and thereby keep open the Supervisorship of this important District, without subjecting the Department to the charge of standing in the way of collecting the revenue and of insincerity in the efforts the Administration is making to suppress frauds in that den of iniquity, the City of New York. I deem it best therefore to Confirm Deuthers [*sic*] nomination. I have no acquaintance with him, but he has the reputation of being a good business man, and a man of integrity. If he is not "right," the reponsibility of the appointment will rest upon the Internal Revenue Bureau, where it belongs.

I have given Messrs Randall Patterson[3] and other friends of the Administration in Pennsylvania, ample opportunity to present a better name, if they could do so, than Southworth[4] for supervisor of the Eastern District of that State. They have not done so, and I do not therefore think it advisable to longer withhold my approval of the nomination of Southworth.

H McCulloch

ALS, DLC-JP.

1. Silas B. Dutcher (1829–1909) was in the mercantile business in New York for a number of years and active in Republican politics. He served as supervisor of internal revenue, and during the Grant administration he was pension agent in New York City. *NCAB*, 2: 174.

2. Kirby (*c*1822–1877) was subsequently listed as assessor and then collector in New York City. *New York Tribune*, Aug. 15, 1877; New York City directories (1871–77).

3. Samuel J. Randall and probably William C. Patterson of Philadelphia.

4. Delos P. Southworth (*fl*1880) was nominated as supervisor of internal revenue for the eastern district; he evidently held that office for a brief time. He subsequently served as city treasurer for Philadelphia. Philadelphia directories (1869–80); *Washington Evening Star*, Nov. 19, 1868.

From Noble D. Larner and John Edwin Mason[1]

Washington, Nov. 20th 1868.

Illustrious Companion:—

We have the honor to transmit to you enclosed, a card of invitation to attend the Second Annual Banquet of Lafayette Royal Arch Chapter of this city,[2] and with it, the congratulations, compliments and esteem, of its officers and members.

In tendering the fraternal welcome of these Royal Arch Masons, we cannot forget the many acts of Kindness received from you, during your administration, and trust that you will give us the opportunity we seek upon this occasion, to express to you our deep sense of gratitude, and appreciation of the services you have rendered to Freemasonry.

Trusting that you will honor us with your presence on this occasion . . .

Noble D. Larner, M ∴ E ∴ High Priest.

Jno. Edw. Mason   Secretary.

ALS (Mason), DLC-JP.

1. Mason (*c*1825–*fl*1892) was a physician who served briefly as a clerk in the General Land Office in Washington. 1870 Census, D.C., Washington, 5th Ward, 45; Washington, D.C., directories (1869–92).

2. The enclosed card indicated that the banquet would be held on the evening of November 24 at Bunker's Avenue Hotel. An account of the banquet claimed that Johnson planned to attend but at the last minute sent his regrets, having been detained by Cabinet business. See the *National Intelligencer*, Nov. 25, 1868.

From Lovell H. Rousseau

New Orleans, La., 20th Nov. 1868.

Mr. President,

Col. Keeler,[1] of my staff, will hand you this & will explain to you fully the condition of affairs here lately & now.

Col. Keeler is a young gentleman of fine talent & well informed of matters in Louisiana. You may rely implicitly upon his judgment and veracity.

I send by him to Washington my annual army report,[2] charging him with communicating to you matters connected with my command in person, which it would be difficult, if not impossible, for me to put upon paper.

I trust the account he will give you of our late disturbances and the manner in which we got through them, will be satisfactory.[3]

My report includes an account of the action of the military during the disturbances here.[4]

Lovell H Rousseau   U.S.A.

LS, DLC-JP.

1. Birney B. Keeler (1840–1886) became 1st lt., 142nd N.Y. Rgt. in September 1862 and eventually captain, receiving four brevets in 1865 and 1867. He remained in the military but never ranked above captain. Arriving in Washington, D.C., on November 24, 1868, he handed over Rousseau's report to General Grant and had interviews with Johnson, Secretary of War Schofield, and some prominent Congressmen on November 25. Frederick J. Seaver, *Historical Sketches of Franklin County* (Albany, 1918), 752; Powell, *Army List*, 407; *Philadelphia Press*, Nov. 26, 1868.

2. Dated October 1868, Rousseau's report can be found as part of the report of the Secretary of War in *Senate Ex. Docs.*, 40 Cong., 3 Sess., No. 1, pp. 302–8 (Ser. 1367).

3. Some of Keeler's information was reported in the *Washington Evening Star*, Nov. 27, 1868.

4. In addition to Rousseau's own report, he enclosed that of Robert C. Buchanan for the period before Rousseau took command. *Senate Ex. Docs.*, 40 Cong., 3 Sess., No. 1, pp. 310–17 (Ser. 1367).

From Alanson W. Kelly

Penn Yan   Yates Co. New York
21st Nov. 1868—

Sir:

I feel at liberty to claim an office at your hands, I would respectfully solicit the Post Office in this village.[1] Not only did I watch and care for your departed son[2] the Dr. but I embalmed him. During your whole administration have I defended you—And offered money to assist in defraying your trial before the senate.[3] With a well fortified petition from our leading Citizens will it avail me any thing to visit Washington?

Col. A. C. Gillem whom I saw not long since says he will, as Sheridan said of Griswold,[4] throw his hat in air if I can only succeed in this application.[5]

A. W. Kelly

ALS, DLC-JP.

1. See Kelly to Johnson, Apr. 25, 1868, *Johnson Papers*, 14: 48–49.
2. Charles Johnson.
3. See Kelly to Johnson, Apr. 25, 1868, ibid.
4. The reference here has not been determined.
5. Johnson nominated Kelly in January 1869, but withdrew the nomination when Kelly demanded another post. See Kelly to Johnson, Jan. 16, 1869.

From Thomas M. Cook

Unofficial

No. 40. West Ninth Street,
New York, Nov. 23, 1868.

Mr. President:—

You were once kind enough to say to me that you would place me in any suitable position within your gift that I might select, and verified the promise by securing me a special Agency in the Treasury Department. This I was able to retain but a few months owing to constant political differences with the Commissioner of Internal Revenue. When I lost that place—1st of January last—I resolved to trouble you no more, and to seek no other political employment. But I now find myself compelled to look beyond literary labor to support my family. I therefore approach you as a friend and ask your assistance.

It has occurred to me that the Custom House in this City must afford some place in filling which I can still pursue my journalistic calling and thus improve my scanty income. Impressed with this idea, and with your kindly disposition toward me, I venture to ask a line from you to Mr. Collector Smythe, commending me to him for employment in the manner indicated. It seems to me your request in my behalf can but be influential with him.

I have no promises to make in reciprocation of the favor I ask. If

your administration is not already assured that it has a warm sympathizer and devoted advocate in me, to the extent of my poor abilities,
I cannot so assure it.[1]

T. M. Cook

ALS, DLC-JP.
  1. There is no evidence that Cook received a position.

From Robert W. Latham

Washington   Nov. 23. 1868

Dear Sir

As an agent of the Union Pacific R. Road, I see with feelings of
deep regret, a disposition on the part of some to obstruct, and retard
the progress of this great National enterprize, by raising frivolous
objections, and throwing unjust obsticles in the way of its speedy
completion. I do not wish to charge improper motives upon any one
thus engaged, but in the absence of Doctor Durant[1] Vice President,
and General Manager, I consider it a duty I owe to him, and to all
connected with the company, and also to the great National interest
involved, to call your special attention to the Subject, relying with
implicit confidence upon your high sense of impartial justice, to afford that relief which you alone can give, as the faithful, and responsible head of the Nation.

In order that evenhanded, and equal justice, shall be meted out to
each portion of this great National work, I respectfully, and earnestly
request, that you will appoint a *new Commission* of three experienced,
practical, business Rail Road men, to examine the Union Pacific Road,
the Central Pacific Road, and the Union Pacific Road, Eastern Division, carfully, and in detail, and to report direct to you at the earliest practicable moment. In the mean time order the subsidy paid to
the Central, and the Union Pacific Roads equalized and then, either
continue to pay both Roads upon the completion of each 20 miles,
or withhold payment from each, until the Commission shall report
to you, thus dealing impartially with both alike.

I am satisfied you will see the propriety, and even necessity, of
having all the Roads examined by the same commissioners, who shall
be men of the most extensive Rail Road information. Men of character and reputation, in that Department of business; whose report
would be received with entire confidence by the whole community.

I deem it best, and most desirable, that you personally shall select this commission, from the class of practical, and experienced men refered to. Men in whom you can confide, and whose report shall be made direct to you, instead of to one of your Departments. In this peculiar, and unexpected opposition, emanating from a source, whose every honorable, and patriotic impulse, should lead it in the opposite direction; this company can only look to You, for that impartial, and unpredjudiced action, which has ever characterised your private, and public conduct.

I am satisfied that any Goverment official, who is engaged in throwing impediments in the way of the rapid progress, and speedy completion of this work, whether from predjudice against the Union Pacific Roads, or partiality in favour of the Central Road, or from motives stronger than either,[2] so that the Union Pacific Road may be crippled, or suspended, so as to enable the Central Company to build one or two Hundred miles, which would otherwise have been built by the Union Pacific Company; will be considered by you totally unworthy of a place in your administration, and an enemy to the Nation's progress and prosperity.

Why is it that the Central Road receives its subsidy upon a telegram, stating that 20 miles has been completed, when the subsidy due the Union pacific Road, on over one Hundred miles is withheld. The Department gives me as a reason for this, that there are no charges, or complaints against the Central Road. This is certainly not the true reason.

While at Salt Lake City a few weeks ago, I was informed by parties who had traveled over both Roads, that the Union Pacific was decidedly the best of the two.

I made a careful examination of the Road myself, and I pronounce it the best Road in the United States, except the Michigan Central Road, and for machine shops, Station Houses, Hotel accomodations &c &c it is superior to any Road from New York to New Orleans.

The idea that this company intend to make all out of it they can in the building, and when finished, turn the Road over to the Goverment, and abandon all their stock in the same, is perfectly ridiculous.

The men interested in this Road, are among the most wealthy, cautious, sagacious business men in the country, and they understand fully the vast business, and accumulating profits which await the completion of the work. In a short time after the Road is finished, you may expect to see the company engaged in laying down a double track, in order to accomodate and facilitate the increasing volume of trafic which will pass to, and from the Pacific Coast.

Hoping that this equal, and impartial request, may meet your unqualified approval, and receive your prompt action . . .

R. W. Latham

ALS, DLC-JP.

1. Thomas C. Durant.

2. Probably an indirect reference to Secretary of the Interior Browning, who refused to release bonds to the Union Pacific Railroad for its completed sections until the track had been inspected by the special commissioners. This caused a financial crunch for the railroad. Williams, *Great and Shining Road*, 221.

From John D. Perryman

Washington   Nov. 23rd 1868

Dear Sir.

My apparrel will not admit of my calling on you. Every body who gets an office here pays somebody to aid him. You can put some money in my pocket by a word to Mr. McCulloch. Green[1] of California whom he has rejected is a personal friend of mine and a great admirer or yours, and deserves the place of Supervisor. He can reconsider the case. Boucher[2] of N. Orleans is an especial friend of mine & I know ought to have the place. And Col. Crane[3] for Southern Ohio. You will pardon this to friendship & necessity.

J. D. Perryman

ALS, DLC-JP.

1. James G. Green (b. *c*1814) was rejected by McCulloch as supervisor for California, Arizona, Nevada, and Utah; instead, Charles L. Wiggins was nominated. Alan P. Bowman, comp., *Index to the 1850 Census of the State of California* (Baltimore, 1972), 182; *Washington Evening Star*, Nov. 19, 23, 1868.

2. Probably Adolph Bouchard, candidate for collector for the Third District of Louisiana.

3. Possibly John C. Crane.

From Thomas Shankland

Brooklyn N.Y.   Nov. 23, 1868

If the President who once said to me, "if I can ever do any thing for you, let me Know" can find no one to fill the office of naval officer of the New York Custom House, he can do much for me by nominating me for that office, & taking the chances of rejection or confirmation by the Senate.[1]

Thos. Shankland

ALS, DLC-JP.

1. Johnson did not nominate Shankland, and Congress did not confirm any of the President's choices; deputy naval officer Cornell S. Franklin filled the post until the Grant administration. See Henry A. Smythe to Johnson, May 27, 1868; Anne M. Deen to Johnson, July 3, 1868; Charles Peters to Johnson, July 3, 1868, *Johnson Papers*, 14: 123–24, 307–9, 460.

From David Shirpser et al.[1]

[Alaska, ca. November 23, 1868][2]

We most urgently beg your influences to recommend the early establishment of civil government for the Territory of Alaska. The doubts no longer exist that Gold, Coal, Copper, and other minerals, are to be found in the Territory in paying quantities, and that emigration will soon follow these discoveries to the Territory, and that military government will be inadequate for the imergency.

We complain that there are abuses in fur trade, and that an unwise policy is pursued to advance the progress of the country.

As merchants and traders we recommend the protections of our fisheries as well as the fur bearing animals from the ravaging destruction of wild adventurers—whose sole object is imediate speculation.

We cheerfully endorse Mr. W. T. Ballon[3] as being Capable, Honest, and loyal to his country to fill the position as our first governor for the Territory.[4]

Trusting your influence to promote the welfare of the Country that it may be self sustain[ing] and that your influence may be used for the purpose above described, we beg as Citizens of the Territory of "Alaska" to Subscribe ourselves . . .

Pet, DNA-RG59, Misc. Lets., 1789–1906 (M179, Roll 291).

1. Shirpser (*fl*1881) was a San Francisco merchant. Eight other men of various occupations also signed the letter. San Francisco directories (1869–81).

2. The letter is stamped received November 23, 1868. Presuming it was written in Alaska, it would have taken some weeks to get to Washington, D.C., but the exact date of its composition cannot be known.

3. William T. Ballon (*fl*1876) was a San Francisco merchant who had spent considerable time in Alaska. In the mid-1870s he was a shipping and commission agent in Seattle. Ibid. (1867); Seattle directories (1876); Jesse D. Carr to Johnson, Dec. 23, 1867, Lets. of Appl. and Recomm., 1861–69 (M650, Roll 3), William T. Ballon, RG59, NA.

4. Alaska's first governor, John Henry Kinkead, was appointed by President Chester A. Arthur in 1884. McMullin and Walker, *Territorial Governors*, 3–4.

From W. G. Ford[1]

Washington, Nov. 25. 1868.

Surrounded as you were, I had opportunity this morning only of presenting you with a map showing the route of the "International Pacific Rail Road" and asking that you dignify the measure by your official commendation of it to the Congress in your Message. Neither your Administration or your own great fame has been or will be linked with a measure more National in its character, more beneficent in its results or more enduring in its importance. The distance is 800 miles nearer from New York by this route than by any other, through a country abounding in its *whole and entire length* in agricultural & mineral wealth.

The bill now before the Congress[2] asks a subsidy, secured by a mortgage upon the Road, to the extent of $16,000 pr mile.

The Democratic Conventions of 1860 were pledged to a Southern Pacific Rail Road route as feasible, cheaper & direct, since when the Government has subsidized the Union Pacific & Central Roads over a much greater distance & with aid of $32,000 pr mile & mammoth land grants. The International is sectional to the South & Great West, but is National to the United States.

The patriotic & impartial course which have characterized & distinguished your policy, prompts me to request your favorable mention in your Message of 7th proximo.

W G. Ford

ALS, DLC-JP.

1. Washington, D.C., directories (1866–71) do not show Ford as a resident of the capital. It is possible that this is William G. Ford (*c*1826–*fl*1878) of Memphis, who was a cotton factor and commission merchant and in the 1870s became president of the Memphis and Kansas City Railroad Company. Given that the proposed International Pacific Railroad line would provide additional linkage for lines emanating out of Memphis, Ford would certainly have had an interest in such a proposed line. 1860 Census, Tenn., Shelby, 5th Dist., Memphis, 111; (1870), 4th Ward, Memphis, 32; Memphis directories (1859–60, 1872–74); *House Reports*, 45 Cong., 2 Sess., No. 667 (Ser. 1824); *Senate Reports*, 44 Cong., 1 Sess., No. 26 (Ser. 1667).

2. Senate Bill No. 603 or House Bill No. 847. See Columbus B. Guthrie and Henry G. Marquand to Johnson, Nov. 10, 1868.

From George W. Greene[1]

Goshen, N.Y.   Nov. 26 1868

Mr. President:

A personal interest connected with some of the persons engaged in the Fullerton & Courtney controversy,[2] has brought me in contact with persons, who, when Speaking upon the subject make, very gross, (and as I most certainly believe) unfounded charges of corruption, affecting members of your Cabinet and even your Excellency.

The charges come from such a source and are made under such circumstances, that, aside from all personal interest, I should feel it to be my bounden duty to apprise your Excellency of them. The charges come from the mouth of the brother[3] of Ex Judge Fullerton and were stated to me as the results derived by him from a very recent conversation with his brother, the Ex Judge.

Through the public prints Ex Judge Fullerton claims to hold to your Excellency the position of your recognized & retained counsel on the part of the Government; and yet his failure to secure the removal of Mr Courtney is accounted for, upon the ground, that your Excellency has never been in earnest in the prosecution of the plunders of the public Treasury. That many high in office, including, as I have stated, members of Cabinet, were, (as the proof is claimed to show) engaged in these same scheems of plundering—but not having *divided* fairly with your Excellency,—hence the pretended prosecution to secure such division. So gross and so terrible charges ought not to go unnoticed. I am responsible for what I write.

Now, my personal interest: I have just been elected over General Van Wyck to represent the 11th Congressional Dist. of the State of New York in the 41st Congress.

He proposes to contest:[4] I have reason to believe that he & the Fullertons here shook hands. The place of Courtney to go (as was hoped) to the Ex Judges brother, & my seat to the general.

If you desire to have this matter of the charges in detail be good enough to communicate such desire at an early day.

Geo. W. Greene

ALS, DLC-JP.

1. A former school commissioner and Orange County, New York, judge, Greene (1831–1895) had just been elected to Congress. He only served until 1870, but later was elected to the New York state assembly (1885–88). *BDUSC.*

2. William Fullerton and Samuel G. Courtney. See N. E. Paine to Johnson, Nov. 15, 1868.

3. Possibly Stephen W. Fullerton (*c*1823–1902), district attorney of Orange County and later county judge there. He was a one-time partner in the New York City law firm of Fullerton, Knox and Crosby, probably some permutation of the firm Fullerton and Knox, to which William Fullerton belonged. *New York Times*, Sept. 21, 1868, Apr. 5, 1902.

4. Charles H. VanWyck was heading the congressional subcommittee that was investigating the government's handling of the whiskey cases. He successfully contested Greene's victory, and in February 1870 replaced Greene in Congress. *BDUSC*.

From Samuel Agnew[1]

No. 821 Chesnut Street
Philadelphia   Novr. 27th, 1868

Hon. Sir:

I am collecting material illustrative of the recent civil war in our Country, and to add to the interest of the collection I am adding letters & Autographs of the Authors &c. My collection will most probably be deposited in the Library of the Presbyterian Historical Society, & possesses therefore more importance than that of an individual designed for personal use. I prefer receiving from parties whom I thus desire to honor their own sentiments expressed with the PURPOSE *before them*, rather than secure letters written with no design of perpetuation, and often unjust to the Author to be thus used. I have in the numerous works collected, a copy of Savage's Life of yourself,[2] & another work issued anonymously in the west. Will you Kindly gratify me in a laudable purpose, by writing me a few lines over your Autograph to be placed in this volume? *And also*, your simple Autograph with date upon another sheet, to be placed with the other volume alluded to.

Samuel Agnew
No. 821 Chesnut St.

ALS, DLC-JP.

1. Agnew (1814–1880) was associated with the Presbyterian Board of Education and the Board of Publication in Philadelphia. Earlier a successful book publisher in Philadelphia, he became one of the founders of the Presbyterian Historical Society and served as its librarian and treasurer for nearly thirty years. Philadelphia directories (1865–75); *NUC*; Samuel Agnew biographical file, Presbyterian Historical Society, Philadelphia.

2. A reference to John Savage, *Life and Public Services of Andrew Johnson*, published in 1866.

From Laura B. Ihrie

Washington, Nov. 27th [1868][1]

My dear kind friend:

To-day being what my husband[2] calls one of "God's days," I wish to remind *you* that it is just what your photographer requires for a *perfect* picture![3]

Cannot you make it convenient to give him a sitting to-day?

I will not be able to see you till next Sunday evening.

Hoping you enjoyed your "thanksgiving" sermon and dinner yesterday . . .[4]

Your Aff. adpt. daughter.

AL, DLC-JP.

1. The year is suggested because Laura Ihrie was in Washington in November 1868; moreover the reference to Thanksgiving Day on "yesterday" fits with 1868, because Thanksgiving was on November 26 that year.

2. Brevet Brigadier General George P. Ihrie.

3. On Wednesday, November 25, Ihrie had gone with her uncle, Orville H. Browning, when he sat for a photograph at Whitehurst's gallery, so the idea was fresh in her mind. Randall, *Browning Diary*, 2: 228.

4. No information on Johnson's Thanksgiving Day activities has been located.

From Dennis Wadsworth[1]

Nov 27th 1868

The humble petition of Dennis Wadsworth colored man, respectfully sheweth that he was convicted at the late term of the district court of the united states for Pamlico North Carolina—was fined $200, and is now imprisoned in the common jail of Craven County N. C. for said fine.

The judicial officer[2] who presided, considering your petitioners case of the most mitigated character imposed the *minimum fine* only. In addition to this favourable view taken by his Honer the presiding judge petitioner begs leave to aver most solemnly that the whiskey (the conclusion of which was the '*gravamen*' of the charge) was sent to the house occupied by his family in his absence without any previous concert with the distiller or with any other person and without knowing indeed from whom it came—That it was kept by him without any effort or purpose to conceal it, and he had no knowledge of any law which he was violating by so doing.

The petitioner further represents that he is very poor and utterly unable to pay said fine.

He has a family consisting of a wife & 1 child, who are dependant upon his daily labour for bread and who are now suffering in consequence of his imprisonment.

Petitioner is informed by his friends that they will pay the *costs* (about $70) if the fine could be remitted.

Petitioner therefore humbly prays your Excellency to pardon or remit the said fine[3] and thus set your petitioner at liberty—and as in duty bound will ever pray.

Dennis Wadsworth

LS, DLC-JP.
1. Wadsworth (c1831–f1870) was a farmer in Craven County. 1870 Census, N.C., Craven Twp., New Brunswick, 14.
2. George W. Brooks (1821–1882) was a longtime lawyer who became a large landowner and slaveholder in North Carolina. Appointed federal district judge by Johnson in 1865, he served until his death. *DAB.*
3. For support of Wadsworth, see Matthias E. Manley to Johnson, Nov. 28, 1868. What action, if any, that Johnson took in this matter has not been uncovered.

From James M. Cavanaugh

Washington— D.C.   Nov 28th— 1868—

Sir,

Understanding that Hon Green Clay Smith—is about resigning his office of Governor of the Territory of Montana[1]—I very respectfully beg leave to Cordially recommend Robert B. Parrott[2]—a resident of said Territory,—as his successor.

Mr. Parrott is very very well qualified for the position. He is a lawyer of ability—popular with the people—and one of the earliest settlers of the Territory.

I do not ask for the appointment, should Governor Smith conclude not to resign—for he has been and is a most excellent and popular officer.[3]

James M. Cavanaugh   Delegate

ALS, DNA-RG59, Lets. of Appl. and Recomm., 1861–69 (M650, Roll 37), Robert B. Parrott.
1. Smith, whom Johnson appointed governor of the Montana Territory in 1866, had returned to Washington, D.C., during the summer of 1868 to try to straighten out some problems with territorial finances. He did, in fact, resign his post, but remained in office until April

1869. *BDUSC*; Michael P. Malone et al., *Montana: A History of Two Centuries*, rev. ed. (Seattle, 1991 [1976]), 105.

2. Parrott (*c*1830–*fl*1904), formerly from Iowa and a resident of Helena, was admitted to practice before the Supreme Court of Montana in December 1864. He apparently discovered the Parrott Mine at Butte, Montana. *Historical Sketch and Essay on the Resources of Montana* (Helena, 1868), 153; *History of Montana, 1739–1885* (Chicago, 1885), 321; 1860 Census, Iowa, Clark, Osceola Twp., Osceola, 1; *New York Times*, Aug. 27, 1904.

3. Johnson did not name Parrott to any post. In January 1869 he nominated Nathaniel P. Langford for the governorship, but he was not confirmed. Earl S. Pomeroy, *The Territories and the United States, 1861–1890* (Seattle, 1969 [1947]), 138.

From Matthias E. Manley[1]

Newbern NC   Nov 28th 1868

Sir

Believing that the petitioner Dennis Wadsworth has been by reason of his credulity & ignorance, the victim of fraudulent & designing men I feel constrained to appeal to your Excellency specially in his behalf.

The persons who have signed a memorial in his favour are among the very best of our citizens of all classes & parties.[2]

Dennis had merited a good reputation in life and your Excellency's clemency could not be bestowed on a worthier object in his sphere of life.

I hope & trust your Excellency will not deem it inconsistent with requirements of public position to remit the fine of $200. Tho' small it is very difficult to raise here in the empoverished condition of our people.

M E Manley

ALS, DLC-JP.

1. Manley (1800–1881) was a prominent lawyer and jurist, who served in the North Carolina legislature in the antebellum period. He began service on the state supreme court in 1859. He was a member of the North Carolina constitutional convention in October 1865 and speaker of the state senate in 1866. According to at least one source, Manley was appointed to the state supreme court by provisional governor Holden in 1865. *NCAB*, 7: 197; Raper, *Holden*, 65.

2. The Wadsworth petition and also the Manley letter were sent to Representative David Heaton, who in turn forwarded them to the President. Like Manley, Heaton also claimed that the persons who signed the Wadsworth petition were among the leading citizens of New Bern. See Heaton to Johnson, Dec. 1, 1868, Johnson Papers, LC.

From William T. Sherman

Saint Louis, Novr. 28 1868.

The U.S. Marshal Col Rogers[1] died today. A Capt John Duble[2] an old school mate of mine, asked me for my signature today in application for the vacancy. He had many good names, and I could not refuse it.

Now at a later time in the same day, I am informed that General Morgan L. Smith is also an applicant. General Smith was for years one of my best Division Commanders, was badly wounded about Christmas 1862 near Vicksburg, but continued to serve till the close of the war, and he would make an excellent Marshal.

I do not wish to be construed as applying for the office on the part of either of these Gentleman, but surely Genl. Smith has my unbounded respect, and the United States cannot too highly repay his past services.[3]

W. T. Sherman   Lt Genl.

ALS, DNA-RG60, Appt. Files for Judicial Dists., Mo., Morgan L. Smith.

1. John B. Rogers (c1828–1868) was appointed and confirmed as marshal of the eastern district of Missouri in the spring of 1866. Earlier he had seen a variety of action during the Civil War with the 2nd (as colonel) and 11th (as major) Regiments of the Missouri state militia cavalry. *Missouri Democrat* (St. Louis), Nov. 29, 1868; Ser. 6B, Vol. 4: 315, Johnson Papers, LC; CSR, John B. Rogers, RG94, NA.

2. Duble (1812–fl1898) commanded a gunboat fleet on the Ohio, Cumberland, Tennessee, and Mississippi rivers during the Civil War. He got in trouble at Memphis when he assaulted one of Sherman's quartermasters, but Sherman intervened subsequently and averted the arrest of Duble. *Centennial History of Lancaster, Ohio and Lancaster People* (Lancaster, 1898), 129–30.

3. On January 20, 1869, President Johnson nominated Smith as marshal of the eastern district of Missouri. On that same day the nomination was referred to the Judiciary Committee. No action was taken, however, until March 3, the last day of the session, when the Senate decided to lay the nomination upon the table. *Senate Ex. Proceedings*, Vol. 16: 448, 451, 505.

From William W. Wales

Baltimore, Nov 30th 1868

Dear Sir:

It has occurred to me that you can do me a particular favor with little trouble to yourself, in furnishing this office with an advance copy of the Message.

Could you do so I pledge myself that it shall not be used outside in any way until we are telegraphed from Washington that it before the House.

It would enable us to get it into type at our leisure, and by so doing, do it justice, typographically, such as extreme hurry often precludes.[1]

Wm. Wales

ALS, DLC-JP.

1. Johnson refused all requests for advance copies of his annual message, because the previous year the press had printed copies prematurely. *New York Herald*, Dec. 7, 1868. See also Robert E. Withers to Johnson, Dec. 2, 1868.

From Mrs. M. E. Webb[1]

Riceville Tenn   Nove the 30 1868

Mr. Presadent Johnston

I will drop you afew lines as I have sent you two letters but cant get no answer; I think if you would have got them I would have got answer.

I wrote to you my condition wich I hope you got my letter. I and my husband[2] are both invalids and we are broke up as I have told you in both of my other letters. There is an account here on my husbands account book against your son Robbert that he got for himself and his boys when he was make up his regment there in Baboursville Ky;[3] if he is there tell him or give him this letter and I know he will pay it as it is not much but me and my little children is in need of clothing and beding. The account is 75 dollars; Mrs Johnson if you have any Clothing you do not want to ware any more I would thak you for them. I do hope Mr Johnson you will assist me if you please; pleas write and let me know whether you got the letter or not.

Mrs M E Webb

ALS, DLC-JP.

1. Possibly Kentucky native Margaret Webb (b. c1826/1827), a mother of nine who lived in the Barbourville area in 1860. 1850 Census, Tenn., Claiborne, 7th Subdiv., 479; (1860), Ky., Knox, Clear Creek Dist., Cumberland Ford, 179.

2. Margaret Lea married Tennessean Larkin Webb (b. c1814/1815) in 1839 in Claiborne County, Tennessee, where they may have resided until 1850. Ibid.; 1850 Census, Tenn., Claiborne, 7th Subdiv., 479; Edythe Rucker Whitley, comp., *Marriages of Claiborne County, Tennessee, 1838–1850 and Campbell County, Tennessee, 1838–1853* (Baltimore, 1983), 4.

3. Robert Johnson organized the 4th Tenn. Vols. (later the 1st Tenn. Cav.) in the Barbourville area in 1862. William R. Carter, *History of the First Regiment of Tennessee Volunteer Cavalry in the Great War of the Rebellion* (Knoxville, 1902), 19.

December 1868

From Ethan A. Allen

New York   Decr. 1st 1868.

Dear Sir.

I feel under very great obligation to you for your many acts of disinterested friendship & kindness to me & be assured Mr President that I shall regard you as my *best* friend during my life.

I sometime since applied to you for the Consulship to Leeds, England & hoping to get it I have secured some Republican influence in the Senate in case you should have felt inclined to send my name in but I perceive by the Baltimore Sun of 26th ulto. that you have appointed Mr. John Savage to that post.[1] As this crushes my hopes in that direction, may I be permitted to ask of you one other favr. as I am dependent on a salary for support which if you will give me I will again trouble you. Please give me an appointment as *Weigher* in the N. Y. Custom House.

A short time since a Mr G H Shirley[2] a Deputy Naval officer in this Custom House was made a weigher & a Mr Doty,[3] private Secretary of Senator E. D. Morgan appointed in his place (they are both Radicals).

I am *now* an Inspector in the Custom House but the pay is only Four Dollars per day, although for this appointment I am very *thankful to you.*

If I cannot get the position of weigher, please ask Mr. Smythe the Collector to give me some position with about $2500 pr year. I am competent to discharge any duties which may be required of me of which fact Mr Wm. W. Corcoran of Washington will satisfy you & I will refer you to Merchants of this City with whom I have been associated.

You will I hope Mr President excuse my anxiety to procure more lucrative position as you know I have recently been married.[4] Hoping soon to have the pleasure of hearing from you . . .

Ethan A. Allen
Box No. 3534 Post Office

ALS, DNA-RG56, Appts., Customs Service, Subofficer, New York, Ethan A. Allen.

1. See Johnson to William H. Seward, Nov. 11, 1868.

2. George H. Shirley (*fl*1901) had been deputy surveyor previously and continued in his new post of weigher until at least 1885. *U.S. Off. Reg.* (1863–85); New York City directories (1867–1901).

3. Lockwood L. Doty (1827–1873) held a variety of secretarial posts with railroads and New York state government officials, including E. D. Morgan. His tenure as deputy customs collector was apparently brief because he resigned to be Morgan's private secretary. Appointed assessor for the 6th District (New York City) in 1869, he soon resigned due to poor health. *New York Times*, Jan. 20, 1873.

4. Allen married Kate A. Cotte in New York City on November 12. *New York Times*, Nov. 15, 1868.

From Chauncey F. Black
December 1, 1868, York, Pa.; ALS, DLC-JP.

Black is particularly disturbed about the reported intention of Secretary Seward to buy or lease Samana Bay from President Baez of San Domingo. He warns that the United States should not enter into any sort of dealings with that country, particularly in light of the controversy over Alta Vela. This was also the position, argues Black, that the legislatures of Pennsylvania, Maryland, and New Jersey took on the matter. Black then reviews the history of the Alta Vela dispute, referring mainly to the statements made by Jeremiah Black, secretary of state at the time the controversy first erupted. The island belongs to the United States and the guano deposits to Abraham D. Patterson and Prudencio de Murguiondo; only the illegal actions of San Domingo altered that arrangement and agreement. Unfortunately, Seward acquiesced in that disruption. In fact, laments Black, Seward still opposes the claims of Americans *re* Alta Vela. The guano discoverers must be protected in the use and possession of that island.

From Samuel F. Cary
                                   Washington, D.C.   Dec 1st 1868.
Sir—

I ask as a *great personal favor* that you appoint John F. Wiltsee[1] Assessor of my District (the 2d Congl. Dist. of Ohio) in the place of C G. Megrue[2] who was recently commissioned by you vice M P. Gaddis resigned. Mr Wiltsee is one of the substantial business men of Cincinnati, of the purest character, universally esteemed and emminently qualified. His appointment would give entire satisfaction to all who desire to see the duties of the office faithfully discharged. He is a Republican but warmly endorsed my vote on impeachment and worked for my re election. There can be no doubt of his confirmation as he has been for years an *intimate* friend of Genl. Grant.

The course of Mr Megrue since his appointment does not entitle him to your continued confidence, and I respectfully but earnestly protest against your sending his name to the Senate for confirmation. I refer you to accompanying papers.[3]

S F. Cary

ALS, DNA-RG56, Appts., Internal Revenue Service, Assessor, Ohio, 2nd Dist., John F. Wiltsee.

1. Wiltsee (*c*1823–*fl*1881) was an undertaker, captain of home guards in 1861, and a long-time officer of Ohio Mechanics Institute. 1860 Census, Ohio, Hamilton, Cincinnati, 14th Ward, 398; Cincinnati directories (1861–81); *Cincinnati Enquirer*, May 4, 1861; Henry A. and Kate B. Ford, *History of Cincinnati, Ohio* (Cleveland, 1881), 228.

2. Conduce G. Megrue (*c*1831–1890), a bookkeeper before the war, was captain and major in the 4th Ohio Cav., USA (1861–63). Sometime after 1870 he moved to New York City. Pension Records, Anna Megrue, RG15, NA; Cincinnati directories (1861–70); *Off. Army Reg.: Vols.*, 5: 7.

3. This letter represents a turnaround in Cary's support for a new assessor of the 2nd district. On September 2 he sent a telegram that "Megrue is the right man for assessor vice gaddis." Megrue was nominated for the permanent assessor position on December 18, 1868, and confirmed January 5, 1869. But he was apparently quickly replaced by the Grant administration. Cary et al. to Johnson, Sept. 2, 1868, Appts., Internal Revenue Service, Assessor, Ohio, 2nd Dist., C. G. Megrue, RG56, NA; Ser. 6B, Vol. 4: 262, Johnson Papers, LC; *U.S. Off. Reg.* (1869). See John C. Crane to Johnson, Dec. 17, 1868, in support of Megrue.

From Alvan C. Gillem

Vicksburg, Miss.   Dec. 1. 1868.

Dear Sir.

Allow me to present to your favorable consideration my friend Judge Jeffords[1] of the High Court of Errors and Appeals of Mississippi. The ability, integrity and freedom from political prejudice which has characterized the conduct of Judge Jeffords has secured for him the confidence of the people of Mississippi. Any statement made by Judge Jeffords is intitled to implicit confidence.

Alvan C Gillem

ALS, DLC-JP.

1. Elza Jeffords (1826–1885) was an Ohio lawyer who served as a quartermaster's clerk in the Army of the Tennessee during the Civil War. He was judge of the state high court (1868–69). Active in Republican party politics, he was elected to the U.S. House and served one term in the 1880s. *BDUSC*.

From Jacob J. Noah

Nashville Tenn   Dec 1st 1868

Nomination urged by Senator Fowler and my brother[1] will materially aid my retention & be personal obligation.[2]

J J Noah

Tel, DLC-JP.

1. Senator Joseph S. Fowler and Lionel J. Noah.

2. Perhaps a reference to Noah's nomination as supervisor of internal revenue for Tennessee, a post from which he resigned in June 1869. Noah had been nominated as U.S. attorney for Middle Tennessee in July 1868 but rejected by the Senate later that same month. See Edward H. East to Johnson, May 15, 1867, *Johnson Papers*, 12: 270; *Nashville Republican Banner*, June 27, 1869.

From Philo Durfee

New York   Decr. 2d 1868

My dear Sir

Mr Fullerton will probably visit you tomorrow on the subject of Internal Revenue frauds.[1] I want to say to you that Mr Fullerton is *honest* & *capable*. I hope you will sustain him and I know in doing so, you will be sustained by the people and discharge a duty to the Country that will bring you support hereafter.

You will I hope draw up this hot bed of curruption in the collection of the Revenue before you leave—no matter upon *whom it falls do it.*

I will try to see you next week.[2] Dont appoint in Courtneys place (Dist' Attorney)[3] now or until I see you. If I can do you any service here write me.

Philo Durfee

P. O. 4466

ALS, DLC-JP.

1. William Fullerton tried unsuccessfully to meet with Johnson the following week. See Fullerton to Johnson, Dec. 18, 1868.

2. There is no indication Durfee visited Washington or met with Johnson.

3. Rumors were circulating that Samuel G. Courtney might be removed, although this did not happen. See N. E. Paine to Johnson, Nov. 15, 1868; James R. Doolittle to Johnson, Dec. 3, 1868; and William Fullerton to Johnson, Dec. 18, 1868.

From Robert E. Withers[1]

Lynchburg, Dec. 2, 1868

Dear Sir—

If it be your intention to furnish copies of your Message to the Press, in advance of its delivery to Congress, I would take it as an especial favor that a copy be sent me for publication in the "News" of this city.[2]

Hoping to have a favorable answer, and with every assurance of my profound respect . . .

R. E. Withers
Editor Lynchburg Daily "News."

ALS, DLC-JP.

1. Withers (1821–1907), a native Virginian and physician, served with the Confederacy and was colonel of the 18th Va. Inf. Immediately after the war he established the *Lynchburg News*. Later he was elected lieutenant governor of Virginia (1873), served one term as U.S. Senator (1875–81), and afterwards was U.S. consul at Hong Kong (1885–89). *BDUSC*.

2. Johnson refused all such requests. *New York Herald*, Dec. 7, 1868. See also William W. Wales to Johnson, Nov. 30, 1868.

From James R. Doolittle

Private

New-York, Dec 3rd 1868

Dear Sir:

Stand fast by Fullerton. Courtney took the Dist. Atty's office poor 3 years ago, lives in a Brown Stone House worth $40,000, and is reputed very rich.[1]

His associates are Shook & Dittenhoffer[2] and Whisky Ring men generally.

The office is not worth over $12,000, a year in the hands of an honest man. The asst Dist Attorney Ethan Allen[3] who has done all the business of the office except the Internal Revenue business, is a much abler man, and a man of undoubted integrity.[4] Appoint him and then with Fullerton you will lay bare the infernal scoundrelism of the officials in connection with the Whiskey frauds upon the Revenue.

In any matter of this kind Mr President I speak only for the country and for the integrity of the Administration.

I have most serious apprehensions that the Whisky Ring reaches high officials at Washington.[5]

J. R. Doolittle

ALS, DLC-JP.
1. See N. E. Paine to Johnson, Nov. 15, 1868, and George W. Greene to Johnson, Nov. 26, 1868.
2. Sheridan Shook and Abraham Dittenhoefer. A high-ranking member of the state's Republican party, Shook (1828–1899), who began as a produce merchant, served as collector of internal revenue before moving into the theatre and brewing businesses. Dittenhoefer (1835–1919), a lawyer, served briefly as a justice of the city court. He became prominent for his career as counsel to actors and theatre. *New York Times*, Apr. 28, 1899, Feb. 24, 1919.
3. This Ethan Allen (no relation to Ethan A. Allen, also a New York City resident) served as assistant district attorney after an earlier career in journalism. See *Johnson Papers*, 13: 520.
4. At least one newspaper did mention Allen as a possible successor, should Courtney be removed. Courtney, however, remained in office. *Washington Evening Star*, Dec. 14, 1868.
5. Some suspected that Commissioner of Internal Revenue Edward A. Rollins, and possibly even Treasury Secretary Hugh McCulloch, were involved in thwarting revenue fraud investigations. See John M. Binckley to Johnson, Nov. 5, 1868, and John H. Gilmer to Johnson, Nov. 11, 1868.

From James B. Olney[1]

Catskill, N.Y., Dec. 4 1868

Sir—

Permit me to say a few words to you relating to the vacancy in the office of the Assessorship of this the 13th District of the State of New York.

It is of the utmost importance to the business and political interests of this community that the vacancy be filled at the coming session of Congress—in order that the interests of the Internal Revenue Department of the government may be fully protected.

Mr. J. At. Cooke[2] is now the acting assessor—but the duties & responsibilities of the office in fact fall upon Mr. F. J. Fitch,[3] long an assistant in the office, & in whose behalf I wish your favorable consideration.

He is a gentleman of ability, a lawyer of conceded reputation in the District, for Eleven years county Judge of the County & whose long familiarity with the duties, & details of each & every department of the revenue service eminently fit him for the performance of the functions of the assessorship. I believe that the loss of his services at this time in view of the many changes which the Revenue laws have undergone, & the numerous adjudications of the Department in regard to the various questions continually arising under the Revenue Laws, would greatly inconvenience and for a long time embarass the collection of the revenue in this District.

Allow me further to say that Mr. Fitchs' character is above reproach, his habits are good, & he is a gentleman of refinement.

During the war, he was a firm supporter of the government in its warfare against Secession & *after* its termination, he was a bold & unflinching advocate of the policy which your Excellency pursued toward the South, being a delegate from this County to the Saratoga Convention which sent delegates to the memorable Philadelphia Convention of 1866.

His appointment to the office of assessor will be satisfactory to the people and business interests of the District.

I have reason to believe that his nomination to that office by you will be confirmed by the Senate.

I trust that his claims to the position will be favorably considered by your Excellency & that he will be appointed.[4]

Jas B Olney

ALS, DNA-RG56, Appts., Internal Revenue Service, Assessor, N.Y., 13th Dist., F. James Fitch.

1. Olney (1833–*fl*1884), an attorney, was the district attorney of Greene County, New York, at the beginning of the Civil War. In 1883 he was elected supervisor of the town of Catskill. *History of Greene County, New York* (New York, 1884), 148–49.

2. In the 1850s J. Atwater Cooke (b. *c*1819) had been a state representative, county clerk, and supervisor of Catskill. Ibid., 51, 122; 1860 Census, N.Y., Greene, Catskill, 576.

3. F. James Fitch (b. *c*1820), a lawyer, had been supervisor of Prattsville (1852) and the county judge of common pleas (1855–63). Ibid., 542; *Greene County, N.Y.*, 34, 36, 381.

4. Johnson did not nominate or appoint Fitch to the assessor's post. Instead, he successfully nominated George H. Penfield in January 1869, whose appointment was confirmed by the Senate in March. *Senate Ex. Proceedings*, Vol. 16: 417, 426, 502.

From Andrew J. Wilcox
"Private and Confidential"

Baltimore   Dec 4th 1868

Mr President

I *beg* of you to do me the very great personal favor *if at all now possible* to make no allusion whatever in your next message to Congress either to me, the letters, or the subject matter of the letters that I have written.[1] In view of the enormous demoralization in every thing, everwhere, and in every place I thought the "times were fully ripe" for a *great and decided reform* and thought that it could be best and most successfully instituted by the Goverment of the United States, the initiatory movement of which was to be the withdrawal of the late Presidential Candidates, the last of those letters were predicated upon this withdrawal, which I and I may say almost every one supposed was an accomplished fact. I viewed the future from that stand point and based my arguments and letters thereupon, but as the Electoral College has now cast its vote and a majority of that vote is for Gen Grant, and he is beyond peradventure, the President of the United States for the next four years at least I find that my presumptions in regard to that matter were wrongly founded, therefore the support of those of my letters since the one advocating that step has fallen and it is my earnest desire that all should fall together in the same chaos and obscurity, and that Gen Grant and the present and next Congress, the majority of whom claim to be his special friends shall have the full benefit of their own views and policy which is no doubt now settled upon and will be strictly adhered to anything that either Your Excellency or myself may say to the contrary notwithstanding, therefore any effort to influence that policy would only be "Kicking against the pricks" or "Casting pearls before swine" or at the most "mixing water with wine," as they "have sown to the wind so let them reapt the whirlwind." But that a merciful God "will temper the wind" the result of their policy "to the shorn lamb" the people of this Country is the earnest fervent prayer of . . .

Andrew J. Wilcox

ALS, DLC-JP.

1. A somewhat prolific writer of letters to Johnson, Wilcox probably refers here to his more recent ones, such as Wilcox to Johnson, Nov. 21, 1868, Johnson Papers, LC; and Wilcox to Johnson, Sept. 18, Nov. 6, 1868.

From Harriet H. Camp[1]

Washington   Dec 5th 1868.

Dear Sir.

I will not trouble you by coming in person to express my gratitude, for words would fail me should I make the attempt; but will resort to the medium of the pen to express my many, many thanks for your kindness to me, a debt of gratitude which I should have acknowledged long ago, could I have learned positively that I was correct in my suspicions, but as another took the credit to himself, I was left in doubt, which is the only cause of my delinquency.

My heart swells with gratitude when I think of the kindness you and your family have ever shown me, but most of all, for the *assistance* rendered me and my sister[2] since our acquaintance with you.

I feel much more than I can find words to express, and realize that it is a feeble attempt I have made to express to you my gratitude, but trust you will make due allowance, knowing it is for the want of ability that I fail.

Miss H. H. Camp.

ALS, DLC-JP.

1. Camp (*c*1830–*fl*1889), a native of Vermont, lived for a time in Greeneville, Tennessee, where she worked as a teacher. She eventually secured an appointment in Washington as a clerk in the Register's office. In the 1880s she was listed as one of the proprietors of a boarding house in Montpelier, Vermont. 1850 Census, Vt., Washington, Montpelier, 372; (1860), Tenn., Greene, 10th Dist., Greeneville, 87; Washington, D.C., directories (1867–69); *U.S. Off. Reg.* (1867); *Gazette of Washington County, Vt., 1783–1889* (Syracuse, 1889), 121.

2. The sister's name was rendered variously as Emerline, Emlen, and Emma Camp (*c*1834–*fl*1889). Like her sister, Harriet, she taught for a time in Greeneville and moved afterwards to Washington, where she became a clerk in the Dead Letter Office of the Post Office. Along with Harriet and other relatives, she owned a boarding house in Montpelier, Vermont, in the 1880s. Ibid.; *U.S. Off. Reg.* (1867–71); 1850 Census, Vt., Washington, Montpelier, 372; (1860), Tenn., Greene, 10th Dist., Greeneville, 87.

From John F. Coyle

Washington, Dec 5, 1868.

Mr. President:

As there seems to be an evident disposition to create public opinion in favor of the Union Pacific Railroad Company, in their demands for full payment of the Government subsidy due them on the completion of the road, and against what is beleived to be your action to protect the interest of the public by insuring a first class road;— and desiring to write understandingly upon this subject which is now attracting so much attention, and maintain this and another evidence of your devotion to the rights of the people, we request you will allow us access to the full report of the commission headed by General Warren and also the report of General Williams.[1]

The synopsis of the Commissioners report which has been furnished to the Press is not sufficiently full or fair to justify us in basing an article upon it. I will call if you desire and obtain these reports or send a Gentleman in our employ, (confidentially) to make such extracts from them as will enable us to commend your action, and do justice to the public interest, which is so involved in the proper completion of this Great National Enterprise.[2]

John F. Coyle

ALS, DLC-JP.

1. During the summer of 1868 Jesse L. Williams had reported on deficiencies in the construction of the Union Pacific Railroad. This was followed by an investigation by a three-man committee, including Gouverneur K. Warren, which reported on even more problems. See Thomas C. Durant to Johnson, Oct. 11, 29, 1868; Robert W. Latham to Johnson, Nov. 23, 1868. See also Orville Browning to Johnson, Dec. 5, 1868, Johnson Papers, LC.

2. On December 7, 1868, the *National Intelligencer* printed an article titled "Pacific Railroad," which discussed the standards for the railroad, established in 1866, and the ways in which the ballast, bridges, rails, and ties, among other things, did not meet these standards. There is sufficient detail in the article to suggest that Johnson probably granted someone the requested access.

From Thomas B. Florence

December 5 1868
2. P.M

My Dear Sir,

The Assessorship of Internal Revenue in the Second District of Pennsylvania IS VACANT by the DEATH of the late incumbent.[1]

I desire the position. If you will assent to it, the Secretary of the Treasury will send the Commission to you to day.[2]

I need the place very, very much. It will last over three months and if given me will be a GOD SEND.

Thomas B. Florence

ALS, DLC-JP.

1. Clifford S. Phillips (c1808–1868) died at his residence on December 3 as a result of accidental gunshot wounds received while on an expedition in Maryland. *Philadelphia Evening Bulletin*, Dec. 2, 3, 1868.

2. The President immediately gave a temporary appointment to Florence to replace the deceased Phillips. Evidently, Florence received quick assurances that he would get the appointment, for fifteen minutes after he wrote the letter published here, he wrote another one thanking Johnson for the appointment! But the formal nomination for permanent appointment was not made until January 13, 1869. Florence's nomination was referred to the Senate Finance Committee on January 19 but no final action was taken on it before the session ended. *Philadelphia Press*, Dec. 7, 1868; Ser. 6B, Vol. 4: 91, Johnson Papers, LC; Florence to Johnson, Dec. 5, 1868, Johnson Papers, LC; *Senate Ex. Proceedings*, Vol. 16: 430, 442.

From Robert W. Johnson

Dec 5th 1868

I certify that the above is a copy of the Original in my hands, just recd.:[1] and that James Timms,[2] the writer, is a Northern man, & was loyal & true to the United States during all the Secession Rebellion: that he is a former citizen from Pittsburg or the vicinity; that he has been engaged for full 20 years, in trade, commerce, & transportation between the Ports on the Ohio & the Ark River Valley & Towns & well known to me all the time; & for the last eight or ten years has made his home & investments in Little Rock & Ark. That he commands universal esteem & respect—, always as an active & honest man of business, now fully 60 yrs of age; & is entitled to be believed, with or without oath.

R. W. Johnson.

AES, DNA-RG107, Lets. Recd., Executive (M494, Roll 109).

1. "The above" was a letter from James Timms of Little Rock, dated November 25, 1868, in which he lamented that "our people are paralyzed or powerless" to protect their property and lives against the marauding state militia. If the people act in self-defense Congress may consider them as "Outlaws and Traitors." Timms wanted the recipient of his letter (not specified) to urge Andrew Johnson to protect the citizens from the militia. Robert W. Johnson wrote his note at the end of Timms's letter. James Timms to unknown, Nov. 25, 1868, Lets. Recd., Executive (M494, Roll 109), RG107, NA.

2. Timms (c1812–1869), a native of Virginia, was a steamboat captain who, since 1845, operated boats on the Arkansas and Mississippi rivers. After occupation of Arkansas by Union troops, Timms headed south, eventually to Mexico. He returned at war's end and became the owner of a gas works in Little Rock. *Arkansas Gazette* (Little Rock), Oct. 20, 1869.

From Simeon M. Johnson

Washn.   Dec 5. 1868

My dear Sir—

It appears to me I can be of some service in Newyork in connection with the Fullerton complications,[1] and I propose to go tomorrow night. I would like to see you a moment on the subject before I go,[2] not to get authority to act for you or speak for you, but to be sure in advising for myself, I am not advising against your policy. In truth, I doubt the policy of a too rigid enforcement of penalties, under the Revenue laws, in the face of the fact (alleged) that so many revenue officers, have instructed persons to commit frauds; and in many cases, doubtless, *been paid* for it. I fear the Fullerton proceeding has merely created a fierce controversy, which has served to stimulate special prosecutions; and so I thought, perhaps, I might do something as aid of justice by going to Newyork.[3]

S. M. Johnson

ALS, DLC-JP.

1. William Fullerton. See James R. Doolittle to Johnson, Dec. 3, 1868.

2. No evidence of a meeting has been found.

3. Evidently, Simeon Johnson did get to New York City sometime in December, for one of the newspapers there reported his residence at a hotel. See the *New York Herald*, Dec. 21, 1868.

From Jacob W. Morgan[1]

St Louis Mo   Dec 5 1868

Judge Treat[2] authorizes me to say my appointment as Marshal will be satisfactory so also the entire bar of St Louis with few exceptions.

J W Morgan

Tel, DLC-JP.

1. Morgan (*c*1823–*fl*1870), a native of Delaware, had been deputy U.S. marshal for the eastern district of Missouri for a few years. Evidently he served as acting marshal in 1869. In early February, he wrote to Johnson asking that his name be forwarded to the Senate for appointment as marshal, given that Morgan L. Smith could not be confirmed. However, in 1870 he was still deputy marshal. St. Louis directories (1866–69); 1870 Census, Mo., St. Louis, Carondelet City, 128; Morgan to Johnson, Feb. 3, 1869, Johnson Papers, LC.

2. Samuel Treat (1815–1902) served as federal district judge in Missouri for thirty years (1857–87). He was also one of the founders of Washington University in St. Louis. *DAB*.

From George S. Fisher[1]

Buffalo   Dec. 7. 1868

Sire

I beg to lay before you the fact that on November 26th 1866 by the burning of the Consulate at Kanagawa, Japan, I met with severe personal loss.[2]

The fire was purely accidental and such as could neither be guarded against by Insurance or otherwise.

By the greatest personal danger and efforts I saved all the public property books and papers of the Consulate—as well as my own law library therein—but the believed fire proof Japanese Government building in which they were placed also soon afterwards took fire & burned destroying everything within it.

The fire was specially detailed to the State Department and the loss sworn to is on file before the Senate, I believe referred to the Hon. Committee on Commerce.

I asked Mr. Secretary Seward to make the same recommendation in my case that he proposed in the alternative to do to Congress when the Legation was burned up in Yedo in 1863,[3] for Minister Pruyn, but he peremptorily refused.

You, perhaps, also know (though you may not) how through Mr. Scty Seward, Mr Pruyn finally got an indemnity of $10,000 Mexicans—then equal to $20,000 United States Currency out of the Japanese Government for his loss by that fire—not to be compared in value to my law library alone—as well as have heard something of the immense jobbing operation between Mr. Pruyn, Mr. Seward and the Japanese Govt, whereby they have realized between them scarcely less than $600,000 to $800,000 more.

If not, with your leave I propose to put these matters in such shape as shall make them—the whole facts—as clear as a sun beam, and lay before you & the world the most astounding revelations if not outrageous ministerial jobbing operations ever perpetrated by public Ministers of this or any other Government, and one that I believe is incomparable and as huge as it is disgraceful to our true policy towards the Japanese of all other foreign nations. No page of history to my knowledge reveals such scheming and immense money making out of an innocent people & Government by foreign Ministers and no paralell to its audacity & cuningly covered up wrong from its inception in 1862 to the termination of the Imperial Commissioners work in 1867, (and specially & only sent on by the Japanese Government to get its contracted ships or money back,)[4] can probably be found among a civilized not to say christianized nation, and certainly not in all our diplomatic intercourse from the organization of our Government to the present date.

In the matter of my own actual loss I only ask Congress to do just as it has in numerous instances for Military & Naval officers paymasters, soldiers and sailors in cases of losses by ship-wrecks, fire, and robbery, believing that civil officers in the service of our Government in Foreign Countries where they cannot insure against loss by fire floods &c have claims upon the Government equal in every respects with those in the Military & Naval service and that justice may only be done to me and mine.

If proper, I ask therefore, as the Secretary of State has refused, that the President will simply recommend the adjustment and payment of my just loss, whatever it may be found to be, in the same way as similar losses have been under acts of Congress heretofore appropriated and paid to our Military & Naval officers & men for their personal losses.[5]

Geo. S. Fisher

ALS, DNA-RG59, Misc. Lets., 1789–1906 (M179, Roll 292).

1. Fisher (c1823–fl1896), an Ottawa, Illinois, banker and lawyer, lived in San Francisco before serving as consul at Kanagawa in the 1860s, and as a diplomat at Beirut, Turkey, in the 1870s. Afterwards he resided in Washington, D.C. 1850 Census, Ill., LaSalle, Ottawa, 180; Washington, D.C., directories (1877–96); Elmer Baldwin, *History of LaSalle County, Illinois* (Chicago, 1877), 250; *History of LaSalle County, Illinois* (2 vols., Chicago, 1886), 1: 522; *NUC*; J. M. Sturtevant to Abraham Lincoln, June 4, 1861, Lets. of Appl. and Recomm., 1861–69 (M650, Roll 17), George S. Fisher, RG59, NA; *House Reports*, 46 Cong., 2 Sess., No. 1258 (Ser. 1937); *Senate Misc. Docs.*, 51 Cong., 1 Sess., No. 91, pp. 1–2 (Ser. 2698).

2. According to reports, Fisher lost all of his personal belongings, furniture, clothing, etc., as well as his law library in the fires. *House Reports*, 42 Cong., 3 Sess., No. 9, pp. 1–2 (Ser. 1576).

3. For an account of the 1863 disturbances at Yedo during Robert H. Pruyn's tenure, see Van Deusen, *Seward*, 519–20.

4. Undoubtedly a reference to the visit by two Japanese commissioners to the United States in 1867. The purposes of the trip were to purchase a warship from the United States (which was accomplished) and to negotiate a compromise settlement over the earlier prices paid to Pruyn and others for the ship, *Fusiyama*. Seward agreed to refund the Japanese a half million dollars on the original price of the *Fusiyama*. Ibid., 521.

5. Fisher's attempts to be reimbursed for his losses in 1866 dragged on for years. In 1873, for example, the House Committee on Foreign Affairs recommended that Fisher be compensated $4,000 for his losses. But seven years later the Committee urged rejection of the bill to compensate Fisher. In 1890 Congress was still dealing with the Fisher claim. Early in that year Fisher presented a petition to Congress still seeking compensation; but in the summer the House Committee on Foreign Affairs issued an adverse report on the matter. *House Reports*, 42 Cong., 3 Sess., No. 9, pp. 1–2 (Ser. 1576); 46 Cong., 2 Sess., No. 1258 (Ser. 1937); 51 Cong., 1 Sess., No,. 2797 (Ser. 2815); *Senate Misc. Docs.*, 51 Cong., 1 Sess., No. 91, pp. 1–2 (Ser. 2698).

From Augustus H. Garland

Little Rock, Ark., Decr. 7th 1868

Mr. President:

Our state is in a most critical condition at this time. I have never known it worse at any time in our history. Of this, in great measure, you must have already been informed. It is not worth while now to criticise the acts or motives of the one man or the other—of one party or the other, but the fact is, if something is not done it will not be long before we will be in open & active collision here. The Governor[1] has called out his militia to put down insurrections where I am satisfied none exist, and in several counties he has declared martial law, where, to say nothing of his authority to do this in any event, there is, in fact, as much necessity for such a step as there would be to declare martial law in Washington City. With all this, the Governor will not hear any complaints or petitions from our people only through the militia officers here & there in the state, and all offers & efforts made by them (the people) to come to a proper understanding with the Governor, & the authorities are vain & futile, & we are actually without relief in every possible shape.

Doubtless there have been acts of violence and infractions of the law, but I do know every one of them could have been disposed of by agencies of the civil law as well & in fact better than by the means here resorted to. And indeed immediately after the election on 3d. ult without appealing to the people in a friendly & amicable manner, and without invoking the aid of the civil law, martial law is at once proclaimed over some ten counties, and the militia is sent into places where all was peace & quiet, and our people absolutely do not know what they can or should do. Affairs are in an alarming condition. If insurrection exists here can not the U S authorities take hold of the matter & send troops here? They would be hailed with joy by our people, and they would, by their very presence, quiet matters, if there is trouble. I beseech you, Mr. President, to look into this, & to take some steps to avert this coming thing. I feel satisfied that the U S military commander here[2] sees no necessity for this, & that he would confirm what I here state to you.

As a sample of what our people offer, & are willing to do, I send you a slip with an address[3] of some of our prominent men as delegates from their counties, calling on their people to conform to the requirements of the Governor here—and sent the offer & tender on all sides & by all persons.

And I am as well satisfied as I can be of anything, that his facts are not *facts*, and that he is mistaken & has been imposed upon.

True, or false however, the great damage is progressing, and in my humble judgment, if this thing continues his works longer bloodshed, war & anarchy all over this state will be the consequence. And I appeal to you in the name of every high & patriotic consideration to move at once in correcting these things, otherwise they will correct themselves in a manner that will be so terrible to behold.

A. H. Garland

PS—The letter of Dr. L T. Cully[4] herewith sent is from an old &

highly respected citizen. It has just come to hand, & is but one of hundreds of a like character that we receive here daily.

A. H. Garland

ALS, DNA-RG107, Lets. Recd., Executive (M494, Roll 109).

1. Powell Clayton.

2. Charles H. Smith.

3. Enclosed is a published letter, dated December 3, to the people of Arkansas from prominent representatives from five different counties. They had conferred with the governor who assured them that it was absolutely necessary to send militia into various counties in order to ensure peace. The letter writers urge the people to cooperate.

4. Lewis T. Culley (c1806–fl1870) was a physician and farmer. Culley's letter is found enclosed. Dated December 2, the letter is addressed to Garland and two other men. Culley reports on atrocities committed by Governor Clayton's militiamen, and says that a delegation has been sent to Washington to seek U.S. troops for the region's protection. Culley asks for help from all Arkansas citizens. 1850 Census, Ark., Hempstead, Saline Twp., 502; (1860), Lafayette, Red River Twp., Rondo, 104; (1870), 17.

From William A. Garner

Nashville, Dec. 7th 1868

Dear Sir

On Saturday 9 A.m. at Lesters Station in Giles County—Tenn. an armed mounted masked Klan of 25 or 30 men: Broke into Capt Kings House[1] and Robed Him of Him Arms attempted to Rob Gen. Harrison[2] but He resisted and a fight began which was kept for Some time late at Night. They Had His House surrounded, I do not Know what has been finally done; but Mr. President I fear that these Good men have as hundreds of other good men have been in our state assassinated: These are the very best of citizens and at the mercy of a band of assassins. The organization is a powerful one most dangerous in its character continuously committing of depidations in many counties in the state. Some thing must be done and that soon or your Excellency may Expect to hear of serious crimes from Tennessee.

These bands are to be put down And I do not see how it can be done by the Civil authorities of the state. Hoping that your Excellency will take some steps to crush them out.

I close as your friend and fellow Citizen.

W. A. Garner

ALS, DLC-JP.

1. John W. King (1826–1910) was captain in the 4th Ohio Cav. (1861–64). After the war, he was a farmer in Giles County but eventually returned to Ohio. Newspapers carried accounts of the December 5 Klan attack in Giles. 1870 Census, Tenn., Giles, 2nd Civil Dist., Pulaski, 10; Pension Records, John W. King, RG15, NA; *Off. Army Reg: Vols.*, 5: 7; *Pulaski Citizen*, Dec. 11, 25, 1868; *Nashville Press and Times*, Dec. 7, 8, 12, 1868.

2. Thomas J. Harrison (1824–1871), a lawyer in Indiana before the war, became a farmer in Giles County afterwards. Later he served as U.S. marshal for the Middle Tennessee district. Hunt and Brown, *Brigadier Generals*; *Nashville Union and American*, Sept. 29, 1871.

From John A. McClernand

Springfield, Ill.   December 7th 1868.

Gen. Edwin S. McCook whom you caused to be appointed Collector of Internal Revenue for this District[1] and who, I think, has discharged his duty faithfully, has some apprehensions that a movement has been inaugurated for his removal. I trust, he will be retained unless for cause to the contrary. It may be that in the discharge of his duty, he was brought into disagreeable contact with some of his original surities—resulting in the giving of a new bond. I think if there is any trouble he is entirely prepared, satisfactorily, to explain it.[2]

John A. McClernand.

ALS, DNA-RG56, Appts., Internal Revenue Service, Collector, Ill., 8th Dist., E. S. McCook.

1. Initially nominated for the collectorship of the 8th district in Illinois on January 20, 1868, McCook's name was withdrawn four days later. However, when he was renominated on July 13, McCook was confirmed and commissioned on the same day. Ser. 6B, Vol. 4: 305, Johnson Papers, LC.

2. There is no evidence of any attempt to remove McCook during the rest of Johnson's term; however, by the fall of 1869 he had been replaced by a Grant nominee. Ibid.; *U.S. Off. Reg.* (1869).

From Edmund G. Ross

Personal

Washington. Dec 8 1868

Dear Sir

I desire to make application for a leave of absence for Gov. R. B. Mitchell of New Mexico to take effect on the 1st of January next. I have some railroad projects in mind in which his Territory as well as the West generally, is deeply interested & I very much desire that he should be here to assist them.[1]

E. G. Ross

ALS, NRU.

1. Mitchell received permission for a two-month leave beginning December 11, 1868. However, he did not actually decide to take it until February 4, 1869, when he abruptly departed for Washington, D.C., in a move designed partly to keep his territorial secretary, H. H. Heath, from taking his own leave. Mitchell subsequently resigned his office on March 30, but had to return to New Mexico to continue as governor until a qualified successor arrived in August. Calvin Horn, *New Mexico's Troubled Years: The Story of the Early Territorial Governors* (Albuquerque, 1963), 129–31.

From Moses N. Wisewell

Washington D.C.   Dec. 8th 1868

Mr President.

I have on file an application to be appointed Commissioner of Internal Revenue, in the success of which, I conceive that not I alone, but the Administration, and the whole country have a deep interest. You will agree, that I come before you, with as numerous, and as responsible endorsers, as perhaps any applicant for office ever had. But in addition to this strong and general support from all classes of men, in all parts of the country, I deem it eminently proper, that I should disclose to you without reserve, the considerations which have induced me to encourage an effort so extensive, and formidable in my behalf.

I am sincerely, honestly, and earnestly, your friend. Your friend, because I believe you are the only man living, who has the power, and with it the will, to save the country from impending ruin. And if you desire to clothe your arm with power to strike an effective blow, as well for the relief of the burdened people, as for yourself; your friends can see, no place where you can begin, with a better prospect of success, than with the head of the Internal Revenue Bureau.

As it is, the Treasury is losing annually, millions upon millions of dollars, by the collusion of corrupt officials, with dishonest manufacturers and dealers. Upon whose head must the suffering public visit the guilt of these enormous crimes? A people, who are already so maddened with the weight of taxation, and official corruption, as to discuss without a tinge of shame, the propriety of repudiation, will have no doubtful answer to these very reasonable questions. Accordingly Mr. McCulloch, by indirection, Mr Rollins in his sworn testimony, and the whole Radical party, with one voice, lay the responsibility at your door. But Sir, you have it in your power to furnish a practical, unmistakable, and crushing reply, by removing the present incumbent, and putting in his room a man who *will* collect the Revenue, *strike down the thieves,* and administer his great office for the benefit of the Treasury, and the country. You have then delivered the nation from the "body of this death" which consumes the substance, and debauches the morals of the people. You are then fairly in the field with that rallying cry always welcome to the people but doubly welcome now, *reform, economy, and official integrity.* This one thing alone will give you the unlimited confidence of the people, and enable you to accomplish your great purpose, of restoring the Union, and all its parts, to the Government of the Constitution. I have studied with great care the laws relating to the Internal Revenue, and the machinery by which it operates, with a view to see whether the nature of the system itself permitted the complete, and radical reformation which I contemplated. I am absolutely certain Mr President that I can achieve it, and if you should chance to agree with me, I want no more splendid opportunity of signalizing my name, in the annals of the time, or of serving the cause of good good government, and Constitutional principals.

This is my sole ambition, and furnishes the only apology, for the application now before you. Should I be appointed, I shall hand you my resignation to take effect when accepted; expecting that it will be accepted, should I prove recreant to the views or fail to acomplish the results herein set forth.

M. N Wisewell

ALS, DLC-JP.

Fourth Annual Message

WASHINGTON, *December 9, 1868.*
Fellow-Citizens of the Senate and House of Representatives:

Upon the reassembling of Congress it again becomes my duty to call your attention to the state of the Union and to its continued disorganized condition under the various laws which have been passed upon the subject of reconstruction.

It may be safely assumed as an axiom in the government of states that the greatest wrongs inflicted upon a people are caused by unjust and arbitrary legislation, or by the unrelenting decrees of despotic rulers, and that the timely revocation of injurious and oppressive measures is the greatest good that can be conferred upon a nation.

The legislator or ruler who has the wisdom and magnanimity to retrace his steps when convinced of error will sooner or later be rewarded with the respect and gratitude of an intelligent and patriotic people.

Our own history, although embracing a period less than a century, affords abundant proof that most, if not all, of our domestic troubles are directly traceable to violations of the organic law and excessive legislation. The most striking illustrations of this fact are furnished by the enactments of the past three years upon the question of reconstruction. After a fair trial they have substantially failed and proved pernicious in their results, and there seems to be no good reason why they should longer remain upon the statute book. States to which the Constitution guarantees a republican form of government have been reduced to military dependencies, in each of which the people have been made subject to the arbitrary will of the commanding general. Although the Constitution requires that each State shall be represented in Congress, Virginia, Mississippi, and Texas are yet excluded from the two Houses, and, contrary to the express provisions of that instrument, were denied participation in the recent election for a President and Vice-President of the United States. The attempt to place the white population under the domination of persons of color in the South has impaired, if not destroyed, the kindly relations that had previously existed between them; and mutual distrust has engendered a feeling of animosity which, leading in some instances to collision and bloodshed, has prevented that cooperation between the two races so essential to the success of industrial enterprise in the Southern States. Nor have the inhabitants of those States alone suffered from the disturbed condition of affairs growing out of these Congressional enactments. The entire Union has been agitated by grave apprehensions of troubles which might again involve the peace of the nation; its interests have been injuriously affected by the derangement of business and labor, and the consequent want of prosperity throughout that portion of the country.

The Federal Constitution—the *magna charta* of American rights, under whose wise and salutary provisions we have successfully conducted all our domestic and foreign affairs, sustained ourselves in peace and in war, and become a great nation among the powers of the earth—must assuredly be now adequate to the settlement of questions growing out of the civil war, waged alone for its vindication. This great fact is made most manifest by the condition of the country when Congress assembled in the month of December, 1865. Civil strife had ceased, the spirit of rebellion had spent its entire force, in the Southern States the people had warmed into national life, and throughout the whole country a healthy reaction in public sentiment had taken place. By the application of the simple yet effective provisions of the Constitution the executive department, with the voluntary aid of the States, had brought the work of restoration as near completion as was within the scope of its authority, and the nation was encouraged by the prospect of an early and satisfactory adjustment of all its difficulties. Congress, however, intervened, and, refusing to perfect the work so nearly consummated, declined to admit members from the unrepresented States, adopted a series of measures which arrested the progress of restoration, frustrated all that had been so successfully accomplished, and, after three years of agitation and strife, has left the country further from the attainment of union and fraternal feeling than at the inception of the Congressional plan of reconstruction. It needs no argument to show that legislation which has produced such baneful consequences should be abrogated, or else made to conform to the genuine principles of republican government.

Under the influence of party passion and sectional prejudice, other acts have been passed not warranted by the Constitution. Congress has already been made familiar with my views respecting the "tenure-of-office bill."[1] Experience has proved that its repeal is demanded by the best interests of the country, and that while it remains in force the President can not enjoin that rigid accountability of public officers so essential to an honest and efficient execution of the laws. Its revocation would enable the executive department to exercise the power of appointment and removal in accordance with the original design of the Federal Constitution.

The act of March 2, 1867, making appropriations for the support of the Army for the year ending June 30, 1868, and for other purposes, contains provisions which interfere with the President's constitutional functions as Commander in Chief of the Army and deny to States of the Union the right to protect themselves by means of their own militia.[2] These provisions should be at once annulled; for while the first might, in times of great emergency, seriously embarrass the Executive in efforts to employ and direct the common strength of the nation for its protection and preservation, the other is contrary to the express declaration of the Constitution that "a well-regulated militia being necessary to the security of a free state, the right of the people to keep and bear arms shall not be infringed."

It is believed that the repeal of all such laws would be accepted by the American people as at least a partial return to the fundamental principles of the Government, and an indication that hereafter the Constitution is to be made the nation's safe and unerring guide. They can be productive of no permanent benefit to the country, and should not be permitted to stand as so many monuments of the deficient wisdom which has characterized our recent legislation.

The condition of our finances demands the early and earnest consideration of Congress. Compared with the growth of our population, the public expenditures have reached an amount unprecedented in our history.

The population of the United States in 1790 was nearly 4,000,000 people. Increasing each decade about 33 per cent, it reached in 1860 31,000,000, an increase of 700 per cent on the population in 1790. In 1869 it is estimated that it will reach 38,000,000, or an increase of 868 per cent in seventy-nine years.

The annual expenditures of the Federal Government in 1791 were $4,200,000; in 1820, $18,200,000; in 1850, forty-one millions; in 1860, sixty-three millions; in 1865, nearly thirteen hundred millions; and in 1869 it is estimated by the Secretary of the Treasury, in his last annual report, that they will be three hundred and seventy-two millions.

By comparing the public disbursements of 1869, as estimated, with those of 1791, it will be seen that the increase of expenditure since the beginning of the Government has been 8,618 per cent, while the increase of the population for the same period was only 868 per cent. Again, the expenses of the Government in 1860, the year of peace immediately preceding the war, were only sixty-three millions, while in 1869, the year of peace three years after the war, it is estimated they will be three hundred and seventy-two millions, an increase of 489 per cent, while the increase of population was only 21 per cent for the same period.

These statistics further show that in 1791 the annual national expenses, compared with the population, were little more than $1 per capita, and in 1860 but $2 per capita; while in 1869 they will reach the extravagant sum of $9.78 per capita.

It will be observed that all these statements refer to and exhibit the disbursements of peace periods. It may, therefore, be of interest to compare the expenditures of the three war periods—the war with Great Britain, the Mexican War, and the War of the Rebellion.

In 1814 the annual expenses incident to the war of 1812 reached their highest amount—about thirty-one millions—while our population slightly exceeded 8,000,000, showing an expenditure of only $3.80 per capita. In 1847 the expenditures growing out of the war with Mexico reached fifty-five millions, and the population about 21,000,000, giving only $2.60 per capita for the war expenses of that year. In 1865 the expenditures called for by the rebellion reached the vast amount of twelve hundred and ninety millions, which, compared with a population of 34,000,000, gives $38.20 per capita.

From the 4th day of March, 1789, to the 30th of June, 1861, the entire expenditures of the Government were $1,700,000,000. During that period we were engaged in wars with Great Britain and Mexico, and were involved in hostilities with powerful Indian tribes; Louisiana was purchased from France at a cost of $15,000,000; Florida was ceded to us by Spain for five millions; California was acquired from Mexico for fifteen millions, and the territory of New Mexico was obtained from Texas for the sum of ten millions. Early in 1861 the War of the Rebellion commenced; and from the 1st of July of that year to the 30th of June, 1865, the public expenditures reached the enormous aggregate of thirty-three hundred millions. Three years of peace have intervened, and during that time the disbursements of the Government have successively been five hundred and twenty millions, three hundred and forty-six millions, and three hundred and ninety-three millions. Adding to these amounts three hundred and seventy-two millions, estimated as necessary for the fiscal year ending the 30th of June, 1869, we obtain a total expenditure of $1,600,000,000 during the four years immediately succeeding the war, or nearly as much as was expended during the seventy-two years that preceded the rebellion and embraced the extraordinary expenditures already named.

These startling facts clearly illustrate the necessity of retrenchment in all branches of the public service. Abuses which were tolerated during the war for the preservation of the nation will not be endured by the people, now that profound peace prevails. The receipts from internal revenue and customs have during the past three years gradually diminished, and the continuance of useless and extravagant expenditures will involve us in national bankruptcy, or else make inevitable an increase of taxes, already too onerous and in many respects obnoxious on account of their inquisitorial character. One hundred millions annually are expended for the military force, a large portion of which is employed in the execution of laws both unnecessary and unconstitutional; one hundred and fifty millions are required each year to pay the interest on the public debt: an army of taxgatherers impoverishes the nation, and public agents, placed by Congress beyond the control of the Executive, divert from their legitimate purposes large sums of money which they collect from the people in the name of the Government. Judicious legislation and prudent economy can alone remedy defects and avert evils which, if suffered to exist, can not fail to diminish confidence in the public councils and weaken the attachment and respect of the people toward their political institutions. Without proper care the small balance which it is estimated will remain in the Treasury at the close of the present fiscal year will not be realized, and additional millions be added to a debt which is now enumerated by billions.

It is shown by the able and comprehensive report of the Secretary of the Treasury that the receipts for the fiscal year ending June 30, 1868, were $405,638, 083, and that the expenditures for the same period were $377,340,284, leaving in the Treasury a surplus of $28,297,798. It is estimated that the receipts during the present fiscal year, ending June 30, 1869, will be $341,392,868 and the expenditures $336,152,470, showing a small balance of $5,240,398 in favor of the Government. For the fiscal year ending June 30, 1870, it is estimated that the receipts will amount to $327,000,000 and the expenditures to $303,000,000, leaving an estimated surplus of $24,000,000.

It becomes proper in this connection to make a brief reference to our public indebtedness, which has accumulated with such alarming rapidity and assumed such colossal proportions.

In 1789, when the Government commenced operations under the Federal Constitution, it was burdened with an indebtedness of $75,000,000, created during the War of the Revolution. This amount had been reduced to $45,000,000 when, in 1812, war was declared against Great Britain. The three years' struggle that followed largely increased the national obligations, and in 1816 they had attained the sum of $127,000,000. Wise and economical legislation, however, enabled the Government to pay the entire amount within a period of twenty years, and the extinguishment of the national debt filled the land with rejoicing and was one of the great events of President Jackson's Administration. After its redemption a large fund remained in the Treasury, which was deposited for safe-keeping with the several States, on condition that it should be returned when required by the public wants. In 1849—the year after the termination of an expensive war with Mexico—we found ourselves involved in a debt of

$64,000,000; and this was the amount owed by the Government in 1860, just prior to the outbreak of the rebellion. In the spring of 1861 our civil war commenced. Each year of its continuance made an enormous addition to the debt; and when, in the spring of 1865, the nation successfully emerged from the conflict, the obligations of the Government had reached the immense sum of $2,873,992,909. The Secretary of the Treasury shows that on the 1st day of November, 1867, this amount had been reduced to $2,491,504,450; but at the same time his report exhibits an increase during the past year of $35,625,102, for the debt on the 1st day of November last is stated to have been $2,527,129,552. It is estimated by the Secretary that the returns for the past month will add to our liabilities the further sum of $11,000,000, making a total increase during thirteen months of $46,500,000.

In my message to Congress December 4, 1865, it was suggested that a policy should be devised which, without being oppressive to the people, would at once begin to effect a reduction of the debt, and, if persisted in, discharge it fully within a definite number of years.[3] The Secretary of the Treasury forcibly recommends legislation of this character, and justly urges that the longer it is deferred the more difficult must become its accomplishment. We should follow the wise precedents established in 1789 and 1816, and without further delay make provision for the payment of our obligations at as early a period as may be practicable. The fruits of their labors should be enjoyed by our citizens rather than used to build up and sustain moneyed monopolies in our own and other lands. Our foreign debt is already computed by the Secretary of the Treasury at $850,000,000; citizens of foreign countries receive interest upon a large portion of our securities, and American taxpayers are made to contribute large sums for their support. The idea that such a debt is to become permanent should be at all times discarded as involving taxation too heavy to be borne, and payment once in every sixteen years, at the present rate of interest, of an amount equal to the original sum. This vast debt, if permitted to become permanent and increasing, must eventually be gathered into the hands of a few, and enable them to exert a dangerous and controlling power in the affairs of the Government. The borrowers would become servants to the lenders, the lenders the masters of the people. We now pride ourselves upon having given freedom to 4,000,000 of the colored race; it will then be our shame that 40,000,000 of people, by their own toleration of usurpation and profligacy, have suffered themselves to become enslaved,

and merely exchanged slave owners for new taskmasters in the shape
of bondholders and taxgatherers. Besides, permanent debts pertain
to monarchical governments, and, tending to monopolies, perpetu-
ities, and class legislation, are totally irreconcilable with free institutions. Introduced into our republican system, they would gradually
but surely sap its foundations, eventually subvert our governmental
fabric, and erect upon its ruins a moneyed aristocracy. It is our sacred
duty to transmit unimpaired to our posterity the blessings of liberty
which were bequeathed to us by the founders of the Republic, and
by our example teach those who are to follow us carefully to avoid
the dangers which threaten a free and independent people.

Various plans have been proposed for the payment of the public
debt. However they may have varied as to the time and mode in
which it should be redeemed, there seems to be a general concurrence as to the propriety and justness of a reduction in the present
rate of interest. The Secretary of the Treasury in his report recommends 5 per cent; Congress in a bill passed prior to adjournment on
the 27th of July last,[4] agreed upon 4 and 4 1/2 per cent; while by
many 3 per cent has been held to be an amply sufficient return for
the investment. The general impression as to the exorbitancy of the
existing rate of interest has led to an inquiry in the public mind
respecting the consideration which the Government has actually received for its bonds, and the conclusion is becoming prevalent that
the amount which it obtained was in real money three or four hundred per cent less than the obligations which it issued in return. It
can not be denied that we are paying an extravagant percentage for
the use of the money borrowed, which was paper currency, greatly
depreciated below the value of coin. This fact is made apparent when
we consider that bondholders receive from the Treasury upon each
dollar they own in Government securities 6 per cent in gold, which
is nearly or quite equal to 9 per cent in currency that the bonds are
then converted into capital for the national banks, upon which those
institutions issue their circulation, bearing 6 per cent interest; and
that they are exempt from taxation by the Government and the States,
and thereby enhanced 2 per cent in the hands of the holders. We
thus have an aggregate of 17 per cent which may be received upon
each dollar by the owners of Government securities. A system that
produces such results is justly regarded as favoring a few at the expense of the many, and has led to the further inquiry whether our
bondholders, in view of the large profits which they have enjoyed,
would themselves be averse to a settlement of our indebtedness upon

a plan which would yield them a fair remuneration and at the same time be just to the taxpayers of the nation. Our national credit should be sacredly observed, but in making provision for our creditors we should not forget what is due to the masses of the people. It may be assumed that the holders of our securities have already received upon their bonds a larger amount than their original investment, measured by a gold standard. Upon this statement of facts it would seem but just and equitable that the 6 per cent interest now paid by the Government should be applied to the reduction of the principal in semi-annual installments, which in sixteen years and eight months would liquidate the entire national debt. Six per cent in gold would at present rates be equal to 9 per cent in currency, and equivalent to the payment of the debt one and a half times in a fraction less than seventeen years. This, in connection with all the other advantages derived from their investment, would afford to the public creditors a fair and liberal compensation for the use of their capital, and with this they should be satisfied. The lessons of the past admonish the lender that it is not well to be overanxious in exacting from the borrower rigid compliance with the letter of the bond.

If provision be made for the payment of the indebtedness of the Government in the manner suggested, our nation will rapidly recover its wonted prosperity. Its interest require that some measure should be taken to release the large amount of capital invested in the securities of the Government. It is not now merely unproductive, but in taxation annually consumes $150,000,000, which would otherwise be used by our enterprising people in adding to the wealth of the nation. Our commerce, which at one time successfully rivaled that of the great maritime powers, has rapidly diminished, and our industrial interests are in a depressed and languishing condition. The development of our inexhaustible resources is checked, and the fertile fields of the South are becoming waste for want of means to till them. With the release of capital, new life would be infused into the paralyzed energies of our people and activity and vigor imparted to every branch of industry. Our people need encouragement in their efforts to recover from the effects of the rebellion and of injudicious legislation, and it should be the aim of the Government to stimulate them by the prospect of any early release from the burdens which impede their prosperity. If we can not take the burdens from their shoulders, we should at least manifest a willingness to help to bear them.

In referring to the condition of the circulating medium, I shall merely reiterate substantially that portion of my last message which relates to that subject.[5]

The proportion which the currency of any country should bear to the whole value of the annual produce circulated by its means is a question upon which political economists have not agreed. Nor can it be controlled by legislation, but must be left to the irrevocable laws which everywhere regulate commerce and trade. The circulating medium will ever irresistibly flow to those points where it is in greatest demand. The law of demand and supply is as unerring as that which regulates the tides of the ocean; and, indeed, currency, like the tides, has its ebbs and flows throughout the commercial world.

At the beginning of the rebellion the bank-note circulation of the country amounted to not much more than $200,000,000; now the circulation of national-bank notes and those known as 'legal-tenders' is nearly seven hundred millions. While it is urged by some that this amount should be increased, others contend that a decided reduction is absolutely essential to the best interests of the country. In view of these diverse opinions, it may be well to ascertain the real value of our paper issues when compared with a metallic or convertible currency. For this purpose let us inquire how much gold and silver could be purchased by the seven hundred millions of paper money now in circulation. Probably not more than half the amount of the latter; showing that when our paper currency is compared with gold and silver its commercial value is compressed into three hundred and fifty millions. This striking fact makes it the obvious duty of the Government, as early as may be consistent with the principles of sound political economy, to take such measures as will enable the holders of its notes and those of the national banks to convert them, without loss, into specie or its equivalent. A reduction of our paper circulating medium need not necessarily follow. This, however, would depend upon the law of demand and supply, though it should be borne in mind that by making legal-tender and bank notes convertible into coin or its equivalent their present specie value in the hands of their holders would be enhanced 100 per cent.

Legislation for the accomplishment of a result so desirable is demanded by the highest public considerations. The Constitution contemplates that the circulating medium of the country shall be uniform in quality and value. At the time of the formation of that instrument the country had just emerged from the War of the Revolution, and was suffering from the effects of a redundant and worthless paper currency. The sages of that period were anxious to protect their posterity from the evils which they themselves had experienced. Hence in providing a circulating medium they conferred upon Congress the power to coin money and regulate the value thereof, at the same time prohibiting the States from making anything but gold and silver a tender in payment of debts.

The anomalous condition of our currency is in striking contrast with that which was originally designed. Our circulation now embraces, first, notes of the national banks, which are made receivable for all dues to the Government, excluding imposts, and by all its creditors, excepting in payment of interest upon its bonds and the securities themselves; second, legal tender, issued by the United States, and which the law requires shall be received as well in payment of all debts between citizens as of all Government dues, excepting imposts; and, third, gold and silver coin. By the operation of our present system of finance, however, the metallic currency, when collected, is reserved only for one class of Government creditors, who, holding its bonds, semiannually receive their interest in coin from the National Treasury. There is no reason which will be accepted as satisfactory by the people why those who defend us on the land and protect us on the sea; the pensioner upon the gratitude of the nation, bearing the scars and wounds received while in its service, the public servants in the various departments of the Government; the farmer who supplies the soldiers of the Army and the sailors of the Navy; the artisan who toils in the nation's workshops, or the mechanics and laborers who build its edifices and construct its forts and vessels of war, should, in payment of their just and hard-earned dues, receive depreciated paper, while another class of their countrymen, no more deserving, are paid in coin of gold and silver. Equal and exact justice requires that all the creditors of the Government should be paid in a currency possessing a uniform value. This can only be accomplished by the restoration of the currency to the standard established by the Constitution, and by this means we would remove a discrimination which may, if it has not already done so, create a prejudice that may become deep-rooted and widespread and imperil the national credit.

The feasibility of making our currency correspond with the constitutional standard may be seen by reference to a few facts derived from our commercial statistics.

The aggregate product of precious metals in the United States from 1849 to 1867 amounted to $1,174,000,000, while for the same period the net exports of specie were $741,000,000. This shows an excess of product over net exports of $433,000,000. There are in the Treasury $103,407,985 in coin; in circulation in the States on the Pacific Coast about $40,000,000, and a few millions in the national and other banks—in all less than $160,000,000. Taking into consideration the specie in the country prior to 1849 and that produced since 1867, and we have more than $300,000,000 not accounted for by exportation or by returns of the Treasury, and therefore most probably remaining in the country.

These are important facts, and show how completely the inferior currency will supersede the better, forcing it from circulation among the masses and causing it to be exported as a mere article of trade, to add to the money capital of foreign lands. They show the necessity of retiring our paper money, that the return of gold and silver to the avenues of trade may be invited and a demand created which will cause the retention at home of at least so much of the productions of our rich and inexhaustible gold-bearing fields as may be sufficient for purposes of circulation. It is unreasonable to expect a return to a sound currency so long as the Government and banks, by continuing to issue irredeemable notes, fill the channels of circulation with depreciated paper. Notwithstanding a coinage by our mints since 1849 of $874,000,000, the people are now strangers to the currency which was designed for their use and benefit, and specimens of the precious metals bearing the national device are seldom seen, except when produced to gratify the interest excited by their novelty. If depreciated paper is to be continued as the permanent currency of the country, and all our coin is to become a mere article of traffic and speculation, to the enhancement in price of all that is indispensable to the comfort of the people, it would be wise economy to abolish our mints, thus saving the nation the care and expense incident to such establishments, and let our precious metals be exported in bullion. The time has come, however, when the Government and national banks should be required to take the most efficient steps and make all necessary arrangements for a resumption of specie payments.

Let specie payments once be earnestly inaugurated by the Government and banks, and the value of the paper circulation would directly approximate a specie standard.

Specie payments having been resumed by the Government and banks, all notes or bills of paper issued by either of a less denomination than $20 should by law be excluded from circulation, so that the people may have the benefit and convenience of a gold and silver currency which in all their business transactions will be uniform in value at home and abroad.

Every man of property or industry, every man who desires to preserve what he honestly possesses or to obtain what he can honestly earn, has a direct interest in maintaining a safe circulating medium—such a medium as shall be real and substantial, not liable to vibrate with opinions, not subject to be blown up or blown down by the breath of speculation, but to be made stable and secure. A disordered currency is one of the greatest political evils. It undermines the virtues necessary for the support of the social system and encourages propensities destructive of its happiness; it wars against industry, frugality, and economy, and it fosters the evil spirits of extravagance and speculation.

It has been asserted by one of our profound and most gifted statesmen that—

[']Of all the contrivances for cheating the laboring classes of mankind, none has been more effectual than that which deludes them with paper money. This is the most effectual of inventions to fertilize the rich man's fields by the sweat of the poor man's brow. Ordinary tyranny, oppression, excessive taxation—these bear lightly on the happiness of the mass of the community compared with a fraudulent currency and the robberies committed by depreciated paper. Our own history has recorded for our instruction enough, and more than enough, of the demoralizing tendency, the injustice, the intolerable oppression on the virtuous and well-disposed of a degraded paper currency authorized by law or in any way countenanced by government.[']

It is one of the most successful devices, in times of peace or war, of expansions or revulsions, to accomplish the transfer of all the precious metals from the great mass of the people into the hands of the few, where they are hoarded in secret places or deposited under bolts and bars, while the people are left to endure all the inconvenience, sacrifice, and demoralization resulting from the use of depreciated and worthless paper.

The Secretary of the Interior in his report gives valuable information in reference to the interests confided to the supervision of his Department, and reviews the operations of the Land Office, Pension Office, Patent Office, and Indian Bureau.

During the fiscal year ending June 30, 1868, 6,655,700 acres of public land were disposed of. The entire cash receipts of the General Land Office for the same period were $1,632,745, being greater by $284,883 than the amount realized from the same sources during the previous year. The entries under the homestead law cover 2,328,923 acres, nearly one-fourth of which was taken under the act of June 21, 1866, which applies only to the States of Alabama, Mississippi, Louisiana, Arkansas, and Florida.

On the 30th of June, 1868, 169,643 names were borne on the pension rolls, and during the year ending on that day the total amount paid for pensions, including the expenses of disbursement, was $24,010,982, being $5,391,025 greater than that expended for like purposes during the preceding year.

During the year ending the 30th of September last the expenses of the Patent Office exceeded the receipts by $171, and, including reissues and designs, 14,153 patents were issued.

Treaties with various Indian tribes have been concluded, and will be submitted to the Senate for its constitutional action.[6] I cordially sanction the stipulations which provide for reserving lands for the various tribes, where they may be encouraged to abandon their nomadic habits and engage in agricultural and industrial pursuits. This policy, inaugurated many years since, has met with signal success whenever it has been pursued in good faith and with becoming liberality by the United States. The necessity for extending it as far as practicable in our relations with the aboriginal population is greater now than at any preceding period. Whilst we furnish subsistence and instruction to the Indians and guarantee the undisturbed enjoyment of their treaty rights, we should habitually insist upon the faithful observance of their agreement to remain within their respective reservations. This is the only mode by which collisions with other tribes and with the whites can be avoided and the safety of our frontier settlements secured.

The companies constructing the railway from Omaha to Sacramento have been most energetically engaged in prosecuting the work, and it is believed that the line will be completed before the expiration of the next fiscal year. The 6 per cent bonds issued to these companies amounted on the 5th instant to $44,337,000, and additional work had been performed to the extent of $3,200,000.

The Secretary of the Interior in August last invited my attention to the report of a Government director of the Union Pacific Railroad Company who had been specially instructed to examine the location, construction, and equipment of their road. I submitted for the opinion of the Attorney-General certain questions in regard to the authority of the Executive which arose upon this report and those which had from time to time been presented by the commissioners appointed to inspect each successive section of the work. After carefully considering the law of the case, he affirmed the right of the Executive to order, if necessary, a thorough revision of the entire road. Commissioners were thereupon appointed to examine this and other lines, and have recently submitted a statement of their investigations, of which the report of the Secretary of the Interior furnishes specific information.[7]

The report of the Secretary of War contains information of interest and importance respecting the several bureaus of the War Department and the operations of the Army. The strength of our military force on the 30th of September last was 48,000 men, and it is computed that by the 1st of January next this number will be decreased to 43,000. It is the opinion of the Secretary of War that within the next year a considerable diminution of the infantry force may be made without detriment to the interests of the country; and in view of the great expense attending the military peace establishment and the absolute necessity of retrenchment wherever it can be applied, it is hoped that Congress will sanction the reduction which his report recommends.[8] While in 1860 sixteen thousand three hundred men cost the nation $16,472,000, the sum of $65,682,000 is estimated as necessary for the support of the Army during the fiscal year ending June 30, 1870. The estimates of the War Department for the last two fiscal years were, for 1867, $33,814,461, and for 1868 $25,205,669. The actual expenditures during the same periods were, respectively, $95,224,415 and $123,246,648. The estimate submitted in December last for the fiscal year ending June 30, 1869, was $77,124,707; the expenditures for the first quarter, ending the 30th of September last, were $27,219,117, and the Secretary of the Treasury gives $66,000,000 as the amount which will probably be required during the remaining three quarters, if there should be no reduction of the Army—making its aggregate cost for the year considerably in excess of ninety-three millions. The difference between the estimates and expenditures for the three fiscal years which have been named is thus shown to be $175,545,343 for this single branch of the public service.

The report of the Secretary of the Navy exhibits the operations of that Department and of the Navy during the year. A considerable reduction of the force has been effected. There are 42 vessels, carrying 411 guns, in the six squadrons which are established in different parts of the world. Three of these vessels are returning to the United States and 4 are used as storeships, leaving the actual cruising force 35 vessels, carrying 356 guns. The total number of vessels in the Navy is 206, mounting 1,743 guns. Eighty-one vessels of every description are in use, armed with 696 guns. The number of enlisted men in the service, including apprentices, has been reduced to 8,500. An increase of navy-yard facilities is recommended as a measure which will in the event of war be promotive of economy and security. A more thorough and systematic survey of the North Pacific Ocean is advised in view of our recent acquisitions, our expanding commerce, and the increasing intercourse between the Pacific States and Asia. The naval pension fund, which consists of a moiety of the avails of prizes captured during the war, amounts to $14,000,000. Exception is taken to the act of 23d July last,[9] which reduces the interest on the fund loaned to the Government by the Secretary, as trustee, to 3 per cent instead of 6 per cent, which was originally stipulated when the investment was made. An amendment of the pension laws is suggested to remedy omissions and defects in existing enactments. The expenditures of the Department during the last fiscal year were $20,120,394, and the estimates for the coming year amount to $20,993,414.

The Postmaster-General's report furnishes a full and clear exhibit of the operations and condition of the postal service. The ordinary postal revenue for the fiscal year ending June 30, 1868, was $16,292,600, and the total expenditures, embracing all the service for which special appropriations have been made by Congress, amount to $22,730,592, showing an excess of expenditures of $6,437,991. Deducting from the expenditures the sum of $1,896,525, the amount of appropriations for ocean-steamship and other special service, the excess of expenditures was $4,541,466. By using an unexpended balance in the Treasury of $3,800,000 the actual sum for which a special appropriation is required to meet the deficiency is $741,466. The causes which produced this large excess of expenditure over revenue were the restoration of service in the late insurgent States and the putting into operation of new service established by acts of Congress, which amounted within the last two years and a half to about 48,700 miles—equal to more than one-third of the whole amount of the service at the close of the war. New postal conventions with Great Britain, North Germany, Belgium, the Netherlands, Switzerland, and Italy, respectively, have been carried into effect. Under their provisions important improvements have resulted in reduced rates of international postage and enlarged mail facilities with European countries.[10] The cost of the United States transatlantic ocean mail service since January 1, 1868, had been largely lessened under the operation of these new conventions, a reduction of over one-half having been effected under the new arrangements for ocean mail steamship service which went into effect on that date. The attention of Congress is invited to the practical suggestions and recommendations made in his report by the Postmaster General.

No important question has occurred during the last year in our accustomed cordial and friendly intercourse with Costa Rica, Guatemala, Honduras, San Salvador, France, Austria, Belgium, Switzerland, Portugal, the Netherlands, Denmark, Sweden and Norway, Rome, Greece, Turkey, Persia, Egypt, Liberia, Morocco, Tripoli, Tunis, Muscat, Siam, Borneo, and Madagascar.

Cordial relations have also been maintained with the Argentine and the Oriental Republics. The expressed wish of Congress that our national good offices might be tendered to those Republics, and also to Brazil and Paraguay, for bringing to an end the calamitous war which has so long been raging in the valley of the La Plata,[11] has been assiduously complied with and kindly acknowledged by all the belligerents. That important negotiation, however, has thus far been without result.

Charles A. Washburn,[12] late United States minister to Paraguay, having resigned, and being desirous to return to the United States, the rear-admiral commanding the South Atlantic Squadron[13] was early directed to send a ship of war to Asuncion, the capital of Paraguay, to receive Mr. Washburn and his family and remove them from a situation which was represented to be endangered by faction and foreign war. The Brazilian commander[14] of the allied invading forces refused permission to the *Wasp* to pass through the blockading forces, and that vessel returned to its accustomed anchorage. Remonstrance having been made against this refusal, it was promptly overruled, and the *Wasp* therefore resumed her errand, received Mr. Washburn and his family, and conveyed them to a safe and convenient seaport. In the meantime an excited controversy had arisen between the President of Paraguay[15] and the late United States minister, which, it is understood, grew out of his proceedings in giving asylum in the United States legation to alleged enemies of that Republic. The question of the right to give asylum is one always difficult and often productive of great embarrassment. In states well organized and established, foreign powers refuse either to concede or exercise that right, except as to persons actually belonging to the diplomatic service. On the other hand, all such powers insist upon exercising the right of asylum in states where the law of nations is not fully acknowledged, respected, and obeyed.

The President of Paraguay is understood to have opposed to Mr. Washburn's proceedings the injurious and very improbable charge of personal complicity in insurrection and treason. The correspondence, however, has not yet reached the United States.

Mr. Washburn, in connection with this controversy, represents that two United States citizens attached to the legation[16] were arbitrarily seized at his side, when leaving the capital of Paraguay, committed to prison, and there subjected to torture for the purpose of procuring confessions of their own criminality and testimony to support the President's allegations against the United States minister. Mr. McMahon,[17] the newly appointed minister to Paraguay, having reached the La Plata, has been instructed to proceed without delay to Asuncion, there to investigate the whole subject. The rear-admiral commanding the United States South Atlantic Squadron has been directed to attend the new minister with a proper naval force to sustain such just demands as the occasion may require, and to vindicate the rights of the United States citizens referred to and of any others who may be exposed to danger in the theater of war. With these exceptions, friendly relations have been maintained between the United States and Brazil and Paraguay.

Our relations during the past year with Bolivia, Ecuador, Peru, and Chile have become especially friendly and cordial. Spain and the Republics of Peru, Bolivia, and Ecuador have expressed their willingness to accept the mediation of the United States for terminating the war upon the South Pacific coast.[18] Chile has not finally declared upon the question. In the meantime the conflict has practically exhausted itself, since no belligerent or hostile movement has been made by either party during the last two years, and there are no indications of a present purpose to resume hostilities on either side. Great Britain and France have cordially seconded our proposition of mediation, and I do not forego the hope that it may soon be accepted by all the belligerents and lead to a secure establishment of peace and friendly relations between the Spanish American Republics of the Pacific and Spain—a result which would be attended with common benefits to the belligerents and much advantage to all commercial nations. I communicate, for the consideration of Congress, a correspondence which shows that the Bolivian Republic has established the extremely liberal principle of receiving into its citizenship any citizen of the United States, or of any other of the American Republics, upon the simple condition of voluntary registry.

The correspondence herewith submitted will be found painfully replete with accounts of the ruin and wretchedness produced by recent earthquakes, of unparalleled severity, in the Republics of Peru, Ecuador, and Bolivia.[19] The diplomatic agents and naval officers of the United States who were present in those countries at the time of those disasters furnished all the relief in their power to the sufferers, and were promptly rewarded with grateful and touching acknowledgments by the Congress of Peru. An appeal to the charity of our fellow-citizens has been answered by much liberality. In this connection I submit an appeal which has been made by the Swiss Republic, whose Government and institutions are kindred to our own, in behalf of its inhabitants who are suffering extreme destitution, produced by recent devastating inundations.[20]

Our relations with Mexico during the year have been marked by an increasing growth of mutual confidence. The Mexican Government has not yet acted upon the three treaties celebrated here last summer for establishing the rights of naturalized citizens upon a liberal and just basis, for regulating consular powers, and for the adjustment of mutual claims.[21]

All commercial nations, as well as all friends of republican institutions, have occasion to regret the frequent local disturbances which occur in some of the constituent States of Colombia. Nothing has occurred, however, to affect the harmony and cordial friendship which have for years existed between that youthful and vigorous Republic and our own.

Negotiations are pending with a view to the survey and construction of a ship canal across the Isthmus of Darien, under the auspices of the United States. I hope to be able to submit the results of that negotiation to the Senate during its present session.[22]

The very liberal treaty which was entered into last year by the United States and Nicaragua has been ratified by the latter Republic.[23]

Costa Rica, with the earnestness of a sincerely friendly neighbor, solicits a reciprocity of trade, which I commend to the consideration of Congress.

The convention created by treaty between the United States and Venezuela in July, 1865, for the mutual adjustment of claims, has been held, and its decisions have been received at the Department of State. The heretofore-recognized Government of the United States of Venezuela has been subverted.[24] A provisional government having been instituted under circumstances which promise durability, it has been formally recognized.

I have been reluctantly obliged to ask explanation and satisfaction for national injuries committed by the President of Hayti.[25] The political and social condition of the Republics of Hayti and St. Domingo is very unsatisfactory and painful.[26] The abolition of slavery, which has been carried into effect throughout the island of St. Domingo and the entire West Indies, except the Spanish islands of Cuba and Porto Rico, has been followed by a profound popular conviction of the rightfulness of republican institutions and an intense desire to secure them. The attempt, however, to establish republics there encounters many obstacles, most of which may be supposed to result from long-indulged habits of colonial supineness and dependence upon European monarchical powers. While the United States have on all occasions professed a decided unwillingness that any part of this continent or of its adjacent islands shall be made a theater for a new establishment of monarchical power, too little has been done by us, on the other hand, to attach the communities by which we are surrounded to our own country, or to lend even a moral support to the efforts they are so resolutely and so constantly making to secure republican institutions for themselves. It is indeed a question of grave consideration whether our recent and present example is not calculated to check the growth and expansion of free principles, and make those communities distrust, if not dread, a government which at will consigns to military domination States that are integral parts of our Federal Union, and, while ready to resist any attempts by other nations to extend to this hemisphere the monarchical institutions of Europe, assumes to establish over a large portion of its people a rule more absolute, harsh, and tyrannical than any known to civilized powers.

The acquisition of Alaska was made with the view of extending national jurisdiction and republican principles in the American hemisphere. Believing that a further step could be taken in the same direction, I last year entered into a treaty with the King of Denmark[27] for the purchase of the islands of St. Thomas and St. John, on the best terms then attainable, and with the express consent of the people of those islands. This treaty still remains under consideration in the Senate. A new convention has been entered into with Denmark, enlarging the time fixed for final ratification of the original treaty.[28]

Comprehensive national policy would seem to sanction the acquisition and incorporation into our Federal Union of the several adjacent continental and insular communities as speedily as it can be done peacefully, lawfully, and without any violation of national justice, faith, or honor. Foreign possession or control of those communities has hitherto hindered the growth and impaired the influence of the United States. Chronic revolution and anarchy there would be equally injurious. Each one of them, when firmly established as an independent republic, or when incorporated into the United States, would be a new source of strength and power. Conforming my Administration to these principles, I have on no occasion lent support or toleration to unlawful expeditions set on foot upon the plea of republican propagandism or of national extension or aggrandizement. The necessity, however, of repressing such unlawful movements clearly indicates the duty which rests upon us of adapting our legislative action to the new circumstances of a decline of European monarchical power and influence and the increase of American republican ideas, interests, and sympathies.

It can not be long before it will become necessary for this Government to lend some effective aid to the solution of the political and social problems which are continually kept before the world by the two Republics of the island of St. Domingo, and which are now disclosing themselves more distinctly than heretofore in the island of Cuba. The subject is commended to your consideration with all the more earnestness because I am satisfied that the time has arrived when even so direct a proceeding as a proposition for an annexation of the two Republics of the island of St. Domingo would not only receive the consent of the people interested, but would also give satisfaction to all other foreign nations.

I am aware that upon the question of further extending our possessions it is apprehended by some that our political system can not successfully be applied to an area more extended than our continent; but the conviction is rapidly gaining ground in the American mind that with the increased facilities for intercommunication between all portions of the earth the principles of free government, as embraced in our Constitution, if faithfully maintained and carried out, would prove of sufficient strength and breadth to comprehend within their sphere and influence the civilized nations of the world.

The attention of the Senate and of Congress is again respectfully invited to the treaty for the establishment of commercial reciprocity with the Hawaiian Kingdom entered into last year, and already ratified by that Government.[29] The attitude of the United States toward these islands is not very different from that in which they stand toward the West Indies. It is known and felt by the Hawaiian Government and people that their Government and institutions are feeble and precarious; that the United States, being so near a neighbor, would be unwilling to see the islands pass under foreign control. Their prosperity is continually disturbed by expectations and alarms of unfriendly political proceedings, as well from the United States as from other foreign powers. A reciprocity treaty, while it could not materially diminish the revenues of the United States, would be a guaranty of the good will and forbearance of all nations until the people of the islands shall of themselves, at no distant day, voluntarily apply for admission into the Union.

The Emperor of Russia[30] has acceded to the treaty negotiated here in January last for the security of trade-marks in the interest of manufacturers and commerce.[31] I have invited his attention to the importance of establishing, now while it seems easy and practicable, a fair and equal regulation of the vast fisheries belonging to the two nations in the waters of the North Pacific Ocean.

The two treaties between the United States and Italy for the regulation of consular powers and the extradition of criminals, negotiated and ratified here during the last session of Congress, have been accepted and confirmed by the Italian Government.[32] A liberal consular convention which has been negotiated with Belgium will be submitted to the Senate.[33] The very important treaties which were negotiated between the United States and North Germany and Bavaria for the regulation of the rights of naturalized citizens have been duly ratified and exchanged, and similar treaties have been entered into with the Kingdoms of Belgium and Wurtemberg and with the Grand Duchies of Baden and Hesse-Darmstadt. I hope soon to be able to submit equally satisfactory conventions of the same character now in the course of negotiation with the respective Governments of Spain, Italy, and the Ottoman Empire.[34]

Examination of claims against the United States by the Hudsons Bay Company and the Puget Sound Agricultural Company, on account of certain possessory rights in the State of Oregon and Territory of Washington, alleged by those companies in virtue of provisions of the treaty between the United States and Great Britain of June 15, 1846, has been diligently prosecuted, under the direction of the joint international commission to which they were submitted for adjudication by treaty between the two Governments of July 1, 1863, and will, it is expected, be concluded at an early day.

No practical regulation concerning colonial trade and the fisheries can be accomplished by treaty between the United States and Great Britain until Congress shall have expressed their judgment concerning the principles involved. Three other questions, however, between the United States and Great Britain remain open for adjustment. These are the mutual rights of naturalized citizens, the boundary question involving the title to the island of San Juan, on the Pacific coast, and the mutual claims arising since the year 1853 of the citizens and subjects of the two countries for injuries and depredations committed under the authority of their respective Governments. Negotiations upon these subjects are pending, and I am not without hope of being able to lay before the Senate, for its consideration during the present session, protocols calculated to bring to an end these justly exciting and long-existing controversies.[35]

We are not advised of the action of the Chinese Government upon the liberal and auspicious treaty which was recently celebrated with its plenipotentiaries at this capital.[36]

Japan remains a theater of civil war, marked by religious incidents and political severities peculiar to that long-isolated Empire. The Executive has hitherto maintained strict neutrality among the belligerents, and acknowledges with pleasure that it has been frankly and fully sustained in that course by the enlightened concurrence and cooperation of the other treaty powers, namely, Great Britain, France, the Netherlands, North Germany, and Italy.

Spain having recently undergone a revolution marked by extraordinary unanimity and preservation of order, the provisional government established at Madrid has been recognized, and the friendly intercourse which has so long happily existed between the two countries remains unchanged.[37]

I renew the recommendation contained in my communication to Congress dated the 18th July last[38]—a copy of which accompanies this message—that the judgment of the people should be taken on the propriety of so amending the Federal Constitution that it shall provide—

First.   For an election of President and Vice-President by a direct vote of the people, instead of through the agency of electors, and making them ineligible for reelection to a second term.

Second.   For a distinct designation of the person who shall discharge the duties of President in the event of a vacancy in that office by the death, resignation, or removal of both the President and Vice-President.

Third.   For the election of Senators of the United States directly by the people of the several States, instead of by the legislatures; and

Fourth.   For the limitation to a period of years of the terms of Federal judges.

Profoundly impressed with the propriety of making these important modifications in the Constitution, I respectfully submit them for the early and mature consideration of Congress. We should, as far as possible, remove all pretext for violations of the organic law, by remedying such imperfections as time and experience may develop, ever remembering that "the constitution which at any time exists until changed by an explicit and authentic act of the whole people is sacredly obligatory upon all."[39]

In the performance of a duty imposed upon me by the Constitution, I have thus communicated to Congress information of the state of the Union and recommended for their consideration such measures as have seemed to me necessary and expedient. If carried into effect, they will hasten the accomplishment of the great and beneficent purposes for which the Constitution was ordained, and which it comprehensively states were "to form a more perfect Union, establish justice, insure domestic tranquillity, provide for the common defense, promote the general welfare, and secure the blessings of liberty to ourselves and our posterity." In Congress are vested all legislative powers, and upon them devolves the responsibility as well for framing unwise and excessive laws as for neglecting to devise and adopt measure absolutely demanded by the wants of the country. Let us earnestly hope that before the expiration of our respective terms of service, now rapidly drawing to a close, an all-wise Providence will so guide our counsels as to strengthen and preserve the Federal Union, inspire reverence for the Constitution, restore prosperity and happiness to our whole people, and promote "on earth peace, good will toward men."

ANDREW JOHNSON.

Richardson, *Messages*, 6: 672–91.

1. See Veto of the Tenure of Office Act, Mar. 2, 1867, *Johnson Papers*, 12: 95–101.

2. See Johnson's comments on the act in Johnson to the House of Representatives, Mar. 2, 1867, ibid., 77–78.

3. See Message to Congress, Dec. 4, 1865, *Johnson Papers*, 9: 479–80.

4. For more on the funding bill, see *Congressional Globe*, 40 Cong., 2 Sess., Appendix, pp. 483–84; Alexander Campbell to Johnson, July 20, 1868, *Johnson Papers*, 14: 385.

5. The following paragraphs are directly quoted from Johnson's Third Annual Message, Dec. 3, 1867. See *Johnson Papers*, 13: 295–98.

6. Treaties were presented concerning the Osage, Kiowa, Commanche, Apache, Arapahoe, Cheyenne, Crow, and Chippewa. Richardson, *Messages*, 6: 598, 635, 637–38.

7. The government director was Jesse L. Williams. For more about the commission and the problems with the Union Pacific Railroad construction, see Thomas C. Durant to Johnson, Oct. 11, 1868; John F. Coyle to Johnson, Dec. 5, 1868.

8. Congress did reduce the army's size in "An Act making Appropriations for the Support of the Army for the year ending June thirtieth, eighteen hundred and seventy, and for other purposes," which became law March 3, 1869. *Congressional Globe*, 40 Cong., 3 Sess., Appendix, pp. 318–19.

9. See section 2 of "An Act making Appropriations for the Payment of Invalid and other Pensions of the United States for the year ending June thirtieth, eighteen hundred and sixty-nine," passed July 23, 1868. Ibid., 40 Cong., 2 Sess., Appendix, p. 543.

10. See *American Annual Cyclopaedia* (1868), 632, for the specific advantages of these postal treaties.

11. For details of the long war between Paraguay and Brazil, Argentina, and Uruguay, see ibid., 609–16; *Senate Ex. Docs.*, 40 Cong., 3 Sess., No. 5, 3 pts. (Ser. 1360).

12. Washburn (1822–1889) was a California newspaper editor before becoming U.S. commissioner (1861–63) and minister (1863–68) to Paraguay. *Who Was Who in America, Historical Volume 1607–1896* (Chicago, 1963).

13. Charles H. Davis.

14. Luís Alves de Lima e Silva (1803–1880), military hero, stout Conservative, and twice prime minister of Brazil, was commander during the Paraguayan war (1865–70). Barbara A. Tenenbaum, ed., *Encyclopedia of Latin American History and Culture* (5 vols., New York, 1996), 3: 420–21; *House Reports*, 41 Cong., 2 Sess., No. 65 (Ser. 1437).

15. Francisco Solano López (*c*1826–1870), considered a megalomaniac, served Paraguay as a diplomat to Europe, minister of war, and president (1862–70). *The New Columbia Encyclopedia* (1975).

16. Porter Cornelius Bliss, an American, and George F. Masterman, an Englishman, were attached to the legation. Bliss (1838–1885), a prominent journalist, had been employed by the U.S. minister to Brazil, by the governments of both Argentina and Paraguay, and as private secretary to Charles Washburn. He later served as secretary to the legation in Mexico (1870–74). Masterman is not otherwise identified. *DAB*.

17. Martin T. McMahon.

18. In 1862 Spain began a futile attempt to regain its former American empire. See Hubert Herring, *A History of Latin America* (New York, 1972), 597, 653–54.

19. For one report, see Ann S. Stephens to Johnson, Dec. 26, 1868.

20. In 1868 the entire southeastern or alpine half of Switzerland experienced the severest flooding in over fifty years. *American Annual Cyclopaedia* (1868), 718.

21. These three conventions were signed in July 1868, but the Mexican congress, in its September–January session, only ratified the two treaties dealing with naturalization and claims adjustments, for there was serious opposition to that dealing with consular regulation. Ibid., 490, 492.

22. While Caleb Cushing did negotiate an agreement in 1868, the Colombian senate rejected it and the U.S. Senate subsequently dropped it. See William H. Seward to Johnson, Feb. 4, 1867, *Johnson Papers*, 12: 8–10.

23. The U.S. had ratified the Nicaraguan treaty in January and it was proclaimed in August 1868. Van Deusen, *Seward*, 517.

24. From 1863 to 1870 Venezuela experienced intermittent civil war between the Conservatives and Young Liberals. Herring, *Latin America*, 516.

25. Sylvain Salnave (1832–1870) engaged in revolutionary activities for many years before being elected president of Haiti in 1867. Discontent with his despotic rule led to further insurrection. Salnave was finally captured and executed. *Appleton's Cyclopaedia*.

26. Both countries were involved in civil wars. *American Annual Cyclopaedia* (1868), 339–40, 687. See also Gideon Welles to Johnson, May 29, 1868, *Johnson Papers*, 14: 135–37.

27. Christian IX (1818–1906) had succeeded his father, Frederick VII, as king of Denmark in 1863. *Columbia Encyclopedia*.

28 A treaty was not agreed upon until 1917. See Third Annual Message, Dec. 3, 1867, *Johnson Papers*, 13: 305.

29. The reciprocity treaty was first placed before the Senate in July 1867 but was tabled. In 1868 and 1869 the Senate rejected it and in 1870 it failed to get the necessary two-thirds vote. Its failure is attributed to the Hawaiian market's insignificance and the country's reluctance to take on new responsibilities. Van Deusen, *Seward*, 533–34.

30. Alexander II.

31. See Charles I. Bevans, comp., *Treaties and other International Agreements of the United States of America, 1776–1949* (12 vols., Washington, D.C., 1868–74), 11: 1220–21.

32. Ibid., 9: 70–79.

33. Ibid., 5: 478–82.

34. See George Bancroft to Johnson, Jan. 21, Feb. 9, 1868, *Johnson Papers*, 13: 488–89, 539–40, concerning the North German treaty, and the Bavarian and Baden treaties in Charles Munde, *The Bancroft Naturalization Treaties* (Würzburg, 1868), 71–78, 116–19. For some of the others, see Bevans, *Treaties*, 5: 476–77; 8: 53–55, 117–20.

35. By mid-January 1868, U.S. minister Reverdy Johnson had negotiated a naturalization

protocol, a claims treaty, and a treaty calling for Swiss arbitration of the San Juan Island boundary. The Senate rejected the claims treaty, delayed the naturalization protocol, and refused to act on the San Juan arbitration. Van Deusen, *Seward*, 508–10.

36. Chinese minister Anson Burlingame and his associates negotiated a treaty with William Seward which was ratified by the U.S. Senate on July 16, 1868. The treaty's eight articles were additions to the 1858 treaty between the U.S. and the Ta-Tsing Empire. Munde, *Bancroft Naturalization Treaties*, 120–23.

37. In September 1868 Queen Isabella II was overthrown, but fighting continued until year's end. The U.S. was the first to recognize the provisional government. *American Annual Cyclopaedia* (1868), 700–709.

38. See Message *re* Proposed Constitutional Amendments, July 18, 1868, *Johnson Papers*, 14: 375–79.

39. The quotation is not identified.

From James W. Simonton[1]

N. York, Dec 9 1868

Pomeroys Democrat[2] which has no connection with us boast fully published your message in an Extra at nine 9 this morning.

All our copies intact.

J W. Simonton
N. Y. Associated Press.

Tel, DLC–JP.

1. Simonton (1823–1882) enjoyed a long and illustrious career in journalism, first in New York and then in California. In 1867 he returned to New York City as the general agent for the Associated Press, a post he held for fourteen years. *DAB*.

2. Marcus M. Pomeroy had been associated in recent years with Wisconsin newspapers; but in 1868 he went to New York City and, with the prompting of Thurlow Weed, established the *New-York Democrat* and also a weekly, called *Pomeroy's Democrat*. He sold it two years later. *DAB*.

From David Looney

Memphis, Tennesse   Dembr 10th 1868

Mr. President

I am here on important business, and it gives me very great pleasure to say your message merits the hearty approval of all good men.

I send you an Editorial from the Memphis Avalanch, Col. Galloways paper.[1] Will return to New York next week.

David Looney

ALS, DLC–JP.

1. Matthew C. Gallaway. No editorial was found enclosed, but Looney is obviously referring to the one that appeared in the December 10, 1868, issue of the *Memphis Avalanche*. This essay was highly laudatory of Johnson's annual message and also of his presidency in general.

From William H. Wesson

Summerville So. Ca   Decr. 10 1868

I had the pleasure of reading your late message this morning: Allow me to say that he is neither a true patriot or a democrat that does not heartily endorse it; indeed, in my opinion if your other acts have not fastened your name *to Posterity*, this message must do it; and the name of Andrew Johnson will equal if it does not excel that of Andrew Jackson.

W H Wesson

ALS, DLC-JP.

From James E. English

New Haven, Dec 11- 1868.

Sir

My friend and neighbor, Hon. F Betts,[1] being about to leave for Washington, where he will spend some little time before going South, I gladly avail myself of the opportunity to introduce him to you and to your acquaintance, and commend him to your civilities while he may be at the capital. Judge Betts, is one of our most respectable inteligent and wealthy citizens, and is thoroughly in accord with our frinds in all Constitutional measures connected with the Government. He is truly a representative man of the conservative Democracy of Connecticut. I commend him to you.

James E. English.

ALS, DLC-JP.
1. Frederick J. Betts (1803–1879) was an active lawyer in New York and then Connecticut. According to one account, Betts visited Virginia in 1868 and held a temporary appointment as a county judge. Afterwards, he returned to New Haven and resumed his legal career. *New York Times*, Oct. 15, 1879.

From J. Montgomery Peters[1]

Baltimore, Decr. 11th 1868.

Dear Sir,

I had the honor during the progress of the Impeachment trial to submit some views to you to enter into the cause which you were pleased to think well of.[2] I am encouraged by this manifestation of your favor to ask you if there is any place within your gift, not already promised to which you can assign me. Nothing, I assure you, but *poverty* could induce me to ask this of you, as I am certainly not in the professional sense an office seeker.

Should it suit you to entertain this application at all, I will produce any required amount of recommendation from responsible citizens.

I have no particular place to name, but leave that entirely to your own selection.[3]

Montgomery Peters,
No. 624, West Lombard St. Balt.

ALS, DLC-JP.

1. Peters (*fl*1871) was an attorney. During the Civil War he had written to Jefferson Davis with advice about how to invade Maryland. Baltimore directories (1871); Peters to Davis, Aug. 17, 1861, in *OR*, Ser. 1, Vol. 51, Pt. 2: 238–39.

2. Probably his letters of April 25, May 8, 18, 1868, Johnson Papers, LC.

3. There is no evidence that Johnson gave Peters a post.

From Ann S. Stephens

National Hotel   Dec. 11th [1868]

My Dear Sir.

If ever there was a selfish, thoughtless, unreliable person I am that individual. I came to you yesterday in order to speak of several things in which my friends were interested and like a traitor forgot them all.

First there is Gen. Burbridge[1] and the commissionership. His interest I particularly wish to advance for he is I really think, *the only* man who would be heartily taken up by the Senate and who will act as your subordinate and as the friend of your friends. *You can hurt this man.* He is honest and true as steel. I spoke with Gov. Morton[2] about him last night. The Governor is warmly his friend and would urge his claims in person if he did not feel that it would be indelicate for him to ask favors of you. He said this to me and I can understand that the feeling is a natural one. He will support Burbridge in the Senate and believes that he will be generally acceptable. When he calls, if you should do him the honor to ask his opinion, he will give it I know.

Then there is Doctor Spencer,[3] my good old friend, who wishes so much to be made Surveyer Gen of New Mexico. Do send him there! He is a thoroughly good and entirely compliant man. I was a wretch to forget him when it was, and is, so important that he should go.

My daughter[4] desires me to say that she is coming in behalf of her friend Lupton[5] and expects you to be very, very good and perfectly charming in the way you will utter that pretty word "Yes." Do be merciful for the young lady has resolved to break her heart if she is disappointed and I cannot spare her yet. Gov Morton wants Lupton appointed very much indeed but cannot ask it of you in person from the very proper feelings that I have spoken of. I really do not think that any other man will be sure of confirmation and to send a man in who will not be confirmed is to have him smothered in the committee and run the appointment into the next session which will do no one good.

Pray take all these things into consideration and be prepared to save me the expenses of that young woman's funeral.

Ann S. Stephens

I enclose two articles from our friend Hoover's Papers.[6] I hope you will be able to call on him. He is better but still keeps his room.

ALS, DLC-JP.

1. Stephen G. Burbridge wished to be Commissioner of Internal Revenue. Despite many recommendations, he was never nominated. See John Welsh to Johnson, July 30, 1867; Stephens to Johnson, Aug. 7, 1868, *Johnson Papers*, 14: 461, 489–90. See also Burbridge to Johnson, Jan. 4, 1869.

2. Oliver P. Morton.

3. Probably Thomas Rush Spencer (d. *c*1871), a New York physician. Although Johnson nominated someone else (unsuccessfully), Spencer did get the surveyorship under Grant and served until his death. *U.S. Off. Reg.* (1869–71); New York City directories (1867–70); Ser. 6B, Vol. 4: 371, Johnson Papers, LC.

4. Ann Stephens (b. 1841) was the older of the two children of Ann S. and Edward Stephens. Edward T. James et al., eds., *Notable American Women, 1607–1950: A Biographical Dictionary* (3 vols., Cambridge, Mass., 1971).

5. Not identified.

6. Jonah D. Hoover edited the *Washington Evening Express* from sometime in 1868 until his health forced his retirement. He died in June 1870. No articles were found enclosed. *Washington Evening Star*, June 6, 1870.

From Samuel M. Harrington[1]

Wilmington Del   Decr. 12th 1868

Dear Sir

I perceive that the newspapers throughout the country continue to report that Mr Rollins wishes to vacate the Internal Revenue office, and that your Excellency will appoint a successor during your term of office. I presume there would be great difficulty in getting any one confirmed by this Radical Congress who is not identified with the Republican party, and if the appointment is defered until after Grant is inaugurated President, an extreme Radical will fill that position for four years more and if a conservative Republican could be confirmed during your term I think he would be continued through the incoming administration and I would present to your notice a man whom I think in evry respect competent for said position who would if appointed fill the office with credit to himself and the General Government. I refer to Robert C Fraim Esq,[2] who is at present Register of Wills at New Castle Delaware. His time of office has now almost expired. Mr Fraim is about 40 years of age. He is a strong vigorous man of good natural abilities. He is entirely *self made* working his way up to his present position from the humblest walks of life. His father was a poor mechanic. Mr Fraim himself served an apperticedship to House carpentering, he served his time faithfully and for some time after he was of age followed this employment for a livelihood; he however was not laboring in his proper sphere. He soon relinquished his proffession of House carpenter and commenced teaching school. This he followed some four or five years, during which time he was a hard student. At the breaking out of the war Mr Fraim entered the army and served nine months as First sergeant of his company. Shortly after his return from the army he was placed in his present position which he has held for over four years. This office he has filled with marked ability gaining the approbation of all political parties. His time will soon expire, and as political party faction runs very high here, the Governor[3] will have to appoint a man of strong party proclivities in Mr Fraim's position. Mr Fraim after the appointment of Register read Law in this county with Wm. C Spruance[4] of the New Castle Bar. Mr. Fraim's moral character is beyond reproach, he uses no intoxicating liquor; and for many years has been an active member of the Methodist Episcopal Church. He is also a worthy Member of the Ancient and Honorable Order of A Y. M. in fact a first class man in every respect, in politics he is conservative. He is opposed to negro sufrage and favors the repeal of the Tenure of Office Act. He is in favor of giving to the Southern people all their rights and of placing them upon equal status with the people of the Northern and Eastern states. Although conservative he has the respect and confidence of both political partys here, and his appointment to the office of Commissioner of Internal Revenue would where Mr Fraim is known give universal satisfaction. Before selecting please consider the matter. For reference I name Thomas F Bayard Esq. Victor duPont Esq. General Henry du Pont Esq Col Henry B Judd Esq[5] and His Excellency Gove Saulsbury Governor of Delaware—; all of whom are distinguished citizens of this state.

Samuel M Harrington

ALS, DNA-RG56, Appls, Heads of Treasury Offices, Robert C. Fraim.

1. Harrington (1840–1878) was admitted to the Delaware bar in 1861. The following year he became adjutant general of the state and afterwards the secretary of state. Harrington was active in Republican party politics, including a term on the national executive committee. *Biographical and Genealogical History of the State of Delaware* (2 vols., Chambersburg, Pa., 1899), 2: 1387–89.

2. Fraim (*c*1830–*fl*1881) was a lawyer who held the post of register of wills in Wilmington for several years. Subsequently, he was in the china and glass business there. 1870 Census, Del., New Castle, Wilmington Subdiv. 1, 93; Wilmington directories (1867–81).

3. Gove Saulsbury (1815–1881) had been elected governor of Delaware in 1866 and served until early 1871. He served in the state senate prior to his election as governor. A physician by professional training, Saulsbury was active in Democratic party politics at the state and national levels. *DAB.*

4. Spruance (1831–1913) was an eminent lawyer in New Castle and after 1871 in Wilmington. He served on the Delaware state supreme court. During 1876–80 he was federal district attorney for Delaware. *New York Times*, Mar. 13, 1913; *Biographical and Genealogical History of Delaware*, 2: 1296.

5. Bayard (1828–1898) was admitted to the bar in Wilmington in 1851. He was elected to the U.S. Senate in 1869 and served until 1885. Thereafter he was President Cleveland's secretary of state. Victor Du Pont (1828–1888) studied law and became a Wilmington lawyer in 1849. He also was involved in the banking and insurance business there. Henry Du Pont (1812–1889) became head of E. I. Du Pont de Nemours & Company in 1850, a post he held until his death. Judd (*c*1816–1892) was a West Point graduate and a career officer until his retirement in 1861. Afterwards he helped organize volunteer troops and was brevetted a lieutenant colonel. *DAB*; *NCAB*, 21: 408–9; J. Thomas Scharf, *History of Delaware, 1609–1888* (2 vols., Philadelphia, 1888), 1: 588; *New York Tribune*, July 28, 1892.

From Moses Keokuk et al.[1]

WASHINGTON, D.C., Dec. 12, 1868.

To his Excellency the President:

The undersigned, chiefs from the Sac and Fox tribes of the Mississippi, respectfully represent to your Excellency that their agent, Albert Wiley,[2] having been guilty of misconduct in office, should be removed for the following reasons.

1. For giving the exclusive right to trade with their tribe to one William Whistler, who charges them exorbitant prices for the necessaries of life, amounting to twice or three times as much as the same articles cost outside the Reservation.

2. That beside refusing any other person license to trade with the tribe, the agent removes, or threatens to remove the chiefs, for not advising their people to trade with the licensed monopoly, and that the agent represents to their people that the Government wishes them to pay such exorbitant prices.

3. That when they desired to come to Washington to obtain redress for their grievances, the agent declared that he would deprive Keokuk of his position, which he has held for 20 years, and would arrest the whole party.[3]

4. That Agent Wiley followed them to Lawrence, Kansas, and procured their arrest and imprisonment, not for any crime, but because they desired to represent their wrongs to the Department.[4]

5. For misrepresenting to us that our last treaty was ratified, and requesting and influencing us to sign a deed for a strip of land two and a quarter miles wide and four miles long, during the absence of the United States Interpreter, thereby taking us unprepared, and forcing us to convey valuable property to the detriment of the tribes.[5]

For these gross outrages of the agent, and for his collusion with the trader, we, the chiefs of the Sac and Fox tribes of the Mississippi, respectfully ask you to remove both the agent, Albert Wiley, and the trader, William Whistler, and appoint an agent with instructions to license at least two traders for the tribe. We come to your Excellency claiming protection against the rapacity of those who desire to swindle us out of the little we have. We have full faith that the Government desires to do us justice, and we beg you will grant our prayer and see justice done us.[6]

New York Tribune, Dec. 14, 1868.

1. Along with three other chiefs, Moses Keokuk was also joined by his son Charles Keokuk (d. 1904), who was an interpreter, and George Powers (b. c1826), formerly a sergeant in the 5th Infantry stationed at Fort Harker, Kansas, who was the official government interpreter. 1860 Census, Kans., Ellsworth, Ft. Harker, 4; Ida M. Ferris, "The Sauks and Foxes in Franklin and Osage Counties, Kansas," *KSHS Coll.*, 11 (1909–10): 374, 385.

2. Wiley (*c*1824–*fl*1870), a native of Ohio, became agent for the Sacs and Foxes in March 1867. By 1870 he was a druggist. 1870 Census, Kans., Osage, Agency Twp., Olivet, 45; Edward E. Hill, *The Office of Indian Affairs, 1824–1880: Historical Sketches* (New York, 1974), 153.

3. When Wiley reported to his superiors that Keokuk and other chiefs wanted to go to Washington to discuss their grievances, Charles E. Mix, acting Commissioner of Indian Affairs, quickly wrote to Kansas Indian Superintendent Thomas Murphy stating that Congress had not appropriated any funds to cover the expenses of visiting Indian delegations. Thus, none was to come, unless specifically ordered to do so by the Indian Affairs office, which Mix did not do. Wiley read the letter to Keokuk and the other chiefs. Mix to Murphy, Oct. 16, 1868, in Ferris, "Sauks and Foxes," 377.

4. Murphy ordered Wiley to take any steps necessary to prevent the Indians from visiting Washington. Moses Keokuk announced that he would pay for the trip himself. The delegation left on November 22, 1868, but was arrested in Lawrence the next day. Keokuk refused to pay bail so the Indians spent two days and a night in jail before they were released on a writ of *habeas corpus*. Their attorneys sued Mix, Murphy, Wiley, and the local deputy U.S. marshal for false arrest. Ibid., 377–78; *New York Tribune*, Dec. 14, 1868.

5. This may have been the main motivating grievance. Ferris, "Sauks and Foxes," 377.

6. The Indian delegation visited Johnson on December 6 and 12. However, Johnson did not remove Wiley, who remained in office until Grant replaced him in June 1869 with Thomas Miller. Eventually, Keokuk was awarded one thousand dollars damages in his suit against Wiley. *Philadelphia Press*, Dec. 7, 1868; *Washington Evening Star*, Dec. 5, 12, 1868; *New York Tribune*, Dec. 14, 1868; Ferris, "Sauks and Foxes," 378–79; Hill, *Indian Affairs*, 153.

From Samuel H. Allen[1]

Waterloo [N.Y.]   Dec 15th 1868

Dear Sir

I have the honor of the pleasure to extend to you an invitation to be present at an Inauguration Ball, given in honor of Hon. John T. Hoffman Governor elect, at the Academy of Music, in this place on the Evening of December 31st and the honor of your presence is earnestly solicited, and I can assure you Sir, that nothing would afford the Young Democracy of this County more pleasure than to welcome you here on this occasion, that by so doing we might express to you our thanks for the brave and strenuous efforts you have made in trying to preserve and defend the Constitution of our Country, and for which the people of little Seneca will for ever look upon you with pride.

Samuel H Allen

ALS, Johnson-Bartlett Col., Greeneville.
1. Not identified.

To Hugh McCulloch

[Washington, D.C.]   December 15, 1868.
The principal applicants for this place—Messrs. Smith[1] and Stanton[2]—seem well recommended. Believing, however, that preference should be given to the one who served as a soldier during the rebellion, the President requests the Secretary of the Treasury to send for his signature a nomination in favor of Daniel H. Stanton.

Andrew Johnson

ES, DNA-RG56, Appts., Internal Revenue Service, Assessor, N.Y., 17th Dist., Daniel H. Stanton.

1. William T. Smith is not further identified.

2. Stanton (1830–1897) was a printer by trade prior to the Civil War. He saw active duty during the war and was severely wounded in combat. In July 1868 Johnson had nominated him as assessor for the 17th District of New York, but the Senate rejected him. On December 17 the President once again forwarded Stanton's name to the Senate. He was eventually commissioned to that post. Later he became a successful land surveyor and in 1876 became county treasurer. Seavor, *Franklin County*, 778; Ser. 6B, Vol. 4: 47, Johnson Papers, LC; *U.S. Off. Reg.* (1869).

From Willard Warner and George E. Spencer[1]

Washington. Dec. 16 1868.
We learn that Captain David Humphreys proposes writing the life of Andrew Johnson President of the United States.

We take pleasure in saying from a long personal acquaintaince with Mr. Humphreys, that we think him eminently well qualified by education and experience for such a task, and that his industry and scholarship will insure completeness and accuracy and his high personal character, is a guarantee of his fidelity in the execution of such a work.

We doubt not that such a work skillfully narrating the history of one whose life has been so eventful and so conspicuous, will be of great and general interest.

Willard Warner

Geo. E. Spencer

ALS (Warner), DLC-JP.

1. Warner (1826–1906) was an Ohio native who had an active career there in business and state politics before moving to Alabama after the war. He represented the latter state in the

U.S. Senate (1868–71), and afterwards served as collector of customs for Mobile. Subsequently, Warner moved to Chattanooga, where he was in banking and other businesses, and served in the Tennessee legislature. Spencer (1836–1893) was an Iowa lawyer who moved to Alabama after the war and practiced law in Decatur. He represented Alabama in the U.S. Senate (1868–79), and retired to Nevada afterwards. *BDUSC.*

From Paul Bagley

Washington, D.C., Dec. 17, 1868.

Mr. President.

In presenting this paper,[1] of which I have the honor to be the bearer, permit me, in the name of the signers and the millions of their constituents, to present to your excellency the deep and abiding interest that is felt in the subject it commends to your consideration.

It is, sir, for amnesty we plead—for that amnesty without which it is *impossible* for a portion of your once disloyal subjects ever to return to their allegiance to the government.

And in making this request, sir, we come to lay down no line of policy for the President to pursue, but simply ask that he will pursue his past policy in this regard unto the end that we have prayed.

The eyes of the world have looked with amazement, sir, at the development of that policy of mercy which has been pursued by the President towards those whose hands were red with rebellion. While China has sent her ranks on ranks of rebels to the grave, while Britain has shot her Sepoys from the cannon's mouth, or Mexico has made a Maximilian her exponent of universal anarchy and blood, it has remained to this glorious republic to close one of the greatest rebellions in the history of the world without shedding one drop of the blood of war when once had arrived a time of peace.

And now, sir, believing that the President will be pleased to take this occasion of extending the amnesty desired, and that God will defend the right, and praying the peace of the President, the government and the people through the Prince of Peace, I have the honor to be . . .

PAUL BAGLEY, Missionary, &c.

Savannah Morning News, Jan. 5, 1869.

1. He presented a petition, signed by numerous members of Congress and dated December 17, which entreated the President to extend "amnesty to all persons recently engaged in rebellion against the government, who are now under *presentment* or *indictment.*"

From John C. Crane

Washington D C   Dec'm 17 1868.

My dear Friend

Permit me to call your valuable attention to the case of Major Megrue assessor of Internal Revenue 2d Disct of Ohio Cincinnati, Ohio.[1]

In the year of 1867, The Major was instrumental in causing the election of Gen'l Cary to the 40th Congress, which compliment the Gen'l then, fully appreciated.

During the recent campaign the Major aided the Gen'l in a *substantial* way to re election. Yet it seems the Gen'l has seen fit, to interfere with the Majors nomination, for action of the Senate.

The Major served with distinction in the Army, and would have given Gen'l Cary his personal services, in 1868, but from the fact of his holding the position of assessor and *for him to have acted for the Gen'l* would *ruined* his *Confirmation.* When Cary voted against Impeachment, Megrue was the *first man* to address him Congratulating him for his Act. The Major *was* and *now* is your *personal friend* and admirer and is deserving of your consideration.

The Sec'y of the Treasury being so well satisfied with Megrues administration, and having signed the Nomination (Gen'l Carys Influence to the Contrary notwithstanding) and forwarded the same to you for action, I do most earnestly *ask you to sign the same* and if possible forward to the Senate for action tomorrow.

I am well aware of Gen'l Cary's interference or requests, in the premises, but I do assure you My dear friend that you never made a more just selection than in the nomination of the Major, and I do most earnestly entreat you to sign and forward his nomination at once.

Personally to me it will renew my obligation of one of whom I have allways carried the highest respect for.

Jno. C. Crane
Willards Hotel Wash D C

ALS, DNA-RG56, Appts., Internal Revenue Service, Assessor, Ohio, 2nd Dist., Conduce G. Megrue.
    1. See Samuel F. Cary to Johnson, Dec. 1, 1868.

From L. Q. Washington[1]

Washington, D.C.   December 17th 1868

Sir;

Will you allow me to offer for your consideration the propriety of selecting next Christmas Day for an unconditional amnesty of all persons participating in the recent rebellion, naming no individual, and excepting none whether by name, or class, or description of any sort. I have thought much of it and I am within bounds in saying that this step would be cordially approved by a large majority of the American people, *acceptable* to, at least, two thirds of them, and in Europe would be hailed by all as a graceful, humane and statesman-like act.

I have always believed that you did not intend to close your Presidential term without such an act, and I sincerely trust for the sake of the country and your own fame that you will not allow this, the fittest occasion, for a general amnesty to pass.

L. Q. Washington

ALS, DLC-JP.

1. Washington (1825–1902), a District of Columbia native and prosecutor of claims, served as chief clerk in the Confederate State Department. Afterwards he returned to Washington and worked as a correspondent and journalist. *New York Times*, Nov. 5, 1902; *Washington Post*, Nov. 5, 1902.

From Anne M. Deen

New York City   Dec 18. 1868.

Sir

My health has been so badly lately, that I have been prevented from visiting Washg'n or even writing to you in regard to the Naval officer at this Port; but understanding that a pressure is being made upon you to nominate a gentleman, I am constrained to rise from my sick bed, and beg to remind you that Mr Deen is still before you;[1] and I know not Mr President, why, you delay in sending in his name, as he has every qualification, and has presented you with reccommendatory letters, sufficient as you have said, to satisfy you, certainly. No candidate has presented more—or from more respectable sources. Beside, Mr Deen, Sir: is a friend of you, and no man has done more for you, or defends you and your past acts more energetically. As you have several times promised to give him the nomination; we hope and trust, that no one will persuade you to again give preference to any other candidate.

I feel that Mr Deen would be confirmed by the Senate. But should you send his name in, and he be rejected, you would be relieved from further importunings—your promises would be fulfilled, and we would consider you free to give thought and trial to any other candidate.

This is a matter Mr President about which I have worried a great deal, and I have accepted the remarks and promises, you have made to me, at different times, as inferrencies that you would make the nomination.

In closing Mr President, permit me to express the hope, that you will not disappoint us, in the nomination,—and to say that if the friends you have around you, had been as faithful as is Mr Deen, much of the trouble, care and abuse, so unjustly heaped upon you, would have been turned to torment the inventors, and they would have realized the truth of the ancient adage, that: Curses, like young chickens, always go home to roost.

Mrs A M Deen
4. East 30th St.

ALS, DNA-RG56, Appts., Customs Service, Naval Officer, New York, John L. Deen.
1. In January, Johnson finally nominated John L. Deen for naval officer of New York, but he was not confirmed. See Anne M. Deen to Johnson, July 3, 1868, *Johnson Papers*, 14: 307–9; Deen to Johnson, Feb. 17, 1869.

From James B. Eads

N York   Dec 18 1868

I will be glad to have R M Johnson[1] nominated for Marshal in Missouri and believe your friends will receive it with favor.

Jas B Eads of St Louis

Tel, DLC-JP.
1. Probably Gen. Richard W. Johnson, who retired from active military service in October 1867 and afterwards became professor of military science at the University of Missouri. *DAB*; *History of Boone County, Missouri* (St. Louis, 1882), 300–301.

From William Fullerton

No 11 Pine St. N.Y.   Dec. 18, 1868.

Mr. President

I spent most of the day yesterday in fruitless attempts to see you. Being compelled to return to New York last night, it seems necessary that I should address you by letter.

I am well assured that I have arrived at a point in my investigations of revenue frauds, where I should pause and ask action on the part of the President. I have collected a vast amount of evidence implicating Government officers in frauds, but I cannot, in justice to the persons furnishing that evidence, use it so long as Mr. Courtney is the U.S. District Attorney here. Past experience proves that the power he possesses is used to persecute those who give information, and not to punish the guilty.[1] Every man who thus far has given me information which has been used, has been indicted. This admonishes me that I may look for a like course to be pursued with future witnesses.

Being unwilling to work against such great disadvantages, and subject men to such perils, I have concluded to suspend all further labors until Mr. Courtney is removed.

With a new and friendly District Attorney I am certain that I can, within the remaining few months of your administration, break up and disperse this body of men who have hitherto defrauded the Government with impunity. It is for you to determine whether that shall be done or not. It is easy to nominate a man in Mr. Courtney's place who will be acceptable to the Senate, and he will be confirmed at once. Then I can resume my labors, and your administration, and not Genl. Grant's, will get the credit which will result from them.

I have a deep interest in this matter, but mine is not to be compared with yours. What you do will pass into history, whilst my connection with it will be forgotten, except that the records of the Courts will show for all time to come that I was indicted for serving you faithfully.

I ask for the removal of Mr. Courtney on no personal grounds, but simply and only because my work cannot be accomplished without it.[2]

If the President is satisfied to leave matters as they are, I will not complain, but wait patiently for a more auspicious hour, when I can be enabled to reach those who are now permitted to use the courts to shield them from merited punishment.

William Fullerton

LS, DLC-JP.

1. In addition to the removal of Binckley from the whiskey fraud case, followed by the dismissal of the government's case altogether, a series of arrests further derailed the government's investigation. John D. McHenry, George B. Davis, and George A. Fitch, all government witnesses, had been indicted, as had Fullerton himself. See John M. Binckley to Johnson, Oct. 7, 1868, Jan. 8, 1869; and George W. Greene to Johnson, Nov. 26, 1868.

2. Courtney was not removed. For other complaints about Samuel G. Courtney, see N. E. Paine to Johnson, Nov. 15, 1868.

From John Ray

Treasury Department. Decr. 18th 1868

Sir

I most respectfully and earnestly recommend to your favorable consideration for the office of Assesser for the 3rd District of Louisiana *James Hart*[1] formerly of Tennessee but for many years a resident of Louisiana. Mr Hart's character for honesty, capacity and Patriotism is unquestioned and of the highest order.

I think it probable you may be personally acquainted with Mr Hart.

I would here say, that Mr Hart does not know of this application being made in his behalf but I feel confident Mr Hart would accept this position. He is in no sense a mendicant for office. He is a man in good circumstances.[2]

Jno Ray

L, NHi-Misc. Mss. Johnson, Andrew.

1. As there were many James Harts in Tennessee and Louisiana, it has not been possible to identify the correct one.

2. At the bottom of Ray's letter, Frank Morey endorsed the candidacy of James Hart. Johnson nominated Hart for the assessor post on the very day of Ray's letter. On the last day of the Congressional session, however, the Senate decided to lay Hart's nomination on the table. *Senate Ex. Proceedings*, Vol. 16: 416, 505.

From Rufus P. Spalding

Washington   Dec. 18th 1868

Sir

I am informed that Richard C. Parsons[1] of Cleveland, Ohio, aspires to the responsible office of Commissioner of Internal Revenue through your nomination and appointment.

Mr. Parsons is one of my constituents and *I know him well*. He is, in my Judgment, a very unsuitable person to be placed at the head of the Internal Revenue Bureau. Some years since I gave him a recommendation for this very position; but then I believed him *honest*, now *I do not*, for I have had evidence to convince my understanding to the contrary.

But aside from this important consideration of capacity & honesty, I beg leave to remind you that, in 1866, I was opposed by this very man, for a seat in the 40th Congress for the reason, mainly, that I was "a Johnson man," as he termed it, and during the impeachment trial last spring, he took strong ground against you, as he was then a candidate for nomination to Congress himself. He even went, so far, on the stump, as to repudiate the course of his friend the Chief Justice.

I very respectfully ask you, Sir, to consider these matters before you act in the premises.[2]

R. P. Spalding

ALS, DLC-JP.

1. Parsons (1826–1899), a Cleveland lawyer, served in the state legislature prior to the Civil War. He was collector of internal revenue at Cleveland (1862–66) and then marshal of the U.S. Supreme Court (1867–72). Parsons served one term (1873–76) as U.S. Representative. *BDUSC.*

2. The President endorsed the envelope of Spalding's letter, "Letter to be preserved for special purpose." He did not nominate Parsons for appointment as internal revenue commissioner.

From Edmund W. Cole[1]

Metropolitan Hotel   Washington D.C.
19th Decr. 1868

Dear Sir

I am on my return from New York to Nashville. Sorry I could not see you in person again. I called this evening, but you was engaged.

I thank you for the interview on last Saturday[2]—and your expressions of Sympathy for our strugling Corporation. I have filed our papers—asking a settlement of this case—with the sec'y of war. The absence of the Sec'y[3] prevents a present hearing of the case before him. But he promised to give the matter attention on his return. If the sec'y of war, feels that he has no authority to make a compromise in the settlement of the bond—Could it be done through the Cabinet?

We feel that our proposition is just to the Government and certainly all that we are able to do.

I expect to return here, some time in January and if the matter can not be reached in any other way—Congress might pass a resolution authorizing or directing the sec'y of war, to settle the matter upon principles of equity and justice.

I take the liberty of enclosing you, a copy of the memorial of the board of Directors to the Government, which I beg you will read.[4] I had a few copies printed that it might be read the more easily. If upon consideration of the premises, the settlement we propose meets your sense of equity & justice—the Corporation will greatly appreciate your influence in consumating it—as we believe a law suit, would be alike unproductive of good results to the Government and the Rail Road Company.

E W Cole   Prest.

ALS, DLC-JP.

1. Cole (1827–1899) had been in the railroad business in Tennessee since the early 1850s. He left the state during the war; in late 1865 Cole was elected general superintendent of the Georgia Railroad and Banking Company. But in August 1868 he became president of the Nashville and Chattanooga line, a post he held for the next twelve years. William S. Speer, ed., *Sketches of Prominent Tennesseans* (Nashville, 1888), 70–72; William Waller, ed., *Nashville in the 1890s* (Nashville, 1970), 312.

2. The interview has not been verified. See Edward H. East to Johnson, Dec. 2, 1868, Johnson Papers, LC.

3. John M. Schofield was gone from Washington December 12 through 20 to attend a Chicago reunion of the western Union armies. *Washington Evening Star*, Dec. 11, 12, 16, 19, 21, 1868.

4. Enclosed is a printed version of Cole's letter to the War Department, dated November 18, 1868. In it Cole discussed in detail the financial arrangement and obligations of the railroad company, particularly with regard to the $1.5 million federal government bond. Cole claimed that many of the sums charged against that bond for equipment, buildings, etc., were exaggerated or overpriced. Moreover, he asked for credits to the company for certain government use of the railroad during the war. In conclusion Cole offered to give the federal government $400 thousand in coupon bonds of the state government and requested the federal government to deduct the cost of property it sold to the railroad company. See also East to Johnson, Nov. 9, 1868.

From Charles J.M. Gwinn[1]

Balto: Dec. 19. 1868.

Dear Sir:

I beg to call your attention to the course of Mr Chandler on the Copper Bill.[2]

That Bill does not even exempt from the increased duty cargoes actually ordered before the passage of the law.[3]

It is a measure of mixed greed and vengeance. It has no other purpose except to drive from the market the products of a Maryland establishment.

You will perceive that the Senate committee against the wish of its chairman,[4] has denied a hearing to parties in interest.

It is for you to arrest the progress of the Bill, if it passes the Senate.[5]

It can properly be vetoed and it ought to be vetoed as

1. an impost of doubtful propriety, looking to the shipping interest of this country.

2. as a bill which improperly segregates one item of imposts from the general body, thus disturbing the relation of duties established in the act of March 2. 1861.[6]

C.J.M. Gwinn
for Balto. Copper Co.

ALS, DLC-JP.

1. Gwinn (1822–1894) was a lawyer and son-in-law of Reverdy Johnson. In the 1850s he had been a member of the Maryland House of Delegates and also the state attorney. He later served two terms as the state attorney general (1875–83). *Baltimore Sun*, Feb. 12, 1894.

2. Senator Zachariah Chandler of Michigan was a chief proponent of a bill "regulating the duties on imported Copper and copper ores," which drastically raised the duties on such imports. Opponents argued the bill would cripple many smelting companies which relied on imported ores, while Michigan's copper interests would reap the only benefits. *Congressional Globe*, 40 Cong., 3 Sess., pp. 144, 158–61; Gwinn to Johnson, Jan. 11, 19, Feb. 8, 1869. See also Robert B. Minturn, Jr., to Johnson, Feb. 10, 1869.

3. For a similar complaint, see James Corner & Sons to Johnson, Feb. 10, 1869.

4. Senator John Sherman, chairman of the Committee on Finance, had informed interested parties that the bill would not be reported until after the holidays. However, despite the December 16 report from the committee and Chandler's urgings, the bill was not discussed until January 18, 1869. *Congressional Globe*, 40 Cong, 3 Sess., pp. 98, 144, 415.

5. The bill passed the Senate on January 19, 1869, and the House on February 8. Johnson vetoed it on February 22, but the veto was overridden and the bill became law on February 24, 1869. Ibid, pp. 451, 978, 1489, 1509. See also Veto of Copper Bill, Feb. 22, 1869.

6. See *Congressional Globe*, 36 Cong., 2 Sess., Appendix, pp. 328–33.

From William P. Wells

Personal.

Detroit Mich. Dec 19 1868.

I earnestly recommend the appointment of Frederick Carlisle as Asst. Secy of the Treasy.[1] He will make a most faithful and efficient officer and his appointment will be much to defeat Chandlers return to the Senate.

Wm. P. Wells

Tel, DLC-JP.

1. Carlisle (*c*1832–*fl*1899) held a variety of posts and jobs in Detroit. He worked for several years in the customs house there in diffrent capacities. But by the 1870s he was in the real estate business. *NUC*; Detroit directories (1862–81); 1870 Census, Mich., Wayne, Detroit, 5th Ward, 214.

2. Zachariah Chandler was reelected to the U.S. Senate. *BDUSC.*

From George Work[1]

New Orleans   19 Decr /68

Sir

I know you have forgotten me but all the time you were speaking for Jackson in Tenn. I was doing the same agt. Clay in my native State (Ky.) & believing you to be a Jackson Democrat, pure and undefiled, I induced my old friend Gov. Matthews of Miss.[2] to go with me to Tenn. to help you to beat my classmate and best personal friend Gustavus Henry. We thought we were helping the cause of human liberty, Alas "now dead on the Globe." My property (1/2 million) was burnt 10 July '63 & I have at 3 score & 10 with 4 broken ribs lost teeth & eyes become a Junior apprentice of the law as Randolph said to Grundy.[3] In the burning my houses & stealing of my property, 20 most complimentary letters from Andrew Jackson to me were taken not to be heard of till the morning of the resurrection, but Genl. Jackson on 5 March '38 wrote Van buren to supercede Trist[4] by my appointment, Consul at Havana.

In June & July 65 I wrote 1/2 doz letters to the State- Dept, saying I would release my claim for the outrage committed on me for the letter of Jackson that for 50 years I have considered the greatest & best man of this world. This *letter* even I cannot get, because I suppose I have lived since 35 at Jackson Miss in the County called for his special friend Genl. Hinds.[5] Tho a Democratic Jackson Babtist for 40 years I am incapable of whyning appeals to any man but I hope you will send me Jacksons letter. I have sympathized with you in your conflicts with the Puritanical Psalm—singing hypocrites of *New* England ([?] than *old* England) as Mr. Jefferson well called them.

Geo. Work

ALS, DLC-JP.

1. Work (*c*1800–*fl*1870) was a lawyer in Hinds County. 1870 Census, Miss., Hinds, Clinton, 14.

2. Joseph W. Matthews (1812–1862) was a surveyor and farmer who turned to politics and served in the Mississippi legislature in the 1840s. In late 1847 he was elected governor of the state and served one term. Sobel and Raimo, *Governors*, 2: 809.

3. The alleged statement from John Randolph to Felix Grundy has not been identified. Randolph (1773–1833) was a long-time U.S. Representative and briefly U.S. Senator from Virginia. He also served one year (1830) as minister to Russia. *BDUSC.*

4. Nicholas P. Trist was consul at Havana (1833–41). *DAB.*

5. Thomas Hinds (1780–1840) achieved military distinction at the Battle of New Orleans. He served as a U.S. Representative from Mississippi (1828–31). *BDUSC.*

From Sidney Lindsay Clagett [1]

Washington   Dec. 20th, "68

Mr. President

The undersigned respectfully asks your consideration of the following statement. Something more than two years ago it was deemed essential to the public interests that a competent & experienced Clerk should be sent to Houston Texas to take charge of the Post Office there. Mr. Minor Bawsel[2] of this City, who had been for fourteen years in the Post office Department was selected & sent. A year ago himself & wife[3] died of Yellow fever leaving three little children, the eldest but five years of age, without any means of support. These little children have since been cared for by their Grandmother,[4] the Mother of Mrs. Bawsel an elderly widow Lady of extremely limited means, utterly inadequate to the proper support of the three little orphans. It has been suggested by many friends that I the Aunt of the children should make an application for appointment as Clerk in one of the Departments. Hence this application. Should it be granted the salery received therefor would be devoted to the care & maintenance of the little Orphans. As my Brother in law died literally in the service of the Goverment & had ever been an Officer of the best reputation for more than a dozen years, it would seem his children have some claims upon the Goverment to the extent at least of employing some one the proceeds of whose labour would be sacredly applied to their support! May I not hope Mr. President for your kindly interposition in their behalf! It is their sole reliance. Mr. Bawsel was a Mason in good standing & much esteemed by all who knew him.

Trusting this application may meet with favourable consideration.[5]

S. Clagett.   359 F St.

ALS, DNA-RG56, Appls., Positions in Washington, D.C., Treasury Offices, S. Clagett.

1. Clagett (b. *c*1832) was the wife of Joseph E. Clagett, a longtime Baltimore physician. They had one daughter. *History of Baltimore, Maryland* (n.p., 1898), 912–13; 1860 Census, Va., Jefferson, Harpers Ferry, 202.

2. Bawsel (*c*1837–1867), a post office clerk in Washington since at least 1853, was sent to Houston, where he served briefly (*c*1866–67) as a postal clerk. *U.S. Off. Reg.* (1853–67); Washington, D.C., directories (1858–66); 1860 Census, D.C., Washington, 3rd Ward, 46.

3. Helen Bawsel (*c*1841–1867) was the daughter of Lewis and Nancy Lindsay and a native of Virginia. Ibid.

4. Nancy Lindsay (*c*1802/1810–*fl*1870) ran a Washington boarding house with her daughter Lydia after the death of her husband about 1862. 1870 Census, D.C., Washington, 3rd Ward, 359; Washington, D.C., directories (1860–69).

5. Evidence of an appointment for Mrs. Sidney Clagett has not been uncovered.

From Robert Looney[1]

New York, Dec 20th 1868

Dear Sir

Seeing your daily nominations, in the different papers I take the liberty, to address you in behalf of my Father, Col, David Looney, who applied to you for an office.[2] My Mother, has written you on the subject,[3] and both my Mother, & Father have been over to see you. My Father is very reduced in circumstances and has no prospect of buisness. If you will give him an office I will regard it as a personal favor and hope to repay you at *some* future day.

Robert Looney

ALS, DLC-JP.

1. Looney (*c*1850–*fl*1900) apparently worked for a time as a mason, and later as a clerk and merchant, in New York City. 1860 Census, Ky., Jefferson, Louisville, 4th Ward, 97; New York City directories (1870–1900).

2. See David Looney to Johnson, Oct. 5, 1868.

3. See Mary Looney to Johnson, Aug. 1, 1868, *Johnson Papers*, 14: 469.

From Louis Schade

Washington D.C.   Decbr. 20, 1868.

Sir

The bearer of this, General Theodore Trauernicht, Editor of the Nashville (Ten.) Democrat, the only German democratic paper in that state, will state to your Excellency the necessity of supporting his journal. The Radicals do every thing for the other German paper,[1] published in Nashville, and it is not more than just that we democrats should follow this example. General Trauernicht, whom you know as a brave officer of our army during the last war, is a gentleman of high intelligence, and will certainly be of great service to you and the party in your State.

Louis Schade

ALS, DLC-JP.

1. Possibly a reference to the *Tennessee Staats Zeitung*, published in Nashville from 1866 to 1868; it was Republican in its political leanings. John Wooldridge, ed., *History of Nashville, Tennessee* (Nashville, 1890), 359–60.

From Edward W. Serrell[1]

64 & 66 Broadway
New York   20 Dec 1868

Sir

As suggested by your Excellency at the interview of Thursday last[2] I have the honor most respectfully to apply for the rank of Major General by Brevet U.S.V.

As I then stated to you I was Colonel of the 1st New York Engineers, for over three years and subsequently received a commission, Brig. Genl. by Brevet U.S.V. Several who were with me and some who served under me had the rank of Brevet Major Genl. conferred upon them.

I was several times recommended by my commanding General for promotion in the time during the war, but in each case was urged not to accept promotion because, as I was told, I could not be well spared from the command of the Engineer troops I then had.

I should much like, if consestent with the interests of the service, that the commission I seek should bear date from some special action, such as the Battle of James Island, the affair at Church flats, The Siege of Charleston, The erection of the "Swamp Angel" Battery, The Siege of Petersburgh The Battle of New Market road, The Capture of Fort Harrison, or the Union of the Army of the Potomac with the army of the James, in each of which I took part as in many other affairs.

I have no longer any connection with the army, but my children after me will take an interest in these things.

I trust therefore your Excellency will favorably consider my application.[3]

Edward W. Serrell
Bvt. Brig. Genl. U.S.V.

ALS, DNA-RG94, ACP Branch, File S-1616-CB-1864, E. W. Serrell.
1. Serrell (1826–1906) was a prominent civil engineer and technical author, with a specific interest in the isthmian canal. Hunt and Brown, *Brigadier Generals*; *NUC*; *New York Times*, Apr. 26, 1906.
2. Confirmation of an interview between Johnson and Serrell has not been found.
3. There is no evidence that Serrell received an additional brevet from the President.

From Milton Crane[1]

Vergennes, Vermont, Dec 21st 1868

Sir—

I take the liberty of addressing your Excellency for the purpose of informing you that on, or about, the first of August 1866, in conversation with E. D. Ellsworth,[2] Military Store Keeper of the Champlain Arsenal in this city, he denounced the President of the United States, as "the man who accidentally occupies the Presidential chair, and as the sole cause of the New Orleans riot, and massacre," and in comparing his Loyalty to that of Jeff Davis, failed to give the former the preference. Also, that Mr Ellsworth took the New York herald, until its editor said the President had done no wrong, he then discontinued it, & took the Times until Mr Raymonds[3] approval of the President and his Policy, after which, he discarded it and took the Tribune.

Should your Excellency deem it expedient to make an exchange in the appointment of Military Store Keeper at the Vergennes Arsenal I respectfully solicit the appointment on nomination.

The first year of our Rebellion, I was appointed by our then Secretary of War, S Cameron to take charge of the Arsenal, and until May 1862 discharged the duties of the office satsifactorily to the Department, and was then discharged for no other reason than to make room for the present incumbent.

On the first of April last, there was a paper sent to the Secretary of War, E. M. Stanton, reccommending me as a suitable person for Military Store Keeper at this post, signed by our most respectable citizens, including Hon F. E. Woodbridge, M C, Hon J Pierpoint, Chief Justice of Vermont, Hon E. Seymour, Ex State Senator, Hon J. E. Roberts, Mayor, of Vergennes, Gen. Geo. W. Grandy, Presidential Elector, and others.[4]

Milton Crane

ALS, DNA-RG94, ACP Branch, File C-483-CB-1868, Milton Crane.
1. Crane (b. c1796) was a prewar sheriff. Vermont directories (1858–59); 1860 Census, Vt., Addison, Vergennes, 253.

2. Ephraim D. Ellsworth (1809–1889) was a tailor for many years at Mechanicsville, New York. For about ten years he served as military storekeeper at Vergennes, Vermont. Afterwards, he returned to Mechanicsville. Nathaniel B. Sylvester, *History of Saratoga County, New York* (Philadelphia, 1878), 356; ACP Branch, File 1900-ACP-1871, E. D. Ellsworth, RG94, NA.

3. Henry J. Raymond.

4. Frederick E. Woodbridge (1818–1888), John Pierpoint (1805–1882), Edward Seymour (b. *c*1811), John E. Roberts (b. *c*1813), and Grandey (b. *c*1813). All were lawyers and former state legislators except Roberts, who was a lumber dealer. In addition, Pierpont was chief justice of the state supreme court (1865–80), and Grandey was several times mayor of Vergennes (1855, 1864, 1871, 1880). *BDUSC*; H. P. Smith, ed., *History of Addison County, Vermont* (Syracuse, 1886), 136–37, 161, 691–92; 1870 Census, Vt., Addison, Vergennes, 2, 10, 17.

From Perry Fuller, James B. Steedman, James O. Nixon

N. Orleans   Dec 21 1868

The appointment of C A. Weed as collector of Int'l Revenue would give satisfaction to the citizens of New Orleans and we recommend his appointment.[1]

Perry Fuller

Jas. B. Steedman

J. J. Nixon [*sic*]

Tel, DLC-JP.

1. Weed was not nominated. For an earlier, and negative, opinion of Weed, see William M. Daily to Johnson, June 19, 1868, *Johnson Papers*, 14: 234–35.

From Henry Frederick Liebenau

241 West 49th Street

New York   Dec 21st 1868

Mr President

I beg your Excellencys pardon for again trespassing on your valuable time. But if you remember sometime ago, you was very kind to me and sent me your Likness with your own autograph, which I prised, but as we all have our troubles I have had mine. My House took fire and Every Article was distroyed and with them your Excellency's Likness which was framed and hung up in my porlor! I now most respectfully ask your Excellency to grant me an other one for it is prised by all my family. With many thanks for your past Kindness . . .

Col. H. Fredk. Liebenau.

ALS, DLC-JP.

From John Bigler and Thomas J. Henley

San Francisco Cal   Dec 22, 1868.

We respectfully recommend Henry Baker[1] as successor to Dr Gunn,[2] Internal Revenue assessor first (1st) District California whose resignation takes effect thirty-first (31st) instant.

The appointment is a good one and will be confirmed by Senate.[3]

John Bigler

T. J. Henly[sic]

Tel, DLC-JP.

1. Although there were several Henry Bakers in San Francisco, Bigler and Henley may have been referring to the Henry Baker (fl1872) who was variously a cashier, clerk, or other office holder at the mint or the customhouse. San Francisco directories (1862–72).

2. Lewis C. Gunn.

3. Johnson made no apparent attempt during the rest of his term to nominate anyone to be assessor of internal revenue for the first district of California.

From Lewis D. Campbell

Hamilton O.   December 25, 1868.

Dear Sir:

I am right glad you issued your amnesty proclamation of this date. My opinion is perhaps of little consequence to any one, still it seems to me preposterous that Davis, Breckenridge and others, who were honest believers in the infernal doctrine of secession, should be prosecuted longer for *their* treason, whilst the radicals are making Senators, representatives, Judges, &c. of *other traitors* who are doubly injurious. Your document comes forth, too, on an appropriate day—the anniversary of the birth of the Savior, who, when on earth inculcated Heaven-born principles of mercy and forgiveness. As a matter of course the canting, pharisaical Radicals who assume to be *par excellence*, the representatives of *loyalty* and the champion-defenders of *"great moral ideas"* will abuse you from pulpit and from press. I presume you can still stand their ravings.

I observe they have pitched into your annual message vigorously—especially the financial part. It is easy to indulge in hard words, but I am watching for the Statesman among them who can now devise a policy that will steer the nation clear of repudiation of some sort. If, three years ago, Congress had adopted a rigid economy and had admitted representatives from the Southern States, we should not only now have had "peace"; but the productions of that fertile region would have become powerful auxiliaries in relieving us of the financial embarrassments entailed by the War. But their wicked policy and their gross corruptions and extravagance makes some sort of repudiation a certainty of the future. It is only a question of time. Sherman[1] may get up funding bills—Morton[2] may make "great speeches" (so called)—and Greeley[3] may write about "consels"; but all these wont bring us the "solid rocks" wherewith to pay in coin what the government owes. Until the government can do that it is idle to expect individuals to be able so to pay. Their idea of fixing a day in the *future* to pay in coin and continuing their *present policy* that is certain to *keep it out of the nation's power to perform*, is simply ridiculous. Morton and old Spinner[4] might get up a bill promising that the Mississippi should run *up stream* after July 1, 1871;[5] but when that time arrives I imagine their bill would be found as impotent to change Nature's law as Butlers Dutch Gap Canal[6] or Grant's excavation at Vicksburgh. The mighty "father of waters" would still flow *downward* to the Gulf. The Nation can only recuperate as indivudals do under adversity, viz, by practicing a rigid economy and by the sweat of the brow producing wealth from the soil and natural resources. So long as it takes *more than all of our revenues* to pay interest, salaries of office holders and the stealings of their pets, it is idle to fix a time to pay in gold and silver.

Lewis D Campbell

LS, DLC-JP.

1. Senator John Sherman had sponsored the ill-fated Funding Bill which Johnson had pocket-vetoed in July. See Alexander Campbell to Johnson, July 20, 1868, *Johnson Papers*, 14: 385–86. See also Horace M. Day to Johnson, Sept. 7, 1868.

2. On December 14, 1868, Senator Oliver P. Morton introduced a bill requiring the treasury to hoard gold until enough reserves accrued to begin the redemption of bonds in specie. Two days later he delivered his major speech on this topic. The bill was tabled in January 1869 in favor of another financial proposal. *Congressional Globe*, 40 Cong., 3 Sess., pp. 61, 101–6, 413–14.

3. In a published letter to Senator Morton, dated December 21, Horace Greeley proposed the sale of government consols (a contraction of consolidated annuities) which would shore up treasury holdings and allow the redemption of bonds to begin immediately. *Webster's New Universal Unabridged Dictionary*, 2nd ed.; *New York Tribune*, Dec. 21, 1868.

4. At least two letters from Treasurer of the U.S. Francis E. Spinner had recently appeared in the newspapers. Both proclaimed the need for repayment in specie and deplored the support given to various greenback approaches. Ibid., Dec. 8, 1868; *Cincinnati Enquirer*, Dec. 18, 1868.

5. Morton's redemption bill set July 1, 1871, as the day specie repayment would begin on U.S. bonds. *Congressional Globe*, 40 Cong., 3 Sess., p. 61.

6. In the winter of 1864–65 General Benjamin Butler failed in his attempt to bypass the James River by digging a canal. Long, *Civil War Almanac*, 618.

Fourth Amnesty Proclamation

[December 25, 1868]

Whereas the President of the United States has heretofore set forth several proclamations offering amnesty and pardon to persons who had been or were concerned in the late rebellion against the lawful authority of the Government of the United States, which proclamations were severally issued on the 8th day of December, 1863, on the 26th day of March, 1864, on the 29th day of May, 1865, on the 7th day of September, 1867, and on the 4th day of July, in the present year; and

Whereas the authority of the Federal Government having been reestablished in all the States and Territories within the jurisdiction of the United States, it is believed that such prudential reservations and exceptions as at the dates of said several proclamations were deemed necessary and proper may now be wisely and justly relinquished, and that an universal amnesty and pardon for participation in said rebellion extended to all who have borne any part therein will tend to secure permanent peace, order, and prosperity throughout the land, and to renew and fully restore confidence and fraternal feeling among the whole people, and their respect for and attachment to the National Government, designed by its patriotic founders for the general good:

Now, therefore, be it known that I, Andrew Johnson, President of the United States, by virtue of the power and authority in me vested by the Constitution and in the name of the sovereign people of the United States, do hereby proclaim and declare, unconditionally and without reservation, to all and to every person who, directly or indirectly, participated in the late insurrection or rebellion a full pardon and amnesty for the offense of treason against the United States or of adhering to their enemies during the late civil war, with restoration of all rights, privileges, and immunities under the Constitution and the laws which have been made in pursuance thereof.

In testimony whereof I have signed these presents with my hand and have caused the seal of the United States to be hereunto affixed.

Done at the city of Washington, the 25th day of December, A. D. 1868, and of the Independence of the United States of America the ninety-third.

ANDREW JOHNSON.

Richardson, *Messages*, 6: 708.

From Bernard O'Kane
Worthy your attention

Boston, Mass.   Dec. 25. 1868

Dear Sir;

No doubt, by special orders from you, your Secretary consigns to the waste basket many communications which should otherwise command attention. I am led to this conclusion from the fact, that as a friend, I have privately made known, by letter, facts which have not created any action thereon.

You cannot doubt for a moment the sincerity of my intention in communicating with you in this private manner, as my public declarations defending you, in good report & bad report, are well known, since August 1866, in the columns of the "Catholic Telegraph," published in Cincinnati. Of course this was a voluntary act on my part, and unsolicited by you. Yet this does not make any difference, as my voluntaryism only proves the act more worthy of appreciation, in consequence of seeking no reward in the past. Neither can I expect any thing at this time; but one favor I am about to ask, & I beg of you to give it your attention; it is of interest to you & to me & to all your friends. It will serve to remove charges held against you, of continuing in office, bad men who were recommended for removal. I therefore solemnly and earnestly request you to remove William H. McCartney,[1] Collector of Internal Revenue, for the 3d. Mass. Dist. This notorious individual has been repeatedly complained of to Commissioner Rollins, who has recommended his removal by you.

McCartney is a shrewd & tricky fellow: at one time he is an administration man, at another he is a Congressional advocate. He has played well, the game which the absurd Tenure of Office bill gives scope to. When Mr Rollins sent in his name with General King's,[2] the Assessor of the same District, for removal, he goes on to Washington, carries six thousand dollars with him, which he places in Simon P. Hanscom's hand for purposes best known to those who withdraws his name, while poor King who has no money to spend is removed.

For fear some respectable name should be presented to Congress, and that the Senate might confirm it, he ignores his administration trick and takes the stump for Grant; on which occasion he unblushingly relates his experience in purchasing his position through the office broker alluded to.

This notorious scamp, McCartney, has been plundering the Government & the people too long. Let him be removed at once, that you, Dear Sir, may escape the odium which he dares to put upon your benignity.[3] If delayed till President Grant is inaugurated he will surely be removed.

Bernard O'Kane

ALS, DLC-JP.
1. For O'Kane's earlier condemnation of McCartney, see O'Kane to Johnson, July 23, 1868, *Johnson Papers*, 14: 414–15.
2. William S. King.
3. For a discussion of the outcome of the McCartney matter, see ibid., 416.

From Lawrence Sangston[1]

Baltimore   Decr. 26th 1868

Dear Sir

The proclamation of amnesty which greeted the people of our country on Christmas morning was a glorious addition to that Holy day of festivity and rejoicing it was a noble duty—well performed.

There yet remains something undone. The prisoners at the Dry Tortugas. They have suffered long and severely and at this moment there are but few of either party who believe them to be guilty of any complication with the murder of Mr. Lincoln but rather regard their conviction and imprisonment as a matter of State or political policy at the time.

While perhaps no one would doubt the justice of releasing them it would still require much of that rare virtue—moral courage.[2]

Your record gives abundant proof that you posess it—equal to any emergency or the performance of any duty.

I have not the honor of a personal acquaintance with you beyond a mere introduction at the laying of the Corner Stone of the Masonic Temple[3] being the Senior Grand Warden of our Grand Lodge but assured of your Kindness I feel I shall be pardoned if there is any impropriety in my addressing you on the subject.

Lawrence Sangston

ALS, DLC-JP.
1. Sangston (*c*1813–1876) was a merchant and president of the Maryland Fertilizing and Manufacturing Company. J. Thomas Scharf, *History of Baltimore City and County* (Philadelphia, 1881), 807; Baltimore directories (1868–72).
2. Imprisoned at Dry Tortugas were Dr. Samuel A. Mudd, Samuel B. Arnold, and Edward Spangler. Significant pressure was being exerted for clemency for these men. Mudd and Arnold,

sentenced to life imprisonment, were pardoned by Johnson on February 8 and March 2, respectively. Spangler, sentenced to six years, was also pardoned on March 2. *Washington Evening Star*, Feb. 4, 11, 15, 17, Mar. 2, 3, 1869; *New York Herald*, Mar. 4, 1869. See also Jacob Thompson to Johnson, Dec. 26, 1868; Pardon of Samuel Mudd, Feb. 8, 1869; Leonard Koons to Johnson, Mar. 4, 1869.

    3. Johnson visited Baltimore on November 20, 1866, for this Masonic ceremony. John S. Berry to Johnson, Nov. 17, 1866, *Johnson Papers*, 11: 466–67.

From Ann S. Stephens

National Hotel   Dec. 26 1868

My Dear Sir

    Gen Cary[1] has left town and I do not know when he will return. I cannot force myself to address Mr Stillwell[2] in any way that might seem like asking a favor, after the deception, to use no harsher word— that he has practiced upon you or upon me.[3] Nor can I ask you again to withdraw his name without some action on his part or on the part of his friend.[4] I do not wish you to violate one feeling of honor or consistency for my sake. Heaven knows I have never been selfish enough for that. But you can hardly understand how important it is that my son[5] should have some good position now and how great a disappointment it will be to us all if he fails to attain one. There are but two vacancies in South America Venzuela and Equador. The latter is scarcely desirable since the earthquake[6] and I have a terror of it but if everything else fails we have no choice. Still I do not wish to ask for that while there is a chance for the mission to Venzuela.

    If Mr Stillwell goes in as his name now stands, will you hold back the nomination to Equador until he is confirmed, or rejected, or his name withdrawn?[7] Otherwise there will be no chance for my son in anything.

    I do not think that Stillwells name will be acted upon at all. If it is not by the tenth of January it never will be. Then if you are so kind as to nominate my son I have little doubt that he *will* be acted upon and confirmed, but if, by what I think an unprobable chance, Stillwell should be taken up and confirmed, then I ask you to nominate my son for Equador. To nominate him for this place before would be to give up Venezuela at the onset. Let me be plain I hope you will make no nomination for Equador until that of Venezuela is filled.

    I was surprised and delighted with the proclamation.

Ann Stephens

ALS, DLC-JP.

1. Samuel F. Cary.
2. Thomas N. Stilwell.
3. See Stephens's letter of January 22, 1869, for her explanation of Stilwell's deception.
4. Unknown.
5. Edward Stephens.
6. On August 13, 1868, a severe earthquake hit Ecuador and Peru, desolating large parts of both countries, with aftershocks persisting for two weeks following the initial disaster. *National Intelligencer*, Oct. 7, 16, 1868. For requests for aid, see, for example, Jose Ribon and Jose Muñoz to Johnson, Oct. 14, 1868, Johnson Papers, LC.
7. Stilwell's name had been sent in for the third time on December 18 as minister to Venezuela, in which capacity he had operated between August 1867 and June 1868. In April 1869 James R. Partridge filled this position. In late January 1869, Shelah Waters of Tennessee was nominated as minister to Ecuador. Ser. 6B, Vol. 2: 312, 314, 317, 372, Johnson Papers, LC; *Register of the Department of State* (1872), 74.

From Jacob Thompson

Montreal. D.C. [Dominion of Canada] Dec. 26th. 1868

Sir

As a Citizen of the South, I thank you for your late Christmas proclamation: and upon the reading of it this morning, I determined to write you this letter, which, I hope, you will read and act upon before you leave office.

When you entered upon the discharge of your responsible duties, the waves of popular excitement were rolling high. The assassination of President Lincoln had raised a storm in the public mind which could not be easily quelled, and the people as well as their officers in high places gave ready credence to every marvellous statement which reached their ears. As that excitement culminated, you were induced to issue a proclamation which inculpated me in the "taking off" of your predecessor.[1] That nomination of me, has been the cause of much embarrassment & annoyance and has done me a vast deal of injury. This is now for the most part, passed away, and cannot be repaired. But, in this connection, I have a favor to ask of you, and I hope, you will not leave office without granting it.

I was abroad when your proclamation was issued. Regarding it in the light of an edict of banishment, I have remained abroad ever since: and I feel I am in honor bound to do so, until the proclamation is in some way revoked. I am convinced now that you must be fully persuaded that all the evidence on which it was originally based was a tissue of perjury or at all events, untrustworthy and unreliable. If you are not convinced, I have not a word more to say. I will endure to the end what I have patiently borne for near four years and wait until the truth can be made manifest. But if you are convinced that a wrong has been done me, and of this fact the public mind every where is thoroughly satisfied. (Moreover I swear to you before High Heaven, I never knew any one of the parties engaged in the assassination and never had any communication with any one of them or with any person for them, directly or indirectly, either before or after the act.) Then I will ask the favor at your hands, to send for the original proclamation which I suppose to be filed in the State or War Department and enter upon its face over your own signature some expression which will signify to those who succeed you and to the historian that in its issuance an injustice was done me. Such an expression as this: "This proclamation was issued improperly" or "issued on perjured testimony" or "issued on testimony which subsequent events demonstrated to be unreliable"—or a simple order revoking the proclamation, if made public and the reasons stated for the revocation, would be better.[2]

My public career is ended. In adhering to the principles which I conscientiously believed to be right, true & in accordance with the teachings of the fathers, I have stranded my little boat. But for eighteen years, my name is found scattered through all the public records. This is the only blot that any where attaches. You alone can wipe it out, and that must be done while in office. I cannot and will never ask any successor to do this act of justice not to me only, but to yourself also.

I have been out of the Country during the whole term of your Administration, but I have witnessed your whole bearing with interest, not unmixed with admiration. The nerve and lofty independence with which you have asserted truth and right and vindicated a strict compliance with the fundamental principles of our Government in the face of the most unscrupulous opposition and in despite of the revilings of infuriated partizans have led me to prefer this request, and have induced the belief that you will allow no stigma to rest on my name which has been unjustly placed there, although it may have been done by your own hands.

Please let me know that you have received this letter & also what you deem it proper to do or not to do in the premises.

J. Thompson

P.S. If there be one fact in relation to this whole affair on which you deem a statement or explanation by me desirable or necessary, I would be greatly obliged to you for an opportunity of making it.

J.T.

ALS, DLC-JP.

1. See Proclamation of Rewards for Arrest of Sundry Confederates, May 2, 1865, *Johnson Papers*, 8: 15–16.

2. While Johnson never revoked the proclamation accusing Thompson and others of inciting and procuring Lincoln's assassination, Stanton revoked the rewards on November 24, 1865, and much of the supportive testimony had been withdrawn by late 1866. Supposedly all of the accused were covered by Johnson's last amnesty proclamation on December 25, 1868. Jonathan T. Dorris, *Pardon and Amnesty under Lincoln and Johnson* (Chapel Hill, 1953), 270–71, 279; Hanchett, *Lincoln Murder Conspiracies*, 75–89.

From Charles C. Carpenter[1]
Private

Kansas City, Mo   December 27 1868

Dr Sir

I have resently been informed by the friends of the late member of Congress from Pa the Hon Charles Denison,[2] who was a Nephew of mine his mother,[3] is my Sister, now 92 years old, Claimed to be a blood relation of yours, on the femal Side of the House. My mothers[4] maiden name was *Ferrier*. I find on examing the family Record that She was born in Orange County New York in 1753. She has three sisters, *Anna*—the one whom the relationship is claimed, married a man by the name of *"John Johnson"*[5] shortly after his marage left orange County and Emigrated to One of the Carolina's from there to Kentucky located in Christian County Hopkinsville. On examining a file of old letters of my father Benjamin Carpenter[6] dated back behind fifty years, I find a family correspondence between my father and a John Johnson a brothern Law, dated at Hopkinsville Christian County Kentucky that of my fathers at the Vally of Wyoming Pa. Uncle Johnson mentions or speaks of two Sons one named John and the other Thomas. John at that time was acting as Sherriff of the County.[7] Hopkinsville was then the County seat. Thomas[8] was going to a Town in Tennessee call Sparta to take charge of a female Seminary. This is all the information I have on which the friends of mine claim blood relationship. If you are of that family of Johnsons[9] our mothers were sisters and of Irish desent, and of course we mite claim relationship, unless this matter on final investigation Should turn out as unhapily as that of the Irishmans who came across his brothe in America. Patrick said he had never seen his brother James, but once since he left Sweet Ireland and then he meet him one day upone one of the streets of New York. His brother was glad to see *him* and he was glad to see his *brother* but when they come to talke the matter over they found out that it was not neither "*him*" nor his "*brother*." Let this matter be as it may, I regard you on the account of your firmness, in dischargin what you suppose to be your duty as the Chief Magistrate of the nation.

Charles Carpenter

P S   As to my character and standing I would refer you to Gen Thomas Ewing. In my profession an Attorny at Law I was one of the Presidential Electors for the State of Missouri 1864 voted for Lincoln & Johnson.

C C

ALS, DLC-JP.

1. Carpenter (*fl*1871) was a lawyer. Kansas City directories (1865–71).

2. Denison (1818–1867), a Wilkes-Barre, Pennsylvania, lawyer, was elected to the U.S. House of Representatives three times but served only from 1863 until his death in June 1867. *BDUSC*.

3. Elizabeth Carpenter (*c*1776–*fl*1868) married Lazarus Denison in 1802. They had eight children of whom Charles was the youngest. Horace E. Hayden et al., eds., *Genealogical and Family History of the Wyoming and Lackawanna Valleys, Pennsylvania* (2 vols., New York, 1906), 1: 153–54.

4. Not identified.

5. Neither Anna Ferrier Johnson nor John Johnson have been otherwise identified.

6. Benjamin Carpenter (*fl*1810) was appointed justice of the peace and judge of the Court of Common Pleas in Luzerne County, Pennsylvania, in 1787. He was a representative in the Pennsylvania legislature in 1794. He moved to Wyoming Valley, Pennsylvania, and in 1810 to Sunbury in Delaware County, Ohio, where he became an associate justice. He had at least one other daughter. George B. Kulp, *Families of the Wyoming Valley* (3 vols., Wilkes-Barre, Pa., 1885–90), 1: 208; 3: 1047.

7. James M. Johnson was sheriff of Christian County (1808–10). Charles M. Meacham, *A History of Christian County, Kentucky, from Oxcart to Airplane* (Nashville, 1930), 30.

8. Not identified.

9. Andrew Johnson was not related to this family.

From Sanford E. Church

Rochester   Dec 28. 1868

Dear Sir.

I am inclined to believe that it would be wise to appoint Mr. Fred Carlilse Asst Secy. of the Treasury.[1] He is entirely competent, and on many accounts his appointment would be a good one.

I understand that he is making war on Chandler of Michigan with every prospect of defeating him.[2]

S. E. Church

ALS, DLC-JP.

1. For an earlier recommendation of Carlisle, see William P. Wells to Johnson, Dec. 19, 1868.

2. Zachariah Chandler won another term as U.S. Senator.

From Robert H. Kerr

Pittsburgh, Dec 28th 1868

Dear Sir.

Please find inclosed the resolution I had the honor to present which was adopted by the Democratic Committee.[1] This noble act will do more to bring Peace to the whole Country than thousands of men in arms. You will have the gratitude of Millions of Americans, while your enemies will only live to be execreated by the people. If Great Britian will only follow the example and open wide the Prison doors of the *Irish political Prisoners*, who are enduring cruel indignities which no other civilised nation in the world would inflict for loving their native land "Not wisely but too well,["][2] it will do more for the tranquility of *Ireland* than the Power of England in arms. Let Queen Vic—go & do what you have done. You have my thanks & gratitude! And I am confident that every true man will say "well done thou good & faithful Servant."[3]

R. H. Kerr

ALS, DLC-JP.

1. Not found, but internal evidence suggests it might have related to Johnson's recent Fourth Amnesty Proclamation, Dec. 25, 1868.

2. From Shakespeare's *Othello*, Act. 5, sc. 2.

3. Matt. 25:21.

From William S. Rosecrans

unofficial

United States Legation at Mexico

December 28. 1868

Your Excellency was so kind as to grant me the privilege of selecting my own Secretary of Legation in the place of Mr Plumb[1] who has resigned.

As he thought it incompatible with the dignity of having been chargé ad interim even temporarily return to the position of Secretary it became necessary to have immediate assistance, from the best available. I appointed Acting Sec' of Legation John A. Gadsden[2] nephew and private secretary here to Gen. Gadsden[3] our former Minister, a gentleman of many years residence here, familiar with the language and people of the country and with the Legation records.

His character and several positions are both high and his appointment which I respectfully ask would essentially advantage the public service.

I am actively at work mastering the language and condition of the people. Effective service, in such circumstances as now and prospectively are likely to obtain in this country demands all this and more.

W. S. Rosecrans

ALS, CLU-S/C.

1. Edward L. Plumb.

2. Gadsden (b. c1827), a planter, had represented the St. James Santee section of Charleston District in the South Carolina house of representatives in 1852. Johnson nominated Gadsden in mid-January 1869 to the post as secretary of the legation. The Senate took no action, however. 1850 Census, S.C., Charleston, Parishes of St. Philip and St. Michael, 364; *Charleston Courier*, Oct. 25, 1852; *Senate Ex. Proceedings*, Vol. 16: 432, 442.

3. James Gadsden (1788–1858) was actively involved in railroad promotion in the 1830s and 1840s. During the Pierce presidency, he became minister to Mexico and engineered the purchase of territory from Mexico, known as the Gadsden Purchase. He returned to Charleston in 1856. *DAB*.

From S. Carson Bowers [1]

Roanoke College   Salem, Roanoke Co. Va.
December 29th 1868.

Honored Sir.

I write to ask a favor of you, and I hope you will pardon my presumption, and grant it.

I want the *Agricultural Reports* issued since 1859, also the Mechanical Reports since same date;—if you will please have them sent to me, I will be greatly obliged by you. You know we Southern people have no opportunity of getting those things through the usual channel, and we (at least many of us) regard *you* as *our* friend. Any of those public documents intended for gratuitous distribution, will be thankfully received and highly appreciated, if it is your pleasure to send them to me.

Without wishing to appear to you as a sycophant or a flatterer, I speak the sentiments of many of our best people, and particularly my own, when I say we owe you an infinite debt of gratitude for your past kindness to us as a people. When we want any thing we go to you as we would to a kind father. Please excuse me, and believe me one of the warmest of your many sincere friends.

With my best wishes for your future prosperity and happiness . . .

S. Carson Bowers.

ALS, DLC-JP.

1. Bowers, apparently from Rockingham County, Virginia, was captain of Co. E, 58th Militia Rgt. in 1861–62. Lee A. Wallace, comp., *A Guide to Virginia Military Organizations, 1861–1865* (Richmond, 1964), 272–73.

From Peter Fairchild[1]

New Orleans   Dec 29th 68

Sir

Does your Proclamation of the 25th inst "General Amnesty and Pardon" Pardon me, for what aid and comfort I may have given the late rebellion. If so, has this State, or, the Government therof, any right to require any test oath, as a qualification, to hold office. An answer, as early as convenient with your Public duties, is desired by many of your true friends, in this City.

P. Fairchild

The above oath,[2] this State requires at the present time. That portion, giving aid to the Rebellion, and taking an Oath to Support the Constitution U.S. I cannot take. About 12 months, I was a non commissioned officer in the Confederate army,[3] and under Van Buren and Polk Administrations I was a Clerk in the Custom House.[4]

I have an appointment under this State Goverment, and cannot enter upon the duties. In case my disabilities are not removed please send me a full pardon—and your Petitioners will ever Pray. I took the oath of allegiance to the U.S. immediately after the Surrender in Mobile Ala in May, 1865—and have been a true and loyal citizen up to this time. I can furnish other testimonials if required. I am 64 years of age.

P Fairchild

ALS, DNA-RG60, Office of Atty. Gen., Lets. Recd., President.

1. Fairchild (c1806–fl1878), a native of New York, was a clerk. New Orleans directories (1870–78); 1870 Census, La., Orleans, New Orleans, 2nd Ward, 67.

2. The rest of this letter was written on the bottom and back of a printed "Oath of Eligibil-

ity" form. The oath was an "iron-clad" type listing a number of things which the signer had to swear he had never done.

3. Fairchild served in the 1st La. Cav. as a private and then ordnance sergeant from March 1862 to November 1863. Andrew B. Booth, *Records of Louisiana Confederate Soldiers and Louisiana Confederate Commands* (3 vols., Spartanburg, 1984).

4. Fairchild had held a post in the New York custom house for three years. Fairchild to James K. Polk, June 30, July 21, 1845, Lets. of Appl. and Recomm., 1845–53 (M873, Roll 27), Peter Fairchild, RG59, NA.

From William S. Groesbeck

Cincinnati   Decr. 29. 1868.

Mr. President:

I take the liberty of recommending Genl. Gordon Granger to the vacancy made by the resignation of Genl. Hooker. I have been requested to make this recommendation, but I make it just as unqualifiedly and heartily, as if it were done without request; for I consider Genl. Granger an excellent officer for the place and fully entitled to it. I earnestly hope he may get it, and I think his nomination by you will be as acceptable to your friends, as any you can make.

With the best wishes for you personally and officially . . .

W. S. Groesbeck.

ALS, DNA-RG94, ACP Branch, File G-273-CB-1868, Gordon Granger.

From Charles C. Dame[1]

Private

Salem Mass.   Dec. 30. 1868.

Dear Mr. President,

I understand that Gen. George H. Peirson[2] is an applicant for the position of Post Master in this city.

As I am well acquainted with Gen. Peirson, and know him to be a man worthy of such an appointment. I take great pleasure in commending him to your favorable consideration, with the hope that he may be successful in obtaining the position he seeks.

Gen. Peirson was actively engaged with the army during the war, rising by his own merit through successive grades to that of Brigr. General, and still holds that rank in the militia of our State. He is very popular, and deservedly so, among the citizens of Salem.

I may properly add that his appointment would be very acceptable among those through whose influence I first had the honor of meeting you. He has held a prominent position among us, by my appointment, during the past three years.

Charles C. Dame.

ALS, DLC-JP.
    1. Dame (1819–*fl*1898) had a somewhat lengthy career as a school teacher before becoming a lawyer in 1859. He served for a number of years as collector of internal revenue of the 5th District of Massachusetts. Dame was a very prominent Mason and eventually became, in the late 1860s, the Grand Master of the Massachusetts Masons. *Biographical Review Containing Life Sketches of Leading Citizens of Essex County, Massachusetts* (Boston, 1898), 235–38.
    2. Peirson (b. 1816) was colonel of the 5th Mass. Inf. during the Civil War. He was active in the Masonic order, serving several times as Master of the Essex lodge. A blacksmith by trade, he was nominated as postmaster on January 12, 1869, but apparently the nomination was not acted upon before the end of the congressional session. Williams Leavitt, "History of the Essex Lodge of Freemasons," *Historical Collections of the Essex Institute*, 3 (1861): 262–63; *Off. Army Reg.: Vols.*, 1: 154; Ser. 6B, Vol. 4: 25, Johnson Papers, LC.

From Charles E. Stuart

Kalamazoo Michigan   Decr. 30, 1868

Sir

I am advised that Frederick Carlisle Esq of Detroit is an applicant for the position of Asst. Secy. of the Treasury.[1] Personally I am not acquainted with him, but from his reputation and from what I learn of him from gentlemen whose opinions are entitled to the highest respect I am satisfied of his entire fitness for the place and that his appointment would be promotive of the public interests. I hope therefore that he may be appointed.

The local effect of it in this state would prove very beneficial.

Chas. E Stuart

ALS, DLC-JP.
    1. For earlier recommendations of Carlisle, see William P. Wells to Johnson, Dec. 19, 1868; Sanford E. Church to Johnson, Dec. 28, 1868.

From William S. Groesbeck

Cincinnati   Decr 31. 1868.

Mr. President:

Allow me, if Mr. Stilwell[1] should be rejected for Minister Resident at Ecuador, to recommend for nomination, Mr. William J. Kuhns of Columbus, Ohio.[2]

I do not know Mr. Kuhns personally, but he is highly esteemed by those in whose opinion I would trust, and I have no doubt he is in every way, well qualified for the place. I am assured, moreover, that he is warmly recommended by your friends. Genl Mungen[3] is anxious for his nomination, and if you should think it right to make it, I shall be much pleased on his account.[4]

W. S. Groesbeck.

ALS, DNA-RG59, Lets. of Appl. and Recomm., 1861–69 (M650, Roll 27), Wm. J. Kuhns.

    1. Thomas N. Stilwell. See Ann S. Stephens to Johnson, Dec. 26, 1868.

    2. Kuhns (b. c1820) was a longtime Columbus merchant. 1860 Census, Ohio, Columbus, 3rd Ward, 233; Columbus directories (1856–67).

    3. William Mungen to Johnson, Dec. 17, 1868, Lets. of Appl. and Recomm., 1861–69 (M650, Roll 27), Wm. J. Kuhns, RG59, NA.

    4. There is no indication that Kuhns was appointed to any post.

From Madison C. Johnson

Lexington, Dec 31 1868

Dear Sir

This will be handed you by Col H K Milward,[1] whom I beg leave to introduce as a Gentleman and as a tried soldier of the Union Army.

Col Milward is a Native of this City and I have known him and all his family since his boyhood. He and his family enjoy an enviable position in the respect and esteem of our community for uprightness and open sincerity in all their relations of life. They have been from the beginning firm and zealous supporters of the Union cause.

Col Milward entered the U S Army with the first Kentucky Volunters, and was active in organizing the Regiment, to the command of which he was finally promoted for his soldierly merits. He was with Sherman in his march to the sea, and took honorable part in all battles fought under Buell, Rozencranz and Sherman. He continued in the service to the close of the war.

As all public emoluments in our State are denied to men of his opinions, he presents in my opinion peculiar claims for any proper official appointment from the general Government. He desires a consulship to Honolulu. To that or a superior position I consider his claim for public service and his full ability to discharge all the duties fully entitle him. I therefore cheerfully give him my fullest recommendation.[2]

M C Johnson.

ALS, DNA-RG59, Lets. of Appl. and Recomm., 1861–69 (M650, Roll 33), H. K. Milward.

1. Milward (1835–*fl*1885) entered the newspaper business at the conclusion of the war, first in Lexington and subsequently in Louisville, Kentucky. He returned to Lexington in the early 1870s and established a business firm, Milward & Co. Shortly thereafter he became postmaster at Lexington. Robert Peter, *History of Fayette County, Kentucky* (Chicago, 1882), 659; *U.S. Off. Reg.* (1877–85).

2. Several prominent Kentucky officeholders, including members of Congress, signed Madison Johnson's letter to endorse Milward. But he did not receive the appointment sought.

From J. B. Stephens [1]

New York   Dec 31' 1868

Dear Sir

We have organized the Bondholders association expressly for mutual protection.

Also we have imployed the best financial talent in this State to make a systomatic Report on a few principles that cannot be invaded or invalidated with impunity. We loaned our money to the government for a purpose—this you know. But those controleing it are also using it for their purposes—*this* you also know.

How are we to have the Dollars—lawful money Refunded to us again—this *is* the vital question of the hour.

Senator Morton's theory of Specie[2] only means to perpetuate the Bonded Debt and not one Statesmen has made any direct efforts to Refund Dollars to the Bondholders. All efforts up to date are only adding Burdens and Disabilities to tax payors without Refunding Dollars to bondholders. The Laws and usury interest already enacted must create universal Bankruptcy in less then ten years & most likely Repudiation unless arrested by Refunding at least some $200,000,000 yearly. But this is not perpetuating political power & patronage.

The Refunding theory is the ony one to avoide taxation and Bankruptsy and the direct road to specie payments. Please consider these unavoidable Deductions as detailed in our Documentary[3] & accept the same as our New Years Gift.

J. B. Stephens   Chairman

ALS, DLC-JP.

1. Possibly John B. Stevens [*sic*] (d. *c*1891), a New York lawyer. New York City directories (1868–92).

2. See Lewis D. Campbell to Johnson, Dec. 25, 1868.

3. Not found enclosed.

January 1869

From Henry H. Haight

Sacramento, [ca. January 1869][1]

Mr President

I consider it my duty to address your Excellency in behalf of a large number (several hundred) of the farmers and others of this State who have settled upon and improved tracts of land embraced within the limits of rejected Mexican grants.[2] Some of these grants were grossly defective and some spurious and fraudulent. They have been examined and adjudged void by the courts but it is reported currently here that a combination is formed to procure the passage of some bill by Congress validating several of them after they have been finally rejected. A large number of worthy and industrious people are either settlers upon or purchasers of these lands or have made costly improvements upon them holding adversely to the pretended grants. For Congress now to impart validity to such grants would be to ruin most of these persons who have every equity and at present all the law in their favor and would be an act of injustice as flagrant as could well be perpetrated in any civilized country. I am not using words without measuring their purport. It is impossible to believe that any legislative body under a republican government would commit such a spoliation unless it was either misled by interested parties or else lost to all sense of justice and propriety and it would be culpable in me were I to remain silent and see hundreds of the pioneer settlers of this State deprived of their homes, the fruits of many years of toil and exposure, for the benefit of speculators in doubtful or spurious titles. One of these pretended grants which it is said to be galvanized into existence covers a large tract within the limits of the city of San Francisco. Another embraces an area of agricultural land large enough to constitute a respectable county and has on it a population of several hundred persons mostly farmers.

In short no language would be too harsh to fitly characterize a measure of the character referred to and I assume that it could never become a law except by overcoming the opposition of the senators and representatives from the Pacific States. Should any such bill pass I most earnestly and respectfully request your Excellency to withold your approval and thereby save hundreds of worthy people from spoliation and ruin. It is needless to say that I have no personal interest whatever in the subject of this letter but I consider it my duty to appeal as I do with undoubting confidence to the sense of justice of your Excellency to prevent the consummation of any such wrong as that referred to in the event that the rumors now prevalent on this subject should prove to be well founded.[3]

H H Haight
Governor of Cal.

LS, DLC-JP.

1. We have assigned a January 1869 date to this document, because the cover sheet of the copy in the Interior Department files indicates that the Haight letter was filed on January 25, 1869.

2. Legal questions concerning Mexican land grants were an issue in California from the end of the Mexican War into the 1880s. Often poorly dealt with, these problems caused periodic disputes over real or potential injustice. For a survey of the issue, see Hubert H. Bancroft, *History of California* (7 vols., San Francisco, 1884–90), 6: 529–81.

3. Johnson had written an endorsement on the original asking that the Secretary of the Interior "be kind enough to read the letter ... and return the same me." See Haight to Johnson, ca. January 1869, Lands and Railroads Div., Misc. Lets. Recd. (1840–80), RG48, NA.

From Benjamin C. Brown et al.[1]

Memphis Tenn   Jany 1, 1868 [1869][2]

Three hundred 300 negro militia are at Marion Ark robbing stores private houses stealing horses and insulting ladies. Have five 5 citizens in jail threatening to hang them and arrest others. They are building stockades and breastwork.[3] Will not the U.S. protect the people. For our standing we refer to Albert Pike and Robt W Johnson.

Tel, DLC-JP.

1. Nine other persons joined Brown in sending this telegram to the President. Brown (c1806–1875) was a Paris, Tennessee, lawyer, who also occasionally lived and practiced in Memphis. He served before the Civil War as Henry County circuit court clerk and clerk and master of the chancery court. 1850 Census, Tenn., Henry, 1st Dist., 485; (1860), 8; (1870), 2; Memphis directories (1859–74); *Henry County, Tennessee Inscriptions in Stone* (2 vols., Paris, Tenn., 1989), 2: No. 298; Goodspeed's *Henry County*, 821, 824.

2. Internal evidence clearly indicates that this is an 1869 telegram.

3. For published accounts of the December atrocities reputedly committed by Governor Clayton's militia in Arkansas, see *Memphis Appeal*, Dec. 22, 1868; *National Intelligencer*, Jan. 8, 1869.

From Frederick M. Clarke[1]

Washington, D.C.   January 1st 1869

Sir:

I have the honor to apply for appointment as U.S. Consul, at Leeds England.

A citizen of Iowa I was at the outbreak of the war, completing my studies at Kneller Hall College near London, England, which place I left in 1861, and returning to Iowa, at once entered the service from which I was discharged in 1866 with an honorable record of nearly five years service. My familiarity with British customs and character, acquired from personal observation and intercourse during a four years residence in Great Britain, together with the experience of three years in an Executive Dept at the National Capital have led me to solicit this appointment feeling confident that the duties of the office would meet at my hands that promptitude and courtesy, which must ever obtain the approbation of our government.[2]

It may be proper for me to add that I am thirty years of age— married—and have visited every state of our Union, and a majority of the European nations including East India.

Fredk. M. Clarke

ALS, DNA-RG59, Lets. of Appl. and Recomm., 1861–69 (M650, Roll 10), Frederick M. Clarke.

1. Clarke (c1845–fl1880) served as a clerk in the Pension Office in Washington. Prior to that position, he had been a clerk in the Interior Department. Although his letter claims that he was thirty years old, the 1870 census lists him as being only twenty-five years old in that year. He served in the Civil War in the 38th Iowa Inf. Washington, D.C., directories (1867–71); 1870 Census, D.C., Washington, 3rd Ward, 170; *Off. Army Reg.: Vols.*, 7: 299; Clarke to Garfield, Nov. 24, 1880, James A. Garfield Papers, LC.

2. There is no evidence that Johnson nominated Clarke for the Leeds post.

From Thomas Cottman

New York   Jan'y 1st 1869

It had been my intention to have paid the compliments of the season in person, but an indisposition interfering with the trip to Washington I have concluded to pay my respects epistolarily—and wish you the fruition of your desires, peace & quietude after so much toil & trouble. Judging from the newspaper reports Louisiana still gives you trouble. I wish you a happy riddance of her. I think you have made a poor trade in swapping Tisdale for Bouchard.[1] I perfectly well recollect the reply made to you when you asked me my opinion of Tisdale "He would do better for himself than the government." Of Bouchard I would say a worse selection could not possibly have been made. The selections for Louisiana have been most unfortunate: but you could not be held responsible for them as they were I presume imposed upon you by recommendations of parties in whom you had confidence. Though living here I can not fail to feel a very lively interest in Louisiana. She has nominally Representatives in either branch of the Federal Legislature, but what they represent is beyond my ken.

Thos. Cottman

ALS, DLC-JP.

1. Eugene Tisdale was to be replaced by Adolph Bouchard as collector of internal revenue for the Third District of Louisiana. Bouchard had been nominated on December 21, 1868, but the Senate took no further action. Ser. 6B, Vol. 4: 204, Johnson Papers, LC.

From William Thorpe
Private

Headquarters of Gen. Hancock,
New York, Jan. 1, '69.

Dear Sir:—

I send you my first New Year's greeting, and heartily congratulate you upon the prospects of a happy future for you and yours. No man that I ever heard of ever passed through such fiery storms as have burst over you. None ever exhibited more magnificent courage.

You have made mistakes, which I have deplored or condemned, but I do not forget that there was but One—and he more than man—who was infallible.

People, long estranged, begin to turn toward you again. The bitter passions of the hour are passing away. They cannot forget your heroic courage in the Senate,—your wise and sagacious career in Tennessee—your patient courage and endurance under the most malignant partizan attacks.

Rest assured, dear sir, posterity will do you full justice. The great acts of your administration will be your enduring monument, and the great doctrines of Constitutional Government enunciated or defended by you will constitute your laurel crown. To us younger men your example will be of priceless value.

Within a few days you will surrender your high office to an untried successor; and, I presume, retire to the comforts of a private life. In the pleasant days before you, I hope at times to be kindly remembered. You deserve, now, all that life can give.

Wm. Thorpe.

ALS, DLC-JP.

From Arkansas Citizens[1]

Memphis Tenn, Jany 2, 1868 [1869][2]

We, citizens of State of Arkansas earnestly implore your interference to put an end in some way to the oppressive course now pursued by Gov. Clayton. We feel warranted in saying that the people of that state desire only and will execute the civil law and unless Gov Clayton is arrested in his course the state will be involved in open war and bloodshed which is now imminent. Many good citizens have been compelled to leave their homes.[3]

Tel, DLC-JP.
1. Eight persons joined in sending this telegram to Johnson.
2. Internal evidence makes clear that this is a January 1869 document.
3. See also Benjamin C. Brown et al. to Johnson, Jan. 1, 1869.

From Henry R. Jackson et al.[1]

Savannah Ga   Jan 2d 1869

The Sheriff of this county[2] has been violently resisted in the effort to arrest a number of negroes charged with crime.

The negroes in the neighborhood are overwhelming in number, are well supplied with arms and ammunition and hold military occupation of a large district of country. The sheriff has called out the police and proceeded with them the day before yesterday to the scene of insurrection but wholly failed to effect arrests. The citizens are forming an organized force for the purpose of aiding the sheriff as a possee. The danger of violent collision is great. The intervention of a small force of United States troops would quell the insurrection and enforce the laws but prompt action is absolutely necessary.[3]

S   Henry R. Jackson
W. W. Kirkland
G M. Sorrell [*sic*]

Tel, DLC-JP.
1. All the signatories were former Confederate brigadiers. William W. Kirkland (1833–1915) served in both the Army of Northern Virginia and the Army of Tennessee. Afterwards, he was for a time a merchant in Savannah before moving to New York City and then Washington, D.C. Gilbert Moxley Sorrel (1838–1901) was a longtime member of General Longstreet's staff before his own promotion to brigade command. At the conclusion of the war he was a merchant in Savannah with his brothers and later was associated with a steamship company. Warner, *Gray*; Savannah directories (1866–81).
2. James Dooner (*c*1821–*fl*1881), a lieutenant in the 1st (Olmstead's) Ga. Inf., CSA, during the war, was later alternately sheriff, deputy sheriff, and justice of the peace in Chatham County. 1870 Census, Ga., Chatham, Savannah, 305; Savannah directories (1866–81); *Savannah Morning News*, Jan. 12, 1869; Lillian Henderson, comp., *Roster of the Confederate Soldiers of Georgia, 1861–1865* (6 vols., Hapeville, Ga., 1958–64), 1: 115–16.
3. According to various reports, several planters and overseers, as well as their families and some sympathizing blacks, had been violently driven off their plantations by roving bands of blacks. Four companies of U.S. troops were ordered to the area, arresting some of the leaders of the unrest and permitting the sheriff's posse to disband. *Savannah Morning News*, Jan. 2, 4, 5, Feb. 1, 1869; *National Intelligencer*, Jan. 4, 5, 1869.

From William P. Wells

Detroit, 2 Jan. 1869.

To the President:

I have heretofore telegraphed my recommendation of the appointment of Mr. Frederick Carlisle as Assistant Secretary of the Treasury.[1] I now beg leave to renew the same by letter. Mr. Carlisle will make a most efficient and valuable officer, and his abilities and energy have been already manifested, in the discharge of duties connected with the Treasury Department, in such a way that no mention of them on my part is necessary.

I beg to add, that if it shall be Your pleasure to give him the appointment, speedy action may contribute to secure results in Michigan which are extremely desirable.[2]

William P. Wells:

ALS, DLC-JP.

1. See Wells to Johnson, Dec. 19, 1868.
2. Probably a reference to the January 6 senatorial election, which resulted in the reelection of Republican Zachariah Chandler. See ibid.; *Chicago Tribune*, Jan. 6, 7, 1869.

From Andrew J. Wilcox

Baltimore   Jany 2nd 1869

Mr President

On the 18th of September last I had the honor of writing[1] and sending Your Excellency several copies of the Sun newspaper published here containing articles published by me. In that letter I asked Your Excellency to make those articles a part of your message to Congress provided it would convene on the following Monday and you should deem it necessary to send in a message to Congress on that day & I also in that letter asked Your Excellency, "to institute such a line of policy in regard to the other matters referred to in those Articles as should seem to you best to accomplish the ends desired." One of those desired ends was the withdrawal of the Presidential Candidates then before the people and the substitution of Chief Justice Chase and the Hon Reverdy Johnson for both tickets. Immediately afterwards I and many others understood that an effort with that end in view was made by Your Excellency. If not too much trouble I now ask your Excellency to do me the very great favor to furnish me with a brief and correct history of that effort to be made use of by me in the publication of the work I design publishing and with any other facts relating to that election or events that have lately transpired which you may deem of interest to the public to know or of being preserved as a matter of political history for which I shall be under many obligations.

Andrew J. Wilcox

ALS, DLC-JP.
1. See Wilcox to Johnson, Sept. 18, 1868.

From Allen C. Beach[1]

Albany   Jany 4, 1868 [1869][2]

Dear Sir

I am sure that the appointment of Fred Carlisle[3] as asst secy of the Treasury would be very gratifying & encouraging to the conservative men of New York for these reasons. They believe him to be incorruptibly honest & eminently qualified. They understand that he opposed impeachment & that his influence will be exerted against the radicals. I have no doubt he would be confirmed & hope he may be appointed soon.

Allen C Beach   Lt. Govr., N.Y.

ALS, DLC-JP.

1. Beach (1825–1918), a lawyer prominent in the state Democratic party, was elected lieutenant governor of New York in 1868 and 1870 and secretary of state in 1877. *New York Times*, Oct. 19, 1918; *NUC.*

2. Internal evidence concerning the recommendation of Frederick Carlisle indicates that this is an 1869 document.

3. For other recommendations of Carlisle, see William P. Wells to Johnson, Dec. 19, 1868, Jan. 2, 1869; Sanford E. Church to Johnson, Dec. 28, 1868; Charles E. Stuart to Johnson, Dec. 30, 1868.

From Stephen G. Burbridge

Washington D.C.   Jan 4th 1869

Should Mr. A Cummings not be confirmed as Commissioner of Internal Revinew[1] I would most respectfully call your attention to my application not wishing to annoy you upon this subject but again to assure you that if honored with the appointment that I shall always feel myself under personal obligations to you, and that my intercourse with you will be of the most pleasant character. And you shall be consulted and your wishes carried out as far as in my power so long as I may remain in the possition.[2]

S. G. Burbridge

ALS, DLC-JP.

1. Johnson first nominated Alexander Cummings in July of 1868, then renominated him on December 14. The Senate finally tabled his nomination on March 3, 1869. *Senate Ex. Proceedings*, Vol. 16: 363, 387, 501–2. See also Ann S. Stephens to Johnson, Jan. 22, 1869.

2. Burbridge was not considered for the position.

From James A. McCauley et al.[1]

Washington D.C., Jan'y. 4, 1869.

Sir:

The Anniversary of the Missionary Society of the Methodist Episcopal Church will be held in this city, on Monday the 11th inst.[2] The occasion will be one in which the members of our church take a very lively interest. As many of these are in the employ of the Government, it is very much desired to obtain for these such release from duty on that day as will enable them to participate in the celebration.

The undersigned are a committee, instructed by the pastors of our churches in the District, to solicit your friendly offices, in such way as your judgment may approve, to secure release, on that day, from duty, of members of our church employed in the several Departments of the Government.

Your favorable action, in the case, will be highly appreciated.[3]

> J. A. McCauley,
> B. Peyton Brown,
> A. H. Ames, Comte.

L, DLC-JP.

1. McCauley (1822–1896) was a longtime Methodist pastor and served as presiding elder of the Washington district. In 1872 he began a career as president of Dickinson College, where he served for the next sixteen years. B. Peyton Brown (1830–*fl*1895) was pastor of the Foundry Methodist Church for several years and of other Methodist churches in Washington and Georgetown. In 1878 he became presiding elder of the Washington district. Alfred H. Ames (*fl*1901) was pastor of Wesley Chapel and subsequently of Eutaw Street Church in Baltimore (1871–74). Much later he served as superintendent of a deaconess home and training school in Baltimore. Washington, D.C., directories (1868–1901); *NCAB*, 6: 464–65; *The Biographical Cyclopedia of Representative Men of Maryland and District of Columbia* (Baltimore, 1879), 540–41; Scharf, *Baltimore City and County*, 575–76.

2. An account of the fiftieth anniversary of the missionary society, held at the Foundry Methodist Church, may be found in the *Washington Evening Star*, Jan. 11, 1869.

3. Johnson urged the different Cabinet members to consider the request from the Methodist committee "as may be consistent with the public interests." See January 7 note from William G. Moore appended to the copy of this letter found in Lets. Recd., Executive (M494, Roll 109), RG107, NA.

From Joseph W. Spoor [1]

Confidential

Newark N.Y.   Jan. 4. 1869

Dear Sir.

I have read with interest the Proclamations you have been pleased to issue, the last of which I perceive is regarded by the various Publications of the day as a *General* Proclamation of Amnesty. Still in what I have read & I believe I have them all—I fail to see embraced

in any of your Proclamations the Tens of thousands of our own soldiers, who for some cause or another have been led to desert from
the Ranks of our Armies which have fought our Battles, achieved
our victories, & defended our Country. I would not for a moment
justify their Course, any more than that of our enemies who openly
fought agains us. Yet it seems to me if the one should be pardoned
the other should be euqally entitled to mercy.

Now Sir as you have it in your power, I entreat you, exercise your
clemency towards them & extend the remedy to the fullest extent of
the disease.

I hold that these soldiers have aready suffered sufficiently for their
errors & to restore them again to the right of Citizenship will not
only lift them up to the ranks of manhood where they can breath the
air of freedom—but you would releive the hearts of many Parents,
Brothers & sisters of that anguish which secretly lingers there. The
Cause of which if *publicly* known, they fear would entail great disgrace upon *them*, as well as those who have been the unfortunate
Cause of it.

I write you as a Minister of the Gospel engaged as such in master
service & entreat that you will take this subject into your heart, &
give it that due consideration which I hope will secure your immediate
action.

J. W. Spoor

P.S. I happen to be one of these *few* ministers who esteem it their
duty to stand with the "*old Democrasy*" & on the account of which "*in
Certain directions*" I get more Curses than Coppers.

J.W.S.

ALS, DLC-JP.
1. Spoor (*c*1811–*fl*1874) was a Baptist clergyman who lived in Rochester for several years.
1860 Census, N.Y., Monroe, Rochester, 5th Ward, 38; Rochester directories (1861–68); *NUC*.

From Ann S. Stephens

National [Hotel]   Jan 4 1869

My Dear Sir.

I have seen Gen. Cary[1] who informs me positively that Mr. Stilwell[2]
does *not* intend to go to Venezuela but only wishes a confirmation
and will resign as soon as his nomination is confirmed. He expressed

every kind feeling with regard to my son[3] and seems, in good faith, to wish him to have the position.

Gov Moreton[4] is also certain that Stilwell only wishes the triumph of a confirmation and will resign directly after he gets it. He promis to do his utmost for my son when he comes before the senate. But Stilwell himself is not here and any delay in his resignation would be disastrous to us if we had nothing to fall back upon.

May I ask you again to hold back the nomination to Equador till this for Venezuela is disposed of, so far as Mr. Stilwell is concerned. We much prefer Venezuela, but trust that you will kindly hold the other in reserve if anything should prevent, or materially delay the promised resignation. I know this is asking a great deal; but I have unbounded faith in your generosity as you may have in my gratitude—which, believe me, will not be for a day but for all time.

I have very little doubt that Edward will be confirmed without trouble. On New Years day many senators called on us and were friendly as possible. Even your sudden and ardent friend Butler[5] could not have been more cordial when he pressed your hand.

I was at the White House yesterday hoping to say all this in person, but came home disappointed, blue, and dreary as the weather. So much depends on success to us that a thought of failure almost terrifies me and but for my faith in your kindness I should sometimes dispond. Pray stand my friend now and the future shall prove how truely I shall be yours.

Ann S Stephens

ALS, DLC-JP.
  1. Samuel F. Cary.
  2. Thomas N. Stilwell. For earlier communication about this appointment, see Stephens to Johnson, Dec. 26, 1868.
  3. Edward Stephens.
  4. Oliver P. Morton.
  5. Presumably Benjamin F. Butler.

From William H. Seward

Washington, 6 January 1869.

The Secretary of State, to whom was referred a Resolution of the House of Representatives passed on the 16th of December last in the following words: "Resolved, That the Secretary of State; of the Treasury; of the Department of War; of the Interior; of the Navy;

the Attorney General; and the Postmaster General, each be, and are directed to report to the House as soon as practicable what reduction can be made, compatible with the public interests, in the number of officers and employees, salaries and expenses in their respective Departments, or in the service connected therewith," has the honor to submit the following report.

The business of the Department may be divided into three classes, namely, the Civil; the Diplomatic; and the Consular parts. The first, the Civil Department, includes a Secretary of State; a First and a Second Assistant Secretary of State; an Examiner of Claims; a Chief Clerk; a Disbursing clerk; twenty-three other clerks, and fifteen messengers and laborers. These officers, messengers and laborers are maintained under the provisions of an Act of Congress, entitled "An Act making appropriation for the civil and diplomatic expenses of the Government," approved 22d April 1854. Vol. 10 Statutes at Large, page 669. The force thus authorized is notoriously inadequate, and, for this reason, an annual appropriation has been made during the last six years for temporary clerks, messengers and laborers, in order to expedite the business of the Department, and protect the Department buildings and the archives against casualties by fire and otherwise. The Secretary is of opinion that no reduction of the force of this branch of the Department, or of its incidental expenses could be made without injury to the public service.

The second division, the Diplomatic, embraces Ministers Plenipotentiary, Ministers Resident, chargé d'Affaires, and Consuls invested with diplomatic powers. The United States have recently come to be regarded as an influential power by all nations, and, as such, they exercise a continually increasing influence in the promotion of commerce, freedom and civilization, especially on the American Continent. Adventurous citizens of the United States are continually sojourning or domiciled in every foreign country with which this Government maintains diplomatic relations. The Department of State is unremittingly engaged in extending protection to those citizens against arbitrary proceedings or revolutionary violence. Necessities are continually occurring for negotiating new treaties. The power vested in the Department for this purpose needs to be increased rather than diminished.

In regard to the third division, namely, the Consular service, it is perhaps only necessary to say that this branch of the service yields a large income to the Government. Any reduction or diminution of its forces—would probably work a reduction of the revenues of the Treasury.

The Secretary of State is not aware that the salary paid to any officer, agent or laborer in the Department of State exceeds the rate of compensation which is necessary to secure intelligent, reliable and effectual service.

For these reasons the Secretary of State is unable to specify any reduction that can be made compatible with the public interest in the number of officers, employees, and the salaries and expenses of the Department of State.

William H. Seward.

LBcopy, DNA-RG59, Misc. Corres., Reports to President and Congress.

From Susan Smith[1]

Jan— 6th— 69

Mr. Johnson

With reverence I take my sete this morning to address you with a few lines to gratify my dear old Mother. She is now in her 79 years. She thinks you are her uncle Richard Johnsons son her Mothers Brother. She wishes to know if your father had a sister Mary that Marryed a gentleman by the name of henry Shelton. You need not be asaned to own them they are all very respectable people some in very hi standing. My dear old Mother is an Angel on earth. The Most of her conversation is about religion. She has a great sermon book and carryes it with her. She wishes to hear something from her mothers people before she dyes. Pleas answer. Direct your letter to Floyd knob Floyd Co. Ind.

Now I shall bring my letter to a close by a request of an answer. Pray for me when it goes well with thee and I shall do the same for the.

Susan Smith

ALS, DLC-JP.

1. None of the people mentioned in this letter could be identified, but they were not related to Johnson.

From Charles W. Woolley
Personal

Cincinnati Ohio   Jany. 6th 1869.

To the President

At the request of several of your personal friends in Ohio, that I should give you my opinion of the Hon. Wm. Penn Nixon,[1] of this City, I have the honor to write you, that he is a person of unblemished character, has filled many public trusts unexceptionably, possesses fine intelligence, is a Lawyer of high attainments, and will be immediately Confirmed by the Senate for any office to which you may be pleased to appoint him. My reasons for saying that he can be confirmed ought not to be questioned, as I am supposed to have had intimate relations once with the members of the Senate, (Vide Butlers Report).[2] In fact, Mr President, I believe that Butler will wager upon anything I may predict of the action of that body. But jesting aside, my assurances are from the Finance Committee directly—also, from other and influential republican Senators. There is no combination in regard to procuring Mr Nixon's appointment, other than such as would be made by the gentlemen who recommend him, as *none others* know that this application is to be made to you. The Senators I alluded to above have been sounded but not confided in. Mr Nixon has made but one promise, and that is to take care of your interests and my good friend Warden,[3] in the way most agreable to him. For this reason and those before given, and in order that you may at last succeed by ousting Rollins,[4] in defeating the schemes of Grant, Schenck[5] etc. is to the Revenue Department, and before retiring from office give to the Country a Commissioner highly creditably to your administration. I hope the appointment will be made. Mr Nixon belongs to the Sherman[6] or Conservative republicans in Ohio, and is therefore anti-Schenck.[7]

Mrs Woolley[8] sends you by express with her best regards a case of "Bourbon," which she has kept locked up from me for eleven years past. Your friends here will insist that you shall tarry with them long enough when you return to Tennessee, to enable them to satisfy in person the high regard they entertain for you.

C. W. Woolley

ALS, DLC-JP.

1. Nixon (1833–1912), a lawyer and member of the Ohio state legislature (1864–68), had

established the *Cincinnati Chronicle* in 1868 with his brother. In 1872 he moved to Chicago and edited the *Inter Ocean* until 1897. *DAB*.

2. Benjamin F. Butler's report, "Raising of Money to be Used in Impeachment," issued July 3, 1868, concerned alleged efforts by Woolley to bribe senators to acquit Johnson. *House Reports*, 40 Cong., 2 Sess., No. 75, passim (Ser. 1358).

3. Probably William W. Warden.

4. Edward A. Rollins.

5. Ulysses S. Grant and Robert C. Schenck.

6. John Sherman.

7. There is no evidence that Nixon was nominated for any post.

8. Mary F. Woolley (*c*1836/38–*fl*1880), a native of Ohio, had married Charles Woolley by 1860. The couple had at least three daughters. 1860 Census, Ohio, Hamilton, Cincinnati, 1st Ward, 104; (1880), 5th Ward, 125th Enum. Dist., 45.

From James Brooks

Washington D.C.   Jan 7- [1869]

Dear Sir

Senator Grimes[1] desires to converse with you on matters connected with the Union P. R. Road, and to have me accompany him as Gov't Director.[2]

As the Senator does not like to move, without a certainty of seeing you, I write to ask, if you could see us at 7. or 7 1/2 P.M. this evening.[3]

James Brooks

ALS, DLC-JP.

1. James W. Grimes.

2. Brooks became a government director of the railroad in October 1867 and remained in that post until the summer of 1869, when he became a regular director until 1873. Ames, *Pioneering the Union Pacific*, 178, 240, 425.

3. It is not known whether Grimes and Brooks visited Johnson.

From R. Weakley Brown

Nashville Tennessee   January 7, 1869.

My Dear Friend.

Your time is so much occupied that I will only trespass a few moments. Your views on reconstruction and finances contained in your last message are most highly patriotic and statesmanlike. But your late general Amnesty Proclamation issued as it was on the birth day of the "Prince of Peace"—I hail as a most auspicious event. Although elected Vice President as an ultra radical yet when you acceded to the Presidency, your sagacious mind and great liberty loving heart,

soon convinced you that Radicalism must be restrained or Constitutional liberty would soon be swallowed up in a Military Despotism,
and for more than 3 years, you have battled for *Constitutional* liberty—with a heroism—and moral courage—worthy of Andrew Jackson—or Rome's old Cato. And to day you have the proud consciousness of knowing—that you have—to the best of your
ability—supported, protected, and defended the Constitution the
great Magna Charta of American Liberty. As an humble citizen of
Tennessee—and a sincere personal friend, I say—"*Well done good and
faithful servant.*"[1] Unprejudiced patriots of this day—apprecate your
devoted patriotism, and thousands of unborn freeman will generation after generation hail the name of Andrew Johnson as the great
Tribune of the People and defender of Constitutional liberty.

Often have I prayed that God in his infinite goodness and mercy
would bestow upon you every blessing temporal and spiritual. And I
hope you may be the *Providential instrument to redeem Tennessee from
Radical—bondage* and *misrule.*

I am your friend, and I look forward to the day that I can not only
take you by the hand as a *brother patriot*—but as a *brother christian.*
To imitate the example of the "Prince of Peace is the highest duty of
man"[2]—and the religion of Jesus christ, is the only thing that will
satisfy the cravings of the human heart.

With my best wishes and prayers . . .

                                                        R. Weakley Brown

ALS, DLC-JP.
    1. From the parable of Jesus concerning the servants given different amounts of talents, as
reported in Matthew 25.
    2. Quotation not identified.

From Bernard O'Kane
Please Answer

                                                        Boston   Jan. 7. 1869
Sir:

I transmitted to you several weeks ago, by advice of counsel, a state-
ment[1] of the extraordinary proceedings of the United States District
Attorney Hillard, and Commissioner Hallett, in the case of one
Minon[2] charged by me for attempt at bribery, and gross violation of

the Internal Revenue laws; and am very desirous to know *what action* will be taken thereon?

The Commissioner and Attorney were evidently influenced by Collector McCarthy[3] in rendering a decision against the law, the evidence, and Government. McCarthy is a notorious character for intrigue, compromise and corruption in office; but he manages to hold on, through payment of money to parties in Washington, and he has the effrontery to boast of it. Commissioner Rollins has piles of complaints on file in his office against this man, some of which have been examined in a loose manner, & then covered up.

For instance, when charges have heretofore been preferred against him, the modus-operandi of investigating them was, to send on a special agent, who merely went to McCarthy & asked him if the charges were true, first making him acquainted with all the secrets in the case; the consequence was he could, like the boy in the fable, "laugh at the man throwing grass" at him. When the semi-quasi judiciary, or lower courts, and United States atty's are open to bribery & corruption, well may *Justice* sigh and the Country mourn. The power of compromise is the bane, the antidote, to take it away.[4]

Bernard O'Kane

ALS, DNA-RG60, Office of Atty. Gen., Lets. Recd., President.
    1. O'Kane to Johnson, Nov. 16, 1868.
    2. George S. Hillard, Henry L. Hallett, and Michael G. Minon.
    3. William H. McCartney.
    4. For more on McCartney, see O'Kane to Johnson, July 23, 1868, *Johnson Papers*, 14: 414–16; O'Kane to Johnson, Nov. 16, 1868.

From Connally F. Trigg and Davidson M. Leatherman

Memphis, Tenn.   Jan. 7, 1869

Dear Sir—

We have the honor to address you upon a subject in which very many of your friends feel considerable interest. We are friends of Genl. Gordon Granger, and of course feel interested in his welfare.[1] As an officer and a soldier we decline to say any thing as Your Excellency knows him so well. We only wish to ask of you Mr President that you will appoint him to the position vacated by major Genl Hooker.[2] By doing so you will confer a favor, and will gratify not only ourselves, but quite a number of the friends of both yourself and the General. In the hope that our request may receive a favorable response . . .

Connally F. Trigg.

D. M. Leatherman

ALS (Trigg), DLC-JP.
    1. See John F. Leftwich to Johnson, Oct. 10, 1868, for another recommendation of Granger.
    2. For other documents concerning Hooker's replacement, see Horatio Seymour to Johnson, Sept. 24, 1868; Alvan C. Gillem to Johnson, Sept. 30, 1868; James W. Nesmith to Johnson, Oct. 13, 1868; Robert A. Hill to Johnson, Nov. 6, 1868; William L. Sharkey to Johnson, Nov. 7, 1868; and Joseph S. Fowler to Johnson, Nov. 13, 1868.

From Edwin R. V. Wright

New York   Jany 7" 1869

I beg of you to restore Capt J. W. Boyce[1] to his position in the Custom House to which he was appointed on your express recommendation. His removal is wholly Inexplicable.

E.R.V. Wright

Harvest Home   N.J.

Tel, DLC-JP.
    1. Not identified.

From John M. Binckley

Washington, 8 January, 1869.

Mr: President:

I have the honor to submit herewith two letters,[1] one just received from Henry D. Lapaugh[2] Esq. of New York, on behalf of one, George B. Davis,[3] alleged British subject with the following remarks:

I have never seen and have no knowledge of Mr. Davis beyond two letters from him which are, I believe, still in my possession, and from conversations with persons who are acquainted with him, including Wm. Fullerton, Esq. The representations made by Davis in his letters were highly important if true, and I thought proper therefore to communicate with him. As the Attny General[4] had informed me that he had imparted authority to Mr. Fullerton to pledge the Government's protection in all proper cases of disclosure and confession, a facility which in his better judgment was not requisite for my operations, the only manner in which I felt competent to further the object was to endorse the few facts stated by Mr. Fullerton in his note to Davis[5] and to disburse the necessary travelling expenses of the messenger—the sum of $150. I consented to the selection of Mr. Yeaton[6] for the bearer because the principal letter from Davis, which had been addressed to the President, had been brought to me by Mr. Yeaton in an open envelope superscribed with my name in the President's hand. I have, of course, no knowledge of the instructions of Mr. Yeaton from Mr. Fullerton or other public agents, in the premises, nor have I had in any way any connection with the matter since the date of my endorsement of Mr. Fullerton's note, of which the above is a necessary explanation.

The letters of Mr. Davis' counsel herewith contain all additional pertinent information under my control; though a communication over Davis' name in the New York Herald[7] (of one of the last days of December) which I remember to have seen, may be worthy of notice.

It is evident that in addressing me for his relief, Mr. Davis is under some misapprehension as to my agency in his affairs, but I deem it due to him to invite your Excellency's early and serious notice to his case—for ought I to forbear the following deliberate expression:

Disclaiming all knowledge of Davis' guilt or innocence in the present or any other prosecution or charge against him, I am of opinion, after a highly instructive experience in a corrupt atmosphere last summer, that his duress was intended to operate and does operate for the protection of numerous, powerful and dangerous scoundrels.[8]

John M Binckley
Solictor of Internal Revenue

ALS, DNA-RG60, Office of Atty. Gen., Lets. Recd., President.

1. Enclosed were two letters from Henry D. Lapaugh to Binckley, dated January 4 and 6, which complained that George B. Davis had been arrested, despite William Fullerton's guarantees to the contrary. Davis had been charged with perjury after allegedly finding improprieties in the office of revenue collector Joshua F. Bailey. Fullerton had offered Davis immunity if he would return from Canada to testify. New York Herald, Dec. 30, 1868; New York Tribune, Mar. 15, 1869. For Bailey's accusations that Davis was cooperating with whiskey distillers, see Joshua F. Bailey to Hugh McCulloch, Oct. 31, 1868, Johnson Papers, LC.

2. Lapaugh (c1826–fl1875) had been a lawyer in New York City since the mid 1850s. New York City directories (1854–74); 1870 Census, N.Y., New York, New York, 20th Ward, 13th Dist., 56.

3. Not identified.

4. William Evarts.

5. According to Lapaugh's January 4 letter to Binckley, Fullerton had written to Davis on October 1, promising immunity from prosecution in exchange for his testimony.

6. Charles C. Yeaton was assisting in the government's investigation. See Charles C. Yeaton to Johnson, Sept. 28, 1868, and K. L. Hodges to Johnson, Nov. 6, 1868.

7. Writing from jail on December 28, Davis claimed he was just another victim of the "whiskey ring," and expressed dismay that those individuals were powerful enough to defy the government's promise of immunity. *New York Herald*, Dec. 30, 1868.

8. Davis was convicted of perjury, and sentenced on July 1, 1869, to five years' imprisonment. Lapaugh did appeal, but nothing further is known about Davis and his fate. *New York Tribune*, July 2, 1869.

From Robert C. Buchanan

New Orleans   Jan. 8" 1869

It is my painful duty to inform you of the death of General Lovell H Rousseau at Eleven 11 o clock last night of Congestion of the Bowels. He was taken sick of monday night last.[1]

Robt. C. Buchanan
Bvt Maj Genl Comd'g

Tel, DLC-JP.

1. On January 4 Rousseau suddenly became very ill and three days later died at his home in New Orleans. Some of his doctors blamed his fatal illness on the change of climate the previous September when Rousseau moved from California and Alaska to New Orleans. *New Orleans Picayune*, Jan. 8, 1869, morning; Pension File, Maria A. Rousseau, RG15, NA.

From Peter Donan[1]

New York, Jan. 8th 1869

Sir,

On this anniversary of the memorable victory achieved by your illustrious brother Tennesseean,[2] I think it neither impertinent nor inappropriate, to write to you personally, to express my honest admiration of your manly, independent and patriotic course, in the last twelve months. I have no personal ends to promote, in thus addressing you. I was a "rebel," and fought to the end, for what I believed to be right. My paper was the first in the country, to perceive and recognise, your real devotion to the old Union and Constitution of our fathers. I expect before long, to take charge of a paper in Tennessee, and if at all consistent with your wishes, I would like to raise your name, for the Governorship of the State. I am aware that there is no precedent for such a step. But these are times that demand a frequent stepping aside, from established usage. The condition of your own State, is today far worse than that of any other *in*, or *out* of, the Confederation, except perhaps, Missouri. Your name would carry a weight in the State, greater than that of any other public name, in the country. I'm satisfied that with it, to rally around, the whole wretched condition of affairs, could be revolutionized forthwith; and Peace, Order, and Law once more resume their sway in the old "Volunteer State." There is no earthly doubt, that if you will permit the use of your name, it will be the beginning of a brighter day for Tennessee.

Hoping that the idea will meet with your approbation; and assuring you of my profound respect and regard . . .

P. Donan.

Late Editor   Record & Vindicator

ALS, DLC-JP.

1. Donan was affiliated in the late 1860s with the Lexington, Missouri newspaper, the *Caucasian*. During a visit with a Nashville newspaper office, Donan was referred to as the "startling, dashing, scathing, Radical-devouring editor. . . ." William Young, *Young's History of Lafayette County, Missouri* (2 vols., Indianapolis, 1910), 1: 294–95; *Nashville Union and American* Aug. 7, 1869.

2. A reference to Andrew Jackson's victory at the Battle of New Orleans in 1815.

From Peter W. Strader

Cincinnati   January 8th 1869

Dear Sir.

William Penn Nixon, of Ohio, whose name will be presented to you for the office of Commissioner of Internal Revenue, is well qualified to fill that position. He is a Lawyer of fine attainments, has held several important positions of public trust, and his integrity is unquestioned.

He is a conservative republican, and as it seems impossible to secure the confirmation of a democrat, I trust he may secure the appointment. I believe that if he is appointed and confirmed, he will go into the office untrameled by pledges and will discharge the duties of the office satisfactorily to yourself and the country.[1]

P. W Strader

ALS, DNA-RG56, Appls., Heads of Treasury Offices, Wm. Penn Nixon.

1. See also Charles W. Woolley to Johnson, Jan. 6, 1869.

From Thomas Swann

Baltimore   Jan: 8th 1869.

My Dear Sir,

Some months ago, I urged very strongly, the reognition of the services of Genl Brooks,[1] by conferring upon him the brevet rank of Maj. General. His recommendations were such as to make it a case of no ordinary interest; and I took great pleasure in presenting his papers to the favorable consideration of your Excellency. Since then you have placed him in command of the Department of Washington. I feel it due to a gallant officer, that I should bring him again to your notice, and ask that you would gratify his many friends by this small act of justice.

Tho Swann

ALS, DNA-RG94, ACP Branch, File 214-ACP-1894, Horace Brooks.

1. Horace Brooks (1814–1894) served during the Civil War as lieutenant colonel, 2nd U.S. Artillery, and then as colonel, 4th U.S. Artillery. A graduate of West Point and a career military officer, he retired in 1877. Johnson nominated Brooks for a major generalship on January 13; the Senate acted favorably upon that recommendation on March 3. Hunt and Brown, *Brigadier Generals*; *Senate Ex. Proceedings*, Vol. 16: 439, 504.

From Edwin L. Brady[1]

Jersey City   Jan 9th 69

Dear Sir

I enclose slip cut from News Paper.[2] Gen Gran says he dont *intend to resign* untill *a few days previous* to his inaguration.

Now Mr President *supose* You *dont see* fit on such *short notic* to *accept* that resignation or if You *are not prepared* to act on *so important* matter as the acepance of the resignation of the great Commander of Armies untill *after the* 4 of Mach. what becomes of his inagural address and all the ect. If You dont accept his resignation before Mach 4th he cant be President on *that day* and if not on that day I dont think any other other day will answer. And I seriously think that Congress would not get Grant out of such a scrape under any known Constitution.

Please excuse presumption of so humble a person in the afairs of the nation.

Edwin. L. Brady

formerly   Senior Chief Engineer U S Coast Survey

Box 84 Jersey City

LS, DLC-JP.

1. Brady (*fl*1888) was a civil engineer at Jersey City for several years. By the late 1880s he had moved to Stamford, Connecticut, but operated his business as a consulting engineer out of offices in New York City. Jersey City directories (1872–76); Brady to Daniel S. Lamont, Mar. 16, 1885; Brady to "Friend," Mar. 10, 1888, Grover Cleveland Papers, LC.

2. The enclosed clipping from an unidentified newspaper carried a brief report, "The Rank of General Not to be Abolished." This account indicated that Grant wished the rank of general to be continued after his elevation to the presidency. In fact, so the essay indicated, Grant wanted Sherman to be his successor and the next lieutenant general to be Philip Sheridan. Grant would keep the places ready for Sherman and Sheridan by waiting until the very last minute before submitting his resignation as general.

From Richard D. Goodwin

Kirkwood Mo   Jan 10th 1869.

Most Worthy President, A. Johnson.

You have had my best wishes during your administration.

My only regret, is that, you ever sanctioned the death of *Mrs Surratt*,[1] which in my estimation was as cold-blooded a murder, as that of my friend President Lincoln.

I will not recount the wrongs in her case, they cannot be righted. But it is yet in your power to make some atonement, and I now ask you, as a friend to humanity, in the name of Justice and in God's name; do not let the fourth day of March pass, before you pardon Dr. Mudd, and Spangler, now suffering worse than death, on the "Dry Tortugas."

Give them their liberty, as one of the last of your noble acts, as president.[2] Thus having done all you now could, thousands of noble hearts will bless you, both in this, and after generations, and your petitioner will ever pray.

R. D. Goodwin

ALS, DNA-RG204, Pardon Case File B-596, Samuel A. Mudd.

1. Mary E. Surratt.

2. Johnson did pardon Samuel A. Mudd and Edward Spangler, as well as Samuel B. Arnold. For further particulars, see Lawrence Sangston to Johnson, Dec. 26, 1868; Pardon of Samuel A. Mudd, Feb. 8, 1869; Leonard Koons to Johnson, Mar. 4, 1869. Goodwin's letter was one of many requesting a pardon for Mudd. See Pardon Case File B-596, Samuel A. Mudd, RG204, NA.

From Charles J.M. Gwinn

Baltimore, Jan. 11. 1869.

I observe that Mr. Chandler of Michigan[1] has returned, having received the reward of his labors in behalf of the copper interest of Lake Superior; and we may expect that he will, at the earliest moment, call up his copper bill in order to pass it.

I take it for granted that there is no chance of defeating that bill in the Senate, but I am advised that it cannot pass, if your Excellency vetoes it;[2] and that in addition to the many objections which may be argued against the bill, there are few which will weigh more potently with Senators than those contained in the leter of Consul Morse[3] of which I send the extract relating to this subject.

I enclose you the leter of the President of the Baltimore Copper Co,[4] which I prepared at his request as the regular counsel of that company.

I beg also to enclose you a pamplet prepared by me[5] in relation to the R.R. questions which are assuming such great proportions.

Charles J.M. Gwinn

ALS, DLC-JP.

1. Zachariah Chandler had been reelected to the U.S. Senate a few days earlier. *Chicago Tribune,* Jan. 6, 7, 1869.

2. See Veto of Copper Bill, Feb. 22, 1869.

3. Politician and diplomat, Freeman Harlow Morse (1807–1891) had served in the Maine legislature, as mayor of Bath, Maine, and in the U.S. House (1843–45, 1857–61). President Lincoln appointed Morse consul at London in 1861, and President Grant promoted him to consul-general in 1869; he was forced into retirement in 1870. *DAB.* The enclosed clipping, cut from the *Baltimore Sun* of January 11, warned that an increase in copper prices would severely damage the American shipbuilding industry, at a time when British and French governments were scaling back taxes on building materials to assist their construction industries.

4. Although not filed with Gwinn's letter, the Johnson Papers contain at least three letters from Henry Martin (*fl*1873), president of the Baltimore Copper Company and later proprietor of the Baltimore Chemical Works. The item to which Gwinn refers is probably a January letter from Martin to the Senate, providing technical details on copper smelting and explanations for why the use of imported ores is cheaper, more efficient, and more productive. Henry Martin to the Senate, Jan. 2, 1869, Ser. 20, Johnson Papers, LC; Baltimore directories (1868–73).

5. Not found.

From Horatio Seymour

Utica   January 11, 1869.

My dear Sir:

Capt. Charles Weston[1] is very anxious to have an order made by President Lincoln promulgated as it relieves him from an unjust discredit growing out of the action of Mr. Stanton.[2]

It seems to me that it is due to Mr. Weston that he should have the benefit of Mr. Lincoln's action.[3] Mr. Stanton's action strikes me, as harsh and unjust. I hope you will find it consistent with your duties to look into this matter and to grant the request of Mrs. Weston.[4]

Horatio Seymour.

Copy, DNA-RG60, Office of Atty. Gen., Lets. Recd., President.

1. A native of Maine, Weston (b. c1822) had been appointed military storekeeper in November 1861 by President Lincoln. In September 1862 he was dismissed for neglecting duty and disobeying orders. Lets. Recd. (Main Ser.), File O-170-1862 (M619, Roll 124), RG94, NA; Powell, *Army List*, 665; Weston to Abraham Lincoln, Mar. 30, 1863, Lincoln Papers, LC.

2. Despite Weston's protestations and explanations, Secretary of War Edwin Stanton concurred in the Chief of Ordnance's decision to remove Weston without a hearing. In a February 1863 meeting with Weston, Stanton again refused to reverse the dismissal. Ibid.; Lets. Recd. (Main Ser.), File O-170-1862 (M619, Roll 124), RG94, NA.

3. Lincoln revoked the order of dismissal. Weston wrote to him in August of 1863 claiming that he had "never doubted, if you [Lincoln] examined the case, you would do me justice." Nothing further has been learned about the case, and it is not known why it remained active. Basler, *Works of Lincoln*, 5: 458.

4. Possibly Hagar J. Weston, who wrote to Lincoln in July 1864 complaining of her "disgrace." She may be the same "Mrs. Weston" who demanded in January 1868 that President Johnson turn the case over to the attorney general. Nothing further is known about her, or about Weston's predicament. Hagar J. Weston to Lincoln, July 10, 1864, Lincoln Papers, LC; Mrs. Charles Weston to Johnson, Jan. 9, 1868, Tels. Recd., President, Vol. 6 (1867–68), RG107, NA.

From William W. Wales

January 11th 1869.

Dear Sir:

The Mexican Congress having ratified the Seward-Romero treaty, signed in Washington July 4th 1868 for an adjustment of claims of citizens of the two Governments,[1] (the same having been ratified by the United States Congress and provision made to carry out the same, and for the appointment of a Commissioner on the part of the United States), I suggest, and earnestly solicit the appointment of, Col. David M. Talmadge[2] of Flushing, Queens County, New York, as eminently

competent to fill the position. He was our late commissioner under a
similar treaty with Venezuela,[3] and notwithstanding the peculiar
combination of adverse circumstances and events transpiring and
surrounding him in Venezuela (internal discord and revolution, overthrow of Government &c) he conducted the business in hand *within*
the time stipulated in a manner highly creditable to himself and satisfactory to claimants, who owe to his indomitable energy and perseverance—under the most adverse and complicated circumstances
possible—added to his knowledge of the language and character of
the people and government with whom he had to deal, *all and every*
the success and benefit attained.

Col. Talmadge is not a politician, but a gentleman of high attainments, clear and comprehensive mind, and of high social position,
and by education position and experience, eminently qualified to
conduct and conclude in the most satisfactory manner the Convention made with Mexico which is of similar character to that of late
with Venezuela. Moreover, apart from his recent creditable service
he deserves well of his country as he was Colonel of one of the regiments first called out by Mr Lincoln in his first call for 75,000 men
to suppress the rebellion, a regiment he [patrotically?] equipped at
heavy expense to himself.[4]

The appointment now solicited would be agreeable to him and at
the same time reflect the sentiments of approval which yourself and
all others must feel as to his efficient conduct of the late Venezuela
mission.

I earnestly solicit his appointment as United States commissioner upon
the convention just concluded between United States and Mexico.[5]

<Testimonials justifying what I have said of him—from eminent
citizens, are now on file in the State Department.>

                                                        Wm. Wales

ALS, DNA-RG59, Lets. of Appl. and Recomm., 1861–69 (M650, Roll 48), David M.
Talmage.

1. The ratification was completed in January 1869. *New York Times*, Jan. 6, 1869.

2. Talmadge (*c*1827–*ff*1885) was a wealthy merchant and broker. 1870 Census, N.Y., Queens,
Flushing, Bay Side, 285; Brooklyn directories (1861–86).

3. This commission was in session August 1867 to August 1868. *Senate Ex. Docs.*, 40 Cong.,
3 Sess., No. 14 (Ser. 1360).

4. Talmadge was the colonel of the 56th Rgt., N.Y. Militia. *OR*, Ser. 1, Vol. 27, Pt. 2: 219;
Henry R. Stiles, *The Civil, Political, Professional, and Ecclesiastical History and Commercial and
Industrial Record of the County of Kings and the City of Brooklyn, N.Y., from 1683 to 1884* (2 vols.,
N.Y., 1884), 2: 1203.

5. Since the act to put the convention into effect was not passed by Congress until April 1869,
Johnson did not appoint Talmadge. *Congressional Globe*, 41 Cong., 1 Sess., Appendix, p. 37.

From R. Weakley Brown
Private

Nashville Tenn   January 12 1869

My Dear Friend

I enclose you a recent letter of Hon A J Fletcher Secy of State which I think you will cordially approve.[1] In March 1866 I visited Gov. Brownlow at his private chamber to see if there was no way to prevail on him to approve of your course. I soon found *nothing* could be done. He then said nothing unkind about you, but I could easily discern the drift of his thoughts. Before leaving Secry. Fletcher came in. He said he was for disfranchising the rebels as a matter of safety, until they had time to cool. I then doubted his [motives?] and have had nothing to do with him from that time until this morning. When I read his letter this morning I repaired to the capitol and thanked him in behalf of the people for his manly and patriotic letter. He said he accepted his re-election with reluctance—and was induced to stand for re-election as a matter of pride and to vindicate his course.[2] He said he did not wish his name to be coupled with the extreme and objectionable powers of the state administration. I apologized to him for having suspected his motive in March 1866, and thanked him again on behalf of the people and told him the approval of his own *conscience* and the *approbation of Heaven*, were of worth more than the plaudits of radical orators or the encomiums of the radical press. (At least this was the substance of my remarks.) I gave him a good book. When I find a man is trying to do right I always have a strong hope he will ultimately become a christian. Mr. Fletcher said he was once a member of the Methodist Church and had 2 uncles who were preachers. I said but little to him about you—knowing he had always been a Whig. I thought I had better say but little to him about you. I think the split in the Republican party in this state will continue to widen—and I hope ere long a truly *conservative restoration* policy will be adopted and we shall once more have peace and good will in Tennessee.

I wish to see the great body of the people *rally once more* to *your standard*.

R Weakley Brown
41 Union Street

(In haste)

ALS, DLC-JP.

1. Fletcher wrote a letter to the *Nashville Press and Times* editor, dated January 9, which was widely published in various newspapers. The letter represented one of the parts of Fletcher's break with Governor Brownlow; in fact he admits as much in the letter itself. Fletcher claimed that his disagreements with Brownlow were not personal but instead concerned policies. He noted his regret that the disfranchisement of ex-Rebels had become "sweeping and perpetual" and "excessively severe." The disfranchised did not, argued Fletcher, take pride or interest in the government. *Nashville Republican Banner*, Jan. 12, 1869.

2. Fletcher was reelected secretary of state by a vote of both houses of the legislature on November 20, 1868. *House Journal . . . 1868–69*, 53–55.

From Thomas Cottman

New York Jany 12th 1869

Mr. President

I see by the papers that you have appointed Sidney Robertson Collector of Internal Revenue for the second District of Louisiana.[1] He is a gentleman & an old respectable citizen of the state. This looks like reconstruction in *earnest*, when the respectable citizens of the State receive the consideration to which their qualifications & position entitle them.

Thos. Cottman

ALS, DLC-JP.

1. On January 11, Johnson nominated Algernon Sidney Robertson to replace E. M. Bouligny, who was to be removed. The Senate eventually placed Robertson's nomination on the table, however. *Senate Ex. Proceedings*, Vol. 16: 429, 442, 501. See also Robertson to Johnson, Sept. 5, 1868.

From Thomas Ewing, Jr.

Washington Jany 12. 1869

My dear Sir:

I take the liberty of suggesting that you order all civilians, now held in confinement in the Southern States under sentence of military Commissions, to be brought forthwith to Fort Warren, Fort McHenry, or some other fort in the northern states, where their friends can freely & readily test by judicial proceedings the legality of this detention; and can obtain their release if the courts ajudge it.

I think this would be an act of humanity, & justice, and respect for law, that would add honor to your illustrious administration among all lovers of constitutional liberty in the land.

Thomas Ewing Jr

ALS, DLC-JP.

From George Watson Prescott[1]

No. 48 Green Street   Charlestown Mass.

Tuesday   Jany. 12th 1869.

Dear Sir

Pardon my presumption in thus intruding myself, an humble individual, upon your valuable time, but like our friend and bro.' B. P. Shillaber Esq.,[2] I cannot, for the life of me, help it. Like him also I have no favor to ask at your hands other than a kind remembrance by you as one of your most sincere friends and an admirer, generally, of your public acts and unvarying stedfast devotion to the preservation, intact, of the constitutional bulwark of our liberties (alas! how shattered by fanatical zeal and what seems to me a waning of *true patriotism* so absolutely essential to the preservation of constitutional liberty) through scenes of the most aggravating nature and amid trials that would have crushed one whose principles were not, as were yours, founded upon the rock of *right* against *might* and who, happily, was endowed with physical and mental strength to resist all.

I thank the "great architect of the Universe" that my country has bourne Andrew Johnson, to whom posterity will point with pride and possibly *with bitterly regret* that his counsels were not heeded.

As our Bro.' says of himself I have long wished to open my heart in gratitude to you for the sacrifices you have made, the trials endured, like a martyr for the cause and support of no less a principle than the perpetuation of the liberties of our common country, which have been so ruthlessly assailed by extreme and internal (infernal) foes.

May the reccolection of the giant efforts you have made in the cause of popular liberty, prompted as they were by the purest love of country and the welfare of *all*, bring peace to your declining years as they must bring praise from a grateful posterity unless posterity becomes so shackled by *party*, or besotted with selfish pursuits that it is blind to great truths and noble impulses.

In presuming to address the retiring Chief Magistrate of our land I claim that "important privelidge" by being "a man, free born, of good report" and, if need be, "proporly vouched for."

Geo' Watson Prescott

ALS, DLC-JP.

1. Prescott (*c*1823–*fl*1881) was a Charlestown bookkeeper. Boston directories (1868–1881); 1860 Census, Mass., Middlesex, Charlestown, 284.

2. Benjamin P. Shillaber (1814–1890) had edited the *Boston Post* before beginning the humor magazine *Carpet-Bag* in 1851. Shillaber authored several books, and contributed humor-

ous essays to journals and newspapers, often under the name "Mrs. Partington." His letter to Johnson, dated January 5, praised the President for his courage and fidelity in defending the Constitution. *DAB*; Shillaber to Johnson, Jan. 5, 1869, Johnson Papers, LC. This letter, or at least portions of it, was made public in the newspapers. See, for example, the *Richmond Dispatch*, Jan. 11, 1869.

From Maria A. Rousseau[1]

New Orleans   Jan. 12th 1869—

Mr. Johnson.

Knowing the kind feeling existing between yourself and my deceased husband[2] I take the liberty of asking a very great favor of you. My oldest son Richard wishes to be put back in the army.[3] Enclosed, I send you his Petition.[4] I also ask if there is a vacancy at *West Point* will *you if you please* give it to my younger son who is now seventeen (*in three months*) years old.[5] Mr. Johnson will you *for the sake of one* who considered it the *highest* honor to be classed amongst *your* friends, help me if you can. I am compelled to look to my boys for help as we are left with a large and *helpless* family.

Mrs. L H. Rousseau

ALS, DLC-JP.

1. Maria Antoinette Dozier (*c*1829–*c*1897) married Lovell H. Rousseau on July 5, 1841, in Bloomfield, Indiana. The couple had two sons and two daughters. Pension File, Maria A. Rousseau, RG15, NA; *New Orleans Picayune*, Jan. 8, 1869, morning.

2. Lovell H. Rousseau had died on January 7. See Robert C. Buchanan to Johnson, Jan. 8, 1869.

3. Richard H. Rousseau (*c*1846–1881), appointed a second lieutenant in the 1st Cavalry on May 3, 1867, resigned as of February 14, 1868, because of poor health. Powell, *Army List*, 565; 1860 Census, Ky., Jefferson, Louisville, 6th Ward, 92; Richard H. Rousseau to Johnson, May 1, 1867; Richard H. Rousseau to Secretary of War, Dec. 25, 1867, ACP Branch, File R-7-CB-1869, Richard H. Rousseau, RG94, NA.

4. Enclosed were both a letter from Richard, asking that his resignation be revoked, and a petition with the same request from ninety New Orleans citizens. Johnson endorsed Richard's letter, "Let the appointment be made. Father is noteworthy." Rousseau was nominated to be second lieutenant in the 4th Regiment, U.S. Cavalry, on January 23, a nomination which the Senate referred to its Committee on Military Affairs but otherwise ignored. Richard H. Rousseau to Johnson, Jan. 12, 1869; Citizens of New Orleans to Johnson, Jan. 12, 1869, ACP Branch, File R-7-CB-1869, Richard H. Rousseau, RG94, NA; *Senate Ex. Proceedings*, Vol. 16: 465, 474; *House Reports*, 44 Cong., 1 Sess., No. 238, p. 2 (Ser. 1708).

5. George L. Rousseau (1852–1882) did not receive an appointment to West Point. For more about his career, see Maria A. Rousseau to Johnson, Jan. 14, 1869. Powell, *Army List*, 565.

From Henry H. Howard[1]

Orford [N.H.]   Jan 13 1869

Dear Sir

You may think it not only presumtive but impertinent for an obscure individual among the granite hills of New Hampshire to thus address you. Please excuse me for I only graitify an irresistible desire to express my admiration of the noble stand you have taken and maintained under trials and difficulties no other has been called to experience. With unwavering fidelity to the constitution of the fathers and the best interest of our beloved country no love of popularity or power no selfish considerations have been able to *sway* you from the path of *right* and *Justice*. Undaunted and fearless you have defied the whole clique of radical disunionists. Every lover of his country can but admire your devotion and firmness. *Posterity will do you Justice.* As you retire from your high position you will have the *prayer and kind wishes* of at least one for many Years of Health and happiness.

Henry H Howard

ALS, DLC-JP.
    1. Howard (b. *c*1806) was an Orford merchant. 1860 Census, N.H., Grafton, Orford, 597.

From Esther Amelia C. Shedden[1]

Mooers Clinton County
New York   Jan 13th 1869

Dear Sir

Nothing that I have heard for a long time has made me so glad as your amnesty proclamation.[2] May God bless you for it. Have the offending not suffered enough and why should not the exile from his native soil rejoice that he may once more return without fear of molestation.

"To err is human
To forgive Divine"

And allow me sir to mention another thing which certainly must have afforded infinite pleasure to the three hundred children of

Washington invited to the White House for a Christmas party.[3] It
was a happy thought and would only have arisen in a kind heart.

But this was not the object of my writing this letter. Some two
years since I made my first request of the Government the pardon of
Capt S M Cooper[4] of the rebel army. Whither he was pardoned at
that time I suppose I shall never know. I have only heard that he was
living in very reduced circumstances at his home near Alexandria.
Now Sir will you pardon me for asking some promotion or favor or
notice in some way for three others who were *rebels* I suppose during
the war.

Just before the war I was in New York on my way to Fortress
Monroe. I had taken passage for that place on the Ship Roanoak just
before it was to sail. I went out into the city accompanied by a woman
and her children (from Conn[)] on her way to Richmond to join her
husband Master of a *sail boat*—I think—on her return she lost all
her money. She was in great distress. What should she do. I stated
the case as rapidly as possible to the purser. No she could not go on.
The ship was about to sail when two young gentlemen came forward and *nobly* paid her passage money to R——. One left the ship
directly but I heard the name *Martin* from South Carolina. G W
Simmons[5] says it was probably Robert Martin[6] whose elegant buildings were burned and lost all in Sheridans raid.

The other was a son[7] of Mr. Mason[8] minister to the French Court
who had just died. He had come on to meet his mother[9] and sisters
just returning from Paris.

The other name is one well known and highly respected in South
Carolina—James H Hallonquist.[10] While at the Fortress one day I
saw a man sitting with an air of great sadness. I asked the cause. He
said he was sick and wished so much he could return to his mother
in Philadelphia. I very soon raised the means. Mr Hallonquist sent
me five dollars with thanks for *asking him* (*not very usual*). He was
then just from West Point. The thought was suggested to me to ask
this of you before retiring thinking some good might come of it.
Perhaps my dignified brother,[11] now a member of Congress might
not quite approve my taking this liberty. But if wrong I hope to be
forgiven. I suppose it would be contrary to all the rules of Presidential etiquette to answer this letter but I would so like to know that it
was not disapproved.

Mrs. E A C Shedden

ALS, DLC-JP.

1. Shedden (c1809–fl1870) was the wife of Bushrod Shedden, a grist mill owner in Clinton County. 1870 Census, New York, Clinton, Mooers, 1; Amnesty Papers (M1003, Roll 58), Va., Samuel M. Cooper, RG94, NA.

2. See Fourth Amnesty Proclamation, Dec. 25, 1868.

3. Johnson and his family hosted a children's Christmas party on December 29, 1868. *National Intelligencer*, Dec. 30, 1868.

4. Possibly the Samuel Cooper (c1838–fl1870) living as a farmer in Fairfax, Virginia, in 1870. Cooper had been in the U.S. Army since 1857, but resigned his commission in 1861 to fight for Virginia during the war. He took the loyalty oath on June 20, 1865, but there is no evidence that he received an individual pardon. Mrs. Shedden had written on his behalf at least two other times, but the dates of those requests are unknown. Amnesty Papers (M1003, Roll 58), Va., Samuel M. Cooper, RG94, NA; 1870 Census, Va., Fairfax, Falls Church Twp., 33.

5. Not identified.

6. Not identified.

7. Either John Y. Mason, Jr., who is unidentified, or Lewis E. Mason (1822–1897), who is listed in the 1860 census as a "gentleman." First Search-World Cat.; 1860 Census, Va., Southampton, West Side Nottoway River, Jerusalem, 49.

8. Lawyer, congressman, and diplomat, John Y. Mason (1799–1859) served in the Virginia legislature (1823–31) and the U.S. House of Representatives (1831–37). He was Secretary of the Navy under Presidents Tyler and Polk (and also attorney general under Polk), and served as minister to France from 1853 until his death. *DAB*.

9. Mason married Mary Anne Fort (c1804–fl1860) in 1821. Ibid.; 1860 Census, Va., Southampton, West Side Nottoway River, Jerusalem, 49.

10. A West Point graduate, Hallonquist (c1835–1883/1884) resigned his commission in 1861 to join the Confederacy, where he served as an artillery instructor, ordnance officer, and eventually chief of artillery for the Army of Tennessee. His performance was mediocre at best, and his postwar life, marked by drinking and financial problems, was no better. *Register of Graduates and Former Cadets of the United States Military Academy: Cullum Memorial Edition* (West Point, 1970), 252; Larry J. Daniel, *Cannoneers in Gray: The Field Artillery of the Army of Tennessee, 1861–1865* (University, Ala., 1984), 78–79.

11. Not identified.

From Thomas Black[1]

Izard County Arks.   January 14th 1869.

Sir

The undersigned would most respectfully represent to your Excellency that the adjoining county of Fulton in this state is almost entirely devastated and laid waste; so complete is the distruction that the people are reduced to greater extremes than during the whole four years war. Many of the best citizens have fled for safely leaving their all behind and many others have been arrested and kept in camps as prisoners without even knowing for what cause. Several men have been shot down either at their homes or after being carried off prisoners. A large number of horses have been taken and carried off to Missouri and so thorough is the devastation that scarcely a cabin within the county has escaped plunder. This work has been done by the Arkansas Meilitia under the immediate command of Col Dale[2] and has been going on for more than two months with almost incredible shamelessness. The only cause or pretext for this terrible work is the murder of Capt Simpson Mason[3] on the Missouri border on the 19th day of Sept last by unknown parties. There has not been since the surrender the slightest resistence or demonstration on the part of the citizens of Fulton or any of the adjoining counties against the civil law or any other authority but the peace has been frequently disturbed by lawless raids from Missouri and a considerable number of these raiders are now in Col Dale's command. Several weeks elapsed after Mason's death before Col Dale entered the County during which the officers of the law had every facility and assistance offered them by the citizens and the Civil [wage?] was in full force in the whole county at the time of his entrance. Neither has there been a gun fired or a hand raised in resistance to Col Dale in all his outrageous operations. This man Mason for whom the Country is suffering such tortures came from Georgia to this State about the commencement of the war, was about forty years old, had lived a roving life from his youth, was never married and was a homeless vagabond. During the war he was a notorious murderer and robber behind the Federal lines on the Missouri & Arks. border. He never belonged to either army, but under a Meilitia Capt's commission from Gov Murphy[4] he organized about twenty Arkansas refugees in Missouri after the surrender and on the 13th day of June 1865[5] when the whole country was in entire peace crossed the state line and commenced an indiscriminate plunder, robbing every house not even exempting old widow women. They mounted armed and equiped themselves, arrested citizens, killed stock and insulted menaced and threatened, took two men from their plows in the field and carried them into the woods and shot them. After two days operations they were disbanded by Col Matson[6] then commanding U.S. forces in North Arks. (No redress for these outrages was ever had nor no retaliation offered and the men are now in Col Dale's command and some of them in high official places.) Soon after this he was appointed Superintendent of the Freedman's Bureau—then President of the board of Registration and in August last was again commissioned to organize a Malitia company and had got together a squad of men and commenced his former career when he was secretly waylayed and shot.

Among the many innocent sufferers by Col Dale's atrocities is Samuel Gentry[7] a man of nearly sixty years, an emigrant from Bedford County

Tenne. to this state in 1851, an exemplary member of the Presbyterian Church for more than thirty years, was never tried for any violation of law, took no active part in the late war and although he neither refugeed North or South but remained at home was not put under arrest by either party during the whole war. Soon after Col Dale entered Fulton Co. A scout went to Mr Gentry's house arrested him together with all his horses since which he has been held a close prisoner and has been carried off South probably to Little Rock with several other prisoners. No person is even allowed to know the nature of the charges, against any of these prisoners. All the avenues by petition or any other means are closed against the country at Executive head Quarters except such as come through the Meilitia commander and the sole object of this communication is to inform you of these facts and to ask your official interference to stay the onward progress of these tyrannies perpotrated as they are upon defenceless and unoffending people; and particularly to implore your aid and influence in behalf of this poor old man Gentry—that he may be allowed to come home to his distressed wife[8] and children and remain at pease amenable only to the laws of the country.

You will at once see that the foregoing part of this Communication is not in my hand writing. It was done by a friend at my instance. The foregoing is an unvarnished statement of facts as they have occured and I cannot too strongly urge their early consideration by your Excellency and such relief as you in your wisdom may think proper to grant in the premises.

I hope you will pardon me for troubling you with this communication for it is my nature to releive suffering humanity when ever it is in my power to do so.

I have been deprived of the pleasure for a long time of corresponding with you owing to the disturbed condition of our once happy country. The cause of these troubles I will not now undertake to mention, they are in the past. Nothing would give me more pleasure than to read a letter from your own pen in which I would be glad to have your opinion as to what we should do to restore peace and prosperity to our whole country such as was enjoyed by the people when you represented Green County and I represented Bedford County in the Tennessee Legislature when and where we formed our first acquaintance when quite young men. You will please direct your letters to Wild Haus Izard County Ark. I am well aware of the great number communications that comes before you for your consideration which admonishes me to come to a close. I must be permited to say this leaves me and mine in good health. Hoping

when this comes to hand it will find you and family in the enjoyment of good health.

Thos. Black

LS, DLC-JP.

1. Black (c1807/1808–f1870), a Democrat, served four terms in the Tennessee House of
Representatives (1839–47). By 1850 he and his family had moved to Izard County, Arkansas,
where he was a farmer. *BDTA*, 1: 49; 1850 Census, Ark., Izard, Rocky Bayou Twp., 14; (1860),
2; (1870), Millcreek Twp., 20.

2. George W. Dale was an Independence County farmer who had been in Arkansas since
about 1863. He served in the constitutional convention in 1868, strongly favoring the disfranchisement of former Confederates. Eugene G. Feistman, "Radical Disfranchisement in Arkansas, 1867–1868," *AHQ*, 12 (1953): 142–43, 161.

3. Mason (c1821–1868), who was a boot maker in 1860, left Arkansas with Union forces in
1862 and returned after the surrender. Opinion seemed to be divided along partisan lines over
whether he was a desperado, as Black claimed, or a Unionist officer who was "laboring . . . to
restore order and quiet in that part of the State." 1860 Census, Ark., Fulton, Union Twp., 23;
St. Louis Missouri Democrat, Sept. 30, 1868; various Arkansas newspapers quoted in Powell
Clayton, *The Aftermath of the Civil War in Arkansas* (New York, 1915), 90–91.

4. Isaac Murphy.

5. Mason wrote to Gen. J. J. Reynolds from Rolla, Missouri, on May 24, 1865, promising to
be in Batesville, Arkansas, two counties south of Fulton, by June 12 or 15. *OR*, Ser. 1, Vol. 48,
pt. 2: 583.

6. Hans Mattson (1832–1893), was a Swede who settled in Minnesota, where he practiced
law, served as agent to encourage Scandinavian emigration to the state, was secretary of state,
and edited several Swedish-language newspapers. During the Civil War he was colonel of the
3rd Minn. Inf., and in 1865 was stationed with them in Arkansas. Ibid., 612, 733; *DAB*.

7. Samuel Gentry (b. c1810) was a Bedford County blacksmith at the time of the 1850
census; by the time of the next census, he was an Arkansas farmer. He does not appear in the
1870 census. 1850 Census, Tenn., Bedford, 4th Dist., 117; (1860), Ark., Izard, Mill Creek
Twp., 57.

8. Probably Mary Gentry (c1807/08–f1870), a native of Tennessee, who was evidently a
widow by the time of the 1870 census and was listed as keeping house. By 1870 the only
"children" living in the household were two adults and one teenager. Ibid.; (1870), Fulton, Big
Creek Twp., Pilot Hill, 36.

From Benjamin F. Jones[1]

Winona Missi   Jan'y 14, 1869.

Respected Sir—

Your correspondent would respectfully represent that he is a citizen of Mississippi, and has no representative in Congress to address,
therefore look to you as our representative.

The Bankrupt Law[2] is deficient in this respect. It permits the Principal of a debt to take the Bankrupt Law and yet holds the securities
responsible for the Debt. Would you be so kind as to recommend to
Congress an amendment to the Law by which the securities on debts

be released at the same time the Principal is discharged. I think this but just and proper & hope it will meet with your cordial opprobation & that you will at once recommend in a special message the above amendment.

B. F. Jones

ALS, DLC-JP.

1. Jones (c1832/1834–f/1870) was a farmer and miller. 1860 Census, Miss., Carroll, 4th Police Dist., Carrollton, 9; (1870), Twp. 21, Range 6E, 11.

2. Probably a reference to the Bankrupt bill that was passed by Congress in March 1867. For a discussion of this act, see Charles Warren, *Bankruptcy in United States History* (Cambridge, Mass., 1935), 104–9.

From Maria A. Rousseau

New Orleans   Jan. 14th 1869—

I *respectfully* ask for an Appointment as Second Lieutenant in the 20th Regiment United States Infantry for my second son George. I understand there are several vacancies in that regiment.

Acting upon the advice of friends a few days ago I asked for an Appointment at West Point.[1] Upon reflection (were I *so* fortunate as to have received *that* appointment for him) I would not be able to incur the expense of his admission as I am left poor[2] with a large and helpless family to take care of. This, *other*, Appointment should your Excellency have in your power to give *him* would enable *him* to be of assistance to me *at* once. The 20th Regiment was my son in Law Gen. L D Watkins[3] old command—now *Gen.* Sykes.[4] Knowing the *kind* feeling existing between yourself and my husband *Mr.* Johnson I take the liberty of asking *this* favor of you.[5]

Mrs L H. Rousseau

ALS, DNA-RG94, ACP Branch, File R-6-CB-1869, George L. Rousseau.

1. See Maria A. Rousseau to Johnson, Jan. 12, 1869.

2. Her poverty was such that her husband's staff members were raffling off his horses to raise money and various New Orleans citizens appointed a committee to prepare some sort of testimonial. On March 14, 1869, Congress granted Maria Rousseau a monthly pension of thirty dollars. *Memphis Appeal*, Jan. 16, 1869; *House Reports*, 44 Cong., 1 Sess., No. 238, p. 1 (Ser. 1708).

3. Louis D. Watkins married Mary E. Rousseau on August 4, 1864, in Louisville, Kentucky. He had died in New Orleans of a stroke on March 29, 1868. Pension File, minor children of Louis Watkins, RG15, NA.

4. George Sykes (1822–1880), an 1842 graduate of West Point, was a Civil War corps commander and career army man. He had become colonel of the 20th Infantry in 1868. Warner, *Blue*.

5. Johnson acceded to Maria Rousseau's request, asking the secretary of war for a board to examine George's qualifications and, at the last moment, nominating him as second lieutenant in the 20th Infantry on March 2, 1869. But the Senate merely sent the nomination to a committee, where it remained. Finally, in 1875, however, George was appointed to the desired rank and regiment, becoming a first lieutenant in 1880. But a year later he was dismissed from the military. Powell, *Army List*, 565; *Senate Ex. Proceedings*, Vol. 16: 498, 500; *New York Times*, Oct. 8, 1882; Robert Morrow to Maria A. Rousseau, Jan. 22, 1869, Johnson Papers, LC; William G. Moore to Secretary of War, Feb. 5, 1869, ACP Branch, File R-6-CB-1869, George L. Rousseau, RG94, NA.

From Thurlow Weed

New York, Jan 14 [1869][1]

Dear Sir,

Col Tracey,[2] the U.S. District Attorney, has Prosecuted several Radical Revenue Officers to conviction. He is a capable, fearless man, and would, as Commissioner, collect the Revenues. And believing that such a Commissioner would reflect credit upon your Administration I cordially recommend his Appointment.

Col Tracy is a Conservative Republican, acting with Mr Raymond[3] and myself. But he would like to discharge the duties of Commissioner solely for the Govment, doing nothing for Party as between a Radical and Democratic nominee.

Though late, please accept my heartiest congratulations upon your triumph over the Impeachers.

Thurlow Weed

ALS, DLC-JP.
   1. Internal evidence suggests 1869 as the correct year.
   2. Benjamin F. Tracy. Weed recommends him for appointment as commissioner of internal revenue.
   3. Henry J. Raymond.

From John M. Smith[1]

Chesterfield District So. Ca
Piney Grove   Jany. 15th 1869

Hon'd. Sir,

You no doubt may be surprised to recieve a letter from one who is an entire stranger to you; especially with regard to the subject of which I am about to write. But first, let me introduce myself as a relative of some of your acquaintances in Tennessee.

Neil S. Brown ex Governor of Tennessee was the grandson of the late Neill Smith[2] of Robeson County N. Ca. who was my fathers[3] brother.

About fifty years ago I served an apprentiship under John L. Smith[4] Governor Browns uncle, who emigrated to Tennessee something over forty years ago.

So much for an introduction. It was my misfortune to have lived in the midst of where Shermans raid passed who applied fire and fagot with a most bountiful hand and striped me nearly of every thing I possessed left me without a horse and I have not been able since to purchase one. I had three daughters married before the beginning of that cruel war all left widows with families of little children. I left my home in Anson County N.C. in the autum of 1863 to assist my eldest daughter[5] being then a widow and in delicate health. Most of my effects I left in care of my only son[6] a practising Physician living in the little Vilage of Morven. Kilpatricks[7] core encamped at the place for several consecutive days and when they left burned every building on the premises and about 1000 dollars worth of my property consisting mostly of carriage trimmings, springs, paints, one buggy a Barouche, timber & tools. My son being absent from home at the time on a professional visit to a relative some forty miles distant or in all likelihood the wretches would have burned him with his buildings.

Now can you give me any pecuniary aid, if you can not, can you give me the office of Collector of Internal Revenue. Most of the offices in this section from the Governor of the State down to the least important are filled with Radicals, Carpet baggers, Scallawags and foreigners.

I know not that you have any acquaintance in this section to whom I could refer you for my character. Judge John A Inglis recently of Cheraw but now of Baltimore M.D. is a personal friend of mine. Some years ago we were members of the same church in Cheraw in this State.

I wish to call you attention to another subject before I close. You are well aware of the measures which have been taken to reconstruct the Constitution and that there were Registrars appointed to register the names of all persons entitled thereto. It was my misfortune to be chairman of the board of registrars for Jefferson Division in this District. I say misfortune because they have not paid me all for my services. My claim is about Sixty dollars, for services rendered in April last. My Voucher and the Voucher of one of my co-adjutors, were forwarded in the same envelope to J. W. Nichols[8] paymaster U.S. army head qrs Charleston. My associate recd. his pay long ago. The officials at head qrs profess to know nothing of my Voucher. It was probably missplaced passing through so many hands. The question now is how am I to get my money.

John M Smith

My address is Mount Croghan Chesterfield Dist So. Ca.

ALS, DNA-RG56, Appts., Internal Revenue Service, Collector, S.C., 1st Dist., John M. Smith.

1. Smith (c1797/98–ff1870), a former carriage maker, was currently a blacksmith. 1850 Census, N.C., Anson, Morven Dist., 172; (1870), S.C., Chesterfield, Mount Croghan, 15.

2. Smith (c1757–1817) was a Robeson County resident but his occupation is unknown. Peggy T. Townsend, comp., *Vanishing Ancestors: Cemetery Records of Robeson County, North Carolina* (3 vols., n.p., 1975–92), 3: 187.

3. Not identified.

4. Not identified.

5. Not identified.

6. John C. Smith (b. c1832) was a teacher before becoming a physician. 1850 Census, N.C., Anson, Morven Dist., 172; Mary L. Medley, *History of Anson County, North Carolina, 1750–1976* (Wadesboro, N.C., 1976), 234.

7. Judson Kilpatrick.

8. Before the Civil War, James W. Nicholls (c1829–ff1876) was a teacher at the Nashville Academy. Recommended during the war by Military Governor Johnson for an additional paymaster's position, he served in that department until 1875. ACP Branch, File 2976-ACP-1875, James W. Nicholls, RG94, NA; 1860 Census, Tenn., Davidson, Nashville, 5th Ward, 152; Nashville directories (1859).

From Orville H. Browning

Washington, D.C.   January 16 1869.

Sir,

I have the honor to transmit, herewith, a copy of a letter addressed to this Department, on the 15th instant, by the Commissioner of Indian Affairs, and a copy of a communication to him, from Col. E. W. Wynkoop,[1] "recommending that the widow of 'Black Kettle'[2] late chief of the Cheyenne tribe of Indians, be released from the military captivity in which she is now held."

I have no reason to doubt that "Black Kettle" was the faithful and unwavering friend of the whites, and that his death was unfortunate for the government.

I can conceive of no good to be attained by holding his widow, now an old woman, as a prisoner of war. Indeed her captivity is well calculated to alienate from the government the friendship of such of her tribe as have heretofore been peaceful in temper and dutiful in conduct.

Justice and humanity alike require that she should be released from captivity and permitted to return to the protection of her daughter.[3]

If you concur in these views I respectfully request that the necessary order for her release may be given.[4]

O H Browning   Secretary.

LS, DLC-JP.

1. Neither the letter from Commissioner of Indian Affairs Nathaniel G. Taylor nor the January 11, 1869, letter to Taylor from former Indian agent Edward W. Wynkoop has been found. See W. A. Nichols to Chauncey McKeever, Jan. 29, 1869, Lets. Recd. (Main Ser.), File I-9-1869 (M619, Roll 710), RG94, NA.

2. Black Kettle (c1803–1868), a southern Cheyenne chief in Colorado, led the band massacred in 1864 at Sand Creek. He was engaged in various peace efforts with the whites but was killed by U.S. troops at the Battle of the Washita in November 1868. His wife, Medicine Woman Later (d. 1868) was a Ponca Indian who had married into the Cheyenne tribe. She was wounded nine times at Sand Creek but survived that attack. *New Columbia Encyclopedia*; Stan Hoig, *The Peace Chiefs of the Cheyennes* (Norman, Okla., 1980), 111; George E. Hyde, *Life of George Bent: Written from His Letters* (Norman, Okla., 1968), 155, 248, 253, 297, 316.

3. In the spring of 1866, Magpie, usually listed as the niece of Black Kettle whom the childless chief treated as a daughter, married the half-Cheyenne interpreter George Bent, son of Colorado trader William Bent. The couple lived with Black Kettle but were absent at the time of the Battle of the Washita. Ibid., 253, 315–16; William T. Sherman to E. D. Townsend, Jan. 28, 1869, Johnson Papers, LC.

4. The request made its way through various military channels until it reached Fort Hays, Kansas, where the Cheyenne were imprisoned. The "widow" of Black Kettle was not there and the Cheyenne women told the interpreter that she had died during the Battle of the Washita. Apparently she and Black Kettle had been killed together while trying to escape the attack on horseback. Chauncey McKeever to W. A. Nichols, Feb. 13, 1869, Lets. Recd. (Main Ser.), File I-9-1869 (M619, Roll 710), RG94, NA; Hyde, *Life of George Bent*, 316.

From Perry Fuller

New Orleans   Jan 16th 1869

Sir:

I take great pleasure in recommending S. H. Torry, Esq. to your favorable consideration, as a warm and devoted friend to your administration. His removal therefore, allow me to suggest, has created much surprise among your supporters.[1]

Knowing him well, I cheerfully endorse him.

Perry Fuller

LS, DLC-JP.

1. Torrey was removed as U.S. district attorney of Louisiana and replaced in early January 1869. See Christian Roselius and John A. Campbell to Johnson, June 13, 1868, *Johnson Papers*, 14: 215.

From Alanson W. Kelly

Penn Yan   Yates Co. N.Y.
16th Jan, 1869

Sir:

I notice by the newspapers that you have complimented me by placing my name in nomination to the Senate for Postmaster.[1] I thank you. I do not desire this office & if I did the *Radical Ring* would decline to ask the Senate to confirm me, and I could only get it by a hard fight, if at all. Yet they make me the promise that if I will quietly withdraw they will support me in an appointment to a consulship. I am advised that Havana & Yedo Consulates are vacant and I would greatly pleased with an appointment to either.[2] I think I have richly earned *something* at your hands—through thick & thin I have supported you & you well know that I have offered my pecuniary assistance—unasked—& for the reason my sympathies have been in your interest ever since I knew you in Nashville.

I have made public speeches & written [?] articles for you often since I first met you. Should I come before you well fortified with letters of recommendation will it avail me in this matter. I shall be certain of confirmation—will I hope be able to retain any position you may give me through the next administration. My political antecedents are identical with those of Senator Doolittle.

A. W. Kelly

In haste.

ALS, DLC-JP.

1. Johnson had nominated Kelly on January 12. For details about the nomination and its withdrawal (on January 20) by the President, see Kelly to Johnson, Apr. 25, 1868, *Johnson Papers*, 14: 48. See also Kelly to Johnson, Nov. 21, 1868, in which letter Kelly indicated his desire for the postmaster appointment.

2. Two days later Kelly again wrote to Johnson requesting the withdrawal of the postmaster nomination and nomination instead as consul at Havana or at Yedo (Tokyo). Kelly to Johnson, Jan. 18, 1868, Johnson Papers, LC.

From Absalom A. Kyle

Rogersville Ten: 16th Jany 1869

My D'r. Sir,

I tender my thanks, for the Courtisies, & hospitality to my daughter Lucy[1] during my stay at Washington. On Friday evening the 8th I went up to the "White House" & expected a good long interview with you looking a good deal more to your interest than my own. I want you to run for Govr. & wanted to talk to you about it—but, suffering from sick head ache—only waited an hour to see you, & came off regretting that, I could not see you. Bob Love,[2] came off with me,—told me, that he had, had a long interview with you, & that, *with half a chance, you would run*. Should the franchise be settled in our favor, there will be no trouble.

I arrived at home on Sunday the 10th remained, Monday & Tuesday went to Knoxville to attend the Federal Court. Whilst there, I talked with very many of our Conservative friends about your running for Govr. and they are all for it—& think you can, by canvassing the State, create a revolution. This is, the universal sentiment, so far as I can gather it.

I regret, exceedingly, that, I did not have an interview with you.

I visited the Govr. (Brownlow) whilst at Knoxville, had 1 1/2 hours interview with him. *He's the full wreck* of an ill-spent life—nervous system entirely shattered muscles of face & eyelid & lips all in rapid motion. He cant live more than 1 or 2 years.[3] I think the next Legislature will have to elect his successor—& I think with a proper settlement of the franchise law, this winter, you can succeed, Brownlow—and nothing would give me more pleasure. You are too young, to retire on the "Henderson Farm" or any other. Yo've been right all the time, altho. overpowered & put in the shade.

Netherland[4] & Wm Kyle have spent the day with me, in my office & they fully agree with *me*.

The whole Conservative sentiment at Knoxville, & I think I can safely say, through out East Ten: is in favor of your running for Govr. in Augt next. Think of these things and shape your course accordingly.

A. A. Kyle

ALS, DLC-JP.

1. Lucy (1848–*fl*1900) continued living at home through 1870; in 1877 she married a

Rogersville dentist, Frederick A. Shotwell. Speer, *Prominent Tennesseans*, 433; 1870 Census, Tenn., Hawkins, 10th Dist., 10; (1900), 85th Enum. Dist., 4A.

2. Possibly the Col. Robert Love (1819–1876) who was a farmer and a lawyer, first in Carter County and then in Washington County. 1860 Census, Tenn., Carter, 2nd Div., Elizabethton, 165; (1870), Washington, 9th Dist., Johnson City, 9; Bennett and Rae, *Washington County Tombstone Inscriptions*, 1: 141.

3. Kyle's dire prediction was off by several years; Brownlow lived until 1877.

4. John Netherland of Rogersville.

From John M. Schofield

War Department, Jany. 16th 1869.

The Secy. of War, to whom was referred the Resolution of the Senate of the U.S., dated Dec. 19th 1868, has the honor to submit to the President the accompanying report of the Qr. Mr. Genl. of the Army,[1] as to the amount of money paid as rent for the building known as the *Libby Prison*, in the city of *Richmond* and to whom paid.

Rent has been paid for all private property used by the War Dept. in the late rebellious States, since April 2, 1866, and the authority of law for the payment is the same in this as in all other such cases.

J. M. Schofield   Secy. of War.

LBcopy, DNA-RG107, Lets. Sent, Mil. Bks., Executive, 59-B.

1. Montgomery C. Meigs's report of January 11, 1869, was transmitted to the Senate by Johnson on January 20. It is found in *Senate Ex. Docs.*, 40 Cong., 3 Sess., No. 24, pp. 1–8 (Ser. 1360).

From Thomas Ewing, Jr.

Washington, D.C.   Jny 17 1869.

My dear Sir:

I sincerely hope, as your friend & the friend of Gen Gordon Granger, that you will nominate him for one of the vacant Brigadierships in the regular army. He will be honored by the nomination whether confirmed or not: and his record as a soldier, as well as his manly adherence to you & the cause, make him more worthy of the honor than any other applicant: while your failure to nominate him will subject him & yourself to much disparaging criticism.

He would probably be rejected—so will anybody who even professes to be your friend & has not carried water on both shoulders. He does not ask the nomination with much hope of confirmation—but rather for the honor of being selected by you as worthy of the promotion. I hope you will not think me too urgent in this matter. I am as anxious for your sake that you should make the nomination as for his.

Thomas Ewing Jr.

ALS, DLC-JP.

From James B. Steedman

New Orleans, La.   Jany 17. 1869.

To the President,

It affords me pleasure to introduce to you Col. James F. Casey,[1] of New Orleans, one of our most worthy and respectable citizens—a brother-in-law of Genl. Grant,[2]—whom your friends here, very earnestly desire to put in Col Fuller's place as Collector, and as Col. Fuller himself has expressed to me a wish that Mr. Casey should be his successor,[3] I take the liberty of recommending Col. C. to you as a conservative man, a highly honorable gentleman, competent, honest, energetic, and very popular with the people of New Orleans.

Your friends in this city, who feel a deep interest in your future, are extremely anxious to succeed in this matter, for the reason, that the appointment of Col. Casey will defeat the efforts of the violent obnoxious men who are seeking the position and expect to use its influence to sustain their negro supremacy.

I have no doubt, as the Col is a brother-in-law of Genl Grant, that if he were in the position, he would be permitted to remain.

If you can consistently do this, it will give universal satisfaction to the people of New Orleans.[4]

James B. Steedman.

ALS, DNA-RG56, Appts., Customs Service, Collector, New Orleans, James F. Casey.

1. Casey (c1830–fl1878) was a brother of former Kentucky congressman Samuel L. Casey. No record of his military service has been found. 1870 Census, La., Orleans, New Orleans, 10th Ward, 368; New Orleans directories (1874–79); Simon, *Grant Papers*, 15: 344; *BDUSC*.

2. Casey had married Emma Dent, sister of Julia Dent Grant, in February 1861. Ishbel Ross, *The General's Wife: The Life of Mrs. Ulysses S. Grant* (New York, 1959), 127.

3. Perry Fuller, interim collector of customs since September, had had a fairly stormy tenure in office and his nomination for the permanent post was in jeopardy in January. Fuller also wrote a letter of recommendation for Casey. See Fuller to Johnson, Jan. 17, 1869, Appts., Customs Service, Collector, New Orleans, James F. Casey, RG56, NA. See also Fuller to Johnson, Sept. 30, 1868; Hugh McCulloch to Johnson, Oct. 20, 1868; Edmund G. Ross to Johnson, Jan. 20, 1869.

4. Although Johnson did not appoint Casey to the customhouse, Grant did in March 1869. Apparently a conservative Democrat, Casey survived a Republican attempt to remove him in 1870, was reappointed by Grant in 1873, and served until some time in 1877. Endorsement on Steedman letter; New Orleans directories (1877–78); *Senate Ex. Docs.*, 41 Cong., 2 Sess., No. 109, pp. 1–18 (Ser. 1407); William B. Hesseltine, *Ulysses S. Grant, Politician* (New York, 1935), 346; *U.S. Off. Reg.* (1875–77).

From M. Elizabeth Young

[Nashville]   Tuesday Morng   Jan 17" /69

A Petition is before Congress asking a Pension for my Aunt Miss Sommerville[1] predicated upon the death of her two brothers[2] in the service of their country. Will you use your influence in favour of the Bill, you know personally her condition and the necessity of some aid being extended to her. She is entirely destitute and my means are entirely expended.

Admiral Farragut who I see dined with you yesterday was a contemporary of her oldest brother[3] was in the same vesel with him in the expedition against the Pirates in 1823 under the command of Comodore Porter.[4] If you will take the trouble to ask him he will recall the circumstances. I have written to him asking his recognition of the fact. Your knowledge and friendship for the lady combined with his for the brother may accelerate the passage of the Bill. Be assured she needs it very much—or I should not trouble you again. The Bill was presented by Senator Fowler and referred to the Comittee on Pensions.

M E Young

ALS, DLC-JP.

1. In July 1868 Senator Joseph Fowler presented a petition in behalf of Martha Somerville seeking a pension for her. There is no evidence in the remainder of the 40th Congress to indicate that the Senate took any action on this request. *Congressional Globe*, 40 Cong., 2 Sess., p. 4346.

2. Probably Pierce B. Somerville (d. 1838) and George W. Somerville (d. 1832). The former served in the Florida campaign of the mid-1830s, contracted an illness there and steadily declined until his death in January 1838. George died of yellow fever at Thompson's Island. Jill K. Garrett and Iris H. McClain, *Old City Cemetery: Nashville, Tennessee Tombstone Inscriptions* (Columbia, Tenn., 1971), 89; Callahan, *Navy List*, 511; *Nashville Republican Banner*, Jan. 3, 1838.

3. George W. Somerville was with Farragut and Porter in the Caribbean in 1823, where they pursued pirates. See Charles Lee Lewis, *David Glasgow Farragut* (2 vols., Annapolis, 1941–43), 1: 156–59.

4. David Porter (1780–1843) was a renowned naval officer who had been in the U.S. Navy since 1798. He was actively engaged in South American naval actions during the War of 1812.

In 1823 he became commander-in-chief of the West India Squadron; he was court-martialed in 1825, however, and later served in the Mexican navy and then in diplomatic posts for the United States. *DAB*.

From R. G. Crow[1]

New York   Jan 18 /69

Dear Sir,

You remember, perhaps, that, on the 22d of July, or thereabouts, 1861, you introduced into the Senate, (you being then a Senator from Tennessee) a resolution reciting that the war was caused only by the disunionists of the South, &c.[2] This resolution was quickly passed. In the House, Mr Crittenden[3] introduced a like resolution, which was passed likewise. And, sir, I have been bold enough to address a letter to you, asking you to tell me why Mr Crittenden introduced such a resolution; because, on the eve of the war, some compromise measures of that gentleman, looking to maintaining the Union, were lost chiefly through the Republicans in Congress. Now, why did Mr Crittenden introduce that resolution that the war was caused only by disunionists of the South. Was it done on the spur of the moment—in the excitement caused by the Bull Run defeat. Perhaps you might be able to inform me. My reason for asking you is this: I am writing a history of the late war, and am somewhat confused at Mr Crittenden's course and your own also. *Do* you believe that the war was caused only by Southern disunionists. I am only a boy of 18. I entreat of you sir to pardon my boldness and answer this letter.[4]

R. G. Crow

Post Office Box 650   New York N.Y.

ALS, DLC-JP.

1. Possibly Raymond (or Ramon) G. Crow (*fl*1900), a bookkeeper residing in Brooklyn. Brooklyn directories (1873–1900).

2. See Remarks on War Aims Resolution, July 25, 1861, *Johnson Papers*, 4: 597–98.

3. John J. Crittenden. On July 22 the House passed the Crittenden Resolution, indicating that the war was being fought to defend the Constitution and to preserve the Union. Long, *Civil War Almanac*, 100.

4. There is no record of a response from the President.

From William E. Niblack

Washington City   Jany 18th 1869.

Sir

I hand you herewith a despatch from New Orleans[1] which I received last night in reply to a despatch to Mr. Sproule[2] which you were kind enough to dictate on Saturday night. Of course you will give it such consideration as you think the circumstances entitle it to.[3]

W. E. Niblack

ALS, DLC-JP.

1. The message was a telegram from Robert S. Sproule in New Orleans which claimed that Perry Fuller objected to being nominated as collector of customs in New Orleans, which post he was then filling. "He never authorized any one to ask his name sent in." Fuller had been nominated on January 13 and wanted the nomination withdrawn. Ser. 6B, Vol. 4: 204, Johnson Papers, LC; Sproule to Niblack, Jan. 17, 1869, Johnson Papers, LC.

2. Robert S. Sproule (c1828–f1875), a former government clerk and editor of the *Evansville (Ind.) Times*, may have been a clothing merchant in New Orleans. 1860 Census, D.C., Washington, 4th Ward, 276; (1870), La., Orleans, New Orleans, 2nd Ward, 67; Washington, D.C., directories (1858–60); New Orleans directories (1868–75); Sproule to Johnson, Mar. 12, 1866, Johnson Papers, LC.

3. Fuller's nomination was withdrawn on January 20. Ser. 6B, Vol. 4: 204, ibid. See also Edmund G. Ross to Johnson, Jan. 20, 1869.

To the Senate

WASHINGTON, D.C., *January 18, 1869.*

To the Senate of the United States:

The resolution adopted on the 5th instant, requesting the President "to transmit to the Senate a copy of any proclamation of amnesty made by him since the last adjournment of Congress, and also to communicate to the Senate by what authority of law the same was made," has been received.

I accordingly transmit herewith a copy of a proclamation dated the 25th day of December last. The authority of law by which it was made is set forth in the proclamation itself, which expressly affirms that it was issued "by virtue of the power and authority in me vested by the Constitution, and in the name of the sovereign people of the United States," and proclaims and declares, "unconditionally and without reservation, to all and to every person who, directly or indirectly, participated in the late insurrection or rebellion, a full pardon and amnesty for the offense of treason against the United States, or of adhering to their enemies during the late civil war, with the restoration of all their rights, privileges, and immunities under the Constitution and the laws which have been made in pursuance thereof."

The Federal Constitution is understood to be and is regarded by the Executive as the supreme law of the land. The second section of article second [*sic*] of that instrument provides that the President "shall have the power to grant reprieves and pardons for offenses against the United States, except in cases of impeachment." The proclamation of the 25th ultimo is in strict accordance with the judicial expositions of the authority thus conferred upon the Executive, and, as will be seen by reference to the accompanying papers, is in conformity with the precedent established by Washington in 1795, and followed by President Adams in 1800, Madison in 1815, and Lincoln in 1863, and by the present Executive in 1865, 1867, and 1868.

ANDREW JOHNSON

Richardson, *Messages*, 6: 697.

From Charles J.M. Gwinn

Baltimore   Jan. 19th '69

Sir:

The debate in the Senate on the Copper Bill shows that the interests intended to be crushed by the Chandler bill[1] must rely for their maintenance on the exercise of your veto power.

The papers in the case have already ben forwarded to you.[2]

It is for you to determine whether Mr. Chandler shall be allowed to crush the interests which are really so essential to the commerce of the country.[3]

Chas: J.M. Gwinn.

ALS, DLC-JP.

1. The bill on copper duties, designed to help the constituents of Michigan Senator Zachariah Chandler, passed the Senate this same day. *Congressional Globe*, 40 Cong., 3 Sess., p. 451.

2. It is not known to what papers Gwinn refers. See Gwinn to Johnson, Jan. 11, 1869, about items he had forwarded earlier, as well as Baltimore Copper Company to the Senate, Dec. 10, 12, 1868, Johnson Papers, LC.

3. Johnson vetoed the bill. See Veto of Copper Bill, Feb. 22, 1869.

From Collis P. Huntington[1]

No. 54 William Street
New York   January 19th 1869

Sir

On the 20th of October 1868 the Secretary of the Interior[2] approved a location by the Central Pacific Rail Road Company of California from "Monument Point" to "Echo Summit" according to a Map and Profiles filed in the Department of the Interior in conformity to law.[3]

We commenced our work at Sacramento in the month of February 1863 and have since pushed steadily forward with all the force which could be worked to advantage, always keeping strictly to the exact line previously located and approved by the Secretary of the Interior, and in good faith conforming to the requirements of the acts of Congress under which we were authorized to construct our Railroad—believing that the government subsidies granted to us should be faithfully applied to the construction of such a rail road and telegraph line as should by their permanence and durability prove to the satisfaction of the government and the people that the subsidies so liberally granted to us had not been misapplied.

In doing this we were engaged with heavy forces for more than four years in crossing the Sierra Nevada Mountains, employing much of the time more than 10,000 men, excavating fifteen tunnels—and portions of the line costing upwards of $200,000 per mile *to grade*.

While we were building about Seventeen (17) miles in the Sierra Nevadas, the Union Pacific R.R. Co built about four hundred (400) miles across the plains, with a force not so large as that employed by us. This proves the difficult nature of that portion of our work on which we were so long engaged.

Besides, all of our rails spikes & other iron material and rolling stock had to be transported from New York, around Cape Horn to Sacramento, a distance of about Eighteen thousand miles, with the exception of a few locomotives and cars purchased in California, and also a few locomotives &c sent across the Isthmus of Panama, at a heavy cost to expedite the construction and equipment of the road.

In confirmation of this statement and as to the manner in which our road thus far has been constructed and equipped, we confidently refer to the report of the commissioners appointed by the Government to examine our road dated December 3d 1868.[4]

On the other hand the Union Pacific Rail Road Company by tem-

porary and superficial construction of portions of their road, by passing around elevations which will require to be tunnelled to be fit for
permanent use—by placing men to work at different points from 50
to 350 miles in advance of their permanent work; by departing from
the location approved by the Secretary of the Interior, and constructing the road without regard to any approved location, are seeking to
take advantage of the delays to which our company was subjected in
the mountainous region, and thus gain possession of portions of the
proposed road, which they would not be able to reach in advance of
us, if their road was substantially built, and upon the permanent line
approved by the Secretary of the Interior.

The purposes of the Union Pacific R R Co in adopting this course
are probably three-fold.

1st   To obtain the government subsidies on that portion of the
line located by us and approved by the Secretary of the Interior.

2d   To divert the trade of Salt Lake City and vicinity to their
road which otherwise would naturally come to us.

3d   To reach and claim certain coal mines (necessary to us for
fuel) lying in the Wasatch Mountains.

All these we can reach *first* and become fairly entitled to, if the
Union Pacific Rail Road Company are required to build their road
in a substantial manner as we have built ours, and to keep strictly to
the permanent line approved by the Secretary of the Interior.

Had we chosen by hasty and incomplete construction to push on
our work in order to gain the Government subsidies, and preoccupy
the ground, we might have gone aside from our location in many
instances; built temporary tracks around mountain elevations, and
tunnelled them at our leisure, by so doing we might have saved a
year or more in time, and met the Union Pacific Rail Road East of
the Wasatch Mountains. But should we have complied with the law,
or fairly and in good faith earned and used the government subsidies? We think not.

We have expended large sums of money in the purchase of rails
and other materials and for work on that portion of the road located
by us, and approved by the Secretary of the Interior, lying between
the present eastern terminus of our rails, and Echo Summit—and
we shall be necessarily subjected to heavy loss, if the Union Pacific R
R Co are permitted to pass around, or over their heavy work eaven
temporarily, and occupy ground adjacent or parallel to that already
located by us, and approved by the Secretary of the Interior, on which
we are now at work with a large force.

We only ask that the Union Pacific R R Company be required to construct their road in a like substantial manner to ours—to excavate tunnels, and not lay temporary tracks around, at points where tunnelling will for permanent use be necessary, and to construct their road on the line approved by the Secretary of the Interior, by which their rails *permanently laid* extending Westward from Omaha will *meet and connect* with ours advancing Eastward, and thus form a continuous line as required by the acts of Congress.

Until this course is adopted and their line put in good and substantial order—We respectfully submit and insist that the Union Pacific R R Company are not entitled to, and should not receive any subsidies, either of bonds, or lands, on any work done, or road constructed by them, West of Echo Summit.

In accordance with these views we respectfully present this our *Protest*.

We further submit and insist that if we build our road to Echo Summit upon the line of our approved location, and according to the provisions of the acts of Congress, we ourselves shall be entitled to receive the subsidies granted, and incident thereto, to that point.

In conclusion we say that as we have endeavored in good faith to apply the subsidies granted to us by the Government, as well as the aid received from the State of California and some Eight and a half millions of dollars of our own means in the construction and equipment of a road which the government commissioners above referred to certify in their report "is being constructed in good faith, in a substantial manner without stint of labor materials or equipment, and is worthy of its character as a great national work" we trust that our rights will be protected by the Government.

We want nothing from the Government to which the Union Pacific R.R. Co are fairly entitled, but only that equal and exact justice be meted out to us and to them. This we do want and have the reasonable right to expect at the hands of the Government.

C. P. Huntington   Vice President

LS, DLC-JP.

1. Huntington (1821–1900) was the Central Pacific's eastern agent responsible for purchasing and shipping supplies and raising finances. He was later in leadership of the Southern Pacific Railroad, and the Chesapeake and Ohio Railroad, as well as other railroad lines and several steamship companies. *DAB.*

2. Orville H. Browning.

3. In another letter to Johnson, Huntington strongly protested any attempt to change this accepted line location. Huntington to Johnson, Jan. 20, 1869, Johnson Papers, LC.

4. The Central Pacific had been inspected by Sherman Day (surveyor general for California), Lt. Col. Robert S. Williamson (Army Corps of Engineers), and Lloyd Tevis (engineer for the Southern Pacific Railroad). Williams, *Great and Shining Road*, 224.

From Sam Milligan

Washington City
January 19. 1869

Dear Sir:

The accompanying application[1] speaks for itself, and I feel bound, both on account of an old debt of gratitude I owe to Mr Hoss, and on account of his eminent qualifications to fill the position he seeks, in good faith, to recommend his appointment, should the office he asks be created.

His handwriting exactly suits a public record, and his accuracy will enable him to keep a set of books unsurpassed by any one. He is poor, and needs the office; so give it to him, if you can consitantly do so.[2]

Sam Milligan

ALS, DLC-JP.

1. The enclosed was apparently a letter from Alfred Hoss, asking to be appointed recorder of deeds for the District of Columbia "in view of the probable creation" of that office. Hoss (*fl*1892) had a long career in government service, including clerking in the Quartermaster General's Office, the Adjutant General's Office, the Surgeon General's Office, and the Records and Pension Division. *U.S. Off. Reg.* (1865–91); Washington, D.C., directories (1868–93); Alfred Hoss to Johnson, Jan. 9, 1869, Johnson Papers, LC.

2. Apparently both Hoss and Milligan misunderstood the bill before Congress, which did not create a new position, but only renamed an existing one. Thus, the acting register of deeds, William G. Flood, became the acting recorder of deeds. Hoss was not nominated for this or any other position. *Congressional Globe*, 40 Cong., 3 Sess., pp. 145, 205, 226, 248–49, 262, 1788, 1819, 1835, 1867, Appendix, pp. 326–27.

From Jefferson C. French

Nashville Tenn.   Jany 20 1869

Regarding united states Grant as an Incubus on the Body politic I respectfully ask you not to leave the functions of Government without its constitutional provisions.[1] The union men of the north and south will enforce this measure. Liberty or monarchy.

Jefferson Coe French

Tel, DLC-JP.

1. The President's office was notified through a subsequent telegram that French, "though a very Intelligent Gentleman when Sober, is very drunk when writing this." C. A. Tinker to William G. Moore, Jan. 20, 1869, Johnson Papers, LC.

From Edmund G. Ross
Private

Washington. Jan 20 1869

Mr President

Upon consultation with the friends of Maj Fuller[1] & more definite information as to his own desire, I ask that his name be withdrawn if you can do so consistently.[2] I fear that unless it is done at once, the opposition to Mr Fuller will force action, & cause his rejection. The case is now in the hands of the committee, which will doubtless report to-day.[3]

E G Ross

ALS, DLC-JP.

1. For an earlier document from Ross concerning Perry Fuller's appointment, which the Senate rejected in July 1868, see Ross to Johnson, June 23, 1868, *Johnson Papers*, 14: 258.

2. In a letter to Johnson recommending another candidate, Fuller mentioned that Senator Ross had his resignation, to be used in case Johnson preferred to support James F. Casey. Ser. 6B, Vol. 4: 204, Johnson Papers, LC; Perry Fuller to Johnson, Jan. 17, 1869, Appts., Customs Service, Collector, New Orleans, James F. Casey, RG56, NA. See also James B. Steedman to Johnson, Jan. 17, 1869; William E. Niblack to Johnson, Jan. 18, 1869.

3. Johnson withdrew Fuller's nomination on the same day Ross requested it. Ser. 6B, Vol. 4: 204, Johnson Papers, LC.

From Ralph W. Newton

Washington D.C.   Jan 21 1869

My dear Sir.

I may possibly live down the loss of my own reputation & the humiliation caused by the apointment of Somebody for Naval Officer of New York,[1] but the confirmation of my friend Smythe would have been certain had Mr. Anthony[2] been nominated & it is impossible, unless, that nomination is made.

R W Newton

confidential

I congratulate upon the beleif that your nominee will be confirmed as he was a pet of your Enemies during your trouble.

ALS, DLC-JP.
    1. On January 20 Johnson had nominated John L. Deen for the position. See Anne M. Deen to Johnson, July 3, 1868, *Johnson Papers*, 14: 309.
    2. Newton was convinced that the nomination of James L. Anthony would help Henry A. Smythe win confirmation as minister to Russia. Smythe's nomination, made in December 1868, was tabled in March 1869. See Smythe to Johnson, May 27, 1868, ibid., 124.

From L. Bradford Prince[1]

67 Wall St.   New York

January 21st 1869

Dear Sir:

I am about arranging an article on the "Civil Service Bill" taking ground in favor of the reform, not only on account of the benefit to the service, but the *relief of the Executive*, in the matter of appointment.

Can you, without too much trouble, give any approximation to the *amount* of time, or the *proportion* of official time, which the President has necessarily to give to the demands of office seekers and those recommending them.

It appears to me that the subject is one of interest and much public importance, and I should be glad, while not wishing to tax your time and attention, of any suggestions or information bearing upon it.

L. Bradford Prince

ALS, DLC-JP.
    1. Prince (1840–1922), a lawyer by training, was active in Republican Party politics. In the 1870s he served in the New York legislature; at the end of the decade he was appointed chief justice of the New Mexico Territory. Ten years later (1889) President Harrison appointed Prince as governor of New Mexico, a post he held for four years. *DAB*.

From Ann S. Stephens

National Hotel   Jan 22d [1869]

My Dear Sir.

The Secretary that Mr Stillwell has talked so much about has at length arrived. He is a lawyer from Michigan, named Murrey,[1] and married the sister of Stillwell's wife, I am told. He went to Venezuela under the name of Secretary, but in fact as a claim agent to act before the Commissioners sitting there last year. This business I suppose he is ready to complete now under the protection of Stillwell's commission, for that gentleman has all along expressed himself unable to give a positive answer as to the exact time of his promised resignation until this man came. Last evening my son[2] went to Stillwell and asked him to state a definite time when he would resign. He replied that *he* did not intend to go to Venezuela at all but would hold the commission till the claims agreed upon were settled. He said that the interest would become due on the first of February; but he would not resign before the middle of that month. Thise claims are the reason of his wanting the place. *Why* is he and his relation so particularly anxious about them? Mr Stillwell pledged himself to me in person—that he would resign in time for another appointment to be confirmed. His brother in law, Gen Cary,[3] did more. He promised that the resignation should be sent in ten minutes after his confirmation. Now he, Mr Stillwell, coolly informs us that he will resign on the middle of Feb and this will be his earliest time. Is this fair?—is it honorable?

I state these facts and leave them with you. I cannot come in person to urge one step in our favor; to do this is always painful to me. The last time I saw you it seemed to me that you were a little impatient with my anxiety and I came home more grieved than you will think a woman of my age should be at so slight a cause. Under the influence of these feelings I shrink from troubling you so soon again, but I remember how keenly my boy is disappointed and feel that I must not have him sacrificed for want of a just understanding of the case. This thing is certain if Stillwell is confirmed and commissioned to Venezuela. Edward Stephens can never be, nor will any one go there unless it be this Mr Murrey. Stillwell has been cruelly trifling with us from the first.[4] Since yesterday I have been trying to use a little influence in favor of Cummings[5] with some success I think, but this interview with Stillwell has completely disheartened me.

Ann S Stephens

ALS, DLC-JP.

1. Actually, William P. Murray (1827–1910) resided in St. Paul, Minnesota, where he had been alderman for sixteen years and would eventually serve as city attorney (1876–89). Murray had been in the territorial legislature and was elected several times to the state house and state senate. *NUC*; C. C. Andrews, ed., *History of St. Paul, Minn.* (Syracuse, 1890), 190–95.

2. Edward Stephens.

3. Samuel F. Cary.

4. See Ann S. Stephens to Johnson, Oct. 16, Dec. 26, 1868, Jan. 4, 1869. Also interesting is that four days after this letter, the *Evening Star* reported Thomas N. Stilwell's announcement of his candidacy for the congressional seat from Indiana's Eighth District. *Washington Evening Star*, Jan. 26, 1869.

5. Alexander Cummings was the current nominee under consideration by the Senate for commissioner of internal revenue.

From William M. Evarts

January 23, 1869, Washington, D.C.; ALS, DNA-RG94, ACP Branch, File A-10-CB-1869, Attorney General.

Evarts responds to a question posed by Johnson on December 30, 1868: whether an army captain who has been sentenced by a court-martial to reduction in rank, "by having his name placed lower down on the list of officers of the same grade," would be restored to his former place if his penalty were remitted by a presidential pardon.

According to military regulations, rank among officers of the same grade is determined by date of commission and all vacancies to colonel "are required to be filled by promotion according to seniority." The interruption of rank by court-martial verdict would only remain while the penalty was in effect. In Evarts's opinion, a pardon would restore the officer to his previous rank in the list, with the exception that he would have lost any opportunities for promotion that occurred while the penalty was in effect.

The case of an officer reduced in rank, however, is different from one who has been dismissed from the service. The latter cannot be restored in any way except by a new appointment and confirmation by the Senate, since his dismissal "entirely dissolves his connection with the service" and reduces him to the same status he had before he ever got a military commission. But an officer reduced in rank does not need to be reappointed.

Evarts has examined some previous cases concerning "the restoration of officers from the reserved to the active list, their transfer from one regiment to another, and kindred subjects" and none of them "supports a different conclusion" from his own.

From Conrad C. Dumreicher [1]

Washington City D.C.   January 26th 1869.

Sir.

By the decision of a General Court Martial, held in San Antonio Texas in April & May 1868 I was dismissed from the service of the United States as an Asst. Surgeon.[2]

Notwithstanding the General Orders from the Head-Quarters of the Army, approving and publishing that decision, state; that the proceedings of that Court had been submitted to you, and had received your approval, I feel compelled in vindication of my personal and professional reputation most respectfully and earnestly to call your attention again to the subject with a view to restoration by means of my re-appointment and confirmation by the Senate for the post of Assistant

Surgeon in the Army in accordance with the Act of July 20th 1868, approved July 20th 1868.

I would not to this extent trouble your Excellency but that I have failed in all my efforts before the Secretary of War and the Judge Advocate General of the Army[3] for a reopening and reconsideration of my case and it is therefore as a last resort, that I venture to take up a moment of your Excellency's time, believing that you will never refuse to do justice to even the humblest of your fellow-citizens.

I feel that I am innocent of the charges preferred against me, and that the only case truly made out on the trial was a conspiracy by unworthy persons to get me out of the service.

Not to worry your Excellency with a lengthy review of the case I beg to enclose herewith for your perusal an argument, which I recently addressed to the Judge Advocate General of the Army,[4] and to ask of you that measure of *justice* in the premises, which I am sure it will always be your pleasure to grant to all, who call upon you for Justice.[5]

C. C. Dumreicher.

ALS, DNA-RG94, ACP Branch, File P-38-CB-1869, C. C. Dumreicher.

1. Dumreicher (b. 1839) graduated from medical school about 1861. After serving as assistant surgeon with the 1st Ill. Cav. and at various points in the eastern U.S., he was assigned to duty in the Washington Territory. Mustered out of the volunteer service in June 1865, he became an assistant surgeon in the regular army in February 1866, serving the 4th Cav. at several forts in Texas. Powell, *Army List*, 291; Papers of Physicians and Surgeons, Conrad C. Dumreicher, RG94, NA.

2. Dumreicher was court-martialed for being drunk on duty on the night when a cavalry captain died, and for disobeying an order to remove his horse from its stable and to vacate his own quarters. He was found guilty and cashiered from the service. General Court-Martial Orders No. 28, June 17, 1868, ACP Branch, File P-38-CB-1869, Conrad C. Dumreicher, RG94, NA.

3. John M. Schofield and Joseph Holt. See Holt to Schofield, Nov. 5, 1868, Jan. 2, 18, 1869; Dumreicher to Holt, Nov. 11, 1868, Jan. 9, 1869, ibid.

4. Perhaps the letter of Dumreicher to Holt, Jan. 9, 1869.

5. On February 3, 1869, Johnson referred the Dumreicher material to Schofield for examination and report. On February 8 and 11, Dumreicher wrote to Johnson complaining that the War Department had done nothing about his case since Schofield "re-concurred in his previous opinion." On February 15, having read the War Department's reply to Johnson, Dumreicher lamented that Holt had never looked at the case himself but had left it to his subordinates. He asked Johnson to read the papers himself and grant him justice. The President, however, refused to take any further action and sent the correspondence back to the War Department. Dumreicher to Johnson, Feb. 8, 11, 15, 1869; Wright Rives to Schofield, Feb. 19, 1869, ibid.

From John H. McClung[1]

Marshallville Ga.   Jany 27th 1869

Sir

You will please excuse this address from a Stranger personally and from an obscure and poor man, but thank God one that has a Soul to appreciate honorable upright acts and motives from his fellowman.

Sir I have not language to express my feelings to you as I would wish, but I cannot concientiously let you retire from the Presidential mansion of the country without thanking you from the bottom of my heart for the noble and manly Stand that you have made for my downtrodden fellow country man of the South during your eventful career as President.

Sir I am no politician nor place hunter never have been nor never will be, but claim the priviledge of tendering the thanks and congratulations of an honest heart and which I honestly believe is cordially responded to by an overwhelming majority of all upright thinking men from the "Potomac to the "Rio Grande" though they may not have the boldness to thus publicly express themselves.

May the Great Judge of the hearts of all men be with you shield and protect you and yours is the sincere prayer of your fellow countryman.

John H. McClung

ALS, DLC-JP.

1. McClung (1822–*fl*1880) was a merchant and farmer. William McClung, *The McClung Genealogy* (Pittsburgh, 1904), 189; 1870 Census, Ga., Macon, Montezuma Dist., Oglethorpe, 264; (1880), 38th Enum. Dist., 56.

From John P. White

Nashville, Tenn., Jany 27th, 1869

Dr. Sir

Mrs Calvin Jackson,[1] a neighbor of mine & resident of Edgefield informs me that she has a claim against the gov for two Horses pressed for the service by Col Hepburn[2] in 1863 and[3] she says that she has had frequent conversations with you on the subject of getting pay for the same while you was here and she has determined to send the papers in the case directly to you. Mrs Jackson I know to be an elegant lady the widow of Calvin Jackson[4] who died in 1860 or 61, and has been made destitute by the war and is at this time in want and other claims of the same kind for Horses pressed at the same time having been paid I am in hopes that she can get this to supply her present wants and any thing you can do for her by your indorsment of the claim or recommendation will be appreciated by her and be doing a favor to one who needs it.[5]

John P White

ALS, DLC-JP.

1. Jane B. Green (b. c1823) married Calvin W. Jackson in 1840. They had one son. 1860 Census, Tenn., Davidson, Edgefield, 29; Edythe Rucker Whitley, comp., *Marriages of Wilson County, Tennessee* (Baltimore, 1981), 171.

2. William P. Hepburn (1833–1916) practiced law in Iowa prior to and after the Civil War. During the war he served in the 2nd Iowa Cav. and rose to the rank of lieutenant colonel. For a time he served as inspector of cavalry for the Army of the Cumberland. He was a U.S. Representative from Iowa for several terms (1881–87, 1893–1909). *BDUSC; Annals of the Army of the Cumberland* (Philadelphia, 1863), 49.

3. Beginning with this word and continuing through the word "for," it appears that White, or someone else, has marked through these words. However, the sentence makes little sense without these words so we have retained them in our rendering.

4. Jackson (c1822–c1860–61) was a Davidson County farmer by the time of the 1860 census; he had resided in Wilson County earlier. 1860 Census, Tenn., Davidson, Edgefield, 29; Thomas E. Partlow, comp., *Wilson County, Tennessee Miscellaneous Records, 1800–1875* (Easley, S.C., 1982), 233; Thomas E. Partlow, comp., *Wilson County, Tennessee Deed Books N–Z, 1829–1853* (Easley, 1984), 306, 401.

5. In a letter to Johnson, Mrs. Jackson referred to a statement made by then military governor Johnson to Jane Jackson's sister that she should be compensated for the horses. One of her friends also entreated the President to cause the claims of Mrs. Jackson to be paid. Any action that Johnson may have taken in this matter has not been uncovered. Jane B. Jackson to Johnson, Jan. 1869; Jesse Frazer to Johnson, Jan. 25, 1869, Johnson Papers, LC.

From Mordecai J. W. Ambrose[1]

No. 47 Everett St. Cincinnati, O.   January 29, 1869.

Sir:

A few days after your inauguration I presented you with a recommendation duly endorsed, for the speciality of U.S. Chaplain. But your excellency declined to honor it. This has been greatly to my injury in every sense of the word; and I should not now renew my application to you for any thing—preferring to die under the frowns of those whom I have assisted to elevate and sustain, and the ingratitude of my country which I have unwaveringly labored to preserve. These things have taken all I had and left me destitute.

I now renew my application; not that I expect a Chaplaincy, notwithstanding it is my preference.

I trust I may receive some appointment that may give me *life* again. Pension agency, collectorship, Gubernatorial chair of some one of the territories, consulate, inspector, or any appointment of some worth that may be in your power to make. I can forward you the necessary recommendation at any time.

This I certainly would not now ask but for the reason that I saw you in a dream last night in your office room; some two or three gentlemen were present, and in due time you gave me audience, and your countenance soon lost its austerity toward me, and I again saw the President with a pleasant countenance in familiar conversation with me, and extending his hand I accepted it cordially, when you gave me the grip of an entered apprentice mason, passed to that of a fellow-craft, and then to that of a master mason, all of which I responded to, when we mutually approached and gave the true word of a master mason in the lawful way. You then gave the sign of distress of a Royal Arch Mason which was recognized and answered by me as I best could without its being recognised by those for whom it is not.

When I took my leave, you eschorted me to the door and pleasantly and cordially gave me an appointment. "*So mote it be.*"

Please do not misinterpret the spirit of the man from this little narative of an act of sleep.[2]

M.J.W. Ambrose, M.D.
Late Chaplain U.S.A.

ALS, DNA-RG94, ACP Branch, File A-17-CB-1869, M.J.W. Ambrose.

1. Ambrose (1815–1903), a Methodist minister who served as chaplain of two Kentucky regiments during the war, continued to reside in Cincinnati where he was listed in the directories as physician and dentist. CSR, Mordecai J.W. Ambrose, RG94, NA; Pension Records, Mordecai J.W. Ambrose, RG15, NA; Cincinnati directories (1867–81).

2. Ambrose received no appointment from Johnson.

From Robert H. Kerr

Pittsburg   January 30th [1869][1]

My Dr. Sir/

You will please find inclosed the proceedings of the Democratic Convention.[2] We have spoken out for the man who can defeat the enemy.[3] The Convention was largely attended by the very best men of the Party. When I spoke of you my remarks were hailed with loud demonstrations of Applause. When you come to retire from office

Fortieth Congress U.S. Second Session
SENATE CHAMBER.

MAY 16TH AND 26TH 1868.

The vote of the Senate, sitting as a High Court of Impeachment for the trial of **ANDREW JOHNSON**, President of the
United States, upon the 11th, 2nd and 3rd Articles.

S.P. Chase, Chief Justice.   *J.W. Forney,* Secretary.

Guilty.

1 H.B. Anthony
2 H.W. Corbett
3 Cornelius Cole
4 J.C. Conness
5 Wm M Stewart
6 J.W. Patterson
7 Justin S. Morrill
8 James W. Nye
9 Timothy Howe
10 Henry Wilson
11 A.H. Cragin
12 W. Sprague

13 Jas Harlan
14 O.S. Ferry
15 Aly. Ramsey
16 John Conness
17 Gust Edmunds
18 Fredk T. Frelinghuysen
19 H. B. Anthony
20 Jm. Howard
21 S.C. Pomeroy
22 W.J. Willey
23 Richd Yates

24 Charles Sumner
25 Aaron H. Cragin
26 Geo H Williams
27 Z. Chandler
28 E.D. Morgan
29 John Sherman
30 John M. Thayer
31 Roscoe Conkling
32 O.D. Drake
33 Simon Cameron
34 T. W. Tipton
35 O. P. Morton

Not Guilty.

1 T.A. Hendricks
2 b A Buckalew
3 Doolittle
4 Doolittle,
5 Tho. C. McCreery
6 George Vickers

7 J.P. Henderson
8 Lyman Trumbull
9 E.G. Ross
10 W. P. Fessenden
11 Garrett Davis
12 J.A Bayard
13 Jos. S. Fowler

14 Jos Grimes
15 Daniel S. Norton
16 Willard Saulsbury
17 Reverdy Johnson
18 P.G. Van Winkle
19 James Dixon

James D. McBride's "impeachment chart."
Courtesy Special Collections, University of Tennessee Library

can you not take this place en route to Tennessee? We the Democracy would be glad to take you by the hand and bid you welcome, trusting you will be spared for many years to come and hoping to find you in the Councils of the Nation, representing your State in the Senate.

R H Kerr
Chairman of the De Com

ALS, DLC-JP.

1. Internal evidence makes it clear that this is an 1869 document.

2. Nothing was found enclosed. The Democratic county convention, of which Kerr was president, met on January 26 to nominate a candidate for governor. *Pittsburgh Post*, Jan. 27, 1869.

3. The county convention supported George W. Cass, but he lost the nomination to Asa Packer at the state convention in July. Ibid.; Erwin S. Bradley, *The Triumph of Militant Republicanism: A Study of Pennsylvania and Presidential Politics, 1860–1872* (Philadelphia, 1964), 345–46.

From James D. McBride[1]

New York, Jany 30th 1869.

Sir:

The "Impeachment Charts" shown to you, are offered for sale together with autograph letters from several members of both Houses of Congress, establishing their authenticity. These two documents of State, showing the action of the Senators, and members who took part in the trial as accusers, and judges. As such they will be interesting mementoes of that historical event, and become objects of great interest, and in time valuable. Your expressed admiration of them, has urged me to bring the matter to your attention. They are valued at two thousand dollars.

James D. McBride   75 Mercer St:

ALS, DLC-JP.

1. A sergeant in 1861, McBride (1842–1932) ended the war as a lieutenant colonel with the 8th U.S. Colored Heavy Arty. and a brevet brigadier general of volunteers. Along with being a lawyer, inventor, and publisher, McBride also produced ornate placards that listed Senators' names, in their own handwriting, along with their votes at the impeachment trial. Hunt and Brown, *Brigadier Generals*; Powell, *Army List*, 459.

February 1869

From Thomas Cooper[1]

Washington D.C.   [ca. February] 1869[2]

Sir

Permit me to trouble you with a line ere my pleasant and to me agreeable service as a domestic under your personal employ terminates in acknowledgement of my heartfelt gratitude for the kindness of your placing my Step son John J Crawford[3] in a position in the Hon Sect. Office Note Division Treasury Department of which I trust he will ever prove worthy of the position he was so kindly recommended. For your kindness to me at all times I am humbly and truly thankful and with the hope that health and happiness may continue to abide with you and family for ever . . .

Thos. Cooper

LS, DLC-JP.

1. Cooper (*c*1820–*fl*1893) had been a coachman in the President's stables since at least July 1866. Cooper moved into the fancy goods-variety store business in the 1870s, but was again operating coaches in the 1880s. Washington, D.C., directories (1866–93); 1870 Census, D.C., Washington, 2nd Ward, 43; A. Hyde to Thomas Cooper, July 17, 1866, Ser. 10, Johnson Papers, LC.

2. Internal evidence, plus the absence of Cooper's name on stable receipts in early 1869, make this date a reasonable assumption. See Thomas Cooper to C. A. Dougherty, Nov. 1, 1868; Johnson to Dougherty, Jan. 1, Mar. 2, 1869, Ser. 10, Johnson Papers, LC.

3. Eventually, Crawford (*c*1854–*fl*1921) would have a long career in government service. He remained in the Treasury Department until the late 1870s, and afterwards worked in the Pension Office until at least 1921. Washington, D.C., directories (1868–1901); 1870 Census, D.C., Washington, 2nd Ward, 43; *U.S. Off. Reg.* (1905–21).

From Vinnie Ream

Washington   February 1869

Sir:

If it were not for the kindness that you have already shown me, and for which I am profoundly grateful, I should not venture to hope that you will be pleased to visit my Studio at the Capitol, and examine the model in plaster of the Statue of the late President Lincoln, which Congress in 1866 commissioned me to execute.[1]

I need not say how much your approval of this work would cheer and encourage me. I have so many anxious doubts and fears. You are both good and great; and if you approve, the criticisms of others would not so much dishearten me.

Vinnie Ream

LS, DLC-JP.
1. See Daniel W. Voorhees to Johnson, May 13, 1867, *Johnson Papers*, 12: 266.

From Anne M. Deen

New York City   Feb 1. 1869.

Dear Sir—

We returned to New York last Thursday and regret that we could not see you before we left Washington. The day after I saw you last I started for New York and did not return to Washington untill Wednesday morning. On Wednesday evening Mr Deen and myself called upon you, and were sorry that you were not in your room, and as we were obliged to and did leave Washington Wednesday evening, we were necessarily deprived of the pleasure of seeing you again.

As you are probably aware, the Senate refused action in our nomination,[1] and, after we had exhausted our *personal* efforts, we of course were forced to return to New York, to enlist other influences. We are hard at work, and hope soon to present so great an array of influences, that the Senate will make our case an exception to their caucus resolution.

We have to thank you my dear Sir, for your many acts of kindness, and trust that God will reward you not alone for your personal kindness, but for the consistent, conservative honest and patriotic course, which has marked your conduct, while in the Presidential chair. Conscious of, and firm in the honesty and integrity of your official acts, those who live after us, will render you the justice which so many of the present deny to you.

Hoping you will pardon us for not remaining longer to see you before we left Washington, and ever praying for your prosperity and happiness . . .

Mrs A M. Deen
4 East 30th Street   New York City.

ALS, DLC-JP.
1. Johnson finally nominated John L. Deen for naval officer of New York on January 20. The nomination was referred to the committee on commerce, where it died. See Anne M. Deen to Johnson, July 3, 1868, *Johnson Papers*, 14: 307–9.

From Martha McCook[1]

Steubenville   Feby. 1st 1869

Considering the nearness of the close of your administration I send my daughter Mrs Baldwin[2] to ask the simple act of justice by Breveting my living and dead sons. Of course we have nothing to expect from Genl. Grant and I earnestly beg that you will Brevet Gen Robert L. McCook (mortally wounded) in his ambulance,[3] Major General of Volunteers. My son Gen Daniel McCook also Major General of Volunteers by Brevet and my eleventh son Charles Morris McCook[4] private in company F second-Ohio Volunteers and killed the first battle of Bulls Run 21st of July/61 please Brevet him a first Leut of Volunteers and last but not least Captain John J. McCook[5] a Col. of Volunteers whose recommendations Mrs Baldwin will present to you.

I ask this favor Mr. President knowing it will cost the goverment nothing and be a great comfort to me.[6]

Allow me to present to you my congratulations that you are so nearly through your troublesome administration and my thanks for your various acts of kindness to my family. May you blessing of God as you have mine.

Martha McCook

ALS, DLC-JP.
1. A native of Washington, Pennsylvania, Martha Latimer (1802–1879) married Daniel McCook in 1817. The latter and the couple's eight surviving sons all served in the Union army with fatal results for the father and three of the sons. C. S. Speaker et al., *An Historical Sketch of the Old Village of New Lisbon, Ohio* (Lisbon, 1903), 69, 73.

2. Mary J. McCook Baldwin.

3. On August 5, 1862, McCook, who was riding on a bed in a carriage because he was ill, was attacked by a band of Rebel soldiers in Tennessee. They shot McCook in the abdomen and he died the next day. Warner, *Blue*.

4. A Kenyon College student, McCook (1843–1861) was the only one of the "fighting McCooks" who did not hold an officer's commission. He actually turned down a nomination as lieutenant in the regular army to serve as a private in the volunteers. Surrounded by Confederate soldiers at First Bull Run, he was shot when he refused to surrender. Speaker et al., *Historical Sketch*, 81, 83.

5. McCook (1845–1911) left his studies at Kenyon College, as did his brother Charles, to

join the 6th Ohio Cavalry. Advancing to the rank of captain, he was wounded at Shady Grove, Virginia, in 1864. He became a lawyer after the war. Ibid., 83; *Who Was Who in America*, 1: 803.

6. Johnson attempted to do as Martha McCook requested, nominating her son Daniel for brevet major general, John for major and lieutenant colonel, and Robert for brigadier general and major general, all on February 8. He did not nominate Charles. When the Senate received the nominations on February 11, they referred them to the Committee on Military Affairs from which they did not emerge. John may have received at least the brevet of lieutenant colonel at some other time. *Senate Ex. Proceedings*, Vol. 16: 471–72, 474.

From Narcissa P. Saunders

Melrose, Near Nashville   Feb 1st, 1869

Dear Mr. President,

It has been a long time since I have had the pleasure of writing to you, but, I have refrained from carrying out my *inclination* simply because I knew, that your time was so engrossed, with public business and cares of state. But, let me, assure you, that although *silent*, *Ma*,[1] and myself have *never ceased* to feel, a *deep* interest, in your welfare—prosperity and success,—and moreover—are delighted that we are soon to have you on Tennessee soil—once more. We, with many others, feel that your *presence* and *influence* will be of *great help*, and benefit to our distressed people, for in some way we think, that your *name* is a tower of strength—and so we are rejoiced, at the idea of your coming among us. Ma requests me to return her thanks for your message and sincerely hopes, that your wise measures—may be *at last* adopted and your concluding words—prevail throughout the land. She also says (and I am sure I join her) that when you return to Tennessee—that you and your family must make us a *special visit*— for we will be very happy to meet you—and can tell you much that will interest you. If Mrs Johnson *cannot come*—some of you can, at least; we will not take *any excuse* from *you*. And now, dear Mr President, after making a *request* that I am *under promise* to do—I will bring my letter to a close. Mrs Davis, of Washington wrote me word of her daughter, Clara, having met you and your kindness &c.[2] They are a most amiable, worthy family but much reduced by the war and other causes—and are greatly in want of means—and if their son *William*[3] could through *your* influence get some appointment under the government the family would be under everlasting obligations— and would be able to live at least in comfort. Will you not—if possible give young Davis *some* appointment? I know—that you will— if in your *power*. They are so anxious and so reduced in circumstances—that I feel a great *deal* of *sympathy* for them. But, I must not trespass any longer on your time. Ma unites with myself in sending cordial regards—while I *remain* your *truly attached friend*.

Narcissa P. Saunders

Please remember us to your family.

ALS, DLC-JP.
  1. Cynthia Pillow Saunders Brown.
  2. Mrs. Davis and Clara have not been identified.
  3. Not identified.

Speech to Georgetown College Cadets

WASHINGTON, Feb. 1, 1869.

I thank you for this visit, and for the kind and courteous address you have presented me.[1] You are all young and intelligent, and starting out to begin the struggle of life. At this particular juncture I may be pardoned if I make some remarks, to which I invite your consideration, as being of that character and importance you will sooner or later learn to appreciate. In a short time the care of the constitution and all that concerns the government, its administration and laws, pass into your hands. It must then be incumbent on your part to prepare yourselves seriously for this high and sacred duty, and to do so it is above all things essential to place your thoughts upon the right basis. As you have deemed it proper to allude to my public career it will not be amiss if I make some allusion here to the fundamental tenets that I laid down for myself in yielding a strict adherence to the constitution of my country, and to that constitution I invite your attention on this occasion. It is important in taking charge of this government that you should draw a marked distinction between its organic and its statute law. Bear ever in mind that it was framed not for the few but the many, and that we acknowledge no superior but one. Instead of having a sovereign in one man we have sovereignty in all. The people are the masters, and individuals elevated to places of trust and power are but their servants. Let me also impress on your minds that the constitution, in which more human wisdom is embraced than in any other instrument that was ever framed, recognizing the infirmity of man and drawing experience from the lessons of history, places limitations on the exercise of power—for one man is not to be trusted. Hence the forethought of the framers in extending protection to the rights of minorities. How deeply important it is to shield this great charter of our liberties from undue encroachment and unprincipled attack must at once strike the mind when it is for a moment considered that the constitution once broken down and trampled upon the barrier of republican liberty is overthrown and the day of freedom closes in night forever. If it is to be amended let it be done in the manner prescribed by the instrument itself. No intelligent person supposes it was designed to remain forever unalterable; but any one can readily perceive that it was made to adapt itself to every condition of the country, subject to the will of the sovereign people and done in the manner and mode pointed out by itself. Any change wrought in the constitution that does not conform to this rule is fatal to its integrity, and robs the people of protection first, and finally destroys their liberties. If I could make a lodgment of the principles of the constitution in your minds, to be taken up and digested hereafter, I feel that I should have done a great deal of good. I think there ought to be a professor in every college in the land to teach its pupils a correct understanding and appreciation of the principles of the constitution, and to hold it next in reverence and importance to the Bible, for it is as much the groundwork of our government as the other is the foundation of our holy religion. Then, let it be your study. It represents all the States. It is our political Bible. It is the basis of our political system. Let all of us come up cheerfully to its support, and prejudice and party malice throughout the land will soon subside. Let us lay our differences on one common altar and say the constitution must be preserved though all things else sink in the dust. I thank you for the very kind and courteous allusions you have made to my services. A man should be very dull, indeed, and his mind very barren of sentiment if he did not feel some patriotic inspiration at seeing so many intelligent and ardent young men coming up to the support of their country and its government. You are beginning the journey of life: I am drawing near its close. You are ascending the hillside, with its dazzling summit before you: I have arrived at the foot of the other side. I will now conclude by thanking you again for this manifestation of your kindness.

New York Herald, Feb. 2, 1869.

1. The address, presented during the visit of senior and junior cadets to the White House, thanked Johnson for his "good feeling towards" Georgetown and the faithful and honorable discharge of his official duties. *New York Herald*, Feb. 2, 1869.

From Bromfield Ridley

Murfreesboro T.   2nd Feby 1869

You are a man of the People & so am I. I have felt for some time like writing you a letter, not on fine vellum paper like Members of Congress & Foreign Ministers. But on such paper as we the people can get in these times of high taxes. I am an old man 65 years old & now that you are about to retire from the Presidency I wish to say a few words which will hurt no body, for I have long since ceased to have feelings that would make me offensive to any human being. I served with you in the Legislature of Tennessee in 1865–66[1] & since that time your promotion has been rapid though not unexpected to me.

From the fact that you were allways at your post & no action of the Legislature escaped you I predicted your success in the world. I did not like your conduct as Military Govr of Tennee at the time. But subsequent events have satisfied me that "all was right." And since you have demonstrated your love for the Union and your profound devotion to the Constitution, I am satisfied that you are a Patriot & a Statesman.

I have been particularly attracted by your veto messages in which you have shown yourself to be the profoundest Constitutional Lawyer in America, for no man could have equalled those messages. Those messages at once gave you the character of the first intellectual man in America. And although you have been surrounded by the great men of the nation, none of them have answered your arguments & to day they will go down to posterity unanswered & and [?]. You have been a *blessing* to the South, our great *breakwater*. Without you we would have been lost without redemption. No man comes at this time to vindicate you. The gust of passion & of antagonistic bitterness precludes impartial judment. None but posterity will do you justice & the People the Sovereign People, will not fail to do you ample complete substantial justice.

Come home to us the people in Tennee. We are your friends & know how to appreciate you. We are still ready to exalt you & to show that we regard you as our friend, the friend of the People & of the Government. I have no fulsome adulation to bestow. But, I trust you will excuse me for saying that the great masses of Tennessee are still your friends through all the evil reports of this corrupt Congress & that we will receive you to our arms as our best friend & greatest benefactor.

Bromfield Ridley

ALS, DLC-JP.
    1. Ridley and Johnson served together in the lower house during 1835–37.

From William S. Jackson [1]

Pittsburgh   February 3d 1869

Hon. Sir

During your Tour in the month of September 1866, while in our City a Reception Committee, having been appointed, came to me, I, being in the Livery business at the time, and engaged Carriages for the use of Your Excellency and party. My bill for these amounted in all to ($271.00) Two Hundred and Seventy One 00/100 Dollars, the greater portion of which I was compelled to hire and have since paid for, and these parties, being the U.S. officials of the City and County, have left unpaid, and there is still due me on that account the Sum of ($116 00/1"") One Hundred and Sixteen 00/1"" Dollars. I have already given them credit with the subscription I proposed to make being the sum of Fifty 00/100 Dollars, leaving the Balance due as above stated. Your Excellency would confer a great favor by seeing the account paid. Hoping you will give the above your attention I subscribe myself . . .

W. S. Jackson

102 Wood Street   Pittsburgh Pa.

ALS, DLC-JP.
   1. Jackson (c1830–fl1888) was associated with a livery establishment in Pittsburgh for a long time but, beginning in the late 1870s and continuing for at least a decade, he worked for a railroad line. Pittsburgh directories (1861–88); 1870 Census, Pa., Allegheny, Union Twp., Green Tree, 7.

To Hugh McCulloch

Febry 3, 1869

Some time since I understood the Secretary to say that he had determined upon Mr. McCartney's removal, and that he would suggest the name of a suitable person as his successor.[1] No nomination however, has in the meantime been sent to this office, & I hope he will submit one without delay.

Andrew Johnson

ES, DNA-RG56, Appts., Internal Revenue Service, Collector, Mass., 3rd Dist., Geo. H. Kingsbury.
   1. On February 8, Johnson nominated George H. Kingsbury to replace William H.

McCartney as collector of internal revenue for the third district of Massachusetts. The nomination was referred to the Finance Committee but evidently no further action was taken before the end of the Johnson presidency. *Senate Ex. Proceedings*, Vol. 16: 468, 474.

From Chauncey H. Snow[1]

Echo City   Utah Territory   February 3d 1869

Sir

I sent a telegram from Rawlings Springs on the 2nd inst,[2] stating that "in my opinion no more money should be paid to the Union Pacific Rail Road Co, until the road is better constructed & managed." The manner in which this road has ben constructed, and the gross negligence, and carelessness, with which it is managed, were in my opinion good reasons for so doing.

From Omaha to Cheyenne the road is in good order, but the grades are heavier and curves sharper than is necessary or practicable. The ties are mostly of cottonwood, or mountain pine, neither of which are considered by practical Engineers, fit for that purpose. Since leaving Laramie on Sunday Evening, until I arrived at this place this morning; they have disabled four Engines, with the train I came by. Two were run off by a land slide, smashing them & 2 cars completely. (The land slide occourred, from the fact of there not having been the proper amount of Earth removed from the cutting.)

The other two engines; one was disabled from some cause unknown to me, and the other was run so long without oil, that the axel of the trucks broke off.

The cuttings and fillings, have not ben brought to the grade shown on the profiles of the company at Washington & New York. And cuttings are not wide enough, nor have they slope enough to prevent land slides. Between Wasatch and Echo, there is ten miles of road that has ben accepted by the commissioners, upon which, the grading is not yet completed, and there is not a cross tie or a rail yet upon the ground. The great interest the Government has in this road, as well as the security of passengers, demands, in my opinion, that the road should be placed in better order, and more care taken in its operation. The property of this road, upon which the Government has so large a claim, should not be destroyed, and the lives of passengers jeopardized, by the incompetency, or gross negligence of its managers. From Bryson to this place the road is unsafe, at the speed of 12 miles per hour, and the road is lined with broken cars that have run off. The location of the road in this vicinity is upon land, (I am informed by men who have travelled this country for years) that is under water from May to August. It is not enough for this company to say they intend to make all necessary repairs at some future day.

The interest of the Government is not protected and the lives of passengers are constantly endangered, and something should be done to compel this company to comply with the laws under which they were chartered. On my return I shall make a full report.[3]

C. H. Snow, Director

LS, DLC-JP.
  1. Johnson had appointed Snow, who had earlier surveyed and located some western railroad lines, a government director of the Union Pacific Railroad in early January 1869. He was removed, however, by Grant in March. *Washington Evening Star*, Jan. 9, Mar. 10, 1869; *National Intelligencer*, Jan. 11, 1869.
  2. Not found.
  3. Snow's report on problems seems to fit quite well with other reports on the railroad, but there are no comparable reports about equipment destruction. One later historian called him a "crackpot," and alleged that he was involved in trying to blackmail the Union Pacific. Williams, *Great and Shining Road*, 223; Ames, *Pioneering the Union Pacific*, 300–301. For Orville H. Browning's response, see Browning to Johnson, Feb. 12, 1869.

From Anna E. Surratt

[ca. February 3, 1869][1]

The undersigned most earnestly and respectfully addresses Your excellency on a matter which has been for more than three years to her a source of great affliction. She seeks the privilege of removing the remains of her deceased mother, to have them interred in consecrated ground.

She fondly hopes that your Excellency will not allow your authority in the premises to expire without granting this request, prompted only by filial love and devotion to the memory of her dear Mother.[2]

Anna E. Surratt

Copy, DNA-RG94, Lets. Recd. (Main Ser.), File S-112-1869 (M619, Roll 746).
  1. A notation on the letter indicates it was received on February 4.
  2. According to endorsements, on February 5 Johnson ordered the remains of Mary E. Surratt delivered to her daughter. The order was sent on February 8 and the body was disinterred at the Washington Arsenal. Mary Surratt was buried at Mount Olivet Cemetery, Washington's oldest Catholic cemetery, on February 9. George D. Ramsay to E. D. Townsend, Feb. 9, 1869, Lets. Recd. (Main Ser.), File S-112-1869 (M619, Roll 746), RG94, NA; *Washington Evening Star*, Feb. 9, 1869; Stephen M. Forman, *A Guide to Civil War Washington* (Washington, D.C., 1995), 166.

From Francis H. Gordon

Jenning's Fork P.O.   Smith Co. Ten,
Febuary 4th 1869.

You will probably remember the writer of this letter, as a Tennessean, who devoted a good deal of his former life, to the advancement of Agriculture and the Mechanic Arts. You will remember too—that I was among the union men who stood by you in maintaining the Union, while you were military Governor, but claimed the right due all free men to think for myself & freely express my opinions. And you may remember me as a Whig of former days, though ever a private citizen, & never seeking or filling office. I premise thus, because I wish you to know what citizen appeals to you, & what are his antecedents.

My object is to present to your mind what need Tennessee has for you in the future. We all know that *you can crush the despotism which oppresses Tennessee.* We believe we can make you Governor of this State next August, by an overwhelming vote; & by your help elect a conservative Legislature & all officers by the free choice of the people. When this is done, we can send you to the U S Senate, where you can still defend the constitution, in the spirit of your able messages. Having brought your own State fully back to the Constitution, you will have more influence on other States, & on the whole nation.

Should all Tennessee ask you to take the course indicated, can you refuse? All former parties will call on you. A hand full of Radicals under Brownlow, will alone oppose you. Strip them of the Militia & their power is gone. This is their only means of holding Tennessee in bondage, to be continually plundered. The great mass of our people ardently desire the union, the Constitution & the enforcement of all constitutional laws. Give us these, & we will have peace. Till this is done, there will be no peace. No man can do as much to this end, as you can.

No doubt the subject of this letter has already been presented to you by others; but I desire to be *sure* that it be considered by you early, even before you leave Washington & the Executive Office. It may be in your power to shape your course to some advantage before you come to Tennessee in March. Of course I do do ask you to answer my letter, or to publish your intentions. The time has not come for this. April will be soon enough. Mean time it is right for you to hear from all our citizens. I know the masses will sustain you. No higher object could be presented a patriot, than the good of the whole, whether he be Governor, Senator or President.

F H Gordon

ALS, DLC-JP.

From Thomas Ewing, Sr.

Washington   Feby 6 /69

Dear Sir

Lewis Wolfley of the revenue service New Orleans,[1] has gotten into some controversy with his superiors who accuse him of insubordination. I know nothing of the merits of the controversy, but knowing Wolfley well, am confident he has done nothing dishonest or dishonorable, but would by no means vouch for his prudent use of language. I hope you will not remove him, as there are many of your friends who take an interest in him, and there is no possible danger of the public service suffering in his hands.[2]

T. Ewing

ALS, DLC-JP.
    1. Assessor of internal revenue for the 1st district of Louisiana.
    2. For a contrasting view urging Wolfley's removal, see John F. Coyle to Johnson, Feb. 19, 1869.

From Charles J.M. Gwinn

Baltimore   Feb 8th 1869

Sir

It is proper to return to the House of Representatives the Copper Tariff Bill, without your signature, for the following reasons.[1]

It is not a revenue bill, but is, on the other hand, intended to *exclude* foreign copper ores from the ports of the United States, and therefore, will yield little or no revenue.

It is not expedient to approve it upon any theory of *protection* to America industry, for while it may promote the intersts of those engaged in working the Lake Superior Mines, it seriously injures the interests of those who are busied in developing the Copper Mines of Vermont, Maryland, New Jersey and California.

The increased duty imposed by the Bill will add, moreover, largely, to the cost of the construction of the shipping of the United States, and will, to this extent, disable our people from competing with foreign Ship-Builders. It is certainly not expedient to check in any way the increase of Ship-building in this country.

The Bill would not only have this effect, but it would also add largely to the cost of many necessary manufactures in which copper is used.

As the statistics of the Country, moreover, show that we are under the existing system, large *exporters* of copper, there can be no pretence of for claiming the protection of an increased duty.[2]

Chas: J.M. Gwinn.

LS, DLC-JP.

1. The bill, designed to increase duties on imported copper ores, had just passed the House, having passed the Senate on January 19. *Congressional Globe*, 40 Cong., 3 Sess., pp. 451, 978. For opposition to the bill, see Gwinn to Johnson, Dec. 19, 1868, Jan. 11, 19, 1869; James Corner & Sons to Johnson, Feb. 10, 1869; Robert B. Minturn, Jr., to Johnson, Feb. 10, 1869. For a favorable view, see Henry R. Linderman to Johnson, Feb. 13, 1869.

2. See Veto of Copper Bill, Feb. 22, 1869.

From Natus J. Haynes & Sons[1]

Franklin, Tennessee. February 8th 1869

Dear Sir:

The "Weekly Review," published by us, Some months ago hoisted your name at the head of its columns as a candidate for Govenor of Tennessee. We did this because we felt and believed that the present critical condition of affairs in this State demanded that you should, on your retirement from your present position, heed the wishes of an outraged and oppressed people, and consent to assume the arduous task of their deliverance. Before the late Civil War our Journal was earnestly and honestly opposed to you. Since the cessation of hostilities we have watched, with the liveliest interest, your firm and unflinching adherence to the Constitution; And in all your struggles you have had our keenest sympathy and admiration for your heroism and Statesmanship. While in the City of Nashville, on yesterday, we learned from some of your friends that our course, and that of other members of the "Press" in this State, in placing your name at the head of our columns, was distasteful to you.

Our object in writing this letter is to learn from you, personally, your views in regard to the matter. What we have done was done in the purest of motives, and meets the hearty endorsement of our people. If any indiscretions have been committed, or any plans of yours been thwarted, by the course of the "Press" in Tennessee, we ought to know it. If the canvass is to be made, the universal wish is to leave the whole matter in your hands, and we shall shape our movements thereby. It is needless for us to say that it is the heartfelt wish and earnest prayer, of every lover of the State, that you may come back to us, strengthened, both physically and mentally, to achieve our redemption. Your coming will be hailed with joy and unbounded gratification, by your fellow citizens in evey part of the State. As much as we desired your nomination at New York, the People now look upon it as Providential, in permitting you to return to the bosom of a State which has always delighted to honor you, and which now so sorely needs the benefit of your enlarged experience and unerring sagacity. We pray you to pardon us for this honest appeal to one who has never turned a deaf ear to the common people.

Any communication from you on this Subject shall remain Strictly private and confidential, unless otherwise ordered.[2]

Hoping you may pardon us for this intrusion, we subscribe ourselves with high respect . . .

N. J. Haynes & Sons
Editors and Proprietors of Weekly Review.

AL, DLC-JP.

1. Haynes (1820–1877) and his son, Thomas E. Haynes (1841–1913) jointly published the Franklin newspaper. But by 1870, Natus Haynes was a grocery merchant. Virginia McDaniel Bowman, *Historic Williamson County Old Homes and Sites* (Nashville, 1971), 152–53; *Directory Williamson County, Tennessee Burials* (3 vols., [Franklin] Williamson County, 1973–91), 2: 85; 1870 Census, Tenn., Williamson, 9th Dist., 28.

2. See Johnson to Natus J. Haynes & Sons, Feb. 15, 1869.

Pardon of Samuel A. Mudd

[February 8, 1869]

Greetings:

Whereas, on the twenty ninth day of June in the year 1865, Dr. Samuel A. Mudd was by the judgment of a Military Commission, convened and holden at the City of Washington, in part convicted, and in part acquitted, of the specification wherein he was inculpated in the charge for the trial of which said Military Commission was so convened and held, and which specification in its principal allegation against him, was and is in the words and figures following, to wit:

> And in further prosecution of said conspiracy, the said Samuel A. Mudd did, at Washington City, and within the Military Department and military lines aforesaid, on or before the sixth day of March, A. D. 1865, and on divers other days and times between that day and the twentieth day of April, A. D. 1865, advise, encourage, receive, entertain, harbor and conceal aid and assist the said John Wilkes Booth, David E. Herold, Lewis Payne, John H. Surratt, Michael O'Laughlin, George A. Atzerodt, Mary E. Surratt and Samuel Arnold, and their confederates, with knowledge of the murderous and traitorous conspiracy aforesaid, and with intent to aid, abet, and assist them in the execution thereof, and in escaping from justice after the murder of the said Abraham Lincoln, in pursuance of said conspiracy, in manner aforesaid;

And, whereas upon a consideration and examination of the record of said trial and conviction and of the evidence given at said trial, I am satisifed that the guilt found by the said judgment against the said Samuel A. Mudd was of the receiving, entertaining, harboring, and concealing John Wilkes Booth and David E. Herold, with the intent to aid, abet and assist them in escaping from justice after the assassination of the late President of the United States, and not of any other or greater participation or complicity in said abominable crime;

And whereas it is represented to me by intelligent and respectable members of the medical profession, that the circumstances of the surgical aid to the escaping assassin and of the imputed concealment of his flight are deserving of a lenient construction as within the obligations of professional duty, and thus inadequate evidence of a guilty sympathy with the crime or the criminal;[1]

And whereas in other respects the evidence, imputing such guilty sympathy or purpose of aid in defeat of justice, leaves room for uncertainty as to the true measure and nature of the complicity of the said Samuel A. Mudd, in the attempted escape of said assassins;

And whereas, the sentence imposed by said Military Commission upon the said Samuel A. Mudd was that he be imprisoned at hard labor for life, and the confinement under such sentence was directed to be had in the Military Prison at Dry Tortugas, Florida, and the said prisoner has been hitherto, and now is, suffering the infliction of such sentence;

And whereas, upon occasion of the prevalence of the yellow fever at that military station, and the death by that pestilence of the medical Officer of the Post,[2] the said Samuel A. Mudd devoted himself to the care and the cure of the sick, and interposed his courage and his skill to protect the garrison, otherwise without adequate medical aid, from peril and alarm, and thus, as the officers and men unite in testifying, saved many valuable lives and earned the admiration and the gratitude of all who observed or experienced his generous and faithful service to humanity;

And whereas, the surviving families and friends of the Surgeon[3] and other officers who were the victims of the pestilence earnestly present their dying testimony to the conspicuous merit of Dr. Mudd's conduct, and their own sense of obligation to him and Lieut. Zabriskie[4] and two hundred and ninety nine non commissioned officers and privates stationed at the Dry Tortugas have united in presenting to my attention the praiseworthy action of the prisoner and in petitioning for his pardon;[5]

And whereas, the Medical Society of Harford County, Maryland, of which he was an Associate, have petitioned for his pardon, and thirty nine members of the Senate and House of Representatives of the Congress of the United States have also requested his pardon;[6]

Now, therefore, be it known that I, Andrew Johnson, President of the United States of America, in consideration of the premises, divers other good and sufficient reasons me thereunto moving, do hereby grant to the said Dr. Samuel A. Mudd a full and unconditional pardon.

In testimony whereof, I have hereunto signed my name and caused the Seal of the United States to be affixed.

Done at the City of Washington, this Eighth day of February, A. D. 1869, and of the Independence of the United States the Ninety third.[7]

Andrew Johnson

Copy, DNA-RG94, Lets. Recd. (Main Ser.), File P-88-1869 (M619, Roll 734).

1. See, for example, C. S. Goodrich to Johnson, Jan. 21, 1869, Pardon Case File B-596, Samuel A. Mudd, RG204, NA.

2. Joseph Sim Smith.

3. See Lizzie P. Smith to Johnson, Apr. 13, 1868, *Johnson Papers*, 14: 32–33.

4. During the latter part of the Civil War, 1st lt. Edmund L.G. Zalinski (1849–1909) served on the staff of Gen. Nelson A. Miles and then as second lieutenant in the 2nd N.Y. Arty. Appointed to the 5th U.S. Arty. in 1866, he served with them at Fort Jefferson (Dry Tortugas), where he became sick with yellow fever. He invented several pieces of military equipment,

Edward Spangler

Samuel Arnold

Dr. Samuel A. Mudd

Three assassination conspirators pardoned by Johnson in 1869.
From Osborn H. Oldroyd, *The Assassination of Abraham Lincoln:*
Flight, Pursuit, Capture, and Punishment of the Conspirators
(Washington, D.C., 1901), 141, 147–48

Anna B. Surratt and Edwin Booth, both of whom petitioned
Johnson for the return of their deceased relatives' remains.
Photos by Mathew B. Brady.
Courtesy National Archives

including a "pneumatic torpedo gun," and retired from the army in 1894 with the rank of captain. Powell, *Army List*, 694; *New York Times*, Mar. 11, 1909; *New York Tribune*, Mar. 11, 1909; E. L. Zalinski to Lorenzo Thomas, Aug. 15, 1868, Lets. Recd. (Main Ser.), File Z-12-1868 (M619, Roll 673), RG94, NA; Zalinski to Thomas, Feb. 1, 1869, ibid., File Z-1-1869 (M619, Roll 767), RG94, NA.

    5. The petition has not been found.

    6. Neither petition has been located.

    7. The pardon arrived at Fort Jefferson on March 8, 1869, on which date Mudd was released. Three days later he was transported to Key West and arrived home on March 20. Henry J. Hunt to Adjutant General, Mar. 15, 1869, Lets. Recd. (Main Ser.), File P-88-1869 (M619, Roll 734), RG94, NA; Samuel Carter III, *The Riddle of Dr. Mudd* (New York, 1974), 335, 337.

From Maria Louisa Hollis[1]

Darkesville   February 9th 1869

Berkely County West Virginia

My Dear Sir

    Promted by the all mighty to ask a favour of you thrue my old unkel Thomas Foster[2] wee are at a los to know what to do. The judge of West virginia[3] has gave our church to two famelies in this village. Wee the people of this comunity built it and paid all but four hundred dollars. It cost us two thousand. Jump[4] the radical carpet gager interseded and paid the ballance and took it. Wee are out intierly. Wee have one hundred children hear for Sunday School upwards of a hundred members. Wee ocupide the church up to last monday. During the war our prechers kept it and two famelies was on the radical side. They held their meeting every two weeks in the church. They could get no congregation so they left of all to gather. Now they come and take the church. Thare is not a room in this village will hold our children or our congregation. If it was warm wether wee could go to the woods. Wee aske in the name of the all mighty for a little assistence to help build us a place to worship in. I hoap god will strenghten you to help us now in time of need. The people are all genealy poor and kept down. Wee have no say in enny thing but pay tax. Thare are but three men that can voat in this town and a bout three hundred inhabitence and one of thoes men is an Idiot has been Living of the county all his life. He has bin the means of a great deal of trouble hear during the war. Wee lost seven thousend dollars by his reporting. Wee cant be mad to think a like. The sitizens hear are honest people. Wee want to dye that way. Wee cant belong to the radicals and live as wee ought. I cald on mr Will Lammon[5] at his mothers at bunkerhill. He will subscribe if it is even so little wee will be thankfull. Wee imbibe simpothy in our unborn children for a

troden down people. Wee have a school house hear but the radicals
have given it to the blacks to preach in. No other place in this town.
Thare never was but the one church hear and to that every body
belonged. Two famelies drew out and took the church. Wee have the
ground and four hundred dollars subscribed. Wee are all with you
praying one for you and yours. Wee have not bin getting justice for
some time back but in god wee trust. Wee are ever your humbel
friends. Your name shall be handed down to the last generation threu
wee the people of this comunity. May the lord bless you and yours
for ever. Wee dont let the right hand know what the left one does. If
you will aid us in enny way please let us know soon. Unkel will wright
to me.[6] God bless the old man he has bin spared for some wise purpos
so long. The radicals have taken our country our church our voat our
school house next will be our land. God forbid.

Mrs Maria Louisa Hollis

ALS, DLC-JP.

1. Perhaps the wife of Jacob R. Hollis, a Martinsburg, West Virginia, hotelkeeper in 1870.
Hollis (c1820–f1870) was a West Virginia native. 1870 Census, W. Va., Berkeley, Arden Twp.,
Martinsburg, 13.

2. Foster (c1791–1870) had been a messenger for the Treasury Department for a number of
years, and eventually a clerk for the 3rd auditor's office in Washington, D.C. Washington,
D.C., directories (1853–71); 1860 Census, D.C., Washington, 2nd Ward, 60; (1870), 173;
Washington Evening Star, Oct. 3, 1870.

3. Perhaps John J. Jackson, Jr.

4. Perhaps Albert Jump (c1840–f1870), a Delaware-born minister serving in Shepherdstown,
West Virginia, in 1870. 1870 Census, W. Va., Jefferson, Chaplin Twp., Shepherdstown, 43.

5. There were several William Lemmons or Lemens in Berkeley County at various times,
but the correct one cannot be determined.

6. There is no known response from Johnson.

From Joseph H. Thompson

Shelbyville Tennessee   Febry 9th 1869

Dear Mr President

I reached home on Sunday and will on tomorrow start to carry out
the instructions given me by Mr McCulloch so far as they relate to
Tennessee. These instructions simply require me to inquire or look
into the solvency of the securities upon the bonds of the several Internal Rev Collectors of this State. To do this will take some ten
days, and the moment I am through with the matter I want to come
to Washington and desire to be there before the *first* March. For that
reason I beg that you have an order issued "for me to report to you in

person the moment I have carried out my instructions so far as they relate to Tennessee." And as I am under orders to go to Kansas Nebraska &c. I can see no reason why such an order might not be granted. I dislike to annoy you with such little matters but to me at least such an order would be very gratifying.

I have to thank your daughter Mrs Stover for her kindness to me on her journey homeward.[1] With her and your grand children I had a most delightful trip and am glad to tell you that I left them all at Greeneville in fine health.

The Conservatives of Tennessee are nearly crazy to see you a candidate for Govenor in August.

Mullins Arnnell & Nunn[2] are in a bad fix in Tennessee—and as if to add insult to injury some of the Republican papers are calling on Mullins to become a candidate for Govenor. The extremists are much afraid that you will be a candidate for Govenor and in doing so that you will unearth the "school fund" completely.[3]

Please have the order issued I ask for, viz "that when I have completed my investigations in Tennessee I report to you or the Dept in Washington."

Joseph H Thompson

ALS, DLC-JP.

1. Johnson's daughter, Mrs. Mary Stover, and her children left Washington for Tennessee on February 5. See *Washington Evening Star*, Feb. 5, 1869.

2. James Mullins, Samuel M. Arnell, and David A. Nunn.

3. A reference to the state's school fund that had been deposited in a Memphis bank which thereafter folded. The state treasurer, R. L. Stanford, resigned in December 1866 and then committed suicide. In December 1868 the lower house of the legislature created a special committee to investigate all matters surrounding the deposit of the school fund at the Tennessee National Bank in Memphis. On February 2, 1869, this committee submitted its report to the House. E. Merton Coulter, *William G. Brownlow: Fighting Parson of the Southern Highlands* (Chapel Hill, 1937), 381–82; Alexander, *Reconstruction*, 242; *House Journal . . . 1868–69*, 145, 320. For the report itself, see "Report of the Special Committee in Relation to the School Fund of the State of Tennessee," *House Journal . . . 1868–69*, Appendix, 131–222.

From Edwin Booth[1]

PRIVATE.

N.Y. Febry 10th 1869

Dear Sir—

May I not now ask your kind consideration of my poor Mother's[2] request in relation to her son's remains?

The bearer of this (Mr. John Weaver)[3] is sexton of *Christ Church*,

Baltimore, who will observe the strictest secrecy in this matter—and you may rest assured that none of my family desire its publicity.

Unable to visit Washington I have deputed Mr. Weaver—in whom I have the fullest Confidence, and I beg that you will not delay in ordering the body to be given to his care.

He will retain it (placing it in his vault) until such time as we can remove other members of our family to the *Baltimore Cemetery*, and thus prevent any special notice of it.

There is also (I am told) a trunk of his at the National Hotel—which I once applied for but was refused—it being under seal of the War Dept., it may contain relics of the poor misguided boy—which would be dear to his sorrowing mother, and of no use to anyone. Your Excellency would greatly lessen the crushing weight of grief that is hurrying my Mother to the grave by giving immediate orders for the safe delivery of the remains of John Wilkes Booth to Mr. Weaver.[4]

Edwin Booth

ALS, DLC-JP.

1. Booth (1833–1893) was an accomplished actor and John Wilkes Booth's brother. *DAB*.

2. Mary Anne Holmes (1802–1885) married Junius B. Booth, first illegally in 1821, then properly in 1851 following his divorce from his London wife. She and Junius had ten children. *DAB*; Gene Smith, *The Story of America's Legendary Theatrical Family—Junius, Edwin, and John Wilkes Booth* (New York, 1992), 22, 96, 245; Stephen M. Archer, *Junius Brutus Booth: Theatrical Prometheus* (Carbondale, Ill., 1992), 66–67, 196–97, 213, 296.

3. John H. Weaver (c1811–c1878) was also an undertaker and cabinet maker. *Washington Evening Star*, Feb. 19, 1869; 1870 Census, Md., Baltimore, Baltimore, 9th Ward, 436; Baltimore directories (1868–79).

4. The endorsement indicates that on February 15 Johnson ordered Booth's body be turned over to the representative sent by his family. The order was carried out that same day. His body was to be held in a vault in Greenmount Cemetery in Baltimore until it could be interred with some other family members, which was not done until June 26. There is no indication that Booth's trunk or personal effects were returned to the family. George D. Ramsay to E.D. Townsend, Feb. 16, 1869, Lets. Recd. (Main Ser.), File S-112-1869 (M619, Roll 746), RG94, NA; *Washington Evening Star*, Feb. 18, 19, 1869; Terry Alford, ed., *John Wilkes Booth: A Sister's Memoir by Asia Booth Clark* (Jackson, Miss., 1996), xvii.

From James Corner & Sons[1]

Baltimore   Febry 10. 1869

Dear Sir.

The "Copper Bill" which has just passed both Houses of Congress—and now awaits your Signature, contains some points which directly affect us as Merchants engaged in the importation of ores from the West Coast of So America, to which we beg leave to call your attention.

We despatched one of our vessels the Barque Serene in August last to the West Coast, and directed our Agent at Valparaiso to purchase a Cargo of Copper ores for her return to the States. The Ores (about 500 Tons) were purchased on the twenty third of December, to be delivered at Tougay, Chili, and our vessel will not get them on board until after the *twenty eighth* of January—the Bill includes all Ores not on shipboard on the *nineteenth* January—requiring us to pay an additional Duty of Some Eight thousand dollars.

We think it unjust to make so decided a change in the Tariff of any article without giving timely notice, or without extending the time, to cover all orders or purchases. Owing to the long distance & length of time required in communicating with these ports we were unable to countermand our orders.

Apart from this direct interest which we have in the Bill, we believe that its effect will be injurious to the best interests of commerce & of the whole country—and we hope you may find other & ample reasons for withholding your signature, and for vetoing the Bill.

Jas Corner & Sons

L, DLC-JP.

1. This letter may have been enclosed in another, from Sen. William P. Whyte of Maryland, who asked Johnson's "kind consideration" for a request from "the oldest commercial house in the shipping trade" of Baltimore. Whyte to Johnson, Feb. 12, 1869, Johnson Papers, LC. James Corner, a leading commission merchant in the 1820s and 1830s, had founded the company, but was apparently deceased by this time. Baltimore directories (1833–42, 1868–72).

From Simeon M. Johnson

N York   Feb. 10 1869

I will see you in Respect to the Fullerton papers sent to Attorney General and give you my views of the whole case.[1]

S M Johnson

Tel, DLC-JP.

1. What papers Johnson alludes to are unknown, but probably involved the charges and evidence against William Fullerton. About this time Attorney General William Evarts ordered the trial delayed, and not until Revenue Commissioner Edward A. Rollins protested in March did proceedings commence. The reason for the suspension of proceedings is unknown. The attorney general even evaded a congressional request for an explanation. *New York Tribune*, Feb. 11, Mar.

12, 1869; *Senate Ex. Docs.*, 40 Cong., 3 Sess., No. 51, pp. 1–9 (Ser. 1360). See also N. E. Paine to Johnson, Nov. 15, 1868, and George W. Greene to Johnson, Nov. 26, 1868.

From Mary Custis Lee[1]

Lexington   February 10th 1869

Mr. President

Encouraged by your kind attention to a former application & prompted by my friend Capt May[2] I now venture to request that you will direct *all* the articles taken from Arlington & deposited in the Patent office to be restored.[3] They are relics from Mt Vernon bequeathed to me by my Father[4] & consequently of great value & interest to his family.[5]

Mary Custis Lee

ALS, DNA-RG48, Patents and Misc. Div., Lets. Recd.

1. Mary Anne Randolph Custis (1808–1873), the only surviving child of George Washington Parke Custis and Mary Lee Fitzhugh, married Robert E. Lee on June 30, 1831. Edmund Jennings Lee, ed., *Lee of Virginia, 1642–1892* (Philadelphia, 1895), 453–55.

2. Perhaps James May (*fl*1873), the steamboat captain and commission merchant who lived in Pittsburgh in the 1840s. He had met Robert E. Lee in St. Louis in the 1830s and was living in Illinois when he tried to help Mary Custis Lee get her possessions back. Pittsburgh directories (1839–50); Douglas Southall Freeman, *R. E. Lee: A Biography* (4 vols., New York, 1962 [1935]), 4: 383; Margaret Sanborn, *Robert E. Lee: The Complete Man, 1861–1870* (Philadelphia, 1967), 340; *DAB*; James May to Johnson, Sept. 6, 1873, Johnson Papers, LC.

3. The articles from Arlington were stored at the Patent Office in 1862 by direction of Gen. Irwin McDowell. Freeman, *R. E. Lee*, 4: 382.

4. George Washington Parke Custis (1781–1857), a grandson of Martha Washington, was adopted as an infant by George Washington after the death of Custis's father. He built the mansion at Arlington and bequeathed it to his daughter Mary Custis Lee. Lee, *Lee of Virginia*, 453, 460.

5. Captain May sent Mrs. Lee's letter to Secretary Browning, whose department included the Patent Office. On February 23 Browning presented the request to Johnson and the Cabinet who unanimously agreed that the articles should be returned. However, before this decision was carried out, the *Washington Evening Express* erroneously claimed that Robert E. Lee was trying to regain his property. This caused a furor in Congress which resulted in passage of a resolution that "the Washington relics were the property of the United States," and therefore not to be handed over to General Lee. Years later in 1901, President William McKinley ordered the items restored to the family. It was expected, however, that these articles would actually remain in the Smithsonian but the family would be compensated for them. Freeman, *R. E. Lee*, 4: 383–84; Randall, *Browning Diary*, 2: 241; *New York Times*, Apr. 27, 1901.

From Robert B. Minturn, Jr.[1]

New York, Feb'y 10. 1869.

The American Free Trade League respectfully represents, that every artificial increase in the price of materials is a burden upon the Industry of the Country, already greatly suffering from the onerous taxation which the necessities of the Treasury have caused to be imposed directly and indirectly. The Free Trade League further represents that it is a well-known fact that the American Mercantile Marine is steadily decreasing, owing to its inability to compete successfully with foreign Shipping, in consequence of the high prices here of all materials used in the construction of vessels.[2]

In view of these well-known facts, the American Free Trade League most respectfully but most urgently requests that, in the interest of the American People, you will veto the Bill just passed by Congress increasing the duties upon Copper, its ores and chemical compounds; as the effects of this measure would be most injurious to the interest of the great mass of the Community.

The above Representation to the President of the United States was adopted by the American Free Trade League, and it was today resolved that it be forwarded to the President, attested by the undersigned.[3]

Robert. B. Minturn
Corresponding Secretary

LS, DLC-JP.

1. Minturn (1836–1889) was a New York City merchant. As a young man he published an account of his travels to India. New York City directories (1869–71); *NUC.*

2. A similar argument against the copper duties bill can be found in Charles J.M. Gwinn to Johnson, Jan. 11, 1869.

3. The "Committee of American Free Trade League," of which Minturn was a member, sent Johnson a letter of gratitude following his veto. See American Free Trade League to Johnson, Feb. 1869, Johnson Papers, LC.

From Joseph H. Thompson

Shelbyville Tennessee   Febry 10th 1869

Dear Mr President

Although I wrote you a day or so ago I beg to hand you the inclosed slips from the Nashville Daily Banner. The letter from Washington you will of course recognize as coming from my own pen.[1] The letter from Fletcher was written to me in reply to a note in which I approved of his view as expressed in a former published letter.[2] The comments on each as well as the comments in regard to yourself are editorials from the Banner of this date.

Since my return home I find the *people*—the masses—more than anxious to see you a candidate for Govenor. Some of our more prominent friends however are disposed to run Fletcher or some other man of that sort—Fowler for instance—*with the view of having you returned to the Senate at once.* By some it is thought an arrangement might be effected by which Senator Fowler could take a position under Grant and thus leave a vacancy to be supplied by you in October when our new Legislature assembles. With you in the field I cannot do not doubt that our next Legislature will be overwhelmingly anti-radical and such in fact is the prevailing opinion.

But notwithstanding this—unless Senator Fowler can be induced to make the race for Governor *or in some other* way be induced to make room for you in the Senate, I have no hesitation in saying that it is not only mine but the wish of every democrat and Conservative union man of my acquaintance that you make the run for Govenor in our next election.

You will of course think of all this and act as your better judgment may dictate.

The lower House of the Legislature have passed a resolution asking Brownlow to disband his milita but I do not believe the resolution will be adopted by the Senate.[3] I go to Memphis at once in obediance to my instructions from Mr. McCulloch. I then return here hoping to find an order to report at Washington as suggested in my note a day or so ago.

Before you go out of office could you not place me in some special position by which I could make some "bread and meat" and which Grant and his advisors would not likely observe for some time to come? Failing in this why not give me a special charge as bearer of despatches to Rosecrantz in Mexico,[4] or something of that sort. Please give the matter a thought—as I want something to do until our summer campaign in Tennessee opens. When that time comes, I should be found everywhere in Tennessee hard at work for Andrew Johnson for whatever position he will accept whether candidate for Govenor or Senator.

Joseph H Thompson

It is believed that Brownlow will never reach Washington. Whether he does or not he cannot live much longer. His health is bad—very bad. Should he die the people of Tennessee will rise *en masse* to make you his successor.

ALS, DLC-JP.

1. There are no enclosures found with Thompson's letter. His published letter from Washington to the *Banner* editor carries the date of February 7, but it was written probably on February 4 (the reference to the pending departure of Mrs. Mary Stover constituting the principal clue about its date). Thompson deals primarily in his letter with consideration of Johnson's political future in Tennessee, especially a possible campaign for governor in 1869. See *Nashville Republican Banner*, Feb. 11, 1869.

2. A. J. Fletcher's letter to Thompson, dated January 29, 1869, was published in the *Banner*. In it, Fletcher refers to the need for peace in "this distracted commonwealth." He professes to be willing to unite with all persons to bring about this desired end. Moreover, Fletcher denies that he has any political ambitions. Ibid. The earlier Fletcher letter to which Thompson refers is the one the secretary of state wrote to the *Nashville Press* editor on January 9. At that point Fletcher announced his formal break with the Brownlow administration. See R. Weakley Brown to Johnson, Jan. 12, 1869.

3. The joint resolution of the lower house called for the disbanding of the state militia, because "the finances of this State are in a crippled condition, and the organization and maintenance of a Militia force, will necessarily greatly add to our indebtedness." It passed on February 10. *House Journal . . . 1868–69*, 371–72.

4. An obvious reference to Gen. William S. Rosecrans, who was serving at this time as a commissioner to Mexico.

From Lewis Cooper

25 North 7th Street.
Phila.   February 11th 1869.

My Dear Sir.

I know (to my sorrow) your term of office, as our President, is fast drawing to an end: And up until within a short time, I had intended never to ask for any personal political consideration, but ill health for the past two years and pinching necessity together with exceedingly dull times here, has driven me to ask a favor, Provided you can grant it without compromising in the least your own streight forward course of justice, and the good of the country; if it is only for a few weeks or months.

I think my self competent for almost anything in the U.S. Mint,— or Custom house, or many other positions here. Those named first in rotation are my first choice.[1]

I know too this is not the regular way of getting those offices, but

I suppose you could direct a course, if pursued, would accomplish the desired end.

For the past year and an half I have labored much with my pen, (as I suppose you have some evidence of) against Radicalism and the impeachment and I feel that more than once my labor was not in vain, Although my grandest object I failed in, viz. your re-election, And for this I feel I have lost favor with those coming into power. My highest hopes are for the great good of the country, for this I have labored day by day, without any pecuniary compensation, from any quarter directly, or indirectly. I have written for News papers, all over the land, to Senators, and representatives in Congress, of both parties, quite a number of articles, and to your self. Very many of my articles perhaps never came to the light. But I shall continue my effort stil strugling for the good of the country, as I hope honestly.

My Dear Sir, If I am too late making this move, or If you cannot do me a favor as asked, here in, without compromising your principles, do not do that.

Lewis Cooper

ALS, DNA-RG56, Appts., Customs Service, Subofficer, Philadelphia, Lewis Cooper.
    1. Although Cooper's letter was forwarded to the Secretary of the Treasury, it does not appear that he received any position.

From Benjamin Eggleston et al.[1]

Washington, D.C.   11 Feby 1869

Mr President:

J. W. Shaw[2] desires to be reinstated in the Army. We regret the difficulty he is in and if you can consistently with duty reinstate him we respectfully ask you to do so. He served well his Country during the war, and we believe sustained a good character as a soldier & citizen. Until the charges made on which he was dimissed we never heard any thing derogatory to his character. Personally we know nothing of his guilt or innocence of the charges but we earnestly hope you may find the circumstances such as to render it proper to reinstate him.[3]

LS, DNA-RG94, ACP Branch, File L-12-CB-1869, J. W. Shaw.
    1. Others among the dozen signatories were George W. Julian, James M. Ashley, Oliver P. Morton, and Thomas A. Hendricks.
    2. James William Shaw (c1839–1879) entered the war as a private in the 11th Ohio Vols., and was mustered out in 1865 as a major in the 8th Ohio Cav. In 1866 he reenlisted in the 28th

U.S. Inf., but was dishonorably discharged in December 1868 for "embezzlement" and "conduct unbecoming an officer and a gentleman." He eventually moved to Washington, D.C., and worked as a lawyer. Washington, D.C., directories (1875–77); ACP Branch, File L-12-CB-1869, J. W. Shaw, RG94, NA; Pension File, Henry B. Shaw, RG15, NA; Francis B. Heitman, *Historical Register and Dictionary of the United States Army, from Its Organization, September 29, 1789 to March 2, 1903* (2 vols., Washington, D.C., 1903), 1: 878.

3. Johnson forwarded the letter to the secretary of war with the endorsement, "Let the appointment be made if there is a vacancy." Shaw received an appointment on March 1, 1869, but it was promptly cancelled, for an act passed two days later forbade any new commissions or enlistments pending consolidation of the infantry regiments. ACP Branch, File L-12-CB-1869, J. W. Shaw, RG94, NA; *Congressional Globe*, 40 Cong., 3 Sess., Appendix, pp. 318–19.

From Sam Milligan

[Washington]   Feb 11. 1869

Mr President.

The pilgrim fathers were driven, through religious persecution, from the old world, to seek freedom to worship God in the new. Their first Act when they landed on the American shores, was with open Bible, in the wild woods, to kneel down, and reverentially dedicate themselves and the whole land to the freedom of religion.

This scene is commemorated, and on Canvass, hung up to the eyes of the Nation, in rotunda of the Capital.

Under this influence nearly all the States have incorporated in their Constitutions or laws some expression, or clause which recognizes the Christian religion, and makes the belief in a God, and future rewards & punishments, a prerequisite to all the rights & privileges of full citizens.

Religious tests are not required; but belief in a God and future rewards and punishments, is recognized as fundamental in the constitutions & laws of all the States.

Now by the proposed amendment to the U.S. Constitution,[1] evry man of whatever creed he may be, may hold office in any state.

He may by his creed deny the existence of a God,—that is, he may be an Atheist, and still have Constitutional approval of his Creed.

The question of religious tests, I know is a delicate one, but could you not, on this point, arouse all the religious denominations against it?

I think it could be made a powerful engine in your favor even delicately hinted at. Think of it!

Sam Milligan

ALS, DLC-JP.

1. Exactly what amendment Milligan is referring to here is not clear. In February, several

members of Congress submitted petitions from their constituents which called for a constitutional amendment that would require recognition and acknowledgment of God as the source of authority and power in civil government. Such petitions seemed to have been routinely forwarded to the judiciary committees of the respective houses. These proposals would have been supportive of Milligan's view. See the *Congressional Globe*, 40 Cong., 3 Sess., pp. 973–74, 1158.

From Orville H. Browning

Washington, D.C.   Febry 12 1869

Mr President

The enclosed paper[1] was laid on the table for me to read, when at Cabinet this morning, and I unintentionally brought it away with me. It is herewith returned.

Some of its statements seem almost incredible.

There is something wrong some where, but where I dont exactly know.

O H Browning

ALS, DLC-JP.
 1. Chauncey H. Snow to Johnson, Feb. 3, 1869.

From John A. Dix

Paris   12. February 1869.

My dear Sir:

I forward to you today, through the State Department, my resignation as Minister to France. My private affairs require my presence at home; and I am desirous for many personal reasons of terminating my residence abroad.

I cannot quit my post here without expressing to you my grateful sense of the kindness and confidence, which you have shown to me during your administration. I shall never cease to carry the remembrance of them with me.

In terminating my official connection with you and your administration, I beg you to accept my sincere wishes for your health and happiness.

John A. Dix

ALS, CSmH.

From John Vaughan Lewis[1]

St. Johns Church   Washington D.C.

12" Feby. 1869

Sir:

In behalf of the family and relatives of James Harold[2] deceased I respectfully request that the body of the said Harold, (now in the custody of the United States Authorities at the Washington Arsenal, if I am rightly informed) may be delivered to me or to such other person as may be designated by me, under such restrictions and guarantees as may seem to you, Sir, advisable.

I need hardly say that I make this request solely as a Christian Minister, and with no other purpose in view but that of comforting the hearts of a worthy and sorrowful family by securing to the remains of James Harold the rites of Christian burial.

It seems to me, Sir, unworthy of Christian civilization that the vengeance of human law, however righteous, should be carried into the grave, whence it can punish none but survivors. The family of James Harold belong to the same Communion with myself, a Communion which craves Christian burial for its dead as a precious privilege, at least, for the living in their bereavement. The long denial of this privilege has been a bitter addition to the afflictions of the family in whose behalf I plead. I pray you therefore, Sir, seriously to consider whether whatever propriety has hitherto required that denial be not now sufficiently fulfilled, and, (if you think my petition just) to issue the order which I have requested, as a kindly act of national relenting toward an afflicted and unfortunate family.[3]

sgd.— John Vaughan Lewis
Rector of St. John's Parish
Washington D.C.

Copy, DLC-JP.

1. Lewis (c1835–ff1879), rector of St. John's Episcopal Church, was a native of Massachusetts. 1870 Census, D.C., Washington, 1st Ward, 362; Washington, D.C., directories (1869–80).

2. Lewis was, of course, referring to David E. Herold.

3. On February 13 Johnson referred Lewis's letter to Secretary of War Schofield requesting that the body be released to Lewis. Joseph Gawler, an undertaker, retrieved the body. On February 15, after Lewis had conducted a service for family members, Herold was buried in the Congressional Cemetery, next to the grave of his father. *Washington Evening Star*, Feb. 15, 1869; Michael W. Kauffman, "David Edgar Herold: The Forgotten Conspirator," *Surratt Society News* (Nov. 1981), 23–28.

From John Savage

Paris   12th February 1869.

Mr President

I duly received the appointment of Consul at Leeds from the Department of State[1] and beg to return my sincere thanks for the desire exhibited by your Excellency—in conformity with your expressed intention just preceding my departure—to throw the Aegis of our Flag over me, and the eclât such distinction might confer, on my travels. As I told your Excellency, I had no inclination whatever for a consulate, and certainly could not have dreamed of being sent to an English one. If I had taken advantage of what seemed a plausible chance, and gone unthinkingly at once to Leeds I would have drawn ridicule on the American character by courting a cheap martyrdom without the possibility of bringing any disputed point to a test: for the incoming administration might or might not feel disposed to give *practical* attention to a case which possibly might seem was created for its embarrassment.

The case of Burlingame was before me:[2] with the difference that my relation to England involved more positive antipathies than his with Austria when sent to that country. Mr. Burlingame had simply exercised his Congressional influence to elevate the international position of the American representative to Sardinia.[3] I began life in arms against England, and would end it in the same manner if I did not hope to outlive the capacity of England for interference in American affairs, or for oppression anywhere. Our government tacitly acquiesed in the expression of opinion against receving Mr. Burlingame at Vienna. It withdrew him from the Austrian Mission, and sent him to China, in whose interests and those of a progressive era he is now unlocking the treasury of the Ages to the general enterprise and friendly competition of more demonstrative civilizations.

I would therefore have declined the appointment at once, but that to have hastily done so might have been misconstrued as a discourtesy toward the best intentions of the Chief Magistrate of my country. Besides the peculiarity of the appointment afforded the opportunity of hovering over the British Channel, so to speak, and perplexing the managers of British affairs with *their own* speculations as to the intentions of my government in displaying me there. I had to postpone the growing idea of presenting myelf in England for reasons stated in my communications of the 2nd and 3rd inst's. to the Secretary of State: to which I beg to refer.[4]

I find very little interest taken here in American affairs. I fear the thinkers and writers of France do not see many American papers or periodicals, and take their intelligence from English sources, or from *Galignani's Messenger,* a concentration of the most English, and consequently most anti-American, of English opinion.

The majority of Americans here, and I have mixed largely with them, grow "more American" by contact with foreign people and ideas. Some there are who become fascinated by gilded exteriors, and would base an argument for the annihilation of the American system on the "order" evinced in the street-sweeping of Paris, but they are exceptions. A very positive feeling exists among our citizens here against Mr. Minister Johnson's course in England.[5] The English are managing that good gentleman with great tact, but on the Anaconda plan. They are slavering him all over preparatory to swallowing him. I trust his effect on them as a pill, will be different from that as a politician, and that he will *disagree* with them *then* at least. The reported expressions of General Grant on the Alabama claims[6] gave great satisfaction to his countrymen here; between whom and their cousins from over the Channel there is a very ill-concealed distemper raging.

When, nearly ten months ago, it seemed settled that your Excellency would confer on me one of the vacant missions to the South American Republics[7] I did not think circumstances would have so disposed themselves as to prevent my receiving the benefit of your intentions. A strong sense of duty binding me to work then in hand interfered with your promise; and so continued until I had to come here for the benefit of my health. Now the opportunity has probably passed away for ever. I regret that I was not able to re-cross the Atlantic before your retirement and place within your power the fulfillment of your kind and frequently repeated desire and design to recognize my services. The fact that they were freely given would have made the rcognition all the more welcome. However Mr. President on your retirement I beg to tender you my respect, and to wish you long life free from the exasperating cares of a station you have dignified with eminent purity of character.

John Savage

ALS, DLC-JP.

1. Johnson nominated Savage on January 19, but the commerce committee returned an adverse report on January 28. His nomination was tabled on March 3. His claim that he somehow received an appointment has not been substantiated. *Senate Ex. Proceedings*, Vol. 16: 431, 442, 464, 502.

2. Anson Burlingame had been confirmed as minister to Austria in March 1861, but was recalled that June in response to Austrian protests. As a leading Fenian, Savage is drawing parallels between Austria's action and the probable response by Great Britain to his nomination. Ibid., Vol. 11: 315, 318, 328; *New York Times*, June 13, 15, 1861; *DAB*.

3. In 1860, while a congressman from Massachusetts, Burlingame introduced a bill elevating the status of the foreign mission to the Kingdom of the Piedmont and Sardinia. Burlingame sought first class status for the Kingdom, partly as a result of recent territorial gains which came at Austria's expense. *Congressional Globe*, 36 Cong., 1 Sess., 1824; *New York Times*, July 10, 1861.

4. These items have not been found.

5. Reverdy Johnson, U.S. minister to Great Britain, was negotiating naturalization issues and the *Alabama* claims. Many Americans criticized him for being too cordial with the English, who had provided ships to the South during the Civil War. *DAB*; *New York Times*, Nov. 11, Dec. 17, 1868.

6. It was rumored that President-elect Ulysses S. Grant opposed ratification of the *Alabama* treaty. Signed in early January by Reverdy Johnson and his British counterparts, the treaty met with general criticism in the U.S.; the Senate refused to ratify it. Ibid., Jan. 26, 1869; Brian Jenkins, *The Fenians and Anglo-American Relations during Reconstruction* (Ithaca, 1969), 288–89. For the text of the treaty, see *New York Times*, Jan. 22, 25, 1869.

7. Nothing has been found concerning another appointment for Savage.

From Ethan A. Allen

New York   Feby 13 /69

Dear Sir.

I feel deeply indebted to you for your kindness to me.

I still hold the position of an Inspector in the Custom House.

I understand that a long list has been sent to the Secy of the Treasury of names for removal. May I beg of you the favr to see that I am *not* removed as this position is to me a matter of vital importance. As for the present I have no other income. & a loss of my position would embarras me very much indeed.

I discharge my duty promptly & with fidelity to the Government.

I am well known to the Inspectors as a Johnson man & the larger portion of the Inspectors are Republicans.

Please protect me in my position & much oblige.[1]

Ethan A. Allen
Box No 3534 Post Office.

ALS, DLC-JP.

1. Apparently Allen continued as inspector for a short time longer, until April. See Allen to Johnson, Feb. 3, 1868, *Johnson Papers*, 13: 520.

From John C. Atzerodt[1]

Washington D.C.   Febr 13, 1869

Sir

In behalf of my mother[2] and other relatives as well as of myself I respectfully beg you to be kind enough to give an order to have the remains of my late brother, George A. Atzerodt, delivered up to me.[3]

John C. Atzerodt.

for himself, his mother Victoria Atzerodt and several sisters.

LS, DNA-RG94, Lets. Recd. (Main Ser.), File S-112-1869 (M619, Roll 746).

1. Atzerodt (*fl*1880), the older brother of Lincoln assassination conspirator George Atzerodt, was a carriage painter by profession, but served as a detective in Maryland during the Civil War. Washington, D.C., directories (1869–81); James O. Hall and Edward Steers, "George Andrew Atzerodt," *Surratt Society News* (November 1981), 29–32.

2. Victore (Anglicized to Victoria) F. Hahn (*c*1805–*fl*1869) married Johann H. Atzerodt in Prussia. They moved to the United States in the 1840s and lived at various places in Maryland and Virginia. On Mrs. Atzerodt's behalf Louis Schade had also requested George Atzerodt's remains two days earlier. Ibid.; 1850 Census, Va., Westmoreland, Washington Parish, 643; Louis Schade to Johnson, Feb. 11, 1868, Johnson Papers, LC.

3. On Monday, February 15, John C. Atzerodt and Louis Schade visited Johnson to get his order to the War Department releasing the body of Atzerodt's brother. In turn Atzerodt gave the order to J. W. Plant, an undertaker, who actually retrieved the body on the next day. Plant took the remains on February 17 to the vault at Glenwood Cemetery until other members of the family could be present for the burial. *Washington Evening Star*, Feb. 15, 16, 17, 1869.

From William M. Evarts

February 13, 1869.

Sir:

In the matter of the application for pardon of John Devlin,[1] the fact that, while at the bar in New york, I defended Devlin, as one of his counsel, upon the trial at which he was convicted, induces me to lay the matter before you more formally than is usual in giving my advice as to the exercise of Executive clemency.

Devlin was sentenced to two years imprisonment in the Albany Penitentiary for exercising the business of a wholesale liquor dealer without having taken out a license. The efforts made by his counsel to introduce evidence at the trial that he had taken steps to procure a license and that the delay in its issue by the Revenue Officers arose from accident were unsuccessful and the prisoner was convicted.

The severity of the sentence, however, can hardly be accounted for upon the record of this trial, and the circumstance that the Government was obliged to forego the trial of some other indictments against the prisoner though it explains, does not, as it seems to me, justify the aggravation of the punishment of the offence for which Devlin was tried and convicted by an imputation of offences for which he has not been tried.

The prisoner has been in confinement for a year, and his conduct in prison has been exemplary, and is highly commended by the Warden[2] of the Penitentiary who joins in the application for his pardon. His health is represented to be seriously affected.

His position in life has been respectable, and his pardon is solicited by many persons of repute and distinction.

Upon this statement, and upon the papers, I beg leave respectfully to submit the case to the President without further advice on the subject of a pardon.[3]

Wm. M. Evarts.   Attorney General.

LBcopy, DNA-RG204, Lets. Sent in Pardon Cases, Vol. A.

1. Devlin (b. c1837), a Brooklyn plumber, had been convicted in March 1868 of selling liquor without a license. 1860 Census, N.Y., Kings, Brooklyn, 5th Ward, 266; Pardons and Remissions, Vol. 9 (T967, Roll 4), RG59, NA.

2. A career prison administrator, Amos Pilsbury (1805–1873) had been warden of the Connecticut state prison before becoming warden of the Albany penitentiary, where he remained until illness forced his resignation. Pilsbury is considered one of the nation's first professional wardens. DAB.

3. Johnson granted Devlin a "full and unconditional" pardon on February 16, 1869, citing that Devlin had attempted to procure a license, and that his conduct in prison had been "uniformly good." New York Tribune, Feb. 18, 1869; Pardons and Remissions, Vol. 9 (T967, Roll 4), RG59, NA.

From Henry R. Linderman

Philadelphia, Feb. 13. 1869

My Dear Sir,

Our people are awaiting with much interest the fate of the Copper Bill, now in the hands of the Executive. They have invested very largely in the Copper business, both as to mining and smelting, and have suffered severely. Men of unquestioned fairness & intelligence represent to me the vital importance of the Bill becoming a law. Without it they say the Lake Superior region must go under. I hope you may find it consistent with your convictions of duty to approve the Bill.[1]

Excuse the liberty I have taken in writing on this subject. I will only add that the condition of our finances requires that our mines &c should all be made to contribute towards the wealth of the nation.

H R Linderman

ALS, DLC-JP.
1. See Veto of Copper Bill, Feb. 22, 1869.

From Nathaniel P. Sawyer

Pittsburg Pa   Feb 13 1869

Your friends here are exceedingly anxious for you to sign the copper Tariff Bill.

N P Sawyer
Editor of the Republic

Tel, DLC-JP.

Veto of Washington and Georgetown Schools Act

WASHINGTON, D.C., *February 13, 1869.*

To the Senate of the United States:

The bill entitled "An act transferring the duties of trustees of colored schools of Washington and Georgetown" is herewith returned to the Senate,[1] in which House it originated, without my approval.

The accompanying paper[2] exhibits the fact that the legislation which the bill proposes is contrary to the wishes of the colored residents of Washington and Georgetown, and that they prefer that the schools for their children should be under the management of trustees selected by the Secretary of the Interior, whose term of office is for four years, rather than subject to the control of bodies whose tenure of office, depending merely upon political considerations, may be annually affected by the elections which take place in the two cities.

The colored people of Washington and Georgetown are at present not represented by a person of their own race in either of the boards of trustees of public schools appointed by the municipal authorities. Of the three trustees, however, who, under the act of July 11, 1862, compose the board of trustees of the schools for colored children, two are persons of color. The resolutions transmitted herewith show that they have performed their trust in a manner entirely satisfactory to the colored people of the two cities, and no good reason is known to the Executive why the duties which now devolve upon them should be transferred as proposed in the bill.

With these brief suggestions the bill is respectfully returned, and the consideration of Congress invited to the accompanying preamble and resolutions.[3]

ANDREW JOHNSON.

Richardson, *Messages*, 6: 705.

1. The Senate passed the bill (No. 609) on July 10, 1868. *Congressional Globe*, 40 Cong., 2 Sess., p. 3900.
2. Not found.
3. The House passed the Senate bill on February 5, 1869, and the enrolled bill was signed by the Speaker the next day. On February 13, the Senate received Johnson's veto message and responded by placing the message on the table and taking no steps to override the veto. Ibid., 3 Sess., pp. 919, 935, 1164. The preamble and resolutions referred to by the President have not been located.

To Natus J. Haynes & Sons

Executive Mansion   February 15th, 1869

Gentlemen:

I have received your letter of the 8th instant and thank you sincerely for the many warm expressions of friendship toward and confidence in me, which it contains.

In answer to your inquiry, I can only say that I have not expressed, nor have I authorized any one to express for me any wish or opinion, negative or affirmative, in the matter referred to; and that the present circumstances are not such as to render it desirable or proper for me to form or publish an opinion thereon, either one way or the other.

With assurances of my appreciation of your friendship and hearty sympathy with your wishes for the redemption of Tennessee and her restoration to peace, prosperity, and good government.

Andrew Johnson

Copy, DLC-JP.

From Joseph Holt

Washington, D.C., Feby. 15, 1869.

Respectfully returned to His Excellency the President.

The within case,[1] reported upon by this Bureau on Dec. 17th last,[2] is again referred upon new evidence and papers produced by the accused.

The new matter consists of:—1. An alleged statement in regard to the condition of the accused, the merits of the case, &c., by Col. Marshall S. Howe.[3] 2. Two certificates or opinions of medical gentlemen, one a civil physician, and the other an assistant surgeon of the army.[4] 3. A testimonial by Hon. G. M. Dodge, late Major General U.S.V. 4. Statements and arguments by the accused, and by his brother in his behalf.[5]

The certificate of Grafton Taylor, M.D.,[6] of Georgetown, D.C., as to the illness of Hoffman, subsequently to his dismissal from the army, was filed prior to the former report of the Bureau and has been therein considered.[7]

The testimony of the medical men above mentioned is as to the effect which a certain stated amount of morphine and quinine taken by a person would have upon his mind and body. It is claimed by Hoffman, that, at the time of his offences and of his trial, he was so much under the influence of these drugs, (administered—as he asserts—by an army surgeon) as not to be able to be tried by a court martial or properly to defend himself thereat.[8] The medical testimony is to the effect that a person taking the medicines stated by Hoffman to have been taken by himself, would, as a general rule, be so affected and incapacitated as not to be conscious of or responsible for his actions. The certificates are based upon his individual representations. If these representations are true and cover the ground, then the certificates are evidence bearing upon the merits of the case; otherwise not.

That these representations fail to convey the actual or entire facts must—it is believed—be concluded upon the testimony. In his full statement to the Court, with which the record of the trial concludes— a statement which, as he pleaded guilty, is to be viewed as containing *prima facie* his whole defence at that time—there is no reference or allusion to his being under the influence of or affected by medicines at the time of his arrest or trial, or at any period prior thereto. The only influence which he mentions is that confessed in his pleas to the specifications of drunken and disorderly conduct—viz. the influence of intoxicating liquor. Thus in accounting for his conduct on the occasion of his principal offence, he says—that having been refused by four different officers to whom he applied for the use of a horse for the purpose of going from the camp to Little Rock—"this was too much for me to bear, and being somewhat under the influence of liquor, I became mad, literally mad; cursed the officers, &c."[9]

The record not sustaining the present allegations of applicant, there remains to be examined the statement of Col. M. S. Howe, Comdg. the regiment at the time of Hoffman's trial. This statement is not made by Col. Howe over his own signature, but is offered by the brother of applicant who claims that he took it down from the Colonel's lips. As presented it goes to sustain the present defence and particularly the claim that accused was not in possession of his senses at the time of trial on account of the use of morphine, or he would not have pleaded guilty; and that had he pleaded otherwise, the charges could not probably have been sustained.

Col. Howe, having been furnished by this Bureau with the statement offered as his own by the brother of Hoffman, and requested to remark thereon, fails altogether to confirm the same. Col. Howe denies that he said he did not believe the charges could have been sustained had the plea been not guilty;[10] states that he told the party that he could not say anything in behalf of accused; that what he said in regard to the character of accused as a soldier was—"if Lieut. H. could have kept from liquor, I could have him attend to duty, but *liquor was his ruin*"; that, what he said about Hoffman's being under the influence of morphine was—that "if the statement of the Lieut. before the court *was true*, he ought not to have plead guilty, but prove by the medical officer that his mind was affected by drugs"— which was not attempted. He remarks of the narrative generally— "Something he," (Hoffman's brother,) has stated I did say, but *not in the light he has represented*," and adds that he "had no idea of furnishing any paper in behalf of" Hoffman.

The only witness produced to corroborate the averments of the applicant having thus failed to sustain him, and the record of trial giving no support to his present defence it is *held* that the representations of the party are not borne out by the evidence. Upon the testimony as it stands the conclusion cannot be avoided that it is entirely or chiefly to the use of intoxicating liquor that are to be attributed the disgraceful offences of the accused; and, notwithstanding the terms of the testimonial of General Dodge, no favorable action in his behalf can be recommended.

It is to be noted that having been duly dismissed by the formal approval of the sentence of a competent court, he could not in any event be restored to the army, except through a new appointment confirmed by the Senate.[11]

J. Holt
Judge Advocate General

LS, DNA-RG94, ACP Branch, File H-53-CB-1865, Wm. G. Hoffman.

1. William G. Hoffman (c1844–ff1893) was a native of Virginia and resident of Georgetown. (Two other reliable sources indicate his birthdate as c1838 or c1840.) In 1861 he became a 2nd lieutenant in the 3rd U.S. Cav. During 1863 and much of 1864 he was assistant commissary for musters for the 16th Army Corps. After he rejoined his regiment, then in Arkansas, Hoffman was accused of being drunk on duty, threatening his superior officers, and refusing to obey their orders. He was dismissed from the service on December 31, 1864, but upon Hoffman's promise to reform, President Lincoln disapproved his dismissal. He was therefore reinstated in February 1865. However, in July and August 1865, Hoffman got into similar altercations with some of the same officers; he was brought before a court-martial which ordered that he be cashiered from the service, effective September 6, 1865. 1860 Census, D.C., Georgetown, 2nd Ward, 54; (1870), 1st Ward, 504; Washington, D.C., directories (1869–93); Hoffman to Simon Cameron, Jan. 10, 1862; Joseph Holt to Edwin M. Stanton, Feb. 1, 1865; Court-martial proceedings, ACP Branch, File H-53-CB-1865, Wm. G. Hoffman, RG94, NA.

2. Holt had remarked that too much time had elapsed since the original case to revoke, set aside, or modify the sentence. The only action Johnson could take would be to pardon Hoffman, which Holt did not recommend. Holt to Johnson, Dec. 17, 1868, ibid.

3. Howe (c1805–1878) became a 2nd lieutenant in the army in 1836 and advanced to lieutenant colonel by the time of the Civil War. Made colonel of the 3rd Cav. in 1861, he remained in that post until he was retired for age in 1866. Powell, Army List, 384; E. D. Townsend to U. S. Grant, Aug. 23, 1866, ACP Branch, File H-767-CB-1866, Marshall S. Howe, RG94, NA. Howe's statement is in John W. Hoffman to Johnson, Jan. 12, 1869, ACP Branch, File H-53-CB-1865, Wm. G. Hoffman, RG94, NA.

4. None of these papers has been found. The assistant surgeon has not been identified.

5. John W. Hoffman (c1846–ff1870) was a clerk in Georgetown by the time he wrote two letters to Johnson on January 12, 1869, defending his brother. Ibid.; Washington, D.C., directories (1869–70); 1860 Census, D.C., Georgetown, 2nd Ward, 54.

6. Grafton Tyler (1811–1884), a physician in Georgetown, was on the board of or served as consulting physician for a number of medical organizations and institutions in the D.C. area. NUC; William B. Atkinson, ed., The Physicians and Surgeons of the United States (Philadelphia, 1878), 238.

7. Tyler had certified that he treated Hoffman for "Typhomalarial fever" upon his return to Georgetown after his discharge. Holt stated that "this fact occurring at such date, can hardly excuse or explain offences committed some time previous." Holt to Johnson, Dec. 17, 1868, ACP Branch, File H-53-CB-1865, Wm. G. Hoffman, RG94, NA.

8. This was hardly a new argument by Hoffman, since he had already used it in a letter to Johnson of November 7, 1865. Ibid.

9. Hoffman explained that he was too ill to write his defense himself and so it was done by his friend, Lieutenant Buchanan of the 3rd Mich. Cav. He did not remember reading the defense in the court-martial, and indeed was so ill with "camp fever" and jaundice that "death would have been a welcome relief." Hoffman to Johnson, Nov. 7, 1865, ibid.

10. Howe's original comments have not been found.

11. On February 16 Hoffman wrote to Johnson again asking that his sentence be modified to allow him to resign so that at some point he could hold an office if he had the opportunity. On February 20 Johnson instead removed "the disability resulting from cashiering." This would have permitted Hoffman to hold some other office, but there is no evidence that he ever did so. He remained in the D.C. area as a carpenter into the 1890s. Hoffman to Johnson, Feb. 16, 1869, ibid.; Washington, D.C., directories (1869–93).

From John Vaughan Lewis

St John's Church   Washington D.C.
15 Feb. 1869.

Dear Sir

You will let me say a word or two that I wanted to say at our interview on Thursday, and would have said, but that I was asking a favour of you at the time, and that is, that I deeply regret the expiration of your official term, and have watched with growing respect and admiration your disregard of popular clamour in matters of State, the sincerity and earnestness of your convictions, and your unflinching courage in obeying them, your irreproachable integrity in office, and your scrupulous regard for right, even in what other men would call trifles.

I am little versed in politics, but it has always seemed to me that you were greatly misunderstood by the majority, and grossly misrepresented. Perhaps, as prophecying is more in my line, I may venture to predict that ten years from this the Country will wish you were back again in the Presidential Chair to save us all from the mischiefs that you have boldly striven to avert. I am glad to believe the current rumour that you do not mean to retire from public life and I heartily wish you success and prosperity in the future. I am sorry, now, that I have not sought your acquaintance more carefully than I have. I assure you my seeming negligence has arisen solely out of the unconquerable repugnance I have to even seeming "to pay court" to those in high station. I should have liked to have had you attend St John's Church, and, as you reside in my Parish, I should have called upon you about it, long since, I suppose, if you had been in lower degree in the nation. I ask your pardon for this pastoral neglect, and hope that when Tennessee, or the country, sends you back to Washington, I may have the opportunity to repair the Errour.

I have not often troubled you with "Applications" but you have never given me occasion for importunity, and for all your kindness and readiness to grant my requests, I offer you my sincere thanks.[1]

John Vaughan Lewis.

ALS, DLC-JP.

1. Three days earlier, Lewis had asked Johnson to release the body of David Herold for purposes of reinterment. See Lewis to Johnson, Feb. 12, 1869.

From H. Melville Myers, Jr.[1]

Barnwell C H   So Ca   Feby 15th 1869

My dear Sir

It may be that this letter, coming from an apparent stranger, will much surprise you. But I trust you will bear with me in thus presuming to address one who occupies, so properly, & honorably, the highest office within the gift of the American People.

My motives in addressing you, are not political, but altogether of a *private* & personal nature—*in brief,* I am driven by *stern necessity* to ask a *favor* at your hands.

My parents[2] now reside in Nashville Tenn. They formerly lived near Kingsport East Tenn. where my Grandfather, Mr Jacob Myers[3]—resided for many years. My uncle who married my fathers Sister,[4] now lives near Knoxville, Tenn.—Col C W Hall—whom you may know. I have often heard him speak of you, and I had the honor of meeting you many years ago at Ross' Camp Ground, during a Democratic Convention (I think in 1845 or 6). Col L C Haynes whom you are doubtless well acquainted with has charge of several important cases of my father, in the courts of Tenn. Also Mr. Deadrick[5]—Dr. F A Ross, who now lives in Huntsville Ala. and before his sad reverse of fortune, lived near Kingsport E. T. as you may also remember—who is also an uncle of mine. I came South several years since and married in this place, a connection, and relative of Genl Hagood,[6] & the late Judge Butler.[7] I am a Lawyer by profession, & practice. But the late sad and disastrous war has swept from me every thing which I possessed, save a valuable Law Library, and a few weeks since my house and lot were sold at a sacrifice. And I am now apprehensive that my Books will have to share the same fate. Were I a single man or even without a family, I would not regard these afflictions & troubles as any thing—but I have a wife[8] & *five small children* helpless & depending on my exertions, for their daily bread, and I do truthfully assure you, that there are times when their *daily wants have been often unsupplied.* This has been the result of no cause of mine—but simply the chief cause resulting from political, Radical *disfavor* as the within enclosed papers may indicate.[9] I have not only been *unjustly removed from office without cause,* but I have been unable; in a great measure from the same cause, to get one cent for all my past services & hence I have been left with my family in a very destitute condition, with not even the means to supply their necessary wants.

The recent legislation of the State has pretty well, for the present destroyed the practice of the Law, should the state Laws continue in force.

Such my dear sir is my own embarrassing condition, and I fear it may be *presumptious in me*, to annoy you with my troubles—but the only apology is that, for *you*, I have always cherished the highest feelings of regard, previous to your entering upon the high duties of the Executive. I have followed you in your political career, ever since. I (a mere boy—) first listened to your eloquent appeals to the Democracy—which assembled en mass at Ross' Camp Ground, up to the present time. I know that you can feel and sympathise with those who will strive by their *own industry* & energy—to attain a worthy and honorable position in life—for "verily every kindness we do our fellow men, will bring its own reward."

You may have forgotten me, & all my family in Tenn but what Tennessean does not know, and will remember the name of Andrew Johnson? A name not only identified with the history of *Tenn*, but intimately associated and identified with the whole history of the country.

It is with much difficulty, I do assure you, that I have brought my mind to consent to make an appeal to you for assistance. Nothing but *sheer necessity* & my needy condition has led me to this course—and be assured that should you take into favorable consideration my cause, it will not only be cherished, by me & my family with remembrances of grateful emotions, but, whenever fortune may kindly favor me, in the future, your kindness will indeed be repaid—not only returning the amount and interest, but also in whatever way my poor service may command.

Hoping to hear from you, at your earliest convenience.

H. Melville Myers Jr.

ALS, DLC-JP.

1. Myers (c1834–fl1880) was a Virginia native and lawyer. 1870 Census, S.C., Barnwell, Barnwell Twp., 21; (1880), 24th Enum. Dist., 4.

2. H. Melville Myers, Sr. (c1810–fl1870), a physician, and Caroline Myers (c1809–fl1870) had lived in Nashville since at least the late 1850s. 1870 Census, Tenn., Davidson, Nashville, 8th Ward, 77; Nashville directories (1859).

3. Myers (c1770–fl1850) during the 1830s was one of the largest landowners in Sullivan

County, Tennessee, and also a property holder in Virginia and Kentucky. For many years he was also a saltpeter manufacturer. 1850 Census, Tenn., Sullivan, 1st Div., 32; Muriel M.C. Spoden, *Kingsport Heritage: The Early Years, 1700 to 1900* (Johnson City, Tenn., 1991), 159, 223, 263, 264.

4. Rebecca H.C. (sometimes Caroline R. on the census) Myers (1810–1888) married Crawford W. Hall in 1829 and they had five children, of whom only two survived to adulthood. [C. W. Hall], *Three Score Years and Ten* (Cincinnati, 1884), 49; *Knox County Cemetery Records* (n.p., 1973), 66; Spoden, *Kingsport Heritage*, 266; 1860 Census, Tenn., Hawkins, 10th Dist., 11.

5. Probably James W. Deaderick, a prominent upper East Tennessee lawyer and judge.

6. Johnson Hagood (1829–1898), a lawyer, was a Confederate brigadier in Virginia until late 1864 when he was transferred to North Carolina. During the postbellum era he served as South Carolina's comptroller general and governor. Warner, *Gray*.

7. Probably Andrew P. Butler (1796–1857), a lawyer, who served as judge of the South Carolina court of appeals before becoming a U.S. Senator (1846–57). *DAB*.

8. Marion S. Smith (*c*1837–*fl*1880) had married Myers in early 1859. Brent H. Holcomb, comp., *Marriage and Death Notices from Baptist Newspapers of South Carolina, 1835–1865* (Spartanburg, 1981), 85; 1870 Census, S.C., Barnwell, Barnwell Twp., 21; (1880), 24th Enum. Dist., 4.

9. Not found.

From Fernando Wood

Capital   Feb 15, 1869.

The papers properly endorsed and sustained by the attorney General in favor of the pardon of N Henry[1] have been forwarded to you. Will you oblige me by acting upon them today?[2]

Fernando Wood
House Representatives

Tel, DLC-JP.

1. Nicholas Henry (*c*1831–*fl*1901) had been a baker and flour dealer before going into distilling. By the early 1870s he was operating stables in New York, and continued to do so until at least the turn of the century. 1880 Census, N.Y., New York, New York City, 20th Ward, 349th Enum. Dist., 24; New York City directories (1861–1901); *New York Times*, Nov. 18, 19, 20, 1868.

2. In November 1868 Henry had been convicted of attempting to defraud the government. On February 16 Johnson signed a pardon, citing improper evidence and several recommendations for clemency, including ones from the prosecuting attorney and the jury. Pardons and Remissions, Vol. 9 (T967, Roll 4), RG59, NA.

From David W. Standeford[1]

Shelbyville [Ky.]   Feb 16 1869.

My father William Standeford[2] Postmaster at this place died last evening. It is the wish of a large portion of this community that

Travis Wilson[3] now Acting Deputy should be appointed. He is honest faithful & capable. Please take no steps until you hear from him by petition and from me by letter.

                                                        D W Standeford

Tel, DLC-JP.
  1. Standeford (c1826–fl1880) was a Lexington carpet dealer. 1870 Census, Ky., Fayette, Lexington, 3rd Ward, 251; (1880), 66th Enum. Dist., 68.
  2. Standeford (c1797–1869), a merchant, had been postmaster since 1861. 1860 Census, Ky., Shelby, 1st Dist., 85; George L. Willis, Sr., comp. and ed., *History of Shelby County, Kentucky* (Hartford, Ky., 1979 [1929]), 227.
  3. Wilson (c1805–fl1880) was a Shelbyville sadler. He was not appointed postmaster. 1870 Census, Ky., Shelby, Shelbyville, 7; (1880), 191st Enum. Dist., 14.

From Anne M. Deen

                                        New York City   Feb'y 17. 1869.
Dear Sir

Your telegram is just received[1] and I hasten to say: that: there is we think very great probability of Mr Deen confirmation, if the Senate go into Executive Session. In fact it is almost a certainty.[2]

I hope Mr President, that you will not be persuaded—now that Mr Deens name is before the Senate—either to withdraw it—or to send in the name of any one else for the position of Naval officer. Mr Deen is the man for the position and if your Excellency will but give us time, he will be confirmed. I will send your Excellency with this, a copy of the "Industrial American"—containing a notice of Mr Deen, that you may see he is all he has been represented to be.

Again Mr President permit me to hope that you will continue Mr Deens name before the Senate.

Either Mr Deen or myself or both of us, will be in Washington next week, when we shall do ourselves the honor of seeing you, and explaining why there is no doubt of Mr Deens confirmation.

Ever praying for your Excellency's health and prosperity . . .

                                        Mrs A M Deen   4 East 30th St

ALS, DLC-JP.
  1. Johnson's telegram to John L. Deen asked: "Have you any reasonable prospect of confirmation." See Johnson to Deen, Feb. 17, 1869, Johnson Papers, LC.
  2. See Anne L. Deen to Johnson, Dec. 18, 1868.

From Blanton Duncan[1]

372 E. St.   Feb. 17 1869

Sir

In accordance with the instruction which you gave me to report what answer was returned by the Secy of War,[2] upon an application for the return of Genl Beauregard's[3] papers, taken after the surrender of the Confederate Armies; & of which the originals had already been surrendered by Genl J. E Johnston at Charlotte N.C., I submit the Enclosed letter from Adj. Genl Townsend[4] affirming the previous refusals of Secy. Stanton to deliver what is claimed by Genl Beauregard to be private property, & copies of which he is beside willing that the Government shall have now or at any other time.[5]

Blanton Duncan

ALS, DNA-RG94, Lets. Recd. (Main Ser.), File S-1521-1865 (M619, Roll 413).

1. Duncan (c1827–ff1892), a Kentucky planter and member of the state house of representatives before the Civil War, went south with troops for the Confederate army and briefly served as a colonel in 1861 and a volunteer aide in 1863. During 1862 he had a contract for printing Confederate treasury notes, but in 1864 he went to Europe for the rest of the war. Pardoned October 12, 1866, under the $20,000 exception, Duncan became a lawyer in Louisville, Kentucky, removing to Los Angeles, California, in the 1890s. 1860 Census, Ky., Jefferson, 5th Ward Louisville, 120; Louisville directories (1875–92); Amnesty Papers (M1003, Roll 25), Ky., Blanton Duncan, RG94, NA; *OR*, Ser. 1, Vol. 51, pt. 2: 66; Lewis Collins, *Collins' Historical Sketches of Kentucky. History of Kentucky*, rev. by Richard H. Collins (Louisville, 1877), 357.

2. John M. Schofield.

3. Pierre G.T. Beauregard.

4. Edward D. Townsend's letter of the previous day was in response to Duncan's of February 11, renewing the request for General Beauregard's papers. Townsend to Duncan, Feb. 16, 1869, Lets. Recd. (Main Ser.), File S-1521-1865 (M619, Roll 413), RG94, NA.

5. Although Beauregard had received one trunk, one box, and some books back in November 1866, he never received his papers which were retained and published in the *Official Records*. T. Harry Williams, *P.G.T. Beauregard: Napoleon in Gray* (Baton Rouge, 1955), 259. See also Beauregard to Johnson, Oct. 12, 1866, *Johnson Papers*, 11: 343–44.

From J. Rutherford Worster

Charleston Ill.   Feb. 17. 1869.

The inclosed papers—herewith transmitted, received from the War Dept. some weeks since,[1] I beg to lay before you. My son[2] was a Serjeant Major in 3rd. Illinois Cavalry and was killed at the Battle of Pea Ridge; he left a widow and two children,[3] whose support naturally devolved on me. The widow died, over a year ago and one of the children a little previous; her last request was that the remains of her brave husband might be buried beside her and her child; and to carry out this wish, is my present object, if the papers can be renewed and the same facilities granted as before proffered.[4]

The reason I did not avail myself of the kind consideration of the Govt. at that time, was because the country was infested with Bushwhackers and cuthroats and the probabilities were vastly preponderant of disaster for the undertaking.[5] It would hardly strengthen my application, were I to say I never called upon by the Govt. for one Dollar for any services of mine and have been volunteer Surgeon; was sent up to the army in front of Richmond with incendiary shells, &c and many others I might name. I therefore would most respectfully ask the President to renew the documents and from any funds he can appropriate furnish the means to accomplish the object.

I beg to state that the papers, from the War Dept. ordering Gen Halleck, to give me every facility for recovering the body of my son, is mislaid, among papers at Washington but was substantially as here represented.[6]

J. Rutherford Worster

Please address me at Charleston, Ill. for 30 days.

ALS, DNA-RG107, Lets. Recd., Executive (M494, Roll 109).

1. The "enclosed papers" were apparently letters from Congressman Cornelius L.L. Leary of Maryland, Sen. James R. Doolittle, and Elisha Whittelsey of the Treasury Department, written to Edwin M. Stanton or Abraham Lincoln in March or April 1862, requesting that Worster be given transportation to retrieve his son's body. Lets. Recd., Executive (M494, Roll 109), RG107, NA.

2. James W. Worster (c1831–1862) enrolled as a private in the 3rd Ill. Cav. in September 1861. On March 7, 1862, he was shot during the Battle of Pea Ridge, Arkansas. CSR, James W. Worster, RG94, NA.

3. Martha E. Tucker (c1837–1867) married James W. Worster in October 1857 at Rock Island, Illinois. The children were Victoria J.K. (1860–fl1876) and Adale Worster (1861–c1866). Pension Records, Victoria Worster, RG15, NA.

4. Apparently he had been given a railroad pass and orders to the military to facilitate his mission. J. Rutherford Worster to John M. Schofield, Jan. 5, 1869, Lets. Recd., Executive (M494, Roll 109), RG107, NA.

5. In addition, General Carr, commanding in the area at the time, thought that it would require a flag of truce to get to the body. CSR, James W. Worster, RG15, NA.

6. The War Department had already told Worster that there was no longer any appropriation available to pay the expenses of Worster's transportation to Arkansas. E. Schriver to Worster, Jan. 4, 1869, Lets. Recd., Executive (M494, Roll 109), RG107, NA.

From Charles Davis[1]

Philadelphia Penna.   Feb. 18th 1869

Dear Sir,

As you will retire from office in a very few days, permit me, as one of the many thousands who have stood by you and sustained your Official Course, to add a parting tribute to your able and Constitutional administration of the laws of our government. You must be fully aware that for your manly defence of our Constitution and the holding sacred the land-marks of the laws, as taught by the noble and illustrious men of this Country, you have made, as might be naturally expected under our modern Republicanism, many, very many enemies. But, honored President, you have, in the minds of the good men of the Nation, and the true men, triumphed over all your enemies, and can proudly say, at your retirement, that you have done not only well, but nobly. As a citizen, and an admirer of your bold and rightful course, I would that every right-minded citizen of the United States would, on the 4th day of March next, rise up, assert his manhood, and extend to you his hand in token of your Constitutional course as President of a great people. But I am afraid that many a good man whose heart would be more outspoken than his tongue, is kept down by a political prejudice which sooner or later will be the curse of this people, and therefore whilst many a man's heart would accord to you all honesty and integrity of purpose, his tongue refuses to give utterance to his thoughts and a neighborhood pride will stay the hand which else would be extended.

It has always been my pleasure to defend you as the President of the Nation, and now that you will so soon retire, to make room for another to succeed you in the arduous and trying duties of your Office, I cannot refrain from addressing you these simple lines.

I know you will depart from the scenes of your thousand trials, with the prayers and kind wishes of thousands of the American people. Many are wrong, even radically, but still a large class of citizens are well disposed, and such will do you full justice.

Accept, honored President, these simple expressions of gratitude.

Charles Davis
345 North 6th Street

ALS, DLC-JP.
1. Davis (1828–*f*1901), a former merchant and now a lawyer, actually resided in Mont-

gomery County, Pennsylvania. But for decades he maintained a law office in Philadelphia. Ellwood Roberts, ed., *Biographical Annals of Montgomery County, Pennsylvania* (2 vols., New York, 1904), 1: 72; Philadelphia directories (1869–1901).

From William H. Hooper[1]

Washington, February 18 1869

Sir

Please accept the package of dried Peaches which I have instructed the expressman to deliver to you. They reached here yesterday from home and I trust may prove as acceptable to your taste as the like have proven to us in our far off Mountain home.

W H Hooper

ALS, DLC-JP.
1. Hooper (1813–1882), a merchant and, eventually, banker, moved to Utah in 1850, where he was territorial secretary (1857–58) and delegate to Congress (1859–61, 1865–73). *BDUSC.*

From William Kennedy[1]

Washington   Feb 18th 1869

Dear Sir;

Allow me to call your attention to some of the acts of the present Sec'ty of the Interior[2] who has brought the only odium of corruption that has sullied the term of your Administration. For whatever faults your enemies may find with you, they cannot put the blot of corruption or dishonesty on your official character. You were right in your *first* conception of this man when you expressed some doubts of him (privately) soon after you made him a Cabinet officer; as he forced on you that reprobate and corrupt rascal Huestis[3] as Warden of the Jail who wronged friends of yours, who were tried friends of yours, of years and years standing; friends who had befriended members of your family, and did every thing to reclaim and Sheild the faults of such from the public. Friends who were the first to prevent and to *point out to you the plot of manufactors testimony to impeach* you, such friends of yours this Sec't. of Interior and Huestis took pleasure in doing injustice to, and the name of these men will sink into infamy and oblivion. But your friends believe tho you had bad men about you still you will get return to the U.S. Capitol in triumph over all your enemies and traducers, Is the sincere wish of those who know and respect you.

William Kennedy

ALS, DLC-JP.

1. There were several William Kennedys in Washington, D.C., during the period. Perhaps he was the Irish native (c1832–f1878) who was a liquor dealer and eventual restaurant owner. 1870 Census, D.C., Washington, 2nd Ward, 344; Washington, D.C., directories (1866–79).

2. Orville H. Browning.

3. William H. Huestis had just been indicted on more charges of misconduct in office. *Washington Evening Star*, Feb. 18, 1869. For background on Huestis, see Isaac Newton to Johnson, Sept. 2, 1868.

From John E. Tuel[1]

New York, Febry 18, '69

Dear Sir:

I write to state that Mr. Smythe did not make the appointment which you requested,[2] and that after many disappointments I withdrew it yesterday. I write also to thank you for your kind interest in the matter, and to express my hopes for your future prosperity and happiness.

J. E. Tuel

ALS, DLC-JP.

1. Tuel (f1877), who had been in the general land office in the 1840s, wrote novels and historical works. He also found employment as an editor and later a correspondent. *U.S. Off. Reg.* (1843); Albert Johannsen, *The House of Beadle and Adams* (2 vols., Norman, Okla., 1950), 2: 274; Washington, D.C., directories (1878).

2. Nothing has been found regarding Tuel's appointment to the New York customhouse.

From William W. Wales

New York   Feb. 18, 1869

Dear Sir:

Your and my friend, Thayer,[1] has a brother,[2] a rail road man, now in charge of one of the most important roads in the North West, out of Chicago; and as he has seen through the papers that Gen. Barnes,[3] Pacific Rail Road Commissioner is dead, he thought you might perhaps consent to give the place to his brother. I therefore write you by his desire, with the expectation of seeing you shortly. If it suits you to hold it open until my next visit to Washington,—if you can not promptly appoint Mr Thayer—I will be prepared to answer any inquiries in the case.[4] It might be a graceful recognition of his many defenses of your policy. His brother's name is Adin Thayer, his references high in the profession. His address, "Hoosick Falls N. York."

Wm. Wales

ALS, DLC-JP.

1. Probably James S. Thayer.

2. Adin Thayer, Jr. (*fl*1870) was a purchasing agent for the Chicago and North West Railroad, as well as a farmer and breeder of sheep and cattle. *Gazeteer and Business Directory of Rensselaer County, N.Y., for 1870–71* (Syracuse, 1870), 156; Chicago directories (1869–70).

3. James Barnes.

4. Lt. Col. Robert S. Williamson had already been appointed to the commission. Collis P. Huntington to Johnson, Jan. 20, 1869, Johnson Papers, LC; Orville H. Browning to John M. Schofield, Jan. 14, 1869, Lets. Recd. (Main Ser.), File I-6-1869 (M619, Roll 661), RG94, NA.

From John F. Coyle

New Orleans La   Feby 19. 1869.

On consultation with our friends here I find the desire for the removal of Woolfley[1] is universal. He is most obnoxious to every friend here and his complicity in the doings of the whiskey ring is in my hands and therefore justifies his removal. I haven't seen any friend of yours here but what urges this man's removal. I would esteem it a personal favor, from all I learn here for this action. The Gentleman recommended by every friend you have here is Genl. McMillen[2] who served with distinction during the War. He is a through republican and consequently if THEY refuse to CONFIRM him they add to the troubles already brewing in the "Camp of the Enemy." Mr. Kellogg[3] will recommend most earnestly Genl. McMillen and, I presume Mr McCulloch will recommend him, and they say he can be confirmed—failing to do so it only renders *them* disatisfied. I most earnestly recommend this action to your Excellency, and the action will give satisfaction to the many friends you have here.[4] The difficulty of agreeing upon Genl. Steedman's successor[5] is so great that I cannot really make a decision between the numberless candidates at this time.

John F. Coyle

ALS, DLC-JP.

1. Lewis Wolfley, assessor of internal revenue for the First District of Louisiana.

2. William L. McMillen (1829–1902), an Ohio physician, was colonel of the 95th Ohio Inf. and eventually brevetted brigadier and major general. He became a cotton planter and politician in Louisiana, serving in the state senate (1870–72) and attempting to serve in the U.S. Senate (1872–73) but was not allowed to take his seat. He held several other Louisiana state offices. Paul E. Steiner, *Physician-Generals in the Civil War: A Study in Nineteenth Mid-Century American Medicine* (Springfield, Ill., 1966), 78–80.

3. William P. Kellogg.

4. McMillen was not nominated.

5. James B. Steedman had resigned his post as collector of internal revenue for the First District of Louisiana. Johnson had already nominated three candidates without success. Ser. 6B, Vol. 4: 203–4, Johnson Papers, LC.

From James B. Craig[1]

New York   Feb 19, 1869.

May I ask of you the favor to delay action in regard to the copper bill until I can see you tomorrow.

James B Craig

Tel, DLC-JP.

1. Craig (c1834–1879) was a New York City lawyer, active in Democratic party politics, and in the 1870s involved in mining operations in Colorado. *New York Times*, Oct. 30, 1879.

From Jonas R. McClintock

Pittsburgh   Feby. 19th 1869

Dear Sir,

I turn from the joy's of the family circle, so auspiciously completed by the return of my eldest son,[1] whom your Executive favor and fatherly sympathies snatched from the cruel and not objectless "findings" of a "military court," to thank you, deeply thank you, for the beneficent results of your timely interference.[2]

His presence and frank interchange of sentiment, readily satisfied me that a Father's alarm, had tended to greatly magnify the demorilization of the camp & city, and led me in my candid rehearsal to your Excellency to give it too high a coloring.

His fondness for the dissipations of the new field in which his lot had been cast, proves less reckless than I had anticipated.

I knew his genial qualities, and convivial dispostion, and felt that any dangerous indulgence in "*play*", could only occur in moments of unbridled excitement brought about by others, and I was, even in my moments of deepest sorrow, reluctant to believe, that under any circumstances he would permit *it* to poach on the funds of the Government.

I was in error both as to the extent of indulgence in drink & *play*—not continuous, but at varied intervals, the *latter* following the former, without going beyond his *pay & private means* with the certainty of cause and effect—thus presenting a more encouraging hope for the future.

He freely admits a carelessness, which in a public officer inflicts great injustice on both the Officer and the Country, arising from an occasional reaching for pleasure and devolving duties on subordinates, (————) for which he deserves punishment, equal to not greater than the offence.

The restraint of his "personal liberty["] for more than three months, and the repayment of the parties who so cheerfully assumed *his liabilities* which he intends to make the first great task of his future, his sad experience teaches, should prove ample reparation and punishment for the wrong committed.

In the last interview granted me, in "commuting the sentence to twelve months suspension," you referred to the "record" of sentences, to show the frequency of Executive interference in shortening the time of suspensions, and *remitting it entirely.*

I fear to withhold appeal to further Executive leniency for the incoming Administration, in view of *my* political status since Feby. 1866,[3] and therefore at this late hour, beg you Mr. President to *remit the balance of his sentence*, as *commuted* on the *9th of Jany. with permission to delay joining his Regiment for 60 or 90 day's.*

This delay, will afford time for me in conjunction with my Son, Major McClintock, after the receipt of a copy of the minutes of the "Court" by which he was tried, not only to ascertain how far it is a true record, but to make a searching investigation into the alleged surreptitious taking of the Draft or check for *Five thousand five Hundred dollars*, and the clear and undoubted forgery of a check drawn to his own order (as was the custom) for Two thousand dollars, in all $7,500, which latter he alleges he never issued, & which is neither noted in check book margin or accounts.

I am rejoiced to be able to assure you, in the language of a high toned Christian gentleman—and soldier of the Army of the Platte, in speaking of my Son "His noble qualities are appreciated by all who know him. I have yet to hear the first one in the Regiment speak unkindly of him because of his Conduct."

Should you after glancing over the "statement marked A."[4] accompanying this letter, find it in your official & Fathers-heart to grant my request, I will when the time for joining his Regt. has arrived accompany him thither, for the purposes named in the statement referred too. Whatever your decision Mr. President in this vital matter,[5] you will ever command the High regard & consideration of . . .

Jonas R. McClintock.

ALS, DLC-JP.

1. John McClintock (1842–1910), after serving briefly with Pennsylvania troops, became 1st lieutenant and later captain of the 14th U.S. Inf. (1861–66), after which he was transferred to the 18th Inf. and then the 36th Inf. He earned the brevets of captain and major. Powell, *Army List*, 462; Pension Records, Margaretta F. McClintock, RG15, NA.

2. In October 1868 McClintock had been court-martialed at Fort D. A. Russell, Wyoming Territory, for embezzling over $8,000 as well as "conduct unbecoming an officer and a gentleman." He was sentenced to be cashiered from the service, imprisoned for three years, and fined the amount of the embezzled money with imprisonment for up to an additional two years until the money was paid. When Johnson reviewed the sentence on January 9, 1869, he determined that because of the soldier's "previous good character" and "gallant services," as well as the fact that the money had already been repaid, McClintock's sentence should "be commuted to suspension from rank and pay" for a year. Lets. Recd. (Main Ser.), File M-127-1869 (M619, Roll 718), RG94, NA.

3. While it is not clear what political change McClintock may have made in February 1866, he was an open supporter of Johnson and his policy in March of that year. McClintock to Johnson, Mar. 26, 1866, Johnson Papers, LC.

4. Not found.

5. On February 28 Johnson referred this letter to the War Department asking that the rest of young McClintock's sentence be remitted. However, Grant declined to remit the penalty and John McClintock remained suspended for the entire year. Having been omitted from the army consolidation, he then awaited orders for nearly another year before he was honorably mustered out of the service on January 1, 1871. Pension Records, Margaretta F. McClintock, RG15, NA; Jonas R. McClintock to E. D. Townsend, Apr. 2, 1869, Lets. Recd. (Main Ser.), File M-431-1869 (M619, Roll 719), RG94, NA.

From Alex S. Wilson[1]

Montclair N.J.   Feb. 19th, 1869.

Since you have been in the office you now hold I have followed the course you have pursued, and it has met my entire approbation. Yours has been a term of hardships and trials such as no other President had, or probably ever will have again—a sturdy, upright, honest fight against all the elements set loose by war and fanatacism. For the

present state of the country no sane man will hold you or your administration responsible. I write this because I appreciate you as a
man and a statesman, and to let you see that there are many who
believe that had your policy of reconstruction and fair dealing been
carried out this country would have been in a more prosperous condition financially, and we would have had less of class and sectional
legislation which sooner or later will bring again war, with all its
horrors.

Alex S. Wilson

ALS, DLC-JP.
  1. Not identified.

From Senators and Representatives

Washington   Feb. 20 1869

The undersigned Senators & Representatives[1] respectfully submit
the accompanying article from the New York Tribune[2] with an earnest hope that the President will extend clemency to the subject
thereof irrespective of the legal aspects of the case & that he will
order his discharge at an early day.[3]

Pet, DNA-RG94, Amnesty Papers (M1003, Roll 73), Misc. Northern and Western States,
John C. Brain [sic].
  1. At least two dozen members of Congress signed this petition.
  2. The article contained a recent interview with John C. Braine, and contrasted his plight—
imprisoned without trial since 1866—with the release and pardon of such men as Jefferson
Davis, Alexander Stephens, and Raphael Semmes. New York Tribune, Feb. 20, 1869.
  3. Braine had been arrested and imprisoned for piracy and murder committed during the
war when he seized the ship, Cheasapeake, which was sailing from New York to Boston. Osten-
sibly, he was to be discharged from prison based upon the December 25 amnesty proclamation.
Petitions were sent to the President and visits made to the White House, all importuning in
behalf of Braine. By early March the U.S. district attorney for New York had entered a nolle
prosequi in the federal court, an action which secured Braine's immediate release. He died years
later, in 1906, in Tampa. New Orleans Picayune, Jan. 21, Feb. 16, 1869; New York World, Feb. 24,
26, 1869; Washington Evening Star, Mar. 3, 1869; Chattanooga Times, Dec. 9, 1906.

From William F. Switzler

Columbia, Mo.   Feb. 20, 1869.

Mr. President:
  Your telegram of 16th inst. is received.[1] Lieut. Payne has received

an order of Jan. 30th, from War Department notifying him of his reinstatement in the Army.[2] He has received no orders to report to his Regiment for duty and desires that such order be sent *at once.* You will greatly oblige me by having this done immediately.[3]

Wm. F. Switzler

ALS, DNA-RG94, Lets. Recd. (Main Ser.), File P-80-1869 (M619, Roll 734).

1. Not found.

2. Special Order No. 25 of January 30, 1869, discussed in J. Scott Payne to E. D. Townsend, Feb. 8, 1869, Lets. Recd. (Main Ser.), File P-80-1869 (M619, Roll 734), RG94, NA. For further information on Payne's situation, see J. Scott Payne to Johnson, Nov. 2, 1868.

3. Switzler had already telegraphed Johnson this request on the same day he wrote. However, Payne still received no orders, so he went to join his regiment without them. When he found that their headquarters were still in Washington, D.C., he went to the capital. Switzler to Johnson, Feb. 20, 1869, Johnson Papers, LC; Mary M. Payne to Johnson, Apr. 26, 1869. See also J. Scott Payne to Johnson, Mar. 5, 1869.

From Sarah Y. Jackson [1]
Private

Hermitage   Feb 21st 1869

Dear Sir

You may perhaps consider the liberty I now take as presumption perhaps folly—but whatever it may be you must please forgive. I have always considered you a friend, and trust *now* you will have patience with me and hear me.

The Legislature of this State has again before them a bill for the sale of the Hermitage, and my removal from my dear old home. It has passed in the House and has passed a second reading in the Senate.[2] I have no doubt it will become a law—and I shall be thrown upon the world in my old age—debilitated and in poverty. I have not *one cent* either in property or in money. My only dependence has been the rent of the land here, which has made me a scanty subsistance. I ask your advice. You frequently gave it to my dear husband[3] and I beg you will not with hold it from me. I own the furniture. Most of it belonged to Gen Jackson my affectionate father. I also have many relics, all valued by me as having been presented to me by him, with all of which I shall be compelled to part, to be scattered singly over the country—perhaps for not one half their value. My poverty will make it necessary for me to sell them. My dear father Gen. Jackson made provision for me in his will, and expressed a hope that I would not be disturbed in my right, but of this dependence I have been deprived by the war, and as I before stated I have not one dollar I can call my own. Dear Sir can you instruct me, how shall I commence or how shall I accomplish this heartrending undertaking—all my happiness as well as many of my sorrows I have experienced here in this loved home, and I had hoped to have been permitted to have passed the remnant of a life almost spent, undisturbed, but it is not to be so.

I have made all my arrangements for the coming year—sowed wheat—employed hands &c and was not aware until a few days since that I was to be removed. I have received no notice as yet, but suppose I shall. What shall I do? Where shall I go? What steps shall I take? I cannot dig—and to beg I am ashamed.

My lamented father had many friends, where are they? Can you not dear sir among them find some who will step forward and aid me in this dreadful emergency.[4]

Excuse me for troubling you—but my heart is so full and my sorrows so very trying—to whom can I apply unless to one who has expressed kindness and sympathy in days that are passed, and who I hope and trust still remembers as a sincere friend . . .

Sarah Jackson

ALS, DLC-JP.

1. Jackson (1805–1887), a native of Philadelphia, had lived at the Hermitage since the early 1830s. She and her husband, Andrew Jackson, Jr., had five children, two of whom died as infants. Harold D. Moser et al., eds., *The Papers of Andrew Jackson. Guide and Index to the Microfilm Editions* (Wilmington, Del., 1987), xxix; Linda Bennett Galloway, "Andrew Jackson, Junior," *THQ*, 9 (1950), 215–16, 306–7.

2. As early as November 1866, Governor Brownlow had recommended to the legislature that the Hermitage property, owned by the state, be sold. In the fall of 1867 legislation providing for the sale of the Hermitage began making its way through the General Assembly. It was initiated in the house and eventually emerged as House Bill No. 506 in February 1868; the following month it passed the house on the third reading and was sent over to the senate. That body adjourned, however, shortly after passing the bill on first reading. The state senate took up the bill again in the fall of 1868 and continued wrestling with it in early 1869. In fact, the day prior to Sarah Jackson's letter, the senate heard a report from the Judiciary Committee about the bill. On February 26, the senate finally rejected House Bill No. 506, thereby leaving the Jackson family at the Hermitage. Brownlow's Legislative Message, Nov. 15, 1866, in White et al., *Messages of Govs.*, 5: 536; *House Journal, 35th General Assembly, 1867–68* (Nashville, 1868), 106, 662, 668, 679–80; *Senate Journal, 35th General Assembly, 1867–68* (Nashville, 1868), 468; Ibid., *1868–69*, 11, 204, 205, 283–84, 291, 298–99, 315–16. See also Sarah Y. Jackson to W. A. Scott, Mar. 23, 1869, CU-BANC.

3. Andrew Jackson, Jr. (1808–1865), the adopted son of President Jackson, married Sarah Yorke in 1831. He died at the Hermitage in 1865 as a result of an accidental gunshot wound. Moser et al., *Guide and Index*, xxix; Galloway, "Jackson, Junior," 216, 342–43.

4. Despite the fact that Francis P. Blair appended a note to Sarah Jackson's letter urging involvement by Johnson, he apparently did not take any action. The President curiously did

draft a message to be forwarded to the U.S. House and Senate concerning the disposition of the Hermitage. He urged Congress to accept the earlier offer of the property by the state of Tennessee to the U.S. government. Johnson suggested several possible uses of the property: a cemetery for Union soldiers, an asylum for former soldiers, or even a home for veterans. The President indicated in his draft message that he was responding to "an appeal." There seems to be no evidence that he actually sent this message to Congress and, because of the dates of the documents, there seems to be no connection between his proposed message and the February 21 letter from Sarah Jackson. Yet, he did receive "an appeal" from someone. See Johnson to House and Senate, Feb. 12, 1869, Ser. 5A, Johnson Papers, LC.

From Samuel F. Cary

Washington, D.C., Feb 22nd. 1869.

Sir

At the request of William Tilden Esqr[1] one of the first members of the Cincinnati Bar I write you in regard to the men who sign a paper to be presented to you in behalf of E A. Smith.[2] I know nothing of the merits of the case but I am quite certain that the men who have signed his paper would not have done so in a case without merit. The Hon Edward Woodruff[3] has had an enviable reputation as a Lawyer and Judge in Cincinnati for more than thirty years. Wm B. Caldwell[4] is a distinguished lawyer & has been chief Justice of Ohio, which he resigned. He is over cautious about signing papers of any kind. Indeed I can assure you that the signatures to Smith's papers are those of the first men of Cincinnati irrespective of political party.

S. F. Cary

ALS, DNA-RG94, Lets. Recd. (Main Ser.), File P-191-1869 (M619, Roll 734).

1. In the early 1860s Tilden (d. 1873) had been a law partner of William B. Caldwell, and later in the decade with Edward Woodruff. Tilden became probate judge in 1873, but died in office. *Cincinnati Enquirer*, Aug. 15, 1873; Henry A. and Kate B. Ford, *History of Hamilton County, Ohio* (Cleveland, 1881), 240; Cincinnati directories (1859–69).

2. Smith (*fl*1870) operated livery stables in Cincinnati and provided horses for the army. In 1862 he was convicted by a court-martial of defrauding the government; he paid a $10,000 fine. Another man, C. W. Hall, was convicted as well, but his fine was remitted. Smith's counsel and supporters were attempting to obtain repayment of the money. There is no evidence that they were successful. Lets. Recd. (Main Ser.), File P-191-1869 (M619, Roll 734), RG94, NA; Cincinnati directories (1861–70).

3. Woodruff (*c*1807–*fl*1881), a judge of the probate and common pleas courts, had been practicing law since 1831. Ibid. (1861–81); 1850 Census, Ohio, Hamilton, 5th Ward, Cincinnati, 56th Dist., 424; (1860), Cincinnati, 20; Ford, *History of Cincinnati*, 316, 317.

4. A former law partner of Samuel F. Cary, Caldwell (1808–1876) had been on the common pleas court before moving to the state supreme court in 1849. After resigning in 1854, he returned to private law practice. *NCAB*, 7: 545.

From Louis Schade

Washington D.C.   Febr. 22. 1869.

Sir

At the request of the widow[1] and orphan children of the late Captain Henry Wirz, I most respectfully ask you to give an order to deliver to me the remains of the Captain,[2] now buried at the Arsenal in this city, for the purpose of having them interred in sacred ground.[3]

Louis Schade

ALS, DNA-RG94, Lets. Recd. (Main Ser.), File S-112-1869 (M619, Roll 746).

1. Wirz's second wife, Elizabeth (b. c1824), at this time a resident of Trigg County, Kentucky, had several daughters. 1860 Census, La., Madison, 285; Elizabeth Wirz to Schade, Feb. 16, 1869, Lets. Recd. (Main Ser.), File S-112-1869 (M619, Roll 746), RG94, NA; *Lousiville Courier-Journal*, Feb. 18, 1869; *Washington Evening Star*, Feb. 13, 1869.

2. Schade, who had been Wirz's defense counsel, was acting on behalf of Wirz's family members who could not afford to come to Washington themselves. Ibid.

3. On February 23, Johnson ordered Wirz's body to be turned over to Schade and the latter, with an undertaker, took possession on February 24. Endorsement, Schade to Johnson, Feb. 22, 1869; R. M. Hill to E. D. Townsend, Feb. 25, 1869, Lets. Recd. (Main Ser.), File S-112-1869 (M619, Roll 746), RG94, NA; *Washington Evening Star*, Feb. 24, 25, 1869. For Wirz's reburial, see Schade to Johnson, Feb. 26, 1869.

Veto of Copper Bill

WASHINGTON, D.C., *February 22, 1869.*

To the House of Representatives:

The accompanying bill,[1] entitled "An act regulating the duties on imported copper and copper ores," is, for the following reasons, returned, without my approval, to the House of Representatives, in which branch of Congress it originated.

Its immediate effect will be to diminish the public receipts, for the object of the bill can not be accomplished without seriously affecting the importation of copper and copper ores, from which a considerable revenue is at present derived. While thus impairing the resources of the Government, it imposes an additional tax upon an already overburdened people, who should not be further impoverished that monopolies may be fostered and corporations enriched.

It is represented—and the declaration seems to be sustained by evidence—that the duties for which this bill provides are nearly or quite sufficient to prohibit the importation of certain foreign ores of copper. Its enactment, therefore, will prove detrimental to the shipping interests of the nation, and at the same time destroy the business, for many years successfully established, of smelting home ores in connection with a smaller amount of the imported articles. This business, it is credibly asserted, has heretofore yielded the larger share of the copper production of the country, and thus the industry which this legislation is designed to encourage is actually less than that which will be destroyed by the passage of this bill.

It seems also to be evident that the effect of this measure will be to enhance by 70 per cent the cost of blue vitriol—an article extensively used in dyeing and in the manufacture of printed and colored cloths. To produce such an augmentation in the price of this commodity will be to discriminate against other great branches of domestic industry, and by increasing their cost to expose them most unfairly to the effects of foreign competition. Legislation can neither be wise nor just which seeks the welfare of a single interest at the expense and to the injury of many and varied interests at least equally important and equally deserving the consideration of Congress. Indeed, it is difficult to find any reason which will justify the interference of Government with any legitimate industry, except so far as may be rendered necessary by the requirements of the revenue. As has already been stated, however, the legislative intervention proposed in the present instance will diminish, not increase, the public receipts.

The enactment of such a law is urged as necessary for the relief of certain mining interests upon Lake Superior, which, it is alleged, are in a greatly depressed condition, and can only be sustained by an enhancement of the price of copper. If this result should follow the passage of the bill, a tax for the exclusive benefit of a single class would be imposed upon the consumers of copper throughout the entire country, not warranted by any need of the Government, and the avails of which would not in any degree find their way into the Treasury of the nation. If the miners of Lake Superior are in a condition of want, it can not be justly affirmed that the Government should extend charity to them in preference to those of its citizens who in other portions of the country suffer in like manner from destitution. Least of all should the endeavor to aid them be based upon a method so uncertain and indirect as that contemplated by the bill, and which, moreover, proposes to continue the exercise of its benefaction through an indefinite period of years. It is, besides, reasonable to hope that positive suffering from want, if it really exists, will prove but temporary in a region where agricultural labor is so much in demand and so well compensated. A careful examination of the subject appears to show that the present low price of copper, which alone has induced any depression the mining interests of Lake Superior may have recently experienced, is due to causes which it is wholly impolitic, if not impracticable, to contravene by legislation. These causes are, in the main, an increase in the general supply of copper, owing to the discovery and working of remarkably productive mines and to a coincident restriction in the consumption and use of copper by the substitution of other and cheaper metals for industrial purposes. It is now sought to resist by artificial means the action of natural laws; to place the people of the United States, in respect to the enjoyment and use of an essential commodity, upon a different basis from other nations, and especially to compensate certain private and sectional interests for the changes and losses which are always incident to industrial progress.

Although providing for an increase of duties, the proposed law does not even come within the range of protection, in the fair acceptation of the term. It does not look to the fostering of a young and feeble interest with a view to the ultimate attainment of strength and the capacity of self-support. It appears to assume that the present inability for successful production is inherent and permanent, and is more likely to increase than to be gradually overcome; yet in spite of this it proposes, by the exercise of the lawmaking power, to sustain that interest and to impose it in hopeless perpetuity as a tax upon the competent and beneficent industries of the country.

The true method for the mining interests of Lake Superior to obtain relief, if relief is needed, is to endeavor to make their great natural resources fully available by reducing the cost of production. Special or class legislation can not remedy the evils which this bill is designed to meet. They can only be overcome by laws which will effect a wise, honest, and economical administration of the Government, a reestablishment of the specie standard of value, and an early adjustment of our system of State, municipal, and national taxation (especially the latter) upon the fundamental principle that all taxes, whether collected under the internal revenue or under a tariff, shall interfere as little as possible with the productive energies of the people.

The bill is therefore returned, in the belief that the true interests of the Government and of the people require that it should not become a law.[2]

ANDREW JOHNSON.

Richardson, *Messages*, 6: 705–7.

1. For text of the bill, see *Congressional Globe*, 40 Cong., 3 Sess., Appendix, p. 304. A favorable opinion of the bill can be found in Henry R. Linderman to Johnson, Feb. 13, 1869, while opposition views are voiced in Charles J.W. Gwinn to Johnson, Dec. 19, 1868, and other documents cited in the notes accompanying the Gwinn letter.

2. The House apparently overrode the veto on the following day, and the Senate did likewise on the 24th, the bill becoming law on that day. *Congressional Globe*, 40 Cong., 3 Sess., pp. 1489, 1509.

From William L. Baldwin[1]

CONFIDENTIAL

Reedsburg Sauk Co. Wisconsin
February 23d 1869

Dr Sir & Bro—

As you are about retiring from the laborious duties of official life will you condescend from your exalted position to perform an act of "Masonic Charity" & give ear to the appeal of a "Craftsman" in distress?

On account of failing health I find that it is necessary I should seek a residence in a tropical country but have not the means to defray such an expense. If an appointment to some official position in one of the Central or South American ports could be granted (or if no vacancies exist in those ports then any point where the climate is mild & warm) it would be all I could desire as it would afford sufficient compensation to materially assist in defraying the expense of such foreign residence.

Enclosed I forward the "demit" from my "Lodge" as the best recommend I am in possession of. Within it is combined the united opinion & recommendation of 42 masonic brethren composing the entire membership of the Lodge & which I desire to have returned to me.

My age is 33 & by occupation am an attorney which business I have followed for several years until poor health compels me to give it up for the present. If you can assist me in the manner I have referred to you may be assured that the favor will not be conferred on an unworthy Bro & the recollection thereof when you pass off the "level of time" will tend to assure your hope in the hour of dissolution. Hoping that you will regard this as strictly confidential . . .[2]

Wm. L Baldwin

Post office address Reedsburg Sauk Co Wis.

ALS, DNA-RG59, Lets. of Appl. and Recomm., 1861–69 (M650, Roll 3), Wm. L. Baldwin.
    1. Not identified.
    2. Baldwin did not receive any office, but a notation on the letter indicates that his certificate of recommendation was returned to him.

From James Edmonston

New Orleans, Febry 23rd 1869

Mr. President;

I pray you accept my sincere acknowledgement for the kindly favor you have been pleased to extend to me, by the appointment you have conferred on me; as an Internal Revenue Officer of the 1st District of La.[1]

Permit me Mr. President to express to you the very great pleasure it will ever afford me, to endeavor to merit a continuance of your friendly interest on my behalf. Upon retiring from office you will bear with you the devoted allegiance of every true American as well as the never fading laurels which you have gallantly won in your intrepid defence of the rights of man, and in your Heroic struggle to preserve the constitution of your country.

J. Edmonston

LS, DLC-JP.
    1. Verification of Edmonston's appointment has not been found.

From Sidney Homer[1]

Boston (Mass)   Febry 23d 1869.

Sir

Will you permit one who has thought upon the subject, to thank you for your veto of the Copper bill.

Your reasons are given in a very clear & comprehensive manner, & must be satisfactory to all who can bring unbiased thought to the subject.

This idea of protection to American industry is a mistaken one— it is only a diversion of industry from one pursuit to another—there is no surplus of industry or skill demanding employment—the difficulty, if any, is in its scarcity—& it is a mistaken philanthropy or wisdom to tempt people to work under ground—when they can do well above ground—from agriculture to mining is a poor exchange, & even to a blast furnace, or a Cotton Mill is no improvement.

These changes will come fast enough from natural causes, without the aid of protection.

Goverment as such, has nothing to say, as to the pursuit in which my labour or capital is employed—provided it is moral & healthful—its province is, to collect revenue—which can only be done on foreign goods through importations.

Our return to specie payment is plain—to call in & destroy the paper money—fund them in to 10/40s whenever & as fast as the public desire it, and green backs & specie will soon be at par.

Sidney Homer

ALS, DLC-JP.
  1. Homer had been in the importing business since the late 1840s. Boston directories (1849–69).

From William J. Murphy [1]

New York. Feb 23rd 1869.

Sir,

Myself and associates have in the course of completion a Pilot Boat of the largest class, for this harbor and we desire to name it after you as a slight token of our esteem for you for your appreciation of your oath of office and your firm Defense of that bulwark of our beloved Country "Its Constitution."

Belonging as we do to a body of men Democratic in principle and action many of us have watched your political career as Senator, Governor & president, with gratification and pride.

As New York is the Depot of Emmigration to the major part of those seeking a future home in this our native land, so will the name of "Andrew Johnson" be to them a reminder of that "Constitution" which made this country what it is, and "if *preserved*" what it will be in future years.

I served as a "Drummer boy" during the Mexican War in the 1st regt. N.Y. Vols and from the assault on Fort Sumpter to the close of the rebellion under the flag of our glorious United States.

Wm. J Murphy
N. W. Corner of 76th st & 3rd av.

P.S. I am a brother of state Senator Murphy,[2] and should be pleased at any time to have you during pleasant weather accompany us upon a cruize.

ALS, DLC-JP.

1. Murphy (*c*1832–*fl*1882) had also been an ordinary seaman in the U.S. Navy (1848–49) and private, Company A, 4th N.Y. Inf. (1861). For this latter service he vainly sought a pension. Pension Records, William J. Murphy, RG15, NA.

2. John McLeod Murphy (1827–1871), a civil engineer, served as a junior officer in the U.S. Navy (1841–52, 1863–64), state senator (1860–61), and colonel of the 15th N.Y. Engineers (1861–62). He also was either author or co-author of a number of publications, mainly related to nautical subjects. Ibid.; *Appleton's Cyclopaedia*; *NUC*.

From Joseph W. Pomfrey[1]

Cincinnati, Feb 23 1869

My Dear Sir:

Would you be kind enough to favor me with an autograph letter of yours ere you retire from the Executive Department of our Goverment. Allow me although an humble citizen of the Republic to congratulate you upon the honest & dignified manner in which you have conducted the affairs of a great nation through the perilous conflicts of the last four years. The future historian if truthful will accord to you the honor of saving from utter ruin one of the best Republics the sun ever shone upon. Had it not been my Dear Sir for you & your noble efforts since your induction in office I fear that our Republic would now be numbered among the things that were. The people as a whole will never know the value of the services that you have rendered them. You have shown yourself both a patriot & statesman & would to God we had a few more such men as you at the head of affairs. They would soon bring order out of chaos & unite all sections in the bonds of fraternal affection. Upon your retirement— from the Executive Department of the Goverment—you cary with you my best wishes for your future welfare. Allow me once more to congratulate you on the patriotism & fidelity which you have displayed during your Administration in managing & placing upon a firm basis the great American Republic. I am not the only one by thousands who feel as I do toward you. Hoping that may live long to enjoy the fruits of your labors & when summoned by the Grim Angel death you may be welcomed to your Fathers house with the exclamation "Well done thou good & faithful servant."[2]

J. W Pomfret[*sic*]

Address me as follows: J. W. Pomfret Hamersville, Brown Co., Ohio.

ALS, DLC-JP.

1. Although the writer of this letter *appears* to have signed his name, "Pomfret," a compari-

son of his handwriting with an earlier 1866 letter of his has convinced us that the surname is actually "Promfey." Moreover, we have been able to track a Joseph W. *Pomfrey* in southern Ohio and northern Kentucky but have not been able to locate a Promfret. We thus believe that Pomfrey (*c*1840–*fl*1900), a Virginia native, a newspaperman and publisher primarily in Covington, Kentucky (although he gives a Brown County, Ohio, address in this letter), is the correct person. 1870 Census, Ky., Kenton, Covington, 7th Ward, 61; (1900), 2nd Ward, E Prec., 91st Enum. Dist., B3. See Pomfrey to Johnson, Oct. 2, 1866, Johnson Papers, LC.

2. From Matt. 25:21 and 25:23.

From Nelson Tift[1]

Washington, D.C.   Feb 23, 1869.

Dear Sir

I send enclosed a pamphlet copy of my statement[2] to the Reconstruction committee relative to the case of Georgia noww under consideration by congress beleiving that you feel a deep interest in the welfare of the state & that you will in the future as you have done in the past use your influence for her protection.

I desire personally & in the name of the people of Georgia to thank you for your patriotic efforts to maintain the Constitution & the rights & interests of the people. History will take care of your reputation. May God's blessing remain with you & yours.

Nelson Tift

ALS, DLC-JP.

1. Tift (1810–1891) was a prominent businessman in Albany, Georgia, and for a time editor and publisher of the local newspaper. In the antebellum period he served several terms in the state legislature. He was elected to the U.S. House in 1868 when Georgia was readmitted as a state. His tenure was brief, July 1868 to March 1869. Afterwards he engaged in numerous business ventures. *BDUSC.*

2. Pamphlet not found enclosed. His statement to the House Reconstruction Committee may be conveniently found in the *National Intelligencer*, February 22, 1869. His remarks dealt with, among other things, the claim about ineligible legislators in the Georgia assembly and the question over the denial of the right of blacks to hold office in Georgia.

From Mrs. Perez Dickinson Gates[1]

No. 320, Cumberland Street,   Brooklyn, N.Y.

February 26th 1869.

Would confer a great pleasure, and Honour upon one of his warmest and most ardent political admirers if His Excellency would favour her with his Autograph before retiring from Office.

That your Excellency may understand the reason why the favour is solicited, I will briefly state: I should deem it a great privilege to have the honour of placing your Excellency's Autograph aside of Jefferson's and Jackson's thereby forming a Trinity with the Three Illustrious J's.

The dignity and wisdom with which your Excellency has honoured the office of State, has been the only redeeming Light of the Administration,—Reminding us of That bright Constellation which illumed the political firmament—Andrew Jackson—The man who, like your Excellency, dared to brave the spleen of the ruthless traitors to our sacred Constitution—and have a Just will of his own.

That your Excellency may feel more favourable disposed to grant the request I will introduce myself—Mrs. Perez D. Gates—widow of the late Perez Dickinson Gates[2]—nephew of Perez Dickinson Esqr. Your Excellency's personal friend, of Knoxville Tenn.

Mrs. P D. Gates.

ALS, DLC-JP.
1. Not further identified.
2. Gates presumably was the son of Dickinson's sister, Electra, and her husband Horace Gates, who were married in 1815. He is not otherwise identified. See Reginald Foster, *Foster Genealogy* (Chicago, 1899), 546.

From Joseph Holt

War Department   Bureau of Mily. Justice
Feby 26. 1869.

To the President:

The petition for the pardon of Thomas Jenkins,[1] now confined in the Penitentiary at Jackson, Miss., is respectfully returned with the following report.

Jenkins was convicted by a Military Commission at Vicksburg, Miss., in Oct. last, of "Assault with intent to Kill," and sentenced to be confined in the Penitentiary for the period of three years.

The proceedings and sentence were approved and confirmed by Bt. Major Gen. Gillem, commanding the Fourth Military District.

It is now represented by the petitioners in his favor, that his conviction was procured through perjured testimony, and three affidavits are submitted as a basis of impeachment of the testimony. These affidavits are *ex parte*, and fail to make out the point sought to be established.

The record of Jenkins' trial has been carefully examined, and is believed to clearly and fully justify the findings and sentence. It affords also a striking instance of the injustice and inhumanity of the treatment accorded to the colored people of the section where the crime was committed, by their late masters, and the slight importance attached by the civil authorities to any outrage committed upon them.

The circumstances attending the commission of the offence, were as follows:

On the evening of the 20th July last, as Jefferson Banks,[2] a freedman, was walking to his home in Fayette, returning from a visit to Natchez, he was overtaken by the respondent, who was on horseback and armed with a double-barreled shot gun. Jenkins called on him with an oath to know what the radicals had told him to do to the democrats, and cocked his gun, pointing it at him. Banks seized it and expostulated, when Jenkins said he did not intend to shoot. The latter then said there was a writ out for the former, and commanded him to march before the horse to jail or he would kill him, at the same time urging his horse against him. Banks raised his right arm to ward off the horse, when the respondent discharged the contents of one barrel of his gun into his body and arm, breaking the arm so as to render amputation necessary. He then discharged the contents of the second barrel at the prostrate body of his victim, but without effect—the shots flying over him. The respondent then went into Fayette and entered complaint against himself, before the Mayor, who put him under bail in the sum of *fifty dollars.*

It was this apathy and evident sympathy of the civil authorities with the outrage, that caused General Gillem to order the trial of the accused before a Military Commission.

The circumstances which are thus briefly related, are set forth in the record with much minuteness in the testimony of Banks, who is evidently possessed of more than the ordinary intelligence of his class.

It was claimed by the defence that Banks shot at the respondent with a pistol, and the testimony on that point was, that three shots were heard by the witnesses at one time. It was not shown, however, that Banks owned a pistol; that there was one found at the scene of the assault, or that one could be found at his house, where a search was made. It is believed that the Commission justly conceived that the point was not made up, having the additional advantage to govern them, not attainable in a review of the proceedings, of noting the manner and bearing of the witnesses.

It is evident too, that had Banks shot at Jenkins, he could hardly have missed hitting him, as they were very close together. An additional and convincing fact upon this point is that the shot of Jenkins entered the arm and body of Banks from *behind*.

Petition for a writ of habeas corpus has been denied in the case by His Honor Judge Hill[3] of the U.S. Dist. Court. This application was based upon the failure of the specification to the charge made to technically accord with the law and practice of the State Courts of Mississippi. Upon this it is remarked that military tribunals can not be governed by the laws of practice & pleading as they obtain in civil courts, and it has always been held heretofore that the simplest form of setting forth the facts of an offence, without technical verbiage, was valid and sufficient.

No reason is perceived why the sentence of the Commission in this case, which is thought to be an extremely lenient one, should not be fully enforced.[4]

J. Holt.   Judge Adv. General.

LBcopy, DNA-RG153, Lets. Sent (Record Books), Vol. 27.

1. Census data on Thomas Jenkins are somewhat confusing. In 1860 he is listed as a twenty-nine-year-old planter. In 1870 he was shown twice, as a twenty-eight-year-old carpenter and as a thirty-five-year-old mechanic. All three listings have him born in Kentucky and the husband of Victoria. 1860 Census, Miss., Jefferson, 3rd Police Dist., Fayette, 32; (1870), Twp. 8, 64; Twp. 8, 1E, 74.

2. Jefferson Banks testified at the trial that he lived three miles from Fayette in Jefferson County and was a "laborer." No such person has been found in that county's 1870 census. Court-Martial Records, OO-3637, RG153, NA.

3. Robert A. Hill.

4. Although it is not known what disposition was made of this case, it seems reasonable, in light of Jenkins's presence as a free man on the 1870 census, that he did not serve his entire sentence.

From Patrick J.R. Murphy[1]

Private

Waverly. Iowa   Feby 26 /1869

Most Excellent Sir

Allow me most respectfully to tender you the homage of my most sincere appreciation and gratitude for your many personal and official favors during your term of office.

May I humbly beg leave to assure your Excellency that the affection, the admiration and the prayers of the *truly* patriotic, national and conservative people of the country will accompany you in your retirement from your exalted position. Although your lot has been cast in a perilous and unprecedented hour of the Nation's gloom and affliction yet all honest and good Men will unhesitatingly recognize in your Excellency the Statesman, the Patriot and the Benefactor who merged all his feelings and interests in his Country's weal and prosperity and soared above individual or partizan predilections.

When the gloom of the times is dissipated and the sunshine of National harmony shall have visited our great and noble country your honored name will be associated with the good the pure the patriotic and the most distinguished of any age and Nation.

I am perfectly satisfied that the future historian of America will rank President Johnson *high* amongst the noblest benefactors of the human race and one of the wisest Rulers of this prolific century.

Although you have suffered acutely and intensely, let me recal the truly Divine sentiment of my illustrious country man—William Smith OBrien[2]

> "Whether on the Gallows high
> Or in the battle's van
> The fittest place for Man to die
> Is where he dies for Man."

I have the honor to remain, most Excellent Sir, your very humble servt.

P.J.R. Murphy D D
Catholic Pastor of Waverly, late Chaplin USA

ALS, DLC-JP.

1. Murphy (*c*1823–1869) was pastor of a congregation in St. Charles, Illinois, before he joined the 58th Ill. Inf. as chaplain (February 1863–August 1864) and then was a hospital chaplain in 1865. In 1868 St. Mary's Catholic Church in Waverly, Iowa, completed its first church building during Murphy's pastorate, a tenure which ended when the priest was accidentally killed while boarding a train at Vincennes, Indiana. CSR, Patrick J.R. Murphy, RG94, NA; J. F. Grawe, *History of Bremer County, Iowa* (2 vols., Chicago, 1914), 1: 311; Powell, *Army List*, 809; Records of St. Mary's Catholic Church, Waverly, Iowa.

2. O'Brien (1803–1864) was an Irish revolutionary who served in Parliament and then worked for a free Ireland in the 1840s, activities for which he was convicted of treason and banished to Tasmania for a time. *New Columbia Encyclopedia.*

From Louis Schade

Washington D.C.   Febr. 26. 1869

Sir

When you gave the order to have the remains of Captain Wirz delivered to me,[1] it was certainly your intention that I should get the whole body and not a part of it. The coffin, however, which was delivered to me at the Arsenal, contains only the trunk—the head, right hand and spine being missing.

If they had been retained for the benefit and in the interest of science,[2] I would certainly have no objection to it, nor would the relatives of Captain Wirz, in whose behalf I act. But the skull of Captain Wirz, or some other part of his body, has, about two years ago, been exhibited at the Old Capitol Prison, by a discharged soldier for money. For that reason, and no other, I respectfully ask you to give an order, that the missing parts of the remains of Capt. Wirz, said to be at the Surgeon General's Office,[3] may be delivered to me for interment along with the other parts on Sunday afternoon, at 3 o'clock.[4]

Louis Schade

ALS, DLC-JP.

1. Endorsement of Feb. 23, 1869, on Louis Schade to Johnson, Feb. 22, 1869.

2. In fact, at least some of Wirz's missing body parts had been retained for scientific purposes. In May 1862 Surgeon General William A. Hammond had issued a circular directing medical officers to collect pathological specimens for an army medical museum. Assistant Surgeons W. Thomson and N. Allen attended Wirz's execution and performed an autopsy, collecting specimens from his spine and neck which would show the effects of hanging, and from his right arm to ascertain how damaged it was since certain testimony at Wirz's trial had claimed that his arm was too disabled for him to be able to perform some of the actions of which he was accused. There is no evidence that they collected his skull. Circular No. 2, May 21, 1862, in Robert S. Henry, *The Armed Forces Institute of Pathology: Its First Century, 1862–1962* (Washington, D.C., 1964), 12; Letter from Lenore Barbian, Anatomical Collections Manager, National Museum of Health and Medicine, Washington, D.C., Apr. 21, 1997, in Andrew Johnson Project files.

3. The National Museum of Health and Medicine, the successor to the Army Medical Museum begun by the Surgeon General, still has two of Wirz's vertebrae but the other specimens have long since disappeared. Ibid.

4. Johnson apparently did not respond to Schade's letter. Rev. Father F. X. Boyle of St. Peter's Church conducted services for the burial of Wirz at Mt. Olivet Cemetery, Washington, D.C., on February 28. *Washington Evening Star*, Mar. 1, 1869.

From Julia Gardiner Tyler

Castelton Hill   North Shore
Staten Island   Feb. 26. 1869

My dear Mr President—

I mentioned when I had the pleasure of seeing you in Washington last summer that I thought it would be an interesting addition to the "White House" to have upon its walls the portraits of the ladies who had helped to dispense its hospitalities & that perhaps I would make it a present of mine.

I put into execution my thought of last summer & forward my portrait by Express today.[1] I wished to have sent it as a Christmas present—(a peace offering in every sense) but it has been for some time in the hands of an Engraver at the wish of an Authoress & hence my delay.

I leave it to you, my dear, sir, to select the location for it in one of the lower rooms & only wish it was destined to remain long under your care.

Please, present my kind regards to Mrs Patterson in which my daughter[2] unites & I beg you to accept for yourself the sincere esteem of

Julia Gardiner Tyler

ALS, DLC-JP.

1. The portrait of Mrs. Tyler, painted in 1848 by Francisco Anelli, was the first painting of a First Lady to adorn the White House. *The White House: An Historic Guide*, rev. ed. (Washington, D.C., 1977), 10–11.

2. Either Julia (1849–1871) or Pearl (1860–1947) Tyler. Sandra L. Quinn-Musgrove and Sanford Kanter, *America's Royalty: All the Presidents' Children*, rev. ed. (Westport, Conn., 1995), 66–67, 71.

From Simeon M. Johnson

New York   Feb'y 27 1869

My dear Sir:

I am very anxious that you should pardon James D. Martin,[1] whose papers you referred, on my presentation, to the Atty General.

The letter to you, among the papers, of C B Goodrich,[2] Mr. Ranney[3] & Mr. Morse,[4] give, what I believe to be, a perfectly candid and truthful exhibit of Martin's case. I wrote the att'y General a letter, reviewing the case, and referred to the great array of the best names in Boston, asking that Martin be pardoned.

I have examined the whole case carefully, and convinced, as I am, that Martin's first act, was a mere error, and what followed came of a nervous anxiety through an entirely mistaken judgment, to do what would best secure the money of the Bank, without any purpose or intent to take a cent to himself, I am clearly of opinion that he ought to be pardoned.

I respectfully but earnestly, call your attention to the names asking his pardon; and I trust you will not think it amiss, if I suggest, that the opinion of so many of his neighbors, ought to have great weight, especially in connection with the ceceded fact, that he has, to no extent, sought to use the money of the Bank.[5]

S. M. Johnson

ALS, DLC-JP.

1. A former clerk, Martin (b. 1829) had been a bookkeeper and cashier at the National Hide and Leather Bank in Boston since the late 1850s. He had been convicted in October 1868 of making false entries and defrauding the bank. *Boston Advertiser*, Oct. 8, 1868; *Philadelphia Press*, Oct. 9, 1868.

2. Goodrich (1804–1878) was a longtime Boston attorney. *NUC*; Boston directories (1859–70).

3. A practicing lawyer in Boston since the 1840s, Ambrose A. Ranney (1821–1899) also served three terms in the state legislature (1857, 1863, 1864) and in the U.S. House (1881–87). *BDUSC*.

4. Robert M. Morse, Jr. (1837–1920), a Boston attorney and legislator. *NCAB*, 32: 181–82.

5. Johnson issued a pardon for Martin on March 3, 1869. This pardon, however, only affected his earlier conviction; Martin was still under indictment on other charges. The outcome of his case is not known. *Washington Evening Star*, Mar. 6, 1869; *Boston Advertiser*, Mar. 29, 1869.

From Henry O'Moel Ryan[1]

Executive Mansion   Feb 27th 69

It is with great regret I a humble citizen of this Country learn of your Excellencys so soon resigning the high and exalted Office you have so nobly filled. I fear it will be many a long year ere "we the people" have so true a Champion of our rights. A few months ago Your Excellency kindly referred me to Genl Michler for work which he gave me on the streets as a laborer. The funds has run out And I have had nothing to do for the past two months. Would you ere you quit office procure me some humble employment as I am in the greatest need and nothing can be procured here without interest. Mrs Genl Michler[2] has done all she possibly could in her Christian Charity to obtain me employment. But all has failed. Wishing your Excellency every prosperity . . .[3]

Henry O'Moel Ryan

P.S. I have travelled in Europe and would make an good guide & Servant Or would be grateful for any humble position here.

ALS, DLC-JP.

1. Possibly the Ryan listed simply as a laborer in the 1869 Washington directory. He is not otherwise identified. Washington, D.C., directories (1869).

2. Sarah (or Sallie) Hollingsworth (c1841–fl1881) married Nathaniel Michler in 1861. 1870 Census, D.C., Washington, 1st Ward, 249; *DAB*.

3. Apparently Ryan met with Johnson in March, still pursuing the possibility of employment. See Ryan to Johnson, Mar. 10, 1869.

From Margaret A. Spencer[1]

Hagerstown   Feb 27th 1869.

I hereby tender my resignation as postmaster of Hagerstown Wayne County Indiana and

Recommend to the appointment of said office James. G. Woods[2] for the following reasons, first he being in every way qualified to transact the business of said office, second he has a family to support, third he has no means at his command, fourth he is in poor health and not able to labor at hard work for the mentainance of his family.[3]

M A. Spencer., P.M.

ALS, DLC-JP.

1. Spencer was postmaster at Hagerstown from January 1868 to the end of March 1869. She may have been a widow (b. c1813) with at least six children. *U.S. Off. Reg.* (1869); *History of Wayne County, Indiana* (2 vols., Chicago, 1884), 2: 620; 1860 Census, Ind., Wayne, Hagerstown, 7.

2. In 1865 Woods was a teacher. He may have been the Woods (b. c1837) who in 1870 was reading law and supporting his wife, four-year-old child, and mother. J. C. Power, ed., *Directory and Soldier's Register of Wayne County, Indiana* (Richmond, Ind., 1865), 217; 1870 Census, Ind., Wayne, Hagerstown, 3.

3. Woods was not nominated. Spencer was replaced by Alexander C. Walker, who held the post for the next fifteen years. *History of Wayne County*, 2: 620, 626.

From Fernando Wood

House of Representatives   Feby 27 1869

My Dear Sir

The Democratic members of this House (all your friends) will dine with me *privately* tomorrow at 5 p.m. at Welckers (15th St)[1] and it will afford us all great pleasure to have the honour of your presence. I hope you will do so and advise me of your acceptance.[2]

Fernando Wood

ALS, DLC-JP.

1. A restaurant run by John Welcker (c1836–1875), who had operated restaurants at different locations in Washington since at least the early 1860s and continued until his death. Washington, D.C., directories (1864–74); *Washington Evening Star*, Mar. 29, 1875.

2. Evidence of Johnson's having attended the Wood gathering on February 28 has not been uncovered.

From Lily Gertrude Yeaton[1]

Washington, D.C.   Feb. 27, 1869

Mr President:

I called at the Executive Mansion today, although too late to obtain an audience with you; being solicitous of appealing to you for further favor, in the matter of the appointment which you so kindly bestowed upon my brother.[2]

Mr. Yeaton[3] called at the War Department on the 17th inst., and ascertained that the notice directing my brother to report to the Military Board, for examination, on or before the 1st of April 1869, had been forwarded to his address in Brooklyn, two days previous. I immediately wrote my brother to that effect; but, although upon receipt of my letter he went daily to the post office, he was unable to obtain any information concerning the notice, until the 25th inst., at which time it was handed to him.

According to this notice, "neglect or failure to notify the Department of his acceptance within *ten days* from this date, (15th inst.), will be treated as a declination of the appointment." The ten days having expired when the notice was received, by my brother, his chances for obtaining the position are, of course, virtually destroyed; but feeling unwilling to relinquish the matter, he has forwarded me the enclosed letter addressed, as required by the notice, to the Adjutant General, and I would respectfully solicit that, by your direction, its explanation may be regarded as satisfactory by the Adjutant General, and my brother allowed to accept the appointment.

Lily Gertrude Yeaton.

ALS, DNA-RG94, ACP Branch, File S-74-CB-1869, G. Stafford.

1. Yeaton (*fl*1872) was the second wife of Charles C. Yeaton. They were married sometime between 1863 and 1867 and had at least three children. Letter from Marcia Jebb, Portsmouth Athenaeum, Oct. 21, 1997, Andrew Johnson Project files; Charles C. Yeaton to Johnson, May 9, 1872, Johnson Papers, LC.

2. Guy Stafford, not further identified, had requested appointment as second lieutenant on February 11, 1869. A conditional letter of appointment was sent on the 15th, and apparently, according to a March 3 endorsement, he was granted permission to report to the examining board. For unknown reasons, however, the appointment was cancelled on March 9, 1869. ACP Branch, File S-74-CB-1869, G. Stafford, RG94, NA.

3. Charles C. Yeaton.

From John Quincy Adams

Quincy   February 28. 1869.

Sir

Although the consciousness of a faithful performance of duty is doubtless the most precious as it is certainly the purest recompense which the weary servant of the people can hope to gather in return for his patient devotion to their true welfare yet there are seasons when it is proper for the private citizen however inconsiderable to express particularly his sense of obligation and offer his respectful thanks to the public office however high in place, with the hope that his words may not be unwelcome.

Especially may such a formal expression be unobjectionable if not needful, when it may be that our honest and our able man may close a term of official duty so involved and blinded by one of these gusts of popular disfavor to which all public men are peculiarly exposed that he may retire from his post oppressed by a load of despondency and embittered by a consciousness of injury which a hearty expression of approbation and sympathy from never so humble a source might in some degree mitigate.

And Sir I can only wish it might afford you one instant's satisfaction to assure you, as in all sincerity I do, that I regard the fortitude and firmness with which you have faced the [?] tempest of popular odium and senseless prejudice, in your attempt to settle our fraternal dissentions upon a basis of kindness and magnanimity and establish our government anew upon the only sure and lasting foundation the right of self government under the limitations of the Constitution;

the calm and uncalculating justice with which you have interposed time after time between a frantic faction of politicians and the Constitution of the Founders; and the supreme fealty you have always manifested for that precious charter of real freedom—as worthy a fame as rich and destined to attain a recognition as sure and lasting as that which illustrates the name of Mr. Jefferson and of General Jackson.

For a considerate and tolerably impartial review such reliable judgment it may be necessary to wait for a time more or less remote, but be you well assured, Sir, that unless this people are perversely bent to abandon forever the way of constitutional liberty, and enter those paths of passionate license which with nations as with individuals lead surely to early ruin and untimely death, they must speedily arouse themselves from their dangerous delusions, abandon their blind and reckless guides and return to the old ways of their fathers where alone they can find peace for their souls.

I pray you to accept my thanks for your distinguished public service and my sincere wishes for your happiness in your private station and to believe that I remain . . .

John Q. Adams

ALS, DLC-JP.

From Thomas Ewing, Sr.

Washington, D.C.   28" Feby 1869

Dear Sir

I hope you will retain the Bill[1] passed last night recognizing obligation to pay gold &c & let the next Congress & the next President commit themselves upon it. Your Message[2] on the public debt is not explicit & exact—it has been much assailed especially in Congress. When out of office you can explain it. *I* understand it thus.

When we borrowed our auditors gave us from forty to eight[y] cents for a dollar making an average of fifty cents, on which we agreed to pay & have thus far paid six per cent per annum on one hundred cents. If an individual should borrow a like actual sum, call it a much larger sum & agree to pay interest on the nominal amount, a court of Equity would enquire what was the actual sum borrowed & when the interest paid amounted to the agreed interest on the actual sum,

& to the actual principal would hold the debt paid. This is Equity according to our Courts of justice. In doing this you would make the case analogous to the English *terminable annuities* where the excessive interest for a definite time is made to pay up principal & Interest.

T Ewing

ALS, DLC-T. Ewing Family Papers.

1. In fact, Johnson did pocket veto the "Bill to Strengthen the Public Credit." A modified version was the first act passed under President Grant. *Congressional Globe*, 40 Cong., 3 Sess., pp. 1879–1883; 41 Cong., 1 Sess., pp. 60, 61, 84, 167; Appendix, p. 35; *Washington Evening Star*, Mar. 5, 1869.

2. See Fourth Annual Message, Dec. 9, 1868.

From John Hall [1]

Philadelphia   Feby 28th 1869

Mr President

The uncertain future before me prompts me to urge upon your Excellency, some action in my case before your retirement from official power.

Your arm has been stretched forth in mercy to the broken hearted, and to those who were separated and confined from home and friends. You have said by virtue of your power arise—depart and sin no more. This is power set forth in mercy. Has your Excellency no power for Justice sake? Will it be said that Andrew Johnson who feared not the great Combination, is afreaid of that same Combination when a case of Justice calls to the plummet line.

What has become of that Pamphlet that Swinton[2] the historian wrote about one year ago—and as it was then said, "Shortly to be issued." Why has that document been suppressed or held back; my authority for the above is the Washington correspondent of the Philada. Mercury I have it.

Governor Geary of this state, stated at the Ratification Meeting held in this City last May[3] that Genl. Grant was to be robbed of his victories. I have the speech in my possession. I would like to know what he has, of which he can be robbed, that cannot be shown to belong to some one else.

I can fill sheets of paper with mysterious allusions to my case, this is not necessary. All that is wanted is that the Country and the World shall hear the footsteps of a man. There is something God-like in man, when he summons all his powers in executing Justice.

Will Your Excellency depart, without the Country feeling the touch of Cato?

"There was a Brutus once," but has the United States no Cato? Is the opportunity to slip for Andrew Johnson to open the eyes of the world?

Send to Congress a recommendation for my relief. Tell them I need it badly, or publish the fact in the same way that your Secretary published it to me on the 14th day of January 1868.[4]

John Hall

No 944 South Third st

ALS, DLC-JP.

1. No occupation for Hall (*fl*1893), a longtime resident of Philadelphia, has been found. Philadelphia directories (1867–94).

2. William Swinton published a great many works; it is not known to which one Hall refers.

3. Perhaps a reference to the May 22 National Union Club meeting, when Governor John W. Geary warned that the war had not ended, for Klansmen and Democrats were still trying to "destroy the liberties of the country." *Philadelphia Press*, May 23, 1868.

4. What Hall refers to here is not known.

Interview with New York World *Correspondent*

WASHINGTON, February 28 [1869].

CORRESPONDENT—"I observe, Mr. President, that the papers have laid out for you a busy, and, by inference, a brilliantly successful programme in Tennessee, upon your retirement from the Executive office. I know nothing to sustain or refute these statements, but am sure that the actual power and the retributive significance of your presence in the Senate would rejoice the hearts of all your friends in both parties. Then, too, as if to overturn this hope, it has been stated that you will go to Europe in the spring, where, as you know, such a reception would be accorded you as few other men have ever received."

THE PRESIDENT—"I have no disposition, indeed my temperament, physical strength, and habits, almost forbid me to sink into idleness at the close of my term, and there is much to be done in the country, and much in Tennessee especially, to enlist my solicitude and my efforts. I have no plan personal to myself for the future; I can truly say that I have no further ambitions to realize, and I certainly have no desire to retaliate on any the slights or the burdens which have been imposed on me. I will undoubtedly exert myself to restore the sway of the Constitution over the country, and particularly over my State, but as to any special line on which I may work, that will be wholly controlled by circumstances. As to going to Europe, too, that is entirely in doubt. After I retire from this place, private business will detain me in Washington for a few days, then my family and self will go to Tennessee, and it depends just on them whether we visit Europe or not. Nothing is determined, and we will be governed by circumstances. As to returning to the Senate, I am free to say that I think there is great need there and large opportunity there for any man governed solely by principle. A Senator should have profound convictions of his own and unbending moral and physical courage too, to maintain them. For such men there is a crying necessity in the Senate, and such men could not only in time bring back the sway of the Constitution but would make their mark as benefactors of the country upon the history of the future. In many respects, I think that a Senator of the United States has the highest opportunities of any officer in our government, for while in a sense he represents a State, in a larger and better sense he represents the country as a whole. By his longer tenure of office he survives the petty, stormy issues which biennially change the House, to a degree, and by his more expanded representation he can and should rise to the plane of statesmanship and tolerance. When I remember my first entrance into Congress, I recall as contemporaries Clay, Webster, Wright, Calhoun, Benton, Douglas, Clayton, and Hayne;[1] and such men as being yet above even the average of their times, yet raised by attraction that average to a near level with themselves. I think that it is more than a coincidence that the evils which afflict this country have dated from and have continued along with the deterioration of the character of Congress individually and collectively considered. Small men brought on great evils and great evils have continued small men. The dawn of better times will be signalized by the advent of better men."

CORRESPONDENT—["]Mr. President, have you heard what Wilson[2] really said in the caucus of Radical Senators the other day?"

THE PRESIDENT—"No sir. What?"

CORRESPONDENT—"He said that he thought it unwise to consider the Tenure-of-Office bill this session, because, though persuaded that it would be repealed, if brought to a vote, and though convinced that you would sign the repeal, he yet thought that along with your approval you would send in a message which would rasp Congress more that it would be able to bear at the present time."

THE PRESIDENT—"That's just like Wilson. He has not enough sense to tell a thing in words which do not give his party opponents a handle. The other day he blurted out that he was against submitting the suffrage amendment[3] to State conventions instead of existing Legislatures, because conventions would have to be voted for, and if folks had a chance to vote on the amendment, it would be lost. This confession ought to be sufficient to kill the amendment, though if it kill even Wilson it will be a wonder. However, neither he nor any one else need fear I would send in anything but my name at the bottom of a bill repealing the Tenure-of-Office law. I vetoed that bill, and of course I would approve its repeal, to be consistent, as I have been consistent all through. Nevertheless, if, instead of a repeal, Congress should send me a bill modifying the Civil-Tenure law, or even mitigating it, I would not approve of it, as I am against the whole principle of the act, believing it to be unconstitutional."

CORRESPONDENT—"Mr. Johnson, the Senate will not touch the Civil Tenure law, in my judgment, until General Grant shows his hand, and not then if he display the least sign of independence. As things stand and as they tend it is improbable that the Senate will relinquish a single feature of the law, for the Senate fears and does not trust your successor."

THE PRESIDENT—"I have noticed, sir, that you have made much of the question in THE WORLD. It was right. The whole of the administration hinges upon it. It is the one thing which prevents a President from being President except in name. All the corruption of the service is owing to the existence of this law. It would be useless to suspend men and have their friends and supporters in the Senate pass upon their cases. Besides, corrupt officials so cover up their tracks as to make it impossible directly to prove their guilt in evidence, however strong the moral convictions or suspicions you entertain of their guilt. Then, too, there are hundreds of officials who, without being corrupt, are inefficient. Inefficiency is a matter of judgment not evidence, in most cases, and charges based upon such allegations, however clear to an Executive, are hard to communicate to such a number of men as constitute a Senate. Above all the Tenure-of-Office bill makes suspension a disgrace to a man, whereas, before, removal was no disgrace. Removal, too, or the apprehension of it, is the best weapon an Executive has to insure honest administrators. Let an official only know that the President can remove him without notice, and that operates more powerfully to keep him in good behavior than all the bonds he could have subscribed in his favor. My experience here has convinced me of this: that no President can administer this government as it ought to be administered without such a law upon him. My very literal compliance with it has demonstrated its inefficiency. No man who comes after me can get along with it. General Grant's demand for its repeal[4] shows that he understands this, and the exertions which his friends make for its repeal show that they understand it. They vindicate my veto of the law and my protests against it, and they acknowledge their mistake in passing it. For my part, I would be glad to see that mistake rectified. To be sure the repeal of the law would do me no good now, but as a patriotic man, desirous of having an honest civil service, I would be glad to see the law wiped out of the statute book."

CORRESPONDENT—"Mr. President, don't you think if General Grant inherits all the burdens put upon you, that from your knowledge of his character there will be trouble?"

THE PRESIDENT—"Neither General Grant nor any other man can administer this government with such a law. No man can administer it properly either who has not a plan, or policy, if you will, of his own, founded upon a clear conviction of what the Constitution teaches and means. General Grant will be peculiarly liable to feel restive under this law. It is one thing to sit in headquarters to write orders and have them obeyed, and it is quite another to wish to institute measures and action, and find yourself hampered as no other President ever was before; and to have your executive functions shorn from you, and yourself blamed for the bungling and corruption of others whom you cannot reach. Presidential recommendations will not amount to general orders by any means. If General Grant develops an intelligent understanding of our system, and demands a firm respect of his right, he may, in time, get back the powers to the Executive office which have been taken from it. To do this he must surround himself in his councils with politicians or statesmen who are familiar with administration and with the laws, and to whom can be safely committed the trusts and powers of government. If a President wants a Cabinet of clerks he can get them, but he will find the whole load of government too much for his time and his mind. If he secures experienced statesmen to assist him, he will find that himself and themselves are deprived of all advantage which comes from accord of action by the existence of a law forbidding changes of employes at will. Congress perceives that the people really disapprove of the checks put upon me. The effort the ablest men of the party are making for repeal of the Tenure-of-Office act proves that they keenly interpret how public sentiment calls for it. That clause of the Army Appropriation bill which I protested against, making all the President's orders go through a subordinate officer, whom I might have removed at any time this twelve-month, and might even remove yet for insubordination, has been recommended for repeal. It shows that Congress feels the people are beginning to realize the shackles put upon the Executive, and demand their abrogation. If the people could as thoroughly realize the other difficulties of my situation, and if once the square issues of the Constitution against centralization could be voted upon, the verdict would be just what it will be when the history of my administration is written. But the real issues have never reached the people. The war cries crowded out all other questions, and the history of the past four years has been a history of successful juggling of the real questions and substitution of false ones. There is hope yet. The Constitution of this country will come to the top at last. Even Logan, in a speech yesterday, remembered that there was a Constitution somewhere and began dimly to recall it.[5] This is favorable, though the very resistance of other Presidents against congressional encroachments will hasten the time when the people will remand each department of government to its proper sphere and assure its proper independence. That time can not be far off. No farther off than the period, however early, when the real issues are understood and not covered up."

This record of what the President said, is very nearly word for word. In a portion of the conversation, the President asked what the impression of Grant was, and was answered that the hope of many was in Mrs. Grant's constant assertion that "Mr. Grant was always a very obstinate man." Mr. Johnson smilingly observed that he had heard that some such quality had been attributed to himself, but of course there was nothing in it.

PRESIDENT JOHNSON AND HIS VISITORS.

The President receives every day nearly one thousand people, and a large number of them practically impose upon his time by renewals of many demands for pardons, claims, &c., which have been refused by the Executive before. There is no way to prevent this, as the rule is to admit all who come in the order of their arrival. About fourteen hours of every day are consumed in this manner, and nothing but the wonderful endurance of the President keeps him in health.

MR. JOHNSON'S PART IN THE INAUGURATION.

The President has duly notified General Grant that he will be happy to await his desires in the usual matter of accompanying him to the place of inauguration. The fact that no reply has yet been received may not be significant if a reply should come at any time before Wednesday, but in either event President Johnson has complied with the conventionalities, and that, too, in a sincere spirit. Indeed, in no instance during any conversation has President Johnson been charged with uttering the least word of criticism or comment upon his successor, and he declares that he feels almost a hope that what with Grant's principles of economy, his administration tendencies, and the bold stroke he has made in advance for freedom, that the General, if he does not succeed in making a successful administration, will at least convince the people that the real obstacle to peace and order are in the unaltered unnatural laws of a factional Congress.

New York World, Mar. 1, 1869.

1. Henry Clay, Daniel Webster, Silas Wright, Jr., John C. Calhoun, Thomas Hart Benton, Stephen A. Douglas, and probably Thomas Clayton and Robert Y. Hayne. A Delaware lawyer, Clayton (1777–1854) held a variety of state offices before serving in the U.S. Senate (1824–27, 1837–47). Hayne (1791–1839) had been attorney general of South Carolina before his tenure in the U.S. Senate (1823–32). He later served as the state's governor (1832–34) and then mayor of Charleston (1835–37). *BDUSC*.

2. Probably Senator Henry Wilson of Massachusetts.

3. The Fifteenth Amendment, which prohibited the denial of voting rights because of race, color, or previous condition of servitude, passed the House on February 25 and the Senate on February 26, 1869. It was eventually ratified by the requisite number of states on March 30, 1870. On February 17, 1869, Wilson voted against a motion that would require elected conventions to ratify the amendment, rather than existing legislatures. That proposal failed, but no comments by Wilson have been found. *Congressional Globe*, 40 Cong., 3 Sess., pp. 1314–15, 1563–64, 1641.

4. In an interview with several New York businessmen on February 23, President-elect Grant commented that as long as the tenure of office law was in place, he would be unable to remove objectionable persons from office. A revised tenure act became law in early April 1869, granting the president greater authority to remove or suspend officeholders. Ibid., 41 Cong., 1 Sess., Appendix, p. 37; *National Intelligencer*, Feb. 25, 1869.

5. On February 27 Representative John A. Logan alluded to the power of the federal government to make treaties with the Indians, but it is unclear if this is what Johnson refers to. *Congressional Globe*, 40 Cong., 3 Sess., pp. 1707–8.

March 1869

From District of Columbia Citizens[1]

Georgetown D.C.   March 1st 1869

Your petitioners Citizens of the United States and residents of the District of Columbia, Humbly pray your Honor, in mercy and charity, to extend the high prerogative of your executive clemency in the pardon of Patrick Kelly of Georgetown D.C.[2] who was sentenced oct. 25th 1865 to six years imprisonment in Albany penitentary for assault and Battery.

He bore an excellent character amongst his fellow citizens previous to committing the hasty act, which provocation and the passion of the moment unfortunately led him to commit.

His wife mary Kelly[3] and four helpless children, who were altogether dependant on his daily labor for support, are now in great destitution and earnestly beseach your honor to restore to them that husband and father from whose support they have been deprived for more than three years.[4]

And your petitioners will ever pray &c.

Pet, DLC-JP.

1. The petition was signed by nearly thirty individuals.

2. Kelly (b. *c*1826) was a stone cutter and a native of Ireland who served three years in the U.S. army. He had been convicted of assault and battery with intent to kill. 1860 Census, D.C., Washington, 7th Ward, 159; *Washington Evening Star*, Oct. 26, 1865; *National Intelligencer*, Oct. 28, 1865; Pardon Case File B-388, Patrick Kelly, RG204, NA.

3. Mary Kelly (b. *c*1830), a native of England, held washing jobs. 1860 Census, D.C., Washington, 7th Ward, 159.

4. In August 1868 the Attorney General had declined to recommend a pardon for Kelly but forwarded the files to Johnson. The President returned Kelly's papers to the Attorney General within two days with no recommendation for pardon. Apparently, no further action was taken before the Johnson administration ended. See Pardon Case File, B-388, Patrick Kelly, RG204, NA.

From Sam Milligan

[Washington, D.C.] March 1/69

Mr President,

On reflection, I think, it would give more point to your strictures on the action of Congress in its invasion of the prerogatives of the Executive, to incorporate this idea.

When I assumed the discharge of the duties imposed by the Constitution on the Executive, I found all its ancient powers, and prerogatives intact; but now under the action of a usurping Congress, without default on my part, as my public acts will attest, I am compelled to turn it over to my successor, shorn of the following powers. Here let your strictures *follow*; or *precede* them by a laconic statement, itimised of the prerogatives lost.[1]

The idea is to make Mr Grant feel, that he comes into office with half his powers gone.

This is a mere suggestion, for your reflection.

Milligan

ALS, DLC-JP.

1. Although Johnson's Farewell Address does not contain Milligan's words, certainly there is much in that document to indicate that the President either followed Milligan's advice or else had already thought along those lines earlier. See Farewell Address, Mar. 4, 1869.

To Robert Morrow

Washington D.C.   Mch 1st 1869

You are hereby relieved from duty at the Executive Mansion, and are directed to proceed to Knoxville, Tenn., and, thence, to report by letter to the Paymaster General, U.S. Army for further orders.[1]

(signed) Andrew Johnson

Copy, DNA-RG99, Lets. Recd., 2113/42.

1. Morrow accompanied Johnson, his family, and friends when they departed Washington on March 18. See *Washington Evening Star*, Mar. 18, 1869.

From William F. Phillips[1]

Cincinnati Ohio. March 2d 1869.

My Dear Sir.

Your very many friends and admirers in our city, have requested of me that I write you, and see if some arrangement could not be made, to have you address your fellow citizens in Cincinnati, as soon as it may suit your conveinance to do so. I can secure our large new and

beautiful opera house, any evening you may name. Please write or
telegraph me.

William F. Phillips
P.S. We will cheerfully pay all the expense you may to, in coming to
Cinncinnati.

ALS, Johnson-Bartlett Col., Greeneville.
    1. Possibly Phillips (c1841–fl1872), a Cincinnati clerk. 1860 Census, Ohio, Hamilton, Cin-
cinnati, 5th Ward, 78; Cincinnati directories (1861–73).

From Henry Liebenau

No: 4. Hamilton place.
New York   March 3d 1869.

Excellent Sir

You are about retiring—surrendering all your power and influence,
and, without enjoying any of the many favors you had in your gift,—
without being regarded by you, as worthy of your favor, permit me to
call your attention to this fact, that none of those who were the re-
cipients of your official favors, more earnestly and more sincerely
sustained your measures and your administration, than your humble
servant.

As the Corresponding Secretary of the "Constitutional Union
Association," I made it a speciality to take official notice, by approving resolutions of all your measures based upon the Constitution of
the United States, and, when the attempt was made by a radical
Congress to trespass upon the jurisdiction of the Supreme Court, I
promptly urged our association to call a public meeting at the Cooper Institute,[1] in support of your course, which proved a complete
success, as your friend Mr Wailes[2] can attest.

I did solicit your influence for some position,[3] as my profession
(Artist.) would not yield support for my family,—from *nescessity* and
not from choice I solicited position, but received none.

I now beg leave never-the-less, to bid you a Kind, an affectionate
farewell,—and, with heartfelt sincerity permit me to wish you
health—happiness and prosperity for the remainder of your days,—
may you and your family enjoy undisturbed repose and happiness,—
and may the sun-set of your days be cloudless and serene,—may
providence direct the hearts of our people, to acknowledge the purity of your motives, and the honesty of your intentions.

May our Heavenly Father grant you a long life of still further usefulness and a blessed immortality, is the fervent prayer of ...

Henry Liebenau

ALS, Andrew Johnson Family Papers, TU.
    1. This pro-Johnson meeting was held on January 30, 1868. See Ethan A. Allen to Johnson,
Feb. 3, 1868; Andrew H.H. Dawson to Johnson, Feb. 3, 1868; Liebenau to Johnson, Feb. 7,
1868, *Johnson Papers*, 13: 518–20, 520–22, 535–38.
    2. William W. Wales.
    3. Liebenau had requested an appointment in the New York customhouse. See Liebenau to
Johnson, Mar. 10, Johnson Papers, LC; Liebenau to Johnson, Mar. 16, 1868, *Johnson Papers*,
13: 653–55.

From Hugh McCulloch
Personal

Washington   March 3d 1869

My Dear Sir

Herewith I hand you my resignation of the office of Secretary of
the Treasury, to take effect at the close of the present Presidential
Term.

In thus closing my official connections with the Government, it
affords me sincere pleasure to express to you my high appreciation of
the distinguished ability and of the fidelity to principle which you
have displayed, as the Executive of the Nation during a most eventful period in its history, and to return to you my hearty thanks for
the courtesy and Kindness with which you have treated me as a member of your Cabinet.

With best wishes for your Continued prosperity and happiness ...

Hugh McCulloch

ALS, DLC-JP.

From Cornelius Wendell

Washington, D.C., March 3d, 1869.

Sir:

The peculiar circumstances of the case must excuse this epistle.

Of the expenses attending the Impeachment Trial, a balance of

Ten Thousand Dollars still remains due and unpaid. This amount I was induced to assume at the instigation and by the direction of Hon. A. W. Randall, E. Cooper, and E. D. Webster,[1] Assessor 32d Dist., New York, with the assurance, positive and unequivocal, that, within ten days of the termination of the Trial, the money should be raised.

Efforts the most strenuous have been made by Hon. A. W. Randall and myself to raise the amount, but with only partial success, amounting to our own subscriptions of Fifteen Hundred Dollars. The Collector and Surveyor of New York[2] have, notwithstanding repeated promises, failed us entirely. The Hon. Secretary of the Treasury should, I think, have co-operated more fully with the P.M.G. in the effort to settle the affair.

I was induced, in order to keep the peace, to give my note for Three Thousand Dollars on account of the above, and, being unable to meet it, a suit has been instituted, and that I must pay by law; the balance, amounting to Fifty-five Hundred Dollars, I will pay, if ever able.

You can judge the object of this note.

Should you desire a personal interview, I will be happy to call upon you at any place you may designate, before Friday, at 5 P.M., as I must leave for New York in the evening train of that day.

I will refer you to Mr. Randall for details, should you desire them, although he is not cognisant of this note to you.

C. Wendell.

LS, DLC-JP.

1. Erastus D. Webster (c1827–fl1871), editor of an Omaha, Nebraska, Republican newspaper before the war, subsequently served as a clerk in the State Department and as Seward's private secretary, and then as deputy surveyor of the New York customhouse. 1860 Census, Neb. Terr., Douglas, Omaha, 1st Ward, 5; Washington, D.C., directories (1862–72); U.S. Off. Reg. (1861–67); Philadelphia Press, May 26, 1868; Van Deusen, Seward, 480; Arthur C. Wakeley, ed., Omaha: The Gate City and Douglas County, Nebraska (2 vols., Chicago, 1917), 1: 302.

2. Henry A. Smythe and Abram Wakeman.

From Albert A. Fagala[1]

Trundle's X Roads, Sevier County, Tenn.
March 4th, 1869.

Mr. Andrew Johnson,

On hearing a somewhat supersticiou Radical lamenting the unfa-

vorable aspect of Grant's Administration, as measured by the cloudy
& unfavorable condition of the weather, I am reminded that this is
the last day of your Administration, at least for a time, & is as well
the beginning of another. I could therefore contemplate for you quite
a respite, were it not for the importunities of your friends, both personal and political. Notwithstanding your features are evident to my
mind. I also know much of your history, and especially would I mention that I had the honor of testifying to the weight of your influence, in our State Reconstruction Convention at Nashville.[2] Yet I
am a stranger to you, & therefore DO NOT WRITE with a view of
eliciting an answer. My object is wholely suggestive, & I feel purely
patriotic. It is not therefore intended as dictatorial and mean. Suggestions however made by one, who has never aspired higher than to
be—(or at least to believe himself) a respected citizen of the U.S. in
contradistinction to the *absurd* doctrine of State-territorialism, &
for the consideration of one, who has never been beaten before the
people in his life, & whos Majesty is the crowning honor of the
Nation, would subject me to the charge of arrogance. To avert which
you will allow me to say, that while I frankly accept the appearance;
I most emphatically deny the spirit. Time flies swiftly to the past, &
with it comes the day when your friends hope to see you vis a vis, to
take you by the hand, & to bid you a kind welcome to your home in
Tenn.; where we hope soon to know ourselves the beneficiaries of
your wise counsils in both our Public & Legislative Assemblies. This
being the case, I need not tell you that as the day approaches Newspaper Speculations increase, rumor thickins and your friends become
more & more hopeful. The substance of News-paper spectulations
are; that you will be a candidate for Gov. of Tenn. the coming summer; that you will accept the nomination of no convention; that you
will stand onely upon the *platform of a common country*; and may I
add; reflecting, your former character; that your policy shall be (as to
politics), *First My Country an then my party*. All of which suggests its
self to my mind as worthy & in my Judgment, forms the only shure
nucleus, around which the Conservative Element of the State can
rally with any hope of success. I am also of the opinion that such is
the judgment and the wishes of the conservative Masses in E. Tenn.
In short we want a man Able, experienced, and tried; who has the
courage to stand upon that Constitution—the living existance of
which, no Union Man—however ignorent—ever doubted up to the
advent of Radical Reconstruction, and upon the laws, the rules and
regulations of the Country, held to be subbordinate thereto by the

Supreme Court of the United States in the plenary exercise of all its legitimate & Constitutional rights. We want a man, who knows, who has the ability, and who dares to defend—even in the hot beds of Radicalism those vital principles, which lie at the foundation of our government. We want a man who can, & who will effectually expose the corruptions, the intrigueing, & villanies of the *Special few*, the leaders of that party of high moral ideas, who have by their repeated acts of assumed legislation, declaired in effect that Jefferson Davis did do what the Rebbles in the end failed to discover; dissolve the Union, & who have arrogated to themselves the unquestionable right of leading the one part, & of driving the other. How long these Political Pimps are to succeed in deceiving the people as to the true object of their frequent usurpations, by the deceitful cry of "Rebble! Rebble!" remains to be seen. How long the truely sincere & loyal people of the Nation, & especially of the so called Rebble States will close their eyes to the fact; that by the Radical Reconstruction Measures of Congress, they, *the bona fida* loyalist of the South are outlawed, & discriminated against as enemies to the Federal Government. How long this State of affairs will be permitted to exist, even into living in the future must, & will determine. I allude to the arguments of Senator Sumner recently made in the Senate of the U.S.[3] and reflected in the action of that body touching the claims of the Loyal people of the South—(The Sue P Murphy case)[4] about which I know nothing of your opinion other than from intuition. If however intuition proves a failure for the first time, & such is to remain the settled policy of the Government; I say to you in all candor, Tell it not in Gath, Publish it not in the streets of Askelon[5] lest the Copperheads of the North rejoice least the Rebbles of the South 'triumph'. Now that we want all of this, & even more, you would like to know what it is that we do not want. I answer. We do not want a New York Convention. It's too soon a thing to be repeated in Tenn. We do not want our noble horse Conservative rode to death by the Anti-belligerants of the North, & the leading Rebbles of the South. In short we do not want anything contrary to the principles herein before enunciated in the last two lines on page 2d & the first five on page 3d.[6] We want nothing more, & will willingly accept nothing less. But enough of this. Now I submit: that in the event you will in anyway consent to be a candidate for Gov. Would it not be better— contrary to former practice—to make your first speeches in E. Tenn? I found this proposition upon the fact, that Middle & West Tenn. are competent to take care of themselves, & E. Tenn. being largely

Radical, a RADICAL change must be sought in this end of the State.
To do which effectually, I hold that to forestall, so far possible, an
expression of an opinion on the part of the people, by chokeing off
their unfair comment of the Radical Press, is absolutely necessary; &
that this may be done efficiently I again submit. Would it not be
better to bring the discussion, so far as possible, of the various issues
within the immediate hearing of the people? For be it remembered,
that we are by nature stubborn, & that just so far as this principle is
ingrafted in us, just so far is reason dethroned, & the D——l has
things his own way. Hence a man once committed, will to THIS EX-
TENT defend what he has heretofore said and done, as though the
fate of this Nation hangs upon his consistency.

A. A. Fagala.

May 4th 1869. The above was written upon the day it bares date,
& was intended to reach you before you would leave Washington
City; but in its conclusion I remembered that that was the great day
of your deliverance, & that it would be ungenerous in any one not to
allow you sufficient time to animadvert upon the interest of [?] and
thing about which you were more immediately concerned. So the
matter of sending went over; but now that your emancipation is
complite; that you have returned, & have the [rewards?]; and that
you have witnessed the very agravated, & agravating (almost chronic)
condition of a Revolution long-ago conceived in the minds of such
men as Sumner, Phillips, & co; but never brought into existance
untill the war for the "The Constitution, the Union, & the Enforcement of the Laws" was all over; and as you have mad manifest at
K'lle Nashville, & Memphis your superior knowledge of; & your
unquestioned ability to treat the *case*, I have concluded to send it on,
that you may know that there is at least one—& I say many, even in
the Radical County of Sevier, who in the mane approve your corse.
Our County is largly Radical: Yet I believe that the masses are honest, but deceived. They need but be convinced. In the beginnin of, &
throughout the war, they looked to you as their Polar Star. Will you
revive a memory of those days, discuss the origin, the progress & the
present of our present situation. If so, let us know, at a convenient &
we will have the matter sirculated &c.

ALS, DLC-JP.

1. Fagala (1828–1892) was a farmer. *In the Shadow of the Smokies: Sevier County, Tennessee
Cemeteries* (Sevierville, Tenn., 1984), 260; 1860 Census, Tenn., Sevier, 9th Dist., 73; (1870), 9.

2. Fagala served as a delegate to the Nashville convention of January 1865. *Nashville Dis-*

patch, Jan. 10, 1865.

    3. Probably a reference to Sumner's speech in the Senate of January 12, 1869, in which he discussed the Sue Murphy case. He contended that there were three important considerations involved in the Murphy claim: that she was a resident of a Rebel state, that the property was located within a Rebel state, and that the property was taken under the necessities of war. Therefore, Murphy's claims should not be accepted and compensated. *Congressional Globe,* 40 Cong., 3 Sess., 299–301.

    4. The case absorbed much of the attention of the Senate during December 1868 and January 1869. A resident of Decatur, Alabama, during the war, Sue Murphy claimed that she suffered $7,000 of damages when her house and other property were destroyed by federal troops. The question of loyalty to the U.S. government proved to be the stumbling block and the key issue, for Murphy's loyalty could not be established. See *Memphis Appeal,* Jan. 13, 1869; *Atlanta Constitution,* Jan. 14, 1869; *New York Herald,* Jan. 22, 1869.

    5. A paraphrase of 2 Sam. 1:20.

    6. These lines begin with the words: "In short we want a man Able, experienced, and tried" and end with the words: "in the plenary exercise of all its legitimate & Constitutional rights."

Farewell Address

WASHINGTON, D.C., *March* 4, 1869.

TO THE PEOPLE OF THE UNITED STATES:

    The robe of office, by constitutional limitation, this day falls from my shoulders, to be immediately assumed by my successor. For him the forbearance and co-operation of the American people, in all his efforts to administer the Government within the pale of the Federal Constitution, are sincerely invoked. Without ambition to gratify, party ends to subserve, or personal quarrels to avenge at the sacrifice of the peace and welfare of the country, my earnest desire is to see the Constitution, as defined and limited by the fathers of the Republic, again recognized and obeyed as the supreme law of the land, and the whole people—North, South, East, and West—prosperous and happy under its wise provisions.

    In surrendering the high office to which I was called four years ago, at a memorable and terrible crisis, it is my privilege, I trust, to say to the people of the United States a few parting words, in vindication of an official course so ceaselessly assailed and aspersed by political leaders, to whose plans and wishes my policy to restore the Union has been obnoxious. In a period of difficulty and turmoil almost without precedent in the history of any people, consequent upon the closing scenes of a great rebellion and the assassination of the then President, it was perhaps too much, on my part, to expect of devoted partisans, who rode on the waves of excitement which at that time swept all before them, that degree of toleration and magnanimity which I sought to recommend and enforce, and which I believe in good time would have advanced us infinitely farther on the road to permanent peace and prosperity than we have thus far attained. Doubtless, had I, at the commencement of my term of office, unhesitatingly lent its powers or perverted them to purposes and plans "outside of the Constitution," and become an instrument to schemes of confiscation and of general and oppressive disqualifications, I would have been hailed as all that was true, loyal, and discerning—as the reliable head of a party, whatever I might have been as the Executive of the Nation. Unwilling, however, to accede to propositions of extremists, and bound to adhere, at every personal hazard, to my oath to defend the Constitution, I need not, perhaps, be surprised at having met the fate of others whose only rewards for upholding constitutional right and law have been the consciousness of having attempted to do their duty, and the calm and unprejudiced judgment of history.

At the time a mysterious Providence assigned to me the office of President, I was, by the terms of the Constitution, the commander-in-chief of nearly a million of men under arms. One of my first acts was to disband and restore to the vocations of civil life this immense host, and to divest myself, so far as I could, of the unparalleled powers then incident to the office and the times. Whether or not, in this step, I was right, and how far deserving the approbation of the people, all can now, on reflection, judge, when reminded of the ruinous condition of public affairs that must have resulted from the continuance in the military service of such a vast number of men.

The close of our domestic conflict found the army eager to distinguish itself in a new field, by an effort to punish European intervention in Mexico. By many it was believed and urged that, aside from the assumed justice of the proceeding, a foreign war, in which both sides would cheerfully unite to vindicate the honor of the national flag and further illustrate the national prowess, would be the surest and speediest way of awakening national enthusiasm, reviving devotion to the Union, and occupying a force concerning which grave doubts existed as to its willingness, after four years of active campaigning, at once to return to the pursuits of peace. Whether these speculations were true or false, it will be conceded that they existed, and that the predilections of the army were, for the time being, in the direction indicated. Taking advantage of this feeling, it would have been easy, as the commander-in-chief of the army and navy, and with all the power and patronage of the Presidential office at my disposal, to turn the concentrated military strength of the nation against French interference in Mexico, and to inaugurate a movement which would have been received with favor by the military and a large portion of the people.

It is proper, in this connection, that I should refer to the almost unlimited additional powers tendered to the Executive by the measures relating to Civil Rights and the Freedmen's Bureau. Contrary to most precedents in the experiences of public men, the powers thus placed within my grasp were declined, as in violation of the Constitution, dangerous to the liberties of the people, and tending to aggravate, rather than lessen, the discords naturally resulting from our civil war. With a large army and augmented authority, it would have been no difficult task to direct at pleasure the destinies of the Republic, and to make secure my continuance in the highest office known to our laws.

Let the people whom I am addressing from the Presidential chair during the closing hours of a laborious term, consider how different would have been their present condition had I yielded to the dazzling temptation of foreign conquest, of personal aggrandizement, and the desire to wield additional power. Let them with justice consider that, if I have not unduly "magnified mine office," the public burdens have not been increased by my acts, and other and perhaps thousands or tens of thousands of lives sacrificed to visions of false glory.

It cannot, therefore, be charged that my ambition has been of that ordinary or criminal kind which, to the detriment of the people's rights and liberties, ever seeks to grasp more and unwarranted powers, and, to accomplish its purposes, panders too often to popular prejudices and party aims.

What, then, have been the aspirations which guided me in my official acts? Those acts need not at this time an elaborate explanation. They have been elsewhere comprehensively stated and fully discussed, and become a part of the nation's history. By them I am willing to be judged, knowing that, however imperfect, they at least show to the impartial mind that my sole ambition has been to restore the Union of the States, faithfully to execute the office of President, and, to the best of my ability, to preserve, protect, and defend the Constitution. I cannot be censured if my efforts have been impeded in the interests of party faction, and if a policy which was intended to reassure and conciliate the people of both sections of the country was made the occasion of inflaming and dividing still farther those who, only recently in arms against each other, yet, as individuals and citizens, were sincerely desirous, as I shall ever believe, of burying all hostile feelings in the grave of the past. The bitter war was waged on the part of the Government to vindicate the Constitution and save the Union; and if I have erred in trying to bring about a more speedy and lasting peace, to extinguish heart-burnings and enmities, and to prevent troubles in the South which, retarding material prosperity in that region, injuriously affected the whole country, I am quite content to rest my case with the more deliberate judgment of the people, and, as I have already intimated, with the distant future.

The war, all must remember, was a stupendous and deplorable mistake. Neither side understood the other; and had this simple fact and its conclusions been kept in view, all that was needed was accomplished by the acknowledgment of the terrible wrong, and the expressed better feeling and earnest endeavor at atonement shown and felt in the prompt ratification of constitutional amendments by the Southern States at the close of the war. Not accepting the war as a confessed false step on the part of those who inaugurated it, was an error which now only time can cure, and which even at this late date we should endeavor to palliate. Experiencing, moreover, as all have done, the frightful cost of the arbitrament of the sword, let us, in the future, cling closer than ever to the Constitution as our only safeguard. It is to be hoped that not until the burdens now pressing upon us with such fearful weight are removed will our people forget the lessons of the war; and that, remembering them from whatever cause, peace between sections and States may be perpetual.

The history of late events in our country, as well as of the greatest Governments of ancient and modern times, teaches that we have every thing to fear from a departure from the letter and spirit of the Constitution, and the undue ascendency of men allowed to assume power in what are considered desperate emergencies. Sylla,[1] on becoming master of Rome, at once adopted measures to crush his enemies and to consolidate the power of his party. He established military colonies throughout Italy; deprived of the full Roman franchise the inhabitants of the Italian towns who had opposed his usurpations; confiscated their lands and gave them to his soldiers; and conferred citizenship upon a great number of slaves belonging to those who had proscribed him, thus creating at Rome a kind of bodyguard for his protection. After having given Rome over to slaughter, and tyrannized beyond all example over those opposed to him and the legions, his terrible instruments of wrong, Sylla could yet feel

safe in laying down the ensigns of power so dreadfully abused, and
in mingling freely with the families and friends of myriad victims.
The fear which he had inspired continued after his voluntary abdi-
cation, and even in retirement his will was law to a people who had
permitted themselves to be enslaved. What but a subtle knowledge
and conviction that the Roman people had become changed, discouraged, and utterly broken in spirit could have induced this daring
assumption? What but public indifference to consequences so terrible as to leave Rome open to every calamity which subsequently
befell her could have justified the conclusions of the dictator and
tyrant in his startling experiment?

We find that in the time which has since elapsed human nature
and exigencies in government have not greatly changed. Who, a few
years past, in contemplating our future, could have supposed that in
a brief period of bitter experience every thing demanded in the name
of military emergency, or dictated by caprice, would come to be considered as mere matters of course; that conscription, confiscation,
loss of personal liberty, the subjugation of States to military rule, and
disfranchisement, with the extension of the right of suffrage merely
to accomplish party ends, would receive the passive submission, if
not acquiescence of the people of the Republic?

It has been clearly demonstrated, by recent occurrences, that encroachments upon the Constitution cannot be prevented by the President alone, however devoted or determined he may be, and that unless the people interpose there is no power under the Constitution
to check a dominant majority of two-thirds in the Congress of the
United States. An appeal to the nation, however, is attended with
too much delay to meet an emergency. While, if left free to act, the
people would correct, in time, such evils as might follow legislative
usurpation, there is danger that the same power which disregards
the Constitution will deprive them of the right to change their rulers, except by revolution. We have already seen the jurisdiction of
the Judiciary circumscribed when it was apprehended that the courts
would decide against laws having for their sole object the supremacy
of party, while the veto power, lodged in the Executive by the Constitution for the interest and protection of the people, and exercised
by Washington and his successors, has been rendered nugatory by a
partisan majority of two-thirds in each branch of the National Legislature. The Constitution evidently contemplates that when a bill is
returned with the President's objections, it will be calmly reconsid-
ered by Congress. Such, however, has not been the practice under

present party rule. It has become evident that men who pass a bill under partisan influences are not likely, through patriotic motives, to admit their error, and thereby weaken their own organizations by solemnly confessing it under an official oath. Pride of opinion, if nothing else, has intervened, and prevented a calm and dispassionate reconsideration of a bill disapproved by the Executive.

Much as I venerate the Constitution, it must be admitted that this condition of affairs has developed a defect which, under the aggressive tendency of the Legislative department of the Government, may readily work its overthrow. It may, however, be remedied, without disturbing the harmony of the instrument.

The veto power is generally exercised upon constitutional grounds, and whenever it is so applied, and the bill returned with the Executive's reasons for withholding his signature, it ought to be immediately certified to the Supreme Court of the United States for its decision. If its constitutionality shall be declared by that tribunal, it should then become a law; but if the decision is otherwise, it should fail, without power in Congress to re-enact and make it valid.

In cases in which the veto rests upon hasty and inconsiderate legislation, and in which no constitutional question is involved, I would not change the fundamental law; for in such cases no permanent evil can be incorporated into the Federal system.

It is obvious that without such an amendment the Government, as it existed under the Constitution prior to the rebellion, may be wholly subverted and overthrown by a two-thirds majority in Congress. It is not, therefore, difficult to see how easily and how rapidly the people may lose—shall I not say have lost?—their liberties by an unchecked and uncontrollable majority in the law-making power, and, when once deprived of their rights, how powerless they are to regain them.

Let us turn for a moment to the history of the majority in Congress which has acted in such utter disregard of the Constitution. While public attention has been carefully and constantly turned to the past and expiated sins of the South, the servants of the people, in high places, have boldly betrayed their trust, broken their oaths of obedience to the Constitution, and undermined the very foundations of liberty, justice, and good government. When the rebellion was being suppressed by the volunteered services of patriot soldiers amid the dangers of the battle-field, these men crept, without question, into place and power in the national councils. After all danger had passed, when no armed foe remained, when a punished and repentant people bowed their heads to the flag and renewed their allegiance to the Government of the United States, then it was that pretended patriots appeared before the nation, and began to prate about the thousands of lives and millions of treasure sacrificed in the suppression of the rebellion. They have since persistently sought to inflame the prejudices engendered between the sections, to retard the restoration of peace and harmony, and, by every means, to keep open and exposed to the poisonous breath of party passion the terrible wounds of a four-years' war. They have prevented the return of peace and the restoration of the Union, in every way rendered delusive the purposes, promises, and pledges by which the army was marshalled, treason rebuked, and rebellion crushed, and made the liberties of the people and the rights and powers of the President objects of constant attack. They have wrested from the President his constitutional power of supreme command of the army and navy. They have destroyed the strength and efficiency of the Executive Department, by making subordinate officers independent of and able to defy their chief. They have attempted to place the President under the power of a bold, defiant, and treacherous Cabinet officer. They have robbed the Executive of the prerogative of pardon, rendered null and void acts of clemency granted to thousands of persons under the provisions of the Constitution, and committed gross usurpation by legislative attempts to exercise this power in favor of party adherents. They have conspired to change the system of our government by preferring charges against the President in the form of articles of impeachment, and contemplating, before hearing or trial that he should be placed in arrest, held in durance, and, when it became their pleasure to pronounce his sentence, driven from place and power in disgrace. They have in time of peace increased the national debt by a reckless expenditure of the public moneys, and thus added to the burdens which already weigh upon the people. They have permitted the nation to suffer the evils of a deranged currency, to the enhancement in price of all the necessaries of life. They have maintained a large standing army, for the enforcement of their measures of oppression. They have engaged in class legislation, and built up and encouraged monopolies, that the few might be enriched at the expense of the many. They have failed to act upon important treaties, thereby endangering our present peaceful relations with foreign Powers.

Their course of usurpation has not been limited to inroads upon the Executive Department.

By unconstitutional and oppressive enactments, the people of ten

States of the Union have been reduced to a condition more intolerable than that from which the patriots of the Revolution rebelled.[2]
Millions of American citizens can now say of their oppressors, with
more truth than our fathers did of British tyrants, that they have
"forbidden the governors to pass laws of immediate and pressing
importance, unless suspended until their assent should be obtained;"
that they have "refused to pass other laws for the accommodation of
large districts of people, unless those people would relinquish the
right of representation in the Legislature—a right inestimable to
them and formidable to tyrants only;" that they have "made judges
dependent upon their will alone for the tenure of their offices and
the amount and payment of their salaries;" that they have "erected a
multitude of new offices, and sent hither swarms of officers to harass
our people and eat out their substance;" that they have "affected to
render the military independent of and superior to the civil power,"
"combined with others to subject us to a jurisdiction foreign to our
Constitution and unacknowledged by our laws," "quartered large
bodies of armed troops among us," "protected them by a mock trial
from punishment for any murders which they should commit on the
inhabitants of these States;" imposed "taxes upon us without our
consent," "deprived us in many cases of the benefit of trial by jury,"
"taken away our charters, excited domestic insurrection amongst us,
abolished our most valuable laws, altered fundamentally the forms
of our Government, suspended our own Legislatures, and declared
themselves invested with power to legislate for us in all cases what-
soever."

This catalogue of crimes, long as it is, is not yet complete. The
Constitution vests the judicial power of the United States "in one
Supreme Court," whose jurisdiction "shall extend to all cases arising
under this Constitution" and "the laws of the United States." Encouraged by this promise of a refuge from tyranny, a citizen of the
United States who, by the order of a military commander, given under the sanction of a cruel and deliberate edict of Congress, had
been denied the constitutional rights of liberty of conscience, freedom of the press and of speech, personal freedom from military arrest, of being held to answer for crime only upon presentment and
indictment, of trial by jury, of the writ of habeas corpus, and the
protection of civil and constitutional government—a citizen, thus
deeply wronged, appeals to the Supreme Court for the protection
guaranteed to him by the organic law of the land. At once a fierce
and excited majority, by the ruthless hand of legislature power,

stripped the ermine from the judges, transferred the sword of justice to the General, and remanded the oppressed citizen to a degradation and bondage worse than death.

It will also be recorded as one of the marvels of the times that a party claiming for itself a monopoly of consistency and patriotism, and boasting, too, of its unlimited sway, endeavored, by a costly and deliberate trial, to impeach one who defended the Constitution and the Union not only throughout the war of the rebellion, but during his whole term of office as Chief Magistrate; but at the same time could find no warrant or means at their command to bring to trial even the chief of the rebellion. Indeed, the remarkable failures in his case were so often repeated, that for propriety's sake, if for no other reason, it became at last necessary to extend to him an unconditional pardon. What more plainly than this illustrates the extremity of party management and inconsistency on the one hand, and of faction, vindictiveness, and intolerance on the other? Patriotism will hardly be encouraged when, in such a record, it sees that its instant reward may be the most virulent party abuse and obloquy, if not attempted disgrace. Instead of seeking to "make treason odious," it would in truth seem to have been their purpose rather to make the defence of the Constitution and the Union a crime, and to punish fidelity to an oath of office, if counter to party dictation, by all the means at their command.

Happily for the peace of the country, the war has determined against the assumed power of the States to withdraw at pleasure from the Union. The institution of slavery also found its destruction in a rebellion commenced in its interest. It should be borne in mind, however, that the war neither impaired nor destroyed the Constitution, but on the contrary preserved its existence, and made apparent its real power and enduring strength. All the rights granted to the States, or reserved to the people thereof, remain therefore intact. Among those rights is that of the people of each State to declare the qualifications of their own State electors. It is now assumed that Congress can control this vital right, which can never be taken away from the States without impairing the fundamental principles of the Government itself. It is necessary to the existence of the States, as well as to the protection of the liberties of the people; for the right to select the elector in whom the political power of a State shall be lodged involves the right of the State to govern itself. When deprived of this prerogative, the State will have no power worth retaining. All will be gone, and they will be subjected to the arbitrary will of Congress.

The Government will then be centralized, if not by the passage of laws, then by the adoption, through partisan influence, of an amendment directly in conflict with the original design of the Constitution. This proves how necessary it is that the people should require the administration of the three great departments of the Government strictly within the limitations of the Constitution. Their boundaries have been accurately defined, and neither should be allowed to trespass upon the other, nor, above all, to encroach upon the reserved rights of the people and the States. The troubles of the past four years will prove to the nation blessings if they produce so desirable a result.

Upon those who became young men amid the sound of cannon and din of arms, and quietly returned to the farms, the factories, and the schools of the land, will principally devolve the solemn duty of perpetuating the Union of the States, in defence of which hundreds of thousands of their comrades expired, and hundreds of millions of national obligations were incurred. A manly people will not neglect the training necessary to resist aggression, but they should be jealous lest the civil be made subordinate to the military element. We need to encourage, in every legitimate way, a study of the Constitution for which the war was waged, a knowledge of and reverence for whose wise checks by those so soon to occupy the places filled by their seniors will be the only hope of preserving the Republic. The young men of the nation, not yet under the control of party, must resist the tendency to centralization—an outgrowth of the great rebellion—and be familiar with the fact that the country consists of united States, and that when the States surrendered certain great rights for the sake of a more perfect union, they retained rights as valuable and important as those which they relinquished for the common weal.

This sound old doctrine, far different from the teachings that led to the attempt to secede, and a kindred theory that States were taken out of the Union by the rash acts of conspirators that happened to dwell within their borders, must be received and advocated with the enthusiasm of early manhood, or the people will be ruled by corrupt combinations of the commercial centres, who, plethoric from wealth, annually migrate to the capital of the nation to purchase special legislation. Until the representatives of the people in Congress more fully exhibit the diverse views and interests of the whole nation, and laws cease to be made without full discussion at the behest of some party leader, there will never be a proper respect shown by the law-making power either to the judicial or executive branch of the Government. The generation just beginning to use the ballot-box, it is believed, only need that their attention should be called to these considerations to indicate, by their votes, that they wish their representatives to observe all the restraints which the people, in adopting the Constitution, intended to impose upon party excess.

Calmly reviewing my administration of the Government, I feel that, with a sense of accountability to God, having conscientiously endeavored to discharge my whole duty, I have nothing to regret. Events have proved the correctness of the policy set forth in my first and subsequent messages; the woes which have followed the rejection of forbearance, magnanimity, and constitutional rule are known and deplored by the nation.

It is a matter of pride and gratification, in retiring from the most exalted position in the gift of a free people, to feel and know that in a long, arduous, and eventful public life, my action has never been influenced by desire for gain, and that I can in all sincerity inquire, "Whom have I defrauded? whom have I oppressed? or of whose hand have I received any bribe to blind my eyes therewith?"[3] No responsibility for wars that have been waged or blood that has been shed rests upon me. My thoughts have been those of peace, and my effort has ever been to allay contentions among my countrymen.

Forgetting the past, let us return to the first principles of the Government, and, unfurling the banner of our country, inscribe upon it, in ineffaceable characters, "The Constitution and the Union, one and inseparable."

ANDREW JOHNSON.

PD, Andrew Johnson Project Files, University of Tennessee, Knoxville.

1. Lucius Cornelius Sulla (138–78 B.C.) a Roman general notorious for capturing and murdering some 8,000 prisoners. He subsequently had himself named as dictator in 82 B.C. *Columbia Encyclopedia*.

2. All of the following quoted statements in this paragraph are from the list of grievances found in the Declaration of Independence.

3. Quotation from 1 Sam. 12:3.

From Leonard Koons[1]

York [Pa.]   Mar 4- 1869

As the term of your administration is about to close and many things have yet to be attended to I thought I would remind you of the promise you made to Mr Spangler[2] when in Washington that

you would pardon his son[3] now confined at Dry Tortugas. Please
have him pardoned and relieve his aged Father.[4]

Leonard Koons

ALS, DLC-JP.
   1. Koons (b. c1815) was a York, Pennsylvania, clerk. York directories (1863); 1860 Census,
Pa., York, 1st Div., York Borough, 88.
   2. William Spangler (1783–1875) was the sheriff of York County (1827–30), a laborer, and
the father of eight children. It is not known when he visited Washington. Michael W. Kauffman
to Glenna R. Schroeder-Lein, Apr. 30, 1997, Johnson Project files; Edmund Spangler material, pt. 1, vi, Surratt House Museum, Clinton, Md.
   3. Lincoln assassination conspirator Edward Spangler (also known as Edmund, Edman,
and Ned).
   4. Johnson had already pardoned Spangler on March 1. Spangler material, pt. 2, 168–69.

From Benjamin Rush

St. Germain-en-Laye, France,
4th March 1869.

Dear Mr. President,

Scarcely now more than *eleven* o'clock *here*, and allowing for the
difference in longitude it can scarcely be more than *six* o'clock A.M.,
in Washington, so that you are still President of The United States,
the functions of The Chief Magistate ceasing I think at mid-day, &
I am still therefore justified in addressing you as above. I suspect too
that I am among the *earliest* of your correspondents to-day in any
part of The United States.

May I then be permitted to offer to you on this day, on which The
Executive Authority of our Country, passes, by constitutional limitation, from your vigorous and patriotic grasp, to the hands of another of our fellow citizens, chosen by the People to administer it for
another constitutional term, an humble tribute of admiration, from
one of your constituents, temporarily far away from home, for the
great ability, patriotism & zeal, enlightened boldness & utter fear-
lessness, with which you have discharged your great Trust.

Called suddenly & unexpectedly to the difficult, & as it has proved
in our already short history *dangerous*, functions of the Chief Magis-
tracy, at a moment of intense excitement in all parts of our Country,
caused by the commission of a crime of which the enormity was
without estimate, & happily without example the—*assassination* of
your immediate predecessor; a crime which obliterated, for the time
being, all party distinctions, & caused every good citizen to shudder;

thus called upon, by constitutional requirements as the then second Officer of The Republic, at a moment at which our great Country had barely emerged, by a few days & hours, from the horrors of a Civil war, of frightful atrocity & duration, & of proportions almost beyond belief; when the worst passions were still uppermost, & reason was drowned, throughout the length & breadth of the land; it was your high & arduous & perilous task to assume the reins of government; a task complicated beyond measure by the new & extraordinary emergencies of the period.

Adhering with unshrinking firmness & a sublime courage to the obligations of your oath of office, to preserve, protect & defend the Constitution, & pursuing the elevated & obvious path of duty, with the keen eye & resolute tread of a Patriot & Statesman, directed singly to the honor & interests of the *whole Country*, the restoration of fraternal relations among *all* your fellow citizens, & the prosperity & happiness of *every section* of the distracted Country, by seeking to heal instead of inflame, and thus obliterate the frightful pest, (your noble record throughout which was too well known to excite distrust of your motives) it was nevertheless your lot to be assailed, from the first, by a storm of opposition & torrent of obloquy, which pursued you to the last, & threatened finally to overwhelm you by an organized conspiracy to hurl you from power, by an infamous perversion of constitutional forms, over which you triumphed.

Your attitude of extraordinary firmness & inflexible pursuit of what you believed to be right, throughout this tempest, attracted the attention, & called forth the applause, of enlightened & patriotic men in all part of our country, & of the calm minded & well judging in other countries.

During my residence & travels in various parts of England & Europe for the last two years & a half this last has repeatedly come to my knowlege from the lips of thos who held the sentiment, as the first, for the previous eighteen months, was every where familiar to my eyes & ears at home.

I could greatly extend this letter by repeating only a portion of all I have heard abroad, in proof of what I say, but will simply advert in a word to what you already have from me in writing, as uttered to me in conversation with two of the most enlightened Statesmen of England & France, one of whom (you know whom I mean) said emphatically, slapping his hand on his knee with energy as he sat, "*I can't tell you how I admire that man.*"

And now Sir your task is done.

With a proud consciousness of having faithfully discharged your whole duty to your whole Country, unappalled by stupendous difficulties & unterrified by threats, you return on this day to your great & patriotic State to mingle once more among your fellow citizens in private life, thus giving another illustration of the simplicity & grandeur of our Institutions, which have made us so great a People.

When the voice of reason shall once more triumph over that of passion, & truth shall prevail over error, Posterity sir will do you justice, & History will enrol you as among the most patriotic of American Presidents.

That a long & happy future may be in store for you, & that your Country may yet again have the benefit of your "*sagepe*," of which that great French Statesman spoke to me (& here again you know whom I mean) your enlarged capacity & ripe experience, remembering that you are still in vigorous life, is but the expression of an earnest hope which I am sure I share in common with a large number of your countrymen.

May I add in conclusion that expecting to remain abroad some time yet, for the purpose of visiting other parts of Europe, & particularly Prussia & Austria, with a view to some acquaintance with their systems of Government, to which end I have already had some opportunities in England & France, Belgium, Switzerland & parts of Germany, it would give me very great pleasure to hear from you, should your new leisure & opportunities permit, & to be favored with some of your news of the condition & prospects of our Country.

I have been passing the winter in Brussels with my Family, & am *here* only temporarily, having been called here by the illness of a son at school, but my address, in Europe, will always be "*Care of Holtinguer & Co. 38 Rue de Provence, Paris.*"

                                                Benjamin Rush.

ALS, DLC-JP.

From J. Scott Payne

                                    Washington, D.C., Mch 5th 1869

Dear Sir.

I take this occasion to express to you my profound thanks, for your action in restoring me to the army.[1] Be assured sir, I shall ever be grateful. On my arrival here this morning, I am advised at the War Department, that your action in this matter was illegal, and that I was not *de jure* or *defacto* an army officer. I shall therefore let the matter rest, as I have no favors to ask at the hands of the new administration. The obligation to yourself is none the less great on account of this decision, and I shall always remember with pride and pleasure, that one of the last acts of your remarkable and eventful administration, was connected with myself. May Peace, happiness and prosperity, to our country, for which you have So nobly battled, ensue, and may they ever attend you through life, is the fervent wish of one who will never cease to remember your kindness.[2]

J. Scott Payne

ALS, Johnson-Bartlett Col., Greeneville.
1. See Payne to Johnson, Nov. 2, 1868, and William F. Switzler to Johnson, Feb. 28, 1869.
2. Although rebuffed at this point, Payne was eventually restored to the army in 1873 as a second lieutenant in the 6th Cav. and the next year regained the post of first lieutenant in the 5th Cav. He achieved the ranks of captain and brevet major before he retired in 1886. Powell, *Army List*, 523.

From William H. Owens[1]

Baltimore, March 6 1869

My Dr. Sir

Since I saw you on Thusday the committee have made all prelimary arrangements for your reception on Thursday 11th inst.

I am directed to say to you that a special car, has been provided to leave Washington on or about 9 A.M. which will be at your disposal, also that any of your personal friends would be gladly welcomed.[2]

I will take occasion to say that invitations to be present at the Banqut have been extended to all of the members of your late Cabinet.

It is probable some member of the committee of reception will visit you on Tuesday 9th & communicate further as to arrangements &c.

It would be very graifying if you could bring with you your friend Mr. Coyle.[3]

W. H. Owens

ALS, DLC-JP.

1. Owens (*c*1821–*fl*1877) was a Baltimore merchant who evidently also served on the city council. *Washington Evening Star*, Feb. 20, 1869; Baltimore city directories (1868–77); 1860 Census, Md., Baltimore, Baltimore, 19th Ward, 308.

2. Elaborate arrangements for Johnson's Baltimore visit were outlined in the newspapers. See, for example, the *Washington Evening Star*, Mar. 8, 10, 11, 1869.

3. According to newspaper reports, Coyle did in fact accompany the Johnson entourage to Baltimore. See ibid., Mar. 11, 1869.

From George Dean[1]

139 Plum St.   Cincinnati   March 8th 1869.

Dear Sir:

Now that you have relinquished the robes of office, and have returned to the position of a private citizen, my motive for addressing you cannot be considered as a desire for personal advancement by bringing my name to your notice; so that whatever I may say in approval of your course while you were President of the United States, I hope may be considered by you as an honest expression of opinion, and not influenced by any unworthy motives. I am also induced to write to you, thinking, that perhaps an honest endorsement of your Administration even by a man who only controls one vote—a mechanic, and one of the men who served as a private soldier for three years (who we so seldom hear of now) would be received by you in the spirit in which it is written, and might perhaps be a small source of gratification to you, in coming from a person of my position in society.

Your Administration has been a notable one in the history of the United States; commencing, as it did, at the close of the largest, and most powerful rebellion on record, it was encompassed with many difficulties which were of course entirely new to the American people, and which required very delicate treatment, so as to counteract all the bitter feelings which were manifested during the rebellion—to heal the wounds that had been received, and to bring the entire population of the U.S. together in the bond of unity and brotherly love;— to render us a free and united people, and to confirm us in our reverence for the Constitution, which is the only safeguard of our liberties.

To do all this, would have been very simple, had the distinction of party been laid aside, had there been as hearty a co-operation with the Executive in sustaining the Constitution *after* the war, as it was claimed we were doing *during* the war; but such a co-operation unfortunately for the interests of the country was not given; the Executive was left comparatively alone in his duty of guarding the Constitution, and in trying to restore its benefits to a section which, having acknowledged its error, was lying humiliated on the ground; waiting for forgiveness, and an opportunity of proving that the lesson it had received was not lost. Unfortunately for the Country, mercy and forgiveness were not given to our misguided brothers; instead of being treated as erring members of one family—there acknowledgements received—their promises for the future accepted—contrary to the advice of the Executive, and in opposition to the desires of our most patriotic statesmen, the opposite course was pursued; they were treated as enemies, their rights taken away—their land filled with armed men, and every check that could possibly be put on them to cripple them still more than the war had done was applied, with the result we see to day.

I have faith in the good common sense of the American people, I do not believe that the leaders of a party will always control the votes of its so-called members; I believe that in seeing and feeling the results of a blind adherence to a party which obtained its power by false pretenses, the people will soon think in reality for themselves, and not follow blindly those, whose only object is personal advancement, at the cost of the entire country.

You have the rare priviledge in looking back over your Administration in knowing that throughout the whole period you occupied the Presidential Chair your whole actions were in harmony with the Constitution, that your continued efforts under great discouragements and trials—such as no other President ever had, and which I trust no other one ever will have—were for the lasting benefit of the entire United States, and particularly for a down trodden oppressed people; and that although at this time the course you pursued has not received such an endorsement by the American people, as you were justly entitled to, yet it will not be many years before the bitterness of the present party spirit will have passed away, and the people will be able to do justice to your Administration, and give you the credit of using your best efforts in defence of the Constitution, and for the benefit of the entire people.

As an American Citizen, I thank you for the steadfastness with which you maintained the supremacy of the Constitution which should be guarded with jealous care by every true citizen of the United States, and also for placing on record—every opportunity that you had—your full reasons for objecting to measures which did not accord with the provisions contained in that instrument, also for your last address to the American people, in which you fully sustain your own position and reputation to the satisfaction of every one who is not a blind adherent of party, and who can look at passing results with an eye single to the public welfare. I trust also, that although you have left the highest office in the gift of the American people, that the country will not lose your valuable aid in still bringing before the people the advantages, and the necessity of sustaining and preserving the document, under which the nation has lived and prospered so well, and which would make us the strongest, most prosperous, and most united people on earth, were its provisions lived up to.

As regards your contemplated visit to Europe, I am sure that you will meet with a hearty welcome from all those who have taken an interest in American affairs during your Administration, who must have admired the energy and will, you displayed under most trying and unpleasant circumstances; when apparently you were the only guardian of the interests and rights of the entire American people, and also for the virtue and patriotism you exhibited in using unlimited power when it was almost forced upon you by those whose hostility has pursued you so long.

Not to weary you, I will close by wishing you long life, health and strength, that you may be long heard in the defence of our liberties, and that you may have the happiness of seeing your efforts crowned with success.

George Dean.

ALS, DLC-JP.

1. When Dean penned this letter, he was listed in the Cincinnati directory as a carver. He may be the same person as George P. Dean (c1841–1894) of Madisonville, Hamilton County, Ohio, who served as a private and later corporal in Company G, 2nd Ky. Inf., May 1861 to June 1864. After the war this man became a farmer and fruit grower before serving in the 1880s as the street commissioner of Madisonville. CSR, George P. Dean, RG94, NA; Pension Records, Marilla A. Dean, RG15, NA; Cincinnati directories (1869).

From Henry H. Ingersoll [1]

Greeneville East Tenn.   Monday March 8th 1869.

Dear and Honored Sir,

At a public meeting held in the Court House in Greeneville by citizens of Greene County without regard to party on Thursday, March 4th[2] at which James Britton[3] presided, and James C. Beeks[4] acted as Secretary, there were adopted a series of Resolutions a copy of which is enclosed.[5] They express fully the object and sentiment of the meeting.

In accordance with the last Resolution James Britton, Edwin Henry, H. H. Ingersoll A. W. Walker, and John P. Holtsinger were appointed as a Committee for the purpose therein specified. It is our design to make the occasion of your return a welcome by *the people*: and, that all may participate, it is designed that it may be as free as possible from all partisan allusions. The people of your old home feel an honest pride in the eminent public services of their distinguished fellow citizen, and we wish to give all an opportunity of participating in the events that shall mark your return *home* after so long an absence. If they stand aloof, the fault shall be theirs, not ours.

Your political friends too, are desirous of manifesting their esteem of your brave and fearless defence of the cause of constitutional liberty, either on the evening of the same day or at some subsequent time, acceptable to you.

In pursuance therefore of the Resolutions and by direction of the chairman of our Committee, I address you now, requesting you to inform us, if a public reception or welcome, of the nature before indicated upon your return home will be acceptable to you; and also, as soon as the same will be convenient, upon what day we may expect you here.

Trusting that you are injoying the relaxation which your retirement from the arduous cares and responsibilities of office has afforded, and that the common Guardian of us all, may graciously watch over you and grant you a safe return to your *home*.

H. H. Ingersoll
Sec'y of Com.

ALS, Johnson-Bartlett Col., Greeneville.

1. Ingersoll (1844–1915), a native of Ohio, moved to Greeneville in 1865 and practiced law there until 1878, when he relocated to Knoxville. In Greeneville in 1875 he chaired the committee in charge of the funeral ceremonies for Johnson. After his move to Knoxville, Ingersoll held several different judicial appointments and eventually became dean of the law school at the University of Tennessee. Mary U. Rothrock, ed., *The French Broad-Holston Country: A History of Knox County, Tennessee* (Knoxville, 1946), 432–33; Doughty, *Greeneville*, 259, 261.

2. According to one newspaper account, the Greeneville meeting occurred on Wednesday and Thursday, March 3 and 4. See *Knoxville Press and Herald*, Mar. 12, 1869.

3. A longtime Johnson acquaintance, James Britton, Jr. (1811–1871), was a Greeneville lawyer and attorney general of the circuit court. He delivered the opening address when Johnson returned to Greeneville on March 20. *Knoxville Press and Herald*, Mar. 21, 1869; Buford Reynolds, comp., *Greene County, Tennessee Cemeteries* (Greeneville, Tenn., 1971), 278; Doughty, *Greeneville*, 37, 245, 249–50. See also Speech at Greeneville, Mar. 20, 1869, and Appendix III.

4. Beeks (b. c1839) was a Greeneville lawyer who served as recording secretary of the Farmers and Mechanics Association in 1870. 1870 Census, Tenn., Greene, 10th Dist., Greeneville, 7; Doughty, *Greeneville*, 251.

5. A copy is not found enclosed. The four resolutions adopted on March 4 expressed approval of Johnson's administration, pleasure at his decision to make Greeneville his home, and an invitation to a public meeting and rally on the day of Johnson's return to Greeneville. *Knoxville Press and Herald*, Mar. 12, 1869.

From Edouard E. Bermudez[1]

New Orleans, March 9th 1869.

Most respected sir,

The heroic—resistance which, to the world's admiration, you have opposed to the relentless ursurpations of a fanatical congress & the ever memorable devotion which, likewise, you have evidenced in the vindication of southern rights, while you filled the Presidential chair, have inspired me, as the representative, on this occasion, of a number of distinguished citizens, with the idea of begging from you a signal favor, which I feel assured, you will cheerfully grant, if it be in your power to do so.

The South had a College, which it did justly boast of & which was probably the only one which we could point to, with pride, and that was Spring Hill College, near Mobile Ala. The main building was of brick, measured 325 in length & four stories high, it had an extensive library, museum & laboratory and other important dependencies, with $125,000., all of which was accidentally destroyed by fire on the 4th to the 5th of February last.[2] The amount of insurance on same was $35,000 only; the debts of the Institution amount to upwards of $20,000, but the creditors are disposed to allow time for the payment of their claim.

I am the oldest graduate of the College under its late administration and professionally know that the Faculty have not the means of rebuilding, and am satisfied that, unless they receive some substantial relief, the college will remain a heap of ruins.

The alumni (as you will perceive by the enclosed editorial of one of the City papers)[3] have taken the matter in hands, here & in Mobile; they spare no effort to assist in the rebuilding and are hopeful that, with some cooperation, they may prove of some considerable help. They have opened subscription lists, organized a Concert, a theatrical entertainment, have planned a Fair, and thought of a series of lectures, by Gentlemen of position in the community. This last method will not probably prove successful, unless Citizens of national eminence assist in the accomplishment of the object in view.

To that end it is, Sir, that I come to day to beg you to lend us your mighty support by coming to this City and delivering before our People, one or two discourses on those subjects which *you know must command their attention.*

The mere mention of your great name will secure the attendance of thousands and, assist us signally in the fulfillment of the result we contemplate.

Trusting that you will deign accede to our ardent supplication and thankful for the attention which you will kindly give it . . .

E Burmudez
Chairman   Comee. of S.H.C. alumni.

ALS, DLC-JP.

1. Bermudez (1832–1892), an 1851 graduate of Spring Hill College, became a renowned lawyer and jurist in New Orleans. Although opposed to secession, he served in the Confederate army. In 1867 Sheridan removed him from office as assistant city attorney. Afterwards Bermudez resumed the private practice of law and eventually served on the state supreme court. *DAB.*

2. A report of the fire may be found in the *Mobile Register*, February 6, 1869.

3. The New Orleans paper referred to is not found enclosed. However, one of the Mobile papers reported on some of the fund raising activities of the alumni. See *Mobile Register*, Mar. 17, 1869.

From Henry O'Moel Ryan

Washington, D C   March *10th* 1869

Having had the honor of an interview, with your Excellency yesterday, when I mentioned to your Excellency my desire to proceed with you to Europe in the capacity of servant Having travelled through Europe I flatter myself I would be of great service to you. In hope of meeting your Excellencys approval And humbly begging of Your Excellency a reply.

Praying to Our Almighty Father to grant Your Excellency long life and prosperity . . .

Henry O'Moel Ryan

P.S. Would Your Excellency condecend to reply please address as follows—Henry O'Moel Ryan   Washington D C.

ALS, DLC-JP.

From John P. Holtsinger

Greenville Tenn   Mch 11 1869

What day will you certainly arrive here. Please answer immediately.

Jno. P Holtsinger

Tel, DLC-JP.

From Benjamin C. Howard[1]

No. 220. North Charles Street

Baltimore   March 11. 1869

Respected Sir.

I said to you, in a momentary interview, this morning, that Mrs. Howard[2] had a very interesting Souvenir, which she was anxious to present to you, in person and alone.

The object of this note is to enquire if you can afford her an audience of a few moments before your leaving the city.

Benjn. C. Howard

ALS, DLC-JP.

1. Howard (1791–1872) was a prominent lawyer and politician from Baltimore. Having earlier served in several political offices, he was U.S. Representative in the 1830s. Afterwards he served as reporter of the U.S. Supreme Court (1843–61). He lost a gubernatorial race in 1861. *DAB*.

2. Jane Gilmor (*c*1802–*fl*1890) married Benjamin Howard in 1818. What souvenir she intended to give to Johnson is unknown. 1850 Census, Md., Baltimore, Baltimore, 1st Dist., 278; Baltimore directories (1875–90); *DAB*.

Response in Baltimore

BALTIMORE, Md., March 11. [1869]

GENTLEMEN—

In rising after the resolution has been read and sentiments thereon expressed,[1] it is not for the purpose of making an address, but simply to return my thanks for the compliment. I have no speech to make relative to public affairs but what has been already expressed, and in rising now it is only to tender my thanks. I am free to say that during the last four years, in the arduous struggle going on for constitutional liberty, in its darkest hour, the confidence and encouragement of the State of Maryland has been an encouragement peculiarly sustaining in its character, for when the crisis arrived, Maryland seemed to be always standing for the Constitution and the Union. I repeat my only purpose in rising is to return thanks, but I will say, in retiring from the most exalted position in the gift of a free people, and resuming the position of a citizen, I feel more honored than I would to-morrow in being President. I feel more pride in being an American citizen to-night than I would in being inaugurated President over the ruins of a violated constitution. Yes, my deliverance is the greatest case of emancipation since the rebellion. I stand a free man, and would rather be a free man than be President and be a slave. The speech you have made me to-day and to-night shall be treasured up as long as one pulsation shall be sent from my heart, and carried with me. Accept my thanks, not as simple utterances, but as the expressions of a heart overwhelming with thanks for the kind reception you have given me.

New York World, Mar. 12, 1869.

1. The toast that preceded Johnson's remarks praised the ex-President as "the bulwark of equal rights, the champion of the only true and permanent Union of these States, and the defender and martyr of the Constitution." It moreover expressed hopes about "his future efforts and influence for the liberation of the captive States of the Union." *New York World*, Mar. 12, 1869. Two days prior to the Baltimore dinner, Johnson had been sent a copy of this toast. It was attached to N. Rufus Gill to Johnson, Mar. 9, 1869, Johnson Papers, LC.

From Louis B. Weymouth[1]

North Dixmont [Maine]   March 14th 1869

Dear Sir.

Have just read your valedictory.[2] I cannot let this opportunity pass without expressing my gratitude to you as a faithful servant of the people.

I have watched you faithfully since 1860. I could not in 64 give you my vote. I say this with all courtesy. Your views in regard to the Southern States were sound and patriotic. If ever a President of these United States was ever maligned you are that man. You have manfully and like a true patriot defended the Constitution of your Country amid the peril and excitement of the worst feelings that ever pervaded this Country. You remained faithful to your Country in its darkest days among the faithless. No instance in the history of this Country, unless it be that noble pure Geo B McClellan who refused to become a dog for the rads when he commanded the Potomac Army. When the leader of a great party will break from it, when he is in the highest office within their gift, and realizing fully the consequences. You could not remain with the radicals at the same time be true the Constitution. You had the courage patriotism of your imperiled Country at heart. You did not leave the party they left you. They did not carry out the principles on which they were elected.

In closing this imperfect letter, may your life be long happy and prosperous, may history do you justice. Finally may the people of oppressed Tenn. make you their Representative in the Halls of Congress.

It would gratify me and the Democracy of Maine to have you once more in the U.S. Senate.

Louis B. Weymouth

ALS, DLC-JP.
  1. Not identified.
  2. Farewell Address, Mar. 4, 1869.

Speech at Charlottesville, Va.

[March 18, 1869][1]

He was introduced very happily, by Mr. McKenney,[2] and after repeatedly bowing his acknowledgments to the crowd, who received him with prolonged and vociferous cheers, he commenced by saying: That it was not his purpose to make a speech; that he merely wished to return his thanks for the honor they did him, in thus testifying their approval of his cause; and that he felt more satisfaction and gratification in knowing that he had merited and obtained the approval of his fellow-citizens, than he could have done, had he been a second time inaugurated President upon the ruins of a violated constitution. Turning to the students he begged them that while laying the foundation of their education and future usefulness, they would study the constitution. He said into their hands would soon fall the task of maintaining and defending it, and that a thorough knowledge of its principles was the only means by which they could render those principles perpetual. He urged them to stand by it as the only ark of political safety, and to cling to it as the shiprecked mariner in the night of storms and tempests, clings to the last plank. He said that in returning to private life, he carried with him the proud consciousness of having done his duty; that he had struggled to maintain the constitution of our fathers; that he felt that he had been true to his country, his conscience and his God, and that he was going home to take his place among the ranks of his fellow citizens, and help them bear the burdens that he has been unable to remove from their shoulders, and that in thus returning to the pursuits of private life, that he could say from his heart, varying the quotation slightly—

> "More true joy, Marcellus exiled feels
> Than Caesar with a corrupt Congress at his heels."[3]

He advised the young men to read and study Addison's Cato, that although it was a dry play, (in which opinion we do not agree) that there was a stern virtue and patriotism, pervading the whole of it, which makes it one which every student and patriot should read and study. He insisted that something must be done to curb the fanatical power of worthless majorities; that minorities must be protected in their rights, or the government must go to ruin. He said that he hoped this could be done, that he was going home to do all he could, and that if he could do no more, following the advice of Cato to his son, he could retire to his rural home, and there among his own groves would pray for his country.[4] He closed by again thanking the crowd for their kind demonstrations of respect and approval, and wishing to each and all the brightest blessings of Providence on all their efforts. He retired amid the shouts of the crowd, to the dining-room of the Central Hotel, where Mr. Bailey,[5] no doubt, gave him the best the county can afford.

Charlottesville Chronicle, Mar. 20, 1869.

1. According to newspaper reports, Johnson was in Charlottesville on Thursday; that Thursday would have been March 18.

2. Newspapers disagree on the name of the person who introduced Johnson at the Charlottesville rally. One says that it was Samuel McKenney of Tennessee, who was a student at the University of Virginia. Another account reports that C. H. McKinney introduced Johnson. It seems likely that it would have been Samuel McKinney, identified in an earlier Johnson volume, who graduated from the university and was the son of Robert J. McKinney of Greeneville. *Charlottesville Chronicle*, Mar. 20, 1869; *Richmond Dispatch*, Mar. 20, 1869. See *Johnson Papers*, 7: 329.

3. This is a slight variation of lines from Alexander Pope's *Essay on Man. Epistle IV*.

4. A reference to Cato's advice to his son, Portius. From Addison's *Cato*, act 4, sc. 4.

5. Rice G. Bailey (c1812–fl1870) was a hotel proprietor in Charlottesville. 1870 Census, Va., Albemarle, Fredericksville Parish, Charlottesville, 15.

Speech in Lynchburg, Va.

[March 18, 1869][1]

GENTLEMEN:

It is not my purpose to address you, but to return my sincere thanks for the compliment you bestow upon me in this cordial reception.[2]

I come among you as a private citizen unincumbered by office, with a right to enjoy the civilities and hospitalities of a citizen anywhere in the United States. And I assure you that I enjoy them nowhere more pleasantly than in this place and on this occasion. In allusion to our recent unhappy struggle I have little or nothing to say. As a private citizen there can be no objection to my expressing my feelings of gratitude and pride with which I have enjoyed freedom for the last two weeks. You have heard a great deal about the abolition of slavery, emancipation and the freedmen. I can call your attention to the greatest case of slavery that has ever existed in the United States. For the last four years I have been the completest slave throughout the length and breadth of the United States. And standing here as a free man I thank God that I am a free man, and have the privilege of speaking as a free man and a private citizen. I must be permitted to remark, emancipated as I am from the labors and perils of official position, and stepping from the highest office in their gift into the ranks, to aid them in bearing the burdens that I have not been able to remove, that it afforded me more pleasure and pride to be emancipated and come among then to help bear those burdens, than to preside over the United States and its violated Constitution.

Your attention has been called to the Constitution here to-night. When I came into power and position, I looked to the source of our distress and difficulties—to these shattered and torn States. My greatest anxiety was to heal the breaches, and to bind up the wounds. I commenced to work at the point at which you accepted terms at the conclusion of the disaster, and by aiding and helping in a kind and liberal manner to restore to position and union and harmony and good feeling. But I need not say that my efforts in that direction were futile.

Up to the time of the meeting of the 39th Congress your members were knocking at the door ready to be admitted and enjoy a participation in the privileges of government. But from the assembling of that body distractions and broils have been rife. It is familiar to you all.

I to-night, as your fellow citizen, propose to take that position as a citizen which conduces most to bring about a consummation of the wishes I have expressed as to the prosperity, peace and happiness of our country. Familiar as I am with matters, I am perhaps not as hopeful as some. Yet I have great hope for redemption. I have a great and unfaltering confidence in THE PEOPLE. The recent results may indicate that that confidence has been improperly reposed. That confidence still I have, and my hope and trust is unfaltering that when tyrannical power shall have had its day our Constitution and laws will resume sway. I hope that the people's apathy and indifference and submission, without alarm will give way, and the crust of prejudice will be dissipated.

I repeat that I have enjoyed more real and unfeigned pleasure and satisfaction during the two weeks, since my retirement from office, than during the preceding four years. When I look at the contrast, it is alarming. One department of the government has been resolved into an absolute despotism by the two Houses of Congress for the last four years. They have exercised powers and usurped prerogatives at which Kings and Princes would have shuddered in their separate individual capacity. Acting together in a body one has encouraged another in perpetration of enormities. We have seen the Constitution set aside, and seen Congress exercise all the powers of government, and have a perfect parallel of what Mr. Jefferson described, when, speaking of a State Legislature, he said that "when unlimited authority is conferred on numbers, it was an exact definition of despotic power."[3] Many will do what an individual would shrink from. I trust these evil appearances will soon give way to a better state of affairs.

There is one other thing to which I would invite your attention. We have witnessed an increase of expenditures and taxation. Corruption has permeated into every department of the Government; and in retiring from public office, where corruption has pervaded every department of the Government, I might almost exclaim.

> "When vice prevails and vicious men have sway,
> The post of honor is the private station;"[4]

and if I do no more when I return to my rustic country home, I may adopt Cato's advice to his son, to "retire to his Sabine field and pray for his country."[5] Yes, in retiring from power I feel prouder and feel more honored than I would if I were again about to be President for the next four years.

In conclusion be pleased to accept my sincere thanks for this cordial reception and distinguished manifestations of your kindness and regard. It is peculiarly acceptable to me, I will carry it with me, and so long as I live, will this occasion be remembered.

I thank you, gentlemen, for this kind manifestation of respect.

Charlottesville Chronicle, Mar. 20, 1869.

1. Although the *Charlottesville Chronicle* did not date Johnson's Lynchburg speech, other papers did. *Nashville Union and American*, Mar. 25, 1869.

2. When Johnson reached Lynchburg he was "enthusiastically greeted at the depot, and conveyed in an open carriage to the Norvell House." That evening a banquet was given at the hotel, during which toasts were made to the recent president, and Johnson responded with a short speech. *Nashville Union and American*, Mar. 25, 1869.

3. A slightly garbled rendering of Thomas Jefferson's complaints regarding the Virginia legislature, from his *Notes on the State of Virginia*, query xiii.

4. From Addison's *Cato*, act 1, sc. 1.

5. Ibid., act 4, sc. 4.

From Augustus H. Garland

Little Rock, Ark., March 19th 1869

Mr. President,

Such you were when I first knew you, such you were all the time I have known you, such I wish you were now, and such I hope to see the day you will be again, although now you are not President.

It has been my good fortune to write several letters during your administration, and at all times it was my pleasure to give my feeble aid to your efforts to restore our country to law, peace & prosperity; and I did hope you would be continued in office for another term, but fate decreed otherwise, and now you are in private life *a looker on.*

It would have been to me the finest day of my life, if we could have nominated you at N York last summer, & then elected you: but, a nomination without an election might have crippled you for future usefulness. While, of course, the nomination by your party would have been more than agreeable to you, yet if you had not been elected, both yourself & the country might have suffered from it.

You now return to your own people, without trammel uncommitted save to those great principles for which you have battled all your life—full of energy as ever, and your talents sharpened by experience, observation, & the closest & warmest of contests. You stand on your record, and on it great battles can be fought & won for right

& justice against wrong and injustice. Your farewell to the people has stirred the public heart & moved it to its core—and in time, the people will arouse & come forth under its influence, as the war horse springs at the sound of the trumpet. There can be no mistake of this. If there can be, then "all is lost."

If you can not stem the tide of poison that is now destroying the institutions of the country, no one can; and I religiously believe with your position you can do it. And there is no place so suitable as Tennessee in which to begin the struggle and when the chain is once broken then there is an end of it. The enemies of the constitution will then retire like bats before day-light. To you alone, do we in the distressed south pretend to look; and no language can describe our troubles, our wrongs & our sufferings, and a continuance of them a short time will end the quiet & happiness of this country; and now that you are out of power I know not one friend we can appeal to for relief in our hour of need & dire distress.

It is not for me to advise you & indeed I feel a great delicacy in suggesting anything, but I may express the hope, that you will offer for Governor of Tennessee, & put yourself in place to go into the U S Senate. You are needed *there* and the country wants you there. I do fervently hope this will be your programme—& if it is you will live to see an open endorsement of yourself & course while President. This is a matter of deep & anxious concern to us here—& I do hope nothing will prevent or deter you in this course.

It is reasonable & natural, that now you should desire quiet & repose, but great interests are at stake, & they demand, in my judgment your services and if you are not active in warding off the blows now threatening the liberties of the country, I dare say, our liberties, before another four years, will be lost forever.

On the 15th July 1865 you pardoned me[1] for my sins of rebellion, & I can say, before Heaven, I have been true, in thought, word & act, to the conditions of that pardon, and 9/10 of our people have lived up to this amnesty and for your magnanimous course in this respect, as much as for anything else, are you abused and insulted, and on this issue, I can not (nor can our people) be an indifferent spectator.

Let me urge you then to enter at once into the contest & your name in Tenn will be "a tower of strength."

I wish you would, if convenient, write me. If you do, endorse on the envelope *Private.*

Wherever you are, private or public, accept my thanks for your noble course heretofore, & my best wishes for your future health & happiness.

A. H. Garland

ALS, DLC-JP.
1. See Edward W. Gantt to Johnson, June 29, 1865, *Johnson Papers*, 8: 313–14.

From Caroline Livingston Edmonston

Washington, March 20th 69

Dear and honored Mr. President

Ex. President, if you will, for a time but so far as Pauline[1] and myself are concerned, always, Our President.

We called at Mr. Coyle's the day you left at 10. A M.[2] in the hope that we might once more be favored by a reception. Fancy our disappointment, when we found you had left.

The enclosed from the Chronicle may serve to amuse you[3]—Random Shots of the enemy.

General Grant is still floundering in the mire, but he may possibly extricate himself without suffocating. His present position reminds me of the story of a man who was in mortal dread and terror of rats. He built himself a tower, surrounded by water, and fancied himself safe, and out of their reach. To his horror, and amazement, the next morning they were climbing in myriads, on all sides of the tower, and entering at every possible orivice.

I presented the note of introduction with which you honored me, to Senator Fowler,[4] who cordially tendered his services. The stereotypical expression—How can I serve you?—said he! As a general thing, Mr. Fowler, I replied, Ladies approach the Senators, only to tax them but strange to say, Mrs Edmonston has at the moment, no request to prefer of the Honorable Senator.

Colonel Casey is still awaiting the action of the Senate;[5] There seems to be some difficulty somewhere. We cannot rely at all upon the news-papers for information. They publish startling statements, without any foundation, simply, I believe, to help the news-boys.

Pauline desires me to tender her respectful compliments.

When your thoughts revert to Washington I pray you, do not leave my sister Pauline and myself out of the circle you surround yourself by, in imagination. You made, permit me Mr. Johnson to say, steadfast, and earnest friends of both of us.

Trusting that I may be favored by an answer, at your earliest convenience ...

Mrs C. Edmonston.

ALS, DLC-JP.
1. Her sister Pauline Harris.
2. The Johnsons, who had been staying with John F. Coyle since Grant's inauguration, left Washington at six o'clock on the morning of March 18. *Washington Evening Star*, Mar. 18, 1869.
3. No articles were found enclosed.
4. Joseph S. Fowler of Tennessee.
5. On March 11, 1869, Grant had nominated James F. Casey to be collector of customs at New Orleans. He was not confirmed until March 25, and was commissioned on March 30. Endorsement, James B. Steedman to Johnson, Jan. 17, 1869. See also, *National Intelligencer*, Mar. 24, 26, 1869.

Speech at Greeneville

GREENEVILLE, March 20, 1869.

Fellow Citizens:

In appearing before you, after so long an absence, the reception and cordial welcome I have received incapacitates me from giving proper expression to my emotions. There is no place like home. The poet well exclaims:

> Breathes there the man with soul so dead
> Who never to himself hath said,
> This is my own, my native land?[1]

He spoke of the time, now far back in personal past, when yet young, he had come to Greeneville. Spoke of his early toils and early associations with many of those present, though many more were not there. He said he had always relied upon the people of Greeneville and had never been disappointed. Step by step he had gone the official round. Greeneville had given him the first office he ever filled, in 1835, as Alderman and next Mayor. He then mentioned all the successive offices through which he had passed up to the Presidency, in all of which he had received their support. He spoke of his career as President. He had tried to discharge his duty regardless of the consequences to himself, and he must here be permitted to say, after going all the round of official trust, unparalleled in history that he was proud to be able confidently to ask: "At whose hands have I ever received a bribe throughout this whole routine? I challenge any and all calumniators of mine to place their finger upon a single stain upon my official character. With the consciousness of having done my duty, I can look this audience in the face and ask, whom have I betrayed? Whom have I defrauded?["]

He said he had no intention to make a speech. On returning to their midst, into the ranks of American citizenship, he desired to show his willingness to bear the bonds now resting upon them. He felt more honor in his present position than he would feel to-morrow in a re-inauguration. He had no purpose to talk politics. No time for that now. No parties now. He warned the people that danger approaches the existence of the constitution, already denied, or thrust in the background, by the dominant party and an arbitrary Congress, which assumes its discretion as the limit of power. No longer do old party differences divide us, but it is now a question of Government: of constitution and law, on the one hand, or a despotic power on the other. The people had better have a prince or a king ruling over them than an arbitrary body enacting laws and measures so unwarrantable and terrible in character.

A great deal has been said about slavery and its abolition. He declared that for the last four years he had been the greatest slave on the earth. The fourth of March was Emancipation Day to him. If the constitution is not wrested, within the next two years, from the hands of the usurpers, it is gone and our government is gone, and despotism rules supreme. He alluded to the interesting and trying times of eight years ago and indulged in many pleasant reminiscences of the land of his youth. He was now at home again, his public career had ended. He will labor to relieve his fellow citizens of the bonds now upon them. He will adopt Cato's advice to his son, and if nothing can be done, he will repair to some Sabine Cave and pray for his country.[2]

He concluded with a renewal of his thanks for their very cordial welcome and withdrew amidst the immense cheerings of the people.[3]

Knoxville Press and Herald, Mar. 21, 1869.

    1. From Sir Walter Scott's *Lay of the Last Minstrel*, canto 6, st. 1.

    2. From Addison's *Cato*, act 4, sc. 4.

    3. See also Henry H. Ingersoll to Johnson, Mar. 8, 1869, and Appendix III.

From William C. Davison[1]

No 145 Sixth St.   Buffalo   March 21st 1869

Dear sir

I dressed you several steps to try to awaken you to the Cause of true Liberty, one of which was the disruption of the wheel of Progress. Now frind andrew I can finally forgive for your vetoe adminstration for you thought that you was bound to support the Constitution as it was, but let me assure you that, oppressive Constitutions and Creads will all crumble to pieces under the burning light of the nineteenth Century. Not only the Creads and Constitutions but their supporters to will all be brought low by the Sythe of Equal rights. The Democrats are now in the same condition that the Whigs ware years ago. They then had hold of the Tail of Polatiks and ware trying to hold the ear of Progress and growling and finding fault all the time with what the Democrats done. Whig papers ware onely growling Sheets, like the N York World. The Democrats layed out the work and went about to due it. Now the Republicans have the advance and the Democrats here have got hold of the tail. Some we find holding on to the Tail of that Miserable oald Constitution after the Boddy has gone to the Tomb and its epitaff been writen deep with fire and sword over our land.

Now friend Andrew let the oald Constitution stay in its grave and no more raise its hideous gost to torment and enslave mankind. Let the gosts of the thousands that have died fighting for and against it gurd it there, and let us look ahead to better things that now every man can set under his own vine and fig tree and injoy the fruit of his own hands and none dare make him afraid. There may be some Ku Klux Clans but these will soon be regulated and the union as it is will soon work harmoneously and those old Stars and Stripes will be hailed by all the world as the simbol of Liberty to all mankind.

Please excuse my presumption.

Wm. C. Davison

ALS, DLC-JP.

1. Davison (c1806–1875) was variously a marine inspector, a lake captain, and eventually (by 1870) a retired mariner. *Buffalo Express*, May 18, 1875; Buffalo directories (1861–74); 1870 Census, N.Y., Erie, Buffalo, 9th Ward, 46.

Interview with Cincinnati Commercial *Correspondent* [1]
[March 22, 1869][2]

ANDREW AT HOME

Since his return he has not made his appearance upon the streets, but remains quietly under his own vine and fig tree, receiving visits from his own acquaintances. As might be supposed, his conversation is almost entirely confined to political subjects, and he takes as much pains to explain and defend his course while President, to a neighbor who happens to drop in, as he would to an audience of a thousand people. He says if his policy had been adopted in the matter of reconstruction after the war, that to-day we would be a united and a happy people, without the internal broils and confusion which are too apparent on every hand in the South. He says he regards the American people in the light of a large family, who have unfortunately fallen into a dispute, and where mutual concessions are necessary on both sides. A family may quarrel bitterly, and come to blows, but after it is all over and quieted, through the exercise of a christian and forgiving spirit, each one of that family feel even better than they did before they had the disturbance, for they have the inward consciousness of having forgiven each other their trespasses.

He says that the reason Grant gives so much dissatisfaction in the appointment of officers is, that he is not experienced in public life, and has no chart or compass to go by. Without a man has cardinal points laid out and a harbor to steer to, he will become befogged and confused. It can not be said that he will lose his course, for he has no course to go by, but drifts about at the mercy of wind and wave. Grant, he says, is a man picked up for his great military reputation, and consequently his great popularity. The Radicals had to take him, although they were somewhat in doubt as to his being genuinely Radical, but to save themselves from defeat they took him, and his record as a brilliant commander in the field elected him. He had never held a civil office before—never had been taught in the school of experience, and blunders might be expected in the selection of subordinates. But everything will come around right after a while. The mass of the American people, at heart, are attached to the Union and the constitution as no people ever before, and though they may be led astray by politicians for a while, they will see the danger before it is too late, and rally to the support of the constitution of our fathers. He has an abiding faith in the people, and a faith that has never been shaken. And so the ex-President will talk by the hour to any and all who may call upon him, from the highest to the lowest. None are so humble, or so poor, or so illy-clad, but whom he will take by the hand and converse with. The old citizens of Greeneville say that this is the great reason of his popularity. He says himself that he never so far forgets his own humble origin as to turn away from the poor in purse and low in spirit. At Jonesboro it happened that three little fellows were crowded up right against the platform of the special car. As he came out, he bowed to the crowd and then shook the hands of these little boys, who were evidently astonished at such extrordinary conduct. They at first looked puzzled, but as he spoke kindly to them, their young faces lit up with joy. Doubtless in after years they will look back to the time when they received such tokens of regard from a man who will occupy so large a place in history.

A TALK WITH THE EX-PRESIDENT

I dropped in upon Andy (as he is familiarly called here,) yesterday, and found him alone, which was something remarkable, considering the number that call upon him.

I was shown into a small but neatly furnished parlor, containing a piano, two or three small tables, and other furniture to correspond. Upon the walls hung pictures of Lincoln, Jackson, Washington and Johnson, and several fine pictures representing Swiss scenery.

He immediately entered into conversation. "I am going up to Henderson this evening," he said, "to see how they are getting along there.[3] Before the war I had a very pretty place up there, but I have not seen it since. I think," he continued, "that we have a beautiful country here in East Tennessee, but we need capital and enterprise. As soon as matters get settled a little, I believe that capitalists from the North will come here in numbers, and help to develop the country; but the people are so thrown out of joint, as it were, and unsettled politically, that men of capital seem afraid to come in here; but this state of affairs will not—cannot, in fact—last long, and, in my opinion, East Tennessee has a future as bright as any section of the country. Our superior soil and climate, together with our great mineral wealth, will be sure to attract immigration as soon as we become a little more settled in a political point of view. We want peace and order in the country, and more confidence in each other. I have always been opposed to anything and everything that would breed tumult and disorder; in short, I have always been a peace man, and opposed to war or the shedding of blood when it could possibly be avoided. At the commencement of our late unhappy struggle I took decided grounds against secession because I knew that it would bring war and bloodshed. I said to the people, let us fight this battle in the Union and under the constitution; let it be a battle of words, as it were, and not a battle of swords. I told the Southern people that if they had been wronged they should seek redress in the Union and under the constitution. For taking this stand and doing all I could to kill the secession movement and make the people stand firm by the Union, I was denounced as a traitor and a tory, and forced to leave my home and have my property destroyed. On the 12th of June, 1861, I left this home because I could stay here no longer. I was hooted-at and insulted in every possible way, and my life threatened. Now, some of the very men who were engaged in this, some of the very men who used to denounce me as a traitor and a tory, because I stood by the government, have since turned to be very loyal, and denounce me as a traitor because I want to stand by the constitution, as I stood by the Union. There are two very bad classes of men in the country," he continued, "and they are what might be called Rebel Unionists and Yankee Rebels. By a Rebel Unionist I mean a man who was very much of a Rebel at first, and wanted to drive every Union man out of the country, as they did me, and who have since turned to be so very loyal that they are unwilling that an honest Rebel should have any rights at all. We have many instances of this class of men in this State; men who deserted the sinking fortunes of the rebellion, when they saw that it was sinking, who are now so wonderfully loyal as to denounce everybody as 'Rebels' and 'traitors' who do not happen to believe as they do. In my opinion, as I said before, another bad class of men in the South are Yankee Rebels— that is, men of Northern birth and education, who espoused the cause of rebellion. When the worst came to the worst, and we saw that there would have to be a war, we naturally looked to the Northern residents of the South for assistance, but in a majority of instances they went against their government."

In speaking of slavery he said: "I never bought but two or three slaves in my life, and I never sold one. The fact is," he said, laughing, "I was always more of a slave than any I owned. Slavery existed here among us, and those that I bought I bought because they wanted me to."

In speaking of the country at large, he said: "There never has been such a glorious country on the face of the earth, and if we can only

get along and patiently bear with each other, all will come right finally. If the North and the South understood each other better there
would be nothing in the way of our being united, prosperous and
happy. That is the greatest desire I have—to see the people of all
sections of our country living in harmony and peace. That was one
reason why I was so bitterly opposed to the secession movement; if
successful, it would have divided and forever ruined the country. In
unity there is strength, but in division there is weakness. The war
was waged to preserve our unity—to uphold the constitution. In
other words the war was waged on the part of the Union people to
compel the Southern people to live in the Union. The Unionists
said: 'You can't go, you must live with us.' Well, the war for the Union
was successful, and now isn't it absurd to turn around and say to the
Southern people, 'We spent a good deal of blood and treasure to
make you live in the Union, but you shan't have any more power
than if you didn't exist.' In such a Union there is about as much
weakness as in no Union at all.

There never was," he continued, "such a glorious opening for the
American people, as there is now, if they will only let the past go,
and look to the future. If we will but live together, harmonize, and be
friends, we will become the greatest nation on earth. What a splendid opportunity," he continued, "for young men just starting out in
life, if they will only be true to themselves and use reasonable industry. I don't care whether he is at the bar, or at the plow, a mechanic,
or a medical student, he lives in a golden age, and an age that he can
distinguish himself in, if he will only persevere in the right course.
Young men are sometimes discouraged because they think their reward for patient toil is slow in coming, but if they will keep right
straight ahead, and not allow themselves to be discouraged at any
thing, there is always some one who will discover their merit and
lend them a helping hand.

There is a great deal said about education, and wealth, and family
connection, and all that, but it all amounts to nothing, unless a young
man is determined to make something out of himself. Education is,
of course, a great advantage, but he that depends solely upon that
will find himself outstripped in the race of life. So a young man who
thinks that, because his family is rich and powerful, he must necessarily be so, will find himself mistaken. A wealthy family are liable to
be broken up and their riches scattered to the four winds, and then
what is the condition of the young man who thought nothing else
was needed?

It matters not what pursuit a young man may follow, or what profession he adopts, if he will only be industrious and economize his time, success will be his sooner or later. Never, in the history of the world, has there been such an opening for young men as there now is in America. The ground is already prepared for the seed—all they have to do is to sow good seed, and the harvest will come in due time."

I mentioned his own case as an illustration of the American system which afforded a chance to all, and told him I had been around to see the tailor shop, where he had first got a start in the world.

"Yes," he said laughingly, "the old shop is there yet, but a great many things connected with it are lost. My old, original sign, together with one or two benches or tables, I had in the cellar, but when the Southern troops made a hospital at my house they destroyed them. I also had a pair of the best shears for the purpose of my trade I ever saw; they were large, and so arranged that a man could use them half a day at a time without tiring his hand like other shears. I was very careful of them, but they went the way of my other things. The Rebel troops used my house as a hospital, and conveyed off or destroyed everything movable. I regret the loss of my books. They were not valuable, in one sense of the word, but dollars and cents cannot replace them. There was one in particular that I believe formed a turning point in my life; that is, it caused my thoughts to take a channel which they might not and probably would not have otherwise taken. This book was a volume of extracts from the speeches of Pitt, Fox, Burke and other English orators. When I was learning my trade at Raleigh, North Carolina, a gentleman used to come into the shop and read aloud, and seeing that we tailors enjoyed it so much, he used frequently to come, and finally gave me the book which was the first property I ever owned. How many times I have read the book I am unable to say, but I am satisfied it caused my life to take a different turn from what it otherwise would. I also had a grammar, arithmetic and geography, of which I became the possessor sometime afterward, and which I prized very highly. Of all my books that I left, I have never heard of but one. The soldiers made away with them all. A few years ago, while I was in Washington, a gentleman in Virginia came across one of my old books and knew it by my name being on the fly-leaf. He sent it to me, but requested that I let him keep it, which I did."

In conversation Johnson is very pleasant, talks readily, but with great earnestness. He never seems to hesitate for a word, but words and sentences follow each other in rapid succession, and in a uniform pitch of voice. His hair is now quite grey, but otherwise there is nothing about him that would indicate his being over forty-five. His face is cleanly shaved, and quite pale, as it always is. His eye is dark, and in conversation he looks you square in the face. J. W. Forney said of him many years ago, (that was before Forney got to be a dead duck, or Johnson became the great traitor,) "that any one who gazed into his dark eyes, and perused his pale face, would have seen there an unquenchable spirit, and an almost fanatical obstinacy that spoke another language."

Nashville Union and American, Mar. 28, 1869.

1. Augustus J. Ricks (1843–1906) was the East Tennessee correspondent for the *Cincinnati Commercial* and therefore the person who likely conducted this interview with Johnson. Ricks, a native of Ohio, saw military duty with the 104 Ohio Vols. He eventually was post adjutant at Knoxville and settled there at war's end. President Grant nominated him pension agent at Knoxville, but that was blocked largely by Brownlow, who declared Ricks "personally objectionable." Ricks remained in Knoxville as a lawyer before returning to Ohio in 1875. He continued the practice of law there and eventually became a federal district judge. *Nashville Union and American*, Apr. 18, 1869; *Cleveland Banner*, Apr. 22, 1869; *New York Tribune*, Dec. 24, 1906.

2. Since the report of the interview was dated from Greeneville, March 23, and the correspondent refers to conducting the conversation "yesterday," we have concluded that the interview took place on March 22.

3. The reference here is to the Greene County farm that Johnson had earlier purchased from David T. Patterson, who had evidently bought it from Joseph Henderson at a sheriff's sale in 1867. See Patterson to Johnson, Aug. 31, 1867; Johnson to Patterson, Aug. 31, 1867, *Johnson Papers*, 12: 533–34; Robert Tracy McKenzie, "Civil War and Socioeconomic Change in the Upper South: The Survival of Local Agricultural Elites in Tennessee, 1850–1870," *THQ*, 52 (1993): 177.

From B. Franklin Clark [1]

New York, March 24 1869

Dr. Sir:

Allow me to suggest that the most useful thing for yourself, & the country will be a *correct* history of your administration.

Our mutual friend, Hon. Eli Thayer is of the same opinion.

I directed a similar note to you at Baltimore, but presume it was not recd.

I shall be glad to know if this has been recd.

B. Franklin Clark

LS, DLC-JP.
1. Clark (*fl*1875) was a real estate agent and broker in Brooklyn. New York City directories (1869–72); Brooklyn directories (1869–76).

From Robert Morrow

Knoxville, Tenn.   Mch. 24, 1869.

My dear Sir;

I reached home Saturday afternoon and have enjoyed its quiet more than all the excitement of the past four years.

I enclosed to you the other day an able article from the N.Y. World,[1] wh. sets forth the tendency towards federal centralization and, ultimately, monarchy, more cogently than any that I have seen. The worry over the Tenure of Office Bill still continues in Washington. "Curses, like chickens, come home to roost." I clip the following from Monday's Natl. Intelligencer:[2]

> It was believed last night that the tenure-of-office act would be repealed by a vote of 33 to 30.
> The Republican Senators will hold a caucus this morning in regard to the matter.

I hardly believe the law will be repealed. Revolutionary parties are not apt to (as Senator Morrell[3] says) "*to eat their own words*," and it will be a notable exception to the general rule if a Legislative Assembly should give up a power once usurped and exercised.

There is nothing of interest here, and but little attention paid to national politics. It will take me about two weeks to arrange my mother's affairs[4] properly before going West. By the way, sir, do you remember a reference I made incidentally some time since, that my mother wished to raise two thousand dollars on some real estate, taxed and justly valued at that amount, and was willing to pay the rent of the property, taxes deducted, amounting to at least ten per cent per annum. I find on coming home that it is absolutely necessary to raise this amount and knowing that you had money to invest and that you could not invest this amount more surely or profitably, I have taken the liberty of mentioning. I would be glad if you would let me know, thro' someone, of your opinion of the investment.

If you would cause to be sent to me one hundred or more copies of your *farewell address* I could distribut them easily in good places.

R. Morrow

ALS, DLC-JP.

1. Doubtless a reference to the *New York World*, March 19, 1869, editorial, "Whither We Are Tending." Among other points, it argued that the four years of incessant warfare and strife between the President and the Congress had eroded the balance between the two branches. Ironically, this circumstance could open the way to monarchy in America.

2. *National Intelligencer*, Mar. 22, 1869.

3. Either Justin S. Morrill of Vermont or Lot M. Morrill of Maine.

4. Malinda Armstrong Morrow (1817–1884) had married Samuel Morrow in January 1840. She had been a widow since 1864. WPA, "Knox County, Tennessee Tombstone Records. Old Gray Cemetery" (typescript, 1938), 86; WPA, "Knox County Marriage License Record Book, 1838–1850" (typescript, 1937), 13.

From Joseph Ramsey

Shelbyville   March 24th 1869

Respected & Dear Sir

Seeing that you are Relieved from that Responsibility, & Burden that you hav Ben Labouring under for the Last four years, and are permitted to Retire to private life (for a Season)—I feel Induced to Say to you, that your Labour zeal Energy firmness & untiring Devotion to the preservation & perpetuation of Civil Government & Human Liberty meet my approbation & Approval and in due time the Approval & Admiration of Posterity. It will have Erected A Monument to your Fame more Lasting and Enduring than the Tower of Babel whilst the Conduct of your opponents will likewise have Erected a monument to their everlasting Disgrace. There is a Divinity to be seen and felt (whether Acknowleged or not) in Honesty Candor & Truth and sooner or Later will prevail. Of Course your greatest Reccord is the Approval of a good Conscience which is worth more In point of Real Happiness than all the Applause that an Ignorant Selfish Rabble Can give utterance to.

But Sir Can you now feel that you should sheath your sword whilst Knaves & Tyrants are waging war against Liberty Independence and the Lawful Rights of man. When we look upon our Beloved State In what a Deplorable Condition we find things now to Exist, let me give you an Example of what Transpired here last Saturday. We had what was called an Election in this Town for Constable in which two were to be Elected. After the Farce was gone through with and the votes Counted out Cal Thompson (A full Blooded negro),[1] and a Stranger Recently moved in by the name of Crick[2] Were Triumphantly Elected. This white man the Stranger that was Elected is a man of Doubtful character for Honesty Being charged with Stealing Horses. The Reason of this State of things is this, the Commissioner of Registration old Jim Martin[3] Assistant Door Keeper in 1865 Who Knows About as much of Honesty and Fair Dealing as a Cat does About Religion he Refuses to give Conservative Ticketts under all most any Circumstances. But will place Blanks in the hands of his Friends to give to All negros or other that will vote the Radical Tickett. By this means the negroes who are all called Loyal Except now & then, one that should be called Consevativ here they can Elect whom they please. In this Town District, Sir this Policy is only Calculated to Turn Loyal Angels into Demoned Rebels. Cannot this Evil be Remedied. I would Like to hear your suggestion, in Relation to this Crying Evil. I would Like to see you govern One man in this State. Let us try and hav If Possible a Consevativ Legislature in this state next fall. I am still permitted to Remain in the Position of Collector for which I am Indebted to you. How Long I may Remain I Cannot Tell. You may hear from me again.

Joseph Ramsey

ALS, DLC-JP.

1. Calvin J. Thompson (*c*1840–1903) was a blacksmith in Bedford County and active in Republican party politics, having served in 1868 as a delegate to the party's county convention. 1870 Census, Tenn., Bedford, 4th Ward of Shelbyville 7th Dist., 3; Helen C. and Timothy R. Marsh, comps., *Bedford County, Tennessee Wills* (Shelbyville, 1984), 149; *Shelbyville Republican,* Aug. 7, 1868.

2. Possibly John G. Crick (b. *c*1846), formerly of Franklin County, who in 1866 married a daughter of John J. Mankin of Bedford County. In 1868 Crick and his father-in-law were partners in a Shelbyville livery stable. 1860 Census, Tenn., Franklin, 7th Dist., 143; (1870), Bedford, Shelbyville, 2nd Ward, 1–2; Helen C. and Timothy R. Marsh, comps., *Cemetery Records of Bedford County, Tennessee* (Shelbyville, 1976), 219; Helen C. and Timothy R. Marsh, comps., *Official Marriages of Bedford County, Tennessee, 1861–1880* (Greenville, S.C., 1996), 40, 183.

3. James C. Martin (1804–1874) was a Shelbyville tailor who also served as a justice of the peace. Marsh, *Cemetery Records of Bedford County,* 263; 1860 Census, Tenn., Bedford, Western Div. 7th Dist., 2; (1870), 5th Ward in Shelbyville 7th Dist., 1.

From Perez Dickinson

Knoxville Tenne.   March 25, 1869

Dear Sir

I notice with pleasure, you intend soon visiting Knoxville.

I desire you to make my House your Home during your stay here, and hope it may be agreable to you to spend a few days with me.[1]

I will be glad to see you, and welcome you and members of your family, or friends you desire to accompany you, at my Home.

P. Dickinson

ALS, DLC-JP.

1. Johnson arrived in Knoxville on April 4, made a speech at the Lamar House, and after-wards spent that evening and a subsequent one at the home of Dickinson. *Knoxville Press and Herald*, Apr. 4, 6, 1869.

From Gazaway B. Lamar, Sr.

Savannah   March 25 1869

Sir,

I intend to publish a reply in part to your Valedictory to the people of the U States—and send you a Copy by this mail.

Gov. Jenkins wrote me that you said "that notwithstanding all you had done for me, I could not be satisfied." I most respectfully request to be informed what it was "you ever did *for me*"—& my address will inform you of only a part of the wrongs & oppressions & damages, I suffered, by your orders—& under your Administration.

I shall await your reply, if you think proper to make one, before I publish the Edition already prepared and I will esteem it a favor to be informed by you, the reasons which moved you to treat me & allow me to be treated as you have done in the past four years—and to suppress the whole, if they do you any injustice.[1]

G. B. Lamar Senr.

ALS, DLC-JP.

1. Lamar and President Johnson had had a troubled relationship throughout the presiden-tial administration. Lamar was convicted in early 1866 of defrauding the U.S. government by the theft of bales of cotton and bribery of army officers. He was released after a short impris-onment and subsequently his sentence was remitted. Johnson evidently pardoned Lamar later, but still incurred the latter's enmity. Charles J. Jenkins to Johnson, Feb. 7, 1866, *Johnson Papers*, 10: 48–49; *Washington Evening Star*, Mar. 2, 3, 1869.

From Alexander Delmar

Private

69 William St   New York   March 26. 1869

Dear Sir:

Yesterday's telegrams announcing your illness[1] have afforded me much pain, for I was one of the few who knew what a Contest you maintained and what a fearful expenditure of vital energy it de-manded. I am glad to know today that you are better. I was attacked in the same way last December, but have so far escaped paralysis, and I think, mainly from the use of frequent doses of bromide of potash. I trust soon to hear of your complete recovery. *Rest*—and plenty of it—is what you most need.

Madame and Mrs. Delmar[2] both send their kind remembrances and wishes for your recovery.

Alex Delmar

ALS, DLC-JP.

1. This is one of several communications received by Johnson about reports of his illness and even death. Gideon Welles reported that the former President had a "severe attack of disease of the kidneys." See Beale, *Welles Diary*, 3: 560.

2. The reference to Madame Delmar may be to Belvedere Delmar (*c*1806–*fl*1870), a native of England and a resident of Alexander Delmar's household. Mrs. Delmar was Emily Delmar (*c*1844–*fl*1870), who kept house for her husband and several children. 1870 Census, N.Y., Kings, 21st Ward, Brooklyn, 305.

From James Holden[1]

161 Townhead   Rochdale [England]
MARCH 26. 1869.

Sir

Pardon me, who am almost a perfect stranger, trespassing on your time and notice—again.

Some time ago—4 or 5 months perhaps—I forwarded you a letter requesting your acceptance of a volume of poems—which accompanied the letter, and which I had then recently published.

I sent the volume purely as a compliment, and as some light expression of my admiration of your Character & Abilities.

To that letter however I have received no reply,—though I have looked out every mail for a reply.

I have wondered many times whether the volume & letter in question ever reached you. If they did I am confident your silence must be attributed to an oversight on your part, and to no want of that kindness & courtesy which I have ever considered to be characterstic of you.

I should therefore be highly gratified to learn from you—if you will so far favor me—whether the Book & Letter ever came in your possession.

The Book is entitled *"Poetic Zephyrs"*; has 350 pages; 8 V O; cloth; GILT edges; & antique type.

Trusting, Sir, you will honor me with a reply (which please send *unstamped*) and with expressions of great Esteem . . .

James Holden

ALS, DLC-JP.

1. Holden authored *Poetic Zephyrs*, which was privately published in 1866. He is not otherwise identified. *NUC*.

From John Smith[1]

Atlanta Ga   26th Mar. 1869

My Dear Sir

I perceive by the Newspapers that you are recovering from your indisposition, let me congratulate you, from the bottom of my heart at the prospect of your restored health. Our poor Nigger Stricken, Nigger polluted and Nigger trodden people could not afford to spare you at this time and we hope that a Kind Providence will permit you to live to witness, the utter overthrow of the Black Monster Niggerism and Carpet Baggism.

In my former letter[2] I quoted from Clay and Webster their opinion of the Nigger Beast which now so afflicts this now almost ruined Country and Government. You may think it is apathy in the Northern people to submit thus quietly to the ruinous, desolating and destructive course of the Niggerites. It is not apathy it is the natural propensity of the Puritan Beast to destroy other weaker peoples provided it put money in their pockets—all history of these Yankee Monsters shows that it has been naturally inherent in them for all time.

Nothing that Clay and Webster predicted 30 and 20 years ago in regard to the doings of the infernal Abolitionists has failed to transpire, much worse than they foretold is now transpiring.

The Imps of Seward now in Congress are committing so many diabolical acts that is far beyond the conceptions of men living in the days of Clay and Webster.

Clay & Webser in their day had the very impersonation before them in the person of Seward of all that was diabolical and destructive yet this Devil conducted himself in such a cowering and Gentlemanly manner that they in a manner let the Raschal pass along. Yet they based their whole predictions on the actions of Seward in conducting the Negro party.

My Father told me 30 years ago that Abolition would break up the Union. Your Father must have been of the same opinion and in fact all reflecting men must have been of that opinion. You beleived that Abolition was Secession. Seward intended Abolition to bring about Secession as the only alternative to bring about Irrepressible Conflict.

Churches split up 30 years ago on the Nigger Society Split up on the same question.

Seward took care to have at least one half of the time of Congress devoted to his Nigger Crusade instead of to the benefit of the Country.

Grant so far has exhibited no Statesmanship although he has a peculiar tact of being offered Lands—Houses, carriages, horses, dogs, cigars Suppers, Wines, dinners, &c &c to an unlimited extent and Swallowing the whole down as presents with the voracity of a Starved dog.

Schuyler Colfax is very little removed from a Slabbering Idiot. The best comparison of Schuyler I have yet seen was given by Mack a Washington correspondent.[3] Mack Says Colfax is like a 2 inches Cylinder driving a 6 foot wheel and observes what a vast improvement in machinery if an Engine would be put upon that principle— a boiler with the demensions of a pint of water running a rail Road train—such is the capacity of Colfax. I am really afraid Grant is a two inch Cylinder. If he is, Sewards imps will have little to retard them in their downward course. I regard our travel in that direction as daily increasing with accellerated speed.

During the progress of the war I observed what a Lick Spitte and boot Licker Seward was to the Russian Bear. His motive for this superciliousness was He held the Bear as a Boogaboo to France & England. Occasionally he would pinch the Bears tail in order that the animal might shows his teeth to those powers which implied "I dare you to intervene." Seward's omnipotance was as universal in Europe as it was at home—his carpet Baggers had been spread all over Europe for years poisinging the minds of the people against the South. I hope you will now study Seward every [?] moment. His political career is as great a curiosty as his crusade has been destructive to the County. It takes a long time to destroy such a Country and Government as ours was—in a few years the fatal effects of Seward's work will begin to develope itself. The poison is slow in its work but sure and fatal. A Nigger Union and Nigger States and Nigger equality which degrade the white man to the Negro level will be fatal.

There is no abatement of the Rancarous Malignancy towards you by Sewards Imps and understrappery. In vain have tried to find any *Just cause* for such a Spirit—unless it be that you were unlike Grant in not accepting *Bribes* from the Raschels.

Sewardism Carpet Bagism & Niggerism is one the same thing. What has transpired, what is transpiring and what is to transpire hereafter was foreseen and planed in Seward's mind as early as 1835. Clay saw through it all in 1839. Webster a blue Bellied Yankee saw through in 1850 and had the courage to denounce it right in their faces. What sublime Patriotism.

The memory of Webster does not stand as high in Blue belly land as that of St John Brown.

John Smith

ALS, DLC-JP.

1. Not identified.

2. Smith's earlier undated, lengthy letter was far more rabid than this one. He railed for numerous pages against Seward and virtually blamed him for causing the Civil War. Smith to Johnson, ca. 1869, Johnson Papers, LC.

3. Joseph B. McCullagh of the *Cincinnati Commercial* and *Chicago Republican*.

From Annie Coyle[1]

Washington   Saturday 27th [March 1869]

My dear President

You can not imagine how frighten and distressed we were when the evening Enquirer announced the death of Ex President Johnson. I for one did not beleave it as I was sure some one would have sent a telegram to us and then about 10. P.M. a telegraph from Mrs Stoover[2] arrived and set our fear at rest. If you had only remained with us you would never have been sick. It is the climate of Tennessee that has done this, so that only shows the necessity of coming back in [Florne's?] place in two years.[3] Frank was over from school yesterday,[4] and was frighten almost to death the night before by one of the boys coming in from the city and telling him that his Father was dead, but I told him about the telegraph from Mrs Stoover so he went back to school contented. Grant is behaving very badly to the Army and the Officers are very angry.[5] So much the better say I, and I only hope every body may follow thier example. Poor Gordon Granger I am afraid he will have to wait some time for his orders.[6] General Hancock has not gone yet to Dokato but will go soon.[7] What a nice time he will have there? Col Moore has been stationed in the pay departements here.[8] Mama and Papa send thier best love to you Mrs Johnson, Mrs Patterson Mrs Stoover Col. Bob. and the chrildren also to Col Morrow[9] if he is with you. Good bye dear Mr President. If you have any photographs taken do not forget me. With lots of love to all the family and a kiss for dear little Belle[10] and one for yourself if you will accept it.

Annie Coyle

ALS, DLC-JP.

1. Coyle (*c*1849–*fl*1880) was the daughter of Johnson's friends John F. and Kate Coyle. In late 1873 she married Henry B. O'Neill and resided with him in Port Huron, Michigan, but by 1880 she was a widow. 1860 Census, D.C., Washington, 4th Ward, 266; (1880), Mich., St. Clair, Port Huron, 398; Annie (Coyle) O'Neill to Johnson, Feb. 9, 1875, Johnson Papers, LC.

2. Mary Johnson Stover.

3. Despite the strange spelling, Coyle may have been thinking of Tennessee Senator Joseph S. Fowler whose term would expire in 1871. *BDUSC.*

4. Andrew "Frank" Johnson, Jr., was a student at Georgetown College.

5. On March 5, 1869, the adjutant general, by new President Ulysses S. Grant's command, issued General Orders No. 10, changing the commands of nine senior generals, in the process insulting some of them and sending others where they did not wish to go. Then, on March 16, the War Department announced General Orders No. 16 consolidating the infantry into twenty-five regiments (from forty-five) and specifying how the officers would be consolidated. David M. Jordan, *Winfield Scott Hancock: A Soldier's Life* (Bloomington, Ind., 1988), 229; *Washington Evening Star*, Mar. 6, 16, 17, 19, 1869.

6. Gordon Granger had been colonel of the 25th Regiment; in the consolidation he lost out to Joseph A. Mower, former colonel of the 39th Regiment. Coyle was correct in predicting that Granger would have a long waiting period, for he was not finally assigned to the 15th Regiment until December 1870. Powell, *Army List*, 337; *Off. Army Reg.* (1869), 152; (1870), 128; *Washington Evening Star*, Mar. 17, 1869.

7. As a result of General Orders No. 10, Hancock was banished to the relatively insignificant Department of Dakota. Jordan, *Winfield Scott Hancock*, 213, 229.

8. An announcement of William G. Moore's assignment appeared in the *Washington Evening Star*, Mar. 26, 1869.

9. Robert Johnson and Robert Morrow.

10. Mary Belle Patterson, Johnson's granddaughter.

From Ellison E. Duncan[1]

Detroit   March 27 /69

Dear Sir

I Saw From Detroit Free Press that you had an attack of Gravel and Suffered intense Pain & as I have had that Complaint Some ten years ago I Know how to Feel For those afflicted with it. The Pain is or was beyond discription with me. I thought I would die Shure. I Called on Doct Lee[2] of N. York City & he gave me Some Pills & in about Six wheeks the gravel & Stones Passed out of me & I have never Enjoyed better health in my whole Life than I have Since that time. I was 40 years old at that time and I Feel as though if you will apply to him For medicine he will Cure you Shure. He is no Quack. He dont advertise in anny Paper. He took From Genl Scoot[3] after the Mexican war Some Stones which he has in his Possession. The medicine he gave me was the Lithintriptic Pill. I would Like to get you Cured if Possible as it Seems as though we Could not Possibly get along without you For Some years yet. As you have Labored For the Last 4 years I want you to be reward & you will be in time. I hope you will Excuse me For intruding on you being that I am a Perfect Stranger but a well wisher.

E. E. Duncan

Brother to Ex Mayor Detroit[4]

P S Address S.H.P. Lee 682—6th Ave Between 39 & 40 st New York City.

ALS, DLC-JP.

1. Duncan (*c*1819–*fl*1881) was a maltster for the ale-brewing industry. 1870 Census, Mich., Wayne, Detroit, 3rd Ward, 49; Detroit directories (1867–81).

2. Samuel H.P. Lee, Jr. (*fl*1874), a New York City physician. His father had discovered a "solvent remedy" for kidney stones in the 1790s called "Dr. Lee's gravel specific." New York City directories (1858–74); *NUC*.

3. Winfield Scott.

4. William C. Duncan (1820–1877) settled in Detroit in 1849, where he became one of the leading ale brewers. He served as alderman for five years, then as mayor (1862–63), and as state senator (1863). Melvin G. Holli and Peter d'A. Jones, eds., *Biographical Dictionary of American Mayors, 1820–1880* (Westport, 1981).

From George H. Locey

Springfield Ills.   Mch 27, 1869

Dr. Sir.

The papers this morning announce that you *still live*. I notice this with peculiar feelings of gratification. I greatly hope you may yet be spared, & I hope that your State, which used to be my own, before the war—(for I was a Prof. in the University of Nashville) will place you in a position where your voice may yet be heard in the Senate—& your power felt by those consummate radicals (rascals) who are destroying the popular form of our Govt. & hurrying it on to ruin with a lever of Centralization greater than was ever before known in the history of nations, & whose oath to maintain the Constitution inviolate, is not worth *a rush*. I know it is unprecedented for a *Prest*. again to enter the political arena, but we are past the day of honored precedents, & the Country needs your services again in the Senate. I hope you may live to compel those who would traduce you, to eat their words, & the public, to stamp your course, as that of an honest man—who saw the dangers, that threatened the Country, & tried to avert them.

I had long ago predicted that you would eschew precedents, & again return to the Senate, when you could battle hand in hand with those who sought to cripple, & foil you in your honest efforts, & hope it may be done.

The present pressure for a repeal of the "Tenure of Office Law"[1] commits the radicals to its unconstitutionality—& the desperate resources to which they had resort, to accomplish their purposes. The people need to hear this from the forum of the Senate, & you are the man to ring the alarum in their ears. May your life be spared is the earnest wish, of . . .

Geo. H. Locey

Box 630

ALS, DLC-JP.

1. See John F. Coyle to Johnson, Mar. 31, 1869, for more on the so-called repeal of the Tenure of Office act.

From Stephen B. Robbins & Company[1]

Overton Hotel

Memphis   Mch 28th 69

Dear Sir

Having understood that you intend visiting Memphis, We take great pleasure in extending to you the hospitality of our house. We have the leading house of Memphis. Genls Granger & Upton[2] are with us and many others that you will meet. Hoping you will accept our invitation . . .[3]

S. B. Robbins & Co.

ALS, DLC-JP.

1. Robbins (c1818–fl1877), a New Hampshire native, was one of the proprietors of the Overton Hotel. He also served as a trustee of the Life Association of America. 1870 Census, Tenn., Shelby, Memphis, 2nd Ward, 21; Memphis directories (1869–77).

2. Generals Gordon Granger and Emory Upton. Upton (1839–1881), of New York and a graduate of West Point, had quite a distinguished military record during the Civil War, particularly in various Virginia engagements. He became commandant of cadets at West Point in 1870 and served for five years; subsequently he was assigned to military duty in California. Warner, *Blue*.

3. Presumably Johnson did in fact stay at the Overton Hotel when he visited Memphis in mid-April. He was escorted there upon his arrival in town and his speech on April 15 was delivered outside the hotel. *Memphis Avalanche*, Apr. 15, 16, 1869.

From Sarah Magruder [1]

Washington   March 29th/69

My dear Mr Johnson

You dont know how terribly distressed I was last week at the news of your sickness, & in fact a report of your death! Oh! It was indeed a time of fasting & prayer with me that your life might be spared to us all for years to come. I wanted to sit right down & write to you then but could not do it. While I was crying so bitterly, Minnie[2] came up & said "Mama, Mr Johnson is a great deal better off, & he wont have *these bad men* to bother him any more!["]

The Dr[3] did not believe it all along and tried to comfort me but it was difficult work I assure you. I do trust you are almost quite well again & we shall continue to hear good news from you. With kindest love to Mrs Johnson & your Daughters I am truly your friend

Sarah Magruder

If Greeneville were a little nearer to us I might go to see you all, and hope to some of these days.

Please let me hear from you soon.

I am truly your friend.

Sarah Magruder

ALS, DLC-JP.

1. A native of Tennessee, Magruder (c1835–1913) worked in the U.S. Treasurer's office in Washington from 1877 through 1883. *U.S. Off. Reg.* (1877–83); Washington, D.C., directories (1868–85); *Washington Post*, Sept. 30, 1913; 1860 Census, D.C., Washington, 1st Ward, 184.

2. Magruder's only child at the time was a daughter, Millicent (c1856–*fl*1912). Ibid.; Dorothy S. Provine, *Index to District of Columbia Wills, 1801–1920* (Baltimore, 1992), 124; Robert H. Harkness, "Dr. William B. Magruder," *Records of the Columbia Historical Society*, 16 (1913): 184.

3. Ironically, Magruder's husband, Dr. William B. Magruder (1810–1869) died almost exactly two months from the date of this letter. William Magruder had been a Washington physician since the 1830s, and had also served on the city council and as mayor (1856–58). 1860 Census, D.C., Washington, 1st Ward, 184; *Washington Evening Star*, May 31, 1869; Harkness, "Magruder," 151.

From Cleveland, Tennessee, Citizens [1]

Cleveland, Tennessee, March 30, 1869.

Dear Sir:—

A large number of your personal and political friends in this vicinity are very desirous that you should visit Cleveland, at no distant time, for the purpose of addressing the citizens of this and adjoining counties on the political questions of the day; and to that end, we have the honor to request you to name a day when it will be convenient for you to visit our city for that purpose.[2]

Pet, DLC-JP.

1. This petition was signed by some thirty-three citizens.

2. Johnson actually passed through Cleveland and stopped briefly between his Knoxville speech and his Nashville speech. But he declined to make a speech at this early April Cleveland gathering. Instead, he returned in mid-June to deliver a three-hour speech at Cleveland. *Cleveland Banner*, Apr. 8, 1869; *Nashville Republican Banner*, June 16, 1869.

From John F. Coyle

Washington   March 30th 1869.

My dear Mr. Johnson

By this same mail goes a letter to Col. Berret, enclosing one from Mr Merrick to you,[1] which so fully explains the condition of affairs, that I need add nothing to it, except to say that in addition to the security in the levied judgements I have ordered deed of trust upon the office effects for the amt. Five thousand dollars. The one thousand was appropriated as follows:[2] Wages to Saturday 13th $785.39— and Hill[3] for Paper $200. I am confident, freed from clutches of a receiver, appointed by a Radical Court, I can within the next two or three weeks divest myself of an embarrassing alliance and be able in the future to exhibit my appreciation of your kindness, by a devotion to your interests. With our most affectionate regards to you all.

John F. Coyle

ALS, DLC-JP.

1. The letters, which were probably to James G. Berret and from Richard T. Merrick, have not been found.

2. Apparently Johnson advanced Coyle $1,000 for the struggling *National Intelligencer* sometime earlier in the month. See Coyle to Johnson, June 30, 1869, Johnson Papers, LC.

3. Probably George Hill, Jr. (*c*1814–*fl*1899), a longtime paper maker and Georgetown postmaster. 1870 Census, D.C., Georgetown, 105; *U.S. Off. Reg.* (1867–69, 1873–77); Washington, D.C., directories (1863–99).

From James F. Irvin[1]

Adel   Dallas   Iowa
March 30 /69

Dr. Sir

Inclosed you will find a notice of your Death[2] which has proved to be a lie a Black Abolition lie and I thank God that it has proved its Self to be Such. I hope to See you president of the united States again for you have been an instrument in the hands of God by which our country has been rescued from the hands of toryism.

Dr. J. F Irvin

ALS, DLC-JP.

1. Irvin (c1828–fl1870), a native of Pennsylvania, was a physician. 1870 Census, Iowa, Dallas, Adel, 15.

2. The notice was from the *Dallas Gazette*, dated March 27, 1869. It printed an announcement published the previous morning by the *Register* which claimed that Johnson had died of paralysis at Greeneville, Tennessee, on March 25.

From John F. Coyle

Washington   Mar 31 1869

My dear Mr. Johnson,

I have hardly words to convey to you, the feeling which prevaded the country on recieving the news of your reported death.[1] The papers from all parts of country come back upon us with comments of the kindest character, and evidences of appreciation of your public and private character. The distress it brought us, and your numerous friends here, and in fact this whole community, evidenced, the warm affection entertained for you and yours.

There is no news here of any moment that would interest you. Your successor seeks relief from the pressure upon him by almost daily indispostion from which he recovers happily, time enough for an afternoon ride.[2] You have seen I presume the revocation of Sherman's order placing the whole War Department under his immediate command?[3] This order was obtained by Rawlings, who tendered his resignation[4] rather than act as a mere clerk, to record Sherman's orders. Already a very strong feeling has grown up and is still growing between the members of Grants family (the Dents & Co)[5] and Gen Rawlings proceeding from jealousy of Rawlings influence. The repeal of the Tenure of Office Act remains with the

Committee of Conference, which is composed of such material, that an agrement seems impossible.[6] The recent speeches of Govenor Sprague, which I presume you have read, provoked universal comment.[7] In a conversation of an hour with him a few nights ago he disclaimed any political object such as the election of Judge Chase in 1872.[8] His sole object being to place his theories before the country, convinced as he says they will eventually arouse that attention which will win them success. His speech of yesterday was even more pronounced than his previous ones.[9] He handled without gloves the New England banking interest and all monopolies as destructive of the moral and material interests of the country.

We have removed from our house on Vermont Avenue and it is now being transformed in to a Hotel, as you were informed when here. All of us are well, and hope you have fully recovered from your illness, which so alarmed and distressed us. Mrs Coyle, Anne and myself, send our most affectionate regards to all of you, and to the Judge, and Mrs Patterson, Mrs Stover,[10] and the children. I will keep you advised of whatever transpires here, and if I can be of any service I pray you command me.

John F. Coyle

LS, DLC-JP.

1. See Annie Coyle to Johnson, Mar. 27, 1869; George H. Locey to Johnson, Mar. 27, 1869; James F. Irvin to Johnson, Mar. 30, 1869.

2. In late March, Grant suffered from facial neuralgia and exhaustion. Simon, *Grant Papers*, 19: xxiv.

3. When Grant took office he immediately appointed William T. Sherman to his own former position of General of the Army and on March 5 ordered that all military business requiring the attention of the President or Secretary of War was to be channeled through the General of the Army. On March 26 this order was rescinded with new directions that business for the President or Secretary of War should be submitted through the Secretary of War. Ibid., 143–44.

4. John A. Rawlins, Grant's former military aide, became Secretary of War after the Sherman order was promulgated.

5. Relatives of Grant's wife, Julia.

6. The two houses of Congress, unable to agree on the bill to repeal the Tenure of Office Act, appointed a conference committee on March 30. In fact, the committee finished revising the bill on the 31st and the House passed it that afternoon. The Senate passed it several days later and Grant signed it, but many people expressed confusion about what the new bill actually did and believed that it did not really repeal the Tenure of Office Act. *Washington Evening Star*, Mar. 30, 31, Apr. 2, 1869; *National Intelligencer*, Apr. 1, 3, 6, 1869.

7. For example, the speech of William Sprague of Rhode Island in the Senate on March 24, 1869, was printed in the *National Intelligencer* of March 31. Sprague claimed that the Senate had no constitutional power to interfere with presidential removal of an officeholder.

8. Salmon P. Chase was Sprague's father-in-law.

9. The *National Intelligencer* did not print the complete March 30 speech.

10. David T. and Martha Johnson Patterson and Mary Johnson Stover.

April 1869

From M. C. Cranston[1]

Stony Run, Oakland Co. Mich.   April 2, 1869.

Dr Sir:

As a number of men in this vicinity, are desirous, on account of health, especially of the *lungs*, of finding a pleasant *home* in the *South*; and, as I believe you would be willing to aid immigration into your favorite State, may I ask you to reply to a few questions, to aid us in obtaining a desirable location?

1st   Which part of Tennessee would you prefer for a Northern man to locate, taking in consideration health, facilities for farming, and other advantages, the vicinity of Greenville, Knoxville, or *Murfreesborough*? I hear the latter very highly spoken of.

From your long residence in the State, you must know all parts of the State well. Your preference as to a location, would have great weight with me.

2nd.   As near as you can judge, at about what price can good farms, with good *buildings, improvements, markets* &c, be bought near the above named places?

3rd   Could you inform me as to the chances for experienced Teachers, in your part of the State?

I would like to come South next Autumn, and teach next winter, with my wife, and, in the mean time, look up a desirable farm of 400 or 500 acres, for a permanent home. Could you tell me what *time* to come, to engage a school, what *course* to pursue, and give me the names of some *prominent* and *proper* men in Murfreesborough, Knoxville and Greenville? Men who could aid me in obtaining a good situation, if my *testimonials*, and references, are perfectly satisfactory?

Now, Mr. Johnson if you could find time, to answer the above questions, and give me the required information, you will confer upon me a very great favor.

Now, kind Sir, will you pardon a digression from the above subject?

I was recently much pained to learn of your late painful illness;[2] but was made to rejoice in the fact, that the same paper that informed me of your illness, also informed me of your recovery, so that you were able to speak in public. May you be spared to battle for the

A second photograph of Andrew Johnson
in Knights Templar regalia.
By C. C. Giers of Nashville, April 1869.
From Ray V. Denslow, *Freemasonry and
the Presidency, U.S.A.* (1952), 126

right; to continue to throw the fire brands of *truth* into the ranks of the enemy, until they scatter, as did the foxes of old, under Samson's *fire proof* renovation,[3] and you are triumphantly returned to the U.S. Senate. I wish all your messages, with the *crowning glory*, the *great Farewell Address*, could be compiled into book form, and a copy placed in every family in the Nation.

I have watched your course as President, your *firm, brave* battles for *truth* and *right*, against the JACOBIN host around you, with feelings of *Admiration*.

O, if the people of this country could only see the true course, as you have so noble portrayed it, how far different the result would be. Mr. Johnson, I am not trying to fawn or flatter; but no man, ever occupied the Presidential chair before you, who could take a long, obscure Bill, from Congress, *suddenly* grasp its *contents* and *effect* on the Country, and in a few hours, write out a message, plainly showing its *evil effects* to the country, and trying so *ably*, to restrain the curse of fanaticism.

And the hight of sublimity was reached, when, during the *impeachment farce*, you firmly defied the *Jacobinistic* rabble, by sending in the Nomination of Maj. Gen. Schofield as Sec. of War, in place of Stanton to be removed as much as to say, that if you were not impeached Stanton would leave,—*Glorious*.

How hard they tried to suspend you from the *powers* and *privileges* of your office, during the Impeachment farce. O, did I not rejoice to see you nobly tell them, that you would never allow that *little thing* to be done. How I watched the treachery of Grant, to get the nomination for President.

Mark his putting his relatives into office down to the fourth generation, something unknown before.[4]

Quite a muddle in the Cabinet during the first week of Grantism.[5] U.S. knows so much. What a contrast between your Farewell Address and his *Inaugural*.[6]

I am sure, that the future history of this Country will do you full justice.

Hoping that you can find time to write me, by return mail . . .

M. C. Cranston.

ALS, DLC-JP.

1. Not identified.

2. See Alex Delmar to Johnson, Mar. 26, 1869, and E. E. Duncan to Johnson, Mar. 27, 1869.

3. Samson had attached burning firebrands to the tails of foxes and sent them running into the fields of the Philistines. Judges 15:4–5.

4. Apparently others accused Grant of nepotism as well. See *Washington Evening Star*, Mar. 15, 22, 1869.

5. After only one week in office, President Grant was forced to make two changes in his cabinet. Alexander T. Stewart, who was confirmed as secretary of the treasury, had to resign because of a conflict of interest, and E. B. Washburne, secretary of state, resigned for health reasons. They were replaced by George Boutwell and Hamilton Fish, respectively. *New York Herald*, Mar. 7–12, 18, 1869.

6. Grant eschewed philosophical and patriotic commentaries in favor of a brief, somewhat mundane listing of the political and social issues confronting his administration. *New York Herald*, Mar. 5, 1869.

From John W. Gonce[1]

Anderson Tenn   April 2d. 1869

Most Honored Sir.

Noticing a paper of the 28th ult. I saw an interview between you and a correspondent, wherein you say:—"What a splendid opportunity for young men Just starting out in life, if they will only be true to themselves, and use reasonable industry!"[2] I am one of these young men, a Tennessean. I love my country; and it will be my highest ambition to serve it, should it ever need my humble services. But if it should not need them, like Pericles, I will rejoice that there are worthier men in my state than my-self. Yea, I am proud of my noble State, by reason of its famous Son and patriot, who has Just vacated the White-House; and it will ever be my desire to have him, as my great and illustrious example, that steadily following it, I may, Some-day, be useful, as well to my country, as my-self. Yet, my own unworthiness bids me not think of aspiring to half of your high eminence.

But, you ask, what is the object of my intrusive letter? It is to beseech you to pour into my soul, some of that wisdom that has brought you to highest honors of your Country. I have had neither father, nor mother to guide—neither brother nor Sister to advise, me; yet, my character shows me that I am capable of hearing and following good counsel. Then, I desire to make you my parental monitor (should the charge be agreeable to you). Advise, and I will accept and abide by thy good counsel.

But to give me advice, you should know something of me. I am 19 years of age. I have a common education—an education, such as I have been able to obtain, but not such a one as I would desire. Not being able to share the advantages of a College, I study at home (like you were used to do) knowing that my future depends on my immediate exertions. I have Just finished the third book of Blackstone. I am studying Law, not so much that I may *practice* it, as that I may *know* it. My character is unimpeachable either as to virtue, honesty, veracity, temperance, industry, or perseverance. But you cry out: *What vanity! what egotism!!*

I do not impose upon you; yet it is necessary for me to give you my character, that you may, now, hear my cause and respect me, and, if I prove otherwise, you may Justly abhor me. I do not desire you to believe it. All that I ask of you, is that you advise me, as if these things were true. After considering, I think Mr James White[3] may know enough of me, to testify to the truth of what I say concerning my character. However, You will confer a great favor on me by keeping secret, from him and all others, the fact of my presuming to address you.

Now, I hope you understand my wants. Then be pleased to advise me as to what I should do, to make my-self worthy of my country, and, I assure you, that you will never regret the trouble of having done so.

J. W. Gonce

P.S.   Should you honor me with an answer, you will please send it in a plain envelope, that others may not know its author, and laugh at my presumption.

ALS, DLC-JP.

1. Gonce (1849–1943) became a Jackson County, Alabama, farmer for a number of years. Later he established a lock factory in Chattanooga. 1870 Census, Ala., Jackson, Pleasant Grove Beat 7, Big Coon, 25; (1880), 7th Beat, 97th Enum. Dist., 17; *Chattanooga Times*, Oct. 14, 15, 1943.

2. This is a direct quotation from Johnson's interview with the correspondent of the *Cincinnati Commercial*. That interview was published in the *Nashville Union and American*, March 28, 1869, and also in the *Nashville Republican Banner* of the same date. It is likely that Gonce saw a Nashville newspaper, but which one is simply not known.

3. Possibly the James White of Winchester, Tennessee, previously identified. See John P. White to Johnson, Feb. 16, 1861, *Johnson Papers*, 4: 298–300.

From Anonymous

April 3, 1869

A. Johnson Esq

I congratulate you & the country that you have ceased to be its chief exutive, for the country sake on a/c of its welfare & prosperity for your sake to save you from further disgrace. Now that you have got home I hope you will have sense enough to keep quite, the rest of your cabinett will do that. They will know enough for that. Whether you will or not remains to be seen. What a Jacobin you have made of yourself, what a disgrace to all future history will you name descend. You made a sad mistake when you began to make your bed with rebels. I was aware the Blairs[1] would control you but I supposed they did not intend to go Quite so far as they & you did both go. The Blairs did not care whether they went with Loyal Men or rebels so long as they could control the administration—but you were willing to go with rebels to have your way simply & nothing else. Genl Gillem[2] once said you would your way if it took all the strength of the Government in your hands to do it. This is what we suppose you undertook to do. How miserably you faild must be a constant reflection with you. A Mr Cole of Georgia told me soon after you took the Presidential chair, that you would certainly turn out a demagouge—that it was so natural for you that you could not help it & That he knew you of old, that he could not be deceived with all your special promises of loyalty as you took that chair to various delegations of loyal citizens of the union. No sir you a brave bad man, you believe the course you took would make more popular at the South & that you could hoodwink enough at the North to give you majority, but how beautifully you was mistaken. You drove out loyal men & put rebels in. You pardoned & released rebels thiefs & robers, all in keeping with you task & administration. You made use of your tools, Gordon Granger, Gillem, Steedman[3] & others— but how beautiful they all vanish soon as loyal hands get hold of the ship of state. Gillem gets hurled back to his servitude position. He never will see line of promotion again, all men have their eyes upon. He & you kept Missisppi out of the Union it will always be rememberd. Gillem is a great Sycophint as well as others to you. You ought to have seen this. Every body else saw it though he was the mereist school boy in the Country. Gordon Granger has got his deserts. He was a bad mean devil. Whiskey & woman was all that he wanted & no objection to a negro wench. He did not care a cent for you or anybody else. All he wanted was his way & could do so more by playing pretty with you but you had not sense enough to see it. As for Steedman all he wanted was to make some money out of you or under your administration. You think you have pampered & fed so many Tenessee fellows that you will you be popular when you come before that people again. Of this you will soon see how mistaken you are. The best thing you can do is to be perfectly Quite. Let silence

obtain symphaty for you, or else come out & be a consistant radical
& raise the whole human race according to their merrit & not according to caste. You & the rebel policy is to raise cast & position—
for elevation & success & not merrit the true test of elevation. It
must be a great sourse of embaresement to you when you remember
as you must the great miserey to the liveing the loss of property & of
life you have caused in your administration. That New Orleans riott
which you allowed to get up—which was so disastrious to life. No
one can look any where hardly but they can find the baleful influence
of your administration. Now Mr Johnson we hope you will have
sense enough to keep still the balance of your life. Reflect on all the
miserey you have committed & repent daily & hourly & may your
peace with your God for the great sins you have committed. Dont
show your head any further in public life.

You can posibly have no more influence hearafter except from a
mere fragment of Sycophints like Nelson,[4] Gillem Granger Jones[5]—
they will all be poor tools aid you. Stop think & repent.

Dead Duck

AL, DLC-JP.
   1. Francis P., Francis P., Jr., and Montgomery Blair.
   2. Alvan C. Gillem.
   3. James B. Steedman.
   4. Probably Thomas A.R. Nelson.
   5. Possibly George W. Jones.

Speech at Knoxville

[April 3, 1869]

After receiving the cordial welcome that I have, I confess that if I
were disposed to make a speech concerning the great questions that
agitate the public mind, I should feel almost incapacitated for speaking. I return my most sincere thanks for this cordial welcome. It is
unusually gratifying to me to be welcomed in this manner, after what
has recently transpired during my term as Executive of this great
nation. How pleasing it is to meet here upon a common ground and
to receive your cordial congratulations. The time has been when, as
Whigs and Democrats, we had our bitter contests, but after the contest was over we laid our weapons aside and met again as friends. As
your late honored Representative[1] has said, we differed on questions
of politics and upon the construction of the constitution, but there

was one thing that Whigs and Democrats agreed in, and that was the necessity for a constitutional form of government; and the only difference was that the Democrats contended for a strict construction, and the Whigs wanted a little more latitude to operate the Government in.

How does it stand now? There has another party sprang up. I care not how you call parties. The great distinction is the principle upon which they are conducted. If there ever was a time, now is the time for regarding the principles of parties. In those times, as I have said, we only differed in our construction of the constitution. We defended the constitution at all hazards, even when driven from the State for our devotion to the constitution. I have filled every office in the gift of the people from the highest to the lowest. My ambition is filled, and I have no more to ask for. I have endeavored to protect the Constitution and the result is before you. I am now in your midst to spend the remainder of my days, where as a boy penniless and a stranger, I can truly say, I expected to live, and here I expect to die and be buried. All I ask in returning to your midst is a fair and impartial examination of my past history. If I have reflected honor upon you, it reflects honor upon your State. I intend to devote the remainder of my life as a private citizen, to the vindication of my official life, and of my native State from the foul obloquoy that has been heaped upon us.

Though bent, I have not been broken by the storm which has nearly wrecked the ship of State.

NOT DEAD YET.

In receiving your welcome, I think that I may with some degree of confidence call your attention to some few questions. I feel the responsibility that is resting upon me; I may say that I received yesterday a large number of papers containing my obituary. It may be that I am as one come from the dead, and if so, I trust you will believe one come from the grave. (A voice, "Not so dead yet.") Once we had a Constitution, and now we ought to return to it. Recently we have seen that liberty has almost departed from the land through the neglect of the Constitution. The Government is divided into three departments, each with its appropriate duties. The Executive is the tribune of the people, not to make laws, but to stand with a negative power, and when Congress makes bad laws, to say, "I forbid." The Constitution also provides that when Congress passed a law by two thirds majority, it becomes valid, but it is not a part of the Constitution—a two thirds majority of Congress have tried to wipe the Constitution out of existence. The Constitution prescribes the duties of each department of the Government, and when the Congress of the United States, excited by interest and a spirit of tyranny, transcended the Constitution, I vetoed their bills and sent them back to them. For this I have been denounced as a traitor, and accused of abandoning my party, and of being a traitor to it. If fidelity to the Constitution is treason to party, I say let the party go.

A USURPING CONGRESS.

Let us see how these Departments operate. Each is confined to its sphere. Let us reason together. Where is the danger in the Government? I tell you here to-day, and as one speaking from the dead, *it is in the Legislative Department.* I mean in the Federal Government. Why! Can the executive make a law? He has only a negative power. The judiciary can only expound a law. But the Legislature can pass laws of the most arbitrary character, and under the pretense of law, trample upon the liberties of the people. Those who are trying to undermine the constitution, have given the impression that a two-thirds majority has the power of the constitution. Then they can go on until a Congress—yes a capricious Congress, yes, a despotic Congress, yes, a USURPING Congress—will take away the liberties of the people. But I feel that I stood as a breakwater at the head of the American government and arrested its progress, for a time at least, until the people knew what was going on. And while others may boast of having established a government, I feel that I can without egotism claim the credit of having been efficient in its preservation.

The time has come to talk about the first principles of Government. Take away the restraints which hold back Congress and you have a despotic Government. Wipe out the other two departments of the Government and you have Congress with its discretion, or perhaps I should say, its indiscretion, the measure of its power.

Jefferson describes such a body as this, as the exact embodiment of a despotism.[2] And let me tell you here that a wise and good prince is infinitely better than a usurping, arbitrary, despotic Congress. (Voice—"That's so, Andy. Go it.")

Look at the course of Great Britain towards the colonies, and compare it with that of Congress. Look at the Declaration of Independence, and see how the acts of Congress are similar to the course of Great Britain. Then when that Declaration was made, and the people saw their wrong, they were aroused to gain their freedom. Now, look at our condition. The great writ of Habeas Corpus suspended, and when a citizen of the United States appealed to the Supreme Court, an arbitrary Congress took from him the rights of appeal and deprived him of his liberty.

The young men I see here must look to these things, for we gray headed men are passing off of the scene, and they must soon take our places. We are Governors of States deposed by Lieutenants in the army. Let me tell a story. A party of gentlemen were recently riding through Richmond, the capitol of the Old Dominion, and seeing a house they asked "who lived there?" The driver studied a while and said, "Oh, that's the gentleman that has the State in charge." Think of it, a little military man had the Old Dominion in charge!

SYMPATHY FOR THE DOWN-TRODDEN.

Congress recently, during the latter part of my term, passed a resolution wanting the Government to interfere in the Cretan matter.[3] Yet the Cretes were governed by a King. Still we are hunting up the downtrodden and oppressed. Such, indeed, was our history before. You remember how we sympathized with Kossuth[4] and with Ireland, for struggling for liberty. (Voice, Three cheers for Fenians.) During my time as President an effort was made to acquire St. Thomas, and we have long desired to gain Cuba. But now they have a rebellion there and Congress, seeking out the oppressed and downtrodden everywhere, is in favor of acknowledging the rebels of Cuba as a belligerent power.

I'll make you see what I am driving at. Is there no oppression any where else? We seem to have taken out a roving commission in search of the oppressed, and when we find them, our bowels yearn for them. But here our own brethren, our own kindred, bone of our bone, are found with this same United States standing with mailed heel upon them. I want Cuba annexed, but I want it done in accordance with law. I suppose there are none here but want Cuba annexed and represented in Congress.

NOT A TRAITOR.

They say that I have been a traitor to my party. Where have I violated any pledges? (Voice, never.) Where was I nominated? Was it at a Radical Convention, a Whig Convention? No. It was a Union Convention. It was a Constitutional Convention, and they invited all to come into that Convention. Now examine the platform of that convention. I defy you to put your finger upon one paragraph of that platform that I have violated.

HIS RECORD REVIEWED.

I replied to the letter notifying me of my nomination, and I want the gentlemen who have been falsifying my record to recur to that letter. I accepted it as a war Democrat and I urged my old Democratic friends to come up and join me. I refer to this simply to make the record right. I stand now as I stood then, battling for the Union and the Constitution of our fathers, but where do some of them stand now? I told them that the true place to fight the battle was in the Union and under the Constitution. So I told Jefferson Davis when he left the Senate. After the battle of Bull Run, the country was dismayed, and five thousand troops marching into Washington could have taken the capital, and to restore confidence, Mr. Crittenden[5] introduced a resolution in one House and I in the other, declaring the war was waged for the Union and the Constitution, and that the States had no power to secede. That they were not out of the Union and could not go out of the Union. Well, we fought the war. We conquered, and the defeated bowed to the decision of war and renewed their allegiance to the Government. Was not this all we wanted?

It has been said, and was true, that I had been maltreated, persecuted and insulted, and when I came into power, the malicious said,—now he will carry out his own doctrines; his passions will be his guide and he will seek revenge. Thank God, I am a man, that, when I am fighting I will fight to the last, but when I have conquered and my foe is prostrate, thank God I have too much magnanimity not to lift him up.

I was President when General Lee surrendered.[6] I thought that restoration was needed, and when there were no States to be found I put them into condition. Governors were inaugurated and States reorganized. The work of reorganization was all complete except the admission of Representatives for Congress. The mails were restored, the blockade removed; but the 39th Congress met and said—no. These States shall not be represented. Hence all these laws that have been vetoed. The Freedman's Bureau law, the Civil Right's bill, the military government of the Southern States—all these I vetoed and I would do it again.

I have been accused of abusing the pardoning power. I have pardoned more men than any other executive but I am glad of it, and I only wish I had pardoned many more. Some of those who abuse me so for pardoning, I dare say, need more pardon than any. (Laughter.) At one stroke of my pen I set 65,000 free, cleared the jails and prisons from those confined for political offenses, and I did well, yet for these things I was denounced as worse than a rebel.

But, after declaring that the States could not go out of the Union, this Congress turned around and said they were out. Let me ask this assemblage if these States had been conquered from some foreign power, who would object to admitting them into the Union; yet they are your own neighbors.

A STRIKING CONTRAST.

At last my course in opposition to the civil tenure bill brought me arraigned as a culprit before Congress. Mark the contrast. There was Jeff Davis, President of the Southern Confederacy, arrested and in jail, and this same party came forward and bailed him out and sent him to Europe, while I, who had fought in the Senate and everywhere for the Constitution, was brought before the bar of the Senate as a culprit. I called on my own State, as well as others, to assist me in this case, and I was acquitted, and now I bring my articles of impeachment against this usurping Congress, and I deliver them to my old counsel (Hon. Thos. A.R. Nelson) and if he prosecutes them as ably as he defended me, he will convict them.

The charge has been made that I was a traitor. Traitor to whom? I want to see the man that will say it to my face. It is easy for them to say it in their nooks and corners and in their little 8 x 10's in the country, but I stand here to day and defy the whole pack of them. They call me a traitor! I come home to spend the last years of my life in defending myself and my State.

MOSES.

They say, "Why, yes, our Moses." Let us see. If there is a colored man here to day, I say to him not to let himself be carried away by his prejudices. The time is coming when you will know who are your friends. I told you four years ago—hear me, don't go away—that freedom meant liberty to work and what you earned from your work to spend for your comfort. And this applies to all. Freedom is worthless unless you work. Freedom is not to build up a miserable lazzaroni to be supported by the government. But a word upon the subject of Moses. I want the colored men to listen to me. Who set the colored men free? Was it done by President Lincoln in his proclamation? No, for you will find that Tennessee was excepted from that proclamation. Who was it, who, standing there upon the Capitol steps at Nashville, in the midst of war and tumult and strife, declared freedom to the colored men of Tennessee.[7] Look to the record and you will see that I declared their freedom then, and that after declaring the colored men free, I said if there was none other more capable than I, I would be their Moses and lead them from captivity. Have not they been lead from captivity? I proposed to be if no one else would. Where are these simon pure Moses? Had any one of them urged you to go out West and take 180 acres of land? Oh, no. There's a great many white men out there. But they will take you here and organize you into clubs and secret leagues and make you believe that they are your best friends. But this man Johnson, oh, he is a traitor, and you must beware of him. But where are these other Moses? Have they smote the rocks and has the water gushed forth? Have they brought the manna from on high? Have they gone to Pisgah's top? I suppose they have presented you a blue book? (Laughter.) All they have given you is a blue book, and an oath to support them.

THE NEGRO'S NEW MASTER.

Let me tell you, colored men, and I have never deceived white men or black men, that these men who talk about your old masters, have only delivered you up to new masters. You are slaves to the League. Let me say to you as I said to my old servant—as I told him when I came back. "Sam,[8] the only difference between us is, that I freed you four years ago, and I was only emancipated on the fourth of March." So you see I am addressing you as a *freedman*. (Laughter.)

It was not long since I was accused of favoring negro suffrage. You will see that I sent a telegram to the Governors of the several States in the South, to go as far as some of the States North had gone. Now, what is the charge? That I am against it. Where is the proof of it? When I suggested that the State of Tennessee and others should go as far in one year as other States had gone in fifty years, it was a great advance.

THE WAR MEN NOW.

Now in one more allusion to Moses, I want to take up the account of these new born advocates. It is very easy for men to come in our midst and talk about rebellions, courage and Union, who, while the rebellion was going on were not within the smell of gunpowder, but were in their closets or some secret place, and became war men when the war was over.

I could tell some secrets concerning the state of affairs. Here it was dangerous for a man to be a Union man; there, where these men came from, they dare not be anything but loyal. I should like to take up my sacrifices and compare with these neophytes. I asked a little while ago what they had done for the colored man. Can any of you tell except to get you into the leagues and give you new masters? Don't you know that the leagues are conspiracies against the government? If you are free, did you become any freer to go in the oath bound leagues and become slaves to new masters? Now, when in a free country you see these oath bound leagues you may know they are trying to take away other men's liberties. These leagues will, if allowed to go on, destroy the liberty of the country.

BROWNLOW ATTESTS HIS LOYALTY.

If I have pardoned so many I ought to be pardoned for some of my errors, but I think I have some evidence of my loyalty. I have a paper which I will read:

Received, Nashville, March 24, 1862, of Andrew Johnson, Military Governor of Tennessee, fifteen hundred dollars to aid in the establishment of a Union Press at Knoxville, Tenn. and to defray my expenses while passing from under secession oppression to the city of Nashville.

$1,500   Wm G. Brownlow

Now, here you see, this was for a Union press, and to aid in escaping from the oppression of secession. (Voice—"Who is it?") Why this is signed by no less a man than Wm. G. Brownlow with his own sign manual. But now, I'm the traitor.

ALL SLAVES TO THE BONDHOLDERS.

But, my friends, we must reason together. We must not allow our feelings to deceive us.

So far as my presence here is concerned, I have no other object than to thank you for your cordiality. I have gone the round of all the offices, and so far as the corruption of the government is concerned, my hands are free from it. Here I have come to live, with my wife and my children. I want little. Man wants but little here below, and, like Cato, I return to my little farm.

But this time is full of alarming portents. The country is in danger, and let me lift my warning voice. Look at the taxes. Your debt is nearly three billions of dollars, so far as the Federal Government is concerned. How much it is at home, God only knows. I know how it was when I was your Governor. You had a school fund then. Where is it now? Look at the taxes of the State and of the Federal Government. The Federal Government collects one hundred and fifty millions, three times as much as was necessary a few years ago for the whole expenses of Government, to pay the *bondholders*. You black men might as well know this, that while they have been enfranchising you and disfranchising white men, they have been making you all slaves. Yes, you are all slaves together to the bondholder, who never shed a drop of blood. I would to God that the Government had not the credit to borrow a dollar to carry on a war. If the people had had before hand to pay the cost of the war, we should never have had one. We had a great talk before the war about a negro slave aristocracy. But these negroe slaves were worth $3,000,000,000. The negro has now been freed from one man only to be a slave to another, for it has to come from their toil and from the white man's to pay these bondholders their one hundred and fifty millions. Did they lend it in gold and silver? No: in a depreciated currency. Now, the interest must be paid in gold and silver, extorted from the toil and sweat of white and black.

THE DIFFERENCE.

I asked you a little while ago what these men have done for you, colored men. Why a little while ago in Washington, a colored man came to me and wanted help. I was pretty hard pushed but I gave him $25.00. He went to Mr. Sumner and he said he had not thought much about the matter. (Laughter). Peter Lowery came along for his Labor University.[9] I knew him and I gave him $150. He went to some of the Simon pures and I don't think he got enough to pay his bill. At Charleston, S.C., they wanted to purchase a building for a colored man's University and sent a preacher on.[10] He came to me and I said I would do what I could. I asked him couldn't he go round to the Freedmen's Bureau. General Howard came with him to me, and he said he would give him letters North. He went North and came back. I gave him then $1,000. I did not put it down on paper, to influence others. A great many have subscribed largely, but when called on to pay they would back out. (Laughter). I, afterwards, heard that preacher say in the pulpit at Washington, that that thousand dollars was a larger subscription than he got North of Mason and Dixon's Line. I want these men to compare notes with me.

A MAN OF PEACE.

My friends, the time is now come to consider the condition of affairs. Had my advice been followed at the commencement of the war it would have been better. War is not the natural element of my life. I desire peace, and a peaceful contest within the Union and under the Constitution. Thank God, my march has not been through Golgotha; my honors have not been gained by blood; the widows and the one armed soldiers cannot attribute their wrongs to me. I stand here to-day vindicating the Constitution as it was handed down to me, and here in the last hours of my life, I call upon you all to cling to the Constitution of the country as the mariner clings to his compass.

Let me tell you here to-day that I would rather be in your midst to-day, privileged to advocate the principles of the Constitution, than to be inaugurated President. I would rather wear the honest dust of peaceful toil than the gilded shoulder straps or the sword, crimsoned in a brother's blood, dangling at my side. Yes; I prefer the peaceful badges of a citizen to the insignia of bloody and relentless war. I had rather be in your midst to unfurl the banner of peace and fasten it below the cross, with the inscription, "God first and my country next." My confidence is unaltered, that the people will be true to themselves, reason will be restored, and we shall again have our old form of government.

Fellow citizens. In parting from you, let me thank you for your cordial reception and for the attention you have paid. Hoping that you may live—we that are older and whose heads are gray must soon pass away—let me urge you to come up and understand the Constitution. The soul of liberty is the Constitution, and without the Constitution there is no liberty.

In parting from you, let me invoke the protection of Almighty God upon you, and with the hope that peace may be restored, I leave you.

Knoxville Press and Herald, Apr. 4, 1869.

1. Thomas A.R. Nelson.

2. For an earlier reference to Jefferson's statement about a legislative body and despotic power, see Johnson's Speech in Lynchburg, Va., Mar. 18, 1869.

3. In July 1867, both the Senate and the House passed a joint resolution that expressed

sympathy for the people of Crete who were rebelling against the Turkish government. *Congressional Globe*, 40 Cong., 1 Sess., pp. 727, 747; Beale, *Welles Diary*, 3: 138–39.

4. Louis Kossuth, Hungarian revolutionary, visited the United States in late 1851 and early 1852.

5. Kentucky's John J. Crittenden (in the House) and Johnson (in the Senate) jointly sponsored resolutions in July 1861.

6. Actually, Johnson was not president when Lee surrendered at Appomattox; in fact, he became president six days after Lee's April 9 surrender.

7. See "The Moses of the Colored Men" Speech, Oct. 24, 1864, *Johnson Papers*, 7: 251–53.

8. Sam had been purchased by Johnson in 1842. See Charles Johnson to Johnson, Jan. 29, 1860, ibid., 3: 405.

9. Lowery (1810–*fl*1887) was president of the board of trustees of the Manual Labor School, located in Rutherford County, Tennessee. Also a minister, Lowery pastored one of the Christian churches in Nashville in the 1880s. 1870 Census, Tenn., Davidson, 13th Civil Dist., 45; Nashville directories (1880–87); *Nashville Union and American*, Mar. 6, 1869. See also Samuel Lowery to Johnson, Oct. 20, 1868.

10. Probably the Rev. A. Toomer Porter. See Porter to Johnson, July 28, 1866, *Johnson Papers*, 10: 745; Porter to Johnson, July 29, 1867, ibid., 12: 440.

From Horace H. Day

New York. March [April] 4 1869[1]

Dear Sir

Nothing can be more honorable in you or diserable *to us* the people who are measring our means for the contest than to see you in throwing off the locked harness, to take on the armour of battle for the people you too have, like Sprague of the Senate,[2] Struck the key note. This days Newspaper will herald along the dim future and furnish the Historian with points made yesterday by Andrew Johnson in Knoxville and, Wm Sprague in the Senate words thoughts which will live. Your words are true as Holy writt. Aye more true than all of them. "WE ARE ALL SLAVES TO THE BOND HOLDERS."

The reporters give you credit for this painfuly, disgracefull *truth*. Let us make it a watch word. Read the New York Herald & other papers report of Spragues Speech unless perchance it is published throughout the Country and you see it at home. (I have just been to the newspaper stand and find the same reports in "all the papers"). Spragues 10 pct a month is a true picture. I paid 20 pr ct on a Loan, upon real Estate a few days ago in Boston, property within 4 Hours Travel of the City and was 1 year trying before I succeeded in obtaining the Loan. So you See the pressure is all over the Land and the power for its overthrow will come up from all parts of the Country and we are to < For enclosure see: Printed article "The People for themselves and a word to Southern Men" 1868, Dec 25 >[3] no Sectional Strife, in the Contest upon which we are now Entering. A few months, (aye Even now Comparison is instituted between Andrew Johnsons Administration of the office and feeble one of Grant)—and years will show you, and the world, the greater wisdom which impeled you to hold such a fast grip upon the constitution. G. has already yielded ground after ground and is becoming buried out of sight of the people. Your warning to the people will prove you a prophet. We are drifting rapidly and surely on to the rocks. The Crash is near at hand. I venture to prophesy September will not be passed before the foundation on which the oligarchy is sustaining its multifarious system of Robbry will be shaken and broken with It. All you have Seen and warned the people of will be upon them. Let it come. We have nothing worth supporting left to us—already the people have lost all confidence in their leaders and this will be followed—is now followed with a loss of respect for institutions. The Senate the most corrupt ever existing under the Govermnt—the House another gang of thieves, with scarcely one strong enough to expose them—a picture from which all must turn away in disgust, too. Look for some—any means tending to deliverance. The uprising in Spain—the revolution in Cuba—the Alabama claims—Fenians, any opening door will be rushed into to make a begning. The Rail Road Swindling Exposures, all togeather from, combined are showing the people, their true situation. It must be the work of all of us, to epose and attack the Enemy. Permit a frank word with you, your personal vindication of yourself is unnecessary, rapidly approaching Events will do more in your vindication than a thousand speeches—attack and expose, the doings of your Enemies, and hasten the flood upon them, which shall swallow them up. In this you have the support and co-operation of the millions of the oppressed, who are now feeling the pressure—the suffering which is the fruit the result of the conduct of this money clicque who have controlled Legislation and attack upon you, to cover their acts, turning the Eyes of the people in hostility to you; while they had both hands in our pockets. Grant has already proven himself their Tool. You made a fatal mistake in not grappling and Exposing this money power a year ago, but, no one can blame you. One man cannot fathom all questions—your time was too much taken up to see it. You see it now, the people—feel it and it will overthrow the Government and may launch us into monarchy—*Repudiation* is inevitable. I urge our Labor union to raise the Cry now. Since the law for "imposing the public Credit," Since they repudiated their [Sects?] of the Contract there is no other course for us. *I* am a repudiater, unchangeably persistantly. I have donned Black Cloth, gone into Cheap quarters put on Linsey Wolsey and shall labor night and day till this infernal system of Plunder is rooted out.

The world gave you Credit for Sounding the key note. Pray play the Tune and we the people will keep step with you. Let the Dogs bark . . . the bite will soon be ours. In this way help us to vindicate you—and The Expression "*He intended to devote the remainder of his Life as a private citizen to the vindication of his official Life*" I would read, to mean, that he would devote in the future his Strongest Efforts to overthrow the gang of Theves who cheated & robbed the people while proclaiming against the peoples champion who tried to resist their unholy work.

Horace H. Day

Do me the favor to read what is marked of the Enclosed.

ALS, DLC-JP.

1. Although Day clearly dated his letter March 4, internal evidence (particularly the reference to Johnson's Knoxville speech) indicates that it is an April letter.

2. It is possible that Day refers here to the remarks made by Sen. William Sprague in opposition to a bill to strengthen the public credit that would, in his opinion, repudiate the national debt. *New York Herald*, Mar. 4, 1869; *Congressional Globe*, 40 Cong., 3 Sess., p. 1831.

3. Enclosed was Day's lengthy statement, dated December 25, 1868. In it Day proposed several resolutions, all of which related to the questions of currency, credit and the national debt.

From George G. de Luna Byron [1]

53 South Washington Square, (West 4th Street,)
New York, April 6th 1869.

Sir,

With regret I saw the statement in the papers that you were seriously ill—suffering of an attack of gravel. Although I cannot expect to be remembered by you, Sir, yet *I* can *never* forget your kindness of heart, of which you *once* gave me so prominent proofs. A gratiful feeling induces me to suggest to you the *frequent* & *continued* use of the *Rakoozy* mineral water of Kissingan as a *remedy* & *preventive* of the complaint in question. I have personally derived great benefit from the use of the waters of that Spring, while on the spot; I have also observed the beneficial effect in some hundred patients—belonging to the vine-growing countries— whose light vines generally produce a gravelly deposit in the bladder. Looking over my papers I had the satisfaction of finding a small pamphlet, relating to the Kissingan Spas, which I beg leave to enclose. The *genuine Rakoozy*, imported from Bavaria, can be obtained, I believe, at various places in New York. I obtained once a supply of Mr. *Sattler*,[2] 204 Broadway—but am not quite certain whether he continues to import it. Should you wish to obtain more information in regard to *Kissingan & its Spa*, allow me to point to *Dr. Granville's Spas of Germany*[3]—a work of *standard value*—having passed through more than 20 editions.

In the course of a week or ten days—I shall proceed to Europe, expecting to be absent for a considerable time. It would be an agreeable surprise to me, should you condescend to acknowledge the receipt of these lines, uncertain as I am to your present residence.

Anticipating your pardon for this intrusion . . .

Geo. G. de L.' Byron,
Late Major U.S.V.A. & of Genl. Frémont's Staff.

ALS, DLC-JP.

1. Byron (*c*1810–1882) claimed to be the illegitimate son of Lord Byron. He was a consummate charlatan, living in New York City and other places in the world, and posing as an officer of the British army, the U.S. army, a journalist, a literary writer, a broker, a mining prospector, a spy, a cotton agent, a bookseller, a representative of European mercantile interests, etc. *New York Times*, July 12, 1882.

2. Probably John Sattig (*fl*1875), a New York City liquor dealer and importer. New York City directories (1860–76).

3. *The Spas of Germany*, which went through many editions, was originally published in 1837 by Augustus Bozzi Granville (1783–1872). *NUC*.

From William Flinn

Washington D.C.   April 6, 1869.

My dear Sir:

I read with much pleasure your excellent speech delivered at Knoxville and was highly gratified to hear that you still live. I sincerely wish you may be blessed with health and strength, and live to see the policy of your administration vindicated by the people. I send you a small sheet, The Daily New Mexican[1] in which you will read an obituary of yourself. The initials in pencil are that of H. H. Heath, the Secretary of the Territory. I notice he is removed by President Grant and another person[2] appointed.

Please give my kindest regards to your son Robert and accept my best wishes for your health and happiness and that of your family.

Wm. Flinn   260 F street

ALS, DLC-JP.

1. The issue was not found enclosed. On March 26 the *New Mexican* reported that Johnson had died of paralysis the previous day. The obituary was brief but sympathetic, noting that although Johnson's views were "erroneous," there was "honesty in his purposes." *New Mexican,* Mar. 26, 1869.

2. On April 3 Grant nominated Edward L. Perkins of Pennsylvania to be secretary of the New Mexico Territory. He may be the Perkins (1843–*fl*1901) who was a Philadelphia lawyer. Although the Senate confirmed him on April 9, there is some debate as to whether Perkins actually went to New Mexico, for apparently Heath remained secretary until early 1870. *Senate Ex. Proceedings,* Vol. 17: 77, 79, 98; Hubert H. Bancroft, *History of Arizona and New Mexico, 1530–1888* (San Francisco, 1889), 704; Pomeroy, *The Territories,* 111; George A. Perkins, "The Perkins Family," *Historical Collections of the Essex Institute,* 21 (1884): 56; Philadelphia directories (1869–1901).

Speech in Nashville

[April 7, 1869][1]

MR. CHAIRMAN—[2]

I shall not attempt on this occasion to make a response to the address that you have made, conveying your feelings and sentiments and of all those you have the honor to represent. Even were I disposed to speak, I could not, on account of my health, do more than simply make an apology in reply to what has been given utterance to here; were I able to speak, and desired to do so, the compliments, honors and the cordial welcome shown here to-day are well calculated to incapacitate me for the performance of such a duty. I thank you from my heart for the cordial welcome I have received in returning to the capital of my own adopted State. To receive such evidences of respect is most gratifying to me under the circumstances. During the last four years, as you are well aware, which has seperated us, my time has been devoted to the consideration of the first principles of the Government. This I will not undertake to discuss on this occasion, but, in response to the reference made to the Constitution of my country which I was sworn to support, protect and defend, I would say, that it has been done in fidelity and to the utmost of my ability. <Cheers> And although I might not have been capable of resisting the encroachment upon the first principles of free government and in removing from your shoulders oppressions and burdens too heavy to be borne, and to which I was going to say, you have almost too patiently submitted, <cheers> I will say in this connection, that, although I have not been able to do this, I feel that I have done one thing which would be enough to gratify any individual for having spent his whole life in the endeavor.

When I was inaugurated President of the United States; when I looked to the great ship of state and saw that she was gliding along down with rapid speed to destruction, like the train that is going down the inclined plane, when, with every revolution performed by each wheel its velocity is increased until destruction seemed inevitable, I feel that I succeeded as a break in arresting it from its downward tendency, and the overthrow of the Government for a time at least. I hoped that a change of fundamental principles would be prevented, and that the whole American people would repell and put a stop to these encroachments—and, though exceedingly slow and laboring under an apathy, would yet come to the rescue and save the Constitution and the country.

In appearing before you on this occasion, and in receiving this cordial welcome, it is proper, I think, for me to say that I come before you to ask for nothing. I am no aspirant for office, and ask for nothing at your hands. You, in times past, conferred upon me every position I asked, either state of federal, and I stand before you asking nothing. Pardon me for saying—and it is not the result or promptings of egotism when I say it—that I have filled every office in the gift of the people from the highest to the lowest or from the lowest to the highest, which is without a parallel in this country. This would seem to satisfy the ambition of any man. The measure of my ambition has been surely filled. In returning to you, after having filled all of these positions, stepping, as I have, from the most exalted position in the gift of the people of the United States, down into the ranks of the people, I feel more honor in taking my position and helping to bear the burdens which I have not been capable of lifting from their shoulders, than to be inaugurated President of the United States to-morrow over the ruins of a violated Constitution. <Loud applause>.

Let us rally around the Constitution of our country; let us hold to it as the ark of our country, as the palladium of our civil and religious liberty; let us cling to it as the warrior clings to the last plank between him and the waves of destruction. Upon the maintenance of the Constitution of the United States depends the existence of a free Government.

The time has been when we had two great parties in this country—Whig and Democratic—the two greatest parties that ever existed in any Government. They had their contests in the political forum and while one broke a lance and the lance of the other would be bent when all was over, they met together as friends and supporters of the Constitution of the country. The differences of these two parties were that one contended for a strict and rigid construction of the Constitution, and the other for a more liberal and broader con-

struction of the Constitution. Though they differed in the construction of the Constitution, both agreed in the perpetuation of the
Constitution of the United States and a constitutional form of government. <Applause.>

Who would have thought that the scene would ever come up of
one branch of the Government, attempting to absorb the other two?
That the legislative department, by unconstitutional, by excessive,
by unnecessary, by tyrannical, (I was about to say diabolical), legislation, have attempted to subvert and overthrow the other two departments of the Government? When a mad degenerate arbitrary body
of legislators commits indiscretions under pretense of law, liberty is
at an end and the Constitution is wiped out of existance: and in the
language of the great apostle of American liberty, Thomas Jefferson,
I declare such a body as this Congress, "the precise definition of
despotic power."[3] This is where we are traveling.

The Whigs and Democrats agreed in that great essential—the
Constitution. The question is now whether we will have a constitutional Government or not; whether the Constitution shall prescribe
the limitation of power, as heretofore, of each department of the
Government or whether Congress shall be legislative, executive and
judicial, without limitation. The discretion of Congress has been the
measure of its power and not the Constitution of the United States!
This is the direction in which we are drifting and it is an important
matter to be well considered.

I will not trespass long upon your attention. <Cries of "go on, go
on.">This event—returning to the State that has honored me, and
whose people have taken me by the hand and made me all I have
been, much or little, receiving such a welcome, is a source to me of
peculiar gratification, and I repeat again, that I feel prouder to-day,
standing in your midst priviliged and authorized to advocate in connection with my fellow-citizens those great principles of free government, than I would to be inaugurated President over the ruins of
the Constitution of my country. <Loud applause.>

Though bent by the storms of State, I am not yet broken, and I
thank my God that there is a little of me left <tremendous applause>
still, to vindicate the Constitution, and the rights and privileges of
this people, <cheers> and, God being willing, in the humblest position in which I may be placed, I intend to devote the remainder of
my life, as short as it may be, to the vindication of my own character
and to our State, both being directly and indirectly connected. Yes,
that reputation dearer to me than life, which is to live when I am

gone, let the consequences be what they may. I have come amongst you to spend the remainder of my days, to wind up my existence, and not by force, but by my own voluntary choice, and, if I can do nothing more, I will adopt the manner of Cato. The young men will have to take the places of those who are already well stricken in years. Let them drink in the instruction of Cato; yes—when Caesar was making *his* inroads upon the Courts. "Return to the Sabine fields," and there with a pure, innocent, sincere heart—if you can do nothing more—"pray for Rome."[4] If I can do nothing more, I can retire to my own home with a good conscience, and pray for my country. <Cheers>.

I feel prouder to-day in retirement—yes, I experience a greater sense of joy and relief than before I was emancipated, for—

> Marcellus more true joy in exile feels
> Than Caesar with a corrupt Congress at his heels.[5]

When I accepted the Presidency, I accepted it as a high trust, and one of weighty responsibilities. I did not accept it as a donation, <cheers> or as a grand gift establishment. <Loud applause>. I didn't take it into my hand as a kind of cornucopia, or horn of plenty, filled with sugar plumbs, <laughter> and be indebted here and there to that or this individual that offered the greatest presents and gifts. <Applause and laughter>.

Amidst all the slander and vituperation that utterance has been given to, that has been fulminated and sent forth, I stand before you unscathed and bid the whole pack defiance. I thank God that I can stand before the people of my State and lift up my both hands and say they are clean, and ask in the language of Samuel, "whose ox have *I* taken, whose ass have *I* taken, or whose hands *I* have received bribes from."[6]

I return to you feeling that I have discharged my duty as an honest man and a faithful public officer.

So long as any impression shall remain on the tablets of my memory, so long as blood animates and warms my being, so long as my existence continues to beat one single impulse, will I remember this cordial welcome; yes, going down with me to the grave. I thank you, gentlemen, for this most cordial welcome. May God in his goodness and plenitude of power give us peace and prosperity. <Loud and prolonged applause.>

Nashville Republican Banner, Apr. 8, 1869.

1. Newspaper accounts all indicate that Johnson arrived by train in Nashville on the afternoon of April 7; he was escorted to the St. Cloud Hotel, where he delivered this speech.

2. John C. Gaut gave a fairly extensive welcoming address before presenting Johnson to the assembled crowd.

3. For Johnson's earlier quotation of Jefferson on this matter, see his Speech in Lynchburg, Va., Mar. 18, 1869.

4. Evidently Johnson's first reference to Cato's advice to his son is found in his Speech at Charlottesville, Va., Mar. 18, 1869. He repeated it several times thereafter.

5. Johnson quoted these lines from Alexander Pope in his Speech at Charlottesville, Va., Mar. 18, 1869.

6. 1 Sam. 12:3.

From William J. Anderson[1]

Winona Miss   April 8th 1869

Sir

I was shown by Mr Joe Selby[2] of Holly Springs, a few weeks since, a certificate, of which the following is a true copy, and which he informed me was the original documents by which you were apprenticed to his father James J Selby.

This is to certify that it is my desire that my son Andrew Johnson is bound an apprentice to James J Selby, to learn the tailors trade, and that he is to serve him faithfully until he is twenty one years old.

Andrew Johnson was born in 1808 December 29th.
Novr. 8th 1818

Signed Mary Daughtry
by Turner Daughtry

Mr. Joe Selby, the gentleman who has the paper in possession, is pursuing his trade at Holly Springs, and is recognized as a man of veracity. His statement with reference to the paper, and its general appearance, may, I think, be regarded as pretty conclusive proof of its genuineness. Nevertheless, if upon this point, the shadow of a doubt exists in the minds of those who have seen it, your endorsement would not only remove that doubt, but would give to the paper an appreciative value, in the hands of one who has a passion for preserving such relics, which it cannot possess without it. If, therefore, your memory will enable you to do so, may I ask the favor of you to state whether or not you believe it to be genuine.

I have just read with much interest the published account of your reception and your speech at Knoxville, and am pleased to discover

that the only effect upon you, produced by the fiery ordeal through
which you have passed during the past four years, is, to nerve you to
a more—if *possible*—determined resistance to the enemies of constitutional liberty. The ultimate triumph of your reconstruction principles, is as certain, as is the degrading destiny of the Radical party.

W. J. Anderson

I have enclosed this to your friend Hon A [J?] Brown[3] who will
inform you who I am.

My address is at—Pickensville Alabama.

ALS, DLC-JP.
    1. Anderson (*c*1808–*fl*1870), who had been a major in the Confederate quartermaster de-
partment, was an insurance agent in Pickensville, Alabama. 1870 Census, Ala., Pickens,
Pickensville, 15; W. J. Anderson to E. H. Gregory, Mar. 4, 1863, Lets. Recd. by Confederate
Sec. of War (M437, Roll 80), RG109, NA; *OR*, Ser. 1, Vol. 24, Pt. 3: 617; Vol. 30, Pt. 4: 5–6;
Vol. 52, Pt. 2: 143.
    2. Joseph W. Selby (*c*1822–*fl*1870) was a tailor in Holly Springs. 1860 Census, Miss.,
Marshall, 1st Ward, Holly Springs, 4; (1870), 15.
    3. Possibly Andrew J. Brown of Greeneville, Tennessee.

From Henry A. Smythe

New York   8 Apr 1869.

My dear Sir.

I am about to embark today—on board the "Deutchland"[1]—(for
Southampton & Harrow) to join my family abroad—& only wish
you were to be of the party—which promises to be a very pleasant
one.

I indulge in the hope, that we may have the pleasure of meeting
you abroad, & of travelling with you—& I need not tell you, it will
give evry member of my family great pleasure—to devote ourselves
to you, & to travel with you & yours—in whichever direction you
may desire—& should you carry out your plan, of making this pleasant trip—as I hope & trust you will do—we shall take great pleasure
in making our plans conform to yours.

My address will be—Care Jno Munroe & Co[2] Paris—& whenever you desire to visit Europe I hope you will advise me & we will
gladly join you.

Together with very many others I have been very anxious with
regard to your health & greatly pained to hear it was at one time not
good—but I now hear it is much better & I hope on account of a

more permanent recovery—you will be induced to carry out your former intention of going abroad.

I believe all of the steam ship lines have extended an invitation to you, at all events, I know either will feel it an honor to have you as a passenger.

The line I am about sailing on today—Messrs. Oelrichs & Co[3]— have fine ships evry Thursday—& the French line—evry other Saturday. All are first class.

Please give my kindest regards to Mrs. Patterson & Mrs. Stover as well as to Mrs. Johnson—& accept for yourself—my warmest regards & respect.

H A. Smythe

ALS, DLC-JP.

1. The *Deutschland*, of the Oelrichs and Company line, left as scheduled on April 8. *New York Herald*, Apr. 9, 1869.

2. John Munroe and Company was a banking firm with offices in New York and Paris. *New York Tribune*, Dec. 3, 1904.

3. Oelrichs and Company were shipping merchants and agents for the North German Lloyds Steamship Company. Ibid., June 29, 1875; New York City directories (1863, 1875).

From Julia Gardiner Tyler

Castleton Hill   North Shore P.O
Staten Island   New York   April 10. 1869

My dear Sir

I confess to feeling a little anxiety to know in what condition my portrait reached the 'White House' & *how* you located it.[1]

The only person I have enquired of in regard to it was, the other day, of my friend, & your friend, Mr Evarts. He could tell me nothing as he said he had not been within the Executive Mansion since you left it.

Please let me hear what you can in regard to it, & then I will pursue my enquiries as to how it is treated by the presiding Administration—if not with care & kindness I can but ask for its return.

I must here express my admiration of your noble speech recently delivered. I am sure a few more such speeches must touch & elevate the National heart—& Heaven knows how much that is needed!

I hope your health will long be preserved whether to expand in thankless efforts for the Country or in the advancement of your own private interests. Nothing can be brighter than the halo that is around your head from your glorious use of your pardoning power.

I remain, with best regards to Mrs Patterson, in which my daughter[2] unites . . .

Julia Gardiner Tyler

ALS, DLC-JP.
1. See Tyler to Johnson, Feb. 26, 1869.
2. The Tyler daughter referred to here could be either 18-year-old Julia or 8-year-old Pearl.

From Elizabeth J. Reynolds [1]

Confidential

Nashville Tenn, April 11th 1869

Hon Andrew Johnson

For you persistent, unappalled defence of the Constitution, of the U.S. of America, please accept our unqualified admiration, and heart felt, gratitude. Having borne the Oppressors heel, through four years, of unremitted endeavor, to preserve National Rights intact, we hail you, as the exponent of true Republicanism, broad enough to embody *Ladies Political Rights* as well as those of *all men*.

"The subject of equal rights as applied to *Woman* is becoming the Question of the day.["] Just, and noble men, are arising in every state of the union, irrespective of Party, who demand, that their Mothers Wives, Sisters and Daughters, shall no longer be classed in Law with infants Criminals and idiots. They ask, that freedom of thought and action, shall be accorded to women equally with men in order, that no fetters may prevent *her* emerging from the chrysalis state to which, the condition of the world, during the dark ages necessarily confined her. They ask for fifteen million of women in this Country, opportunity to bring about, a higher Civilization, than man, unaided, *by her*, can achieve. Hon Sir, permit me to affirm, that, no State in this Union, has a Republican government, and that the principles, the grand fundamental *idea*, of Equality & justice embodied in the Declaration of Independence, is not, *even comprehended*, by a majority of our people. Yet it was, the injustice of Taxation, without *Representation* that nerved, our fore fathers—yes our fore mothers too, to engage in, and carry on, the Revolutionary War.

Men, now vote, every where, who own nothing, but women, who hold property, either inherited, or the product of their own industry, are allowed not a whisper, in the disposition of the Taxes, that are levied on them. "We have faith, in the depths, of generosity, chivalry, and self sacrifice, that now slumbers in your souls.["] If we, had to create, a sense of justice, of tenderness, of respect, for Woman we should have little hope. As those sentiments, already exist, all we have to do, is, to call *them out*, by eloquently, pleading our cause, before you. To deny equal rights, to woman, is to degrade *her*, in public estimation. Are not all disfranchised, classes considered degraded? Does not, the very condition of Disfranchisement, educate people, to consider themselves degraded and inferior? See the material effect of this condition, on woman. Not only herself, but her labor, is considered, below par. She recieves, but one half, one fourth, one sixth, the compensation, allowed to man, for the same work. The cry for justice, goes up, all over the land, from women, who have, no fathers, husbands, or brothers, to provide for, or protect them. Women who work, and support, themselves, and the helpless ones, dependent on them, and who, often recieve, at the hands, of their employers, the "stones, and scorpions of insult," instead of the "bread that should feed them." Yet these employers are the Law makers, and profess, to include, womans interests, in Legislating for *themselves*. No class of persons, can represent, or legislate, *rightly* for another class. It is impossible. Woman needs, the Ballot, that, they, may become a Power, to protect, themselves from the rapacity of man. For since, the wolves, and wild Indians, are all cleared out, the only, creature, that woman, needs, protection against, is, the being, who with a "lordly air["] styles himself, her "natural protector." But Hon. Sir, I need not argue, the case, further. The same arguments, that you have used to prove, that it was right and best, to give Suffrage, to the Irish and the black man, will tell, with double force, in the Lady suffrage cause. May we, not hope to *hear you* say to men, give up woman, your *last slave*, at Freedoms call—and you, will, begin, the task, of self government, and learn to rule yourselves?

In the name, of intelligent, educated millions, of your fellow citizens, at the request, of many Ladies, this is submitted, by me, to your consideration.

Mrs. E. J. Reynolds

ALS, DLC-JP.
    1. Reynolds (*fl*1886) was the widow of William Reynolds; beyond that, nothing else has been uncovered about her. Nashville directories (1874–86).

From John Black [1]

                            April 12th 1869   Memphis Tennessee
Dear Sir.

Do not be offended, nor believe these lines are written by an enemy to you, far, very far be it from me, not to rejoice and be Glad,
and contented with the most of your public acts while president.
Two or three points however I will be very glad if you will explain in
a public speech which you are expected to make in Memphis: one;
while you were acting as Military Governor of Tennessee, which you
refer to in your speech in Knoxville; that is this, you say that you
standing upon the capital steps at Nashville amidst war tumult and
strife declared freedom to the colored men of Tennessee. Please tell
us by what Constitutional Authority did have to do this thing. Where
can you find any law of Right founded upon just principles to take
away the property of your neighbour who was as much opposed to
rebellion as you could possibly be. If President Lincoln did not chose
or want to free the negroes, why were you not satisfied to let the
servants of your neighbours alone, as God Almighty has commanded
you to do. Lincoln said he freed the negroes as a war necessity. When
that necessity ceased, why did you not by Proclamation restore all
things as they were, so soon as rebellion ceased to be? The Resolutions in Congress were that the war should be carried on for no
other purpose but to restore the Union. 2nd. Did we not seceed from
Great Britten? Did not the Southern States have a much more just
cause for secession in the late rebellion than we formally did from
Great Brittian? Had the North & the South seperated peacibly; upon
just and honest principles, would it not have been the wisest act of
man kind since God created Man. Save the people and the people
will save the Government. For what is a Government worth without
people. Were not many—a great many of the people engaged in the
late rebellion truly and sincerely in the belief that they were right,
and that their cause was just, and right and true to the principles
which was fought for and won by our fore fathers in the cecession
from Great Britian, and when they were over powered by great numbers and ceased to rebell any longer, and strictly kept their pledge
why have they not been treated like civilized human beings instead
of brutish beasts? "Oh judgement thou art fled to Brutish beasts and
men have lost their reason." Has the U.S. Government got what
they fought for. Have the U.S. Government kept their pledged faith
in one single fact? When? And How was the present Government

formed? Is any one state justly, rightly and Constitutionally bound to support and adhear to the present form of Government? Is not our present Government forced upon the people at the point of the bayonet & mouth of the cannon contrary to the consent of the people? Now President Johnson I will be glad if you will answer and explain these things to the people of Memphis who will gladly hear all that you have to say? Also, I want you to consent to be the next Governor of Tennessee and we the people of the state will overwhelmingly place you in that office. Also I want you (if Alexander Steephens of Georgia is a live) and him to so amend the Constitution of the U.S. with all the necessary bearriers, parts & railing and so stake and Reder it, that do difficulty what ever shall here after ever jar, shake or trouble the people of these U.S. any more for ever.

Take the Ten Commandments written by God himself expressly to guide and govern mankind while on earth, and form your Constitution as near as possible to the meaning of these Commandments and lay it before the people and we will vote for it, and adopt it as our own so long as the world may permitted to remain for the people, but unless something of this kind be done before many years, this world will be destroyed on the account of the awful whirl pool of corruption, so sure as there is a God. Now Ex President Johnson will you do it? You are the man to do it. You can do it, and if you refuse and will not do it I will hold you responsible at the bar of a just God. No more at present.

John Black

ALS, DLC-JP.
   1. Perhaps the John Black (*c*1838–*fl*1878) who was a lawyer in Memphis and a justice of the peace. 1870 Census, Tenn., Shelby, Memphis, 6th Ward, 89; Memphis directories (1869–78).

From Caroline Livingston Edmonston

Washington, April 12 /69.

My Esteemed Friend.

   I am praying that the Supreme Court decide against the Constitutionality of the franchise Law, that your way may be clear to the Senate of the U. States thence to the White House—Again Our President. May the Almighty give you health to carry out your programme, and accord to me the supreme happiness of tendering my congratulations on so auspicious an event.

Assessor Wolfley[1] dealt us a blow, that would have crushed any one but your energetic little friend. He had my Brother[2] removed previous to being ousted himself. I was up, and doing in the twinkling of an eye, and before I left, had matters in train to have him reinstated. Commissioner Delano[3] told me that if Assessor Joubert[4] (colored) would endorse him, that he would be reinstated. There was a quandary! But I managed it adroitly by tacitly ignoring the fact that Mr. Joubert (a very kind hearted and gentlemanly colored person by the bye) was not of pure race.

I placed my Brother's credentials before him, and insinuatingly petitioned for his reinstatement. It was at once promised, and I wrote my brother to send on his application, endorsed by Assessor Joubert, who will be in New Orleans by the time he receives my letter. I shall remain in Washington until I forward his commission, and then return to New Orleans to attend to some business matters there. This done, I shall make my summer quarters in the vicinity of New York, the Paris of America.

My sister Pauline[5] sends her respectful compliments, trusting with myself that we may have the pleasure of seeing you before we leave Washington for the South.

I pray you Mr. President (it may occur to you that I remarked the last time I saw you, that you were always to be our President) pardon my writing so much at length about my own affairs. Did I not know you to be kind of heart, and a sincere sympathizer with the crushed and suffering Southerners, now that they have in good faith laid down the war-club and made the 'amende honorables,' I should have been more brief.

Am I not to be favored by a reply to my missive?

May I ask if you received a few lines from me shortly after you left Washington?

Mr. Ross[6] who voted against the impeachment was snubbed by Genl. Grant. Wishing to know what were the intentions of General Grant for appointments in his state, and understanding very conclusively that the General was vindictive, he unflinchingly told his President to go to, ——— well Tartarus, whereupon he was ordered to leave the White House. Western men don't stand any humbugging when they are in a rage. I see Colonel Moore,[7] very often and we always revert to the halcyon days when you reigned supreme in Washington.

                                                    Mrs. C. J. Edmonston.

ALS, DLC-JP.

1. Lewis Wolfley, assessor of Louisiana's First District.

2. James Edmonston.

3. Columbus Delano.

4. Blanc F. Joubert (c1818–ff1885) was named assessor of the First District, a position he held for several years. Later he served as state tax collector. 1870 Census, La., Orleans, New Orleans, 6th Ward, 192; *U.S. Off. Reg.* (1869–71); New Orleans directories (1870–85); *New Orleans Picayune*, Mar. 18, 1869; *Charlottesville Chronicle*, Mar. 23, 1869.

5. Pauline Harris.

6. Edmund G. Ross.

7. William G. Moore.

From A.O.P. Nicholson

Columbia, Tenn   Apl. 12 1869.

Dear Sir:

I enclose you an invitation to speak here on your return from Memphis.[1] These signatures were procured here to-day in a few hours. I hope you will come. Let me know when you will come. I am just returned from Centerville where I have been for the last week at Court—otherwise I should have been at Nashville to see you. We will try to have a large crowd & I dont doubt we will succeed.[2]

A.O.P. Nicholson

ALS-DLC-JP.

1. The invitation, bearing scores of signatures, is found enclosed. The signers lauded Johnson's "devotion to the constitution" and his "ability to vindicate the constitutional rights of the people against the aggressions & usurpations of Congress."

2. Although Johnson planned to stop and speak in Columbia in late April, en route from North Alabama to Nashville, his trip was cancelled when he learned of his son's death. *Nashville Republican Banner*, Apr. 23, 24, 1869.

From John L. Bartow [1]

Fort Valley Ga   15. Apr 1869

Sir—

I am one of a numerous class of people throughout the South who have hated you cordially in the dark days that are past, and who would have considered it his duty to have slain you on sight.

But Sir, I wish to say—and beg your pardon for this intrusion at the same time—that your course since the late unhappy war, standing as you did solitary & alone, by the old constitutional landmarks, striking for a defeated people when there was nothing to gain, & on the other hand by simply adhering to the powerful dominant party, you might to-day have been President has won for you a host of friends & admirers here among whom although the very humblest, I am proud to rank myself, the warmest. May the good God bless you sir—& strengthen your hands for the coming conflict in Tenn. Wether Andrew Johnson be Governor of Ten., Senator in Congress, or President of the United States or what is grander still a simple citizen, the South can never forget for one moment the Grand old man who interposed his own person, to shield them from the ruthless bolts of radical hate hurled by our powerful enemies at her defenseless head.

With the honest earnest hope that you will be successful & that you will leave no stone unturned to secure that success—for we make common cause with you . . .

Jno. L. Bartow

ALS, DLC-JP.
   1. Bartow (c1834–fl1870), a former Confederate Nitre Bureau superintendent and agent, by 1870 was a resident of Cave Spring, Georgia. 1870 Census, Ga., Floyd, 141st Subdiv., Cave Spring, 14; Confederate Papers re Citizens or Business Firms (M346, Roll 46), John L. Bartow, RG109, NA.

From John Campbell

Philadelphia, April 15th 1869

Dear Sir

I can now afford to address you and I do so with pleasure. You are no longer President, and, therefore what I say cannot be attributed to fawning upon power. I never solicted a favor from you during your presidential term of office. The misfortune that attends a President is that he has much difficulty to know the friend from the toady. I am glad to see that you are at work to purify (if possible) the public atmosphere. In such a course you will have the best wishes of all good men. I need hardly say to you that the Republican party has endevoured to load your policy with odium and that many of the mercenaries who sought your patronage are a curse to any party to which they belong. If we act wisely in 1872 we will wrest power from our present bad and corrupt rulers. I wish you to understand that I have no axe to grind that in the general misrule I can live but I do want your advice to be followed. You are acting like a Philosopher and patriot in endeavouring to arouse the people to a sense of the danger to which they are exposed. Perhaps it is too soon to say who ought to be the next nominee of the Democracy for President. My impression that had we nominated Hancock and Hendricks that we might *perhaps* have elected them. I hope to see you in our next national convention and I also hope to see you again a member of the U S Senate. No matter what mistake you may have made while President every honest man must admit that for honesty and integrity you have never been surpassed. You were no recipient of gifts. Oh how the high and honorable office of President has been already degraded and disgraced by the present office holder who grabs every thing from a fat ox to a furnished mansion. In conclusion I may say that I felt saddened when I heard of your sudden illness. My hope is that you may live many very many years to terrify political knaves and to defend the rights of the people.

John Campbell

ALS, DLC-JP.

From Carl C. Giers[1]

Nashville Tenn.   April 15 1869.

Sir!

I send you by to-days mail some of your photographs which I hope will meet with your approval in regard to likeness and execution.[2] Your friends here think that they are just like you.

With many regards, and kind wishes for your health and prosperity . . .

C. C. Giers

P S. Should you wish more copies please let me know it.

ALS, DLC-JP.

1. Giers (1828–1877), a Nashville photographer, was a native of Bonn, Germany, who had lived in the United States since 1845. In 1873 he was a delegate from Tennessee to the World Exposition at Vienna. Afterwards, Giers represented Davidson County in the lower house of the General Assembly (1875–77). *BDTA*, 2: 333.

2. At least two of Giers's photographs depicted Johnson in Knights Templar regalia, reprints of which appear at two locations in this volume: the *frontispiece* and on p. 560.

Speech in Memphis

[April 15, 1869][1]

Fellow Citizens:

In appearing before you on the present occasion, I do not do so in the character that I have done in times gone by. When I came before you heretofore it was usually in making an appeal to you for some favor which it was in your power to confer. It is not to solicit favors at your hands, so far as individual and personal preferment is concerned, that I am here to day, but only in the character of a citizen having recently retired from the most exalted position in the gift of a free people. In retiring to private life I feel more pride in being an American citizen than in being inaugurated President over the ruins of a violated Constitution.

I know that in the beginning of the present troubles there were differences of opinion between many of you and myself. You had your opinions, and I had mine. Some of you believed that by division and separation of the States, certain things could be accomplished; others, and I for one, thought differently, and thought that the true place to remain was where we were,—under the Constitution, and there fight our battles. That was my opinion. As to how this was to have been accomplished it is not my intention to go into a discussion. The result is before us all, and shows who was right and who was wrong. I believe in maintaining our true position under the aegis of the Constitution. I said there to abide was our position, and time would prove who was most correct, whether to maintain our ground and stand firm, or abandon it and take sides opposite to the Constitution. I refer to this merely to show that differences did exist; but look at the example of Charles V., Emperor of Germany, who wearied with the cares of state, retired to a monastery and resigned his throne to his son,[2] and spent his time in retirement in attempting to regulate the movements of watches and make them keep time exactly together. He made various experiments, and again and again tried and failed in making any two of them keep the same time. This led him to reflect upon the crime and folly of trying by force to make all men of the same opinion as himself. We are led by this reference to see the crime and folly of trying to make men of different opinions agree.

If we differ in opinions, time will prove which was right. Give every man the credit of being honest in his opinions. It is a way that a man understands a question. There can be no debate in a question that we understand. It is the want of understanding questions which causes argument. To quote a couplet which I learned years ago—

> "Never argue what you do not understand,
> Nor worship a God that you can comprehend."[3]

It is the want of understanding questions which causes argument. If questions were understood, there would be no argument. It is the incomprehensibility of God which causes our worship.

Since I became President of the United States, you are no doubt aware of the fierce contest which transpired between the Executive and Congress, and have seen the papers teeming with abuse and misrepresentations and obloquy upon me. I was traduced, misrepresented and accused of everything that could be infamous. The contest was between two departments of the Government.

Government was created for man, and not man for government; government was created for the convenience and protection of man's rights—for this, government was made.

Let me tell you the great problem to be worked out now is whether the Government is to be sustained or overthrown.

In a constitutional government the power emanates from the people. The Constitution is the combined and express will of the people, and limits the powers and functions of those who are chosen agents to execute their will. It was intended to divide the power into three equal divisions—Legislative, Judicial and Executive. When it comes to the Executive-Legislative aggressions under pretence of law, have assumed to themselves.

The Executive branch of the Government is negative. It is not aggressive; it can only say to the law-making power when they are transcending their powers, "thus far shalt thou go, and no further." Remain in abeyance until your action can be submitted to the people, and they shall have an opportunity of considering and determining whether Congress is right. Or, if the measure have a two-thirds majority, he can return it to Congress, and it becomes a law. Where Congress passes a law by a two-thirds vote, it becomes a part of the Constitution. When you go back to the organic law of the land, you see that a law, passed by a two-thirds majority, is no more a law than if simply passed by a majority and approved. Hence, in Congress, you find the various laws passed. You are familiar with most of those submitted to me for my approval.

I, as President of the United States, felt it incumbent on me to veto many, and transmit others back to them with my reasons for the same. My reasons were given to the country.

I have nothing to regret in what I have done. My only regret is that I could not efficiently stop them in their course. (Tremendous applause.) I did what I would do again. I believed they were unconstitutional encroachments and usurpations of power, and as an honest man I vetoed them, and vetoed them again and again.

There are many that think that the passage by a two-thirds vote can change the Constitution. Under this pretense they might usurp all law, wipe out the Executive, and might abolish the Judiciary. Right here is the rock on which the government will split. We may talk about despotic power and despotic governments. There are various kinds of despotisms, and when we come to examine them and understand what government is, let me tell you that to concentrate all power in one body of men is the most rigorous of despotisms, far more despotic than any one man. A body, in the shape of a Congress or Legislature, to whom this power is given, would enact laws and usurp powers that one man would shrink from and shudder at. By association, countenance, friction of persons, they dare do as a body things that one man would shudder at. Hence, when it comes to a Congress or Legislature, with no Executive or Judiciary to restrain them, all power centralized in them, I would much prefer a wiser judiciary and just Prince. Such a body, to use the language of Jefferson, the apostle of constitutional liberty, is the perfect definition of despotic power, and more to be dreaded and feared than any one-man power.[4] Under pretence of law, it absorbs, assumes and usurps to itself all power, and goes forward and wipes out the other branches of the Government. It is the design of some persons to change the character of our Government to this. They are forming the change in various ways, and I tell you that the character of our Government is more in jeopardy than when two armies were in the field.

There are at this time some persons now designing the change. When we examine we see the outcroppings of the scheme. Various schemes have been suggested to consolidate the Government in Washington—either in Congress or a dictator.

What do we see in confirmation of this design in the Congress of the United States? I hold in my hand a copy of a paper recently established and now published in New York entitled *The Empire*— and it has for a heading "The Empire is peace—let us have peace." (Sensation and laughter.) (A voice, "The best in the world.") The Empire is peace—let us have peace! (Reads from the *Empire*):[5]

"The conductors of this journal believe Democracy to be a failure. Though theoretically plausible, in its practical workings it has been found totally inadequate to the wants of the American people.

We believe that the national faith, if left in the keeping of the populace, will be sullied by the sure repudiation of the National Debt, and that an Imperial Government can alone protect the rights of national creditors.

We believe that an Imperial Government, in its paternal relation to the people, will care equally for all citizens, and, while guaranteeing security to the rights of capital, will jealously protect the interests of the industrial classes."

See what an indication is here; it is a mere outcropping of this fixed design. Again:

"We believe that the Republic means lawlessness, corruption, insecurity to person and property, robbery of the public creditors, and civil war; that the Empire means law, order, security, public faith and peace."

The history of the world teaches us that a nation, harassed by war, its resources exhausted, when an ambitious leader comes along, is ready to submit to anything for the sake of peace.

"We hope," continues this paper, "that it will not be so with our beloved America, and that, in the broad blaze of the light of the nineteenth century, our fellow-citizens will not allow blind prejudice and inherited political ophthalmia to prevent them from reading the signs of the times."

"We have had our age of individual uprightness and personal patriotism, but even then we might have read a lesson in the fact that our first revolution was a dismal failure until our fathers made an autocrat of George Washington, for and during that emergency. Some few men did receive a glimmer of light when all the people rallied so enthusiastically around the self-declared dictatorship of Andrew Jackson; but it was left for the revolution through which we have just passed, to open the eyes of hundreds of thousands who never saw before. The war was a failure until we made Abraham Lincoln almost an absolute autocrat, with more power than any other sovereign on earth. We made him such, and all the people said 'Amen! It is necessary. The Republic is well enough in peace, but it is not the thing to ride out a storm in.' And many were content to stop here, refusing to see that the very weakness which was unable to manage the war had made the war possible—nay had made it inevitable. It is with an almost ludicrous unconsciousness of their inconsistency that so many good citizens base their present hopes of peace, not on the wisdom and power of their 'representatives' in Congress assembled, but upon the fact that a man is in the President's chair, from whom they may expect some signs of autocratic firmness and executive consistency."

Now see what is there plainly indicated. This thing is thrown out as a feeler by an ambitious Congress, ready to come forward to usurp our liberties—a feeler to see if we are ready for a dictator. The people are no longer to be trusted with the national honor and credit, and this plan assumes to come forward to establish a secure Government, and secure the payment of the national debt. To continue:

"And we find moreover, that other nations see our weakness, and, for all our wealth, dare not trust so frail a concern as ours, so that we pay for our indebtedness double the interest demanded of the decayed despotisms of the Old World.

This is the ninth year since the beginning of our recent troubles, and the fourth since the nominal close of our war, and are we yet 'at peace?' If so, what may be the meaning of our President's most popular aspiration, and why does it have more meaning to the general ear, coming from his mouth, than it ever did in the voluminous enactments of the people's representatives?

With *what*, permit us to ask, is any one so willfully blind as to overlook the fact that no man any longer considers himself entitled or in duty bound to secure a representation on the floor of Congress? Is it not, patent that, so far as 'representation' goes, three-quarters of our people have forgotten even the doctrines, and that an immense part of them have long since ceased even to care who rules them? We have to preserve but a system of juggling appliances, moral and legal trap doors and false entrances, by which demagogues obtain power and robbers sit in high places.

Let us reassure the timid: Autocracy, in such a system as it is now possible to establish it, shuts out the idea of despotism—nor would tyranny ever be possible among such a people as ours or in such a continent as this. Instead of a thousand masters, there would be but one—and all that any man would lose would be his forty millionth chance of turning up as President."

OPPOSED TO CHANGE.

My countrymen the time has come to recur to first principles. I have nothing to ask of you. My race is run, but I speak to you, as if you were a part of my own flesh and blood. I want no preferment.

My early education was amid struggles for a vindication of a free government, and I am opposed to seeing our government pass into the hands of a dictator. I stand on the Constitution—the express and combined will of the people, and on its battle-field I intend to stand and oppose the advances of despotism upon a great people and a free government. In vindication of myself, so far as my little reputation is concerned, which will be a part of history, I intend to devote the remainder of my life to the advocacy of those principles which I prize more than life itself.

In example of what Congress—but before I proceed to that, I will say, in vindication of the Constitution, that embodiment of wisdom and inspiration; that great chart of American liberty does not deny the privilege of changing it. Look at the Constitution and you will see that the far-seeing sagacity of the farmers [*sic*], in anticipation of the requirements of progress, provided a mode of amending it, if it should be found too small or too large. They provided the mode and the manner how it is to be altered, either by the suggestion of the people to Congress, or of Congress to the people.

This mode should have been adopted before the proposition to exercise powers outside of the Constitution. The time to consider is given, and the amendment can be either made or rejected, with due deliberation.

OLD TIMES.

The Whigs and Democrats had political contests, bitter ones, and they met each other on the stand or through the newspapers. In these contests I met some of you, and shivered a lance upon you, or you broke a javelin upon me, but when the contest was over we met each other as friends and brothers. The contest was in the Constitution. The difference between the two parties was that the Democratic contended for a strict construction of the Constitution.

The Whig contended for a little more latitude, a more liberal construction of government under the Constitution. But both agreed on one point—that there was a Constitution. These two great parties—would to God we had them now—(A voice—Amen! The best in the world.) both moving in the limits of the Constitution, both adhering to it, and only differing in the little more strictness, or a little more latitude. But the great essential was there—a constitutional government.

While I am not a fanatic—would to God I could inspire some fanaticism—I would inspire the people as Peter did, though Peter's inspiration was partly fallacious; but I wish I had the power of Peter when he was preaching the crusades, regardless of Richard and Saladin, when he moved the nations and peoples of Europe, as one man, to preserve the Holy Sepulchre. But I have no such powers. If I had, I would arouse the whole American people to the importance of preserving the Constitution of our forefathers, the combined and expressed will of the people, and would say to the usurping Congress "thus far shalt thou go and no further." (Applause.)

CONGRESS.

When we take this Congress, that has been riding over the Constitution, and ask what it has done, (A voice—"nothing." Another—"tell us, Andy") a friend says nothing! Ah, they have done *worse* than nothing. They have done too much. (Laughter, and cries of "that's so," "the best in the world," etc.)

Let us turn to the history of this majority that has been acting with such utter disregard of the Constitution. While public attention has been carefully and constantly turned to the past and expiated sins of the South, the servants of the people, in high places, betrayed their trust, broke their oaths of obedience to the Constitution and undermined the very foundations of the Government. When the rebellion was being suppressed by the volunteered services of patriot soldiers amid the dangers of the battle-field, these men crept, without question into place and power in the national councils. After the danger had passed, when no armed foe remained, when a punished and repentant people bowed their heads to the flag, and renewed their allegiance to the Government of the United States, then it was these pretended patriots appeared before the nation and began to prate about the thousands of lives and millions of money sacrificed in the suppression of the rebellion. They have since persistently sought to inflame the prejudices engendered between the sections, to retard the restoration of peace and harmony, and by every means to keep open and exposed to the poisonous breath of party passion the terrible wounds of a four years war. They have prevented the return of peace and the restoration of Union; in every way rendered delusive the purposes, promises and pledges by which the army was marshaled, treason rebuked and rebellion crushed; and made the liberties of the people and the rights and powers of the President objects of constant attack.

They have wrested from the President his constitutional power of the supreme command of the army and navy; they have destroyed the strength of the Executive Department by making subordinate officers independent of and able to defy their Chief Magistrate; they have attempted to place the President under the power of a bold, defiant and treacherous Cabinet officer; they have robbed the Executive of the prerogative of pardon; rendered null and void the acts of clemency granted to thousands of persons under the provisions of the Constitution, and committed gross usurpations by legislative attempts to exercise this power in favor of party adherents; they have conspired to change the system of our Government by preferring charges against the President in the form of articles of impeachment, and contemplating, before hearing or trial, that he should be placed under arrest, held in durance, and when it became their pleasure to pronounce his sentence, driven from place and power in disgrace; they have in time of peace increased the national debt by a reckless expenditure of public moneys, and thus added to the burden which already weigh upon the people; they have permitted the nation to suffer the evils of a deranged currency to the enhancement in price of all the necessaries of life; they have maintained a large standing army for the enforcement of their measures of oppression; they have engaged in class legislation; built and encouraged monopolies, that the few might be enriched at the expense of the many; they have failed to act upon important treaties, endangering our peaceful relations with foreign powers. Their course of usurpation has not been limited to inroads upon the Executive Department by unconstitutional and oppressive enactments. The people of ten States of the Union have been reduced to a condition more intolerable than that from which the patriots of the Revolution rebelled. Millions of American citizens can now say of their oppressors with more truth than their fathers did of British tyrants, that they have forbidden the State governments to pass laws of immediate and pressing importance unless suspended until their assent should be obtained. That they have refused to pass other laws for the accommodation of large districts of people, unless these people would relinquish their right of representation in the Legislature, a right inestimable to them and formidable to tyrants only. That they have made judges dependent on their will alone for the tenure of offices and the amount and payment of claims. That they have erected a multitude of new offices and sent thither swarms of officers to harrass our people and take out their substance. That they have affected to render the military independent of and superior to the civil power; combined with others to subject us to a jurisdiction foreign to our Constitution and unacknowledged by our laws; quartered large bodies of armed troops among us and protected them by a mock trial from the punishment of any murders which they should commit on the inhabitants; imposed taxes on us without our consent; deprived us in many cases, of trial by jury; taken away our charters; excited domestic insurrection among us; abolished our most valuable laws; altered, fundamentally, the form of our Government; suspended our own Legislatures; and declared themselves invested with power to legislate for us in all cases whatever. This catalogue of crime, long as it is, is not complete. The Constitution vests judicial power in one supreme Court, whose jurisdiction shall extend to all cases arising under the Constitution and the laws of the United States. Encouraged by this promise, a refuge from tyranny, a citizen of the United States also, by order of a military commander, given under sanction of a cruel and deliberate edict of Congress, had been denied the constitutional rights of liberty of conscience and freedom of the press and of speech, personal freedom from military arrest, of being held to answer for crime only upon presentment of an indictment, of trial by jury, of the writ of habeas corpus, and the protection of a civil and constitutional government. A citizen thus deeply wronged appeals to the Supreme Court for the protection guaranteed him by the organic law of the land. At once a fierce and excited majority, by the ruthless hand of legislative power, stripped the ermine from the Judges, transferred the sword of justice to the General, and remanded the oppressed citizen to a degradation and bondage worse than death.

It will also be recorded as one of the marvels of the times that a party claiming for itself a monopoly of constituency and patriotism, and boasting of its unlimited sway, endeavored by a costly and deliberate trial to impeach one who defended the Constitution and Union, not only throughout the war of the rebellion, but during the whole term of office as Chief Magistrate, but at the same time could find no warrant or means at their command to bring to trial even the chief of the rebellion. Indeed, the remarkable failures in the case were so often repeated that for propriety's sake, if for no other reason, it became at last necessary to extend to him an unconditional pardon.

What more plainly than this illustrates the extremities of party management and inconsistencies on the one hand, and of faction, vindictiveness and intolerance on the other. Patriotism will hardly be encouraged when in such a record it sees that its instant reward may be the most virulent party abuse and obloquy, if not disgrace.

Instead of seeking to make treason odious, it would in truth seem to have been their purpose rather to make the defense of the Constitution and Union a crime, and to punish fidelity to an oath of office.

THE FINANCE.

This is some of their work outside of the Constitution, and because I charge them with their high crimes and violation of the Constitution, they heaped on me vituperation and obloquy.

If I know myself I came here on this occasion to speak to you in the language of soberness and truth, and I have accomplished my intention. I do not want you to think you will hear an orator declaim, in sounding, rounding sentences, I tell you if you did you can let yourselves down. I came here to deal in facts and arguments. Give me your attention:[6]

The population of the United States in 1700 [*sic*] was nearly four millions. The people increasing in each decade about 33 per cent., it reached in 1860 thirty millions, an increase of seven hundred per cent. on the population of 1790. In 1869 it is estimated that it will reach thirty-eight millions, or an increase of eight hundred and sixty-eight per cent in 79 years. The annual expenditures of the Federal Government in 1791 were $4,200,000; in 1820, $10,200,000; in 1850, $41,000,000; in 1860, $63,000,000; in 1865, nearly $13,300,000,000; in 1869, it is estimated by the Secretary of the Treasury, in his last annual report, that they will be three hundred and seventy-two millions of dollars. By comparison of the public disbursements of 1869, as estimated with those of 1791, it will be seen that the increase of the expenditures since the beginning of the Government has been eight thousand six hundred and eighteen per centum, while the increase of the population for the same period was only eight hundred and sixty-eight per centum. Again, the expenses of the Government in 1860, the year of peace immediately preceding the war, were only sixty-three millions, whilst in 1867, the year of peace three years after the war, it is estimated they will be $372,000,000, an increase of 489 per centum, while the increase of the population was only 21 per centum for the same period. These statistics further show that in 1791 the annual national expenses compared with the population were little more than one dollar per capita, and in 1860 but two dollars per capita, while in 1869 they will reach the extravagant sum of nine dollars and seventy-eight cents per capita. It will be observed that all of these statements referred to exhibit the disbursements of peace periods. It may, therefore, be of interest to compare the expenditures of the three war periods—the war with Great Britain, the Mexican war, and the war of the rebellion. In 1814 the annual expenses incident to the war of 1812, reached the highest amount, about thirty-one millions, while our population slightly exceeded eight millions, showing an expenditure of only three dollars and eighty cents per capita.

In 1847 the expenditures growing out of the war with Mexico reached fifty-four millions, and the population about twenty one millions, giving only two dollars and sixty cents per capita for the war expenses of that year.

In 1865 the expenditures called for by the rebellion reached the vast amount of twelve hundred and ninety millions, which, compared with a population of thirty-four millions, gives thirty-eight dollars and twenty cents per capita. From the fourth day of March, 1789, to the 30th of June, 1861, the entire expenditures of the Government were seventeen hundred millions of dollars. During that period we were engaged in wars with Great Britain and Mexico, and were involved in hostilities with powerful Indian tribes; Louisiana was purchased from France at a cost of fifteen millions of dollars; Florida was ceded to us by Spain for five millions; California was acquired from Mexico for fifteen millions, and the territory of New Mexico was obtained from Texas for the sum of ten millions.

Early in 1861 the war of the rebellion commenced, and from the first of July of that year to the end of June, 1865, the public expenditures reached the enormous aggregate of thirty-three hundred millions. Three years of peace have intervened, and during that time the disbursements of the Government have successively been five hundred and twenty millions, three hundred and forty six millions, and three hundred and seventy-three millions. Adding to these amounts three-hundred and seventy-two millions, estimated as necessary for the fiscal year ending the 30th of June, 1869 we obtain a total expenditure of sixteen hundred millions of dollars during the four years immediately preceding the war, or nearly as much as was expended during the seventy-two years that preceded the rebellion, and embraced the extraordinary expenditures already named.

Take the war and peace periods. Corruption permeates every department of the Government. Think of it, and ask yourselves if reform is not needed. You will find upon examination a debt fixed on the country, a debt of more than $2,600,000,000, requiring the payment of more than 150 millions in gold and increasing the taxable burdens of the people to more than 450 millions per year. Congress is in favor of a continuance of this debt, in favor of the bondholder, the corrupt and tyrannical Congress. We see the design of all this. It is usurpation of all power. They are afraid of the people, afraid of repudiation, because they hold the bonds and are personally interested in their redemption. Think of it, 150 millions in gold per year required to meet the interest on this burdensome debt. Out of $500,000,000 collected each year for the purpose of defraying the expenses of the Government, full 150 millions dollars are necessary to pay the bondholders, who represent $2,500,000,000 of debt. The poor man who toils for the Government in its navy yard, arsenals and shops, must take greenbacks for his wages, greenbacks at a depreciation of 35 to 40 per cent. below par, but the rich bondholder, who lives at his ease and rolls in luxurious wealth, gets gold for his coupons gold—and silver. The working man must take paper at a discount of 40 per cent. below par. The man who sweats, and labors, and toils, pays the debt, the soldier too, but the wealthy bondholder must have his gold and silver. I say this in no spirit of demagogueism, but in a spirit of justice. I sent into Congress my views upon this subject. I will read you what I said. Here is what I said:[7]

"The feasibility of making our currency correspond with the constitutional standard may be seen by reference to a few facts derived from our commercial statistics.

The aggregate product of precious metals in the United States from 1849 to 1867 amounted to $1,174,000,000, while, for the same period, the net exports of specie were $741,000,000. This shows an excess of product over net exports of $433,000,000. There are in the treasury $103,407,985 in coin; in circulation in the States on the Pacific coast about $40,000,000, and a few millions in the National and other banks—in all less than $160,000,000. Taking into consideration the specie in the country prior to 1849, and that produced since 1867, and we have more than $300,000,000 not accounted for by exportation or by the returns of the treasury, and therefore most probably remaining in the country.

These are important facts, and show how completely the inferior currency will supersede the better, forcing it from circulation among the masses, and causing it to be exported as a mere article of trade, to add to the money capital of foreign lands. They show the necessity of retiring our paper money, that the return of gold and silver to the avenues of trade may be invited, and a demand created which will cause the retention at home of at least so much of the productions of our rich and inexhaustible gold-bearing fields as may be sufficient for purposes of circulation. It is unreasonable to expect a return to a sound currency so long as the Government and banks, by continuing to issue irredeemable notes, fill the channels of circulation with depreciated paper. Notwithstanding a coinage by our mints, since 1819, of eight hundred and seventy-four millions of dollars, the people are now strangers to the currency which was designed for their use and benefit, and specimens of the precious metals bearing the national device are seldom seen, except when produced to gratify the interest excited by their novelty. If depreciated paper is to be continued as the permanent currency of the country, and all our coin is to become a mere article of traffic and speculation, to the enhancement in price of all that is indispensable to the comfort of the people, it would be wise economy to abolish our mints, thus saving the nation the care and expense incident to such establishments, and let all our precious metals be exported in bullion. The time has come, however, when the Government and National Banks should be required to take the most efficient steps and make all necessary arrangements for a resumption of specie payments. Let specie payments once be earnestly inaugurated by the Government and banks, and the value of the paper circulation would directly approximate a specie standard.

Specie payments having been resumed by the Government and banks, all notes or bills of paper issued by either of a less denomination than twenty dollars should by law be excluded from circulation, so that the people may have the benefit and convenience of a gold and silver currency which in all their business transactions will be uniform in value at home and abroad.

'Every man of property or industry, every man who desires to preserve what he honestly possesses, or to obtain what he can honestly earn, has a direct interest in maintaining a safe circulating medium—such a medium as shall be real and substantial, not liable to vibrate with opinions, not subject to be blown up or blown down by the breath of speculation, but to be made stable and secure. A disordered currency is one of the greatest political evils. It undermines the virtues necessary for the support of the social system, and encourages propensities destructive of its happiness; it wars against industry, frugality and economy, and it fosters the evil spirits of extravagance and speculation.' It has been asserted by one of our profound and most gifted statesmen, that 'of all the contrivances for cheating the laboring classes of mankind, none has been more effectual than that which deludes them with paper money. This is the most effectual of inventions to fertilize the rich man's fields by the sweat of the poor man's brow. Ordinary tyranny, oppression, excessive taxation—these bear lightly on the happiness of the mass of the community compared with a fraudulent currency, and the robberies committed by depreciated paper. Our own history has recorded for our instruction enough, and more than enough of the demoralizing tendency, the injustice and the intolerable oppression on a virtuous and well-disposed of a degraded paper currency authorized by law or in any way countenanced by Government.' It is one of the most successful devices, in times of peace or war, of expansions or revulsions, to accomplish the transfer of all the precious metals from the great mass of the people into the hands of the few, where they are hoarded in secret places or deposited under bolts and bars, while the people are left to endure all the inconvenience, sacrifice, and demoralization resulting from the use of depreciated and worthless paper."

From this we see where we stand in reference to the public debt. Let all be treated alike, as I pressed upon Congress. Instead of hoarding up the gold for the payment of coupons, all should be paid in gold and silver. It is practicable. In 1849, the year after the termination of an expensive war with Mexico, we found ourselves involved in a debt of [$]64,000,000, and this was the amount owed by the Government in 1860, just prior to the outbreak of the rebellion. In the spring of 1861, our civil war commenced. Each year of its continuance made an enormous addition to the debt, and when, in the spring of 1865, the nation successfully emerged from the conflict, the obligations of the Government had reached the immense sum of $2,873,992,909. The Secretary of the Treasury shows that on the 1st day of November, 1867, this amount had been reduced to $2,491,564,453, but, at the same time his report exhibits an increase during the past year of $35,625,102, for the debt on the 1st day of November last is stated to have then been $2,527,129,552. It is estimated by the Secretary that the returns for the past month will add to our liabilities the further sum of $11,000,000, making a total increase during three months of $46,500,000. Has not the country and the Government the capacity, and is there not enough gold and silver to satisfy all alike. Congress passed resolutions condemning the message to which I allude. The immaculate, pure and saintly Congress passed a resolution condemning my message. So much for these important questions. We should understand and see if the evils complained of cannot be righted.

PARDONING POWER.

We will now turn to another subject. I will speak of my exercise of the pardoning power. Some complain that I pardoned too many, and some that I did not pardon enough. If I had it to do over again I would perhaps pardon more. I have pardoned a great many, and I believe a great many of those who make complaint need pardoning a great deal worse than those pardoned. (Laughter). All I regret about it is that I have not pardoned more than I have. Yet I may have

pardoned some that I ought not to have pardoned, and refused some
that should have been granted. It was said that I refused to extend
pardon in one case since ascertained to have been innocent. I may
have erred. It is human to err, divine to forgive. It could not be expected of a fallible man to get along without error. I acted according
to the best dictates of my conscience. I treated all alike—those who
were poor and those high in society. It may be said that I literally
stepped upon the scaffold and prevented the execution of thousands.
Some who, at the outset of the war, followed me with hate, pursued
me and denounced me as a traitor, who even searched the mails for
my correspondence, were subjects of my pardon and my clemency.
Many such expected that I would retaliate and give vent to a personal feeling of revenge; but, thank God that I am a man! (cheers)
and when it comes to acting upon a question of public policy, I can
act magnanimously. I do not regret that it has been in my power to
show that I understood humanity and magnanimity. Would to God
I could pardon the whole world! (Cheers.) There are individuals,
here and there, who need a pardon much worse than those who have
been pardoned.

HIS RETURN TO TENNESSEE—MILITARY TAX.

I returned to my adopted State to learn that, instead of peace, there
was bickering and strife—that the people were quarreling among
themselves and divisions and dissensions had weakened them.

I have heard and read a great deal about the military tax imposed
by me while Military Governor. Where is the man that can say that
filthy lucre has at any time attached to my fingers or adhered to my
person? What I do, I try to understand; and I do always what I think
is right. While the angry strife was raging, while brother was arrayed
against brother, men in Nashville induced others to go into the rebel
service, as it was called, to leave their wives and children dependent
upon the public charity. When Nashville was captured, I, as Military
Governor, found these poor women and children destitute, threatened with being turned out of doors, and with starvation. To prevent
this wrong I levied this tax. I collected this tax from those who were
able to bear it, and kept the women and children of the poor Confederate soldiers from starvation, and in their homes. Every cent of
it was devoted to the poor. I never saw a dollar of it. I said this is the
cause of humanity and justice, and these women must be supported.
I do not regret that I did this. On the contrary, if Military Governor
now, would repeat the operation.

PROCLAMATION OF FREEDOM—MOSES.

I will now turn to another subject, upon which there is a little sensitiveness. But I am addressing an intelligent audience who will understand me. I received a letter upon this subject, so great is the anxiety of some of my friends concerning it.[8] I have only to take care of my record and reputation, and that of my State, and have no ambitions to satisfy. The subject I allude to is that in reference to the emancipation of slaves in Tennessee. All know how this took place. It occurred in Nashville. When I saw that the war was likely to continue, with slavery, I determined that the colored people should be free. It is not what we want, but what we have. I did, on the 24th day of October, from the steps of the Capitol at Nashville, make declaration of freedom to the negroes for the purpose of assisting to terminate the rebellion.[9] And this I want the colored people to understand; I want them to understand who is their best friend. When messengers of death were flying, when men were being shot down in hearing of the shrieks of the wounded and dying, I made this speech and proclamation, which I read from a paper of the day:

"In looking at this vast crowd of colored people, continued the Governor, and reflecting through what a storm of persecution and obloquy they are compelled to pass, I am almost induced to wish that, as in the days of old, a Moses might arise who should lead them safely to their promised land of freedom and happiness.

'You are our Moses,' shouted several voices, and the exclamation was caught up and cheered until the Capitol rang again.

God, continued the speaker, no doubt has prepared somewhere an instrument for the great work he designs to perform in behalf of this outraged people, and in due time your leader will come forth; your Moses will be revealed to you.

'We want no Moses but you,' again shouted the crowd.

'Well then,' replied the speaker, 'humble and unworthy as I am, if no other better shall be found, I will, indeed be your Moses, and lead you through the red sea of war and bondage, to a fair future of liberty and peace. I speak now as one who feels the world his country, and all who love equal rights his friends. I speak, too, as a citizen of Tennessee. I am here on my own soil, and here I mean to stay and fight this great battle of truth and justice to a triumphant end. Rebellion and slavery shall, by God's good help, no longer pollute our State. Loyal men, whether white or black, shall alone control her destinies, and when this strife in which we are all engaged is past, I trust I know we shall have a better state of things, and shall all rejoice that honest labor reaps the fruit of its own industry, and that every man has a fair chance in the race of life.'"

I want the colored people to hear me. They tell you that the Moses who had proclaimed freedom to whites and blacks had deserted you. Who is it that tells you that I have deserted you? Who is it that tells you that I and the Southern people have deserted you? Who is it, colored people, that tells you that the Southern people are your worst enemies? Who and what are they? Who among them periled their lives and spent their money that now talk about Moses. I want the attention of the colored people who are here. I want them to hear what I said on the steps of the Capitol at Nashville when I proclaimed their freedom. I said: "Colored men of Nashville, you have all heard of the President's proclamation, by which he announced to the world that the slaves in a large portion of the seceded States were henceforth and forever free. For certain reasons which seemed wise to the President the benefits of the proclamation did not extend to you or to your native State. Many of you consequently were left in bondage. The task master's scourge was not yet broken, and the fetters still galled your limbs. Gradually this iniquity has been passing away, but the hour has come when the last vestiges of it must be removed. Consequently I, too, without reference to the President or any other person, have a proclamation to make, and standing here upon the steps of the Capitol, with the past history of the State to witness the present condition to guide, and its future to encourage me, I, Andrew Johnson, do hereby proclaim freedom full, broad and unconditional to every man in Tennessee."

I want this to be remembered, that Tennessee was exempted from the operation of Lincoln's proclamation. It was under these circumstances, let me tell the colored people, that I proclaimed them free. All I promised was performed. Let me ask you where is the modern Moses? Where is the new Moses who has come to lead you? A new set of masters have taken possession of you. Do you remember how long Moses was in delivering the Israelites? Just forty years. You were freed in one night, and have been free four years. When the man who set you free returns, he finds an Aaron in the camp, and a golden calf erected for your worship, to make which you have been called upon to give up your trinkets and ornaments and your money and means. Your new masters only want your labor, your trinkets and your gold. Moses is come to proclaim the truth to you. The Leagues, in which you have become involved, make you take oaths.

I want your attention; I want to occupy my proper place in your hearts. I want to occupy a true place in your hearts. Have these Loyal Leaguers set you free? How much have they given you of freedom, or anything else? I hold in my hand a little

BLUE BOOK.

It is very much worn, but you can see a little blue in it yet (holding it up to the crowd). Well, I will read from this little blue-book. I have considerable reputation in connection with blue-books. I will read and prove to you that every member of the Loyal Leagues is a slave and a conspirator against the Government. I will read you the oath of these Loyal Leaguers. They swear, among other things:

"And I will never make known in way or manner, to any person or persons not members of the U.L., any of the signs, passwords, proceedings, debates or plans of this or any other circle under this organization, except when engaged in admitting new members into this League."

Let me ask, my colored friend, were you free when you went into this Loyal League? If so, what did you get by joining? Did you get anything? Why not act upon your own good sense? You do not need Loyal Leaguers to tell you what to do. Act up to your own conscience and judgment, and do not be guided or dictated to by men who join Loyal Leagues for ulterior purposes and to become your task masters. Does it make you any freer to take this oath? The Loyal Leagues are conspiracies against the Government, the laws and the country. You need emancipation worse now than you did the day your freedom was proclaimed from the steps of the Capitol at Nashville. Your Moses has come to free you again. You remember that Moses did not reach the promised land, but died on Pisgah's top. He lived to be a very old man. He was 120 years old when he died. I am but sixty now. When Moses returned from the mountain, he was amazed to find that a golden calf had been set up for the worship of the children of Israel. These Loyal Leagues want your money for the golden calf they worship. I want you to be free and free of these obligations. When Moses returned from the mount he broke the golden calf, ground it into powder, threw it into the water, and then made the children of Israel drink of their iniquity. He said, standing in the gate, all that are on the Lord's side come to Moses. You are not going after these false gods, not going after these Leaguers, not going after these impostors, these false prophets—come to me. Where is the forty acres and the mule they promised you? If they were earnest in what they have promised, why did they not send you up to the Northwest, where there is plenty of land for settlement and the asking? They did not want you up in that country. They could not get your money and your trinkets if you went up there. They would not, for that reason, permit you to avail yourself of the homestead law. They could not get your trinkets. Now you have nothing—they have taken your money and your trinkets, and you are the slaves of those worse than taskmasters. They have a mortgage upon you and a bill of sale. When I arrived at Knoxville, they told the colored people of East Tennessee I had come to enslave them, but I retorted, and told them to tell their masters that I had come to break their chains. They said that I was coming back to return you to slavery. Is it true? Who have I enslaved? Not one. I am here to assist in the freedom of all—white, black and all. The use these Loyal Leaguers have for you is to get the places and all you have. I trust and hope the colored people will do me justice. I am getting old. In going down, I will occupy a place in the pages of history. I desire to occupy a place in the affections of those I have endeavored to serve. These poor colored people should be placed in the true position, and we should do what we can for them.

PARDONS—THE STATE.

I have done what I thought best, and have pardoned and restored all those whom I found under disability. It is a question to be settled. In law it is good, some of the most profound lawyers having been consulted in regard to it. Look at your own State affairs. When I left the gubernatorial office it was in a different condition. Where is your State Bank? Where is your School Fund? (Laughter and cheers.) And what is the amount of your State debt? How about the militia? In considering this we discover a conflict with the organic law of the land, with the Constitution of the United States, which guarantees a Republican form of government to every one of the States. The power is conferred upon the United States to suppress domestic violence as well as to protect against foreign invasion. It is provided that no State shall keep ships or troops, because the United States provides for the suppression of domestic violence. All sheriffs have authority to call out the civil power. When has any disturbance transpired in the State which the sheriffs of the several counties were not competent to quell? You cannot tell me. Nothing has occurred that could not be paralleled in ordinary times. The States were to be protected and defended in the enjoyment of peace and republican liberty. Where is the sheriff who cannot execute process? I am almost ready to enter into an obligation for the execution of the civil process in almost every county in the State.

How easy then to destroy your form of government. What do you mean by your Governor declaring martial law? If that was permitted in every State our Republican system would shortly be subverted and overturned. If State after State should declare martial law, the civil be subordinated to military law, all indeed would be lost and the "Empire" be established.

RETROSPECTIVE.

In returning as a citizen to the midst of those for whom I have toiled and labored, it gives me more pleasure to become a private citizen than to be inaugurated President of the United States on the ruins of a violated Constitution. (Applause). Yes, I feel emancipated after four years of toil, and I would rather be in your midst as a private individual, with the proud satisfaction of having done my duty, rather the furrows of care and responsibility, on my brow, the dust of the shop and the field on my garments, as badges of peace and prosperity, than to wear the gilded tassel, or the epaulets, or the dangling sword, dripping and red with the bloodshed in cruel civil war. I have filled every office of honor in the gift of the people; I have been the rounds. I do not say it egotistically. I have filled every position in the Government, and the United States does not furnish a parallel case, where a man by his own actions, in regular gradations and advancement. In traveling from the highest to the lowest, from position to position, thank God the road I traveled has not been paved with human souls, nor led by a Potter's field or a Golgotha, nor have the bridges that I passed over been floored with limbs and bodies of companions and kindred. Thank God, the blood of husband nor brother of no sister or wife, no orphan child can be attached to me. My career has been as a civilian and I would rather retire as a civilian to private life. For if can do no more I can follow the advice of Cato to his son in the last extremity in pent up Syracuse, "Go my son to the Sabine fields, and there praise the gods!"[10] I can retire to my humble home, and pray for my country and the preservation of its liberties. If I know myself I love my country; and for serving her I have been denounced for all that is vile. They talk of "treason" and "traitor," about abandoning the party. Where is the principle that I have abandoned? or departed from? If being faithful to my country, if fidelity to the Constitution is treason to my party, then I am guilty of that treason. (Applause.)

In conclusion of what I have said to you in broken and labored words to-day, if we shall preserve the constitution, I ask no more honorable part than in the ranks, redeeming the people from the thraldom in which they have been cast.

If an additional sacrifice is necessary to preserve the Constitution, restoration of lost rights and a return of prosperity, erect your alter and take me, and the blood which warms and animates my veins shall be poured out as a libation on the alter of my country.

Let us gather around and stand like a band of brothers in defence of our alters, or fall and sink in the dust together, but that the Constitution shall be preserved. Take the Constitution and hang it under the cross, let it be litten by the fires of the cross, and inscribe on it, "Peace—the Constitution and Union, one and Inseparable," and ere long the enemies which beset her shall be chased away and our country shall again enjoy peace and prosperity.

Returning thanks for the attention paid him, and hoping that all little feelings of hate or rancor that may have existed, should be forever forgotten, amid the most vociferous and enthusiastic cheering, Mr. Johnson closed, and the crowd dispersed.

Memphis Appeal, Apr. 16, 1869.

1. The date is indicated by numerous newspapers.

2. Philip II (1527–1598) ascended the throne on the resignation of his father, Holy Roman Emperor Charles V. *New Columbia Encyclopedia* (1975).

3. Not identified.

4. Johnson's earlier speech at Lynchburg, Virginia, is the first reference he made to Jefferson's statements about legislative and despotic power. See Speech in Lynchburg, Va., Mar. 18, 1869.

5. The proper title of the paper is the *Imperialist*, a weekly serial of mysterious sponsorship that began publication on April 10. Conservative papers claimed "radicals" and "bondholders" were behind it, since the paper advocated revolution, an "imperial government," and repayment of the national debt. *Cincinnati Enquirer*, Apr. 14, 1869; *National Intelligencer*, Apr. 20, 1869; World Cat database, accession no. 11424082.

6. The following paragraphs are from the Fourth Annual Message, December 9, 1868. There are discrepancies between this newspaper account of the message and the actual message.

7. Again, these quoted paragraphs are from Johnson's Fourth Annual Message.

8. A reference possibly to the John Black letter. See Black to Johnson, Apr. 12, 1869.

9. See "The Moses of the Colored Men" Speech, Oct. 24, 1864. *Johnson Papers*, 7: 251–53.

10. Cato to his son, Portius, from Addison's *Cato*, act. 4, sc. 4.

From James J. Erwin[1]

Petersburg Illinois   April 16th 1869

Dear Sir

In Perusim your Speach Delivered at Koxville Tenn it occured to me that you were doing for the People a good thing in as mutch as a Great many have been Politicaly Fanaticaly and I mite say willfully Blind to the Best interest of the goverment. Power seames to be gone from the Reasoning faculties of the now dominant Party, Except to Plan to Retain Power at whatever Cost. I do not Propose to write a Political letter. I am no Polititon and but a poor shollar yet when I look Back and reflect about the condition of ower Government under ower good old Democratic Rule and compar notes then and now I can not but Conclude that you are doing a good thing for the People and I hope and trust that you will draw the attention of the People to the Danger which is now threatning us as a nation. You told the People at Knoxville that the Legislative Power was the Power that Could take away *ower libertys*. That needs not the filosiphy of a learned man to see that you Could have told them more that these secrete Political societies is where a good many of the legislators make their start and that a Political Party that works in the dark cant very well help being corrupt. They chose darkness rather than light Becaus their deeds ar Evil. The constitution as it was be fore ower late unplesantness I think was Good a nuff and I suggest that a Union Constitutional and Educational Party be Recomended in Every state of the United States that the object of that Party shall be to learn the Constitution and Give to it the Proper meening of what it says. Let there be a one Definition *and that be made Plain so he that* Runeth may read and having red may understand. You will Pleas Excuse the liberty I take in addressing thes few lines to you. My apology for so doing is that I like the Speech you made at Knoxville and hope to see a good many more from the same Source.

James J Erwin

ALS, DLC-JP.

1. Erwin (*c*1825–*ff*1870) was a carpenter. 1860 Census, Ill., Menard, Petersburg, 214; (1870), Athens, 18.

William Cornell Jewett

CINCINNATI, April 18th 1869

Ex President Johnson.

I note your noble work South in opposition to the "Empire" power at Washington.[1]

You will observe by within[2] I have since meeting you—succeeded in the formation of the basis of a people's Reform party.[3] I hope you will be inclined to take part in inaugurating the movement in a portion of the States. You will oblige me by informing me to *my address Baltimore*, if you will address, with me—meetings at some Northern point—or at Richmond & other Southern points—a[t] a future day. You letter will be deemed private.

Wm. Cornell Jewett

ALS, DLC-JP.
1. Probably a reference to Johnson's Memphis speech and his comments regarding the new journal, *The Imperialist*. See Speech in Memphis, Apr. 15, 1869.
2. No enclosure has been found.
3. Jewett helped preside over a meeting of the "People's Reform Party," which convened in Cincinnati on April 16. The platform included repudiation of the debt, and enforcement of American claims and concepts of naturalization. *Cincinnati Enquirer*, Apr. 17, 1869.

From John Edwards

Louisville Ky   April 20 69

Dear Sir

I read your Nashville speech with pleasure and satisfaction. There is one point in connection with the past history of events that is seldom alluded to at the present day—which I regard as an important for the consideration of the public—and I am now induced to call your attention to it from the fact that about the period you assumed the Governorship of Tennessee under Mr. Lincoln, we corresponded together on the question of the preservation of the Union, and the future policy to be pursued.[1] At that time you took the position the act of secession was a nullity, that so soon as insurrection in any one of the seceded states was surpressed it was the duty, and the right of the loyal people thereof to put the civil government under the Constitution in motion to make such changes as the consequences resulting from the war demanded as was done in Arkansas and Louisiana though the advice and direction of President Lincoln.

Near the close of the war—a new doctrine was sprung by the extremists in Congress that the seceded states were to be regarded as conquered provinces. If this doctrine was true then treason was not committed, hence radicals have dodged the issue of trying Rebels for treason before the courts—prefering to form a pretext to force Negro Equality upon the Country.

Your policy was the policy of President Lincoln, and the true one which but a few years will require to show its wisdom.

In connection with the foregoing I have to remark I have traveled recently thru several states North and South, have mixed freely with the people of all classes. I find the people utterly demoralized—everywhere no one has any confidence in the future stability of affairs. Money Money is the cry—patriotism is gone—and we are rapidly hurrying on to destruction.

A majority of those who go with the radicals do so either through sordid motives or fear. The people have no confidence in extreme radicalism or radicals regarding the whole thing as corrupt from begning to end.

The reason why radicalism at the north last fall seemed to be endorsed by such large majorities was not because of the popularity of radical measures. But it was because of the unpopularity and odiousness of most of the leaders of the democratic party. Men who were opposed to the war—Copperheads. While the people are at heart ready to abandon the radicals, they are not willing to flee to the Copperheads for protection.

What is wanted to effect a change to overthrow radicalism is for the old Democratic party to disband its organization—and give us a new organization with a new name. A great blunder was committed in not nominating Judge Chase last fall.

John Edwards

ALS, DLC-JP.
1. See Edwards to Johnson, June 20, 1862, *Johnson Papers*, 5: 490–92.

From Robert Avery

479 E. Street   Washington D.C.
April 24th 1869

Dear Sir:—

I took the liberty of writing to you some ten days ago and of telegraphing to you a week ago in reference to the Army orders of which I spoke to you a year ago and again in January of this year and which you were kind enough to order the Adjt. Genl. to prepare for me.[1] I think you will recollect that I told you why I wished them. It was to obtain reliable matter for my forthcoming "Biographical History of the Rebellion"[2] a book not likely to be popular with some of the present heroes as it "strips of the lions hide" from many of them "and hangs a calf skin on their recreant limbs.["][3] The orders referred are now ready and if you will have the kindness to send me a letter requesting the Adjt Genl., Gen Townsend to deliver them to me I can obtain them, and will be for this as for many favors in the past your grateful debtor.

Rob't. Avery   Late Bvt Maj Gen Vols

ALS, DLC-JP.

1. On April 23, Edward D. Townsend forwarded a set of general orders to Johnson in Greeneville, which the former President (through William G. Moore) had requested. Townsend to Johnson, Apr. 23, 1869, Johnson Papers, LC.

2. There is no record of a publication by this or any similar name produced by Robert Avery.

3. This is a slight variation of lines from Shakespeare's *King John*, act 3, sc. 1: "Thou wear a lion's hide! doff it for shame, And hang a calf's-skin on those recreant limbs."

From Robert A. Bennett

[Gallatin, Tenn., ca. April 24, 1869][1]

Most esteemed Sir

The within invitation[2] was written and handed me to deliver to you at Nashville on the 24th Inst and urge upon you to come to Gallatin and address your fellow citzens of Sumner and adjoining counties. The sudden departure of yourself for Greeneville prevented me from delivering the same. The sad news of your sons death caused you to hasten home. Accept my sincere condolence for the loss sustained. Robt Johnson and myself served in the legislature together in the sessions of 1859 and 60 and I formed a warm personal attachment for him and shall cherish his memory. With a grateful heart allow me now to urge you to accept this invitation of the people of Sumner and to write to me on the subject. We will have an immense assemblage of persons and the people will spare no pains or expense to entertain the vast crowd that we know will be present.

R A Bennett

ALS, DLC-JP.

1. This letter would have to have been written some time after April 23. Internal evidence

about the death of Robert Johnson (which occurred on April 23) suggests that Bennett wrote the letter shortly after that news was received. We have arbitrarily assigned the April 24 date.

2. The enclosed invitation from Gallatin, dated April 23, contained dozens of signatures from Sumner County citizens. As Bennett indicates, the invitation urged Johnson to visit Gallatin soon.

From Joseph C. Bradley

Huntsville Alabama   April 24 1869

Dr. Sir

I herewith send you a slip from the Huntsville Advocate[1] containing the proceedings of the City Authority in regard to your reception. It will explain itself and give you renewed assurance that altho. some of your life long friends may have differed with you in the latter part of your Presidential Administration in regard to your reconstruction policy, yet they never defamed your good name or allowed others to do it in their presence, and may hereafter (when you are out of power) prove more sincere friends to your person & character, than new recruits who seem so much prepossessed with you at present. Your speech was listened to in our City by many Republicans on whom it made favourable impressions, and they expressed a great desire to call on you in a most respectful way but were refused this privilege by the Democratic Ex Committee, which you doubtless perceived were full of ardor & zeal and mostly new converts to the Democratic faith. You have my best wishes for a long & happy life.

Joseph C Bradley

ALS, DLC-JP.
1. Not found enclosed. Johnson had visited Huntsville after his departure from Memphis.

From Sam Milligan

private

Washington City   April 25. 1869

Dear Sir:

I see by this morning's papers, you were suddenly called home, from Athens Alabamma, by the unexpected death of your son, Robert. I hope the telegram is not true; but if it is, you have my heartfelt sympathies. His death was untimely, and therefore the more painful. But it is the common lot of us all, and when it comes, altho always unbidden, we ought not to murmur.

I wished, however to say, that things are going here in a hard gallop to the D——l. The dominant party is now ready of its own corruption to tumble to pieces; and the poor little man in the Presidential Chair, is, from want of intellect, as powerless as a child to hold it together. One year will not pass, before he will sink down into a mere cypher—the tool of tools. He has no ability to stand alone, and his party no common ground upon which it can uphold him. He has not, and never will have, any distinctive policy of his own, and can not, I fear, understand, and carry out that of any other mans. All is at sea, and the whole Government drifting on the most fearful breakers. It ought to be saved from wreck and ruin.

Now, what can be done? The people are honest, and want to do right; but experience has taught me, they are easily misled. Parties, upon principle are not yet formed since the war, certainly not crystilized. And now is the time to open the campaign for 1872. Four years will soon be round, and the work is a heavy one.

I therefore suggest, that one mammoth paper, be established here—at the seat of Government, to be edited by a select, and able corps of Editors, and that under strict organizations, evry other paper, little and big, friendly to the cause of the constitution, should be, as far as possible, induced to strike the same note of the central organ, and that this organ be sent out free, or as nearly so as possible, to evry town and hamlet in the United States. Such a paper, would, under proper organization, be irresistable.

But how can the money be raised to set it on foot? I answer by subscriptions. I believe the sum necessary, apportioned among the states, with sub committees, to act on the Counties, can readily be raised, and the whole put in motion in less than ten months.

To this end, you ought to announce, a short skillfully prepared platform as the basis of the whole. It should rest on fundimental principles, and be broad & general enough to catch evry disaffected man.

To begin it you ought, I think, to come here, and then go to Baltimore, New York, Philadelphia &c.

Now, what do you think of the outline. I dont want any body to speculate in it a single dime; but the whole to rest on patriotism, pure and undefiled. The idea is my own. I have consulted with nobody. I am done—think about it.

Sam Milligan

ALS, DLC-JP.

From Robert Avery

479 E St   Washington D.C.   April 26th 1869

Dear Sir:—

It is but three days since I had the honor of addressing you upon a matter of business,[1] and upon the same day of conversing with our friend Dr. Norris[2] in regard to your own health which I was pleased to learn was good and that you had every prospect of comfort and happiness and now the telegraph brings us the sad news of the death of your son. To those who know you only as a public man, and those who know you but slightly this announcement makes but slight impression but to those who know you as it has been my good fortune to do, and who know your great kind heart full of sympathy for every one, and who have learned to esteem you as I have done for what you are, this announcement brings grief as it does to you. I beg to offer to you and your bereaved family my heartfelt condolences.

Robt. Avery
Late Bvt. Maj. Gen.

ALS, DLC-JP.
1. See Avery to Johnson, Apr. 24, 1869.
2. Basil Norris had served as Johnson's physician in Washington during the presidency.

From Mary M. Payne

Providence Boone Co Mo   26th April 69

Hon Andrew Johnson

Your Excellency my dear sir will excuse the liberty that a suffering sorrowing Mother takes in addressing you.

My son Lt J Scott Payne of the 5th U s Cavalry—telegraphed to you on the 12th of Sept last to give him a leave of absence or to accept his resignation to take effect Decr 1st. You accepted his resignation to take effect from the date of the telegram Sept 12th & not as it was tendered for Decr 1st.

My son at *once* wrote a protest[1] getting Maj Rollins & Col Switzler M C *elect* from this District & they approached the Sec of War & yourself.[2] During the time that you had the matter under advisement & consideration my son sent to your atty Genl Mr Evarts a statement of the grounds upon which he asked reinstatement.[3] Col Switzler states that you gave the case to Mr Evarts for his opinion—

that in cabinet meeting you determined & did reinstate him. My son was with me—impatient miserable at the delay during all the winter. After receving official notice of your order reinstating him—he wrote to Gen. Townsend for *orders* for duty.[4] Not receving any he got Col Switzler to telegraph to you & you promptly on the 13th of Feby replied by telegram "that the necessary orders in Lieut Paynes case have been sent on the 30th Jany."[5] Maj Rollins wrote to Sec Browning—Col Switzler telegraphed to you & also wrote to you[6]—Senator Henderson[7] was there to see that orders were sent—was a friend of my son's urging his reinstatement—but no orders for duty came & finally he set off to join his regiment first—but on reaching St. Louis found the Headquarters was still in Washington & went there—but owing to the anxious delays & hopes & certainty that you would have him ordered to his regiment it was the 4th of March & then Gen Townsend informed him that he had not been reinstated according to law. He went to the Atty Genls, office—found no statement of the case & returned home. He tried to see you at Mr Coyle's[8] but was denied—and upon the ground that you were wearied out with the cares of state & wrote you & after your return to Tennessee again wrote you getting Col Switzler to endorse the letter. Now it does seem to me that you—great in your own [shiny?] intellect with such an adviser as Mr Evarts would never have done any thing illegally. Of course all resignations properly accepted are final. Reinstatement by the President needs confirmation by the Senate. This my son never expected as he knew the Senate would not confirm your appointment in his case—and I think it becomes your duty as a vindication of your own act to state to my son on what grounds *you* Reinstated him & ask for Mr Evarts legal opinion in the *case*. There are many reasons why you should outside of this. This young officer was detailed on duty in Knoxville & because he obeyed instructions and discharged his duty faithfully as a soldier & gentleman *was* misrepresented & shamefully, treated by low politicians in East Tenn—they were the men who despised you & wanted to trade illegally under the disguise of loyalty & who reward noisy secessionist & *condemn* the men who served the *government*—who are faithful from a high sense of duty & patriotism & scorned to overthrow *the papers so* beautifully formed by their forefathers. Go to the Union men of East *Tennessee* & see what estimation this young man is held in—by the law abiding patriotic citizens. Col Abernethy[9] & Col Jno Williams & hosts of others will testify as you know they did in his court martial. He was shamefully outraged by Gen *Tho-*

mas[10]—who during all his trouble professed kind sympathy & again to me & yet so prejudiced Gen Scofield[11] as to cause all this trouble.

If Gen Scofield your sec of war refused to send orders when *you* President of the United States & Com in Chief of the army ordered him—is he not infamous—& you telegraphed that these orders had been sent.

My son was arrested about the 10th of June on his way home to attend his fathers[12] sale & to see to a widowed & despondent mother. He was detained in Nashville two months, without a trial then sent to Washington & tried & acquitted of evry charge—was returned to Nashville & ordered west—& believing that you were friendly to him & would grant his request, he telegraphed for the *leave* & in the event of not getting it for his resignation. He felt lone & miserable & unfriended & that he could *not* fail to see me—he was my only child—his father *just* dead & I alone—unprotected & unprovided for. I lost 37 *valuable* slaves by the war—this young man lost 25,000$ worth—his all in his own right—4 of his men enlisted in the army under Mr Lincolns proclamation for compensation to loyal owners—*he* with only his profession *when* his father & mother & himself were *all* of a large & *wealthy* & influential family that remained true to the government. It is the hardest case I have *known* & you would be serving *humanity* to state to *him* in such terms as you no doubt *can* his true status & his means of redress. No matter how *humble* the *individual* it is a vindication of your own act. I have lived in Mo 12 years—but I had influential friends in Va.—the Confederate Sec of War was a near relation & friend[13]—Mr Wise & Mr. Lyon[14]—all would have done any thing in the prosperous days of the confederacy to serve me. The half brother of my son[15] became at an early age brigadier Genl. & the [Lees?] were nearly [connected?] to him—but I *chose* like yourself for *me* & mine the old flag & *Union*— & I do desire something of my country. My opinions alienated me *from* all ties of blood & ruined our future & with this *fine son* in such trouble. So lately widowed & therefore for my sake you must serve this *son* who is talented & honorable & who never was a politician & only a soldier.[16]

Mary M Payne

ALS, DLC-JP.

1. Not found.

2. James S. Rollins and William F. Switzler. See, for example, James S. Rollins to Johnson, Nov. 26, 1868, ACP Branch, File P-156-CB-168, J. S. Payne, RG94, NA.

3. While the letter to William M. Evarts has not been found, see J. Scott Payne to Johnson, Nov. 2, 1868, for his general complaint.

4. J. Scott Payne to Edward D. Townsend, Feb. 8, 1869, Lets. Recd. (Main Ser.), File P-80-1869 (M619, Roll 734), RG94, NA.

5. Telegram not found.

6. See William F. Switzler to Johnson, Feb. 20, 1869.

7. John B. Henderson.

8. John F. Coyle.

9. James T. Abernathy.

10. George H. Thomas.

11. John M. Schofield.

12. Arthur M. Payne.

13. There were six Confederate secretaries of war, but the two most likely to have been relatives of the Paynes were the Virginians George W. Randolph (Mar.–Nov. 1862) and James A. Seddon (Nov. 1862–Jan. 1865). Mark M. Boatner, *The Civil War Dictionary* (New York, 1959).

14. Henry A. Wise and James Lyons.

15. William H.F. Payne (1830–1904) was the oldest child of Arthur M. Payne and his first wife, Mary M. Fitzhugh Payne. A Warrenton, Virginia, lawyer, he enlisted as a Confederate private, served in the cavalry, and was made brigadier general as of November 1, 1864. He was wounded and captured three times. After the war he resumed his law practice and served one term in the Virginia House of Delegates. Warner, *Gray*; Baird and Jordan, *Fauquier County Tombstone Inscriptions*, 1: 160; John K. Gott, *Fauquier County, Virginia Guardian Bonds, 1759–1871* (Bowie, Md., 1990), 88.

16. There is no known Johnson response to this letter, either to Mary or to J. Scott Payne.

From John Williams, Jr.

Knoxville, April 26th 1869.

Dear Sir:

I have conversed with many of our friends to-day, in regard to political matters in our State.

To-morrow, I am informed that Mr. Thomas Nelson,[1] will declare himself a candidate for the Supreme Bench, in connection with Shackleford & Smith,[2] the two present defeated Judges. They seem to think this is the best plan to get the Court, which met to-day at Brownsville. Two cases they say are before the Court, & if they succede in getting a decision against the Franchise Law,[3] that, then there will be very little difficulty in beating Stokes, with Fletcher.[4] So you see they expect to make one election dependent upon the other. I do not however, see clearly how this will work, for this reason. If the Court decides against the law, then, the Rads will take an appeal to the Supreme Court at Washington; & the case cant be tried until after our August election, which will enable the Rads to hold Gubernatorial, & Legislative elections, under the law as it now stands. Is that not so? Then if this is the correct view, what shall next be done? If Senter[5] goes into the Convention, & is defeated by Stokes, then, he cant run, but perhaps he may be induced to favor Fletcher; & by his canvassing the State thouroughly upon the ideas suggested to you, by him the other night; & for you to aid him by talking to the people upon the general idea of the Rads to change the character of our Government, I think bald faced Billy can be whipped.[6]

Whatever notions you may have from time, to time, I will be pleased to learn.

A big split is brewing here between Maynard & Brownlow,[7] on one side, & the disappointed office seekers on the other. The prospects brightens, & only needs work to consummate the desired end. Would like to hear from you.

John Williams.

ALS, DLC-JP.

1. Thomas A.R. Nelson did in fact publicly announce on April 27 that he would be a candidate for the state supreme court. See *Nashville Republican Banner*, Apr. 30, 1869. Running as a Conservative, Nelson was not successful. Alexander, *T.A.R. Nelson*, 145.

2. James O. Shackelford and Henry G. Smith, both incumbents, were not nominated at the judicial nominating convention in Nashville on April 20. Alexander, *Reconstruction*, 213.

3. Two days after the supreme court election the court rendered a decision at Brownsville declaring Brownlow's setting aside of voter registrations as unconstitutional. Brownlow had acted under terms of the 1866 franchise law. The net effect of the court decision was to open up voting rights to many citizens who had previously been disfranchised. This in turn would enable Conservatives to reap electoral advantages over the Radicals—which is exactly what happened in the summer gubernatorial and legislative elections. Ibid., 214; Alexander, *T.A.R. Nelson*, 145.

4. William B. Stokes and Andrew J. Fletcher. In August Stokes did in fact seek the governor's chair, but Fletcher did not.

5. DeWitt C. Senter, who became the governor upon the resignation of Brownlow. Brownlow resigned in order to take his seat in the U.S. Senate to which he had earlier been elected by the state legislature. Alexander, *Reconstruction*, 198.

6. Stokes was easily defeated in the August gubernatorial election by Senter. Ibid., 218.

7. Horace Maynard and William G. Brownlow, leading Radicals.

From Frederick W. Schneider[1]

Troy, N.Y., April 29th /69.

Dear Sir—

Being a young man, just entering upon the political arena and doubtful of success, I herewith take the liberty of requesting Your Excellency, to whom I have always looked with admiration and more than ordinary respect, to answer me a few questions, which are of vital importance to me at the present time, but may be more so in future. I should never have had the confidence to thus seek for information from one so far above my humble sphere, had not Your Excellency inspired me with a faint hope of meeting with a response.

When, some years since, on the occasion of the erection of a monument in honor of the lamented *Douglass*, Your Excellency passed, on your way to Chicago, through Rochester, N.Y., I had the pleasure and honor, of shaking hands with you.[2] I looked up in your countenance, and the thoughtful, scrutinizing look you then gave me, inspired me with an uncontrollable ambition.

Had Your Excellency at the age of twenty, a determination to make a mark in the world?

And was your success, in a measure, due to such determination?

In your intercourse with other distinguished statesmen, have you discovered their success to have been owing to the same determination on their part?

The answers to the above questions are of great importance to me, and I will at all times cherish a grateful remembrance of you for solving them.

If permitted to give them publicity, I shall not hesitate to do so.

Fred W Schneider.

No. 130 Congress st., Troy, N.Y.

LS, DLC-JP.

1. Schneider (*fl*1873) was a printer in Troy. Troy directories (1870–73).

2. The reference here is to Johnson's famous "swing around the circle" trip through the Northeast and Midwest in August–September 1866.

Appendix I

ADMINISTRATION OF ANDREW JOHNSON (1865–1869)

[Adapted from Robert Sobel, ed., *Biographical Directory of the United States Executive Branch, 1774–1971* (Westport, Conn., 1971).]

Office	Name
Secretary of State, 1865–69	William H. Seward
Secretary of the Treasury, 1865–69	Hugh McCulloch
Secretary of War, 1865–68	Edwin M. Stanton
Secretary of War ad interim, 1867–68	Ulysses S. Grant
Secretary of War ad interim, 1868	Lorenzo Thomas
Secretary of War, 1868–69	John M. Schofield
Attorney General, 1865–66	James Speed
Attorney General, 1866–68	Henry Stanbery
Attorney General ad interim, 1868*	Orville H. Browning
Attorney General, 1868–69	William M. Evarts
Postmaster General, 1865–66	William Dennison
Postmaster General, 1866–69	Alexander W. Randall
Secretary of the Navy, 1865–69	Gideon Welles
Secretary of the Interior, 1865	John P. Usher
Secretary of the Interior, 1865–66	James Harlan
Secretary of the Interior, 1866–69	Orville H. Browning

*From March 13, 1868, when Stanbery resigned, until July 20, 1868, when Evarts assumed office, Browning discharged the duties of attorney general in addition to his functions as head of the Interior Department.

Appendix II

VETOES, PROCLAMATIONS, AND SELECTED EXECUTIVE
ORDERS AND SPECIAL MESSAGES (SEPTEMBER 1868–APRIL 1869)

[Asterisks indicate documents printed in Volume 15; most are printed
in James D. Richardson, comp., *A Compilation of the Messages and Papers
of the Presidents* (10 vols., Washington, D.C., 1896–99), Volume 6.]

Date	Veto Messages	Richardson, *Messages*
Feb. 13	*Veto of the Washington and Georgetown Schools Act	705
Feb. 22	*Veto of the Copper Bill	705–7
	Proclamations	
Oct. 12	*Proclamation *re* Thanksgiving	660–61
Dec. 25	*Fourth Amnesty Proclamation	708
	Executive Orders	
Sept. 12	Order *re* Command of Department of Louisiana	668
Oct. 10	Order *re* Military Interference in Presidential Election	668–71
	Special Messages	
Jan. 18	*Explanation of Fourth Amnesty Proclamation	697
Mar. 4	*Farewell Address	———

Appendix III

ADDRESS BY JAMES BRITTON, JR.[1]

Mr. Johnson,—

As chairman of a committee appointed and especially instructed by the people of Greeneville, of Greene County and Upper East Tennessee, as the vast concourse present will abundantly testify, I am here, sir, to tender you a warm and cordial greeting on your return to your adopted home amid the beautiful blue mountains of your own loved East Tennessee. On behalf of those whom I represent, I am authorized to say to you, welcome, to come and in our midst spend the evening of your life after your laborious and arduous duties in the highest and most responsible trust within the gift of the American people.

You might well adopt the language of Napoleon Bonaparte when he retired to the island of Corsica, "Blindfold, my native hills I would have known." On behalf of your political friends, I will be permitted to say, "Well done, thou good and faithful servant." The conflict that you have just terminated has been a battle for Constitutional liberty that has no parallel in the annals of human history. We well remember, in 1859, when the Southern mind was being instructed; when Southern passions were being inflamed, and a Rebellion of gigantic proportions was being inaugurated, your voice was heard in the Senate chamber of the United States above the voice of all others, louder than a tenfold thunder, in denunciation of treason and rebellion. Then again, in 1861, when the Rebellion had gathered strength, and State after State had gone down in the abyss and whirlpool of secession, your voice of warning was heard, all over East Tennessee, like the prophet Jonah in the streets of ancient Nineveh. Afterwards, when you were made military governor of Tennessee by President Lincoln, and when the city of Nashville had been redeemed by the prowess of Federal arms, and when the city was again surrounded by a fearful rebel army, and the commanding general favored the evacuation of the city, it was your indomitable will, invincible determination, and unconquerable spirit that saved the city from annihilation and the Federal arms from serious reverse.

Shortly afterwards, when you had been elected to the second highest office within the gift of the people, upon the death of President Lincoln, by Constitutional provision you succeeded to the Presidency. As soon as the policy of your Administration was developed, a fierce and bitter war was opened upon you, which continued without cessation or mitigation. Your Constitutional constructions were thrown into a political crucible heated seven times hotter than the fiery furnace into which the Hebrew children were cast, but, like them, you have come out without the smell of fire upon your garments.

We feel assured, President Johnson, that the day that the robe of office fell from your shoulders, by Constitutional limitation, was a prouder day in your history that the coronation of a king, prince, or potentate that has ever been crowned in the Old World, and an infinitely prouder day than the Inauguration-day of the present Chief Executive of the United States. Your Administration has closed; the integrity of your conduct is now in the eternity of the past, and the judgment that prejudice and excitement may have pronounced against you will be reversed by posterity, and history will record the verdict in your favor.

In conclusion, President Johnson, it is our most sincere desire that you may live to enjoy the reward of your labor, until your motives will be correctly interpreted and your struggle for Constitutional liberty will be better understood, and when you come to die, "to shuffle off this mortal coil," and your spirit returns to the God that gave it, there to enjoy the reward of the pure in heart, may your mortal remains be left as a heritage to the people of your adopted home! And when affection and genius shall have reared a monument to your memory, and the curious of future generations come to visit the tombs of the illustrious dead, they will find on Mount Vernon the remains of Washington, who led the armies of the Colonies to victory and independence, whose most exalted trait of character was his pure patriotism; at Monticello they will find the remains of Jefferson, whose immortal pen drafted the Declaration of Independence, whose most prominent trait of character was his great political sagacity; at Montpelier will be found the remains of Madison, whose careful hand drafted the Constitution, with its wise checks and balances, whose most prominent trait of character was his great prudence and caution; at the Hermitage will be found all that was mortal of Jackson, who humbled England's pride, and whose most prominent trait was his courage, physical and moral; and when they come to linger about the tops of some of our beautiful hills, the last resting-place of Andrew Johnson, they will say, There lie the mortal remains of a man that had the patriotism of George Washington, the political sagacity of Thomas Jefferson, the prudence and caution of James Madison, and the physical and moral courage of Andrew Jackson. Such will be the conclusion of those who live in after time, when prejudice shall have died and the memory of truth, virtue, and integrity shall alone remain. Trusting that the sea of life on which you have been sailing may grow more calm, and the evening of your life may be more quiet than it has hitherto been, I will close by repeating that your[*sic*] are welcome, thrice welcome, on your return to your adopted home, and may your days be many to enjoy the harvest of a well-spent life!

James S. Jones, *Life of Andrew Johnson* (Greeneville, 1901), 336–39.

1. Delivered March 20, 1869, on the occasion of Johnson's return to Greeneville. For more on the event, see Henry H. Ingersoll to Johnson, Mar. 8, 1869. Johnson's address is printed as Speech at Greeneville, Mar. 20, 1869.

Index

Primary identification of a person is indicated by an italic *n* following the page reference. Identifications found in earlier volumes of the *Johnson Papers* are shown by providing volume and page numbers, within parentheses, immediately after the name of the individual. The only footnotes which have been indexed are those that constitute identification notes.

Abbott, Joseph C., 54, 55*n*
Abernathy, James T. (11: 382*n*), 622
Abolitionists, 549–50
Adams, John, 395
Adams, John Quincy (10: 667*n*): from, 487–88; to, 70
Agee, James H., 6, 7*n*, 37, 44; from, 45–51
Agnew, Samuel, 256*n*; from, 256
Alabama, 71–72, 78, 84–85, 110, 293, 453, 619
Alabama claims, 175–76, 443, 576
Alaska, 25–26, 31, 253, 300
Albany Penitentiary (New York), 445–46, 497
Alden Typesetting Machine, 205
Alexander II (11: 518*n*), 301–2
Allen, Ethan (13: 520*n*), 267
Allen, Ethan A. (12: 28*n*): from, 263–64, 444
Allen, Kate A. Cotte (Mrs. Ethan A.), 263
Allen, Samuel H.: from, 313
Allen, Samuel P. (10: 558*n*), 66
Allen, William Henry, 100, 101*n*
Alta Vela (island), 230–31, 264
Ambrose, Mordecai J. W., 407*n*; from, 406–7
American Free Trade League, 435
Ames, Alfred H., 355*n*; from, 354–55
Amnesty: requests for, 315, 317, 336–37, 355–56
Amnesty Proclamation (Fourth, 1868), 332
Amnesty proclamations: mentioned, 23, 106, 146, 233, 330, 332, 334, 335, 336–37, 340, 342, 355–56, 361, 377, 394–95; opposition to Fourth, 330; requested, 177
Anderson, Henry T., 5, 5*n*
Anderson, John B., 116
Anderson, Mattie, 5*n*; from, 5
Anderson, W. J., 584*n*; from, 583–84
Annual Message (Fourth, 1868), 281–306
Annual messages: advance copy wanted, 260–61, 267; criticism of, 330; Fourth quoted, 603–7; mentioned, 143, 218, 227, 254, 269, 287, 307, 330, 361; publication of, 306; Third quoted, 290–93

Anthony, James L. (14: 308*n*), 400
Apache Indians, 130–31
Applications: for employment, 525; for government positions, 5, 24, 62, 73, 74, 99–100, 107–8, 111, 115, 118, 120–21, 148, 166, 189–90, 193, 198–99, 236–37, 239, 240, 248–49, 252–53, 263, 266, 272, 274, 280–81, 308, 325, 326, 328, 349, 354, 357, 385, 388, 406–7, 436, 437–38, 473, 484–85; for U.S. Army promotion, 97–98
Appointments: in Alaska, 31; in California, 71, 330; claims commissioners, 175–76; in Colorado Territory, 125; commissioner of internal revenue, 12–14, 280–81, 308–9, 310–11, 320–21, 354, 367, 384, 402; to Cuba, 388; in District of Columbia, 399; to Ecuador, 335, 344–45; to Great Britain, 193, 349, 442–43; to Hawaii, 345; in Illinois, 241, 279; in Indiana, 225, 485; internal revenue, 45; to Japan, 388; in judiciary department, 196, 245, 260, 274, 318; in Kentucky, 115, 455–56; in Louisiana, 24, 96, 107–8, 115, 116, 234–35, 320, 329, 350, 374, 391, 400, 462, 474, 534; in Maryland, 241; in Massachusetts, 343–44, 418; to Mexican claims commission, 33–34, 58–59, 152; in Mexico, 340–41, 371–72; in Mississippi, 189–90; in Missouri, 260, 274, 318; in Montana Territory, 258; in New Mexico Territory, 232, 309; in New York, 31, 88, 152, 153, 163, 197–98, 246, 248–49, 252–53, 263, 268–69, 314, 317–18, 388, 400, 412, 456, 461; in North Carolina, 173–74, 228–29; in Ohio, 45, 264–65, 316; in Pennsylvania, 62, 73–74, 161, 246, 272; in post office department, 225, 248–49, 325, 343–44, 388, 455–56; railroad, 16–17, 134, 203, 461–62; recommended, 58–59, 110–11, 114, 117, 125, 134, 164, 175–76, 201, 203, 209–11, 227–28, 241, 245, 252, 260, 308–9, 316, 320–21, 326, 371–72, 378, 400, 414; to Russia,

The Papers of Andrew Johnson, Vol. 15, was designed and typeset on a Macintosh computer system using PageMaker software. The text is set in Caslon. This book was typeset by Kimberly Scarbrough and printed and bound by Thomson-Shore, Inc. The recycled paper used in this book is designed for an effective life of at least three hundred years.

—